LINCOLN STEFFENS

The Autobiography of
LINCOLN STEFFENS

COMPLETE IN ONE VOLUME

New York

THE LITERARY GUILD

1931

Typography by Robert S. Josephy

PRINTED IN THE UNITED STATES OF AMERICA
BY QUINN & BODEN COMPANY, INC., RAHWAY, N. J.

TO
ELLA WINTER

ACKNOWLEDGMENTS

Chapters of this book have appeared in *The Pictorial Review*, *The Bookman*, and *Plain Talk*. Acknowledgments are made to these publications for permission to reprint. The photograph of St. Basil's Cathedral, Moscow, by Margaret Bourke-White, is one of a series to be published in the fall of 1931 in book form.

CONTENTS

PART III. MUCKRAKING

CONTENTS

PART IV. REVOLUTION

viii   CONTENTS

ILLUSTRATIONS

PART I
A BOY ON HORSEBACK

WHEN I WAS AN ANGEL

EARLY in the morning of April 6, 1866, in a small house "over in the Mission" of San Francisco, California, I was born—a remarkable child. This upon the authority of my mother, a remarkable woman, who used to prove her prophetic judgment to all listeners till I was old enough to make my own demonstration. Even then, even though I was there to frown her down, she was ever ready to bring forth her evidence, which opened with the earthquake of 1868. When that shock shook most San Franciscans out of their houses into the streets, she ran upstairs to me and found me pitched out of bed upon the floor but otherwise unmoved. As she said with swimming eyes, I was "not killed, not hurt, and, of course, not crying; I was smiling, as always, good as gold."

My own interpretation of this performance is that it was an exhibit less of goodness than of wisdom. I knew that my mother would not abandon me though the world rocked and the streets yawned. Nor is that remarkable. Every well-born baby is sure he can trust his mother. What strikes me as exceptional and promising in it is that I had already some sense of values; I could take such natural events as earthquakes all in my stride. That, I think, is why I smiled then; that is why I smile now; and that may be why my story is of a happy life—happier and happier. Looking back over it now for review, it seems to me that each chapter of my adventures is happier than the preceding chapters right down to this, the last one: age, which, as it comes, comes a-laughing, the best of all. I have a baby boy of my own now; my first—a remarkable child, who—when he tumbles out of bed—laughs; as good as gold.

I was well-born. My mother, Elizabeth Louisa Symes, was an English girl who came from New York via the Isthmus of Panama to San Francisco in the sixties to get married. It was rumored about the east that the gold rush of '49 had filled California with men—self-selected, venturesome, strong young fellows who were finding there gold, silver, and everything else that they sought, excepting only wives. There was a shortage of women of the marriageable sort. My mother had highly developed the woman's gift of straight-seeing, practical intelligence which makes for direct action. She not only knew that she, like all girls, wanted a husband; she acknowledged it to herself and took steps to find one. There was no chance for her in the crowded east; competition was too sharp for the daughters of a poor family like hers. She would go west. A seamstress, she could always earn a living there or anywhere. She took one of her sisters, Emma, and they went to the easiest man-market in the world at that time, and there, in San Francisco, they promptly married two young men chums whom they met at their first boarding-house. They paired off, and each married the other's beau; otherwise it turned out just as these two wise maidens had planned. This on the authority of my father, who loved and laughed to tell it thus when my mother was there to hear; it annoyed and pleased her so. She was an amiable, teasable wife. He was a teasing, jesting father with a working theory that a fact is a joke.

My father was one of the sixteen or seventeen children of a pioneer farmer of eastern Canada, who drove west with his wife in a wagon to Illinois, where he bought, cleared, and worked his piece of wilderness, raised his big herd of tall boys and strong girls, and, finally, died in 1881, eighty-one years of age. He was a character, this grandfather of mine. I saw him once. My mother took me and my sister to visit him when we were very small, and I remember how, bent with age and brooding, he gradually looked up, saw us, said "Humph," and went back into himself and his silence. He came to life only one other time for me. I was looking at a duster made of horsehairs that was stuck in a knot-hole on a board fence. It looked just like a horse's tail, and I was peering through a crack to see the horse. My grandfather, watching me, said, "The horse was cut off the tail." I wondered, but he did not laugh, so I believed him.

Besides farming and breeding, my grandfather did some preaching, and when there was no regular teacher he taught the school. Also he raced horses and betted on them. Once, on a wager, he preached on the track between heats a sermon which was remembered long enough for me to hear of it. A favorite indoor winter sport of his was to gather the family around the fireplace and set my grandmother telling a story of some terrible night fight with the Indians. She described the approach of the savages so well that you felt the shivers creeping like Indians up your back, and at the attack, when the varmints broke out of the darkness with their tomahawks raised and ready, when the terror-stricken children turned to see the savages crash at them, a yell ripped the silence—my grandfather's. He chose the moment which he knew—which they all knew—"Mother" was working up to, and springing from his seat he shrieked, as he could shriek, the tearing war-whoop of the wild west. And my father said that though his father and mother played the game over and over, and always in the same way, so that the children not only knew what was going to happen, but were sure they could sit through it, the old folks collaborated so perfectly that, when the yell went up, they all were lifted by fright to their feet to fight, till the war-whoop turned into a laugh. It must have been thrilling; my father could not describe it without some of the old fear in his eyes, the terror which carried over to me, a little boy.

Because my father, the last child of the first "worn-out wife," was small and not strong, his father called him "the scrub" and told him that he probably would not live; and when he did live, the old man said that, anyhow, he was no use on a farm. He let him, therefore, do what he wanted to do: go to town, take a job in a store and courses in two commercial colleges. Working by day and studying at night, my father got his education and saved up enough money to go west. Horace Greeley had been preaching that to the young men of the east, but the old New York *Tribune* was read in the west also, and many a western boy grew up, as my father did, determined to go west.

My father traveled de luxe, for that day: on horseback. He joined a wagon train, led by Colonel Carter, and he and a chum of his, likewise mounted, served as scouts. They rode ahead or off on the flanks of the ox-and-horse train to look out for Indians.

They saw some. There were several skirmishes and one attack which became a pitched battle. When it was over, my father found his chum dead with an arrow in his breast. That arrow was kept along the front of a shelf in the bookcase of our home, and whenever it was referred to, my father would lay down his newspaper, describe that old fight, and show us the blood-stains on the arrow. If we would let him he would tell the whole tale of the long march across the plains, around the edge of the desert up through the Sierras, down into the Valley of the Sacramento River.

MY FATHER JOINED A WAGON TRAIN
From an old sketch by Theodore R. Davis, in *Harper's Weekly*

The overland approach is still an element in the overwhelming effect of a first impression of California. To me as a child, the State was the world as I knew it, and I pictured other States and countries as pretty much "like this." I never felt the warm, colorful force of the beauty of California until I had gone away and come back over my father's route: dull plains; hot, dry desert; the night of icy mountains; the dawning foothills breaking into the full day of sunshine in the valley; and last, the sunset through the Golden Gate. And I came to it by railroad, comfortably, swiftly. My father, who plodded and fought or worried the whole long hard way at oxen pace, always paused when he recalled how they turned over the summit and waded down, joyously, into the amazing golden sea of sunshine—he would pause, see it again as he saw it then, and say, "I saw that this was the place to live."

When the wagon train broke up and scattered, he went on to San Francisco. He was not seeking gold or land but a start in business, and in San Francisco he found it (Sept. 1862) as bookkeeper in the firm of Fuller and Heather, importers and dealers in paints, oils, and glass. That was his job when he married and I was born. But soon thereafter he was offered a quarter interest in a

SACRAMENTO IN 1851
From an old print

branch store which the firm was establishing in Sacramento. He went there, and that is where my conscious life began.

I can recall nothing of my infancy in San Francisco. My memory was born in Sacramento, where it centers around the houses we lived in. Of the first, in Second Street, I can call up only a few incidents, which I think I still can see, but which I may have constructed, in part at least, out of the family's stories of that time. I can see yet my mother with her two hands over her face, and several people gathering anxiously about her. A snowball had struck her in the eyes. It rarely snows in that part of California— once, perhaps, in four or five years—so that a snow fall would have excited those people, all from the east, and they would have rushed out of the house to play in the snow. This I infer from hearsay. But what I see now, and must have seen a bit of then, is my mother standing there in trouble. And the reason I am so sure I recall my own sight of her is that she looks pretty and girlish in this one memory. All my other mental pictures of her are older and—not a girl, not a woman, but just my mother, unchanging, unchangeable, mine as my hand was mine.

I think I see, as from a window, safe and without fear, a wild, long-horned steer, lassoed by three mounted vaqueros who spread out and held him till he was tied to a tree. No one else recollects this scene, but it might well have happened. Sacramento was a

"I THINK I SEE . . ."

center for ranches and mines. Lying in an angle of the Sacramento and the American Rivers, the town was the heart of the life, the trade, and the vice of the great valley of wheat and cattle ranches, of the placer mining of the foothills, of the steamboat traffic with San Francisco and, by the new railroad, with the world beyond. I remember seeing the mule teams ringing into town, trains of four or five huge, high wagons, hauled by from twelve to twenty and more belled mules and horses driven by one man, who sometimes walked, sometimes rode the saddled near wheel-horse. Cowboys, mostly Mexicans and called vaqueros, used to come shouting on bucking bunches of bronchos into town to mix with the teamsters, miners, and steamboat men in the drinking, gambling, girling, fighting, of those days. My infant mind was snapping wide-eyed shots of these rough scenes and coloring and completing them with pictures painted on my memory by the conversations I overheard.

I seem to have known of the gold strikes up in the mountains, of finding silver over the Range in Nevada, of men getting rich, or broke, or shot. I was kept away from this, of course, and I heard and saw it always darkly, under a shadow of disapproval. Other ideas and ideals were held up in the light for me. But secretly I was impatient to grow up and go out into that life, and meanwhile I played I was a teamster, a gun-playing, broncho-busting vaquero, or a hearty steamboat man, or a steamboat. I remember having a leaf from our dining-table on the floor, kneeling on it, and, taking hold of one end, jerking it backward over the carpet, tooting like a steamboat whistle. Three or four big chairs and all the small chairs in the house made me a mountain train of wagons and mules; a clothes line tied to the leader and strung through the other chairs was a rein which I could jerk just as the black-bearded teamsters did. And, of course, any chair is a horse for a boy who is a would-be vaquero.

Horses, real horses, played a leading part in my boyhood; I seem always to have wanted one. A chair would do on a rainy day, but at other times I preferred to escape into the street and ask drivers to "please, mister, gimme a ride." Sometimes they would. I was a pretty boy with lovely long blond curls. This I know well because it kept me from playing with the other fellows of my age. They jeered at my curls and called me a girl or a "sissy boy" and were surprised when I answered with a blow. They were taken off their guard by my attack, but they recovered and charged in mass upon me, sending me home scratched, bleeding, torn, to my mother, to beg her to cut my hair. She would not. My father had to do it. One day when the gang had caught me, thrown me down, and stuffed horse-droppings into my mouth, he privately promised me relief, and the next morning he took me downtown and had his barber cut off my curls, which he wrapped up in a paper as a gift for my mother. How she wept over them! How I rejoiced over them!

No more fighting by day, no more crying by night. The other boys accepted me as a regular fellow, but I got fewer free rides. I have no doubt the drivers liked my angelic locks. Anyway, before they were cut off, drivers used often to take me up in their seats with them and let me hold the reins back of where they held them and so drive real horses. My poor mother suffered so much from these disappearances that the sport was forbidden me: in vain. I went right on driving. I did it with a heavy sense of doing wrong, but I couldn't help going whenever a driver would take me. Once, when I was sitting alone holding the reins to let a team drink at a trough (the driver stood away off at the horses' heads), I saw my father come around the corner after me. I dropped the reins and climbed down off the wagon. My father took my hand and, without a word, led me home. There, at the door, my mother caught me up away from my stern father and, carrying me off into the parlor, laid me across her knees and gave me a spanking, my first. My mother! I had expected punishment, but from my father, not from her; I felt saved when she rescued me from him. And then she did it—hard.

This turned out to be one of the lasting sorrows, not of my life, but of hers. She told it many, many times. She said that my father stood at the door, watching her till she was done with me, and then he asked her why she did it.

"I did it," she said, "to keep you from doing it. You are so hard."

"But," he answered, "I wasn't going to spank him for that. He was having such a good time, he looked so proud up there on that old manure wagon, and when he saw me, he came right down, put his hand in mine, and came straight home, trembling with fear. I couldn't have spanked him. And you— Why did you do it? And why so hard?"

My mother cried more than I did at the time, and she always wept a little when she told it, explaining to the end of her days that she did it so hard just to show that he need not ever spank me, that she could do it quite enough. "And then," she'd break, "to think he wasn't going to do it at all!"

MY SAVAGE STAGE

THE world as I knew it in my angelic stage was a small yard, with a small house on one side of it and a wide, muddy street in front. The street was wonderful, the way to heaven. Astonishing things passed there, horses and wagons, for instance. It led in one direction to "the store," my father's place of business, where it was a rare privilege to go and be cheered and jeered at as the boss's boy. Across the street beyond some uninteresting houses was another street, called Front Street, which had houses only on one side. The other side was the reeling, rolling, yellow Sacramento River—a forbidden menace and a fascinating vision. That's where the steamboats plied, the great, big, flat-bottomed cargo and passenger boats, some with side wheels, some with one great stern wheel. I did not know, I did not care, where they went. It was enough that they floated by day and whistled by night safely on that dangerous muddy flood which, if it ever got a boy in its grip, would roll him under, drown him, and then let his body come up all white and still and small, miles and miles away.

But we moved from that Second Street house to a little larger one 'way over on H Street between Sixth and Seventh. A new and greater world. The outstanding features of it were the railroad, the slough, a vacant lot with four big fig trees, and school. The railroad had a switch line on the levee around the slough on Sixth Street, and I used to watch the freight cars shunted in there. I watched and I wondered where they came from. Unlike the steamboats those cars spoke to me of the world, the whole world. In my Second Street mind the steamboats just paddled up and down, as I did on my table-leaf; but those H Street trains of cars came from somewhere and they went somewhere. Where? I could not read, but sometimes those box cars came in covered with fresh snow, and snow was a marvel to me. All my picture books had snow scenes, sledding and skating, houses alight in the dark covered with glistening white. Not for me, any of this. The only snow I ever beheld I saw from my schoolroom window, far, far away on the mountain peaks. The snow-covered cars came, then, from over the mountains, 'way, 'way over, and I wanted to know

MY BOYHOOD AND SACRAMENTO'S

The above and the three following illustrations are taken from the *History of Sacramento County*, Thompson and West, Oakland, California, 1880

what was 'way, 'way over. They told me in scraps and I remember sitting by the railroad track, trying to construct the world beyond out of the scraps of information people threw me till I was called sharply to come home, and asked what in the world I was mooning there at those cars for. Grown-ups don't understand a fellow.

And they could not understand the fascination of that "filthy old slough, which ought to be filled up" (as it is now). To me it was a lonely place of mystery and adventure. Sometimes it was high with water, and I could hunt mud-hens with my "slingshot." Sometimes it was almost empty, and—sure it stank, but what of that?—I could play scouts and Indians with the other boys in the brush, dodging along the twisting trails made by the mechanics going to and from the railroad repair shops on the other side of the slough.

The lot with the fig trees was next door to us, and there I built a nest and finally a house up among the branches—my savage stage, which a kid has to claw and club his own way through, all alone, he and his tribe. And there, in our hand-made hut in the monkey-land of those fig trees, there I found out about sex.

Parents seem to have no recollection and no knowledge of how early the sex-life of a child begins. I was about six years old when I built that hut, which was a wigwam to me, a cache; it was a safe place in which to hide from and watch the world below. Small animals, birds, chickens, and sometimes people could be seen from it, and it was fascinating to observe them when they were unaware that I, a spy, an Indian, an army scout, could see all that they did. The trouble was that they never did anything much and I never did anything much. It was becoming a bore when one day a big boy—eight or nine years old—came along under my tree looking for figs. He saw my hut; he spied my two spying eyes.

"What ye think you're doing?" he demanded.

"Nothing," I answered.

He climbed up the tree, crept into my hut, looked it over, approving with his nodding head; then he looked at me. I shrank from that look. I didn't know why, but there was something queer in it, something ugly, alarming. He reassured me, and when I was quiet and fascinated, he began there in that dark, tight, hidden little hut to tell me and show me sex. It was perverse, impotent, exciting, dirty—it was horrible, and when we sneaked down into the nice, clean dust of the sunlit ground I ran away home. I felt so dirty and ashamed that I wanted to escape unseen to the bath-room, but my mother was in the living-room I had to pass through, and she smiled and touched me fondly. Horrid!

"Don't, oh, don't!" I cried, and I shrank away appalled.

"Why! What is the matter?" she asked, astonished and hurt.

"I dunno," I said, and I ran upstairs. Locking the bathroom door, I answered no calls or knocks. I washed my hands, my face, again and again till my father came home. His command to open I obeyed, but I would not let him touch me; and I would not, could not explain, and he, suspecting or respecting my trouble perhaps, let me off and protected me for a long period during which I could not bear to have my parents, my sisters—I would not let any one I loved touch me: all signs of affection recalled and meant something dirty, but fascinating, too. I could listen when the other boys (and girls) told one another about this dark mystery; I had to. It had the same lure that I felt in the hut that day. And I can remember a certain servant girl who taught me more, and vividly I can still see at times her hungry eyes, her panting, open mouth, and feel her creeping hands.

I do not remember what my first school taught me. Nothing like this, nothing of life. It was, at the beginning, a great adventure, then a duty, work, a bore that interfered with my boy's business. I can "see" now only the adventure. I was led to the schoolhouse by my mother, who must have known how I felt, the anxious confusion of stark dread and eager expectation that muddled me. She took me by the hand to the nearest corner. There I dismissed her; I must appear alone, like the other boys; and alone I trudged across the street up to the gate where I saw millions of boys playing as if nothing were happening. It was awful. Before I dived in I turned and I saw my mother standing, where I had left her, watching me. I don't remember that she made any sign, but I felt she would let me return to her. And I wanted to; how I wanted to! But I didn't. With more fear than I have ever since known, and therefore more courage than I have ever since had to rally, I walked into that Terror, right through that mob of wild, contemptuous, cruel, strange boys—grown-ups don't know how dangerous big boys are—I ran up the stairs and nearly fell, gasping, hot, but saved, into the schoolhouse. I cannot recall anything that happened there, only that we of the infant class were kept (probably to be registered) about an hour and that I came out and walked home with such a sense of victory and pride as I have never known since. I told everybody I met, even strangers, that "I've been to school."

I boasted my great boast all day and it was well received till, in the afternoon, after the "big classes let out," I repeated it to some big boys as a reason for letting me play ball with them.

"Yea," said the leader, "you bin to school, in the ABC class! Naw, ye can't play with us."

I have met that fellow since; everybody has. He is the killjoy that takes the romance out of life; he is the crusher that keeps us down on the flat; he is the superior person, as I well know. I have been that beast myself now and then. What makes us so?

And what makes grown-ups promise things to children and fail them? Charlie Prodger was the only man, except my father and Colonel Carter, who kept his word with me. He was something of a politician, and I was made to feel that there was something bad about a politician. I did not know what it was that was bad, but I did not care in the case of Charlie Prodger. I loved the sight of him coming dapper and handsome, smiling, toward me; and I had, and I have now, a deep, unreasoning respect for him. What grown-ups call good and bad are not what us boys call good and bad. Charlie Prodger was a good man to me then; he promised me a pair of stilts; other boys had them and could walk on them right through mud and water, over low fences and even up steps. Charlie Prodger did not say he would give me a pair; he was more wonderful than that. He said: "You'll get your stilts. Some day you'll find them on your front porch, and you'll never know where they came from." And sure enough, one day soon I found on the front porch the finest pair of stilts that any boy in our neighborhood ever had, and on them I climbed to heaven for a while—and for always to a belief in the word, not of all men, but of "bad" politicians like Charlie Prodger.

But Charlie Prodger never promised me a horse, and it was a horse I wanted, a pony. When he made good with the stilts I asked him to promise me a pony. I was sure that if I could get a promise out of him I'd get my pony. He laughed; he understood, but no, he said he could not give me a pony; so he would not give me the promise of one.

But there is another sort of fellow: the fellow that not only made promises and broke them, but probably never meant to keep them. A driver my father hired sometimes of a Sunday to drive us down Riverside Drive was, I thought, a great man and a good friend of mine. He let me sit up in the driver's seat with him and not only hold the reins behind his hands, but on a straight, safe piece of road he held behind and I held in front. One day he swung his whip at a pigeon, ringing it around the neck with his lash. That made a deep impression on me. He got down, wrung the bird's neck, and brought it to me. Poor pigeon! Yes. But I admired the driver's skill, and he boasted: "Huh, I can do it every time. I was a teamster in the mountains, and I got so I could snap a fly off the ear of my lead mule." No doubt he turned and winked at my fond parents, sitting in adult superiority on the back seat, but I saw nothing. I wanted and I asked my expert friend to catch me a pigeon—alive. He said he could; he said he would, but he didn't. He didn't on that drive, but he promised to on the next. He didn't. For years, I think, I asked that driver every time I saw him for my pigeon, and always he gave me, instead, a promise.

I must have pestered that poor, thoughtless liar, but the men I drove the hardest were those that I asked to give me a horse. And they were many, everybody that had anything to do with horses, and others besides—they all knew that I wanted a pony. My grandfather, Colonel Carter, my father, my father's partners, all received messages and, later, letters, asking for a pony; and most of them did not say they could not or would not give me one; most of them put me off with a promise. I had a stable of promises and I believed those promises. I rode those promises hard, once to a bad fall. One of my father's partners, who was coming from San Francisco on business, wrote that he was going to bring me either a velocipede or a pony—according as I chose the right one. Which did I want? I wrote that I preferred the pony, and when he came, he had nothing.

"You guessed wrong," he said. "I had no pony to give you. If you had chosen a velocipede—"

I stood there staring at him, and he laughed. He did not know the shock, the crushing agony that kept me still. I could not move. My mother had to pick me up and carry me to bed. I might have had a velocipede. I could use a velocipede. I could have made believe it was a horse, or a steamboat, or a locomotive, and it *was* a velocipede. My regret was a brooding sorrow, speechless, tearless, and that liar laughed.

A MISERABLE, MERRY CHRISTMAS

M Y FATHER'S business seems to have been one of slow but steady growth. He and his local partner, Llewelen Tozer, had no vices. They were devoted to their families and to "the store," which grew with the town, which, in turn, grew and changed with the State from a gambling, mining, and ranching community to one of farming, fruit-raising, and building. Immigration poured in, not gold-seekers now, but farmers, business men and home-builders, who settled, planted, reaped, and traded in the natural riches of the State, which prospered greatly, "making" the people who will tell you that they "made the State."

As the store made money and I was getting through the primary school, my father bought a lot uptown, at Sixteenth and K Streets, and built us a "big" house. It was off the line of the city's growth, but it was near a new grammar school for me and my sisters, who were coming along fast after me. This interested the family, not me. They were always talking about school; they had not had much of it themselves, and they thought they had missed something. My father used to write speeches, my mother verses, and their theory seems to have been that they had talents which a school would have brought to flower. They agreed, therefore, that their children's gifts should have all the schooling there was. My view, then, was that I had had a good deal of it already, and I was not interested at all. It interfered with my own business, with my own education.

And indeed I remember very little of the primary school. I learned to read, write, spell, and count, and reading was all right. I had a practical use for books, which I searched for ideas and parts to play with, characters to be, lives to live. The primary school was probably a good one, but I cannot remember learning anything except to read aloud "perfectly" from a teacher whom I adored and who was fond of me. She used to embrace me before the whole class and she favored me openly to the scandal of the other pupils, who called me "teacher's pet." Their scorn did not trouble me; I saw and I said that they envied me. I paid for her favor, however. When she married I had queer, unhappy feelings of resentment; I didn't want to meet her husband, and when I

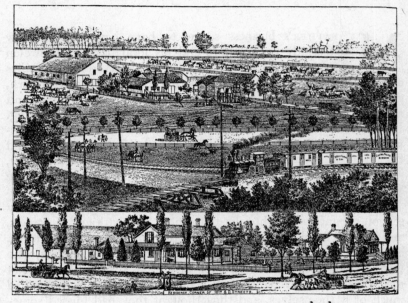

A TYPICAL SACRAMENTO RANCH IN THE '70'S

had to I wouldn't speak to him. He laughed, and she kissed me— happily for her, to me offensively. I never would see her again. Through with her, I fell in love immediately with Miss Kay, another grown young woman who wore glasses and had a fine, clear skin. I did not know her, I only saw her in the street, but once I followed her, found out where she lived, and used to pass her house, hoping to see her, and yet choking with embarrassment if I did. This fascination lasted for years; it was still a sort of super-romance to me when later I was "going with" another girl nearer my own age.

What interested me in our new neighborhood was not the school, nor the room I was to have in the house all to myself, but the stable which was built back of the house. My father let me direct the making of a stall, a little smaller than the other stalls, for my pony, and I prayed and hoped and my sister Lou believed that that meant that I would get the pony, perhaps for Christmas. I pointed out to her that there were three other stalls and no horses at all. This I said in order that she should answer it. She could not. My father, sounded, said that some day we might have horses and a cow; meanwhile a stable added to the value of a house. "Some day" is a pain to a boy who lives in and knows only "now." My good little sisters, to comfort me, remarked that Christmas was coming, but Christmas was always coming and grown-ups were always talking about it, asking you what you wanted and then giving you what they wanted you to have. Though everybody knew what I wanted, I told them all again. My mother knew that I told God, too, every night. I wanted a pony, and to make sure that they understood, I declared that I wanted nothing else.

"Nothing but a pony?" my father asked.

"Nothing," I said.

"Not even a pair of high boots?"

That was hard. I did want boots, but I stuck to the pony. "No, not even boots."

"Nor candy? There ought to be something to fill your stocking with, and Santa Claus can't put a pony into a stocking."

That was true, and he couldn't lead a pony down the chimney either. But no. "All I want is a pony," I said. "If I can't have a pony, give me nothing, nothing."

Now I had been looking myself for the pony I wanted, going to sales stables, inquiring of horsemen, and I had seen several that would do. My father let me "try" them. I tried so many ponies that I was learning fast to sit a horse. I chose several, but my father always found some fault with them. I was in despair. When Christmas was at hand I had given up all hope of a pony, and on Christmas Eve I hung up my stocking along with my sisters', of whom, by the way, I now had three. I haven't mentioned them or their coming because, you understand, they were girls, and girls, young girls, counted for nothing in my manly life. They did not mind me either; they were so happy that Christmas Eve that I caught some of their merriment. I speculated on what I'd get; I hung up the biggest stocking I had, and we all went reluctantly to bed to wait till morning. Not to sleep; not right away. We were told that we must not only sleep promptly, we must not wake up till seven-thirty the next morning—or if we did, we must not go to the fireplace for our Christmas. Impossible.

We did sleep that night, but we woke up at six A.M. We lay in our beds and debated through the open doors whether to obey till, say, half-past six. Then we bolted. I don't know who started it, but there was a rush. We all disobeyed; we raced to disobey and get first to the fireplace in the front room downstairs. And there they were, the gifts, all sorts of wonderful things, mixed-up piles of presents; only, as I disentangled the mess, I saw that my stocking was empty; it hung limp; not a thing in it; and under and around it—nothing. My sisters had knelt down, each by her pile of gifts; they were squealing with delight, till they looked up and saw me standing there in my nightgown with nothing. They left their piles to come to me and look with me at my empty place. Nothing. They felt my stocking: nothing.

I don't remember whether I cried at that moment, but my sisters did. They ran with me back to my bed, and there we all cried till I became indignant. That helped some. I got up, dressed, and driving my sisters away, I went alone out into the yard, down to the stable, and there, all by myself, I wept. My mother came out to me by and by; she found me in my pony stall, sobbing on the floor, and she tried to comfort me. But I heard my father outside; he had come part way with her, and she was having some sort of angry quarrel with him. She tried to comfort me; besought me to come to breakfast. I could not; I wanted no comfort and no breakfast. She left me and went on into the house with sharp words for my father.

I don't know what kind of a breakfast the family had. My sisters said it was "awful." They were ashamed to enjoy their own toys. They came to me, and I was rude. I ran away from them. I went around to the front of the house, sat down on the steps, and, the crying over, I ached. I was wronged, I was hurt—I can feel now what I felt then, and I am sure that if one could see the wounds upon our hearts, there would be found still upon mine a scar from that terrible Christmas morning. And my father, the

UPPER LEFT: "WHEN I WAS AN ANGEL." UPPER RIGHT: LENNIE
STEFFENS, AGED TWELVE. LOWER LEFT: JOSEPH STEFFENS, FATHER.
LOWER RIGHT: ELIZABETH LOUISE SYMES, MOTHER.

practical joker, he must have been hurt, too, a little. I saw him looking out of the window. He was watching me or something for an hour or two, drawing back the curtain never so little lest I catch him, but I saw his face, and I think I can see now the anxiety upon it, the worried impatience.

After—I don't know how long—surely an hour or two—I was brought to the climax of my agony by the sight of a man riding a pony down the street, a pony and a brand-new saddle; the most beautiful saddle I ever saw, and it was a boy's saddle; the man's feet were not in the stirrups; his legs were too long. The outfit was perfect; it was the realization of all my dreams, the answer to all my prayers. A fine new bridle, with a light curb bit. And the pony! As he drew near, I saw that the pony was really a small horse, what we called an Indian pony, a bay, with black mane and tail, and one white foot and a white star on his forehead. For such a horse as that I would have given, I could have forgiven, anything.

But the man, a disheveled fellow with a blackened eye and a fresh-cut face, came along, reading the numbers on the houses, and, as my hopes—my impossible hopes—rose, he looked at our door and passed by, he and the pony, and the saddle and the bridle. Too much. I fell upon the steps, and having wept before, I broke now into such a flood of tears that I was a floating wreck when I heard a voice.

"Say, kid," it said, "do you know a boy named Lennie Steffens?"

I looked up. It was the man on the pony, back again, at our horse block.

"Yes," I spluttered through my tears. "That's me."

"Well," he said, "then this is your horse. I've been looking all over for you and your house. Why don't you put your number where it can be seen?"

"Get down," I said, running out to him.

He went on saying something about "ought to have got here at seven o'clock; told me to bring the nag here and tie him to your post and leave him for you. But, hell, I got into a drunk—and a fight—and a hospital, and—"

"Get down," I said.

He got down, and he boosted me up to the saddle. He offered

to fit the stirrups to me, but I didn't want him to. I wanted to ride.

"What's the matter with you?" he said, angrily. "What you crying for? Don't you like the horse? He's a dandy, this horse. I know him of old. He's fine at cattle; he'll drive 'em alone."

I hardly heard, I could scarcely wait, but he persisted. He adjusted the stirrups, and then, finally, off I rode, slowly, at a walk, so happy, so thrilled, that I did not know what I was doing. I did not look back at the house or the man, I rode off up the street, taking note of everything—of the reins, of the pony's long mane, of the carved leather saddle. I had never seen anything so beautiful. And mine! I was going to ride up past Miss Kay's house. But I noticed on the horn of the saddle some stains like rain-drops, so I turned and trotted home, not to the house but to the stable. There was the family, father, mother, sisters, all working for me, all happy. They had been putting in place the tools of my new business: blankets, currycomb, brush, pitchfork—everything, and there was hay in the loft.

"What did you come back so soon for?" somebody asked. "Why didn't you go on riding?"

I pointed to the stains. "I wasn't going to get my new saddle rained on," I said. And my father laughed. "It isn't raining," he said. "Those are not rain-drops."

"They are tears," my mother gasped, and she gave my father a look which sent him off to the house. Worse still, my mother offered to wipe away the tears still running out of my eyes. I gave her such a look as she had given him, and she went off after my father, drying her own tears. My sisters remained and we all unsaddled the pony, put on his halter, led him to his stall, tied and fed him. It began really to rain; so all the rest of that memorable day we curried and combed that pony. The girls plaited his mane, forelock, and tail, while I pitchforked hay to him and curried and brushed, curried and brushed. For a change we brought him out to drink; we led him up and down, blanketed like a race-horse; we took turns at that. But the best, the most inexhaustible fun, was to clean him. When we went reluctantly to our midday Christmas dinner, we all smelt of horse, and my sisters had to wash their faces and hands. I was asked to, but I wouldn't, till my mother bade me look in the mirror. Then I washed up—quick. My face was caked with the muddy lines of tears that had coursed over my cheeks to my mouth. Having washed away that shame, I ate my dinner, and as I ate I grew hungrier and hungrier. It was my first meal that day, and as I filled up on the turkey and the stuffing, the cranberries and the pies, the fruit and the nuts—as I swelled, I could laugh. My mother said I still choked and sobbed now and then, but I laughed, too; I saw and enjoyed my sisters' presents till—I had to go out and attend to my pony, who was there, really and truly there, the promise, the beginning, of a happy double life. And—I went and looked to make sure—there was the saddle, too, and the bridle.

But that Christmas, which my father had planned so carefully, was it the best or the worst I ever knew? He often asked me that; I never could answer as a boy. I think now that it was both. It covered the whole distance from broken-hearted misery to bursting happiness—too fast. A grown-up could hardly have stood it.

A BOY ON HORSEBACK

M Y LIFE on horseback from the age of eight to fifteen was
a happy one, free, independent, full of romance, adventure, and learning, of a sort. Whether my father had any
theory about it or was moved only by my prayers I do not know.
But he did have some ideas. He took away my saddle, for example.
My mother protested that I had suffered enough, but he insisted
and he gave me reasons, some for himself, some for me. He said
I would be a better horseman if I learned to ride without stirrups
and a saddle-horn to keep my balance. The Indians all rode bareback, and the Comanches, the best horsemen on the plains, used
to attack, clinging out of sight to the far side of their horses and
shooting under their necks.

"We had to shoot a Comanche's horse to get the fellow," he said,
"and even then the devil would drop behind his dead pony and
shoot at us over the carcass."

I consented finally to having my beautiful saddle hung high in
the harness room until I could sit my horse securely. The result
was that I came to prefer to ride bareback and used the saddle
only for show or for games and work that needed stirrups and a
horn, as in picking up things off a box on the ground or handling
cattle (calves) with a rope.

That, however, was but one detail. I had begun about that time
to play boys' games: marbles, tops, baseball, football, and I can
see now my father stopping on his way home to watch us. He
used to wag his head; he said nothing to me, but I knew he did
not like those games. I think now that he thought there was some
gambling in them, and he had reason to dread gambling. It was a
vice that hung over from the mining days in California, and the
new business men were against it. They could not have it stopped

because "Frank" Rhodes, the political boss, was the keeper of a famous gambling-house; he protected business men, but also he protected his own business. They could not fight Frank too openly, but they lost money and they lost clerks and cashiers through the gambling hells. My father had had to discharge a favorite book-keeper on account of his heavy play at the gaming-tables. He may have given me the pony to keep me from gambling games or to get me up off the streets and out into the country. There was an-other result, however, which he did not foresee.

After that blessed pony loped into my life, I never played those trading games which, as I see them now, are the leads not merely to gambling but to business. For there goes on among boys an active trade in marbles, tops, knives, and all the other tools and properties of boyhood. A born trader finds himself in them, and the others learn to like to trade. My theory is that those games are the first lessons in business: they cultivate the instinct to beat the other fellows on 'Change and so quicken their predatory wits. Desirable or no, I never got that training; I never had any inter-est in, I have always had a distaste for, business, and this my father did not intend. I remember how disappointed he was later when he offered to stay in his business till I could succeed him and I rejected the "great opportunity" with quick scorn—"Busi-ness! Never."

My pony carried me away not only from business but from the herd also and the herding habits of mind. The tendency of the human animal to think what others think, say what the mob says, do what the leaders do or command, and, generally, go with the crowd, is drilled in deep at school, where the playground has its fashions, laws, customs and tyrannies just as Main Street has. I missed that. I never played "follow the leader," never submitted to the ideals and the discipline of the campus or, for that matter, of the faculty; and so, ever since, I have been able to buy stocks during a panic, sell when the public was buying; I could not al-ways face, but I could turn my back on, public opinion. I think I learned this when, as a boy on horseback, my interest was not in the campus; it was beyond it; and I was dependent upon, not the majority of boys, but myself and the small minority group that happened to have horses.

I began riding alone. When I mounted my pony the morning

after I got him I knew no other boys that had horses, and I did
not think of anybody else. I had a world before me. I felt lifted
up to another plane, with a wider range. I could explore regions I had not been able to reach on foot. Sacramento is protected
from high water in the rivers by levees which send the overflow
off to flood other counties. I had visited these levees on foot and
wondered what was beyond them. Now I could ride over them
and the bridges to—anywhere, I thought. The whole world was
open to me. I need not imagine it any more, I could go and see.

I was up early to water, feed, and clean the pony before breakfast. That meal, essential for the horse, was of no importance to
me. I slighted it. My father, cautioning me not to work a horse
till he had fed fully, said I had plenty of time to eat myself. But
I could not eat. I was too excited, too eager, and when I was
free to rise from the table I ran out to see if the pony was through
his breakfast. He wasn't. I watched him; he was in no hurry. I
urged him a bit, but he only lost time looking around at me
curiously, and then slowly resumed his meal. My sisters came
out to see me off, and one of them rebuked my impatience with a
crude imitation of a grown-up.

"The *pony* eats like a gentleman," she said, as if I cared about
gentlemen. Something my father had said hit me harder. He said
that teamsters, vaqueros, and Indians fed more and longer when
they were in a hurry to get off on a long, hard run than on other
days; they foresaw that they must be "fortified with food." It
took nerve, he admitted, to eat that way, but those fellows had
nerve. They could control their animals so perfectly because they
had self-control. They didn't force a horse, even in a pursuit.
They changed the gait often and went long stretches at a walk.
And they could shoot straight, especially in a fight or a battle, because they never became fidgety.

I didn't know it then, but I can see now, of course, that my father
was using my horse to educate me, and he had an advantage over
the school teachers; he was bringing me up to my own ideals; he
was teaching me the things my heroes knew and I wanted to learn.
My mother did not understand that. When she came out to the
stable, I was anticipating the end of the pony's meal by putting on
his saddle blanket and surcingle, and telling my sisters where I was
going.

"Don't ride too far the first day," she said. "You will get hungry and sore."

Awful! But I got away at last, and I rode—in all directions. Intending to do one levee that day, and the others in succession the next two days, I rode over them all that morning. I rode over the first one to the American River, and I was disappointed. The general character of the earth's surface did not change much even in that great distance and the change was for the worse—sand and muddy brush. I turned back and rode over the opposite levee, and I could hardly believe it—the land on the other side was like the land on this side. I rode into town again and went across the bridge over the Sacramento River to Yolo County, and that was not different. By that time I was hungry, very hungry, and I came home. Also I was a little hot and uncomfortable in the seat. I was late for lunch, but my mother had kept things warm for me, good things, and she did not ask me very bad questions. Where had I gone? I told her that. What had I seen? I could not tell her that. I had gone to the horizon and seen nothing new, but I did not know that myself well enough to report it to anybody else. Nor could I answer her inquiry for the cause of my depression. Only I denied that I was sore, as she suggested. No, no, not that. I had fed my horse and rubbed him down; when I had eaten I went out and watered and walked him. Then I cleaned him till my sisters came home, and then we all cleaned him.

The next day I was sore, so sore I could hardly sit or walk, but having lied about it, I had to prove it; so I rode off again, in pain, but bravely as a cowboy or an Indian taking torture; only I did not go far. I stopped, dismounted, and let my pony feed on some grass under the trees of East Park. I lay there, and no, I did not think; I imagined things. I imagined myself as all sorts of persons, a cowboy, a trapper, a soldier, a knight, a crusader—I fancied myself as the hero of every story I had read. Not all on this one day. From the day my pony came to me I seem to have spent many, many hours, playing around in my imagination, which became the most active faculty of my mind. For, as I say, I was alone much of the time. I learned to like to be alone, and that pleasure I come back to always, even now. When I am tired of the crowd I go off somewhere by myself and have a good time inside my mind.

As a boy I would ride far, far away to some spot, give my pony a long rope to swing round on, and let him feed on the grass, while I sat and did nothing but muse. I read a great deal. Finding that books fed my fancies, I would take one along, and finding a quiet nook, I read. And my reading always gave me something to be. I liked to change the hero I was to the same thing on horseback, and once wholly in the part, I would remount my pony and be Napoleon, or Richard the Lion-hearted, or Byron, so completely that any actual happening would wake me up dazed as from a dreaming sleep. Dream people lived or lay in wait for me in the brush across the river, so that the empty spaces beyond my old horizon, the levee, became not only interesting but fascinating with dread or glory, and populated with Persons.

"Hey, kid! Don't swim the river there. The rapids'll sweep you clean to San Francisco."

I looked up. It was the bridge-tender, the man that walked the trestle over the American River after every train to put out fires started on the dry sleepers by live coals dropped from the locomotives. I respected a man that filled a responsible place like his, but I slid into the water, swam along shore, came out, and dressed. I could not tell him that Byron swam the Hellespont, which was harder to do than to cross the American at that point; and I did not like to confess that I had a trap set on the other side where the Chinamen had their peanut farm and represented the Saracens to me. When I was dressed, the trestle-walker bade me meet him at the end of the trestle. I did, and a friendship was well started. He didn't scold me, he praised my swimming, but he said that the current was strong at that place and that it wasn't brave, it was foolish, to go in there. "A boy oughtn't to do what a man wouldn't do." He asked me some questions, my name, age, where I lived, where my father's business was. He felt over and approved my pony. I asked him how he could walk so fast on the trestle, having no planks to go on, and stepping from one sleeper to the other.

"Oh," he said, "I can walk 'em fast now because I walked 'em slow at first."

I wanted to try. He took my hand and made me walk slowly, one by one, until I was over my nervousness. When I could do it alone, he invited me to his watchman's cabin, about one-third of the way across. I went, he following. When we reached his little house we sat down, and we had, man to man, a nice, long talk, which became so confidential that I trusted him with the information that I was a trapper and had my traps set for beavers all up and down the river. And my faith was not misplaced. He didn't say that there were no beavers in that river; we both knew there weren't, and we both knew that that didn't matter. All he said was that he was a gold miner himself—and expected to strike it rich some day.

"I don't work at it much," he admitted. "Mostly I tend bridge. But in between trains, when I ain't got a thing to do, I think about it. I think how I came west to find a fat claim and work it and get rich, so I write home that that's what I'm doing, prospectin', and I am, too, and sometimes I play I have struck it and I go home and I spend my money."

After that I caught more beavers, and he and I spent my profits my way. Yes, and after that he struck it richer than ever, and him and me, we went back east and we just blew in his money his way. It was fun. I got a bad name from this. There were grown-ups who said I was a "fearful liar," and no doubt I was unconvincing sometimes. My father asked me questions, and I told him about my bridge-tender. I said that my bridge-tender could run as fast as a train on the trestle, and my father gave me a talking-to for telling such a whopper. I felt so bad about it that I told the bridge-tender.

He thought a moment and then he said, "The next time your father is to take a train out this way, tell me, and tell him to be on the rear platform."

The next time my father was to take a train that crossed the trestle, I told him what to do, and I went out to my bridge-tender. He climbed down off the trestle, disappeared into the brush, and came back with a few ripe cantaloupes. We waited till the train came. Now trains had to go slow on that trestle, and as the locomotive passed, the bridge-tender held up a melon to the engineer and said something about "easy does it." So when the train passed, the bridge-tender jumped out after it and ran and ran; and he caught up to the rear car and he handed that melon to my father, who waved to him and then took off his hat to me.

The bridge-tender and me, we were awful proud. We talked about it and laughed. "That'll fix him," the bridge-tender said, and he wished we could get just one beaver to show 'em. "I'd give good money if I could buy one somewheres."

But I had no trouble about the beavers. Men scoffed, and some boys did at first, but I soon had all my crowd setting and watching traps in the river. And we had a war, too. There was that peanut farm run by the Chinamen who were Turks and Saracens. We boys were crusaders, knights. So when we used to swim over to steal the peanuts, we either got peanuts, which were good, or we had a battle with the Saracens, which was better. They came at us with clods of earth, which they threw. We fired back, and when they came too near we dived into the river, and ducking and diving, swam home to the Christian shore.

My crowd was small and of very slow growth. They were all fellows I met on horseback, an odd lot. First—and last—there was Hjalmar Bergman, a Swedish boy. His father, a potter, and his mother lived in a hut out on the outskirts of the town; they spoke no English and were very poor. Hjalmar had a horse because his father, who had received it in payment of a debt, had no use for it. Black Bess, as I renamed her, was a big mare, high spirited, but well trained in the cattle game. Whenever any dangerous work had to be done the vaqueros would borrow Black Bess, and we boys would go with her and see the fun. Jake Short, who was the best cowboy in town those days, knew Bess well; and she knew him or his business. Once there was a "loco" (mad) steer in a field that had to be shot. We sat on the fence and watched Jake ride out on Bess with his big Colt revolver ready. When Bess caught sight of the steer coming head down at them, she halted, braced herself, and stood fast, moving only to keep facing the crazy beef. Jake dropped the reins, settled his hips to the left in his saddle, and leaned far forward on the right side. The steer came madly on till he was within ten feet of them; then Jake fired and Black Bess leaped bodily to the left, letting the steer fall upon the spot where she had stood. Jake jumped down and finished the steer, and there stood Bess just where he had left her.

"That's what I call a hoss," he said to Hjalmar, and I was proud. Bess was Hjalmar's hoss, but she was in our crowd.

There were other boys with horses, all sorts of boys and all sorts of horses, but mostly they were boys and horses that belonged in one way or another to the cattle and the butchering business. Will

Cluness, the doctor's son, had a pony "just to ride," but he didn't go with us much; he preferred marbles, tops, and the other games on the ground. I invented or adapted games to horse play; Will liked some of them. Hide-and-seek, for example. We found a long, straight stretch of road in old East Park, with paths and brush and trees beside it. There, at the end of a run of, say, an eighth of a mile, we drew a line across the road. The boy who was "it" held his horse on the line while the rest of us scattered into the woods. "It" called out now and then—"Ready?"—until there was no answer; then he rode where he thought we might be. He took care to keep behind him a clear run to the home line, but he had to hunt for us or the sight of us on our horses. Our game was to ride out of sight around him and make a dash for home. If he saw one of us or a horse he recognized he shouted the rider's name, pointed, and, turning, ran his horse for home base. The named rider would start at the same instant, and there was a race.

The horses soon learned this game and would start for home so suddenly at the sight of "it" that their boy was sometimes left behind. I was hiding under a tree one day when my pony saw the white horse of Ernie Southworth, who was "it"; he leaped forward, banging me against a limb of the tree; I clutched the limb, and the pony darted out of the woods, met "it" on the road, raced him, and won. We had a dispute whether the rider had to be on his horse at the finish, and it happened so often that the horse came in alone that we made a rule: a horse, with or without his rider, won or lost the race.

But Will soon tired of this and our other games. He could not fight Saracens that were really only Chinamen, and he held it in great contempt to set traps for beavers that did not exist. There were other boys like that. They were realists, I would say now; practical men. I learned to play with such boys, too, but I preferred the fellows that were able to help create a world of our own and live in it.

I took men into my crowd, too; especially horsemen. The other fellows did not; they said that grown-ups laughed at and spoiled every game. And that was true in the main. But I knew men like the bridge-tender who could play, and there was Jake Stortz, a German who lived and had his barn on the block back of my stable. Jake had the city street-cleaning contract, and he was a fireman and a truck-man. He had lots of horses. His wife, a bare-footed peasant woman, took care of the horses, and she and Jake were my advisers in the care, feeding, and handling of my pony. Jake let me be a fireman. He put a bit on my pony's halter, as he did on one of his own horses, arranged it so that you could with one movement snap it into the horse's mouth, untie, clear, mount him bareback, and so start for a fire the moment the whistle blew. At first I had to ride to the fire with Jake, and he would not wait a second for me, but I soon learned the signals and where to head for. I beat Jake to the fire sometimes, and the firemen knew it. "Where's Jake?" they'd call to me when I dashed up alone.

The first time there was a fire when I was at the dinner table, I upset my chair and frightened the whole family, but I got out and away so fast that nobody could say a word till I came home an hour or so later. Then I had to explain; my father spoke to Jake, and there was no trouble. I could go to fires any time except when I was in school or in bed, and my mother made me a fireman's red shirt.

But there was some unnecessary trouble about a stallion. Mrs. Stortz, who had charge of all the breeding of their animals, took me into all the technique of having colts. I held the mare while she steered the stallion. It was difficult work. The stallion got excited; he never wanted to wait till the mare was ready, and Mrs. Stortz had to hold him off. If the mare was restive and kicked, I had to hang on and make her stand. But we did this so often that we soon had it all down pat. And I had to "watch out" when the foal was due. Mrs. Stortz was responsible but busy, so I had to help; keep my eye on the mare who was left in the pasture field, with instructions to call her at the first sign of the birth.

One day as I was riding out on my pony I saw a mare down and the colt half out, and I couldn't make Mrs. Stortz hear. I let my pony go home; I ran to the mare, and she seemed to have given up. I patted her head, urged her to try again, and then ran and myself pulled out the baby horse. I did it all alone. Meanwhile I had been calling, "Mrs. Stortz, Mrs. Stortz." She came, and when she saw that all was well, she kissed me. And she told Jake and everybody. Jake was so glad. He said that that colt was to be the best horse he ever had and he'd name him after me. And he did. And I watched my colt grow with great impatience. Which was all

all right. My father heard of it, and he spoke of it, but while there was some doubt about something—he wagged his head over it— he did not forbid anything. A couple of years later he came home with a handbill in his hand, and he was very angry. I didn't see why. I had seen the bill myself; it was posted up on Jake's barn; I had one in our stable; and it was in every blacksmith's shop and at the race track. It carried a picture of my colt, full grown and with my name. It was an announcement that "this splendid, high-bred stallion Lennie S. would stand the season for all mares at $50 a throw." My father had a talk with Jake and the handbills were all called in; another bill, with the same horse and the same price, but another name, was put out.

THE SPORTING AGE

THE range a horse gives a boy is wide enough—for a while. I was content—for a while—with the ground I could cover in half a day's riding on a Saturday and from three till six on a school day. If I left home promptly after breakfast on a no-school day and right after school on the other days, I could see a good deal of the world. When I had seen all within that circle I had to repeat; intensive exploration was the result. I discovered then the race track.

The county fair grounds were not far away from our house. I had gone there with my father afoot to see the cattle parades and watch the races. Between the fairs there seemed to be nothing doing. I speeded my pony a quarter of a mile on the fine, but deserted, track—and it was fun to play I was a jockey, ride like one all bent over, and then walk my victorious racer down the stretch before the grandstand, which I refilled with a cheering crowd.

One morning, when I turned in there early, I found out that the fair grounds were not deserted. A string of race horses was being exercised, blanketed, by grooms and jockeys. I tagged on behind. Some of them hooted at me, called me a "kid," and ordered me to keep away. One of them, a colored boy called Smoke, riding the last of the string, turned his head and told me not to listen to them. I listened to him, and when the others bade me again to "sneak," he answered them.

"Ah, leave him be," he said.

On the back stretch I rode up beside him, and he explained that there were some stables open all year round on the fair grounds and that more would soon be arriving to train. I might come to his stable whenever I wanted to.

34

"You jes' as' for Smoke," he said, "say ye're a pal o' mine, an' that'll be enough an' a plenty."

I accepted Smoke's hospitality often after that. The other boys soon were used to me—even the trainers spoke to me. One trainer saw a use for me. Smaller and lighter than any of the jockeys and able to stick a horse without a saddle, he asked me to ride a trotter of his. I was delighted; it was a way to get inside. He brought out his big, fast mare, blanketed and bitted, tossed me up on her back, and ordered me harshly to "trot her a mile, just as hard as she'll trot. And, mind this now, kid," he added like a threat, "don't you let her break. See?"

I did it. I lay 'way back on the small of my back, lifted my knees, and so, balancing with all my weight and strength on the reins, put that heavy trotter around the mile in good time. Fine—for the trotter; for all trotters, and especially for colts. No weight, no harness, as free as in the pasture, and yet held down to a trot. And no wages to pay. Other trainers took me on. It was hard on me; some of the horses were heavy-gaited; they shook me pretty badly, but I could not complain, could I?

STEFFENS, JOSEPH, merchant, Sacramento; was born in York township, Upper Canada, January 15, 1837; his parents removed to Carroll county, Illinois, arriving in May, 1840, where his father, stepmother and two children still reside; he was deemed physically weak, and at the age of nineteen was by his parents advised to leave the farm, attend the Rock River Seminary, Ogle county, Illinois, and Bell's Commercial College, Chicago, to prepare for a mercantile life. After leaving those institutions, and teaching school two or three terms, in 1859 he engaged with G. M. Clayton & Bro., paints and oils, Freeport, Illinois, at $20 per month, where he remained three years. In the summer of 1862 he crossed the Plains, with Levi Carter, now of Stockton, arriving in Sacramento and San Francisco September 9. The last of the same month he secured the position of bookkeeper with Fuller & Heather, paints and oils, San Francisco, at $50 per month; remained with them until the house consolidated with that of Cameron, Whittier & Co., same business, in 1869, under the name of Whittier, Fuller & Co. After one year there he came, in February, 1870, to Sacramento, to take charge of the firm's branch here. He was admitted as partner in this firm in January, 1874, being still a partner in the Sacramento house. January 15, 1865, at San Francisco, he married Miss E. Louisa Symes, of Hoboken, New Jersey, who arrived in that city by the "Moses Taylor" November 27, 1862. They have four children— Joseph Lincoln, born in San Francisco, April 6, 1866; Lulu, in same city, August 24, 1868; Lottie, born in Sacramento, October 26, 1872, and Laura, in same place, June 18, 1874. Store, Orleans Building; residence, southeast corner Sixteenth and K streets.

MY FATHER'S "WHO'S WHO"

Smoke said it was an imposition, and the other jockeys called me a fool of a kid. But the trainers told me that if I kept small, ate little, and worked hard, I might become a jockey some day.

Being a jockey became what being a knight or a poet or a vaquero used to be. I worked hard. I used to do four and five miles a day on four or five horses. I studied and adopted the language, manners, and stubby gait of the jockeys, and I made my way; I was rising fast in racing circles. There was some trouble sometimes at home. I did not eat at all at some meals; others were modified fasts, and—I was hungry. My mother was worried. She couldn't make out what the matter was and appealed to my father, who, as was his wont, eyed me, wagged his head, and said nothing for a week or so. He saw me break my fast now and then, eat ravenously, and, filled up for once, resume my "training." At last he took me aside and spoke.

"What are you trying to do?" he asked. "Fast? I see you refuse all your food, then break down and eat like a pig. That isn't the way to fast, you know. The way to fast is to eat nothing—and that is all right. But what's it all about?"

I told him all about what it was all about: how I was the best bareback rider of fast trotters on the turf and had a great future before me, if I could keep down my weight, as a jockey. He heard me out, asked a few questions: the names of my stables, of the trainers, and of my favorite jockey, Smoke.

"All right," he said. "If you are going in for racing, do it well. But the way to keep down your weight is not to eat nothing, but to diet, taking moderately of plain, simple foods; no sweets, no fats, none of the heavy dough-like things you have always eaten too much of. I'll help you choose and limit your foods, and you tell me from time to time how you are getting on at the track."

That ended my troubles at home. My mother fretted some; not much; a look from my father saved me from eating even the cakes that she made to tempt me. And, as always, she helped adjust my clothes to my new occupation. She changed the fireman's shirt she had made me for the fires to a close, high-necked jockey's shirt, and had high heels put on one pair of shoes. I was a jockey at home, and at the track I was an institution, and not only as a rider and trainer of trotters.

I went to all the races, of course. They let me in, free, at the stable entrance. I used to be sorry for my father and friends, who had to leave me there and go on themselves by the ordinary gate for the public and then sit on the grandstand, while I had the run of the paddocks, the stretch, and the betting-ring. But these were places for between heats. When the horses went up the stretch to start, I climbed up to my post, one of the pillars that held up the grandstand, the one directly opposite the judges' stand, to which the wire was fixed. There, in an angle formed by the pillar and one of its braces, I sat and had the best view of the track on the whole course. It was better than the judges'. I could see as well as they which horse passed first under the wire. The gamblers and touts soon saw that; they knew that I knew the rules, the horses, the jockeys, and so, when it was a close heat and the judges were consulting, the horsemen would call up to me for the result.

"Hey, kid, who takes the money?"

And, promptly and certainly, I would tell them and, climbing down, run off up the track to watch the grooms strip, scrape, sponge, and blanket the horses. Racing was to me what I had heard it called, the Sport of Kings and the King of Sports. I idealized it as I idealized everything, and consequently I had my tragedy of disillusionment—as always—young.

Being in with the stables, I soon began to hear about "fixed races." What were fixed races? The first answer was a laugh, a chorus of hoots from the jockeys. "Say, the kid wants to know what a fixed race is!" I was hurt. Smoke may have seen my humiliation; he came up to me and said, "Never you mind, kid, I'll tell you some day."

"Yes, he will," said another boy. "He knows all right."

And another said: "A fixed race, kid, is a good thing. That is when we get ours, see?"

It was Smoke who explained it to me: that usually at every "meet" there were some races prearranged to have an unexpected horse win over the favorite. Since they, the jockeys, grooms, trainers, and owners, were all betters, they could make "big killings" when they were "in on the know" of a fixed race. Sometimes one crowd knew, sometimes another, and sometimes everybody got in, and then—sometimes—the "fix" was "unfixed" at the last moment and "everybody lost" but the owner, trainer, and jockey.

I didn't bet. I had no wages, and therefore I had no compensation for the heartbreak of this information. I had only the suffering due to the crash of my faith. It was sad to see a rider I knew and liked hold back a favorite that I loved and knew could win. I could cry—I did feel tears in my eyes whenever such a thing happened.

Smoke took it the way I did, and yet one day he told me he had to pull the horse he was to ride, a gelding that the nigger had talked so much about that we both adored the animal. He was a "sure thing," this horse, young, but a coming favorite. All the stables knew that, and they knew how Smoke could get the best out of him. When Smoke told me the stable had sold out this horse he smiled. I was sorry for the horse and ashamed for Smoke. I looked away till I heard Smoke say, "Well, anyway, I've put up a pile of money on the race, all I've got, all I could beg, borrow, or steal."

From my post under the wire I watched that race, and having been "put wise," I saw Smoke pull the horse. He had to. That horse had the habit of winning, and he meant to win again. It became almost a fight between the horse and the jockey. I was afraid others—maybe the judges—would see what Smoke was doing. He got a bad start, which the horse made up on the outside of the first turn, when he took the lead and held it, going slow, all along the back stretch. The quarrel broke out on the far turn. The horse's head flew up twice as if to catch and take the bit, but Smoke kept it and at the beginning of the home stretch he was riding in the ruck. There his horse broke free for a moment and sailed up, easy, to the leaders, only Smoke had him inside against the rail and he couldn't get through. And when he moved out to go around, it was too late. With Smoke holding him hard he could not go, and under the wire he was third. The horse fixed to win was first.

I didn't want to go up the track to see the horses after that race. I sat still, and I saw our favorite come back, champing and angry, I thought, and dazed, to the judges' stand. When Smoke raised the butt of his whip to the judges and got his bid to dismount and came up to be weighed, he jumped down and, do you know, his horse turned his head and looked at him? It was just one glance, and I noticed that Smoke did not return it; he turned his back and ran with his saddle and all up to be weighed. He was ashamed before the horse. And the horse was ashamed, I was sure, before the crowd. He went home, head down, champing, and when the grooms started to rub him down, he kicked at them.

After a while, when I could, I went back to the stables to find Smoke. He was nowhere in sight, but a hostler, seeing what I was up to, winked and tossed his head over toward the rear; and there back of the stables was Smoke, crying.

"It's all right," he blubbered when I came up to him. "It's good business for white folks, an' a nigger don't matter, but—de hoss! A hoss is a gen'leman, kid. It hurts him to lose a race, it breaks him —permanent—to sell a race. You ought to 'a' seen de look he done give me when I got down off'n him. I had to sneak out o' his sight, and I don't see how I kin ever look 'im in de face again."

I began to lose interest in the race track. Racing wasn't what it was cracked up to be, and the bridge-tender, whom I consulted, could not help me much.

"You mustn't feel so bad about things," he said when he had heard the whole story. "The nigger was all right, as men go, and, as he said, the horse is a gentleman. There's something to hang on to in racing, as in everything. This railroad, for instance. It's a crook in politics, but—there's some of us keeps it going straight enough to carry freight and passengers."

He went on to tell me a lot about "the road" and life that I did not understand. All I gathered was that nothing is as it seems, but it's all right somehow. He put the blame on what he called "the suckers": the outsiders that bought stock in the road and bet on the races—blind.

My father noticed that I was cold on the track; I ate all sorts of food and talked of other things. I did not go to the races, except now and then when he took me, and finally I would not go even with him. The reason for this was that the last time I went with him and some of his business friends, he and they were suckers. I left them in the grandstand, went down to the stables, and the boys told me that the principal event of the day was a fixed race, and how, and who was to beat the favorite. Returning to my father's party, I found them betting on the favorite. I felt like warning them, but they thought they knew all about the horses, their records, their pedigrees, owners, jockeys—everything. They were sure the favorite would win. I waited therefore till the horses were started and the books closed. Then I told them which horse would win. They seemed not to hear me, but they remembered when my horse came in first. They turned on me and asked me how I had guessed it. I answered them as I heard a jockey answer such a question once.

"Well, not by pedigree and performance."

"Why didn't you tell us?" they demanded.

"I dunno," I said. I could not tell them that it was because they were suckers and that I did not care for suckers, only niggers, horses, and other gentlemen, like the bridge-tender. My father was angry or thoughtful; he waited till we were alone at home, and then to his questions I answered with the truth, not only about that race, but racing: the whole story of my experience on the track. He did not say much. He just sat there and thought. He often did that: just sat and brooded. I remember how it used to trouble my mother, those long silences. This time he was only an hour or two. I had to go to bed, but when I was almost asleep, he came up, sat on the edge of my bed, and said: "I wouldn't give up racing entirely, if I were you. Horse racing is a fine sport, but bad men get into it as they do in other things, and they try to spoil it all. But they can't spoil it if we who play fair do our part. We have bad men in business, too, but business is all right. No. Drop in on the track once in a while. Don't overdo it, as you did; don't be a jockey, but go on and know all about horses."

This advice struck me as man to man. I took it. I did not go to the races often, but I did go to the track now and then till two incidents came together to me. One morning as I was riding a trotter, my knee breeches worked down, leaving the lower part of my body free, and, as it bobbed up and down with the horse's hard trot, I had a most delicious local sensation, so entrancing that I loosed the reins, relaxed all my muscles, and rolled off the horse, which broke and ran, leaving me on the back stretch. I was not hurt. I was bewildered, and, bewildered, I walked across the fields to the stables. There the trainers and jockeys gathered around me, demanding angrily why the deuce I had turned the horse loose that way. I tried to tell them what had happened, and, after some moments of puzzling, somebody seemed to understand. I didn't, but the crowd passed some key-word that unlocked their minds and their mouths. They burst into a queer sort of jeering laughter, slapped their thighs, and hooted—all but the trainer of the horse. He flew into a rage. "No more of that on my horse," he declared, and the other trainers agreed that I couldn't be trusted to exercise trotters any more. I was a joke. I slunk off on my pony, humiliated and perplexed.

And then came the fall of Smoke. He was the only jockey who did not laugh at the sight of me. He never referred to my humiliation. Smoke had troubles of his own, and shame, too. It seems that he had pulled his horse that day so well that he was called an expert at losing a race and was put up on other favorites to keep them from winning. He who hated it most had to do it most. He came under suspicion, was watched, caught, and ruled off the track.

Poor Smoke! He came to my stable to tell me about it. A little fellow, no bigger than I was, he could not understand. "White folks ain't fair," he said. They told him to pull their horses. They had influence. Any one of them could have gone to the front for him and got him off with a fine. They wouldn't do it. Not a man would speak up for him. "Didn't want to get mixed up into it." No. They asked Smoke not to give them away, and he didn't; and it was partly because he would not confess and betray his stable that he lost his license.

Smoke disappeared. I never saw him again. But my father saw me right after Smoke told me his story. I was sitting on the fence back of the stable, looking into the alley, thinking.

"What are you doing there?" my father asked me gently. "Your mother says you have been sitting up there for an hour or two."

"I was just a-thinking," I said.

"What about?" he asked.

"Smoke was here today," I said. "He's fired off the track."

"For pulling his horse?"

"For doing what his trainer told him to do."

My father stood there, and he thought too. Neither of us said a word. We just thought and thought till my mother called us to supper.

"What's the matter with you two?" she asked.

"Oh, nothing," I answered, and my father backed me up.

"Nothing much," he said, and my mother turned upon me sharply.

"Don't you be like your father," she said. "Don't think, and think, and think—nothing."

A PAINTER AND A PAGE

MY FATHER brought home to dinner one Sunday a painter, W. M. Marple, an artist from "the City," as we called San Francisco. I was excited. I had read about the famous painters; art was one way of being great; and I had been taken to the Crocker Art Gallery in Sacramento. All very interesting, but there was some mystery about pictures. Those that I liked best were scenes in mining-camps or on ranches and, generally, from the life about me. I could not discover anything very great in them. It seemed to me that they weren't even true; they didn't see things as I saw them. It was evident that in art, as in everything else, there was something to learn. And this visiting artist was my chance to learn it.

"I can't tell you anything about art," he said when I put to him at table my eager questions. "Nobody can. But I can show you."

He proposed after dinner to go out and make some sketches. He meant that he was going to paint a picture! And I could watch him at it! Where? What was there to paint in Sacramento? I guessed that he would paint the Capitol; that was the greatest thing in town. But no, I had a triumph, but it was not on my guess of the Capitol.

My father, mother, and others always wondered why I spent so much time over on the American River bottom: a washed-out place, where no one else ever went. Why not ride in the streets or the good country roads? I could not explain very well. The river bottom was all gravel and sand, cut up by the seasonal floods and left raw and bare of all but dead, muddied brush and trees. I remembered how it disappointed me the first time I saw it, the day I rode over there on my new pony. Since then I had filled it up with Indians, Turks, beavers, and wild beasts and made it a beautiful scene of romance and adventure. But I could not tell everybody that! I was ashamed of my taste in natural scenery.

And yet that was Mr. Marple's choice. He asked my father to take him there. He said he had passed by it on a train one afternoon and had seen something he wanted to paint. To my father's astonishment and mine, we had to lead the great painter to my playground. I was the guide, of course, a troubled, but a very proud leader; I could not think myself what Mr. Marple would like to see and paint there. A hole, where I swam because the water was warm, did not suit him. He pushed on deeper into the brush and, forgetting us in a most fascinating way, he moved about, here, there, till, satisfied at last, he unpacked his stuff, set up his easel, put a small square of boarded canvas on it, and went to work without a word.

How I watched! His first movements I could imitate, and I did, to the bridge-tender the next day. That painter looked at the scene in which I could see nothing to paint; nothing; just brush, miles and miles of mud-stained brush and leafless, drowned scrub willows. He studied this with one eye, held up the handle of his brush, and measured something which he dabbed off on his canvas. Then he looked some more, long, hard, while he pinched paints in little piles on his already mixed-up board of many colors. What was he doing? I asked. "Getting the colors right," he said, and with that, he began suddenly to paint. Fast. I lost track of what he was doing, though I did not take my eyes off that easel and the scene. I could not make out what was going on. Whatever it was, he was quick about it, so quick that in a very few minutes he had the whole canvas covered, and then, as he stepped back and I looked, suddenly it became a picture, a picture of the scene; only—

"What is it?" I asked him.

"Oh, the name of it when the sketch is painted," he said, "will be, say, 'A sunset.'"

Yes, that was right. The sun was burning a golden hole in the top line of the brush and the brush under and around the hole was gold, too, old gold; the whole was a golden picture. But— He was looking at it himself, squinting, with his head on one side, then on the other; he touched it here, there, and finally, backing far away, he said, "Not so bad, eh? Not bad."

It was beautiful, I thought, but it wasn't good; it wasn't true. It was bad of the brush; it wasn't brush at all. And I said as much. He laughed, and he answered me with a saying I never forgot.

"You see the brush and the baked mud. All right. They are there. Many things are there, and everybody sees what he likes in this and in every other scene. I see the colors and the light, the beautiful chord of the colors and the light."

Now I did not see the brush either; it was not the baked mud that made me come and play over there; and I told him so. I admitted that I had seen that the first time I rode out there, but after that—after that—

"Well," he encouraged me, "what did you see after that?"

I was caught. I owned up to the Indians, Saracens, elephants, and—he did not laugh. My father did; not the painter. Mr. Marple said that if I were an artist, I should paint Indians or wild animals—"You should paint a princess in the brush if you see her there." I could understand that.

"But your golden light is really there," I said, "and my Indians aren't."

"Your Indians are where my gold is," he answered, "where all beauty is, in our heads. We all paint what we see, as we should. The artist's gift is to see the beauty in everything, and his job is to make others see it. I show you the gold, you show me the romance in the brush. We are both artists, each in his line."

My father bought that picture, and my mother arranged to have me take drawing lessons. I was going to be a great painter for a while and fill the American River bottom with—what I saw there. But my drawing teacher did not teach me the way Mr. Marple did; I could not learn to copy other drawings; all I ever did that was called good was a group of horses' heads. My mother held me to it; she made me take drawing lessons as she made me take music lessons long after I had lost all desire and interest in them. That was her guiding principle of education: that her children were to have a chance at everything; no talent was to be overlooked in us. None.

The proper fruit of Mr. Marple's visit was of another, a similar sort. I was to have a lesson, not in drawing, but in seeing. Mr. Marple's son, Charlie, came to live with us. Maybe that was the purpose of the painter's visit. Anyway, after him came Mrs.

Marple, and from her I learned that her son, a boy a little older than I was, had a promise of an appointment to be a page at the next session of the Legislature. She was looking for a place for him to live, a house where he would be cared for. "Would I like a playmate?"

Would I? I was delighted. I could show him all the places I knew, and he could show me the Legislature. But what was a page? There were pages in my books; they were little boys at court or in the service of knights and ladies. But a page in a Legislature, what was that? A messenger, they said, a boy that carried bills and letters and notes from one member to another on the floor of the House or Senate. I became interested in the Capitol, the Legislature, the government. I read up on, I asked everybody questions about these things, I visited the Capitol, and as always with me, I formed some sort of picture of the machinery of government. Yes, and I had made in my mind also a portrait of Charlie Marple, made it up out of what I had read of stories and pictures of pages at court.

When Charlie came he was no more like my picture than his father's sketch was like my river bottom, and as for the Legislature . . . Charlie was a homely fellow—and weak, physically—not graceful and pretty, and he wasn't so eager for politics as he was to use my pony. He had been told about that; he had been looking forward to riding it; and when we went together out to the stable, his expectations were satisfied. He put his hand cautiously on the pony's rump, and the face he turned to me was alight with pleasure.

"But," he said, "I can't ride; never was on a horse in my life."

"It's easy," I reassured him, and I boosted him up on the pony's back there in the stall. When he found that easy, I untied the horse and led him out around the yard until Charlie learned to sit him without hanging on too hard to his mane. A happy boy he was at the end of his first lesson, and I was proud. I got on and showed how I could ride, up and down, around the block, at any gait. "Easy, see?"

We had to go to the Capitol and to the hotel lobbies to inquire about his appointment, which was only promised; and I worried: I knew what promises were. I went with him and it was his turn to show me things. He seemed to know as much about politics as

I did about my riding, but he was more interested in riding than he was in that Legislature. He made me tell him over and over where he would ride: down the river, up the river, out in the country, to the trestle bridge, to the beaver traps. There was a long delay of his appointment, and I wondered why. The legislators were in town; Sacramento was filled with them; and the Legislature did not meet. Why?

Charlie explained indifferently that they were "organizing." There were committees to "fix up" and a lot of fat jobs to be distributed; not only pages to appoint, but clerks, sergeants-at-arms—everything; hundreds of them, and yet not enough to go around. There were, for instance, three times as many boys promised pageships as there were pages; and a pageship was a petty job. The page got only $10 a day. Some places paid much more than this in salaries, besides what you could make out of them.

"It all depends on who gets the speakership," said Charlie. "Let's go riding."

"But aren't you afraid you'll get left?" I asked anxiously.

He wasn't. His "member" was the San Francisco leader of the Republican railroad crowd which was sure to capture the speakership and thus the whole organization of the House. They could fill any job, but of course they had to give something good to the Democratic railroad gang and "chicken-feed" to the opposition Republicans. That was "good politics."

So we went riding, both of us on the one horse. I rode in front, Charlie holding on to my waist behind. He was glad of the delay. Until the sessions began, we could play all day every day together, and his salary was cumulative—$10 a day! The amount of it impressed me. A boy getting $10 a day was a wonder to a boy like me, who never had more than a dime at a time. Charlie hardly thought of it. His thoughts were on the pony, on learning to ride, seeing the rivers and the country, or playing Indians and crusaders, and trapping beavers.

I wish I could recall all that I went through that winter. It was a revelation; it was a revolution to me. Charlie was appointed a page; we all went to the opening session, where, with a formal front, the Speaker was elected (just as if it had not been "fixed"), speeches made (just as if spontaneously), and the committees and the whole organization read off (just as if it had not been "settled" days and nights before). Then I saw why Charlie wasn't interested in his salary: he got none of it; it all went home; and he had no more money in his pocket than I had in mine. But also I saw that the Legislature wasn't what my father, my teachers, and the grown-ups thought; it wasn't even what my histories and the other books said. There was some mystery about it as there was about art, as there was about everything. Nothing was what it was supposed to be. And Charlie took it as it was; my father took it as it seemed to be; I couldn't take it at all. What troubled me most, however, was that they none of them had any strong feeling about the conflict of the two pictures. I had. I remember how I suffered; I wanted, I needed, to adjust the difference between what was and what seemed to be. There was something wrong somewhere, and I could not get it right. And nobody would help me.

Charlie was forever for getting away from the Capitol. So were the legislators. They kept adjourning, over every holiday, over Sundays, over Saturdays and Sundays, over Saturdays, Sundays, and Mondays. We could ride, therefore, and we did. We made long trips out to the ranches, up and down and across the rivers. Charlie never wearied; he never got enough of our exploration and of our romance. He entered into the spirit of my games of "playing" knight or cowboy. He learned to ride; he could go off alone, but I liked riding, too, and he preferred that we stay together. It was more fun to talk and think together about dangers ahead; it was safer to meet them shoulder to shoulder. I enjoyed our many, many days of free play.

But I enjoyed also the sessions of the House when Charlie had to be on the floor. He found me a seat just back of the rail where I could sit and watch him and the other pages running about among the legislators in their seats. Charlie used to stand beside me, he and the other small pages, between calls, and we learned the procedure. We became expert on the rules. The practices of debate, quite aside from the legislation under consideration, fascinated me. I wished it were real. It was beautiful enough to be true. But no, speeches were made on important subjects with hardly any one present but the Speaker, the clerks, and us boys. Where were the absent members? I did not ask that question often; not out loud. The pages laughed; everybody laughed. Charlie explained.

"The members are out where the fate of the measure debated here is being settled," and he took me to committee rooms and hotel apartments where, with the drinks and cigars, members were playing poker with the lobbyists and leaders. "The members against the bill are allowed to win the price agreed on to buy their vote."

Bribery! I might as well have been shot. Somewhere in my head or my heart I was wounded deeply.

Once, when the Speaker was not in the chair and many members were in their seats, when there was a dead debate in an atmosphere of great tension, I was taken down a corridor to the closed door of a committee room. There stood reporters and a small crowd of others watching outside. We waited awhile till, at last, the Speaker came out, said something, and hurried with the crowd back to the Assembly. Charlie held me back to point out to me "the big bosses" who had come "up the river" to "force that bill through"; they had "put on the screws." I was struck by the observation that one of the bosses was blind. We went back to the House, and quickly, after a very ordinary debate of hours, the bill was passed on the third reading and sent to the Senate, where, in due course, it was approved. It was a "rotten deal," the boys said, and I remember my father shook his head over it. "The rascals!" he muttered.

And that, so far as I could make out from him and from all witnesses—that was the explanation. The Legislature, government —everything was "all right," only there were some "bad men" who spoiled things—now and then. "Politicians" they were called, those bad men. How I hated them, in the abstract. In the concrete —I saw Charlie Prodger often in the lobby of the Legislature, and I remember that some one said he was "one of them," a "politician." But I knew Charlie Prodger, and I knew he was not a "bad man."

And the sergeant-at-arms, who was called "bad"—one of the San Francisco gang—he was one of the kindest, easiest-going men I ever met. He looked out for me; he took care of all the boys. Many a time he let Charlie Marple off to have a free day with me. And there were others: every "crook" I met seemed to me to belong in a class with the bridge-tender, Mr. and Mrs. Stortz, and all the other grown men and women who "understood a fellow"

—did not stick at rules; did not laugh at everything a boy said and frown at every little thing he did.

When the Legislature closed and Charlie Marple went home, I was left to ride around the country alone, thinking, thinking. I asked questions, of course; I could not think out alone all that I had been learning that winter; I could not easily drop the problem of government and the goodness and badness of men. But I did not draw from my friends any answers that cleared my darkness. The bridge-tender said that all Legislatures were like that. And Jim Neely said so too. Ah Hook was not interested.

"What for you askem me fool question," he said. "Chinaman he findee out long time allee government allee samee—big clook."

But there was an answer of a sort about that time, an answer to one of my questions: Why didn't somebody challenge the rascals —if they were so bad? The boss of Sacramento, Frank Rhodes, the gambler, was having one of his conventions of the local ringleaders in a room under his gambling-house. It was at night. There were no outsiders present, none wanted, and the insiders were fighting, shooting men. During the meeting Grove L. Johnson, a well-known attorney in the town, walked in with his two sons, Albert and Hiram, both little more than boys, and both carrying revolvers. They went up to the front, and with one of his boys on one side of him, the other on the other, Mr. Johnson told those crooks all about themselves and what they were doing. He was bitter, fearless, free-spoken; he insulted, he defied those politicians; he called upon the town to clean them out and predicted that their power would be broken some day. There was no answer. When he had finished, he and his sons walked out.

Something in me responded to that proceeding. It was one way to solve my problem. There was no other response, so far as I could see or hear. People said unpleasant things about Grove L. Johnson, and the Rhodes ring went right on governing the town. Later, much later, the boss disappeared, and still later Grove L. Johnson himself was one of the bosses of the Legislature. Albert Johnson died. But Hiram Johnson became a reform Governor of California and a United States Senator.

What struck and stunned me at the time was that this courageous attack by the Johnsons—especially by the boys—had no effect upon the people I knew. I was trying to see the Legislature and government as Mr. Marple saw the sunset through the brush in the river bottom; not the mud but—the gold, the Indians—some beauty in them. The painter said there always was something beautiful to see. Well, Mr. Johnson and his two boys—their defiance was beautiful; wasn't it? I thought so, and yet nobody else did. Why? I gave it up, or, better, I laid the question aside. I had other things to think of, wonderful things, things more in my line.

VII

THE NEELY FARM

WHEN the romance began to fall off the race horses, I looked around for a new interest and there was none within my old range. I had about exhausted the resources of the world within a quarter of a day's ride of home. My circle must be widened; I must go off for all day. What held me? Not my parents; they let me go wild. Not my pony: he was a tough little cayuse. The noonday meal was the stake I was tied to. If I could ride away out into the country till noon, eat there somewhere, and ride back in the afternoon, I could cover miles and miles, see new things, new people. The problem was where to eat and feed my pony.

I tried nowhere at first. I rode half a day, dismounted on the edge of a vineyard, and ate grapes, but there is no grass when grapes are ripe; my pony had to nibble stubble. That was not enough for him, and the grapes were too much for me. I came home with a stomach-ache. My mother, who did not understand a boy at all, said it was the grapes, and she proposed that I take my lunch with me. "Your father does," she argued. Yes, but teamsters, scouts, knights, and vaqueros did not carry a lunch—and I wasn't going to. When my mother insisted and made up a lunch parcel for me I hid it in the stable or ditched it. I would not be weak. I would "find" myself, as my kind of people did.

I consulted the bridge-tender about it. He said I might share his meal whenever I wished, and his fare was good regular food: ham and eggs with black coffee and brown sugar. He could not provide for a horse, however, and the bridge was not far enough out of town. I used his hospitality only for breakfasts when I rose early and could get out to his place by six-thirty A.M.

I made friends with Ah Hook, a Chinese farmer a little farther

51

out. He was hostile at first. Having a patch of melons and another of peanuts, he was suspicious of a boy.

"What for you come catchem eat here?" he asked. "What for you no go home?"

I explained, "Too far," and he asked, "What for you go too far?"

That was an easy question. I had to see what was beyond. He laughed.

"Melican boy, he go lookee see—what? No ting, no ting. China boy, he no go lookee see. He know all-leadee, notting, allee samee."

I answered that: "What for you Ah Hook come allee way China lookee see—Sacramento?"

"Me no come lookee see Sacramento," he replied. "Me come catchem dollar, go home China."

"Yes," I argued, "you come catchem dollar to catchem eat allee samee me."

Ah Hook liked that. He chuckled and surrendered.

"All li," he said. "All li, you come eatee lice here."

And I did once or twice, and Ah Hook put up my pony to feed with his old skeleton of a horse. But his bill of fare was always the same "lice" and tea, both made Chinese fashion, and I didn't like rice. I had to find another road-house.

As my custom was, I made a business of the search, and I turned the business into a game. My youngest sister has turned this trick into a philosophy. "Why work?" she says whenever any one complains of the labor of something. "Make a game of your job and then—play."

I played that I was a fugitive from justice in search of a friend, but I became so absolutely a hunted criminal that I was too cautious. I ran away from the people who might have helped me. I found nothing, and another day was wasted because I was after an enemy and forgot that it was actually a friend I wanted. I avoided everybody. The next Saturday I was more sensible. I was the trusted scout of a general who sent me out to find a base, an advance post where he could quarter and supply his troops; and he ordered me to hunt till I got what we must have. Riding up on a low eminence on the Stockton road, I folded my arms and reconnoitered, and I saw several places that would do. I was judging by appearances; I preferred neat farms. The Duden Farm was spick and span. It was small, but all the buildings were painted; the fences were well made and the fields well tilled. Mr. Duden had a blacksmith's shop on the corner of the main road and a cross road. There he himself always worked; his sons kept the farm. That was an objection. Country boys had an uncomfortable way of looking a city boy contemptuously up and down, asking technical questions, and laughing at the answers. I was desperate, however; the troops must be provided for; the general was a fine chief but a martinet. I considered the Duden place.

Riding on to the blacksmith's shop, I stopped and stared at Mr. Duden. He looked up from his anvil, asked me if I wanted my pony shod, and when I said I didn't, he went on with his work, hammering red-hot irons and spattering the sparks all over everything, even his leather apron and—to my wonder—his own bare, hairy arms. It was a fascinating sight. I wouldn't mind being a blacksmith who shod horses. The glowing splinters burned black spots on the floor, but they didn't burn Mr. Duden. Why? I asked him.

"They know me," he answered, but he did not look up. He went on beating the red-hot irons, ducking them sizzling into water and poking them back in the open fire, just as if I wasn't there. I rode on, therefore, and the Dudens lost for a year or two the chance to know and feed me.

The Duden place was five miles out. Two miles farther there was a cross road that led left to Florin, a railroad station, now the center of a Japanese colony which has been written about many times as an example of the failure of the whites to hold land against the cleverest of the yellow races. In my day the farms were almost ranches in size and the houses few. There was no building between Dudens' and the cross road, none beyond for miles. It was all open fields of wheat, shining hot in the sun. You could see the heat radiating like white flames over the land. I turned down the Florin road because I saw off to the left of it an oasis, a white cottage, with a flying windmill in a small, fenced garden of young trees, and near it a big, unpainted barn. Pretty good. A lane opened off the road; I jogged along it between the yellow wheat and the great, light green vineyard irrigated by windmills, up to the house. I saw that there were flowers in the garden, kept fresh by tiny streams of water, carried all through and around it by a perfect little system of ditches. The whole place was neat, cool, shady, and quiet; and not a sign of a human being till I arrived opposite the cottage gate. There I saw, with a start, a woman standing, wiping her hands on her apron and staring hard at me. It was Mrs. Neely.

Mrs. Neely was the New England wife of William Neely, a

THE NEELY RANCH

tall, straight, gentle man from Mississippi. This I learned later, and indeed a good deal of what I have to tell now of her and me is her story, told afterward to my mother, and all mixed up hopelessly with my own recollections. But I can see still the picture of her at our first meeting; I can feel the straight line of her tight, silent lips, and the gleeful, dancing look out of her watching, inquiring eyes. She drove all thought of my troops out of my head.

"How de do?" I began anxiously.

"How do you do?" she answered.

"I'm Lennie Steffens," I explained, "and I'm looking for some place where I can get lunch for us when I'm off on long trips in the country."

"Us?" she repeated. "Who are us? You don't mean you and your pony?"

"Yes," I said, "and my father says it's more important to feed my pony than me, but he can eat grass, if you have no hay."

"Oh, we have hay," she answered, "but why should we feed a boy and a horse whenever they happen along?"

"I don't know," I said, and I didn't. I was often asked the question; I had even asked it myself; and I never could answer it.

"Where do you and your pony live?" she questioned. "And what do you two do for a living? What are you doing now 'way out here?"

I told her where I lived. I could not tell her what I did for a living, except that I went to school. And as for this trip, I had explained that, but I repeated a little more fully. I was hunting for a place where I could always be sure of regular meals when I was out on the Stockton road.

"Does your mother let you range the country wild like this? And your father! Do they know where you are today?"

"No." I blushed for them. "They don't know where I am to-day. They hardly ever know till I get back. But they don't mind. They let me go anywhere I want to, as long as I am with my pony."

"Umph, I see," she said. "They trust the pony." And she called, "Jim, Jim."

A man stuck his head out of the barn. "Hallo?" he answered.

"Here, Jim," she said. "Come and take this useless boy's good-for-nothing pony; put him in the barn and feed him. Hay, no barley. And you"—she turned to me—"you climb down off that horse and come with me."

Jim came and took the pony with a wondering look at me. I went with Mrs. Neely, who led me to her kitchen and bade me "wash up." She said I was dirty. She went on with her cooking, and when I had washed, we had a long talk. I don't remember what it was all about, but I do recall her interest in my sisters, who did not interest me. They weren't boys and could be used, so far as I had discovered, only on rainy days, when they served pretty well as brakemen and better still as passengers on a train of chairs or a steamboat. Yes, and she asked me about school, which bored me. The only good thing I could tell her about school was that Friday was a short day, closing at two o'clock instead of three, and there was no school from then till Monday. Two days and a half free. In order to use them, however, I had to find places where I could stop and feed up.

She saw, she said. "And when you decide that we will do for one stopping-place, you will go on and look for others farther out."

"Ye-e-e-s," I agreed. I had not thought so far ahead as that, but the moment she mentioned it, I could see it would be well to have other stations. Also I could see that Mrs. Neely could understand—some things; which is very important to a boy, whose life is one long search for people who have some insight; intelligence is so rare, especially among grown-ups.

Dinner was a long time preparing. I thought Mrs. Neely would never stop putting things on the table—wonderful things: cakes and jams, honey and milk and pickles. Long after there was enough even for me she kept baking and cooking and pulling things out of cupboards, cellars, and the oven. And I wasn't the only impatient one. Before she was ready Jim came up to the house.

"Always first—to meals," Mrs. Neely said uncomfortably, but Jim answered her back. "It's late," he said. "That noon train went by long ago." Her reply was a blast on a horn that brought Mr. Neely up to the door. Both men wiped their boots carefully on the door-mat outside the kitchen door, and that made me notice that the house was very clean.

I was introduced to Mr. Neely as "a good-for-nothing boy who has come here on a useless pony for a square meal for both, and he proposes, if the board is satisfactory, to come often, whenever he is passing by—at meal times."

"Then," said Mr. Neely, "I hope that you have a good dinner for him." He said this charmingly, with a polite bow to me, and he gave me a warm handshake. I liked Mr. Neely right then and there. Of Mrs. Neely I could not be sure; she was queer. As for Jim, Mr. Neely's brother—I ranked him where Mrs. Neely put him, at the foot of the table; he was just a regular fella.

"Yes," Mrs. Neely repeated when the men had washed up and we were seated at table, "I have done my best, as you see, with the cooking of this first—a sample meal. For I infer from what he tells me that he won't come to us again unless he is suited, though he says his father says that it is more important that Jim feed his pony well." It was true that I had said all that; only the way Mrs. Neely said it made me feel very uneasy. It was always a puzzle to me why people took what I said and gave it a twist that made it sound preposterous or ridiculous.

I was hungry, however. So were the other men, and the food was not only abundant, it was good. I had chanced upon the best cook in the county; so I ate; we all ate, all but Mrs. Neely, who kept at me with questions, funny questions. How was the election going to go? Who would be our next President? What was playing at the theater? And the opera? (Sacramento had no opera.) When would the next ball be? What were the latest fashions? I didn't answer the questions; didn't have to; nobody did. We just ate and ate, and she asked questions without waiting for answers till I was full, very full, and then Mrs. Neely got me started telling the story of my life—to come. That seemed to interest them all; they sat around listening to what I was going to be, until Mrs. Neely said it was time to go to work. Then Mr. Neely shook hands with me, said good-by, and told me to come again whenever I wanted to.

"That settles it so far as we are concerned," said Mrs. Neely. Mr. Neely was head of the house, and if he said I might come again, I could be sure of a welcome from her.

"But how about you?" she asked me. "Do you want to come again? Does the board suit you?"

I told her it did; I was very sincere on that point, and she was glad. She liked to have a visitor now and then from the great world; liked to hear the news. She complained that some visitors, especially boys, did not know much, had no idea what was going on; and some boys were a lot of trouble, banging around and breaking fences and things, making noises that scared the cattle and fowls. I wasn't like that. She was pleased that I was different. And she seemed to have a grievance against a boy that came, not by himself, but with a horse that had to be fed and cleaned. What would I do with a boy like that? What could such a boy expect? To be taken in and coddled and— I was troubled. It sounded just like me, this part, and Jim grinned. She turned on him and drove him out. "You go on to your work," she commanded angrily, and when he obeyed and was gone, she grabbed and squeezed me.

"You darling," she said, "you darling," and she kissed me, several times, hard, the way my mother did till I had put a stop to the practice. I couldn't stop Mrs. Neely. I saw what looked like wetness in her eyes, and besides, all of a sudden she pushed me out of the house and slammed the door.

Jim was waiting for me. He took me out to the barn. He kept snickering a suppressed laugh while he showed me that the pony had fed well. He put on bridle and blanket, boosted me upon the pony.

"Now, boy," he said, "you come often. We get better meals when you do. The Missis doesn't strain herself every day the way she did today. And Will, he likes you."

"But how about Mrs. Neely?" I asked. "Does she really want me to come?"

"Want you?" Jim exclaimed. "*Want* you! She has wanted a boy like you all her life."

VIII

A PRINCE AND A COWBOY

A BOY's life is pestered with problems—hard ones, as hard as any adult's. There is the whole world to get into your head. You have to make a picture of it; that's easy, but the picture has to correspond somewhat with the world outside, which keeps changing. You have the sun going fine around the earth, and then all of a sudden you learn something more and the earth starts whirling around the sun. This means a complete readjustment. It happens often. Every time I had everything all right and working harmoniously inside so that I could leave it and mind my own business, some fact would bob up to throw it all out. I remember how, when the earth was flat, I had to put China and the Far East to the west of me, no easy task for a boy; and then when I had that done, I studied a book which made the earth round like an orange. Where was one to put China then?

I consulted some of the other boys about that, and they looked dazed for a moment; but they soon turned to the ball and bats and bade me do likewise.

"Ah, play ball," they said in effect.

Our cook, a Chinaman, was contemptuous. "What for you go lookee see find China? China no lost. Fool boy lost, yes, but China all li."

And this, the construction of the universe as a whole, was only the main business of life. There were minor problems. It took me and my crowd days of exploration to discover and map in our minds the confluence of our two rivers, the American and the Sacramento. It took longer to make out how the river steamboats and the railroad trains could start from Sacramento at right angles and arrive both at the same place, San Francisco. Also there were the inhabitants of the earth to understand, the grown-ups who do and say such queer things. They say they love you and yet they balk you like enemies. They tell you to be good and you'll succeed, and the next thing you know they will be chuckling about how dishonest some successful man was. Nor will they explain anything, not seriously. They laugh at a fellow's questions. Or if they pretend to throw a light, they only cast a shadow that darkens and complicates the puzzle. They don't seem to realize how painful your need is to find out just where you are at in a mixed-up world. Sometimes it seemed to me almost as if they didn't know where they were at themselves.

As I was leaving the Neely farm that day I was wondering what Jim Neely meant by what he said about Mrs. Neely wanting a boy like me and what Mrs. Neely meant by being so cross with me and then so soft. If she wanted me why couldn't she take me straight as a regular fellow would? I could not make it out. I thought and thought, but the sun was hot over me and the pony was hot under me. I did what I had to do with many, many questions: I gave them up, for the present; I laid them aside and hung on to the thought that anyhow I had a feeding-station seven miles out on the Stockton road. And before I reached home I had another feeding-station still farther out, and another problem.

Single-footing along the flaming road, I picked up the track of cattle going my way, and pretty soon there was a cloud of dust ahead. Hurrying as much as I could on such a day, I caught up with a cowboy driving a small herd of big calves and young steers to market. I asked if I might help him.

"You betcher life," he answered. "My horse is about in."

No wonder. It was a small drove, and, as the cowboy said, it's easier to handle a big drove. If there's a mob, cattle will herd like humans. But when they're a few, and of mixed ages, they are like a bunch of shooting stars. "Maybe we can do it together," he said. "I'll drive from behind here and you'll ride along the side of the next cross road, doing the dirty work."

It was dirty work. A calf would bleat and bolt. My pony would spring ahead and cut him off. Then a young steer, smelling water, would bellow and go, with others after him, down the road. I had to race to the front, stop short, and hold them. An open lane on one side was easy; the pony would of himself see and take and hold it, but when there was a cross road, open both sides, we had, us two cowboys, alternately to drive and head. I would shoot up, yelling, along one side, then fall back and drive as he galloped up the other side. By good team work we got by. I was sweating, my pony was in a lather, and the cowboy and his horse were caked with the mud of the damp dust. He was pleased, however, and, to keep me with him, he paid me a compliment (the way grown-ups do).

"You know the cattle game, don't you?" he said.

"No," I answered, "but my pony does, and I'm learning it from him. How long you been on the road?"

"All day," he said. "The ranch is about twenty miles out."

Twenty miles out! Just right. I began fishing for an invitation to visit him, asking him questions. The ranch was not a big one, he said; it was mostly a wheat farm, only part hay and cattle. He was one of five or six hands that worked steady on the place.

"Why don't you ride out and see us sometime?" he invited. "You like to work cattle. We'll let you have all you want of it."

I told him about my gang, and he laughed. "Five or six! All kids? Well, you may all come. Why not? Make a week-end of it." A week-end? What was that? He used lots of funny words, and he spoke them very English. And he suggested a date when there would be work for us to do, cattle work.

I liked the idea, accepted it, and I liked this fellow. I stared at him approvingly till he turned away as if embarrassed, and when he looked back at me, he asked me a diverting question.

"Why no saddle?"

I explained that my father wanted me to learn bareback, and that led to the Comanches. I told him all about them, how they rode, fought, and—I must have become so enthusiastic about those Indians that he suspected me.

"I see," he said, "you are a Comanche Indian chief."

This struck me at first as fresh. I did not like to have anybody walk right into my—my privacy, like that, sit down, and stick his feet up on the table. But my second thought was that maybe he was my kind of a fellow, like the bridge-tender. I decided to see.

"No," I said. "I used to be a Comanche chief's son, but that was long ago; several weeks back. I am—something else now. I'll tell you what I am if you'll tell me first what you are."

"Why," he said, "I am, as you see, a cowboy."

I was disappointed. He did not understand. I said as **much.** "Of course, I can see you're a cow-puncher, but that's only your job. I don't mean that. What I mean is, what are you really?"

"Really?" he echoed. "What's really? I'm a real cowboy."

"That's funny," I said, "I thought you'd tumble to what I meant, and you didn't."

I was about to give up, and he seemed to sense that. He looked almost ashamed, and I didn't care. If he wasn't my sort, if he didn't belong to our crowd, he didn't matter. We rode along in a silence that could be felt, like the heat, till a steer charged the fence. "Water," I called as my pony charged at the steer, and I was glad that the rest of the herd joined the attack on that fence. It kept us busy for a while. When we could fall back and ride together, the cowboy had decided to talk.

"I'll tell you about myself," he said. "My name, my cattle name, is Duke. That's what the cattlemen call me from Texas to the Pacific, only they pronounce it Dook. And they name me so, not because I am a duke. My father, as it happens, is a lord, but my older brother will inherit his title. I myself, I am nothing, as you see. I'm called by an English title because I am English, but as a matter of fact, I am a plain American cowboy."

I was thrilled. I had read about the English nobility, books on books, and here for the first time I was seeing one.

"Is that what you mean by 'really'?" he inquired.

"Maybe," I answered, and it was his turn to be disappointed. I was sorry now. It was my turn to talk. I told him about me, to explain what I meant.

I had been reading Scott's novels lately, I said, and lots of other English stories about knights and gentlemen and ladies. I knew what a younger son was and had even thought I'd like to be one.

"Really?" he said, only he said it differently from me.

"Yes-s—" I hesitated. But I decided to trust him. "Yes," I confessed. "I wouldn't have minded being the son of a lord, and, as a matter of fact, I was—not exactly that, but I've been something like that for a good while lately."

"But why?" he asked. "You are in the way of being what I wanted to be when I was a boy, and yet here you are—"

"Nothing," I interrupted, and I poured out my woes.

Here I was, a boy, just an ordinary boy. I wasn't a poor boy, like the boys I had read about in stories, the fellows that started with nothing, no father, no mother, no home. They starved in the streets, picking up now and then a crust of bread to eat, and finding here and there a dark hallway to sleep in, but they begin by selling papers and shining shoes; they are smart, industrious, honest, and brave; so they rise slowly but surely and by and by they are a success. They own the paper they sold or—whatever it is they are at.

"That's great," I summed up. "They are heroes of books. I'd like to be the hero of a book."

But, I grieved, I could not be that. My father and mother did not die when I was young. They are both still living, and they had a home for me. I didn't have a chance; I could not go out and suffer, strive, and become a success.

The Duke saw my predicament. He tried to be encouraging. There were other things I might do.

"What?" I demanded. "I can't be one of those rich men's sons or the son of a duke and do what they do." There were stories about them, too. They had boats and rivers they could row on; not like the Sacramento and the American Rivers: not swift floods or all dried up. They had snow and ice and parks. They could go sledding, and skating, and they had places to go riding in, made on purpose for saddle horses, and grooms to follow them. Not like me. I had to ride over to the river bottom or out on the plains, always with other boys, among farmers and—and—

I halted. I had almost said something that might hurt his feelings. He saw my embarrassment, and like a duke, he bridged it gracefully (the nobility is very graceful, you know).

"And cowboys," he suggested.

"Yes," I said, and to make it easy for him, I explained gracefully that I didn't mean him. I was glad I had met him; I was certainly coming out to his ranch with my crowd to help with his cattle. I had to do something to fill up my time.

"But you can see, can't you," I said, "that working cattle on a ranch isn't what a fellow with ambition would choose to do if he had his choice."

A team was coming toward me. "I'll head 'em," I said, and I rode up and turned our cattle off to the right side of the road. After that there were two cross roads in succession; both the Duke and I were busy, and by that time, the city limit was near. There were other things to think of.

What butcher were his calves for? When he told me, I told him that all would be well. Loony Louie was that butcher's ranchman; he would be on the look-out for us, with the bars down, and there was a pond in his corral. The cattle would turn in of themselves for the water. And this happened. We had a couple of miles of very hard work. The herd split, and half of them got away up one of the many lanes. My pony brought them back, and—well, we worked the whole tired, famished drove to the butcher's place. There was Louie standing out in the middle of the road with his gate wide open. The cattle rushed in, and our horses followed— one mad rush for the pond, and there they all waded in up to their bellies and sank their heads in up to their eyes. And Louie, closing the gate and running after us to the pond, stood and danced there; he laughed and yelled like a maniac at the sight of the drinking animals.

I saw Duke looking astonished at him.

"What's the matter with that man?" he asked, as we rode up out of the water and headed for town. I saw my chance to explain what I meant by "really."

"Well," I said, "Loony Louie is called crazy, but he isn't. He is all right, only he loves stock. You saw how he was glad when your thirsty calves wallowed in the water and drank their fill? Well, he loves that; he loves to see 'em drink and feed. He'll cry if he sees them slaughtered; sure. That's why they say he's crazy: because he loves animals and goes crazy when he sees them drink when they're thirsty and eat when they're hungry; and—and when they're killed he goes crazy too."

"Poor devil!" the Duke muttered.

"No," I corrected, "Louis was in prison once for stealing cattle and once he was in the insane asylum for the same thing. But I know him, and I knew what he wanted: knew he didn't want to own cattle but only to take good care of them, so I got him a job here to take care of the butcher's cattle. It would have been better to put him on a ranch where cattle aren't killed, but no rancher would take a loco cattle-lover. Only this old German butcher could understand about Louie. He gave him the job of priming up his cattle, and he keeps him away as much as he can from the slaughter house."

"Really!" the cowboy exclaimed, and I answered, "Yes, really. And there you have said it yourself."

But he didn't see it even yet. We rode along the city streets, quietly; all you could hear was the flap of his chaps and the clink of his spurs.

"Come again, kid," he said at last.

"Why, don't you see?" I said. "That butcher's man, who has the job of feeding up cattle to be killed, he is really—he is playing he's the friend of those calves of yours, and he'll take 'em into the barn, feed them a lot, pet them, talk to them, and he will listen to them, and—and—"

"And?" the cowboy boosted, and I told him straight how Louie could sit up on a fence with you and tell you how a young calf feels when it is separated from its mother and what a wild steer would like to be—really.

"He does to me," I said. "He has told me stories that are—real about what the cattle tell him."

"Really?"

"Yes," I said, and I told him about the bridge-tender, whose job was to tend the American River trestle. A good job, and dangerous, and he did it up brown. But he didn't care for it. "He's really a prospector who strikes it rich and goes home where his people live, and the girl that wouldn't marry him, and—and—"

"And—" the cowboy said, and I saw he was understanding, so I went on.

"And I go out there and sit in his cabin, and him and me, we go back home rich and spend the money; he just blows it and he makes his folks proud of him, and—and—"

"And—"

I had to go back and explain that the bridge-tender's troubles all came from a certain preacher in his home town who, because the bridge-tender got to dancing and raising the dust, denounced him to his face in a sermon in the church. The bridge-tender was with his girl, and it so shamed her that she wouldn't have him 'round any more.

"See?" I said, and he saw that much; so I trusted him with the whole truth, how, when the bridge-tender and I are alone on the trestle and there is no train due, we make his pile, we go back east to his home. We walk into that church—everybody's there, the girl, too, of course—and the bridge-tender, who has been the talk of the town for a week, he walks up the middle aisle of the church, draws his gun, and makes that preacher come down out of his pulpit, kneel down, and apologize to the girl.

"And she marries the bridge-tender?" the Duke asked.

"Sometimes," I answered. "Sometimes we take her, and sometimes she begs to be took, but we scorn her."

We had come to the corner where there was a small drovers' hotel with a stable next door, the Duke's hotel. We stopped; since the Duke did not seem to see it, I pointed it out to him: "Your hotel," I said.

"Yes, yes," he said. "But let's finish this. Your butcher's man is —really—a cattle-lover; your bridge-tender is a rich miner. Any others like that?"

"Yes," I said. "You know Hank Dobran, the gambler, that runs this hotel and bar where you are stopping tonight? Well, he —this is a secret, of course—when Hank has made enough to be independent—he tells me he is going to turn in and clear up the dirty politics of this town and make a fine, grand town that all the other cities all over the world can copy."

"Any more?" he asked after a while, and I looked at him and he wasn't joshing me. He believed. I answered him, therefore:

"Every fellow I get to really know is that way," I told him. "Every one of them is playing he is really something else besides what his job is. And that's what I mean by really," I said, "and—and that's why I asked you what you were, really."

The Duke did not answer. He just sat there on his horse in front of the hotel stable. We were so quiet that the stableman came out and looked at us—and gave us up. But his wonder brought the Duke to. He spoke.

"I was that way, kid," he said. "I was like you. I read books, as a boy; I read and I wanted to go and be what I read. Only I read stories about the far west, Indians, scouts, cowboys. I read about knights, too, and lords and ladies, kings, queens, and princesses. Yes, but I saw that sort. I knew them as—as you know cowboys. So I didn't want to be a prince or the son of a—duke. I played I was a cowboy. I could ride; I had horses, yes, and—but I hated to ride on our silly little saddles on bridle paths in our fancy parks with a groom behind me—and my sister. I wanted to go west and be a cowboy among cowboys—and really ride—really. And—well —as you see—I did. That's what I am now and have been for ten years. It isn't what I imagined it to be. It is no more what it is cracked up to be than a lord is or the son of a lord. But no matter, here I am, Dook the cowboy—really a cow-puncher."

He seemed to be sad about it, and his sadness put up a problem to me, the hardest puzzle of that day.

"Funny!" I said. "You're a cowboy really—and I—I don't know what to be now, but for a long time lately—weeks—when I rode up to you, I was a prince, the son of a lord, the Black Prince in the Middle Ages."

The Duke didn't laugh the way some men would. He thought and thought, and at last he looked as if he was going to say something. He didn't. He changed his mind, I guess. For all he did was to put out his hand, take mine, and shake it hard, once.

"Good-by, Prince," he said. "It is time to go home. It's time for both of us to go home—really."

"Good-by, Duke," I said, and I rode off home puzzling and puzzling.

IX

I GET RELIGION

DURING the morning recess at school the next Monday, I
gathered my crowd (of horse-boys) on the school steps,
and while we watched the other boys playing leap-frog,
I reported the Duke's invitation to visit his ranch some weeks
hence and my plan to start on a Friday afternoon, stay somewhere
out in the country that night, go on early the next day to the
cattle ranch, and work and play with the cowboys till Sunday afternoon or Monday morning. They were delighted, but where were
we to stay Friday night? I told them all about the Neely farm
for me and they asked me to "ring them in on that." Since there
were five or six of them at that time, I hesitated. They pressed me
to try it. They gave many, but different, reasons for thinking Mrs.
Neely would take us all in.

Hjalmar Bergman said she would because his mother would.
Charlie Raleigh, who was the oldest of us, argued that my account
showed that Mrs. Neely liked me so much she would do anything
I asked. Will Cluness held that she would if we paid her, but that
was no use because we never had any money. Another fellow
thought we might offer to work out our board and lodging; another that we might fix it up with Jim Neely to let me sleep in
the house, and say nothing about the others but sneak them into
the barn, trusting to luck to swipe enough food for supper and
breakfast. By the time school "took in" again, I had promised to
ride out to the farm the next Saturday and see what I could do.

I did that, and all I got was another pretty problem. Jim saw
me coming up the lane. He hailed me from the barn, and he was
so friendly that I felt encouraged to consult him at once, before
I dismounted.

"How many boys did you say?" he asked.

68

"Oh, from five to six or eight—depends on how many can get off."

He grinned. "Wall now," he said, shaking his head, "I think that if I was you, I wouldn't put that up to the old lady."

"Why not?" I appealed. "They are all all-right fellows."

"Sure thing," he said. "The boys are all right, but what's the color of their horses?"

I told him: white, gray, black, etc., and two bays besides mine. He asked for the markings on the other bays. None, I said, all red.

"Um-hum," he reflected. He looked critically at my pony, and he answered in a very peculiar way. "No. It won't do. Mrs. Neely is very particular. She is one of those rare women that likes a boy that rides a bay pony with a white star on his forehead and one white forefoot. She would be furious if you brought her any others."

Now, what could you make of that? I leave it to anybody that that was a puzzle. I sat there on

MR. NEELY'S "WHO'S WHO"

my pony puzzling and puzzling, till Jim called me down, took my pony, and sent me into the house to see Mrs. Neely.

"So," she greeted me, "here you are again. Out for another square meal? All right. This time you have brought me all the news from town, no doubt; the answers to all my questions. Of course. You go and find Mr. Neely; he's ditching in the vineyard; and don't come back till I blow the horn. Then we'll hear the news you have collected for me."

I had no news. I had forgotten her old questions. I never thought of anybody but myself, my mother would say; I could hear her saying it. Maybe it was true. I was ashamed of myself. But Mr. Neely received me gladly, a little too polite; he shook hands with me and said, "How do you do?" which is a strange question to put to a fellow who doesn't know or care how he is. I said I was all right, and I asked him how he was. "Pretty well," he said, of course; you could see he was well. I told him about Mrs. Neely's questions, how I had forgotten them and didn't know what I would do when she asked them at dinner. He only laughed a little and looked away.

"Never mind," he said. "Her questions are for me, not you. She misses theaters, music, church, and her relatives, out here on a farm in the west. Thinks we should have stayed east and lived in a city. And maybe we should; maybe I shouldn't have listened to the tales about California and the golden west. Maybe—"

He was quite sad, like Dook was and the bridge-tender sometimes, and I was sorry, but I couldn't see how it had anything to do with me, the Neelys' coming west. I asked Mr. Neely what I could do, but he only handed me a hoe and showed me how to clear the ditches, opening one side stream and closing another. And it was fine to do. I worked all morning and learned all about irrigating, something about hog and hay raising, a farmer's seasons, markets, and so on. It was very interesting. I had half a mind to be a farmer myself. And why not? If being a prince isn't what it's cracked up to be, why not be a farmer and be done with the terrible problem of choosing a career?

But Mrs. Neely did not want me to be a farmer. She thought it better for me to become a preacher. It was sudden, but I considered it. When she called us on the horn, I ran across fields to water my pony; but I met Jim, who said he had done that; so I came back to the house with him. I noticed how he walked, a sort of plodding gait as if over a plowed field, and I could copy it pretty well. He noticed it.

"You're walking like a regular farmer," he said.

Pleased, I told him I meant to be a farmer, and noted each thing he and Mr. Neely did to prepare for dinner. I washed up as they did, chucked my hat on the bench with theirs, and wiped my feet as carefully on the mat. And at table—crowded with good things—I ate in silence, hungrily. Mrs. Neely sat on the edge of her chair, watching us, helping, rising to fetch us whatever was wanted, without a word. She ate little, but she did not ask me the questions I feared. No. We were at peace till Jim gave me away.

"He's going to be a farmer, that boy," he said as he sat back, sated.

"He is not," Mrs. Neely answered, just like that. I was startled. Mr. Neely smiled, Jim winked at me, but Mrs. Neely sounded so sure that I was convinced. The men left me with her. She had to clear away, and that, her duty, she did silently, quickly, and most thoroughly. She not only washed the dishes, pans, knives and forks, as the Chinese servant did at home; she polished them. She set the whole dining-room-kitchen to rights, thoroughly; then she set herself to rights, took off her apron, and turned to me.

"What time do you start for town?" she asked. I told her about four. "Very well," she said, "let's go out in the garden and talk." We went into the garden and she worked, irrigating and picking flowers and—talking. I can see her now, a slight figure with small, tender, strong hands, kind brown eyes, and firm, straight little mouth, tending her flowers and saying, "I'm their pastor, and they need me as much as they need the sun. It is good to be needed." I can't remember all that she said, but pictures came up in her words, as flowers shine in shrubbery, and I got somehow the story of a little girl who dreamed of being needed in the garden of the world. She met as she grew older and she loved a tall, handsome man who was good, "the best man in the world": generous, kind, faithful. And this prince of simple men, he needed her; he said so, but, clearer still, she saw his need. She took him, gladly, and he took her—he took her far, far away. And it was a beautiful place where they went, a garden indeed, and he was good always. "That girl lived twenty years with that man and she never discovered in him a single fault. There is no other man like that." He was her ideal and "the novels are all wrong; they did not live happy ever after, those two. They lived only at peace for ever. That is what lovers have for ever, true lovers; not happiness, but peace." There could not be happiness for her because the garden was too big; it was a state, and no woman and no one man could tend it. Only many men and many women could irrigate and prune and bring up the flowers in so big a garden. And her man did his part of that. For he was a farmer. But it was not enough for her, because her dream was to be the princess of a prince who tended not land and cattle, but mankind; not wheat and grapes, but souls, the spirits of men and women and children. She could have served with her man in a garden of souls, and he, with his beautifulness, would have been a prince of peace to his fellow men as he had been to her alone and she would have been a gardener to the children of men instead of only to her flowers and her wonderful, wonderful man.

It was a sad, a very sad, happy story, and it had a moral. "Happiness comes from your work," she pointed. "Not from love and not from goodness, but from finding out what you like to do and doing it. And so—don't be a farmer," she snapped with her scissors. "Be a minister."

And because the story was so sad and so happy, I thought I might become a minister. But she wasn't through. She questioned me about what I wanted to be. I gave her the list: Indian chief, cowboy, knight, statesman, locomotive engineer, prince—I didn't tell her all my ideals. I suppressed the jockey stage, and the teamster, the steamboat, and a large number of other ambitions; she did not notice any omissions. She seized upon the prince. That was the thing to be, only not a royal but a spiritual prince. And she got out of me, too, some of my other problems: how the world was made, where children came from, where China was on a spherical globe. She discovered also that these problems troubled me deeply and were driving me to thought and study and worry. And she had the answers to all of them.

"If you will believe," she said—"if you put your faith in God and leave it all to Him, your troubles will be over and you will be at rest. Try it."

And I tried it. She told me the biblical story of the Creation more really than I had ever heard it, and so beautifully. I knew it very well. I had had church and Sunday school regularly, and I did believe in God and Christ. Of course. I had begun of late to have some emotional sense of religion. Religion, however, had been a duty, not a reality; church was, like school, like other requirements, a mere matter of the dull routine of life. My imagination, my emotions, had all gone into my own adventures, experiments, and play. She turned them into religion and made it a part, almost the whole, of my life—for a while. I had from that day's talk with Mrs. Neely a sense of comfort and clearness which she said I might, as a preacher, convey to all mankind.

When I went out to the barn for my pony, Jim, who came to help me, looked at me curiously.

"Going to be a preacher, eh?" he said. "How old are you?" I

told him. "Oh, well, that'll be all right." And he boosted me up on my pony and watched me ride off, as Mrs. Neely did, waving from the garden.

It was an ecstatic time for me. I rode out to the Neely farm whenever there was time. I had begun "going with girls" and to parties. My mother, noticing it, had me and my sisters take dancing lessons, and we had parties in our house. I fell in love. I really loved several girls, besides Miss Belle Kay, whom I called on often. I adored her, and I think now she understood me pretty well. She took me seriously, let me worship her, and played up her part perfectly. She let me tell her about my other girls, whom I merely loved at first; no adoration about that; she helped me to pick one out of the several and encouraged me to intensify my concentrated sentiment. This romantic period was coming to a head when Mrs. Neely discovered and turned it into religion. I still went to dances; I still called on my girl. I still enjoyed all the girls and the parties and the ice cream and cakes. I was happy in all this, but so was I happy at my beaver traps, hunting, swimming, and riding with my friends, men and boys. But happiest of all were the miserable hours I spent weeping over my soul in my bed, praying for it in corners, and going to church where the music was wet even if the sermons were dry. My father eyed me keenly as I developed my sudden interest in church-going; he had just seen me fasting as a jockey, but my mother accepted this, as she did all my conversions, without skepticism, with heartfelt sympathy. She assured me that Mrs. Neely was right, that my prayers would be answered. And the test came soon.

The time was coming for the week-end out on the Duke's ranch. All the boys were ready for it. When I reported that Jim said that Mrs. Neely would take in only boys on red ponies with certain white marks, they went out themselves on their off-colored horses and made other arrangements. Meanwhile I spent all my spare time on the Neely farm, talking religion with Mrs. Neely, farming with Mr. Neely, and life in general with Jim Neely. My father suggested that I change my address, live there, and visit my own family now and then; it would save the pony many a trip, and I said I would take up the subject with the Neelys and let him know. He got a look from my mother which made him snap his paper with his finger and turn to the news of the day.

Each of my parents thought the other did not understand me, and I agreed with both of them. And I preferred it so, because my sisters, who did understand me, abused the power of their intelligence.

"Let's see," said one of them, "you are going out to the Neely farm to work cattle on Saturday and then to the ranch for a Sunday of prayer. Is that the plan?"

We took our horses to school at noon on the Friday of our departure, our horses, guns, and all the dogs of our several neighborhoods. Leaving the animals hitched in the shade of the trees outside the grounds, we went to our classes for the hour and a half which, curiously, was longer than the whole two hours of other days. It was hot; the schoolroom was a bake-oven. The only cool thing in sight was the snow on the Sierras far, far away; the only interesting sight was the face of the clock. The teacher was cross, but hot too and prompt. She also watched the clock; I saw her look at it, and she saw me unlacing my shoes and unbuttoning buttons; she knew why I was undressing, and at 2:29, with a nod at me, she banged the bell and I was the first out of the room, the first into the street, where the dogs greeted me with yelps. The other fellows were close after me, but I was mounted when they arrived and with my dogs (mostly Jake Stortz's greyhounds) was galloping down the street toward the American River. The race was on.

Since Sacramento City is laid out in squares, you could ride out any street you chose and turn wherever you liked. I had my street alone for a while; we always took different streets for the start. But there were only a few places where you could cross the railroad track, and we met in groups at those places, and headed for one spot on the river where we all came together. This day we all crossed the track at the same place, and I was still first; my teacher had seen to that; but through the brush and over the sandy bottom of the river we were in a bunch, a bunch of undressed or undressing boys who dropped their clothes in heaps on the sand and rode naked into the river. As the horses plunged, hot, into the icy water, you had to dive off their backs and swim or wade back to beat them ashore, else they would get away; and so when you were out and had them standing in line, the race was over. I was first.

Tying our horses to the brush, we swam; that is to say, we dived in, swam a few strokes, and came out to roll in the sand—repeating this till we were "used to" the cold water. Then we usually swam across the stream and swiped peanuts and melons from the Chinese farmers, but this day they (the Saracens) were expecting us. There were several of them; we saw them hiding, in wait for us. And besides we had something more interesting than a war with the Saracens ahead of us. We dressed early, after only two hours of swimming, rode back to town, and took to the Stockton road. It was hot, the horses were sweating, the dogs panting, and we were uncomfortable from the sand in our clothes. But we raised a hare a few miles out, and as the dogs charged, we followed over the fence and had a hunt, short but fast. One of Jake Stortz's dogs picked up the hare; he was mine, therefore, and I hung him like a scalp from my belt.

As we approached Florin we separated one by one, each with his dogs for the place he was to stay the night. I rode up the Neely lane, my three dogs after me, and Jim and Mrs. Neely came out to greet me.

"What's this?" she demanded. "Dogs, too? You never said there would be dogs. What can we do with—"

Jim came to the rescue. "I'll find a place for them," he said. I leashed them for him, and he went off with the dogs and the pony. Mrs. Neely was grumbling about the dogs, but she gripped me by the shoulder, and when Jim was gone, she exclaimed at my appearance. A fellow never is neat after a swim, but she scolded me, ran her fingers through my hair, down my neck. "Sand," she discovered. "Sand everywhere. You come with me."

She pulled me over to the big irrigating tub in the garden, yanked off my clothes, and stuck me in the cold water. "You stay there," she commanded, and she shook out my clothes. Hanging them up on the branch of a tree, she darted into the house, and, coming back with soap and a brush, she washed, she scrubbed me, complaining all the time about boys and ponies, and dogs; savages, inconveniences, dirt, and dogs; selfishness, thoughtlessness, inconveniences, and dogs. "Dogs, too!" she would exclaim. But she got me washed, helped me dress in rolled-up clothes of her husband's, and it seemed to me as if she liked us all, boys, ponies, inconveniences, and dogs. She was putting on her indignation, I felt; I wasn't sure, because she was very rough. She would jerk me around; she wouldn't let me dress myself; she wanted to put on every garment, shirt, pants, shoes and stockings. And when I was fully dressed, she brushed my hair and took me by the hand to her kitchen, where I had to sit by the fire while she finished her preparations for supper, which I evidently had belated. Anyhow, Mr. Neely came in uncalled, and when she began to tell him indignantly about me and how I came to them full of sand and dirt and dogs, he smiled and interrupted.

"Yes, yes, but you. How are you?"

"Oh, I'll be all right," she answered impatiently. But he touched her cheeks, and I noticed that they were red. "That's the stove," she said, but he wagged his head and looked anxious.

We ate the hot supper with hot breads, in silence as usual, we three men, and Mrs. Neely hung over me and gave me selected morsels to eat. She ate not a mouthful, as Mr. Neely remarked at the end. "No, I can't," she said, and she rose, and went about clearing the table and the kitchen while we sat silent. There was something the matter, but I began to feel sleepy; I tried to keep awake, but my head nearly sprained my neck, and at last, I remember, Mrs. Neely, having finished her work, spoke up.

"Now, then, you dirty boy, you are tired," she said. "You'll be falling asleep in your chair. Come with me." Mr. Neely offered to take me to my room, but "No," she commanded sharply, "I'm going to put him to bed."

She put her arm around my neck and drew me into the parlor where she had all ready, on the sofa, a piled-up white bed. It looked good, all clean and cool, and I could have tumbled right into it myself, had she let me. But, no, she must undress me, put on me one of Mr. Neely's great nightgowns, and we kneeled together by the bed and prayed. I had no special request to make; so I said a regular prayer, the Lord's, and I hardly could say that, so heavy was I. But Mrs. Neely prayed something about being "spared sickness, which is idleness." Then she rolled me into the bed, drew the sheet close about me, and as I fell asleep, she seemed to be crying quietly. Still on her knees, with her arms out over me, I felt her sobbing.

There was something the matter.

X

I BECOME A HERO, SAVE A LIFE

ONE of the wrongs suffered by boys is that of being loved before loving. They receive so early and so freely the affection and devotion of their mothers, sisters, and teachers that they do not learn to love; and so, when they grow up and become lovers and husbands, they avenge themselves upon their wives and sweethearts. Never having had to love, they cannot; they don't know how. I, for example, was born in an atmosphere of love; my parents loved me. Of course. But they had been loving me so long when I awoke to consciousness that my baby love had no chance. It began, but it never caught up. Then came my sisters, one by one. They too were loved from birth, and they might have stayed behind as I did, but girls are different; my sisters seem to have been born loving as well as loved. Anyhow my first sister, though younger than I, loved me long before I can remember even noticing her, and I cannot forget the shock of astonishment and humiliation at my discovery of her feeling for me. She had gone to Stockton to visit Colonel Carter's family, and in a week was so homesick for me that my father and mother took me with them to fetch her. That was their purpose. Mine was to see the great leader of my father's wagon train across the plains and talk live stock with him. You can imagine how I felt when, as we walked up to the house, the front door opened and my little sister rushed out ahead, threw her arms around me, and cried—actually cried—with tears running down her cheeks, "My Len, my Len!"

I had to suffer it, but what would Colonel Carter think, and his sons? And as it was with my family, so it was with Mrs. Neely. I came to love her, as I did my mother and sisters, but only with great difficulty, because she loved me first, loved me when I was

77

loving not her, but her delicious cooking, and worst of all she loved me as a regular fellow such as I was—a horseman, trapper, scout, knight—cannot afford to be loved. Hence my feelings that night, when, some time after Mrs. Neely prayed me to sleep, Mr. Neely called me. There was something the matter, and I was not sorry, I was almost glad.

"Mrs. Neely is sick," he said. "She has a high fever, and I have to ask you to get up quick and ride into town for the doctor. Will you?"

Would I? "Paul Revere," I thought, and I was up and dressing. No pony express rider ever dressed faster than I did. Nor more gladly. Mr. Neely was telling me what doctor to get, where to find him, what to say, and I heard his directions. Sure. But I was eager to be off on my long, hard night ride—seven miles to go, six, five, four, and so on till, panting and exhausted, the pony and I would knock up that doctor and—

Jim Neely came in. "Your horse is at the gate, ready," he said. Great! Jim said it right, and I answered, "So am I." Mr. Neely turned away. "I must go back to Mrs. Neely," he said, and his face looked anxious, frightened. It was evidently a real emergency. I dashed out, Jim following me to the garden gate, and I seized and jumped up on my horse.

"One moment," Jim called and took the pony by the bit and spoke; he spoke very slowly. "You know, don't you, how to ride fast and far?"

Of course I did, and I wanted to start, but no, Jim wasted precious time talking.

"You start off easy, a gentle lope to, say, the main road. Then you walk the pony a hundred yards or so, then you lope again to about Dudens' place. By that time the pony will be warmed, but a bit winded. Walk again till he's easy, then go it; gallop a mile or so. Walk him again, fast, but walk; then you can run him a bit; not far. Trot half a mile—"

It was awful. Jim was right. That was the way it was done; I knew that; but it was hard; it was not the way the Paul Revere poem did it, nor any of the other poems; all the books let a fellow run the whole way, and that was the fun of it, to run till your horse dropped. But the cavalry, the scouts, Indians, and cowboys, all hurried as Jim said, except when they were drunk. And Jim said I was not to get drunk even on excitement. I had to keep my wits about me and think of everything.

"About your dogs, for example," he said, "and the other boys. What am I to do about them?"

I was glad it was dark, so that Jim could not see that I was ashamed to have forgotten everything. He asked me if it would be right for him to drive down to Florin with the dogs to meet there the gang and tell them to go on alone to the ranch.

"Yes, that'll be all right," I said. "Let go."

But Jim didn't let go. He suggested that I go home after seeing the doctor, have my breakfast there, and come out to the farm again tomorrow, Sunday. Yes, yes, I agreed, only—

"How far can your pony run at full speed?" he asked, and I told him; a quarter of a mile. "Well then, remember that," he said. "He can run only a quarter of a mile, and you have seven miles to go."

By this time I was so dashed, so unheroic, that Jim may have seen my depression. He gave me a boost back up to the poetic. "Now go," he said; "you are going to find out that the hero business is hard work, requiring judgment and self-control, not merely whip and spurs. And," he added, "your friend Mrs. Neely needs you tonight, you and a doctor. Good luck to you."

So I got away, but of course Jim stood and watched me. I had to lope slowly down the lane to the cross road and so on to the main road. It was a faster lope than Jim meant, but I walked the pony halfway to Dudens', and—well, I followed instructions pretty nearly. It was a strain. The hero business was, like everything else apparently, not what it was cracked up to be. I had time to think that; I had time to think of a lot of things out there alone in the dark—pretty dark—on that road all alone. There were some farmers driving to market, but I passed them fast, and so really was out there alone most of the time. And I could not imagine much. Jim had spoiled the game, and my thoughts finished it. For the chief of my thoughts was that Mrs. Neely was really ill, needed me, and—and—this is what hurt: I had been glad she was sick so that I could make an unselfish dash to town for the doctor. What was the matter with me? Did I think only of myself, as my mother said? Was I incapable of love and devotion?

By the time I reached the city limits the light of dawn was breaking, outside and in. It showed up over the Sierras, and it showed up all over my conscience. The light brightened the mountains and the road; it was quietly beautiful outside, but inside it darkened my soul and agitated my ugliness. I was like the rest of the world; I was not what I seemed. I was a sham. And I didn't want to be a sham. No, I didn't.

Religion came to my rescue. As I thought of Mrs. Neely sick and praying, so good to me and expecting so much goodness from me, I remembered that I was to be a preacher, a shepherd of men. Well, here I was, a shepherd. With a wave of emotion, I cut out being a Paul Revere and became a minister, a country preacher, like my grandfather, riding on his horse to get a doctor to come and save a lost lamb or sheep, Mrs. Neely. That seemed to give a meaning to my night ride, an heroic meaning, and I galloped on into the city happy again, happy and sad, a combination which occurred often in my young life. The clatter of my horse's hoofs rattling along the sleeping streets, echoing from the dark, dead houses, gave me the thrill I liked. I met and flew past a milkman, wondering what he would wonder about me and my speed, but I didn't care, really. I bent over my pony's neck, held the reins low down like a jockey, and twisting and turning into the right street, darted at full speed up to the doctor's house. Throwing the reins over his hitching-post, I ran up the stairs, rang the bell, knocked at the door, again and again, till at last a sleepy Chinese servant came to the door.

"Wasser maller you?" he demanded.

"Doctor, quick," I said.

He turned, grumbling, and disappeared. He was gone a long time, and when he came slipping back, he bade me calmly "Come in." He led me upstairs and on into the doctor's bedroom, where the doctor lay deep in bed. When I sank my message down to him, he groaned, was still a moment; then up he came and out, and he dressed.

"Mrs. Neely," he said as he pulled on his boots. "Great, good woman that, a lady, the American gentlewoman. We must save her." And, quickly dressed, he came with me down the stairs. At sight of my horse he paused.

"Oh," he exclaimed. "No buggy. You came a-horseback. Must

have been a dark and lonely ride"—and looking at me—"for a boy." He asked and I told him who I was. "Good boy," he said, "brave boy. And you want to save Mrs. Neely. Well, we'll save her together. You've done your part. I'll go and get my rig, and I'll do mine. What'll you do now?"

"I'll pray for her," I said. "She wants me to."

"Oh, you'll pray, eh? I meant to ask if you'd drive out with me or go home?"

"Jim said I was to go home," I answered.

"Um-hm," the doctor said. "Good. You go home and pray for Mrs. Neely, and I'll drive out and do the rest. And maybe the best I can do will be to tell her you are praying for her."

As he went out to his stable, I remounted and rode home. It was full dawn when I reached the stable. I rubbed down and fed my pony, and that done, I knelt in the stall and prayed for Mrs. Neely. It was an exquisite pleasure, that prayer; so I prolonged it until I was lifted into a state of bliss. Thus moved, I went into the house, up to my room, and tried to sleep, in vain. I prayed some more. I had discovered something, the joy of prayer; and the light of it must have been on my face when I appeared at breakfast. Everybody looked up, and everybody but my father said something.

"Why—?" one sister began, and another, "How—?" "But what ails you?" my mother exclaimed. "Nothing," I answered, but after a while I broke down and told it all, Mrs. Neely's illness, my night ride, the doctor, and—and the prayers. There was universal admiration and sympathy, excepting, as I noticed, on the part of my father. He looked sharply at me for a moment, and he might have spoken if my mother had not caught his glance and warned him: "Now, Joseph." He obeyed. He snapped his morning paper and read it.

The next few days were wonderful. I was exalted. I was melancholy; I worried about Mrs. Neely's condition, which was serious. The doctor shook his head and told me so when he came back from his first visit. He had sent out a nurse with some medicines that afternoon and was going himself that (Saturday) night. I moped around Sunday morning, went mournfully to church, where I joined in the prayers with my whole heart and some tears.

"He's enjoying it," I heard my father blurt to my mother as

we were coming out of the church, and she was shocked, indignant, and shut him up. So was I hurt, and yet I gradually realized that it was true. What did that mean? I was unhappy, I was miserable, and yet—and yet I was happy. I prayed for Mrs. Neely's recovery, I wanted her to get well, and yet—and yet, I saw and I faced the fact that I would not for the world have had her not sick.

That afternoon I was to ride out to the farm. I called, first, on the doctor, who was really worried. "Very, very ill," he said, "but we must save her. We will. You are praying?" he asked. I was. "Good," he said, "I told her you were." And he gave me some medicines to take out, and I rode the long seven miles with the lifting sense that I was really of use to some one at last.

Jim was dressed in his Sunday town clothes and looked scared. Mr. Neely I did not see, nor the patient, of course. The nurse was in the kitchen and she didn't see me. She would not even look at me. I stayed with Jim, who fed and rubbed my horse. As we sat on the top board of the corral fence, he talked beautifully about Mrs. Neely.

"I thought she didn't like you," I commented.

"Huh," he said. "She always pretends to be down on a fellow. It took Will years to believe that she liked him, even him. And you. Remember how she pretended to resent your nerve in coming here just for meals? I tell you that woman is so full-up with love that she has to make out she is down on us, and she is so good and kind that she has to act bad and hard and cold. That woman is one of these here hypocrites, upside down—just the opposite from us."

He was watching the road, and by and by he got down off the fence. "Here they come," he said. I looked and saw Hjalmar Bergman on Black Bess, waving from the end of the lane. Jim explained that he had arranged to have the other boys stop there for me on their way home from the ranch.

He had my pony ready, and as he boosted me up on his back, Jim said: "There is one thing more. The nurse says the crisis will come for Mrs. Neely tonight. The doctor will be here for it, no doubt. I think it would be fine if you would do tonight what she asked you to do—pray."

"I've been praying all the time," I answered.

"I know," Jim said, "but a prayer tonight might be answered, and that would please Mrs. Neely if she gets well."

I promised. And then I almost forgot it. When I joined Hjalmar and he and I rode down to the main road to meet the other fellows, we got to talking about their time at the ranch. It must have been great. They had good hunting on the way out, landed there with fourteen hares and a lot of birds. They were well received; the cowboys messed around with them all afternoon, when they were cutting out some young steers for the market. Saturday night there was a great dinner, drinking and gambling by the gang, and on Sunday—games, racing, roping, shooting—everything. I had missed it!

But the news that hurt me most was that Dook was gone. I would never see him again, and "it was my fault." He had told the other hands about us boys; he had arranged for our reception and entertainment; and then, about a week before we were to come out to the ranch, he up and left. He had a chance to get a boat that was sailing from San Francisco to England, a boat that he knew the captain of; but when the other fellows asked him why he was going home so suddenly, he answered: "It was something that kid said."

"What did the kid say?" they asked him.

"Oh," he answered, "the kid said that there was romance everywhere, even at home."

I was dazed; so was Hjalmar; so were the other boys. "Did you say that?" Hjalmar asked.

I had not. I didn't even know what it meant. "What is romance?" I asked, and the boys didn't know either. We all puzzled awhile, then dropped the problem to pick up a buck hare that rose in the road; he bounded with the dogs and horses after him and twice jumped the fence before the dogs got him.

When we reached town it was dark, and I was late to supper. I was thinking. What did the Duke mean? What is that which is everywhere, even at home? That romance business? And why did the Duke sail for home? Why not a steamship? Why didn't he stop and see me on his way? Was he angry with me? But, chiefly, what is romance? I forgot all about Mrs. Neely and my promise to pray. I fell asleep thinking about the Duke and romance. On Monday I had school, and it was interesting that day; we had the ranch to talk over and over. We were invited to come again. But that afternoon I remembered with a pang that Mrs.

Neely needed me. I called on the doctor; he was not in his office, and he was not expected home till late; had a bad case out in the country that was coming to a crisis that night.

"So," I thought, "the crisis was not last night; it's tonight." I still could pray. And thinking about that, and thinking how thoughtless I had been, I worked myself up into a crisis of my own; I prayed, riding my pony; I prayed in his stall. I was in such a state of repentance and faith at supper that my mother was worried. She tried to have me tell her what the matter was. I wouldn't. I went off alone to my room and there, kneeling down, I prayed and wept for a long, long time, till I saw my mother peeping in at the door.

Indignant, I rose and was about to say something when she put her arms around me and disclosed her belief in me, in prayer, and especially in my prayers. She was so truly, so emotionally sympathetic that I told her what I was praying for: Mrs. Neely and her crisis that night. "Perhaps it is at this very hour," she suggested, and somehow that got me by the throat. I dropped back on my knees, and I prayed aloud, my mother beside me.

The next day I called on the doctor. He was hurriedly leaving his office on a case, another case. "Mrs. Neely?" he called back at me. "Oh, Mrs. Neely, yes, the good woman is all right. She had a sharp crisis; I was there, and I almost gave her up, but about nine o'clock she suddenly came through and fell asleep. And now, last night and this morning, she was on the way to complete recovery."

Nine o'clock! That was the hour. I told my mother, and she and I rejoiced. Nine o'clock was my bedtime; it was the very moment when I had prayed. We were pals, my mother and I, all the afternoon; we talked about my future, the church, and the good I would do in the world. It was great. And I thought my father was going to join in with us. He knew about my prayers; my mother had told him, no doubt, and when he came home that evening he said he had seen Mrs. Neely's doctor and that she was on the road to recovery.

"We know," my mother said. "And the crisis was passed at nine o'clock, just when Lennie was praying."

"Y-e-e-s," my father agreed, "the hour was the same, but the doctor said it was Sunday—"

"Oh, Joseph," my mother cut in, and he stopped. Nothing more was said by any of us—neither then nor afterward—about that, but the tradition grew both at home and on the farm that I had saved Mrs. Neely by my prayers. And it was a pretty tradition, a pleasant belief, which even my father respected. For I remember how once, when I was thinking about the Duke's last words, I asked my father at table what the cowboy meant by saying romance was everywhere, even at home, and my father said, "Well, but it is, isn't it?"

And somehow I knew that he meant that that was true of me and religion, or—something like that. And he was a religious man, too.

XI

I GET A COLT TO BREAK IN

OLONEL CARTER gave me a colt. I had my pony, and my father meanwhile had bought a pair of black carriage horses and a cow, all of which I had to attend to when we had no "man." And servants were hard to get and keep in those days; the women married, and the men soon quit service to seize opportunities always opening. My hands were pretty full, and so was the stable. But Colonel Carter seemed to think that he had promised me a horse. He had not; I would have known it if he had. No matter. He thought he had, and maybe he did promise himself to give me one. That was enough. The kind of man that led immigrant trains across the continent and delivered them safe, sound, and together where he promised would keep his word. One day he drove over from Stockton, leading a two-year-old which he brought to our front door and turned over to me as mine. Such a horse!

She was a cream-colored mare with a black forelock, mane, and tail and a black stripe along the middle of her back. Tall, slender, high-spirited, I thought then—I think now that she was the most beautiful of horses. Colonel Carter had bred and reared her with me and my uses in mind. She was a careful cross of a mustang mare and a thoroughbred stallion, with the stamina of the wild horse and the speed and grace of the racer. And she had a sense of fun. As Colonel Carter got down out of his buggy and went up to her, she snorted, reared, flung her head high in the air, and, coming down beside him, tucked her nose affectionately under his arm.

"I have handled her a lot," he said. "She is kind as a kitten, but she is as sensitive as a lady. You can spoil her by one mistake. If you ever lose your temper, if you ever abuse her, she will be ruined for ever. And she is unbroken. I might have had her broken to ride for you, but I didn't want to. I want you to do it. I have taught her to lead, as you see; had to, to get her over here. But here she is, an unbroken colt; yours. You take and you break her. You're only a boy, but if you break this colt right, you'll be a man—a young man, but a man. And I'll tell you how."

Now, out west, as everybody knows, they break in a horse by riding out to him in his wild state, lassooing, throwing, and saddling him; then they let him up, frightened and shocked, with a yelling broncho-buster astride of him. The wild beast bucks, the cowboy drives his spurs into him, and off they go, jumping, kicking, rearing, falling, till by the weight of the man, the lash, and the rowels, the horse is broken—in body and spirit. This was not the way I was to break my colt.

"You must break her to ride without her ever knowing it," Colonel Carter said. "You feed and you clean her—you; not the stable man. You lead her out to water and to walk. You put her on a long rope and let her play, calling her to you and gently pulling on the rope. Then you turn her loose in the grass lot there and, when she has romped till tired, call her. If she won't come, leave her. When she wants water or food, she will run to your call, and you will pet and feed and care for her." He went on for half an hour, advising me in great detail how to proceed. I wanted to begin right away. He laughed. He let me lead her around to the stable, water her, and put her in the stable and feed her.

There I saw my pony. My father, sisters, and Colonel Carter saw me stop and look at my pony.

"What'll you do with him?" one of my sisters asked. I was bewildered for a moment. What should I do with the little red horse? I decided at once.

"You can have him," I said to my sisters.

"No," said Colonel Carter, "not yet. You can give your sisters the pony by and by, but you'll need him till you have taught the colt to carry you and a saddle—months; and you must not hurry. You must learn patience, and you will if you give the colt time to learn it, too. Patience and control. You can't control a young horse unless you can control yourself. Can you shoot?" he asked suddenly.

I couldn't. I had a gun and I had used it some, but it was a rifle, and I could not bring down with it such game as there was around Sacramento—birds and hares. Colonel Carter looked at my father, and I caught the look. So did my father. I soon had a shotgun. But at the time Colonel Carter turned to me and said:

"Can't shoot straight, eh? Do you know what that means? That means that you can't control a gun, and that means that you can't control yourself, your eye, your hands, your nerves. You are wriggling now. I tell you that a good shot is always a good man. He may be a 'bad man' too, but he is quiet, strong, steady in speech, gait, and mind. No matter, though. If you break in this colt right, if you teach her her paces, she will teach you to shoot and be quiet."

He went off downtown with my father, and I started away with my colt. I fed, I led, I cleaned her, gently, as if she were made of glass; she was playful and willing, a delight. When Colonel Carter came home with my father for supper, he questioned me.

"You should not have worked her today," he said. "She has come all the way from Stockton and must be tired. Yes, yes, she would not show fatigue; too fine for that, and too young to be wise. You have got to think for her, consider her as you would your sisters."

Sisters! I thought; I had never considered my sisters. I did not say that, but Colonel Carter laughed and nodded to my sisters. It was just as if he had read my thought. But he went on to draw on my imagination a centaur; the colt as a horse's body—me, a boy, as the head and brains of one united creature. I liked that. I would be that. I and the colt: a centaur.

After Colonel Carter was gone home I went to work on my new horse. The old one, the pony, I used only for business: to go to fires, to see my friends, run errands, and go hunting with my new shotgun. But the game that had all my attention was the breaking in of the colt, the beautiful cream-colored mare, who soon knew me—and my pockets. I carried sugar to reward her when she did right, and she discovered where I carried it; so did the pony, and when I was busy they would push their noses into my pockets, both of which were torn down a good deal of the time. But the colt learned. I taught her to run around a circle, turn and go the other way at a signal. My sisters helped me. I held the long rope and the whip (for signaling), while one of the girls led the colt; it was hard work for them, but they took it in turns. One would lead the colt round and round till I snapped the whip; then she would turn, turning the colt, till the colt did it all by herself. And she was very quick. She shook hands with each of her four feet. She let us run under her, back and forth. She was slow only to carry me. Following Colonel Carter's instructions, I began by laying my arm or a surcingle over her back. If she trembled, I drew it slowly off. When she could abide it, I tried buckling it, tighter and tighter. I laid over her, too, a blanket, folded at first, then open, and, at last, I slipped up on her myself, sat there a second, and as she trembled, slid off. My sisters held her for me, and when I could get up and sit there a moment or two, I tied her at a block, and we, my sisters and I, made a procession of mounting and dismounting. She soon got used to this and would let us slide off over her rump, but it was a long, long time before she would carry me.

That we practiced by leading her along a high curb where I could get on as she walked, ride a few steps, and then, as she felt me and crouched, slip off. She never did learn to carry a girl on her back; my sisters had to lead her while I rode. This was not purposeful. I don't know just how it happened, but I do remember the first time I rode on my colt all the way around the lot and how, when I put one of the girls up, she refused to repeat. She shuddered, shook and frightened them off.

While we were breaking in the colt a circus came to town. The ring was across the street from our house. Wonderful! I lived in that circus for a week. I saw the show but once, but I marked the horse-trainers, and in the mornings when they were not too busy I told them about my colt, showed her to them, and asked them how to train her to do circus tricks. With their hints I taught the colt to stand up on her hind legs, kneel, lie down, and balance on a small box. This last was easier than it looked. I put her first on a low big box and taught her to turn on it; then got a little smaller box upon which she repeated what she did on the big one. By and by we had her so that she would step up on a high box so small that her four feet were almost touching, and there also she would turn.

The circus man gave me one hint that was worth all the other tricks put together. "You catch her doing something of herself that looks good," he said, "and then you keep her at it." It was thus that I taught her to bow to people. The first day I rode her out on to the streets was a proud one for me and for the colt, too, apparently. She did not walk, she danced; perhaps she was excited, nervous; anyhow I liked the way she threw up her head, champed at the bit, and went dancing, prancing down the street. Everybody stopped to watch us, and so, when she began to sober down, I picked her up again with heel and rein, saying, "Here's people, Lady," and she would show off to my delight. By constant repetition I had her so trained that she would single-foot, head down, along a country road till we came to a house or a group of people. Then I'd say, "People, Lady," and up would go her head, and her feet would dance.

But the trick that set the town talking was her bowing to any one I spoke to. "Lennie Steffens' horse bows to you," people said, and she did. I never told how it was done; by accident. Dogs used to run out at us, and the colt enjoyed it; she kicked at them sometimes with both hind hoofs. I joined her in the game, and being able to look behind more conveniently than she could, I watched the dogs until they were in range, then gave the colt a signal to kick. "Kick, gal," I'd say, and tap her ribs with my heel. We used to get dogs together that way; the colt would kick them over and over and leave them yelping in the road. Well, one day when I met a girl I knew I lifted my hat, probably muttered a "Good day," and I must have touched the colt with my heel. Anyway, she dropped her head and kicked—not much; there was no dog near, so she had responded to my unexpected signal by what looked like a bow. I caught the idea and kept her at it. Whenever I wanted to bow to a girl or anybody else, instead of saying "Good day," I muttered "Kick, gal," spurred her lightly, and— the whole centaur bowed and was covered with glory and conceit.

Yes, conceit. I was full of it, and the colt was quite as bad. One day my chum Hjalmar came into town on his Black Bess, blanketed. She had had a great fistule cut out of her shoulder and had to be kept warm. I expected to see her weak and dull, but no, the good old mare was champing and dancing, like my colt.

"What is it makes her so?" I asked, and Hjalmar said he didn't know, but he thought she was proud of the blanket. A great idea.

I had a gaudy horse blanket. I put it on the colt and I could hardly hold her. We rode down the main street together, both horses and both boys, so full of vanity that everybody stopped to smile. We thought they admired, and maybe they did. But some boys on the street gave us another angle. They, too, stopped and looked, and as we passed, one of them said, "Think you're hell, don't you?"

Spoilsport!

We did, as a matter of fact; we thought we were hell. The recognition of it dashed us for a moment; not for long, and the horses paid no heed. We pranced, the black and the yellow, all the way down J Street, up K Street, and agreed that we'd do it again, often. Only, I said, we wouldn't use blankets. If the horses were proud of a blanket, they'd be proud of anything unusually conspicuous. We tried a flower next time. I fixed a big rose on my colt's bridle just under her ear and it was great—she pranced downtown with her head turned, literally, to show off her flower. We had to change the decoration from time to time, put on a ribbon, or a bell, or a feather, but, really, it was not necessary for my horse. Old Black Bess needed an incentive to act up, but all I had to do to my horse was to pick up the reins, touch her with my heel, and say, "People"; she would dance from one side of the street to the other, asking to be admired. As she was. As we were.

I would ride down to my father's store, jump off my prancing colt in the middle of the street, and run up into the shop. The colt, free, would stop short, turn, and follow me right up on the sidewalk, unless I bade her wait. If any one approached her while I was gone, she would snort, rear, and strike. No stranger could get near her. She became a frightened, frightening animal, and yet when I came into sight she would run to me, put her head down, and as I straddled her neck, she would throw up her head and pitch me into my seat, facing backward, of course. I whirled around right, and off we'd go, the vainest boy and the proudest horse in the State.

"Hey, give me a ride, will you?" some boy would ask.

"Sure," I'd say, and jump down and watch that boy try to catch and mount my colt. He couldn't. Once a cowboy wanted to try her, and he caught her; he dodged her forefeet, grabbed the reins, and in one spring was on her back. I never did that again. My colt reared, then bucked, and, as the cowboy kept his seat, she shuddered, sank to the ground, and rolled over. He slipped aside and would have risen with her, but I was alarmed and begged him not to. She got up at my touch and followed me so close that she stepped on my heel and hurt me. The cowboy saw the point.

"If I were you, kid," he said, "I'd never let anybody mount that colt. She's too good."

That, I think, was the only mistake I made in the rearing of Colonel Carter's gift-horse. My father differed from me. He discovered another error or sin, and thrashed me for it. My practice was to work hard on a trick, privately, and when it was perfect, let him see it. I would have the horse out in our vacant lot doing it as he came home to supper. One evening, as he approached the house, I was standing, whip in hand, while the colt, quite free, was stepping carefully over the bodies of a lot of girls, all my sisters and all their girl friends. (Grace Gallatin, later Mrs. Thompson-Seton, was among them.) My father did not express the admiration I expected; he was frightened and furious. "Stop that," he called, and he came running around into the lot, took the whip, and lashed me with it. I tried to explain; the girls tried to help me explain.

I had seen in the circus a horse that stepped thus over a row of prostrate clowns. It looked dangerous for the clowns, but the trainer had told me how to do it. You begin with logs, laid out a certain distance apart; the horse walks over them under your lead, and whenever he touches one you rebuke him. By and by he will learn to step with such care that he never trips. Then you substitute clowns. I had no clowns, but I did get logs, and with the girls helping, we taught the colt to step over the obstacles even at a trot. Walking, she touched nothing. All ready thus with the logs, I had my sisters lie down in the grass, and again and again the colt stepped over and among them. None was ever touched. My father would not listen to any of this; he just walloped me, and when he was tired or satisfied and I was in tears, I blubbered a short excuse: "They were only girls." And he whipped me some more.

My father was not given to whipping; he did it very seldom, but he did it hard when he did it at all. My mother was just the opposite. She did not whip me, but she often smacked me, and she had a most annoying habit of thumping me on the head with her thimbled finger. This I resented more than my father's thorough-going thrashings, and I can tell why now. I would be playing Napoleon and as I was reviewing my Old Guard, she would crack my skull with that thimble. No doubt I was in the way; it took a lot of furniture and sisters to represent properly a victorious army; and you might think as my mother did that a thimble is a small weapon. But imagine Napoleon at the height of his power, the ruler of the world on parade, getting a sharp rap on his crown from a woman's thimble. No. My father's way was more appropriate. It was hard. "I'll attend to you in the morning," he would say, and I lay awake wondering which of my crimes he had discovered. I know what it is to be sentenced to be shot at sunrise. And it hurt, in the morning, when he was not angry but very fresh and strong. But you see, he walloped me in my own person; he never humiliated Napoleon or my knighthood, as my mother did. And I learned something from his discipline, something useful.

I learned what tyranny is and the pain of being misunderstood and wronged, or, if you please, understood and set right; they are pretty much the same. He and most parents and teachers do not break in their boys as carefully as I broke in my colt. They haven't the time that I had, and they have not some other incentives I had. I saw this that day when I rubbed my sore legs. He had to explain to my indignant mother what had happened. When he had told it his way, I gave my version: how long and cautiously I had been teaching my horse to walk over logs and girls. And having shown how sure I was of myself and the colt, while my mother was boring into his silence with one of her reproachful looks, I said something that hit my father hard.

"I taught the colt that trick, I have taught her all that you see she knows, without whipping her. I have never struck her; not once. Colonel Carter said I mustn't, and I haven't."

And my mother, backing me up, gave him a rap: "There," she said, "I told you so." He walked off, looking like a thimble-rapped Napoleon.

XII

I BECOME A DRUNKARD

FROM the Sacramento valley on a clear day one can see the snow-capped peaks of the Sierras, and when the young summer wheat is stretching happily in the heat of the sun, when men and animals and boys are stewing and steaming, it is good to look up through the white-hot flames at the cool blue of the mountains and let your eyes skate over the frost. All through my childhood I thirsted for those Sierras. They were a scene for daydreams and night wishes. My mother always tried to fulfill our wishes, and my father always yielded to her pressure when time had proven our demand real and strong. We went one summer vacation to the foothills; no snow; the peaks shone and called to us still from afar. After that we went higher and higher, to Blue Cañon, to Summit Station, Lake Tahoe, and, before the railroad was put through up the other way, north to Mount Shasta. I liked the mountains. They were not what I expected. It took several summers and some growth on my part to reach the snow line, and then, to my disappointment, the old snow was "rotten," as the mountain people had told me. There was no sledding, skating, or snowballing on summer snow. But there was, as always, compensation for disappointment. There was something better than what I had looked for and not found: hunting, fishing, swimming, boating, trapping in the woods; lakes, rapids, and the flumes.

My life a-horseback in the valley had prepared me to enjoy these sports with skill, joy, and imagination. Beaver-trapping without beavers had taught me to trap chipmunks and catch them; shooting hares, meadow-larks, and ducks was practice for quail and deer. And my friends in the valley below were introductory to the mountain folk.

Horse play is good business for a boy; schooling a young horse was good schooling for me, and no doubt Colonel Carter had my education in mind when he gave me a two-year-old colt to educate. I became, as he predicted, a good shot; not so good as I pretended and was thought to be, but the training of the colt had developed in me some patience, steadiness, and a degree of self-control which has been of use to me always and served me well in the mountains.

Once, for instance, when I was up on the McCloud River with a party of fishermen I made a chum of an Indian boy about my age. He was shooting fish with a rifle when I came upon him. Standing still on a low bluff over a deep, quiet pool of the river, he watched the school of salmon trout at rest in the dark, cool depths, and whenever a big one rose to the surface, he fired—just before the fish flipped—then he slipped downstream to wade out and pick up the dead or wounded trout. A silent boy—silent as an Indian—he did not greet me; he said nothing at all. I talked. I told him I could shoot too; not fish, to be sure, but deer, bear—anything else. He heard my boastings long, making no comment till we were going back to camp. Then we saw a hawk light on the top of a high pine across the canyon, perhaps two hundred yards away. I thought he was going to shoot it. He adjusted the range of his rifle to the distance and then, without a word, he handed the gun to me.

"Now make good." He might as well have said it; I was caught, and I would expose and humiliate myself, but there was no way out. I took the rifle, aimed carelessly (what was the use?), and quickly fired. And the bird fell! Amazed myself, I am sure I did not show the least surprise. I handed back the rifle and went on talking as if nothing out of the ordinary had happened, and I never mentioned the incident and I never fired a rifle again in that region. Never. That was self-possession. It was educated intelligence. That shot, reported by the Indian boy, won me among the Indians and mountaineers a reputation which could not be bettered and might easily have been damaged. I was a crack shot; only, curiously enough, shooting bored me. I am sure that, if my colt had not drilled me in the control of myself and other animals, I would have shot at something else or referred in some way to that unlucky hawk.

All this character-building, however, had interfered somewhat with my proper school work. I went through the grammar school always near the foot of my class and finally failed of promotion to high. My father blamed the colt. He was not altogether right in this. I was graduated from college, where I had no horse, last or among the last in my class. Something else was the matter, something far more educative, I think now; but horses were enough to account for my backwardness to my parents, and that diagnosis made it hard for them to deal with me. They shared my guilt.

We had become a horsy family. When my colt was broken to ride I turned over my pony to my sisters. There were three of them, and one pony was not enough. My father bought a third saddle-horse. Meanwhile he had acquired for himself and the family in general a carriage and a pair of black trotters, which I broke to the saddle because my mother caught the horseback fever. There we were, therefore, a family of six with three saddle-horses and two carriage horses. Naturally they desired to ride into my life, meet my friends, and visit the places I had talked so much about. Reluctantly, gradually, I introduced them to my circle, beginning with the bridge-tender.

One day we all drove or rode out to the trestle where the bridge-tender-prospector, properly warned, received them well and told them all about me. "All they could stand," he said afterward. "I didn't say much about walking the trestle. I didn't say anything about swimming the river in the rapids. I spoke of the Saracens, but I did not mention the Chinese and peanuts and melons." The bridge-tender was all right, a credit to me; and the family respected me on his account. "Good man," my father said. "A good friend of yours," said my mother.

Ah Hook, whom we visited a week or so later, did not rise so well to the emergency. My father liked him, bought a lot of peanuts from him, and ordered a sackful to be delivered at the store "for the boys." But my mother sought for Ah Hook's appreciation of her son; she liked to hear me admired; and the Chink grinned and gave her his honest opinion.

"Him boy allee same heap damn fool," he said. "Him no sabee; him lucky. Tellem lies all day. Tellem me lies, tellem nother man lies: tellem himself lies too. Him boy big damn fool liar. Yes."

My mother did not care to stay long at Ah Hook's; she could not see what I saw in him. We soon closed that visit and the family never went back. Ah Hook, by his tactlessness, lost his chance to become a connection of our family. There were other disappointments. Loony Louie seemed crazy even to me when my father and mother were presented to him. He had just witnessed a slaughter of veal, and bewailing his calves, he was a crazy sight which I saw through their eyes. Some of the parents of my boy friends were not as acceptable to mine as they were to me. I think that, as a rule (for boys), it is better to keep parents apart and at home.

However, in my case, the Neelys made up for Mr. Hook, Louie, and everybody else. The family visit there was carefully planned and long remembered. We all went, three mounted and three in the carriage, and the Neelys were all dressed up in their Sunday clothes, except that Mrs. Neely wore a dainty apron over her black silk dress. The greetings over, she ran back to her kitchen, and Jim and Mr. Neely and I had the horses to take care of. These chores done, the horn blew, and in we filed, an embarrassing crowd, to a dinner, a wonderful dinner. Mrs. Neely had everything for them that I had ever had and more besides, much more. Jim was delighted; he winked at me. But we all enjoyed it, the food, I mean. I did not care for the conversation. It was all about me, and it took the form of a race between my mother and Mrs. Neely to see who could tell the most. I knew all my mother's stories; so did my sisters, who snickered at me or kicked me under the table. Mrs. Neely's recollections, too, I knew, but not in the form in which she told them that day. She seemed to remember everything I had ever done or said out there, and some of my deeds and especially some of my sayings did not sound the way I had thought they would. Rather fine acts became ridiculous. My mother would exclaim that she was surprised, and my sisters would whisper that they weren't surprised. I don't mean that Mrs. Neely gave me away, or if she did, she covered it up somehow. Things that had annoyed her when they happened became almost all right somehow. The time I fell into the pig pen, for instance, and had to be washed, I and my clothes, "every stitch" —Mrs. Neely was certainly irritated that time.

"All this unnecessary extra work just for you, and you lying clean and comfortable in my nice bed while I slave for you"— that is what she had said to me, and now when she told my mother about it, she just laughed, like Jim, as if she had liked it.

But the most embarrassing subject for me and my father, the most amusing to Jim, and the most happy for my mother and Mrs. Neely, was what they called "the efficacy of prayer." The moment it was broached my father drew Mr. Neely into a discussion of some other themes like the weather, the markets, and the future of farming. Jim listened to the ladies, as I had to, and we heard them compare notes on the hour when I prayed. My mother told her she saw me on my knees and knew it was nine o'clock because that was my bedtime, and Mrs. Neely was sure of the hour because the nurse's record showed it was only a little after nine when her crisis passed. Best proof of all, however, was the sense Mrs. Neely had of relief and that some hand had lifted a great weight from her, and from that moment she began to get well. Jim squeezed my knee under the table and smiled; I didn't know whether to express approval or—what.

When late that afternoon we hitched up and drove away with the carriage full of fresh eggs, vegetables, fruit, cakes, and everything, "a good time had been had by all."

Also arrangements had been made for the regular future delivery at our house of whatever produce Mr. Neely had ready for market. There was a big contract for hay and grain. After that the Neelys, one or other of them, used to appear about once a week at our house, and sometimes they stayed or came back for the noon meal.

The two families were friends for life, even after I was gone away to college. I was in Germany when Mrs. Neely fell ill and died. They cabled me to save her, and I tried, but I couldn't. I wasn't praying those days, but I did pray for Mrs. Neely; and she knew it. It was in vain. Her death nearly ended Mr. Neely. He began to age; he sold the farm, and I don't know what became of Jim, but Mr. Neely moved into the city. My father took charge of his small savings and found him a boarding-place where he was to pay so much a week out of his capital, which they reckoned would last a certain number of years, months, and days. The limit worried Mr. Neely, so my father wrote to me, asking me to send him a written guarantee that, after my friend's own capital was used up, I would pay his board as long as he lived. I did so, and Mr. Neely seemed to be relieved and at peace. But he died just the same when his money was ended; he assured my father, who saw him nearly every day toward the end, that he was willing to accept his board from me, but I had the privilege of paying back only a few weeks—of all the good times he had given me, he and Mrs. Neely.

Mrs. Neely never knew that I took to drink and, from the broad road to the pulpit, turned off into the narrow road to hell. An eastern family of boys came to Sacramento, the Southworths, and they fascinated me and my gang, for the very reason that we despised them and tried to hurt them. They were well dressed. "Us regular fellers," we affected to ignore clothes and, since we had to wear something, preferred such careless garb as farmers and vaqueros and cowboys wore. The Southworth boys were an affront to us; they wore eastern clothes, like those you saw in the illustrated eastern papers; and they wore them without shame, without consciousness. Boys can despise and admire, resent and covertly hate and love at the same time; they are not consistent like grown-ups. We got together to see what could be done, and we decided that, while they could wear good clothes easily, they probably could not ride a horse. We would get them on a horse that would bring them down a peg.

My mother's horse was a mad animal that was gentle with her but so wild under a boy that he would run away. We called him the Yellow Streak. I asked Ernie Southworth if he would like to ride with us some day. He said very politely that he would appreciate our courtesy; so we mounted our horses after school one day and rode to the Southworths' house, I on my colt leading Yellow Streak. We boosted Ernie up on the horse, which whirled and ran away, just as we knew it would. We had to race after the Streak with the boy dude riding high; his hat flew off, his neat coat swelled with the wind, his face went white. The Streak ran to our street, turned so fast that he nearly fell, and made straight for our stable. He was going so wildly that he could not turn into the alley; he tried to but passed by and was stopped by a post at the curb. His stop was like that of a broncho—two or three terrible jerks which pitched Ernie Southworth over the post on his hands and knees.

When we rode up, caught the Streak, and jumped down to enjoy the eastern boy's rage and wounds, he stood up and—he apologized. He didn't mean to let the horse get away like that; he was unprepared for the sudden start; he would try again and, he hoped, do better. It was no fun lynching a fellow like that. We 'fessed up to our game and took him into our gang, which straightway took to drink.

No psycho-analytic novelist could guess or even follow the psychology of our downfall. Only boys will understand the perfect logic of it. Since Ernie Southworth was game about the runaway horse, he had to become one of us, and since he dressed well and we all had to stick together, we began to care about clothes. Having become dudes, we didn't exactly follow the fashions of "the east" (which, in California, meant the eastern U.S.), but we kept just a little ahead of them by copying the styles as caricatured in the comic weeklies. We found them more striking than the tailors' fashion plates. When you are dressed up you do the things that go with dress. We went in for dancing and girls. Now the world of women and dancing and fashion is a world by itself, with its own ideals and heroes. The hero of our new world was a fellow a little older than we were, who danced, dressed, and talked well. He was a favorite among the girls because the day after the dance he could describe to the girls in their technical terms what every well-dressed girl and woman wore. We wanted to be like him, but we could not describe women's clothes; so we had to do something else that he did. And the easiest of his habits to imitate was that of going into a saloon, standing at the bar, and having rounds of drink. We danced and spooned and talked, too, but drink was the thing, as vain as herding cattle or trapping beavers, but as fascinating. Once, for example, as I staggered (a little more than I had to) away from the bar, I overheard one man say to another:

"Those boys can carry some liquor, can't they?"

That was great. But better still was the other loafer's reply: "Yes," he said, "but it's tough to see young men setting out on the down grade to hell that way."

XIII

NAPOLEON

I BECAME a drunkard as I had been a knight, a trapper, and a preacher, not for long and not exactly with my whole heart, but with a large part of my imagination. My stomach saved my heart. I hated what I drank; it made me sick. If I could have taken beer or soda or lemonade I would have liked drinking, but think of walking up to a bar, putting your foot on the rail, your elbow familiarly on the polished ebony—like a man —and then asking the barkeep for an ice-cream soda! Impossible. It wasn't done. Beer, yes, but one drank beer for thirst, and I had no thirst. I was on the road to hell, and nobody would have noticed and grieved over my melancholy fate if I had ordered anything but the shuddering, sickening concoction that was the fashion just then among "bad men": rum and gum. That was what Will Ross, our ideal, took, and the whole town was mourning the downfall of this brilliant young man; so we boys ordered rum and gum, braced ourselves, and gulped it down as if it was medicine, excepting, now and then, when no one was looking, we could spill it. I was clever at this; I was caught at it sometimes, but it was worth the risk. The man who could throw away the most could outlast the others, and the manly game was to drink one another down.

"See that fellow over there?" I heard a teamster say one day, and we looked at a young bank clerk who was a crack billiard player, too. "Well, sir," the teamster continued, "that bloke can carry more liquor than a carload of watered stock."

If only that could be said of me!

We all dreaded our fathers. It seemed to be well known that they would "raise hell" with a son who was going to hell, and that was a stage of the journey. Some fellows had been turned out of house and home, some of the hardest, ablest drinkers. I never did have any luck at home. My father never came up to expectations. When he discovered what I was "up to," he did not "go straight up in the air"; he wasn't even shocked.

One night when I came home late as usual, he walked, night-gowned, white, and silent, into my room, watched me without a word as I undressed, and saw me, also speechless, tumble into bed.

"What is this all about?" he asked then.

"Nothing," I said, as distinctly as I could.

"Oh, I know it's nothing," he answered. "It always is nothing with you, but what kind of a nothing is it? If you keep it up, it will be something, something silly, of course, but you might with practice learn to like to drink."

So he knew; he really understood all about it. How did he come to know more about it—more than I did? I was disappointed and humiliated, but also I was sleepy. He saw that, and with a "Tish"—his expression of contempt—he left me to sleep. He never referred to the subject again. He acted, however.

He announced one day that I was to go to a private school, the military academy at San Mateo, south of San Francisco. I was delighted—a change. His reasons, as I remember them, were that I had failed to be graduated from the grammar school, could not go to the high school at home without repeating the last year at the grammar school, and evidently I could not study by myself at home. I seemed to need a school where there was enough discipline to compel me to work. There was too much liberty and play in my life at home. Hence, a military school.

I was delighted. My new chum, Ernie Southworth, had long had a great advantage over us. He knew all about Napoleon. I knew something about Napoleon and Richard the Lion-hearted, the Count of Monte Cristo, and many, very many, other knights; I knew something about many similarly imitable persons, poets, cowboys, trappers, preachers. My interest was scattered, my parts as various as any mere actor's. Ernie had one steady, high ideal, a hero, Napoleon Buonaparte, and when he, on his old white horse, started telling us about the great modern conqueror, we were still, awed, inspired, but humble. For Ernie, unlike the rest of us, was not himself Napoleon; he only followed him as a marshal might, or a soldier with a marshal's baton in his knapsack—a respectful distance behind, bold, worshipful, obedient.

When, then, it developed that he, Ernie, was to go east to study dentistry, while I was to go west and be trained for a Napoleon, I recovered my happy superiority. Most of the other fellows of my gang were about to go to work or to the local high school. They envied me, and they and the girls and my family made an event of my departure, a happy one for me, therefore. "Going away" to school was a distinction and an adventure.

I was about fifteen years old, but I had not a thought of what I was to learn at the new school, except soldiering, of course. And when I got there I found that the boys, all in radiant gray uniforms, loathed these clothes and everything pertaining to the military side of the establishment. Whether it was a pose with them I could not tell; anyway, it was with me, for I had to pretend not to like the orderly discipline, which fascinated me. My secret enthusiasm counted, and I was soon promoted to be a corporal, and better still, I was made a cadet drillmaster and taught the new boys tactics all the time I was there. Meanwhile I read about Napoleon as if I were reading up on my own future.

This I can remember, and I can recall a good deal of all my private reading; I was carrying on my own education in my own boy's way. But I can remember no more of what was taught me in the classrooms of this school than I can of the other schools I went to at home. It was a pretty good school for that time, probably the best of the so-called private schools in a State where the public schools were the best. But there was no attempt made, so far as I can remember, to interest us in the subjects we studied. They were work, therefore, and our minds ran freely to our play or our own curiosities and aspirations. I was not good at the games played: football, baseball, marbles, tops, hare and hounds. Too much horseback had left my running and dodging muscles undeveloped. I used to wish I could have my colt brought down to school, so as to show the great pitchers and halfbacks that there was something that I could do—besides drill. The only distinction I won in athletics was by chance.

Playing hare and hounds one afternoon, I set out with the hares, and humiliated long enough, I was determined to stay with the leaders for once. We had gone perhaps a mile when I began to fail. My distress was alarming; I thought I would fall down and die. I saw myself being carried back dead to the school, but I picked out a great oak ahead on the road; I would go that far anyway, and to my amazement, just before I got there I broke into a sweat, my breath came easily, and I sprinted up to the leaders and finished with them with a sense that I could go on for ever. They, too, were astonished and could not explain it. I had got my second wind, and counting on it thereafter, I was chosen always for long-distance running.

But I was homesick, not for home, but for my horse and my gang, for my country life games and for my interrupted career as a drunkard. There were vacations. My colt, grown now, bore me out to all my old friends, the bridge-tender, the Neelys, and the rest. That was the best of my life. It was natural; no more poses there, except that I never could be so cruel as to tell Mrs. Neely that I had, not given up, but almost forgotten about being a minister. I talked to her about the Episcopal church services we had at school. I rather liked them, as I liked drill. I must have had a taste for ritual. But to the Neely men and to my other grown-up friends I had become what I was, a schoolboy, the only difference between me and other such boys being that I was to be a great man —somehow; and I suppose that all the other schoolboys shared in that distinction.

My father, who knew me pretty well, I think, drew from me or my teachers at San Mateo enough to seek a cure. To center my interest in the school he suggested that, besides Napoleon, I read *Tom Brown at Rugby*. That had some effect. As he expected, no doubt, I began to emulate Tom Brown. This was difficult in our school. We had no fagging system. I tried to establish one, and the older boys were for it; only the little fellows objected. They had some snobbish objection to blacking our shoes, running our errands, and otherwise becoming our servants. Force was needed, and my luck gave me the power.

The discipline of the school was partly a cadet system. The officer of the day was responsible for the enforcement of the law for his twenty-four hours. One night when I was on duty I heard a soft disturbance in one of the dormitories, and slipping in there, I caught several boys out of their beds. They were with other boys. By threatening punishment, I drew from the smaller boys confessions which revealed an ancient, highly organized system of prostitution. One boy, the son of a general, was the head of it. He had as his white slaves a large number of the little boys, whom he paid with cakes, candies, etc. He let them out to other older boys at so much money, candy, or credit per night.

This appeared to me as a chance to introduce the fagging system. I called together the senior officers in my gang. Some of them owned up that they were as guilty as their juniors, but those of us who were innocent of that crime carried through our plot. We made fags of the young criminals. It was fun. It was a sort of reign of terror, and we tyrants enjoyed our power so much that, like grown-ups, we rather abused it. We could not help letting even the teachers see the craven obedience we could exact and the menial services we required.

There was an inquiry from above. Some of the boys confessed everything, and the headmaster had me up as the head of the whole conspiracy. He was furious, but also he was frightened. I could defy him. I would not tell him anything, but he knew all about it himself, the fagging system and, too, the vice foundation thereof, and he was afraid to have any detail of either evil leak out to the parents. He must have known that such things occur in many private schools in all countries; it is said to be common in the English so-called public schools. He acted, however, as if the scandal were unheard of. I don't know all that he did about it, but he compelled me to witness the whipping he administered to the vice squad, and he forbade fagging. I felt so mean that I would have submitted to any penalty, and I escaped all punishment. My first essay into muck-raking cost me nothing.

My best-remembered punishment was for getting myself and half the school drunk, and out of that punishment came some good and some bad results—a change in me.

XIV

ALL THROUGH WITH HEROISM

T HE Napoleon in me énded, as the emperor himself did, in prison. As a leader I had to find worlds to conquer; so when fagging failed I took to drink, I and my followers. My custom had been to drink only in vacations in Sacramento; in San Mateo I was sober—a sort of double life. When I came back to school for my last term I was drunk, not so drunk as I seemed. I could brace up and be sober in the presence of authority, and I could let down and play drunk for the other boys, who were so astonished, so admiring, so envious, that it occurred to me to introduce the habit into the school.

Biding my time, I made some propaganda. That was uphill work. Some other leader had heard a speech against religion; he had brought with him a lot of literature, a book of Bob Ingersoll's lectures, for example, and he soon had all the boys disputing hotly the claims of revealed religion. I hated it, kept out of it as much as I could, but it was everywhere, and I had to hear some of it. And because I did not debate the question but only listened, I was half persuaded. Indeed I think I was the only boy who had his mind opened to the questions underlying the doubts of the day. But having my own leadership to defend, I could not afford to yield to the passing mania for truth, and I stuck to my guns; I stood always for drink as the solution of all such problems till, at last, when the fever of controversy lessened, my propaganda was heard and considered. A practical question superseded the academic religious issue, to wit: Where could we get the drink to get drunk on? I said I would attend to that. It was not so easy as I thought. No tradesmen dared to sell drink in quantity to schoolboys; I met only flat refusals from the saloon men. But, like all great leaders of men, I found lieutenants to do what I could not myself do.

A fellow who was slow to join our "conspiracy against the good name of the school," when finally brought in, said that he would find the drink. I had been thinking of rum and gum; he thought of beer. A brewery wagon passed our school now and then; he stopped it one day and arranged for the delivery of a keg of beer in a certain remote field the next Saturday afternoon. We were there, twenty or thirty boys; and more wanted to come, but were forbidden by us big fellows. I remember how the smaller boys cried or were indignant at our presumption at closing to them this open road to the devil. But we told them that when they grew up we would take them in with us, and so we left them and went to meet our brewer.

He came, he opened the keg for us, and he lent us a tin can "off'n the wagon." It was a warm day; the field was far from the school; we had a thirst which was not easily slaked by our one borrowed can. We drank and drank, round on round, and when we rolled the empty keg into the hiding-place agreed upon, we were a sight and a sound. I don't know whether the sight and the sound of us did it; I heard afterward that some disgruntled small boy peached on us for revenge; anyway there was a large group of spectators out on the campus to see and to hear us come home. Among the witnesses were some teachers.

There were whippings; there were temperance lectures and sermons; there were stomach-aches; and there was no more drinking at the school in my day. We all were punished, but I, as the Napoleon, was stripped of my sword and rank as cadet officer and condemned to the guard-house in solitary confinement for twenty-two days. Some other old boy, far back in the history of the school, had been locked up for twenty-one days. I must go down on the records with the longest sentence ever suffered, before or after; hence my twenty-two days.

My punishment was a blessing to me. I read. They let me have books, not novels, but histories and solid things. Among them was an encyclopedic tome which was full of statistical information. The chapter on drink was the one I was asked to read, and I did. It showed me so that I never forgot, not only the waste and the folly, but the vanity of drinking. I got this last because I myself had been half aware of the pretentiousness of my drunkenness; it was a pose with me, and when I saw it handled as a pose in men, grown men, the romance went out of it: it went the way of politics, racing, and other illusions. I never could enjoy drinking after that; I was as ashamed of it as I was of being a sucker in the betting-ring.

There was another chapter on religions that told how many of them there had been and how men, grown men, always practiced the one that dominated their day. That fed my doubting mind, and I asked for other books, which I was carelessly allowed to have: Herbert Spencer, Darwin, and others. But the subject that hit me hardest was war. That book—I don't remember the title of it—that most improper book for boys told as a story of idiotic waste the history of all the wars in the whole story of man, and I called for paper and pencil. I had to write an oration for my graduation day, and I wrote one out of that book on the stupidity of war. But what I did not write was a conclusion, tentative but emancipating, that men, the superior grown-up adults that I had always respected, were and always had been mostly ignorant fools whom a boy, even a little fellow like me, need not look up to. I had long felt, deep down, that they did not see straight, that they could not explain things to me because they did not understand them, and now I knew that, if I was to learn anything, I had to find teachers who knew, and even at that, look out for myself.

When I came out of the guard-house, my sentence served to the last minute, I was a hero on the campus—and I might have enjoyed the awed stares of the other boys. But I had seen a light. I was on to my own posings, and also I was contemptuous of the springs of those boys' admiration. They were cub dubs; their respect was worthless. I heard it said, and I do not doubt, that I looked conceited, priggish, but I know now that I was dazed by a new interest, a fixed determination. I was going to college, and I was going there, not to make a record, not, as the headmaster said, to represent the school and make it proud of me—I was going to college to find out the truth about some of the questions that had bothered me. I was not to be put off any longer with the appearances of things. I meant to know, really, and I had no doubt that some of those professors really knew the truth.

An experience I sensed at that time clinched my conclusions and my determination. I was speedily, too speedily, restored to my rank as a captain of cadets. And the reason given, that I was needed as a drillmaster, did not deceive me; I had drilled cadets in the uniform of a private. Another "reason" set my back up again. My father had been notified of my misconduct. He did not hurry to the school; he let them punish me their way, of course. It was not till my sentence was nearly over that he visited me in prison. A memorable day. When they unlocked the pretentious barred doors, threw back the silly bolts with their prison ring, for him, he came in, and turning, dismissed my jailers.

"Feel all right?" he asked. I said I did. "Of course," he said. "Your mother was worried about your health in this cell, but I knew you would take it standing up. And I know you are not going to be a drunkard, too. Your stomach won't let you, for one thing; I've noticed that it makes you sick to drink too much. All that worries me is your posings, the bunk you have seemed always to like. I never saw you do anything for the fun of doing it; you always wanted to tell about it and see yourself and be seen doing it. That's poppycock. It does no harm in a boy, but you'll soon be no longer a boy, and there are a lot of men I know who are frauds and bunkers all their lives. I'd hate to see you go on into that sort of thing. And I don't believe you will, either. I am going to give you every chance, and you can waste or use your chances, as you will. That's up to you. But it's up to you to choose your chance. You can work or study for anything you like, but do, please do, find out what you want to do and be."

So he talked and I was prepared to take it all in just as he said and meant it. I remember thinking that he was as real as the bridge-tender, as much a gentleman as Mr. Neely, as warmly for me as Mrs. Neely, but I answered him in kind. I told him I had done some reading which revealed me to myself, a little; I had seen my vanity, especially in the matter of drink, which I really hated. But also I saw, I said, the posings and the pretensions of, for example, that school.

"They aren't thinking of me and the other boys," I said; "they are doing what they do, punishing us and degrading us, for outsiders to see, for parents to hear of and so believe in the school."

He nodded. "I'll fix that," he said, and I knew by the way he looked that he would give the school authorities an unhappy half hour. And he did. He told them, I suspected then, to restore me to my cadet rank, and afterward he told me that he made it clear to them that neither I nor the other boys were in any danger of going to hell and that it would be wiser for them to drop that pretense and treat us as foolish, but not wicked; young idiots, but not much more so than our teachers and masters.

Fine! But he made a mistake himself. When we had arrived at a perfect understanding, he and I, he broke it to me that in his first anger he had sold my colt. I was appalled. He had not sold one of my sisters; he would not have thought of that. But also he did not think that my colt to me was what a child of his was to him. I loved that horse. I loved that horse as much as he loved me. True, I had no constant use for her; she was eating her head off in our stable, waiting for my vacations. I had thought myself that, when I went away to college, I would have to send her back to Colonel Carter, who appreciated her, could use her properly, and would take care of her. And that colt was used to being loved and needed care. That thought had counted against college; my colt had stayed me from accepting an appointment to West Point. And my father had sold her.

"To whom?" I asked, when I could—when I had some control over my trembling pain and grief. What kind of man was to have the power of life and death over that fine, happy, trustful, spoiled, proud creature? I asked, and I did not want to hear; and he did not answer right away. He lowered his eyes when he told me.

"I don't know. I turned her over to a dealer."

I went rigid. He looked up at me, and I stood and looked at him till he winced and, without a word, went out, leaving the cell door open. He came back later. I was lying face down on the cot.

"Good-by," he said, and he leaned over and took my hand.

"Good-by," I managed to say somehow, and I let him shake my hand.

I never found out what became of my colt. Once from a train I saw a cream-colored horse that looked exactly like her, drawing, head down, a market wagon overloaded with vegetables and driven by a Chinaman.

PREPARING FOR COLLEGE

THE year 1884-85 was a period of great adventure for me. When I came up to Berkeley for the entrance examinations at the University of California I failed in Greek, Latin, and enough other subjects to be put off for a year. My father was alarmed. I was eighteen years old, and he thought, I think, that my failure was his fault; he had chosen the wrong school for me. He had, but the right school for me and my kind did not exist. There were schools that put boys into the colleges, east and west, and at a younger age than mine. I came to know those boys well. They are the boys (and they become the men) that the schools, colleges, and the world are made for. Often I have envied them; more often I have been glad that I was not of them.

The elect were, for the most part, boys who had been brought up to do their duty. They memorized whatever their teachers told them to learn. Whether they wanted to know it, whether they understood it or no, they could remember and recite it. Their own driving motives were, so far as I could make out, not curiosity; they rarely talked about our studies, and if I spoke of the implications of something we had read or heard, they looked dazed or indifferent. Their own motives were foreign to me: to beat the other fellows, stand high, represent the honor of the school.

My parents did not bring me up. They sent me to school, they gave me teachers of music, drawing; they offered me every opportunity in their reach. But also they gave me liberty and the tools of quite another life: horses, guns, dogs, and the range of an open country. As I have shown, the people, the businesses, and the dreams of this life interested me, and I learned well whatever interested me. School subjects which happened to bear on my outside interests I studied in school and out; I read more than was required, and I read for keeps, too. I know these subjects to this day, just as I remember and love still the men and women, the boys and girls, who let me be friends with them then and so revealed to me some of the depths and the limitations of human nature. On the other hand I can remember few of my teachers and little of the subjects which seemed to me irrelevant to my life.

These other subjects are interesting, and they might have been made interesting to me. No one tried to interest me in them; they were put before me as things that I had to have to get into college. The teachers of them did not appeal to my curious, active mind. The result was that I did not really work at them and so got only what stuck by dint of repetition: the barest rudiments of a school education. When I knocked at the college gates, I was prepared for a college education in some branches; my mind was hungry enough for the answers to some profound questions to have made me work and develop myself, especially on lines which I know now had no ready answers, only more and ever more questions: science, metaphysics, etc. I was not in the least curious about Greek, Latin, mathematics, and the other "knowledge" required by the standardization of that day.

My father discovered and put me into the best private school in San Francisco as a special student to be crammed for Berkeley— and he retained one of the teachers there, Mr. Evelyn Nixon, to tutor me on the side. Characteristically, too, my father gave me liberty: a room to sleep and work in, with no one to watch over and care for me. I could go and come as I pleased. And I came and went. I went exploring and dreaming alone around that city as I had the country around Sacramento, and the place I liked best was the ocean shore; there I lived over the lives of the Greek heroes and the Roman generals and all the poets of all the ages, sometimes with ecstasy, but never, as in my boyhood, with myself as the hero. A change had come over me.

Evelyn Nixon formed it. He was the first teacher I ever had who interested me in what I had to learn—not in myself, but in the world outside, the world of conscious culture. He was a fanatic of poetry, especially of the classic poets. When he read or recited Greek verse the Greeks came to life; romance and language sang songs to me, and I was inspired to be, like him, not a hero nor even a poet, but a Greek scholar, and thus an instrument on which

beautiful words might play. Life filled with meaning, and purpose, and joy. It was too great and too various for me to personify
with my boyish imitations and heroism. I wrote verses, but only to
learn the technique and so feel poetry more perfectly. I wanted to
read, not to write; I wanted to know, not to do and be, great
things—Mr. Nixon expressed it.

"I'm nobody," he used to say. "I'm nothing but one of the
unknown beings Homer and Dante, Shakespeare, Caesar, and the
popes and the generals and statesmen have sung and fought and
worked for. I'm the appreciator of all good words and deeds."

A new, a noble rôle, and Evelyn Nixon was a fine example of it:
the receiver, not the giver, of beautiful inventions. He was an
Englishman; he took a double first at Oxford, I heard, and came
for his health to San Francisco. There was a group of such men,
most of them with one story. They were athletes, as well as
scholars at Oxford and Cambridge; they developed muscles and
a lung capacity which they did not need and could not keep up in
the sedentary occupations their scholarship put them into. Lung
troubles exiled them.

"Keep out of college athletics," they advised. "Don't work up
any more brawn there than you can use every day afterward."

Nixon taught me Greek, Latin, and English at school, and at
his house he opened up the beauty and the meaning of the other
subjects I had to cram up for entrance. I worked for him; I worked
more, much more, for myself. He saw this, he saw my craving for
the answers to questions, and he laughed.

"I will answer no questions of yours," he shouted. "Men know
no answers to the natural questions of a boy, of a child. We can
only underline your questions, make you mad yourself to answer
them, and add ours to whip, to lash you on to find out yourself
—one or two; and tell us! That is what youth is for: to answer the
questions maturity can't answer." And when I looked disappointed
and balked, he would roar at me like a demon.

"Go to, boy. The world is yours. Nothing is done, nothing is
known. The greatest poem isn't written, the best railroad isn't
built yet, the perfect state hasn't been thought of. Everything
remains to be done—right, everything."

This said, he said it again and again, and finally, to drive me,
he set our private hour from seven till eight o'clock Saturday

evenings, so that I could stay on into the night with his group
of friends, a maddening lot of cultivated, conflicting minds. There
were from four to ten of them, all Englishmen, all Oxford and
Cambridge men, all exiles and all interested in any and all subjects, which they discussed with knowledge, with the precise information of scholarship, but with no common opinions on anything apparently. There were Tories among them and liberals and
one red: William Owen, a grandson, I think, certainly a de-
scendant, of Robert Owen, the first of the early English socialists.
There was at least one Roman Catholic, who showed me so that
I never forgot it the Christianity of that church; his favorite
thesis was that the Protestant churches were Old Testament,
righteous sects and knew nothing really of Christ's teachings of
love and forgiveness. And there were Protestants there, all
schooled in church history, and when a debate came to a clinch,
they could quote their authorities with a sureness which withstood
reference to the books. I remember one hot dispute of the Catholic's reference to some certain papal bull. Challenged, he quoted
it verbatim in the original Latin. What they knew was amazing
to me, and how they knew it, but what they did not know struck
me harder still. They could not among them agree on anything
but a fact. With all their knowledge they knew no essential truth.

It was conversation I was hearing, the free, passionate, witty
exchanges of studied minds as polished as fine tools. They were
always courteous; no two ever spoke together; there were no
asides; they all talked to the question before the house, and while
they were on the job of exposition any one, regardless of his side,
would contribute his quota of facts, or his remembrance of some
philosopher's opinion or some poet's perfect phrase for the elucida-
tion or the beautification of the theme. When the differences rose
the urbanity persisted. They drank their Californian wine with a
relish, they smoked the room thick, and they pressed their views
with vigor and sincerity and eloquence; but their good temper
never failed them. It was conversation. I had never heard conversation before; I have heard conversation sometimes since, but
rarely, and never like my remembrance of those wonderful Saturday nights in San Francisco—which were my preparation for
college.

For those conversations, so brilliant, so scholarly, and so consciously unknowing, seemed to me, silent in the background, to reveal the truth that even college graduates did not know anything, really. Evidences they had, all the testimony of all the wise men in the historical world on everything, but no decisions. None. I must myself go to college to find out more, and I wanted to. It seemed as if I had to go soon. My head, busy with questions before, was filled with holes that were aching voids as hungry, as painful, as an empty stomach. And my questions were explicit; it was as if I were not only hungry; I was hungry for certain foods. My curiosity was no longer vague.

When on Sundays I would take the gatherings I had made out of the talk of the night before down to the Cliff House with me and sit there on the rocks and think, I formed my ignorance into a system. I was getting a cultivated ignorance, a survey not of the solved but of the unsolved problems in every science from astronomy to economics, from history to the next tricks in versification. I thought of them; I thought, rejoicing, that there were things to do for everybody in every science, every art, every business. Why, men did not know even how to love, not technically, not beautifully! I learned of the damage done me by having my sex feelings separated from love and poetry, and as for astronomy, government, conversation, play and work, men were just crawling on their hands and knees out of their caves.

But the best that I got out of it all was objectivity. Those men never mentioned themselves; apparently they never thought of themselves. Their interest was in the world outside of themselves. I caught that. No more play-acting for me. No more dreaming I was Napoleon or a trapper, a knight, a statesman, or the younger son of a lord. It is possible that I was outgrowing this stage of a boy's growth; the very intensity of my life in subjective imagination may have carried me through it, but whether I would have come out clearly impersonal or no by myself, I don't know. All I am sure of is that their conversations, the attitude and the interest of those picked Englishmen, helped and, I think, established in me the realization that the world was more interesting than I was. Not much to see? No, but I have met men since, statesmen, scholars, business men, workers, and poets, who have never made that discovery. It is the scientific attitude, and some scientists have it—not all; and some others, too.

When I went up for my examination this time in Berkeley I passed, not well in all subjects, but I was admitted to the University, and that fall I entered the University of California with a set of examination questions for the faculty, for the professors, to answer.

XVI

I GO TO COLLEGE

Going to college is, to a boy, an adventure into a new world, and a very strange and complete world too. Part of his preparation for it is the stories he hears from those that have gone before; these feed his imagination, which cannot help trying to picture the college life. And the stories and the life are pretty much the same for any college. The University of California was a young, comparatively small institution when I was entered there in 1885 as a freshman. Berkeley, the beautiful, was not the developed villa community it is now; I used to shoot quail in the brush under the oaks along the edges of the college grounds. The quail and the brush are gone now, but the oaks are there and the same prospect down the hill over San Francisco Bay out through the Golden Gate between the low hills of the city and the high hills of Marin County. My class numbered about one hundred boys and girls, mostly boys, who came from all parts of the State and represented all sorts of people and occupations. There was, however, a significant uniformity of opinion and spirit among us, as there was, and still is, in other, older colleges. The American is molded to type early. And so are our college ways. We found already formed at Berkeley the typical undergraduate customs, rights, and privileged vices which we had to respect ourselves and defend against the faculty, regents, and the State government.

One evening, before I had matriculated, I was taken out by some upper classmen to teach the president a lesson. He had been the head of a private preparatory school and was trying to govern the private lives and the public morals of university "men" as he had those of his schoolboys. Fetching a long ladder, the upper classmen thrust it through a front window of Prexy's house and, to the chant of obscene songs, swung it back and forth, up and down, round and round, till everything breakable within sounded broken and the drunken indignation outside was satisfied or tired.

This turned out to be one of the last battles in the war for liberty against that president. He was allowed to resign soon thereafter and I noticed that not only the students but many of the faculty and regents rejoiced in his downfall and turned with us to face and fight the new president when, after a lot of politics, he was appointed and presented. We learned somehow a good deal about the considerations that governed our college government. They were not only academic. The government of a university was —like the State government and horse-racing and so many other things—not what I had been led to expect. And a college education wasn't either, nor the student mind.

Years later, when I was a magazine editor, I proposed a series of articles to raise and answer the question: Is there any intellectual life in our colleges? My idea sprang from my remembered disappointment at what I found at Berkeley and some experiences I was having at the time with the faculties and undergraduates of the other older colleges in the east. Berkeley, in my day, was an Athens compared with New Haven, for example, when I came to know Yale undergraduates.

My expectations of college life were raised too high by Nixon's Saturday nights. I thought, and he assumed, that at Berkeley I would be breathing in an atmosphere of thought, discussion, and some scholarship; working, reading, and studying for the answers to questions which would be threshed out in debate and conversation. There was nothing of the sort. I was primed with questions. My English friends never could agree on the answers to any of the many and various questions they disputed. They did not care; they enjoyed their talks and did not expect to settle anything. I was more earnest. I was not content to leave things all up in the air. Some of those questions were very present and personal to me, as some of those Englishmen meant them to be. William Owen was trying to convert me to the anarchistic communism in which he believed with all his sincere and beautiful being. I was considering his arguments. Another earnest man, who presented the case for the Roman Catholic Church, sent old Father Burchard and other Jesuits after me. Every conversation at Mr. Nixon's pointed some question, academic or scientific, and pointed them so sharp that they drove me to college with an intense desire to know. And as for communism or the Catholic Church, I was so torn that I could not answer myself. The Jesuits dropped me and so did Owen, in disgust, when I said I was going to wait for my answer till I had heard what the professors had to say and had learned what my university had to teach me upon the questions underlying the questions Oxford and Cambridge and Rome quarreled over and could not agree on. Berkeley would know.

There were no moot questions in Berkeley. There was work to do, knowledge and training to get, but not to answer questions. I found myself engaged, as my classmates were, in choosing courses. The choice was limited and, within the limits, had to be determined by the degree we were candidates for. My questions were philosophical, but I could not take philosophy, which fascinated me, till I had gone through a lot of higher mathematics which did not interest me at all. If I had been allowed to take philosophy, and so discovered the need and the relation of mathematics, I would have got the philosophy and I might have got the mathematics which I miss now more than I do the Hegelian metaphysics taught at Berkeley. Or, if the professor who put me off had taken the pains to show me the bearing of mathematical thought on theoretical logic, I would have undertaken the preparation intelligently. But no one ever developed for me the relation of any of my required subjects to those that attracted me; no one brought out for me the relation of anything I was studying to anything else, except, of course, to that wretched degree. Knowledge was absolute, not relative, and it was stored in compartments, categorical and independent. The relation of knowledge to life, even to student life, was ignored, and as for questions, the professors asked them, not the students; and the students, not the teachers, answered them—in examinations.

The unknown is the province of the student; it is the field for his life's adventure, and it is a wide field full of beckonings. Curiosity about it would drive a boy as well as a child to work through the known to get at the unknown. But it was not assumed that we had any curiosity or the potential love of skill, scholarship, and achievement or research. And so far as I can remember now, the professors' attitude was right for most of the students who had no intellectual curiosity. They wanted to be told not only what they

had to learn, but what they had to want to learn—for the purpose
of passing. That came out in the considerations which decided the
choice among optional courses. Students selected subjects or
teachers for a balance of easy and hard, to fit into their time and
yet "get through." I was the only rebel of my kind, I think. The
nearest to me in sympathy were the fellows who knew what they
wanted to be: engineers, chemists, professional men, or statesmen.
They grunted at some of the work required of them, studies that
seemed useless to their future careers. They did not understand
me very well, nor I them, because I preferred those very subjects
which they called useless, highbrow, cultural. I did not tell them
so; I did not realize it myself definitely; but I think now that
I had had as a boy an exhausting experience of *being* something
great. I did not want now to be but rather to know things.

And what I wanted to know was buried deep under all this
"college stuff" which was called "shop." It had nothing to do
with what really interested us in common. Having chosen our work
and begun to do it as a duty, we turned to the socially important
question: which fraternity to join. The upper classmen tried to
force our answers. They laid aside their superiority to "rush" those
of us whose antecedents were known and creditable. It was all
snobbish, secret, and exclusive. I joined a fraternity out of curiosity:
What were the secrets and the mystic rites? I went blindfold
through the silly initiation to find that there were no secrets and
no mysteries, only pretensions and bunk, which so disgusted me
that I would not live at the clubhouse, preferring for a year the
open doors of a boarding-house. The next great university question was as to athletics. My ex-athletes from Oxford and Cambridge, with their lung and other troubles, warned me; but it was a
mistake that saved me. I went with the other freshmen to the
campus to be tried out for football, baseball, running, jumping,
etc. Caught by the college and class spirit, I hoped to give promise
of some excellence. Baseball was impossible for me; I had been
riding horses when the other boys were preparing for college
on the diamond. I had learned to run at the military academy and
in the first freshman tests I did one hundred yards enough under
eleven seconds to be turned over to an athletic upper classman
for instruction. Pointing up to Grizzly Peak, a high hill back of
the college, he said: "All you need is wind and muscle. Climb that

mountain every day for a year; then come back and we'll see."

I did not climb Grizzly Peak every day, but I went up so often that I was soon able to run up and back without a halt. At the end of the year I ran around the cinder track so long that my student instructor wearied of watching me, but, of course, I could not do a hundred yards much under twelve seconds. Muscle and wind I had, but all my physical reactions were so slow that I was of no social use in college athletics. I was out of the crowd as I had been as a boy.

I shone only in the military department. The commandant, a U.S. Army officer, seeing that I had had previous training, told me off to drill the awkward squad of my class, and when I had made of them the best-drilled company in college, he gave me the next freshman class to drill. In the following years I was always drill-master of the freshmen and finally commanded the whole cadet corps. Thus I led my class in the most unpopular and meaningless of undergraduate activities. I despised it myself, prizing it only for the chances it gave me to swank and, once a week, to lord it over my fellow students, who nicknamed me the "D.S."—damn stinker.

My nickname was won, not only as a disciplinarian, however; I rarely punished any one; I never abused my command. I could persuade the freshmen to drill by arguing that, since it was compulsory, they could have more fun doing it well than badly; and that it was the one exercise in which they could beat and shame the upper classmen whose carelessness was as affected as their superiority. That is to say, I engaged their enthusiasm. All other student enthusiasms, athletics, class and college politics, fashions, and traditions I laughed at and damped. I was a spoilsport. I was mean, as a horse is mean, because I was unhappy myself. I could be enthusiastic in a conversation about something we were learning, if it wasn't too cut and dried; we had such talks now and then at the clubhouse in my later years. But generally speaking we were discussing the news or some prank of our own.

One night, for example, we sallied forth to steal some chickens from Dr. Bonte, the popular treasurer of the university. I crawled into the coop and selected the chickens, wrung their necks, and passed them out with comments to the other fellows who held the bag.

"Here," I said, "is the rooster, Dr. Bonte himself; he's tough, but good enough for the freshmen. Next is a nice fat hen, old Mrs. Bonte. This one's a pullet, Miss Bonte," and so on, naming each of the Bonte girls, till we were interrupted.

There was a sound from the house, the lights flashed in the windows, and—some one was coming. The other fellows ran, and I—when I tore myself out—I ran too. Which was all right enough. But when I caught up with the other thieves I learned that they had left the sack of chickens behind! Our Sunday dinner was spoiled, we thought, but no: the next day the whole fraternity was invited to dinner at Dr. Bonte's on Sunday. We accepted with some suspicion, we went in some embarrassment, but we were well received and soon put at our ease by Dr. Bonte, who explained that some thieves had been frightened while robbing his roost. "They were not students, I take it," he said. "Students are not so easily frightened; they might have run away, but students would have taken the bag of chickens with them. I think they were niggers or Chinamen."

So seated hospitably at table we watched with deep interest the great platter of roasted chickens borne in and set down before Dr. Bonte, who rose, whetted his carving-knife, and turning first to me, said: "Well, Steffens, what will you have, a piece of this old cock, Dr. Bonte? Or is he too tough for any but a freshman? Perhaps you would prefer the old hen, Mrs. Bonte, or, say, one of the Bonte girls."

I couldn't speak. No one could; and no one laughed, least of all Dr. Bonte, who stood there, his knife and fork in the air, looking at me, at the others, and back at me. He wanted an answer; I must make my choice, but I saw a gleam of malicious humor in his eye; so I recovered and I chose the prettiest of the girls, pointing to the tenderest of the pullets. Dr. Bonte laughed, gave me my choice, and we had a jolly, ample dinner.

We talked about that, we and the students generally and the faculty—we discussed that incident long enough and hard enough to have solved it, if it had been a metaphysical problem. We might have threshed out the psychology of thieves, or gamblers, but no. We liked to steal, but we didn't care to think about it, not as stealing. And some of us gambled. We had to get money for theaters, operas, and other expenses in the city. I had only my board, lodging, and clothes paid for by my father, and others had not even that. We played cards, therefore, among ourselves, poker and whist, so that a lucky few got each month about all the money all of the other hard-ups had, and so had all the fun. We played long, late, and hard, and for money, not sport. The strain was too great.

One night my roommate, sunk low in his chair, felt a light kick on one of his extended legs; a second later there were two kicks against his other leg. Keeping still and watching the hands shown down, he soon had the signal system of two men playing partners, the better hand staying in the game. We said nothing but, watching, saw that others cheated, too. We knew well an old professional gambler from the mining-camps who was then in San Francisco. We told him all about it.

"Sure," he said, "cheating will sneak into any game that's played long enough. That's why you boys oughtn't to gamble. But if you do, play the game that's played. Cards is like horse-racing. I never bet a cent except I know, and know how, the game is crooked."

Having advised against it, he took us around to the gambling-houses and the race course and showed us many of the tricks of his trade, how to spot and profit by them—if we must play. "Now you won't need never to be suckers," he said. "And ye needn't be crooks either," he added after a pause. But we had it in for our opponents. We learned several ways to cheat; we practiced them till we were cool and sure. After that our "luck" was phenomenal. We had money, more than we needed. In my last two years at the university I had a salary as military instructor at a preparatory school in the town, and my roommate, the adopted son of a rich gold-miner, had a generous allowance. But we went on playing and cheating at cards for the excitement of it, we said, but really it was for the money. And afterward, when I was a student in Germany, I played on, fair, but hard—and for money I did not need, till one night at the Café Bauer in Berlin, sitting in a poker game that had been running all night, an American who had long been playing in hard luck, lost a large amount, of which I carried away more than my share. The next day we read in the papers that when he got home he had shot himself. I have never gambled since—at cards.

XVII

I BECOME · A STUDENT

IT IS possible to get an education at a university. It has been done; not often, but the fact that a proportion, however small, of college students do get a start in interested, methodical study, proves my thesis, and the two personal experiences I have to offer illustrate it and show how to circumvent the faculty, the other students, and the whole college system of mind-fixing. My method might lose a boy his degree, but a degree is not worth so much as the capacity and the drive to learn, and the undergraduate desire for an empty baccalaureate is one of the holds the educational system has on students. Wise students some day will refuse to take degrees, as the best men (in England, for instance) give, but do not themselves accept, titles.

My method was hit on by accident and some instinct. I specialized. With several courses prescribed, I concentrated on the one or two that interested me most, and letting the others go, I worked intensively on my favorites. In my first two years, for example, I worked at English and political economy and read philosophy. At the beginning of my junior year I had several cinches in history. Now I liked history; I had neglected it partly because I rebelled at the way it was taught, as positive knowledge unrelated to politics, art, life, or anything else. The professors gave us chapters out of a few books to read, con, and be quizzed on. Blessed as I was with a "bad memory," I could not commit to it anything that I did not understand and intellectually need. The bare record of the story of man, with names, dates, and irrelative events, bored me. But I had discovered in my readings of literature, philosophy, and political economy that history had light to throw upon unhistorical questions. So I proposed in my junior and senior years to specialize in history, taking all the courses required and those also that I had flunked in. With this in mind I listened attentively to the first introductory talk of Professor William Cary Jones on American constitutional history. He was a dull lecturer, but I noticed that, after telling us what pages of what books we must be prepared in, he mumbled off some other references "for those that may care to dig deeper."

When the rest of the class rushed out into the sunshine, I went up to the professor and, to his surprise, asked for this memorandum. He gave it me. Up in the library I ran through the required chapters in the two different books, and they differed on several points. Turning to the other authorities, I saw that they disagreed on the same facts and also on others. The librarian, appealed to, helped me search the book-shelves till the library closed, and then I called on Professor Jones for more references. He was astonished, invited me in, and began to approve my industry, which astonished me. I was not trying to be a good boy; I was better than that: I was a curious boy. He lent me a couple of his books, and I went off to my club to read them. They only deepened the mystery, clearing up the historical question, but leaving the answer to be dug for and written.

The historians did not know! History was not a science, but a field for research, a field for me, for any young man, to explore, to make discoveries in and write a scientific report about. I was fascinated. As I went on from chapter to chapter, day after day, finding frequently essential differences of opinion and of fact, I saw more and more work to do. In this course, American constitutional history, I hunted far enough to suspect that the Fathers of the Republic who wrote our sacred Constitution of the United States not only did not, but did not want to, establish a democratic government, and I dreamed for a while—as I used as a child to play I was Napoleon or a trapper—I promised myself to write a true history of the making of the American Constitution. I did not do it; that chapter has been done or well begun since by two men: Smith of the University of Washington and Beard (then) of Columbia (afterward forced out, perhaps for this very work). I found other events, men, and epochs waiting for students. In all my other courses, in ancient, in European, and in modern history, the disagreeing authorities carried me back to the need of a fresh search for (or of) the original documents or other clinching testimony. Of course I did well in my classes. The history professors soon knew me as a student and seldom put a question to me except when the class had flunked it. Then Professor Jones would say, "Well, Steffens, tell them about it."

Fine. But vanity wasn't my ruling passion then. What I had was a quickening sense that I was learning a method of studying history and that every chapter of it, from the beginning of the world to the end, is crying out to be rewritten. There was something for Youth to do; these superior old men had not done anything, finally.

Years afterward I came out of the graft prosecution office in San Francisco with Rudolph Spreckels, the banker and backer of the investigation. We were to go somewhere, quick, in his car, and we couldn't. The chauffeur was trying to repair something wrong. Mr. Spreckels smiled; he looked closely at the defective part, and to my silent, wondering inquiry he answered: "Always, when I see something badly done or not done at all, I see an opportunity to make a fortune. I never kick at bad work by my class: there's lots of it and we suffer from it. But our failures and neglects are chances for the young fellows coming along and looking for work."

Nothing is done. Everything in the world remains to be done or done over. "The greatest picture is not yet painted, the greatest play isn't written (not even by Shakespeare), the greatest poem is unsung. There isn't in all the world a perfect railroad, nor a good government, nor a sound law." Physics, mathematics, and especially the most advanced and exact of the sciences, are being fundamentally revised. Chemistry is just becoming a science; psychology, economics, and sociology are awaiting a Darwin, whose work in turn is awaiting an Einstein. If the rah-rah boys in our colleges could be told this, they might not all be such specialists in football, petting parties, and unearned degrees. They are not told it, however; they are told to learn what is known. This is nothing, philosophically speaking.

Somehow or other in my later years at Berkeley, two professors, Moses and Howison, representing opposite schools of thought, got into a controversy, probably about their classes. They brought together in the house of one of them a few of their picked students, with the evident intention of letting us show in conversation how

much or how little we had understood of their respective teachings. I don't remember just what the subject was that they threw
into the ring, but we wrestled with it till the professors could stand
it no longer. Then they broke in, and while we sat silent and highly
entertained, they went at each other hard and fast and long. It was
after midnight when, the debate over, we went home. I asked the
other fellows what they had got out of it, and their answers showed
that they had seen nothing but a fine, fair fight. When I laughed,
they asked me what I, the D.S., had seen that was so much more
profound.

I said that I had seen two highly-trained, well-educated Masters
of Arts and Doctors of Philosophy disagreeing upon every essential
point of thought and knowledge. They had all there was of the
sciences; and yet they could not find any knowledge upon which
they could base an acceptable conclusion. They had no test of
knowledge; they didn't know what is and what is not. And they
have no test of right and wrong; they have no basis for even an
ethics.

Well, and what of it? They asked me that, and that I did not
answer. I was stunned by the discovery that it was philosophically
true, in a most literal sense, that nothing is known; that it is precisely the foundation that is lacking for science; that all we call
knowledge rested upon assumptions which the scientists did not all
accept; and that, likewise, there is no scientific reason for saying,
for example, that stealing is wrong. In brief: there was no scientific basis for an ethics. No wonder men said one thing and did
another; no wonder they could settle nothing either in life or in
the academies.

I could hardly believe this. Maybe these professors, whom I
greatly respected, did not know it all. I read the books over again
with a fresh eye, with a real interest, and I could see that, as in
history, so in other branches of knowledge, everything was in the
air. And I was glad of it. Rebel though I was, I had got the religion of scholarship and science; I was in awe of the authorities in
the academic world. It was a release to feel my worship cool and
pass. But I could not be sure. I must go elsewhere, see and hear
other professors, men these ·California professors quoted and
looked up to as their high priests. I decided to go as a student to

Europe when I was through Berkeley, and I would start with the German universities.

My father listened to my plan, and he was disappointed. He had hoped I would succeed him in his business; it was for that that he was staying in it. When I said that, whatever I might do, I would never go into business, he said, rather sadly, that he would sell out his interest and retire. And he did soon after our talk. But he wanted me to stay home and, to keep me, offered to

OUR HOUSE IN SACRAMENTO
Now the Governor's Mansion

buy an interest in a certain San Francisco daily paper. He had evidently had this in mind for some time. I had always done some writing, verse at the poetical age of puberty, then a novel which my mother alone treasured. Journalism was the business for a boy who liked to write, he thought, and he said I had often spoken of a newspaper as my ambition. No doubt I had in the intervals between my campaigns as Napoleon. But no more. I was now going to be a scientist, a philosopher. He sighed; he thought it over, and with the approval of my mother, who was for every sort of education, he gave his consent.

XVIII

BERLIN: PHILOSOPHY AND MUSIC

GERMANY meant art and music to me as well as philosophy and science. Ever since the day I had watched as a boy the painter, Mr. Marple, sketch his sunset over the brush of the American River bottom and heard what he said about art, I had wanted to understand and feel painting. I had taken lessons in drawing while at school; at college there was no art in the curriculum, but in my senior year, when I had the direction of outside lectures, I persuaded a well-known painter to come to Berkeley and tell us all about art. He had never lectured before; he probably has never lectured since. He went up on the platform, set up a black and white copy of Millet's "Sower," and I think he thought that he could put into words what his hand could say with lines and colors. He couldn't; he said a few words, and his amazement at his own helplessness was a sight to see.

"Art," he began, "painting—painting is— It isn't pictures, you know. It's—well, now, take 'The Sower' there." He looked at it and began waving his right hand. He looked at us, then at the picture, and then appealingly back at the audience, swinging his hand as if he were drawing a line. "That isn't a sower," he blurted, "nor a picture. It's a—don't you see—it's a line."

And, sure enough, it was a line. It was the same line he was drawing in the air with his eloquent hand; a big, sweeping, speaking, beautiful line. I saw it; I saw one key to the understanding of art. Paintings were not pictures only; they were, among other things, beautiful lines detected in nature and drawn so that all who will can see them.

The painter thought he had said nothing, and he could not go on. With one more wild dumb look at us and another at the Millet, he uttered a cry of despair and came down off the platform amid the shouts of student laughter.

Walking with the humiliated man to the station, I tried to tell him that he had said something to me; and I repeated in my own words what I thought it was.

"That's it," he said. "I didn't know I had said it, but you've got it. And I'll tell you how to go on and get the rest.

"You are going abroad," he said. "You will visit the art galleries, the cathedrals—everything that is beautiful. You will be tempted to read the guidebooks and other books about the arts. Look out. They can keep you from getting art. They will tell you which are the best things, and if you believe them, you will know what is called best, the best to them, but you won't know what is best to you. You won't feel art. You may become a scholar in it, you will never be a judge of art; you'll have no taste.

"My advice is to go without a guide into the galleries, often; walk along slowly, stopping to look only at those things which interest you. I am sure you will choose the wrong things, probably pictures—pictures that a writing man can describe, and describe better than the painter has painted them. No matter. You like what you like. If they are no good as art you'll tire of them; they will end by making you sick, and you'll choose better things, and better and better till finally you like the things that are best to you. You may not have perfect taste; there is no perfect taste; but you'll have taste and it will be yours, not somebody else's, but your very own; and you may not be able to lecture on it any better than I can, but you will have a feel for the painter's art, which is a fine art."

When I arrived in Berlin in the summer of 1889, I walked the galleries in just this way. There was little else to do. The university, the opera, and the theaters being closed, I loafed about the cafés, music halls, took walks in the Thiergarten and around the city. But every forenoon I put in an hour or two walking through the galleries, without a book, looking at the pictures that stopped me, and some of what my painter had predicted came true. In those few months my taste changed; I came to dislike pictures that I had liked at first; I could see and enjoy lines, designs, and even forms, while color combinations came to have as much meaning for me as a chord of music. It was work, however; a gallery is like a library. I was trying to read all the books at once.

In the fall, I was glad of a new interest: music. Hegel and his philosophy of art had threaded the arts upon an historical chain, given them a definite and a general significance, each and all. His was an intellectual key to music. But I applied to this art also the painter's key to painting. Going to the first operas offered, I took the score, and sitting on the dimly lighted stairway back of the topmost gallery, I followed the music as music and knew it well before I allowed myself to sit in a seat and see the stage and hear the words. This method of practicing the hearing of the music alone first I kept up all winter, and my reward was a growing preference for fine concert music over all but a few favorite operas.

There were pictures in music too, and also there were lines and tones, color and composition: business and art!

The university opened when the theaters did, and I was eager and ready to start. I had a small room in the Artillerie Strasse back of the university, and there I had been exercising my college German on the landlady and her son and reading up on my courses, choosing my professors, etc. Ethics was my subject, but I was not intending to study it directly. I would hear and read the men who taught it. I must know what they knew or thought or believed, but I had learned enough of their doctrines to feel pretty sure that they were not scientific; they did not have what I sought; a basis, probably in some other science, for a science of behavior. I was to start, therefore, with pure philosophy and ethics; metaphysics would be my main *Fach*, but all I wanted of it was a lead into other sciences.

Scientists were already discovering that the old, classical categories of knowledge were a hindrance. Physicists were forced into chemistry and back through mathematics to physics. But the German universities, like Berkeley, like all universities, were organized as they still are, not for inquiry and research into the unknown but for the learning (and teaching) of the known. They are scholarly, not scientific, and if I were to take a degree I must choose my categories and stick to them. I had no thought of, I had nothing but scorn for, degrees, but when I appeared for matriculation, I had to pretend to a candidacy; so I announced myself out for a

Ph.D., with philosophy for my major subject, art history and economics for seconds.

The procedure of matriculation had one surprise for me. When I presented my precious papers at the Secretariat, the clerks took my passport, but they looked askance at my bachelor's diploma.

"What's that?" asked one of them, and I told him.

"Oh, an American Doktorat!" he said. "It's worthless here. All we require is the passport," and he scribbled off the data he needed from it, gave me a form to fill out and my receipts for fees paid, and said he would deliver later my certificate of matriculation, an enormous calfskin Latin document.

He despised my degree as much as I did his, and I was hurt, with cause. I had worked, sacrificed my interests—I had cheated for that worthless baccalaureate. My cheating had been open at Berkeley. I had said that I would not half study the subjects that did not interest me and that, since they were required for a degree, which I (thought I) had to have to continue my studies abroad, I would cram for and sneak through the examinations in them. One professor, Colonel Edwards, who heard what I had threatened to do, sent for me and asked me how I could justify such conduct. I told him. His subject was conic sections. I said I did not want to know it, couldn't make head or tail of it myself, and that he, as a teacher, had failed to show me what it was all about. "It's just one of the many things," I said, "in which I find I have to submit to force; so I'll pretend to conform, but I won't really."

Pondering a moment, he asked me if I could prove any propositions. "Yes," I said, "some seven or eight. I know them by heart."

"All right," he said. "I don't want you to cheat; I won't let you cheat. I'll give you a private examination right now. You do two out of three propositions and I'll give you a pass."

Going to the blackboard, he wrote up one. "Can you do that?" I said I could. He wrote another. "That too?"

"No," I said, and he wrote another that I did not know.

"We'll make it three out of five," he suggested, and he wrote up one more and looked at me. I laughed and nodded; I could do it, and slowly he chose the fifth, which I knew. I wrote them out in a few minutes, handed them in, and—he passed me, after a long and very serious lecture on ethics, which I told him was to be my specialty. I was going to Germany on purpose to find out if there was any moral reason for or against cheating in cards, in politics, or in conic sections—"either by the student or the professor," I added.

And it was all in vain. I had been graduated (at the bottom of my class) at this cost, and I did not have to pass at all; I did not have to be a philosophic bachelor; all I had to have to enter the German and the French universities was my American citizenship, which I was born with. And so it was after I had entered. I did not have to work; no one knew or cared whether I heard my lectures or played my time away. There was the university, with its lectures, laboratories, professors, and workers. You could take all or nothing. I was free to study what and when and as my interest dictated, and the result was that I worked hard. I read everything, heard everybody, in my courses and in others. Whenever the students spoke well of a man who had anything to say on any subject, I took some of his lectures, but I held to my own trail of research for an ethics that was not merely a rationalization of folkways and passing laws, forms, and customs; taking for pleasure only music, lots of music, and staged literature, except a few weeks of nights at the poker table in the back room of the Café Bauer.

XIX

HEIDELBERG: THERE IS NO ETHICS

WITH the Black Forest behind it and the Neckar River running through it to the Rhine, Heidelberg is a place of temptation and pleasure, and this wise old university was no spoilsport. All the lectures were on the four working days of the week, Tuesday, Wednesday, Thursday, and Friday, leaving the week-end long and clear for play. Many students go there for fun. I met an American corps student who had been fighting and drinking and idling so long there that he could hardly rally his English to talk with me.

"I must quit this, go to some other university and work," he said when we parted. I had reminded him of some old drowned purpose.

I went to Heidelberg to hear Kuno Fischer, the most eloquent if not the most apostolic of the professors of Hegel's philosophy, and I studied hard with him. Other subjects also I took, continuing my Berlin courses in art history and economics. My semester at Heidelberg was a fruitful season, but it bore flowers too. I made some friends there, and together we had all the fun that was going, in the town, on the river, in the Forest—beer-drinking, dancing, swimming and boating, walking, talking, and exploring the world and one another.

My room was up on the *Anlage*, just above the city park in a little house kept by a Viennese woman who in turn was kept by a local merchant. Her gay days were over; she was a good old mother to her two children and altogether contented with her condition of dependence upon the honor of the gentleman who had "married a lady" and was devoted to her, his proper wife. He only paid, but he paid regularly for his past sins. His old mistress did not regret hers; she loved to talk about them. She took me in as her one lodger to make a little extra money out of the front room, which her small family did not need. An expressive woman with a common story, lived and seen from her Viennese point of view, she served lively entertainment and some light upon ethics with all the meals that I took in my room. These were not many.

Kuno Fischer gave his first lecture, logic, at seven o'clock in the morning; no time for more than a hot cup of coffee at home with a piece of bread, which I finished often as I finished dressing on the way down to the university. Other students also showed signs of haste at 7:15, when, on the dot, the professor began his lecture with a smile for the breathless state of his hearers and the imperfect arrangement of collars and ties. I saw some fellows in slippers, pajamas, and overcoats, looking up with admiration at the professor, neat, composed, and logical. And eloquent; I missed taking many a note to sit and listen to Kuno Fischer's poetical prose. Few Germans can either speak or write German—well. Their language is too rich, variable, and unripe for them. Only the masters can master it, and Kuno Fischer, handsome and intelligent, was a master of German as he was of his own thinking in it. I asked him once how it came that he spoke German so well.

He had a habit which I had of going from his first lecture to the river for a swim. Sometimes we walked together down to the floating bath-house, and many a pleasant talk we had on the way. He chatted as he lectured, in short, clear, incisive sentences, and he liked it that I liked his style. It was by way of a jesting compliment that I put to him my question: "Herr Geheimrat, wie kommt es dass Sie so schön deutsch sprechen?"

"It's because I speak English," he answered in English, and, laughing, he reminded me that Goethe, asked once the same question, replied that his best German was written in the period when he was soaking in French.

After the swim I had breakfast in some café or beer hall, where I completed my notes; then more lectures till one o'clock. The noon meal was usually with some crowd of students in a restaurant, under the stiff forms of the student ritual, the gossip, the controversies, the plans for excursions or fights. Once a week I had an art history course which took us up to the castle to examine the stones and trace their periods, or off to the excavations near by, as far as Wiesbaden. Other days there were other lectures or library work or home study till along about four, when I went forth either to the Schloss or to some other café for coffee or to the river for a paddle. The boatman had several canoes, "left by the English," he said.

Just above the bridge the river is artificially narrowed and deepened, making a rapid, called the Hart Teufel, for about an eighth of a mile, and it's a struggle to paddle up it. I used to do it for exercise and then drive the little craft on up the easy, broad river to some one of the many garden restaurants along shore. After a bath out in the stream, I had an appetite which made the good cooking seem perfect, and a thirst which took beer as the Hart Teufel took water. There was always some other loose student to join for a long, slow supper and a long, highbrow conversation. When the darkness fell, there was the canoe to lie in and the river to float me effortlessly back to town. I could philosophize in the dark; if there was a moon I could romance. Pleasant days, those lonely Heidelberg days. Pleasanter still the friendly days that followed.

Once, when the art history professor had his class out for field work on some ruin or other, a tall young German came up to me, struck his heels together, saluted stiffly, and said: "My name is Johann Friedrich Krudewolf. I am a German; I take you for an American. I want to learn English. I propose to exchange with you lessons in German for lessons in English."

I closed the foolish bargain, and we shook hands on it. There was one lesson in English, one in German, and no more. I did not have to study German; I was learning it fast enough by absorption, and I think now that while he did want to learn English, he was really seeking a friend. Anyhow we became so interested in each other that the conversation, even at the first and last lesson, ran away from the purpose and, of course, ran into the language easiest for both of us to understand. Bad as my German was then, it was so much better than his school English that we always spoke German and soon forgot lessons. His specialty was art history, and I was glad of that; Hegel's history of art gave a philosophic meaning to the subject, and my new friend's interest in the details filled in beautifully my efforts to feel art both in itself and as a border of flowers along the course of our civilization.

Our excursions with the class to churches, castles, and ruins were pleasant recreations for me, so pleasant that we made study trips by ourselves for fun. We foot-toured the Black Forest three days at a time, always to see things Krudewolf wished to examine for art history reasons, but his notes told by the way and the ruined castles illustrated vividly the history of the rise of great German families from robbers to robber knights, to military and social power, to riches, position, and honors. That was the way it was done of old, and I made notes on morals as studiously as my companion did on art.

The best excursion we made, however, was for its own sake. The Neckar River was navigable up to Heilbron, and a curious kind of boat-train operated on it, the *Schlepper*. There was a cable laid in the middle of the stream. The power boat picked up this cable, pulled itself up on it, and passed it out over the stern. By this means the tuglike *Schlepper* schlepped a string of cargo boats up the Neckar to Heilbron and back down to the Rhine. Johann hired a rowboat and sent it on the *Schlepper* up to Heilbron, whither we went by train to meet it. A day and a night in funny old Heilbron, with its old, old stories, and we set out in the rowboat to row (or float) home to Heidelberg. We started early one morning, meaning to go far that day, but by ten o'clock we were passing such tempting restaurants in river gardens that we yielded, stopped and had breakfast, which we thought would do for lunch, too. But we could not pass by the resorts that called to us; we had to see some of them. We chose one for luncheon, a long luncheon, and when we embarked again, chose others here, there, everywhere for beer, coffee, or—something. We could not row; it was a waste, and—even drifting was too fast.

The Neckar, from Heilbron to Heidelberg, is one of the most beautiful stretches of country that I have ever seen—or it seemed so to me then. We stayed our first night at a village inn on the river bank, and while we dined made two important discoveries. This was a *Shaumwein* (champagne) country, with the "fizz" at seventy-five cents the bottle; and this season was a church festival at which everybody drank, danced, and made love. We danced till midnight that night and then took some peasant girls out rowing in our boat. We got away late the next morning and were stopped everywhere by pretty places for coffee or wine or meals or historical sights that Johann had to investigate. We didn't make five miles the second day. That night we danced—every night we danced, and we began to get away later and later in the mornings. We were ten days making a distance that one might have rowed in three or four, and then felt and wondered that we had done so beautiful a journey so fast. And I wonder now that I have never gone back, as I declared and have always been sure that I would "some day," to do the Neckar over again in a rowboat slowly— two or three weeks of it.

Toward the end of the semester a friend of mine, Carlos J. Hittell, came over from Munich to visit me. He was an art student from California. I had known well his brother Franklin at Berkeley; his father, Theodore H. Hittell, the historian, had had more to do with my education than many a teacher. A retired attorney, he had turned to the writing of history, especially of California. He used to work on the dining-room table after dinner while I, his children and their friends, talked as youth will, finally and positively, of all sorts of things. Once he kept me when the others left, and he went into my mind and broke all the idols he found there. He was rough.

"You can't learn if you know everything already," he said. "You can't have a free mind if it's full of superstitions." And he whanged away. I took it pretty well, and because I came back for more, he continued to destroy my images. Every time I went to the house, whether to dinner, to call on his daughter, Catherine, or to sing songs with his sons, he lay for me and drew me into talk and some reading in his good library. A great service this fine old man rendered me. And his son, Carlos, did me another.

When Carlos joined me at Heidelberg, he completed our trio, one student of art history, one of ethics and philosophy, and one of the real thing, art. We played, walking, rowing, swimming, and touring. but also we talked, and the artist, without knowing or meaning it, spoke as one having authority. Johann and I listened to the man who was doing what we were merely reading and thinking about. We saw what the artist had told me at Berkeley, that we were getting scholarship about art, not art. But, like that other artist, Carlos Hittell could not express in our medium, words what he was doing or trying to do when he was painting. We must go and be with art students when they were at work in their studios and see if we could—not hear, but see what art is. When the semester was over, therefore, we all went to Munich to study art instead of art history. No more Heidelberg for either of us.

And no more philosophy for me. There was no ethics in it. I had gone through Hegel with Kuno Fischer, hoping to find a basis for an ethics; and the professor thought he had one. I had been reading in the original the other philosophers whom I had read also in Berkeley, and they, too, thought they had it all settled. They did not have anything settled. Like the disputing professors at Berkeley, they could not agree upon what was knowledge, nor upon what was good and what evil, nor why. The philosophers were all prophets, their philosophies beliefs, their logic a justification of their—religions. And as for their ethics, it was without foundation. The only reasons they had to give for not lying or stealing were not so reasonable as the stupidest English gentleman's: "It isn't done."

This was my reluctant, disappointed conclusion, arrived at after a waste of a couple of good years of conscientious work. I must leave the philosophers and go to the scientists for my science of ethics as I must go to the artists for art. I said good-by to the good kept woman who had kept me so comfortable. She accepted my departure as she accepted everything.

"Men come and men go," she said cheerfully.

"Always?" I asked.

"They don't always come," she laughed, "but always they go, always."

"And that's all there is of it?"

"All? Nay," she protested, pointing to her two. "For me there are always the children, thank God."

XX

MUNICH: THERE ARE NO ARTISTS

A PLAIN old third- or fourth-class café and beer restaurant called the Blüthe was the blooming center of the art-student life of München in my day (the summer of 1890). That is where the Americans I knew and some Germans dropped in when they had nothing else to do. Some of them took their meals there at one long table, which, when cleared of an evening, became the gathering-board for others who dropped in for coffee or later for a drink after the theater. It was around that board that I first heard artists themselves tear to pieces the everlasting question: "Well, and what is art anyhow?"

And if I did not get the answer, it may be in part because at that time there were no artists in Munich, not really. There were men there whose names are now well known and whose pictures are bought and sold as the works of great painters. It's all a mistake. They told me themselves that none of them was an artist. And my German friend, Johann Friedrich Krudewolf, heard the same thing from the German masters and students he met.

We parted, Johann and I, when we arrived together in Munich. He was going to study at the university there; I was going to Leipzig. We might have played around together all summer; our purposes were the same, but I did not think to suggest that. I took a room in the house where Carlos Hittell lived, met his friends, mostly Americans, and when Johann saw that I was among my own, he said he would go off among his countrymen. He looked wistful, I remembered afterward, but he said "Goodby," and I thought he was long and sentimental about it; so I was short and, as he reminded me later, American.

Carlos Hittell wanted to work; so he took me to the Blüthe, introduced me to the crowd there, and I found a fellow who had time to waste talking about art. And he could talk art, too. He showed me through the Pinakothek to illustrate his ideas, and he spoke with inside understanding and authority of the artists repre- sented there. These were very few. Not all of the old masters in that gallery were masters, and of the modern painters there was but one who could paint: Lenbach; and even Lenbach, as you can see, Lenbach himself gave up art for portraiture, for fame and success. I betrayed some interest in the pictures of other men of whom I had heard; he showed me them, he showed me with his cutting thumb and his curling lips and his sneering eyes that, excepting only Lenbach, the other moderns were either merchants and manufacturers or, at best, struggling, unsuccessful students of the art of painting which remains to be revived by—some one.

"Any of the Americans likely to revive the art?" I asked hope- fully.

He laughed himself into a knot. He'd show me. We went calling at all the studios of all the students he knew. Fine fellows, hard at work, they stopped to pull out their canvases one by one. It was pathetic or ridiculous. They looked so hungry, some of them, for a bit of appreciation, their eyes darting from their poor pictures to my poor face. I rather liked some of the "sketches" I saw, and I certainly would have said so, had my guide not warned me.

"Look out, now," he would say, as we climbed the stairs to a studio, "this poor devil is sensitive; he thinks he can paint. And he can draw, a little. But paint? Never. You'll see. But don't— don't hurt his feelings by saying what you think."

Or he would laugh before another door: "This chap, he thinks he's a genius. He is sure he can paint. But I'll tell you how he does it. His fad is Defregger. He goes out around the villages, looking for Defregger peasants in Defregger costumes and De- fregger groupings. If he finds a Defregger picture, he paints it as Defregger painted it; only—nobody but himself can see the like- ness. But he never does find a Defregger in real life; neither did Defregger; of course not; so the student does what his master did: he hires models off the city streets, dresses 'em up, poses 'em, and paints them as Defregger has shown they ought to be. And he sells his things. That's the trouble with art today. Some of these house painters can sell their stuff—to Americans, generally; but they sell it. They live."

And sure enough, this student of Defregger was painting when we went into his studio a Defregger-like group of Tyrolese peasants, using a saucy little wicked street girl dressed up as a peasant Madonna. She and the painter and my friend made jokes and laughed all through the work. And when my guide left me there and I turned the conversation into serious channels, this painter went off into a worship of Defregger till he became so wrought up that he quit work to take me to the gallery to see the Defreggers. He looked at nothing else; he bade me look at nobody else, not even Lenbach.

"Lenbach! Pooh!" he said. "He can paint some, but he can't see. Bring him Bismarck or the Kaiser or some prince and tell him to paint, and he'll make you a likeness, but—that man lives here and sees nothing of the life about him; nothing. I don't believe he ever looked at a peasant, and if he did, what would he see? The character, the life, the truth and beauty of the real people? Never. No. But now look at that Defregger—"

I was in despair. I could not learn to recognize a work of art unless I could see one. I had come to Munich to watch men paint and to see and feel what the painter at work was trying to do. My guide showed me in studio after studio students and painters making, not pictures—only outsiders would call such things pictures; sometimes the man painting at it spoke of it as a picture or a painting—my guide called them sketches, and he let me see and hear that the sketchers did not put their mind on what they were doing. They all talked while they worked, told jokes, laughed, poked fun at the model, flirted with her, made love. No wonder they could not be taken seriously. No wonder they were not and never would be artists; none of them, excepting my guide. We used to go often to his studio to rest, talk, and have a drink. He drank a good deal. But he never worked when I was there, and he never talked about his own things. He merely got them out, one at a time, one for each visit. He would set the picture for the day up on the easel, adjust it carefully in the light, and leave it there. "A work of art speaks for itself," he used to say. "You look at it and just let it work in." So we sat and drank, talked of other things, meanwhile letting the picture speak for itself. I did not care at first for his pictures; they were all sketches, unfinished, but it was amazing how, as he talked about painting for the imagination of the spectator who liked himself to finish what the artist only indicated—it gave one a thirst to see more and more of a line started, until between us, the painter and I, we had made a perfect picture. If I had been buying pictures, I would have bought one or two of my guide's works. As it was I was content to adore them and follow him; and he was satisfied, too. We became fast friends, but I wasn't seeing him at work; and I wanted to see a real master at work.

One night at the Blüthe some one proposed that we all go to Venice to make some sketches. I was delighted, and several voices were willing. Others opposed it, and the conversation became a debate on the subject whether Venice was the most beautiful place in the world or the filthiest, ugliest, most lied about. And the opposition won, so far as I was concerned. At least, I came away with the impression that Venice was a beastly collection of one-time palaces, now slummy tenements set down upon a network of stinking sewers navigated by intelligent rats who lived well upon the garbage dumped into the tideless, motionless drainage of a community of dirty thieves. But the wrong side won, practically. The crowd decided to go to Venice.

They got out a big butcher's book, and as they studied it I realized that its brown paper pages carried addresses, not only for Venice, but everywhere. Whenever a Blüthe student had been off sketching he noted in that book the hotels and restaurants he discovered, with prices and characterizations which were a guide for others. I often used that book. That night those men picked out of it a short list of hotels, pensions, restaurants, and cafés, which we all used in and on the way to Venice. Carlos Hittell copied out of it other addresses for Salzburg, Vienna, Trieste, and when he and I got back to his flat he proposed that we go to Venice, not with the gang direct, but around by Vienna. And so we went, pleasantly and slowly, and I remember that the butcher-book guide put us in good, cheap places all along the line, so cheap, indeed, that we made the whole round trip, all costs included, for $1.50 a day each. I could travel in Europe, as I could study, on my allowance, which was $50 a month. This gave me a sense of liberty, such as a tramp has; the whole world was open to me.

At Venice we joined the sketchers. We found there, as I had at Heidelberg, canoes "left by Englishmen," and we paddled all through the canals, especially the narrow back ways. Carlos and I had good sport at Venice, and after two or three days I began to feel the picturesque beauty of this dirty old tumbledown world-capital. I could see it the better, I think, for having come to it with the hopeless expectation sketched on my mind by the art students in Munich who did not want to go there. Their description was realistic; it served only to prepare me for the worst and so to get the best; one should always be forewarned of the stenches, filth, and wreckage of Venice before his first visit.

I watched the painters paint Venice, one by one, and I saw that they saw and were pointing out the essential beauty of Venice; and the skill, the instinctive taste, and the knowledge they put into their work suggested that my Munich guide could not have been altogether right: some of them were artists of some sort; second-rate, perhaps, or third, but they had something I had not; they could do with colors what I, for example, could not do. I sounded them on the point, however, and each of them agreed with my art master as to the others. "Good fellows. I like them, but—" I wished that my guide, the only painter in Munich, were at Venice; after watching the others at work on their "sketches," I would have liked to see a real painter painting—Venice.

One day I said something like this. It was the day of our departure. The train left about noon, and after breakfast and packing, we sat around doing nothing. Carlos Hittell suggested that we walk to the station.

"Walk!" they shouted. "You can't walk in Venice. We'd get lost."

Carlos said that he would lead all that would follow him to the station without a moment's hesitation at any time. How would he do it? He said any westerner could do it. You fix in your mind the direction of the station and you go that way, turning to be sure, but always keeping your mental compass clear. Several of us offered to follow him; the rest were to attend to the baggage and report us missing in Munich.

"All right now," said Carlos to us, pointing toward the station, far away and out of sight. "That is our direction. Come on." And he started off at a right angle. He darted into a back street, turned here, there, right, left, even back, but swift as an Indian he sped along till all in a whirl after twenty minutes' walk we came out upon the bridge over to the Rialto, where two fellows quit us. There was a steamboat station there; they would stay there till the crowd came. Carlos, with the rest of us, crossed the bridge, dived into the tangle of streets on the other side, and, over another bridge, came upon the station, an hour ahead of time.

How did he do it? We discussed this on the train, and no one would accept Carlos' explanation: that he had the plainsman's sense of direction. I backed him up, telling how Carlos had shot a cork out from between my thumb and finger; which was true. He was a westerner. But that did not explain his knowledge of Venetian streets, not even to me, his co-liar. He would not tell his secret till years afterward: he had observed on the corner of a building he was sketching the sign, "*Alla Strada Ferrata.*" He inquired and was told that that sign marked every turn of the way to the railroad station. He knew his Latin, if not his Italian.

My staunch support of Carlos and their irritation at his feat in path-finding so aroused the wrath of the crowd that on the train they turned upon me, no longer a guest. I came back with comments on their art and, to defend my position, quoted my Munich art guide on the general principles of art.

"I wish," I said, "that he had come to Venice and painted it."

It was awful. I can't remember what they said; they all spoke at once. The judgments that stuck in my mind were that he— "He? He isn't a painter; he's a bum." "Never works, only talks art, drinks, brags, and runs down everybody else." "One of these here beginners. Never finished anything."

It was unanimous. It was convincing. My one, last, only, lonely modern painter was—dead—to me.

XXI

LEIPZIG: MUSIC, SCIENCE, LOVE

THE day before I was leaving Munich for my winter semester at Leipzig (1890-91) I interrupted my packing to go out and drink a glass of cool beer. Turning into a café, I saw a young man sitting alone with his face down on his arms folded on the table. There was something familiar about his head, and looking again, sharply, at it, I recognized my Heidelberg student friend, Johann Friedrich Krudewolf. I touched his shoulder. He threw up his face angrily, and there were tears in his eyes.

"Nu!" I said with a push as I withdrew my hand. *"Was heisst's,* Johann?"

His anger passed, and he, tapping his chest, answered:

"The doctor says I can't stay in Munich."

"Good," I said, gladly. "We will go to Leipzig then."

His face lighted up, but he wasn't sure the doctor would approve of Leipzig either. "Don't ask him," I suggested. Johann did not know whether there was any good professor of art history in Leipzig, and I didn't. But he had in his pocket the fat little paper book which gave all the courses for all the universities. We looked up Leipzig, and Johann said, "I'll go." There was a fine course in his subject. We had our beer with our planning and separated to meet on the train the next day. And there, on the train, we planned to live and study together for a year. A year of art history for both of us, and for me a year of psychology under Wundt, the leader, if not the founder, of the school of experimental psychology. I would take all his lectures and work in his laboratory, as if for a degree, and say nothing of my purpose: to see if I could find in psychology either a basis for a science of ethics or a trail through psychology to some other science that might lead on to a scientific ethics.

We were early; the mob of students had not arrived, so that we had a choice of quarters. We took two connecting rooms in the Petersteinweg. The only other roomers were a working-girl who raised a living on her wages by some traffic in the business of love and a regular old street-walker who made love a business. The landlady was a lone, but not a lonely, old widow woman who envied, loved, and quarreled for fun with the girl. Johann became *Herr im Hause;* he kept order. When the row in the back room became so loud that I went out to see and enjoy it, Johann would come flying out of his room to make the peace. They came to fear him and his just wrath. Me they laughed at or with; I was the crazy American, with the queer, foreign habits. I took a bath every day, for example.

The old woman had agreed to deliver in my room every morning a large vessel of cold water, and she was astonished that I insisted upon and used it, pouring it over me as I stood in my rubber tub. She must have reported this in the neighborhood and to the *Mädel,* as we called the girl in the back room; and I infer that her report was not credited in the market-place. Anyway one morning, as I stood stripped in my tub with the water held high above my head, my door opened, and there were the old woman, half a dozen other old women, and the *Mädel,* all staring wide-eyed, open-mouthed at me, while the landlady pointed proudly, triumphantly, exclaiming:

"Na, und was hab' ich g'sagt? Da staht er. Se'en Sie?" ("Well, and what did I tell you? There he stands. You see?")

Johann protested. He tried to make them respect me. Even though I was a foreigner, and an American at that—queer as I was, I was a human being and not a captive animal to be shown off. It was no use. I was exhibited, with pride to be sure, but my door might be thrown open at any crisis in my life, intellectual or physical, to prove to some market man or a customer of the *Mädel* that their boasts were true. They did have a living American in the house.

The landlady told me the story of her life, often, and all her troubles, and the girl told me several versions of hers with all her passing triumphs, rights and wrongs. Some men treated her dreadfully; some men were treated dreadfully; but all were despised and loathed, except now and then one would be all right for a short while. I liked a pretty baker girl across the street; she looked like the warm rolls she sold me, but Johann took no interest in girls, and he frowned on my flirtations.

"Ah, no," he would say, "don't fool that little baker girl; she is too trustful, too easy."

He found somewhere and brought home one day Guido Peters, an Austrian student of music, who swept us into his enthusiasm and made us also students of music. Leipzig was a music center, and Guido knew everybody and everything in that distinct and devoted world. He got all the concert programs long in advance, gave us lectures on each composer and his work, illustrated. Sitting at his piano, he would pull a piece to pieces, playing it analytically and then straight through, with comments, explanations, and criticism. The weekly event was the Gewandhaus concert on Monday nights. Guido brought home the next program Tuesday, and day by day he would work with us to make us familiar with it till on Friday we all went together to the last private rehearsal to which music students were admitted; on Saturday we heard the public rehearsal; and on Monday night, we were quite ready to appreciate the finished concert. And so with all the other good music given in Leipzig that winter: we had it over and over till we knew it inside and out; harmoniously and mathematically, sensually, scientifically, and artistically.

In return for our interest in his subject, Guido Peters took some in our subjects. He heard a lecture with us now and then, went with us to the art galleries of Dresden and Berlin. He did not care much for the science and the history of art and ethics. He preferred art for art's sake, art's and love's. For he was in love; he was in love, not with any girl in Leipzig, but with many girls at home, in Austria. He wrote love-letters to his several sweethearts whom he loved—"all," he said, "equally. I pour out my whole heart to the one I am writing to, turn to the next, and I pour out my whole heart to her." And he always wanted to read us the last two or three of those letters; and he did, till I stopped him one day.

"No," I protested, "don't read it. Play it on the piano."

He looked uncomprehending a moment, then saw the point, leaped to the piano, and he played the letters. He played them all after that, and finally, by way of an experiment in applied psychology, I got him to play a letter he was full of before he wrote it. The effect astonished him. He didn't have to write it. "Nay," he exclaimed, "I can't write it now." Of course not. When he played a love-letter he was a lover in love; he poured forth his whole heart to us, and after the orgy of it, there was nothing for him or for us to do but go down to the river, take a boat, and row slowly, softly, sentimentally up the river, the pretty little river under the trees, and, in the silence of our hearts, listen to the nightingales.

A serious matter for me, these debauches. To Johann it was merely music; to Guido himself it was art and love; that's all. The Germans are sentimental idiots when drunk like that. But we Americans are a practical race. When we are moved, we are moved to action. If we get drunk, we want to break something. I broke an engagement and married.

Guido and his music and his love for his remote girls were not alone to blame for my conduct. The coming of spring at the wrong time—right after the winter—had something to do with it; and then there were Wundt's lectures and the hard scientific spirit of the experimental laboratory. "We want facts, nothing but facts," he used to declare. The laboratory where we sought the facts and measured them by machinery was a graveyard where the old idealism walked as a dreadful ghost and philosophical thinking was a sin. One day when the good old professor was looking over us and our works, his one seeing eye fell upon William James's great book on psychology, just out. Wundt had almost blinded himself by the abuse of his eyes in experimentation; he had but one tiny spot in one retina that could see. He picked up James, fixed his one spot on the first page, and beginning at once to read, started off like a somnambulist for the door.

Then he remembered, turned, and asked my indulgence. "*Sie erlauben?*" When I "allowed," he went on reading and walking into his own room. The next morning he came back, laid the book on my table, and thanked me.

"You have read it?" I asked, astonished.

"All night long," he answered. "Word for word, every word." And his familiars told me afterward that this was literally true. He had sat down with the book when he got it from me, read it word by word, as he had to with his eye-spot, and finished it the moment he returned it to me. As he was about to leave it with me, I stopped him with a question: What about it?

"Well, and—?" I said. ("*Na, und*—")

"It is literature, it is beautiful," he stammered, "but it is not psychology."

Against this I always like to put a story Wundt's assistant, Külpe, told us after a visit to the neighboring University of Jena to see the aged philosopher Erdmann, whose history of philosophy, in some ten volumes, we all had read and studied. They had a warm, friendly talk, the old scholar and the young scientist, all about the old philosophers and their systems. But when Külpe tried to draw him out on Wundt and the newer school, Erdmann shook his head, declaring that he could not understand the modern men.

"In my day," he explained, "we used to ask the everlasting question: 'What is man?' And you—nowadays you answer it, saying, 'He *was* an ape.'" ("*Er war ein Aff*".")

And yet Wundt had a philosophy, and not only of facts; no, and not only of theories, either. He said that theories were only aids to experiment, which was the test. He taught and I learned from him the discipline, the caution, and the method of the experimental procedure of modern science. But Wundt, in practice, had established facts, he thought, by this method, and he built upon them conclusions which formed a system of philosophy written into several volumes. With an ethics, too; it was all complete. Well we knew it. It was under attack at the time. Some fresh, young men were challenging, with facts, with experimentally determined data, some of the very foundations of Wundt's psychology, which in turn was the basis of Wundt's philosophy. We were working, for the truth, of course, but also we were fighting, and when we got results which confirmed Wundt we were glad, and when we got results that seemed to support the enemy . . .

Some of us were looking over the laboratory records of an American student who had stood high with the Professor and, therefore, with us all. He had gone home, taken a professorship, and was holding high our colors. He became afterward one of the leading men in American science and education. His student papers were models of neatness, and as we looked we saw that they were a masterpiece of caution, wisdom, and mathematical labor. The records of his experiment showed that he got, at first, results which would have given aid and comfort to the enemy and confounded one of Wundt's most axiomatic premises. He must have suffered, that promising young student; it was his thesis for the degree of Doctor of Philosophy, which he needed for his career at home; he must have thought, as a psychologist, that Wundt might have been reluctant to crown a discovery which would require the old philosopher to recast his philosophy and rewrite the published volumes of his lifework. The budding psychologist solved the ethical problem before him by deciding to alter his results, and his papers showed how he did this, by changing the figures item by item, experiment by experiment, so as to make the curve of his averages come out for instead of against our school. After a few minutes of silent admiration of the mathematical feat performed on the papers before us, we buried sadly these remains of a great sacrifice to loyalty, to the school spirit, and to practical ethics.

Ethics! There was no foundation in (experimental) psychology for a science of ethics; not that I could find. There might be some day, when psychology itself is scientific. All I got out of my year of German psychology was a lead into biology on the one hand and into sociology on the other, a curiosity to hear and see what the French thought they knew about such matters, and best of all, a training in the experimental method. I decided to go to Paris for a year at the Sorbonne, and I began to change my subject from ethics to morals; from what ought to be done to what is done, and why. Lightly I say this now, but to me, in the spring of 1891, the conflict of ideas and emotions was a crisis that weighed heavily on me. I had lost time. I had lost myself.

There is no made road across the sciences. To pursue an inquiry from one of them through others into another is like trying to travel 'cross country in England without returning to London. The sciences are laid out within perpendicular lines. The physicists, chemists, biologists, and astronomers now are making tracks across their fields, but in my day they also were fenced in, each man to his own *Fach*. My difficulties and my sense of defeat put me in a state of mind where Johann and his art, Guido Peters and his music and his loves, the river and the nightingales and the spring, and, yes, the baker girl and the *Mädel* in the back room and the funny

old landlady—with the regrets of all of them, and their laughters
—all these were an inspiration to me to go and make love myself
to a pretty American girl who sat just behind me at Wundt's lectures. It was unethical, but I did it; and it was good for some
nineteen years.

XXII

OVER THE ALPS TO PARIS

IT IS related of Frederick C. Howe that when he had laid the finished manuscript of his autobiography proudly before his wife and she had read it, she looked up at him with the humor that is all hers and said, "But, Fred, weren't you ever married?"

"Oh, yes," he answered. "I forgot that. I'll put it in."

I can understand this. A love story is worth writing, I believe, only when it is understood, and a man seldom understands his own romance. I don't understand mine. It seems to me that I can see through a government or a political situation, but human relations are beyond my comprehension. They happen to me; friendship has been the music of my life, but what does music say? And what does love mean? We should be able to answer this question. Love is coming of age as the human mind is, and the two should be decently married. But my intelligence stops where love begins and begins again where love leaves off.

And so it is, I think to observe, with males generally. They can grasp sex; that's what they practice and talk and think they know a bit about, but sex and love are or should be one, as women know, who can navigate cunningly through the storm that blinds their lovers. If there is ever to be a science of love and marriage and if it is to be an applied science, women and such effeminate men as poets will have to make it. Eugenics will be the woman's art as it is her business now.

Anyhow my marriage was none of my business. When Johann, my German chum, and I rowed up the Pleisser River in the autumn the nightingales spoke to us and we to them, of psychology and art history, ethics, philosophy, and music. There was no sentiment about us. Johann had no girl; mine was in America. For I had left America with a "sort of understanding" with a girl at Berkeley. Johann could be soft about anything, and he declared that that was not because he was German. "Americans are just as weak," he said. But I set the tone of our friendship, and whatever of weakness there was in me was hidden in my letters to—"home."

When winter came, closing navigation on the river, we worked till the Christmas season approached. How I hated the German Christmas! The whole world went home, closed the door, and opened the window-shades, leaving the foreigner to wander about in the cold darkness all alone and look in longingly at the light, warmth, and merriment. I had arranged with Johann to ignore Christmas. We studied while the city went silly shopping, and even when the Day fell upon us like a fog, we stuck to our dull labors till, toward evening, I could not stand it. Calling Johann, I took him for a walk in the dusk. The streets were abandoned to us and the dirty, old snow, and to make matters worse, there were the lighted windows with their tinseled trees and the sounds of domestic happiness. I could not stand that either. We went home. I slammed into my room, leaving Johann to go on to his, next door. I sat in the dark, utterly miserable, wondering what Johann had meant by saying that Americans (and the English, too) were as sentimental as Germans, only not so honest about it. He would see, I had said, and I was showing him and his tribe, the Frau *Wirthin* and the sewing-girl and the old street-walker, who held, all of them, that such sentimentality, like love and like murder, would out. I was setting them an example.

I don't know what they had seen, but I had seen quite enough of Christmas when, about suppertime, Johann's door opened and he stood, sharp-cut black in the light that shone from behind him. He stood there a moment, and then, in the dialect he fell into only when he was moved, he said:

"*Du, geh' a mal her,*" which means "Come" but says "Go once here."

I went once, and I saw on his table a pretty little candled Christmas tree, blazing away, with parcels on and under it, and, all around, the plates, bottles, foods, fruits, and candies of a Christmas dinner. It looked good to me.

"Wait," said Johann. "I'll call the others." And as he went out I said, "Wait," and I slipped back into my dark room, got out

from under the bed the gifts I luckily had bought secretly for—
everybody who came, the Frau *Wirthin,* the *Mädel,* and the poor
old smiling wreck of the streets who danced in with Johann,
bringing greetings and parcels, more food, more bottles, and the
odor of a goose cooking joyously in the *Wirthin's* little kitchen.

We sang songs, ate and drank; we drank, sang, and danced.
There was a distribution of presents; then we sang and danced till
late into the night, when we discovered all at once that we so
loved one another that we hooked arms and drank solemnly a
Brüderschaft, the whole mixed five of us. I liked it. I swam and
the others nearly drowned in the Christmas spirit, and it started
something in me, as the old Frau *Wirthin* predicted.

"You'll see," she said to me. "You can't go on loving without
loving."

"Why not?" the street-walker asked, surprised. "Men all love
without loving. That's what I'm there for." ("*Deswegen bin ich
da.*")

"Ach!" the sewing-girl interpreted, "you two use the same
words to say opposite things."

Johann's eyes had become fixed on me. He was seeing in the
light of the women's chatter something that seemed to alarm him.

"Nay," he protested, "you wouldn't, would you? You'll be true
to her that is at home?"

"Long, perhaps," the street-walker answered, "but not forever.
And it's long already, as this Christmas has shown."

She turned to the door; her Christmas was over.

"Where you going?" the *Mädel* asked her, and the street-
walker replied with a look at Johann:

"I am going out to meet some true lover coming home alone
from his lonely Merry Christmas."

The work hardened after the holidays. Wundt's lectures got
down to cases, the laboratory hummed like a factory, and there
were quizzes in pure philosophy. I was busy; so was Johann;
everybody was working. I was restless, too, and Johann noticed it.

"What are you forever looking for?" he asked irritably one day.

"Looking!" I exclaimed. "I'm not looking for anything."

"Seems to me you are a hunter on the hunt," he insisted.

I did not know what he meant, but I was annoyed; so I watched
myself, like a psychologist, and sure enough, something in me was

searching for something or somebody outside of me. And I found her. Toward the end of the winter semester it was that I noticed an American girl at Wundt's lecture, and she saw me. She was a brown-eyed, straight-standing, rather handsome young woman with a singularly direct way of looking at one. The Professor's *famulus* said her name was Josephine Bontecou.

"Why?" he asked, smiling. "Why this sudden interest? She has sat in that same seat all through the semester, and some of us Germans have seen her before." Had they? I went to the English church to meet her. She was not known there. I went for the first time to other places where Americans and the English foregathered. She was not at any of them. Following her out of the lecture one dark evening, I accosted her in the Stadt Park. She understood; she always understood. She let me go with her to her apartment, where I met her mother, a woman I understood—the only one, I think.

Susan Bontecou had divorced her husband, a physician and surgeon of Troy, N.Y. Her daughter took her mother's side, and the two came to Europe to start new lives, Josephine as a student of psychology intending to write fiction, the mother to see the scenes of the history she knew well from her life of imaginative reading. They were a devoted couple, and that devotion which they thought to be their virtue turned out to be their tragedy. They were happy enough when I met them. They must have looked alike, but now in Leipzig, there, the mother was beginning to whiten with the years, and her once straight, strong little body was weakening. Her mind was alert, keen, and kind, like her eyes; she was really a shrewd woman of the world.

When Josephine brought me home to her that first day, we all talked pleasantly along for a while; then the daughter left me with her mother. It was always so. Josephine could not waste her time; she had work to do. It was the mother who, quietly sewing, would listen to my wonderings; she must have sensed my essential youth.

"My daughter is older than you are," she said one day, and I can remember looking into her uplifted eyes with astonishment at the irrelevance of her remark. Our conversations with Josephine all turned around one question: whether she should accept the offer of marriage she had received from a young German *Junker*, a corps student and duelist, who held out to her an estate with a castle to live in and villages of poor peasants to be grand and kind to. I was for it, the mother against it, and Josephine was in doubt; so it seemed to me, and yet here was the mother telling me that her daughter was too old for me.

"Yes?" I answered, and I meant and I must have looked, "What of it?" For the mother added, "Josephine is much older than you are."

There was no answer; I could not make out what this lovely old lady was thinking about. And so with Johann. He also was opposed to what I had not the slightest intention of doing. One night when I told him I thought that the American girl was going to marry "the *Junker*," Johann stared at me so long that I felt my face flush. He hated Josephine; he called her "dominating," and this time he took off his slipper and shook it at me.

"What do I care," I said, "if the *Junker* is ruled by his wife?"

"The *Junker!*" he exclaimed. "The *Junker* is safe," and he went off to his own room.

No one seemed to be able to understand that Josephine Bontecou and I were to have a friendship; no one; not even the nightingales. For when, in the spring, Johann and I went rowing up the river, the birds sang, not, as in the fall, of science and art, but of love and romance, of adventures and new countries and other peoples. I was going to Paris. Josephine and her mother were planning a summer vacation tour through the Alps to end in Paris at the Sorbonne. That had always been my plan, to study in Paris; it just happened to be hers too. Johann knew that, but he pretended to be surprised that I was willing to give up my German doctor's degree "for a year of—Paris." He emphasized "Paris," but I knew what he meant. And he knew, too, how I despised degrees, how psychology was only a road to ethics—a blind alley; and he did not know that Josephine had finally, finally declined the *Junker's* offer of marriage. He never even asked how this came out.

"Your German friend is jealous," Mrs. Bontecou remarked when our train pulled out and left him standing on the platform.

"But what of?" I answered her.

"Of your friendship with Josephine," she said very gently.

I don't remember a single Alp. Years afterward when I traveled in Switzerland it was all new to me; and yet Josephine and I walked it that summer. Her mother was with us, but she took trains or diligences to meet us at the places we tramped to. Josephine saw everything; she was always thorough; but I saw only Josephine, I think. Anyway I fell in love with her in Switzerland, and when we arrived in Paris we were engaged. Johann was right after all. Everybody was; as usual I alone was wrong: all wrong, but all right too.

XXIII

PARIS, LONDON—HOME

PARIS is a loose merger of many, very many, small provincial communities, each of which is self-sufficient and pleasantly or offensively clannish.

"Do you live here?" they will ask in the little local shops, and your answer makes a difference, not only in the prices, but in the service. A policeman won't arrest you if you live on his beat; the accredited street-walker won't pick your pocket; they will see you safely home. Even though you are a foreigner, you may still be a *petit Parisien,* an insider, more French than a Parisian from some other quarter; he is the stranger. Some quarters boast of inhabitants who have never been to Paris—the Paris of the foreigners and the financiers. The *grands boulevards* are a place which the *petits Parisiens* make excursions to, as they visit Versailles, on a holiday, all dressed up, in family or neighborhood sight-seeing groups.

My Paris, the *petit Paris* of my student days, was the Latin Quarter, of course; but the Latin Quarter then was a simple, idyllic, fresh-water college town. Our connection with Paris was by horse busses which made the trip pleasant on a sunny day, but long, halting—a day's work; we dressed up and took the trip only to fetch money from the bank or to call on some tourist friend from home. That and the opera were the only uses we had for the Right Bank. I remember once an enterprising party of reckless fellows ventured with their girls to Montmartre; that was something like; and they had a good time, but they didn't get back till late the next forenoon and were all tired out and wretchedly sobered by the long, long journey. No, our lives were complete in the Quarter, which was the largest of all the Parisian communities, and, we thought, the most important. It had two physical centers, Montparnasse and the Boul' Mich', and it had two lobes to its brain, the Sorbonne (with the university) and the Beaux Arts (with the other private art schools), but the art students and the university students played together, and play and work were all one to them, like truth and beauty, which we all sought merrily together, seriously by day, and at night still more seriously. For gayety and earnestness were undivided, too. Anyway we were one, we, the students and our shop-keepers, our laundresses, waiters, concierges, and our *gens-d'armes*. We had rows among ourselves, but as against the world —the successful, Philistine, spoilsport Paris—we were one big union.

Maybe it is so now. Montparnasse has won out over the Boul' Mich', but I see the same all sorts of students together and I hear them using our phrases to express our ideas. The elements are not changed: wine or women; art and science, or success and business; evolution or revolution. There's a difference, however. There are taxis and the underground; students appear on the *grands boulevards*, and the tourists at Montparnasse, a flood of spectators. There's an audience. We played to ourselves. Our life seems to me to have been simpler, more naïve, much less conscious. It was, like our art, for its own sweet sake. The shop-keepers and the cafés are more businesslike now, the students more—histrionic. I recognize it all. It is just as if the fiction about us had come true. The Latin Quarter today is what it was supposed to be in my day—and wasn't.

My student friends did not feel that they had to "keep some girl or other." Some of them fell in love with the loveliest little woman in the world, and they set out to live happily with her all their lives. They did not do it, not often, but the *ménages* I knew were as real as mine. I lived with Josephine Bontecou just as they lived with their girls. We were married, to be sure, but nobody knew that, and it made no difference to our friends or to us. We had taken rooms in a Montparnasse hotel, Josephine, her mother, and I, and Josephine went to work, her mother went sight-seeing, and I looked around. We were not going to marry till our studies were over and we were back in America. I feared my father would recall me if he heard that I had taken a wife. But after a few weeks of waiting, we stole off to London, lived there the required twenty-two days, and on the twenty-second were married on the way to the boat-train for Paris. I was seasick all that first night of my married life, wretchedly and then restfully sick: it did me good, and the next day, in Paris, I, too, went to work. We told nobody of our marriage, neither at home nor in the Quarter; so we had all the advantages of the law and all the thrills and the prestige of lawlessness.

My work was interesting to me, generally, not specifically. I took all the courses I signed up for, I heard besides every lecture that any student or any book mentioned as "good" in any way, and more besides. I was like those Paris bums who drop in to the Sorbonne lectures all day long just to sit down and be warm; I would join any stream of students going in to any room to hear the lecture on any subject. That was my plan: specifically to look everywhere for a lead to ethics, and generally, to get a sense of the French methods and spirit. I heard some able, thought-breeding men and felt the difference between them and the German professors. The French speak French almost universally as few Germans can speak German: not only clearly, but with a precision and a finish that is charming. The French believe in reason; they experiment, too, of course, and their laboratory work is clean, careful, and productive of results, but they cannot stop their minds from collaborating, as the Germans do. The French are impatient mentally. Their imagination will out, and they love to think about the conclusions they cannot help foreseeing and sometimes anticipating and even forming. Their great fault I felt to be this, their greatest virtue: they worked and thought and spoke like artists, esthetically, and with all their false faith in reason and their trained skill in logic, they used their heads to prove the truth of something that was only very beautiful; and so they would express it beautifully. In any lecture room in the Sorbonne one could find some scholarly actor, with his glass of sugar and water, reciting, even singing, a prose poem on a chemcial or a metaphysical formula. It was usually convincing, too; it was not always science, but it was literature, and when Charcot, for example, was showing on the set stage of his amphitheater what his psychiatric patients could do or suffer, it was drama.

"Go," he said when he was through with a woman patient who had done her stunts, and then as she was passing off the stage, the professor struck the table with a hammer. The cataleptic stopped, stiffened, and stood rigid with her hands half lifted and her face turned back toward us.

"*La femme de Lot*," said Charcot, with a showman's flourish, and sure enough, there stood Lot's wife, a pillar of miraculous rigidity.

Play and work live together in France, like wit and logic, art and science, and men and women. We enjoyed life in Germany, too, but we did not amuse ourselves in the laboratory; we labored there till tired; then for recreation we went out to a beer hall or into the country and, dropping business, played hard. It was pleasant. I liked the German way. But Paris was somehow a release from some sort of repression. It was good to feel free to walk into a laboratory exactly as you would into a café and jest with the other fellows, even about the experiment, speculate upon the possible results, say seriously what might not be true—just to hear how it sounded. And it was good to go to a café and join a frivolous crowd and feel that you could talk shop. It was as if the *verboten* signs had been removed from imagination, intuition, and temperament.

Perhaps my impression of Paris is pointed by the fact that I was living there, freely and fully living, with a wife, and that my friends were mostly artists rather than university students. I had a home, and some of our friends had homes; not all lawful, but warm, happy, domestic. They were French homes; the dining-room was separate—any one of the many restaurants where we met and dined together, and thought and talked and practiced our arts.

"Who can express in the fewest lines the attitude of that waiter to that girl he is serving?"

In words or in pencil strokes on the table-cloth everybody tried it, and discussed the results, graphically, psychologically, poetically, discovering, by the way, that all the arts and the sciences, too, are pretty much all one thing. There was one man, Louis Loeb, who loved this game, and through it we became lifelong friends. He picked me up as my German friend, Johann Krudewolf, had, for a purpose. Josephine had noticed that he always joined our crowd at dinner or coffee and was intensely interested whenever the talk turned to writing or to the parallel of painting and writing. She said that he was after something from me, and one night he declared it. He asked me if I would show him, technically, the difference between prose and verse. An odd question, as he knew, and he went on to justify it, oddly.

"I've never had a college education," he said. He had been a lithographer in Cleveland, Ohio, and made enough money to come to Paris to study art; that was all right; he would be a painter. But he loved music, too, and literature; he read every night, not intelligently. He needed to know the art of writing, as he had heard me say I wanted to understand the technique of painting.

"I'll teach you," he proposed. "I'll teach you painting if you'll teach me writing."

It was like Johann's proposition to exchange German for English lessons; only Loeb got the better of his bargain as I got the better of Johann's. Loeb learned to read. I asked him that night what he was reading. He drew from his pocket a volume of Milton's poems, and I turned to "Il Penseroso" and "L'Allegro." I read out loud to him a few heavy lines of the one, then a few light lines of the other, showed him the choice of words, the difference in cadence, and other tricks of the poet's craft, illustrated in those two poems. He had no prose with him, but I talked a little of the same and other tricks of prose. That was about all. He used to bring me afterward books with marked passages which he read to me as beautiful, and he analyzed them for me. He had it. He came to his reading with taste, with the artist's sense of art, and he was interested; he wanted to know. My few hints were enough, therefore. Taking them as a key, he opened book after book all that winter, all his short life—too short; and he read with much appreciation—all the literatures he had the languages for: English, French, and German. Louis Loeb became one of the best-read men I knew, a thoughtful, cultivated man of the world, far better educated than the average college graduate; but he never ceased expressing in his demeanor and in words his belief that he had missed something; he had never been to college. I argued with him; I introduced to him college-bred dubs to show him that he had taught and trained himself better than college had educated them. In vain. Louis Loeb taught me that it is worth while going through college if only to know what is not there.

That was what I learned and was learning. The universities

of the United States, Germany, and France have a classified body of knowledge, which an obedient, unquestioning student can learn the history of and, if he is clever, can add a chapter to. But if he has a question or a need in his mind he will not readily find the answer. At any rate, all the universities had to offer me by way of ethics was the long story of what man had thought about right and wrong; I felt that I could have gone home and lectured in a college on the successive systems of ethics; I certainly could have taken a degree in my specialty and written text-books for American schools with German thoroughness and French neatness. But I did not want to do that; a career did not attract me; and I did want to discover some basis for a scientific theory of ethical conduct. I could not. The French, like the Germans, had none. The best I had got out of all my scholastic wanderings was the belief, which was probably only a hope, that when there was a science of psychology, a science of sociology, and a science of biology, when we could know how man was born, bred, moved, and to what end, then we might lay out a program for the guidance of his conduct. For example, assuming that men are an evolving species, we might say that all acts, personal and social, that made for development were good, and that all conduct and conditions that hindered growth were bad. I did take that as a loose guide for myself, but to make it scientific, biology has to prove and describe evolution, psychology has to show us human possibilities, sociology has to be made a study of the effects of environment on human psychology; and even then, men have to know the possibilities of their growth and choose among them.

Talking about this and other wide, momentous problems in Louis Loeb's studio, where he was teaching me painting by letting me see him paint, I learned little of painting, not so much as he had learned of reading, but I did learn something. I learned that I could not learn to paint except by painting. Loeb himself had not learned to write, only to read; and I could read painting, some painting. But that was, I found, not what I wanted; I had wanted of painting, not only to feel, but to know what it was to paint. And I could not, without practice. Thinking of this, I applied it to ethics. I could not have even a philosophic ethics without practice; I must first study morals. The thing for me to do, I decided, was to leave the universities, go into business or politics, and see, not what thinkers thought, but what practical men did and why.

This was no revolution. I was about through anyway; my wife was already at work on a novel which, she realized, drew none of its psychology from the courses she had so faithfully worked at, but only from her own sense of personalities and experience. We would go home. I wanted to go to London for a few months' reading in the British Museum; her mother, having lived over all the historical scenes in all the churches, palaces, prisons, and public squares of Paris and much of Europe, was eager to see London; and Josephine felt like a rest. They went to London when the year in Paris was up, while I rushed up into Germany to visit a bit with Johann, who had gone, ill, to a cure for consumptives, an out-of-the-way place which required many changes and some command of German to get to. And I noticed that I had that command. My spoken German was a broken German when I left Germany, and in Paris I had never practiced at all, had not met Germans and spoke not a word of their language; yet here I was, after a year of French and English only, rattling off German like a native. And Johann noticed it.

"But," he exclaimed when we greeted each other at the station, "where have you learned to speak German so well?"

Evidently the brain is like any other muscle. While it is being worked it may not seem to learn or develop very fast the faculty needed; it becomes overtrained, so to speak, as mine was in the two years' constant strain to speak German. Give it a rest, as athletes do their bodies, and the blood-supply and growth go on and have the time to build up what is wanted. Anyhow, after two years of exercise and one year of neglect, I could really speak German, rapidly, easily, and with pleasure.

But I, too, had a cheerful surprise. Johann looked well, as well as I had ever seen him look. His summons to me had been so exigent that I feared he must be nearing the end, but no, his tall straight figure and his strong, good face were as vigorous and expressive as of old. We walked the long way to his hotel, where he introduced me to his new friends, the other patients, and for a week I lived their rather pleasant life in the air and sunshine. One day Johann asked me how bequests for scholarships were made in American universities, what my father's name, age, and birthplace were, what my mother's maiden name was, and then whether, if anything happened to him, I would return to Germany and do something he might want done.

I didn't promise blindly. My answer, after a moment of reflection, was that when I was once in America, I would probably be at work, busy and not free lightly to leave my business to come back to Germany, but that if he would have that in mind and yet ask me to I would promise. He seemed to be satisfied, even pleased, and said no more. We had a pleasant last evening together, and I left him, feeling, as I said, that he had happy, healthy years ahead for his art history researches in Italy, as he planned.

I rejoined Josephine and her mother in London. I went to my reading in the British Museum or sight-seeing with Mrs. Bontecou, who was an informed, imaginative guide; my wife was hawking the manuscript of her novel; and we all went shopping, for, after all, our return home was the chief thing in our minds. I was having all sorts of fashionable clothes made for my start in life; morning suits, evening suits, sporting and even business suits, and hats—high, low, soft, and hard, all English, the latest things. There was even a lounge suit and a cap for the steamer. When I paced the deck of the ship that was taking me "home" to the business of practical living, I was a beautiful thing, tailored and educated, an American boy of twenty-six, dressed outside like an Englishman, and filled up inside with the culture of the American and European universities.

I was happily unaware that I was just a nice, original American boob, about to begin unlearning all my learning, and failing even at that.

PART II
SEEING NEW YORK FIRST

I

I BECOME A REPORTER

WHEN my ship sailed into New York Harbor, my father's agent brought down to quarantine a letter which I still remember, word-perfect, I think.

"My dear son: When you finished school you wanted to go to college. I sent you to Berkeley. When you got through there, you did not care to go into my business; so I sold out. You preferred to continue your studies in Berlin. I let you. After Berlin it was Heidelberg; after that Leipzig. And after the German universities you wanted to study at the French universities in Paris. I consented, and after a year with the French, you had to have half a year of the British Museum in London. All right. You had that too.

"By now you must know about all there is to know of the theory of life, but there's a practical side as well. It's worth knowing. I suggest that you learn it, and the way to study it, I think, is to stay in New York and hustle.

"Enclosed please find one hundred dollars, which should keep you till you can find a job and support yourself."

This letter made me feel as if the ship were sinking under me; I had to swim. I did not know how, not in those waters, but it was not fear that hit me so hard. Nor disappointment. I had no plans to be disturbed. My vague idea was to go home to California and "see" what chance there was, say, at some college, to teach or lecture on the theories of ethics while making a study of morals: the professional ethics and the actual conduct of men in business, politics, and the professions. I could get no academic position in the east, where I was not known, but I might carry on my research as an insider in business just as well as I could as an observer. My wife asked me how I was going to go about getting a job in business and how meanwhile we were to live. For the first time, I think, I realized that I was expected to support my wife and that meanwhile my wife expected my father to help us. And my father would have done it. He said afterward that if he had known that I was married, he would not have thrown me off as he did—for my good, "just to see what you could do for yourself," he said. My wife was for telling him then and there, but I could not. I declared that I would never ask my father for another cent, and I didn't. The next money transaction between us was a loan I made to him.

No, my father was putting me to a test, I said, and I would show him. And my mother-in-law, Mrs. Bontecou, backed me up. She said she would see us through with her little money. Josephine was angry, and, in brief, ours was a gloomy landing-party. I alone was cheerful, secretly; I had an idea. I would write.

At the small hotel Josephine knew, I took pencil and paper and I wrote a short story, "Sweet Punch." That was a Saturday. I did it that day and rewrote and finished it on Sunday. Louis Loeb called that night. He was illustrating for *Harper's Magazine*, and he said he would offer them my story the next day. He sold it to them for fifty dollars. I sat me down to calculate. That story was done and sold in three days. Call it a week. I could make fifty dollars a week, which multiplied by fifty-two was, say, $2500 a year. Enough to live on. But I didn't do another story that week nor the next. Too busy looking for a job, I excused; but the fact was that I couldn't do another for a month, and then the second story was rejected. It was years before I got into the magazines again.

It was weeks before I found a job. I was amazed at the difficulty. There I was, all dressed up in my beautiful morning coat with top hat, answering ads, any ads for anything, from an editorship to errand boy. Literally. The juvenile literature I had read as a boy, about lads who began at the bottom and worked up, had stuck. Here I was, what I had once grieved that I was not, a poor but willing young fellow, without parents, friends, or money, seeking a start in life, just a foothold on the first rung of the ladder: I would, like my boy heroes, attend to the rest. And I couldn't get the chance! I couldn't understand it.

The most urgent ads came from the water front, and I would

go into one of those shabby little dirty, dark shops, where they dealt in ship furnishings or produce—dressed like a dude, remember; especially careful to be in my best to make a good first impression—and showing the clipping from the paper, ask for an opening. The shop-keeper would throw himself back in his chair and stare at me and splutter, "But—but do you think you can do the work? It's hard work and—and—are you—qualified? What has been your experience?" And I answered that I had studied at Berkeley, Berlin, Heidelberg, the Sorbonne! And for some reason that seemed to end it.

Those were the days when business men were prejudiced against a college education. My father's partners had the prejudice. They warned him that his course with me would ruin me, and I think that it was they who advised him to drop me in New York and see who was right, he or they. Business men have learned since that college does not unfit average young men for anything but an intellectual career; they take them on and will tell you that the colleges are the best source in the world for cheap labor. But in my day, next to my clothes and general beautifulness, the heaviest handicap I had was my claim to a college education, and not only one college, but—five. Some employers dropped their hands and jaw and stared me silently out of their sight; others pushed me out, and others again—two I remember vividly—called in all hands to "see this college graduate that wants to clean the windows and run errands."

My father was right. As I went home to my wife and mother-in-law to describe life as I found it and business men as they found me, I had to confess that I was learning something, that life wasn't what I had expected from my reading. My money was all gone, all the one hundred and also the fifty dollars, and I was paying for myself alone. Mrs. Bontecou paid for her daughter, and soon she was paying for her son-in-law too. I became desperate. My father had given me a letter from the supervising editor of all the Southern Pacific Railroad publications, the monthly magazines, weeklies, and daily newspapers that "the Road" owned or subsidized, to an editor of the Century Magazine. I had not used it, because I preferred not to apply "pull." I was for getting my start in life on merit alone. Mrs. Bontecou was with me on that; Josephine was impatient and practical. She pressed me to deliver the letter of introduction, and I did. I asked Mr. Robert Underwood Johnson to give me an editorial position on the *Century*.

He read the letter, pondered, asked me questions, and sized me up. Seeing through my clothes and my story, I guess, he very cautiously asked me if I would be willing to start—just for the practice—to begin my editorial career as—a—reporter. Would I? I certainly would; I would have laid off my top hat to be a copy boy. That cleared the air for him; maybe it stripped off my English clothes. Anyway he offered to get me on either the *Tribune* or the *Evening Post*, and I went home, happy and proud, to dis-

"THE EVENING POST" WHEN I JOINED IT IN 1892

cuss with my family the choice I had between those two New York papers.

I can't recall what decided us, but I think it was only that the *Evening Post* was an evening paper; I could be home at night and so have time to do some literary work. However it was, I took a note from Mr. Johnson to Joseph B. Bishop, an editorial writer on the *Post*. Bishop frowned, but he led me out to the city room and introduced me to Henry J. Wright, the city editor, who looked helplessly at me and, I thought, resentfully at Bishop.

"I don't need any more reporters," he said to Bishop, "but," to me, "you can come in next Monday and sit down out there with the reporters, and as I get a chance, I'll try you out—on space."

I didn't know what that meant, but I didn't care. I had a job. As I described it to my wife and her mother, Josephine was not elated as her mother was, and the next Monday when I sat out there in the city room, ignored, while all the world seemed to be in a whirl, I was not elated either. The next day I saw "Larry"

Godkin, the editor who wrote the leaders I read and re-read, admiring; he passed by the city door. Bishop nodded to me once, but neither Wright nor the other reporters looked my way. Interesting fellows they seemed to be; they must know all the mysteries of a great city. They did not talk much, but I overheard enough to infer that they were familiar and bored with sport, politics, finance, and society. I was awed by the way they would, upon a few words from the city editor, dart or loaf out of the room, be gone an hour or so, come in, report briefly, and then sit down, write, turn in their copy carelessly, and lie back and read, idly read, newspapers.

One afternoon about one o'clock Mr. Wright came into the room, and seeing no one there but me, exclaimed impatiently and went out. A moment later he came back and right up to me.

"See here," he said, "there's a member of a stock brokerage firm missing. Disappeared utterly. Something wrong. Go and see his partner and find out why the man is gone, whether there's funds missing, too."

He handed me a memorandum giving the firm name and address in Wall Street. An assignment! I was to report. I darted out of the office into the elevator, and asking anybody for directions, found my way to Wall Street—Wall Street!—and the office of the lost broker. His partner rebuffed me. "No, I don't know why he skipped. No idea. No, nothing missing. How should there be?" But I wasn't going to fail on my first chance; so I persisted, asking questions, all about the missing man, his character, antecedents, habits, and when that caused only irritation, I asked about Wall Street. The broker soon was talking; we moved into his private office, sat down, and I told him the story of my life; he told me his, and I was thinking all the time how I could write something interesting about the ethics of a stock broker; I had long since been convinced that the missing broker was innocent of anything more than a drink or an escapade with a woman, when all of a sudden the partner sprang up and said:

"Well, you are the most persistent son of a gun I ever met in all my life, and you win. I'll give you what you seem so damn sure of anyhow. My —— partner has not only skipped, I don't know where; he has taken every cent there was in the office, in the banks, and—then some." He named the amount, and I, astonished by the revelation, but satisfied that I had a front-page sensation, ran back to the office, where I astonished my city editor.

"Really?" he said. "You are sure? It's libel, you know, if it's wrong. He told you himself, the partner did? Sure? Umh— Well, write it, and we'll see."

I had pencils all sharpened—sharpened every day—ready for this moment, and I went to work. It was easy enough to report the facts, but I felt I must write this big news as the news was written. That I had studied in my idle hours, the newspaper style, and that was not easy. I labored till the city editor darted out to see what I was doing; he saw; he read over my shoulder the writes and re-writes of my first paragraph, and picking up one, said, "This is enough." And away he went with it. All I had to do was to lie back in a chair and wait to read my stuff in print, a long wait, perhaps half an hour, till three o'clock, when the last edition went to press, and then twenty minutes before the paper came down. And then when it came down, the damp, smelly paper, my paragraph wasn't in it! I searched again and again, with anxiety, hope, dread. I did not care for the money; the space was too short to count, but I felt that my standing as a reporter was at stake, and so, when I was at last convinced that my "story" was left out, I got up and dragged home, defeated and in despair. I told Mrs. Bontecou about it, not my wife, and was comforted some. If I failed at journalism, the old lady argued, there still was literature.

The facts of my story appeared in the morning newspapers, but they were better, more neatly, briefly stated, than I had put them; perhaps I had failed, not as a reporter, but as a writer. And this conclusion was confirmed at the office, where the city editor said "Good morning" to me and, after all the other reporters were gone out, gave me an assignment to ask the Superintendent of Schools something. One more chance.

Braced to make the most of it, I gave that official a bad hour. He had to answer, not only the question the city editor asked, but others, many others. He found himself telling me all about the schools, education and its problems, and his policy. I had some ideas on that subject, and he got them; and he had to accept or refute them. He became so interested that, when he had to break off, I was invited to come back another day to "continue our conversation." Good. I returned to the office and wrote a column interview, beginning with the city editor's question and the answer. This time, when the paper came out it had my story, but cut down to the first question and answer, rewritten as an authoritative statement of fact. My reporting was all right; my writing was not. The next day, a Friday, I had to go out, confirm a reported suicide, and telephone the news, which another reporter took down and wrote.

That afternoon I saw reporters clipping from the cut files of the *Post*. I asked what it was for, and one of them said he was making up his bill. He cut out his own stories, stuck them together in a long strip, and measuring them with a foot-rule, reckoned up the amount of space and charged for it so much a column. I did the same, and my poor little bill of earnings for my first week of practical life was something like two dollars and ten cents. And I was not ashamed of it; I was reassured, if not proud.

Nor was that all. As I was finishing this task the city editor called me up to his desk and bade me rewrite as a separate story for the Saturday paper the interview I had had with the Superintendent of Schools during the week. He suggested the idea or theme to write it around, and I, elated, stayed there in the office till closing-time, grinding out my first long "story." And the next day I had the deep gratification of reading it at full length, the whole thing as I had written it. I measured it, secretly, and it came to four dollars plus—a fine start for my next week.

That Sunday was a bore; I could hardly wait for Monday to go on with my reporting, and talking with my wife and her mother, I developed ideas and plans. There were several promising questions to put to the Superintendent of Schools; the news suggested other men to see and talk to, and no doubt now the city editor himself would ask me to do more. When I walked into the office on Monday morning, eager and confident, I was dashed by the way I was ignored. No greetings from anybody, and as the morning wore on and the other reporters were sent off on assignments, I realized heavily that I was not to be used. I took my hat and told the city editor I would like to go out on a quest of my own. He nodded consent, and I went and had with the Superintendent of Schools a long interview which I wrote and handed in. It did not appear in the paper, and for two days I was ignored and got nothing out of my own assignments. The men I tried to see were not in or would not see me. I had the experience so common for reporters of being defeated, and in an obscure way, too. Toward the end of the week I was sent out to see a Rapid Transit Commissioner and got some news which pleased the city editor: a formal, printed statement, which was printed. That was all. My space bill was about six dollars. But on Saturday, too late to be included, appeared my interview with the Superintendent of Schools.

With this to start with again, I could live over Sunday and was ready to dive on Monday into my journalism. I had to be my own city editor, but I could be, now. I got another school story, which was printed; it was news; and another which was held, I knew now, for Saturday. I called again on the Rapid Transit Commissioner, and he gave me a brief interview which I used to tempt the other Commissioners to answer. That was news and appeared right away. So was a statement by the Mayor which I went for all by myself. Somebody had said something in print that was critical in a small way of some department, and his office being open to the public, I walked in and talked to him about it. My bill that week was something like fifteen dollars.

My system was working, and, I learned afterward, was amusing the staff and interesting the city editor, who described it as I could not have described it. It was a follow-up system, well known in journalism but unknown to me as a method. Every time I was sent to or met a man in a position to furnish news, I cultivated him as a source and went back repeatedly to him for more news or more general views on the news. If there was a news story in the papers, and not too big, I would read it through for some angle overlooked and slip out to the persons involved and ask some questions. My contribution often appeared as a part of some other reporter's story, usually at the end, but several times as the lead. And always there were school news articles from my Superintendent, who was talking policy to me weekly and letting me visit and write about schools. These articles brought letters to the editor, which showed that we were tapping a field of interest. I had a free hand here till, later, there was an education department which included the universities and private schools, and so brought in advertising. But there was the Art Museum, too, to "cover" and report; Rapid Transit with its plans, not only for transportation in the city, but for real estate, park, and street development. Every time the city editor sent me into a field for a bit of news I got what he wanted and went back for more general reports. He used me very little, however, leaving me to my own devices; and his reason came out when, after a few months, my bills were running up to fifty, sixty, and more dollars a week, and the other reporters were taking rather unfriendly notice of me.

One Friday, as I was making out my bill, William G. Sirrene, a fine southern boy who was one of the star reporters, looked over my shoulder and exclaimed, "What's that? Seventy-two dollars! Why, that's nearly three times what I'm getting on salary."

He called out to the others the amount of my bill, and when they also exclaimed, he explained: "Why, you are the best-paid man on the staff!"

I felt like exclaiming myself. It was news to me. I had no knowledge of salaries or earnings on the paper; all I knew was that I was supporting myself and my wife at last, saving a little each week, and driving on for more, and more. And I would have given it all to be a regular reporter like Sirrene or the others, and that is what I was asked to do. I think now that some of the reporters, not Sirrene, "kicked" to the city editor that I, a new man, was being paid more than they were, the veterans. Anyway he sent for me, and explaining that my bills were running too high, asked me if I would be changed from space to a salary, the best salary they paid the ordinary reporter, $35 a week.

"Then," he said, "I can use you more myself on more important news."

I not only consented, I was dazed with the implication of my triumph. All became clear in that short talk with my chief. I had not been sent off on assignments because I was making too much money on my own and I had "made good." Even my first disappointment, the failure to print my news of the defalcation of the missing broker, was to my credit. The city editor did not dare print the report, by a new and untried man, of a piece of libelous news; he had sent an old reporter down to confirm it, and the broker who had talked to me not only repeated what he told me; he had spoken well of me; but by the time the confirmation was delivered, it was too late. The paper was gone to press. I was "reliable, quick, and resourceful," the city editor said, as he made me a regular reporter.

In a word I was a success, and though I have never since had such a victory and have come to have some doubt of the success of success, I have never since failed to understand successful men; I know, as I see them, how they feel inside.

WALL STREET

G ENERAL reporting in New York in my day was a series of daily adventures, interesting, sometimes thrilling, but, on the *Evening Post,* rarely perilous. A conservative three-cent evening newspaper, competing with one-cent papers, it avoided crime, scandal, and the sensational generally. Mr. Lawrence Godkin, the editor-in-chief, was a reformer. Irish in breed, English in culture, his ideals both of journalism and politics were British Liberal. He was against bad government and bad journalism, which he attributed to bad men. His cure was to throw the rascals out and elect good men, regardless of party. Called a Mugwump, he was really an aristocrat. His war in New York was against the boss, Richard Croker, Tammany Hall, and the Democratic city governments, but he fought even more bitterly Boss Platt and the State machine of the Republican party, which sometimes opposed and sometimes traded with Tammany.

The news department of the *Post* had, theoretically, nothing to do with the editorial policy. Reporters were to report the news as it happened, like machines, without prejudice, color, and without style; all alike. Humor or any sign of personality in our reports was caught, rebuked, and, in time, suppressed. As a writer, I was permanently hurt by my years on the *Post.* The editorial page and, to some extent, the book, theater, and music reviews, were the only departments which were really written. I was allowed to "do" the German theaters, and they were, next to the Yiddish, the best in the city; but I was never permitted to say anything like that. After a year or two of the German "first nights," I was used often to cover the second-best English openings under the close control of the dramatic editor, who had a policy. And in general the news reporters, supposed to have no concern with the editorial policy of the paper, were led, somehow—not directly, but by the method of trial and error, we learned to gather ammunition for the editorial writers. Mr. Godkin was no hero to me; I saw very little of him, and that little was not pleasant, but I read him. I found it helpful professionally to con his editorials every day for "tips" as to what to look for in the news and how to write it. His leaders seemed to me to be shallow; clever, forceful, ripping, but personal and not very thoughtful. No matter. Nobody can read a newspaper every day and not be influenced by it; we read "our paper" in our quiet, relaxed moments, when we might be thinking, and thus unwittingly let the editors form our minds. Godkin was mind to me all those years, and I was legs to him, one of his many pairs of running feet, ears, and eyes. There were compensations.

When I was promoted, at reduced pay, from space to general reporter, Mr. Wright, the city editor, did what he said he would do. He gave me assignments every morning, and as I in my eagerness worked, plotted, persisted in getting the news expected of me, my uses became more and more important and various. In the course of a few months I had visited all parts of the city, called on all sorts of men (and women), politicians, business men, reformers; described all sorts of events, fires, accidents, fights, strikes, meetings. It was happy work for me. New York was like a great swimming-hole into which every day I dived, here, there, anywhere, and swam around for something or somebody worth getting. And all the time I had the advantage of interviewing men who gave me some of the respect or fear they felt for "Larry" Godkin.

I came to love New York; I had a sentiment about the people, the business, the politics, and the streets of the great city which cared neither for me nor for itself. My old academic interest in scientific ethics faded; it would come up when some prominent citizen was lying to me. This experience enraged the other reporters; it only set me to thinking that reporters, like judges and prosecutors, had no moral right to the truth, because they would turn it against the truth-teller. And I had to notice that the ethics of business and the ethics of politics are such different cultures that a business man in politics will commit sins appalling to the politician, and vice versa. Morals are matters of trade or profession and form the ethics they are supposed to be formed by.

But science and philosophy, like the theaters and books, seemed tame in comparison with the men and women, the unbelievable doings and the sayings, of a live city. New York was real; and life was "different." Literature and the arts did not show it as it was. So it seemed to me, and before I was sated with it and long before I could write anything about it except in the paper, I was assigned to a department, Wall Street.

One afternoon toward the end of the winter (1892-93) Mr. Wright called me up to his desk and asked me if I would take the place of the Wall Street reporter, an Englishman, who had been called home by the death of his father. Wright said that there was trouble ahead for Wall Street, a period of depression, possibly a panic, and "we" must have a man down there, a special reporter, who would give all his time and thought to the financial news. He knew, he said, that I had had no experience of banking and business, but he had noticed that I worked and read up on any subject I was reporting. My universities had taught me to study. He thought I could learn enough to "cover" Wall Street in the emergency. Anyway, he would take a chance if I would. Would I? he asked.

I was thinking, dazed. Wall Street! I remembered that the Wall Street reporter before he sailed had advised me, if I expected to stay in journalism, to specialize in something: sport, the theaters, finance. I had seen the sense of that. But did I mean to stay in journalism? And if so, would I thrive as a financial expert, I who had always avoided business? My answer to Wright was that I would consider for a day or two and then tell him my decision.

My wife laughed at the thought of me in Wall Street, as my father would have. My wise old mother-in-law listened to all that we said, and at the end, pointed my own instincts. She always saw what I wanted; she usually advised as I desired. Mrs. Bontecou thought that, since I was only taking the place of another man who was coming back in a year or so, I might do very well for myself to have the experience of Wall Street. It would be profitable to me, if not to the paper. The next day I went to Wright with a plan. He was to give me a list of five or six of the commanding Wall Street bankers; I would call on them and see if I could make with them an emergency arrangement by which they were to take care of their favorite paper and help me to the news during the bad times. I think Wright, a Scotchman, saw what I did not: that this would be a shrewd way to enlist the expert, authoritative service of big insiders. And that is what happened; the *Post* had the inside track in that panic. Anyway the city editor approved with alacrity my suggestion; he consulted with the financial editor and handed me a list of leading bankers whom I called on, after banking hours, that afternoon. One by one I saw them, and my Wall Street experience began at once.

My approach to high finance was that of most of the world, I think; it certainly was something like that of the novelists and playwrights I knew. It was the awed approach of a boy brought up in the belief that there are heroes, really giants and great persons, good or evil, to be found in life. I had not discovered any as yet. On the contrary, my boyhood experience had been explosive of illusions, and in the universities, especially in Europe, I had looked for giants under the names of the celebrated philosophers, scientists, and scholars I went hopefully to study with. My experience with them was like one or the other of two experiences I had in Munich. The great professors either destroyed themselves, as the Munich painters flattened my awe of artists by their well-nigh universal contempt for one another, or they let me see them as I saw Henrik Ibsen. I happened to be worshiping that poet-playwright when I was in Munich, and some one who heard me talking about him told me that he was in that city and where I could see him at dinner any day. Off I hurried to Ibsen's restaurant; the god came in due course. He walked up to the little table reserved for him, let the waiter take his stick, but not his hat. That he kept, and when he sat down, he put it upside down between his knees—and stared into it. As he looked, he bowed, smirked, turned his head this way and that way, and tossed his mane. What was in that hat? I had to know. Getting up quietly, I walked over, and as I passed behind him, I looked where he was looking—at a mirror, a little hand mirror.

Vanity has come to be a virtue or at least a useful gift, to my way of thinking now, but at that time it seemed a human weakness, like professional jealousy, and the sight of these and other common faults in the geniuses of Europe helped to send me home with a theory that the great men of my day were probably the masters, not of art and philosophy, but of finance and industry; and especially those of America. My Wall Street assignment was an opportunity to see giants.

The names on my list were all famous in New York; one of them was internationally known; and their banks are great institutions. The bankers received me readily enough, much less formally than a European professor would a young man; they were all *Post* readers, as they said. But when I stated my business, when I mentioned the word "panic," they almost had one themselves. Even when I changed the word, first, to "depression," then to "a strain," they denied it. All was clear and fair ahead. They were lying; I did not mind that; it is moral and not unethical to lie to a reporter. But it is not professional, it is not politic, for a reporter to lie to a banker. So I thought, and so—I passed lightly over their formal, exclamatory corrections of my business.

For some reason, I said, my paper felt that it was very important just then to have a man in Wall Street; the regular reporter, whom they knew, was away, and "we" had no properly trained person to put in his place. I was asked to serve, and I was willing to if the commanding bankers on my list, recognizing the emergency, would agree to trust and help me, not only to get but to understand the news. In return I would promise to keep confidences, and in my reports not reflect in any way the excitement and panic of the—

A list? My editor's list of commanding bankers! They had to see that list, and that list gave them their second shock. Some of them lay back and roared with laughter at my names. Others were serious, but indignant, scornful. "Bankers!" they said in effect. "You call these bankers? And commanding bankers! Who gave you this list? Your city editor! After consulting with the financial editor? I can't believe it. I know the financial editor, and he knows who is who down here."

I recalled the artists of Munich on the other artists of Munich, and I was willing to retreat and admit that my paper's half dozen financiers were not the giants of Wall Street; not all of them. They might, the six, be chosen to cover different regions or departments of financial knowledge and news. That appeased them so much that I was disposed to chuck the whole list into the scrapbasket, but no, that wasn't necessary. Some of my list were all right. And of course, I bethought me, there was always one that belonged, and the one was always willing to acknowledge, however grudgingly, that some other one or two might be of some help to me sometimes. But one of them, by way of my first lesson, bade me get it right up into the front of my brain that in the whole of the United States there were but three bankers; and this banker went so far as to name two of the three, one in Chicago, and the other—the two others, in fact, were in New York. I understood, then, and as I went on with my experience in Wall Street, I was given to understand many times that I was talking to one of the only three bankers—really, professionally bankers—in America.

For I did go on. These men on my list agreed, all but one, to help me "cover Wall Street" during the emergency for "their paper," the *Post*, and the one who only said he would "see" began right away to see. To test me, he gave me a small but important bit of news "confidentially." The trouble with this confidence as a test was that I saw through it; I reported to the city editor what the cunning banker told me and cautioned him that the news was given us to see if we would print it. Of course, Mr. Wright did not use it, and when the banker saw that it was not in the paper the next day, he tempted me again. And again. This man tried me out for a month or more and then, gradually, became my most productive source of news. But the others also trusted me; among them they added to my list, not only bankers, but brokers, speculators, arbitrage traders, money-changers,—specialists and experts of all sorts, who, altogether, gave me a pretty good theoretical schooling in the stock and money market, as well as the daily news.

And there was news. The panic of '93 was one of the great periodic depressions in our financial history, and I used to feel that I was sailing through the storm on the bridge with the officers of the ship. They were glad to have me there. A rank outsider, who did not speculate and had nothing to lose, the panic was an adventure to me, and the falling, failing banks, railroads, and busted pools of speculators were only the action and scenery of a great drama. I could write the news without excitement—if I got it in time, and the bankers soon learned the value of letting me break a bad piece of news, like a big failure, in the cool, dull, matter-of-fact terms of the *Evening Post*, as I had promised. This was made possible by their warning me weeks ahead that such and such a railroad or industrial organization was in trouble. I could gather the facts and figures, write the story, and—many a time we had it all set in type, like the obituary of a dying man, long before the event. "The United States Cordage Company went into the hands of a receiver today," and then a column or two or more of the history of the company—all quietly written and standing in type so that when it happened, I could telephone to the office and on five minutes' notice "release" the whole long story. And such news was usually announced at the close of the stock market, in order to give the traders the night to think it over, permit the banks to support the market, and so avoid too sudden a break in prices. It was, as I say, convenient for the leading financiers to have an evening paper that would report the bad news thus; it was, by the same token, a profitable advantage to the

FINANCIAL

STOCKS CONTINUE TO DECLINE

Railway Stocks Sold Heavily- All De —Attack on Northern Pacific Secu rities—Foreign Exchange Rates Advancing.

In default of further actual bad news, such as demoralized the market yesterday, professional operators for the decline had recourse to-day to rumor. They were not altogether successful. A heavy break there was in the first hour, shared by the general list, but concentrated upon Northern Pacific stock and bonds. Not the least heavy of the week's liquidation, among houses putting themselves in shape for all emergencies, has been in these securities; and from this the story suddenly sprang forth to-day that the company's June interest coupons could not be paid. The rumor was wholly false, and was in fact officially and emphatically denied. That the Northern Pacific has fallen upon unpleasant times for the necessary adjustment of its floating debt, everybody understands. Money accommodation, in the face of a partial money panic, is no easy matter to obtain. It certainly does not reflect unfavorably on the company's general situation that its managers, as is now generally known, have been able to obtain it.

On the denial of this rumor, another demonstration was made against the market by a violent attack on Reading stock. The delay in publishing officially the new reorganization plan was made a pretext for this. It is noticeable, however, that promoters of corporate reorganizations are wisely slow in appealing to shareholders in the present financial situation. Despite a temporary pause, during the noon hour, in operations for the decline, there was little semblance anywhere of actual rally. Like that of yesterday, to-

FROM THE NEW YORK "EVENING POST" DURING THE PANIC OF 1893

evening paper to have not only the news in full, but "beats," and be bought and read as an insider speaking with authority; and neither last nor least, as I saw it, was the credit I won by my "success" in a field where I was so inexperienced and ignorant. But what I prized and most profited by was the picture I was making for myself of Wall Street, its leaders, workers, and followers, their methods, manners, customs, morals, and point of view.

This came later, however. Appreciation of what I see comes usually only after a period of digestion, and I did not understand Wall Street when I was down there. Too busy. I did not try to put in order the facts I was piling up; it was enough that I spoke the language, knew whom to call on for special information or news, and where to find the nearest telephone. The geography of the Street was my chief interest. Of the facts, only those that could be written as news stood out. If a leading financier, at the end of a dark day of disaster, sat tight denying something I was sure of till, worn out, he fell across his desk, weeping and confessing, I picked up not the hysterical man but the confession, and that I wrote without tears, statistically. When a desperate bear asked me into his office, offered to put me short of one hundred—two hundred—three hundred shares of a stock if I would publish information injurious to the company, I would leave his bribe to take, investigate, and, if true, print the news. The human side of Wall Street was only gossip which made good stories to tell in the city room after the paper went to press or to entertain people at dinner. Having no prejudice for or against finance, I had no judgment, no point of view. It was as it was, neither good nor evil, and even when toward the end of my special service there I began to speculate myself, it was partly to learn the ropes and report better. I was only a reporter reporting, and what I reported did not take form in the picture I have of high finance till I had time, while doing other work, to look back and see through what I had seen.

BULLS AND BEARS

WHEN I was a boy, blacksmiths and niggers who had to handle mules and kicking horses used to tell me that the safest place to be in range was close up to the bad animals' heels, and I saw them rush in, pick up a hind leg, and hang on to it, while they shod the hard-hitting hoof. I never tried it myself on a mule, but I did on Wall Street, and there's some truth in it.

The panic of 1893, like all periods of business depression, was a dismal time of radiating destruction. But it had its bright side, inside; it was good for the bears and for my education. The shorts rejoiced in the ruin; they made money, and they were happy. As a reporter on the side lines in the Stock Exchange I could see and hear and feel the wild joy of the bears on a day of tumbling prices, and it was a never-ending surprise to me, because everything I had read, heard, or imagined had pictured the dark depression, despair, and anguish of the losers. And of course there were sufferers, some of them on the floor, others in the banks and brokerage houses, most of all, however, far from the market, out in the country—the public. Among the brokers generally, whether "on the floor" or in their offices, an active market, whether prices are rising or falling, means that business is good; and that's what one felt, and that's what remains to be written—the joy of a panic.

It's like a war, a revolution, a strike—like any crisis in human affairs when men have to walk up and face the consequences of their ignorance, folly, or wickedness—the panic of '93 was a period of bad times chiefly for the innocent. The news of it, the reports printed, are "bad" because they are written by, about, and for bulls. The bears are forgotten and as friendless as the strikers are who rush gleefully forth from the factories to the cafés, or the revolutionists and army officers whose day is come. On the scene

one feels the prevailing spirit of activity. It is the period of recon-
struction that is gloomy and sad; it is so long, so hard, and so
disappointing.

Before the panic had run its course, the regular Wall Street
reporter whose place I had taken came back, and I was turned into
general reporting again, politics and business, chiefly business.
When the constructive work began in finance, the city editor sent
me more into "the Street" to discover and report the plans making
by the bankers, lawyers, and industrialists for the reorganization of
bankrupt concerns and, gradually, for the organization of new
corporations and new combines, even, for example, the U. S. Steel
Company. These schemes began during the panic; they were compelled by the circumstances, and I heard of them, but paid no
heed, while we were in that period when good news was not news.
But after a year or so of failures, while the receiverships continued, good news was becoming news; not the best news, but still
good, secondary news, and that was my part. I was the bull reporter, the other man was the bear. He was seeing my old conservative, more or less suffering, proper bankers who are really
only money-lenders. I had to do with the private bankers who are
the constructive engineering financiers.

Of these last, J. P. Morgan, Senior, was the greatest. I did not
see much of him, of course; nobody did. He was in sight all the
time. He sat alone in a back room with glass sides in his banking-
house with his door open, and it looked as if any one could walk
in upon him and ask him any question. One heard stories of the
payment of large sums for an introduction to him. I could not
see why the tippers with business did not come right in off the
street and talk to him. They did not. My business was with his
partners or associates, principally Samuel Spencer, but I noticed
that these, his partners, did not go near him unless he sent for
them; and then they looked alarmed and darted in like office-
boys. "Nobody can answer that question except Mr. Morgan,"
they would tell me. Well, Mr. Morgan was there; why not go in
and ask him? The answer I got was a smile or a shocked look of
surprise. And once when I pressed the president of one of the
Morgan banks to put to him a question we agreed deserved an
answer, the banker said, "Not on your life," and when I said,
"But why not?" he said. "You try it yourself and see." And I did.

I went over to J. P. Morgan and Company, walked into his office, and stood before him at his flat, clean, clear desk. I stood while he examined a sheet of figures; I stood for two or three long minutes, while the whole bank seemed to stop work to watch me, and he did not look up; he was absorbed, he was sunk, in those figures. He was so alone with himself and his mind that when he did glance up he did not see me; his eyes were looking inward. He was a mathematician, you know. One of the stories told of his life was that he was so gifted in mathematics that the University of Göttingen invited him to stay there to take a lectureship that would lead up to a career in pure mathematics. I thought, as he looked at and did not see me that day, that he was doing a sum in mental arithmetic, and when he solved it he dropped his eyes back upon his sheet of figures and I slunk out.

Somebody stopped me as I was going out through the bank and laughingly asked me what had happened.

"Nothing," I said; "he didn't even see me."

"You're lucky," was the chuckling answer. "You have to call him to wake him up. If you had said, 'Mr. Morgan,' he would have come to. And then—"

"What would have happened then?" I asked.

"Oh," the partner said, "then you would have seen—an explosion."

I believed that; it was generally believed on the Street that J. P. Morgan was a dangerous man to talk to, and no doubt that made it unnecessary for him to be guarded by door men, secretaries, and stenographers. He could protect himself. I know that I came to feel, myself, what others on Wall Street felt, a vague awe of the man.

But I went through that awful circle once. I said, "Mr. Morgan." The paper received one afternoon a typewritten statement from Morgan and Company; it was some announcement about a matter of bonds that had been news for months, and the city editor called me in to read it with him. He could not make it out. It was a long, complicated statement all in one sentence, and I could not read it either. "Take it down to Mr. Morgan and ask him to read it," Mr. Wright said, and I remember I was startled. I asked Wright if he knew what he was asking of me: to go and put a question to the old man himself. "Yes," said Wright, "but it has to be done." I picked up the statement, ran down to the bank, conning the sentence, and ready for the explosion, I walked into Morgan's office and right up to his desk. He saw me this time; he threw himself back in his chair so hard that I thought he would tip over.

"Mr. Morgan," I said as brave as I was afraid, "what does this statement mean?" and I threw the paper down before him.

"Mean!" he exclaimed. His eyes glared, his great red nose seemed to me to flash and darken, flash and darken. Then he roared. "Mean! It means what it says. I wrote it myself, and it says what I mean."

"It doesn't say anything—straight," I blazed.

He sat back there, flashing and rumbling; then he clutched the arms of his chair, and I thought he was going to leap at me. I was so scared that I defied him.

"Oh, come now, Mr. Morgan," I said, "you may know a lot about figures and finance, but I'm a reporter, and I know as much as you do about English. And that statement isn't English."

That was the way to treat him, I was told afterward. And it was in that case. He glared at me a moment more, the fire went out of his face, and he leaned forward over the bit of paper and said very meekly, "What's the matter with it?"

I said I thought it would be clearer in two sentences instead of one and I read it aloud so, with a few other verbal changes.

"Yes," he agreed, "that is better. You fix it."

I fixed it under his eyes, he nodded, and I, whisking it away, hurried back to the office. They told me in the bank afterward that "J. P." sat watching me go out of the office, then rapped for Spencer and asked what my name was, where I came from, and said, "Knows what he wants, and—and—gets it."

He never offered me a partnership, but when Samuel Spencer, the receiver of the Southern Railway, arranged for an interview with him a year or so later, Mr. Morgan remembered and talked to me—"not for publication"—about the south from a financial point of view. The talk was a dry, but convincing, bull prophecy of what has happened since down there, later, much later than the prophet expected; but it was a true prophecy.

Morgan was a bull. "He gets it coming and going," the Street used to say, "but he always says that for the long pull the bull side is the winning side in America. The U.S.A. is a bull country." That is to say, he made money by selling on a falling market; but he bought too on the way down and so ended, he and his bank and his "crowd," in possession of enough stock at sacrifice prices to give him the control. Then he could "reorganize" the railroad and other companies he had chosen as, in the long run, good; he could finance and direct the running of them. He made his bear profits, got his banker's commission on the reorganization, the banker's interest on money lent, the banker's profit on underwriting and floating the new stocks and bonds, and, best of all, the control. This was all common practice and common knowledge when I was in Wall Street; it was talked about as just plain business, and as I heard it all, it seemed to me to be only good business, profitable, proper, and—easy. I used to wonder why men went into any other business than Wall Street if they wanted only to make money, and I declared to myself and to my friends that when I wanted to make money I would not write, or report, or edit, or manage; I would go into Wall Street. I would quit working and—make money.

And, mind you, this was not cynicism; it was plain common sense to me. A student of ethics, I accepted it as the world does, as the business men generally, as bankers, brokers and indeed bishops accepted it as, not only the custom, but moral and wise. Many a time, I have sympathized deeply with a stock operator or a banker who was thrown into the depths of despair because he had not made the millions he had planned to make; he had not lost, he merely had not made his money. I watched men working and lying to smash a company that they were trying to get cheap, the control of it, and I rejoiced with them when they "busted" the old crowd, drove them out ruined, and got the business. I was offered the presidency of one such company. I considered taking it, and when I objected that I knew nothing of business, neither that or any other, the answer was that I did not need to; they would tell me what I was to do; in fact I must consult them. All I had to do, apparently, was to draw a good salary, occupy a fine office, and make a respectable appearance. "You'll get out of reporting and become a man of affairs." I did not grasp what this meant at the time. When I declined to be lifted out of journalism up off the street into high finance with a social and financial position, I did not despise or pity as I do now the successful men who seize such opportunities. My reason was personal: business did not attract me; money was no object; I liked reporting; I did not generalize at all. I did not understand, so I did not condemn, the practices of big business. I was not thinking in those days; life was too, too interesting, the world as it was too fascinating, to stop to question anything but politics, which was all bad, just as business was all good, to me.

James B. Dill was the first man to remind me that I was an intellectual, that I might think as well as see and write. He was a masterpiece. He was the man who put through in the State of New Jersey the laws to enable the organization of trusts and combines, to free corporations, to free them to do whatever they pleased. His was a great name in Wall Street; even the big fellows spoke of James B. Dill with awe and retained him to organize their plans into going concerns. He was the man, for example, who brought Andrew Carnegie and J. P. Morgan together for the purchase and sale of the Carnegie steel properties and so laid the basis of the United States Steel Company, the biggest transaction and the biggest trust of those days. "I put Morgan in one room, Carnegie in another," he recounted, "while I took the third room in between them with my clerks and stenographers. I knew that if they met they would blow up; so I played the part of buffer and negotiator. They could express their opinions of each other to me. I could agree with both of them, sympathize with the generosity and bigness of each one, and share his contempt for the narrow meanness of the other. I was sincere, uninsultable, and true to their agreeable purposes, the one to buy, the other to sell."

Dill was a realist with insight and humor, but hardly any one knew of his humor. He was always spoken of with awe as "James B. Dill." No familiarity with him; Mr. Morgan might be "J.P."; he was called that, but James B. Dill was always and only a name, a mystery, a wonder-worker in those terrible days when the reorganization of the débris of '93 was beginning. No one but the masters ever saw him, and we, who would no more think of approaching him than we would walk in on J.P. himself, we—I thought of him as a silent, thinking, conspiring lawyer who sat still in the big back room of a great suite of offices, with an army commander's staff of almost equally great attorneys-at-law, who all joined their learning and their wits to advise, at huge fees (which rumor named), the brains of big business. He was, in brief, the great black man who showed good Business how to circumvent bad Politics and the anti-trust legislation passed to satisfy the ignorant, envious people.

For there was, at that time, a very general popular discontent, the choral accompaniment of the hard times; and the passion of the day was the anti-trust sentiment, which was a development out of the old anti-monopoly cry of the earlier period. The *Post* was not anti-trust; it was anti-Tammany; but it was for business, except now and then when there was some exceptional scandal, too outrageous to be passed by in silence. The *Post* was sincere, of course; almost everybody was, almost everybody is, sincere. I did not know it, but I can see now that what I needed then was what the world needs all the time, to find some one who was not sincere but intelligent. I found that man in James B. Dill. Bless him.

One day some morning newspaper printed a "roast" of James B. Dill, the author of the criminal New Jersey trust laws. It showed how that State had enacted statutes under which the anti-trust laws of other States could be evaded and American public opinion defied. A sovereign State, Jersey had the right to pass any laws it pleased, and if it enabled the formation of trusts in New Jersey, New York State and the other States had to recognize the creatures of the free State of New Jersey. The article declared that it was James B. Dill who had himself invented and put over this legislation, quietly, almost secretly, in New Jersey, and then it showed in some detail what was permitted: plain financial crimes.

This clipping was handed to me, with instructions to go and see Mr. James B. Dill and get his denial or correction of these charges. So! I was to see the black man! I felt as I did when I was sent to see Mr. Morgan, as an English pressman would if he were sent to interview a minister of the Crown, as a girl feels who is to be presented to the Queen. I was flattered. I was trembling with fear, I was awfully bold, as I went, hurrying and slowing up, eagerly and then dreadfully, downtown and up into the building where the silent councilor of the trusts was hidden away in—not a great suite of offices, but a small, neat set of two or three rooms. A smiling little stenographer and typist took my card, with my name and that of my paper on it, into one of the rooms, and returning instantly, swept me in to Mr. Dill, who met me with a smiling welcome on his rosy, round, happy face.

"The *Evening Post*—at last," he chuckled, and his round little body seemed to laugh as it settled back into its big chair. "I have been wondering," he said, "why you have not called on me. I have been tempted to send for you. The abuses of the Jersey Trust laws must be exposed and stopped. Yes," he added, as he glanced at the clipping I held out to him, the story that I thought would anger and drive him to a furious contradiction, "yes, all that is true, and more, much more."

And to my amazement he opened up the criminal inside of the practices under the New Jersey legislation, a picture of such chicanery and fraud, of wild license and wrong-doing, that I could not, I dared not, take it all down; I was too confused. And Dill saw that, and he laughed; his eyes twinkled and his round little belly shook with the humor of the situation.

"You are astonished?" he said. "And well you may be. But you must write what I tell you. Don't quote me. I am the founder of this legislation, and as such you may name me, but don't say I gave you these facts; it would look odd; it might be suspicious, to make me the authority for an exposure of what I am the enabling founder of, but it is your duty to describe what is done under these laws, and if your editor shows any hesitation, you may tell him to call me up on the 'phone; I will stand back of whatever you print."

I did not write all that Dill told me; not then; I never have. I could not at the time, because, as I have said, I was too imbued with the Wall Street spirit and view of things to speak as this lawyer did of the holies of the holy. Upton Sinclair learned from him; he was a socialist. I was a Wall Street man myself, unconsciously, but literally. That's how I came finally to understand what corruption is and how it gets a man, not as the Reds and the writers think, but as the Whites and the Righteous are: rogues outside, but inside, honest men. However, that's for later. When James B. Dill told me first about Wall Street and his Jersey laws, and he saw that I would not, could not, take it in, he made merry with me, laughing and quizzing and telling me ever more and more.

"Why, didn't you ever hear how they wiped out Richmond Terminal?" he would say, and he would tell me that story. "And you didn't know that? A Wall Street reporter, and you don't know that! And this—" He told me something else that I had never heard of; and then something else. "Nor that? Never knew that? What do you know?

"I say," he said, when I rose to go after that first interview, "I must know you better. And my wife and daughter; they must know you." He invited me to his house; he took me there, and thus began a friendship that lasted as long as James B. Dill himself in the body. He had incorporated himself and his fortune under his Jersey laws as "The James B. Dill Corporation"—I think that was the title of it—he told me about it with glee, a corporation with five shares—or three, which he controlled, he laughed; one share to his wife, one for his daughter (in escrow), the rest (and the control) for him. "Avoids taxes and all sorts of troubles when I die." So "The James B. Dill Corporation" may be immortal, but my jolly little imp of a Santa Claus, my mischievous professor of financial law, my good friend James B. Dill, died, a loss, a real loss, but not till he had made me see Wall Street and Business and Politics and Law as he saw them, from the inside out; and not, of course, till he had explained to me why he, of all men, had led and inspired and provided the ammunition for the exposure of the James B. Dill laws of New Jersey.

"Why, Dr. Innocent," he said, "I was advertising my wares and the business of my State. When you and the other reporters and critics wrote as charges against us what financiers could and did actually do in Jersey, when you listed, with examples, what the trust-makers were doing under our laws, you were advertising our business—free. For financiers are dubs, as you know yourself now; don't you? They have to be told, and they have to be told plain so that they get it, and so, as I say, while I gave you the facts to roast us with, what you wrote as 'bad' struck business men all over the United States as good, and they poured in upon us to our profit to do business with us to their profit. The only drawback was that when Delaware and New York and other 'bad' political sovereigns saw what Jersey was doing and how we made money and friends out of our trust policy they copied us, and they went further than we did, or, to be exact, they tried to."

And so saying, Dill laughed and laughed and laughed; not cynically; not wickedly; but merrily, with his whole body and soul. James B. Dill was one of the "wisest," wisest and, yes, about the rightest man I ever met.

"Trusts are natural, inevitable growths out of our social and economic conditions," he said often. "You cannot stop them by force, with laws. They will sweep down like glaciers upon your police, courts, and States and wash them into flowing rivers. I am for clearing the way for them. Let them go, and if they cannot be brought into social use, why—then—then"—he would laugh— "then I would be for exploring their origin and dealing with—I mean closing up—their source."

THE POLICE

EVERY newspaper that I know anything about suffers from politics, "newspaper politics." The men on it decide on some question of policy or control or places, and everybody becomes more or less involved. Joseph Pulitzer, the founder, owner, and editor of the New York *World*, cultivated warring factions. Whether his theory was that disloyalty to one another made his heads of departments loyal to him or that rivalry developed the advantages of competition, he had a business manager who did not speak to some editors, who did not all speak to one another. Charles A. Dana had the most united staff; his competition was between his morning and evening papers, but we used to hear of quarrels and contempts even on the morning edition which was the *Sun*. Godkin may never have heard of parties on the *Evening Post*; the division was not sharp and open, but Henry J. Wright, and the publisher, J. S. Seymour, were, however quietly, against Linn, the managing editor, who represented instinctively the taste and policy of the editor-in-chief. He was for keeping all police and sensational news out of the paper, and in the main he had his way. Wright and Seymour, who wanted to build up circulation and business by printing all the news, had one great victory, and it was most profitable for me.

One afternoon when I was back on my general reporting the city editor called me up to his desk and asked me if I would like to cover police headquarters. A startling suggestion. The *Post* had never had a man in Mulberry Street, where the heads of the police and detective service had their offices. It was the source of crime news—and Mr. Wright said, quick, that I was to pay no attention to crime; I was to cover the activities of Dr. Parkhurst, whom I had already interviewed several times for the paper.

The Rev. Dr. Charles H. Parkhurst was discovering the corruption of the police and denouncing the force from his pulpit. He
sounded like a prophet of old in his sermons, but personally he was
a calm, smiling, earnest, but not unhumorous gentleman who
frankly enjoyed his notoriety and his exposures. He knew some
of the doings of the police; they were dangerous facts to allege;
libelous. He had to be careful, and he was cautious, but he was
persistent, methodically, thoroughly. He organized in and out of
his congregation a society to investigate the police, procure evidence, and put him in a position to describe New York police
methods and their relations with Tammany Hall, the liquor
interests, and criminals. The *Post* was interested, of course, in anybody that came out openly against Tammany; there was some
suspicion of a clergyman who "profaned his pulpit with police
filth," even as against Tammany; and my first assignments to see
Parkhurst were reluctant. Dr. Parkhurst talked moderately, sen-
sibly, briefly, and, as I reported him, in tone with the paper.
Following up a police news lead, as I always did, I called on him
every few days; we became rather friendly, and I was soon able
to warn my chief of news to come; which came—at police headquarters. Mr. Wright had seen, I think, that Dr. Parkhurst offered
him a good excuse for assigning a reporter to police headquarters:
to report the police side of an opening controversy; and since
the clergyman and I seemed to get along well together I was the
man to go.

"Not to report crimes and that sort of thing," said Wright, in
effect. "You will keep in touch with Dr. Parkhurst, know what
he is doing, and work in with him for the purpose of reporting his
findings with the police department for a background." But I got
from him somehow the idea that, if I could find a way, not a
sensational, conventional, but, say, a political, a literary, way to
write about robberies, murders, etc., I might try putting some
crime into the *Post*.

No urging was needed to make me accept the assignment. I was
eager for it. "The police" meant to me a dark, mysterious layer
of the life of a great city into which I had not yet penetrated. My
experience in Wall Street, especially my mocking relations with
James B. Dill, had driven it into my consciousness that it was
possible to think that I knew all about something and yet be an

innocent ignoramus. Dill had taught me that back of my bankers and brokers and their news of Wall Street there was a world which I had not even glimpsed and which the Wall Street men themselves did not really picture as it was. Few of them ever saw it. My reports of "the American X & Y Company receivership," columns long, were not "the" story, as Dill told it afterward. I had never got and printed the truth back of the financial news. It was probably so with the police news; there was probably a still greater truth back of the petty, monstrous abuses Dr. Parkhurst was disclosing. And then there were the murders, fires, robberies, and politics. I might not write, but I could learn all about such events. I went to police headquarters as I had gone to Wall Street, as I had gone to Europe, and as I had come home to America, with the suppressed ardor of a young student and with the same throbbing anxiety that an orator feels just before he rises to speak.

But, first, I called on Dr. Parkhurst to tell him of my assignment and make with him the kind of agreement I had had with my Wall Street bankers: to work together with him and exchange news and confidences. He was interested, of course; it meant support for him by the *Evening Post,* and he spent several forenoons describing his plans, methods, and best of all, the police chiefs and their system of corruption, as he knew and could not yet prove. As it turned out, Dr. Parkhurst knew well what he knew, but he did not know the system as it was exposed later by the Lexow Committee; nobody had pictured that; and that, even that, was not all. However, after a few talks with Dr. Parkhurst I felt that I knew both the chief police officers and their worst crimes, and so, with no little dread and a solid foundation of certainty, I went one morning early to police headquarters with my card to present to the Superintendent of Police, Thomas F. Byrnes.

It was his hour for receiving citizens with complaints, his inspectors, captains, heads of departments with reports, and "the press." His small outer office was crowded with people, uniformed and in plain clothes. I was embarrassed, but I handed my card to the chief's favorite sergeant, Mangin, and as he bade me wait my turn, a tall, handsome inspector of police, whom I, of course, did not know, spoke out loud into the silence.

"A reporter from the *Evening Post,*" he said, clear and distinct like a pistol shot. "The *Post* has always despised police news, true police news, but now when we are under fire they are to have a man up here to expose and clean us all out, us rascals."

I felt as if his shots had hit me, and I sank wounded into a chair; the man was not through. Sneering and pointing at my red-hot face, he said, "We'll see how long he stays here."

The challenge braced me. I asked Sergeant Mangin, "Who is that man?"

Mangin hesitated, glanced at my foe, and then said, softly but audibly, "Inspector Williams."

I knew that name. Dr. Parkhurst had told me of the audacity and force and badness of the "clubbing inspector," so I rallied to him.

"Oh," I said, "Clubber Williams. I know about him," and to him I made my bluff. "I shall stay here till you are driven out."

There was a sense of quick excitement. Mangin darted through the swinging doors into Superintendent Byrnes' inner office, an officer came out, and I was bidden to enter—out of my turn. Mangin undoubtedly had told Byrnes what had happened. The Superintendent rose to meet and greet me, reading my name from the card in his hand, and adding, "The *Evening Post.*" Indicating a chair beside his desk, he said in his most formal fashion that I was welcome at police headquarters. The force was irritated, naturally, being subjected just then to criticism from places where "the finest" might expect support.

"When you stop to think that it is we, the police, who protect your lives and property, guarding you not only from thieves and robbers, but from strikers and mobs, you can see, no doubt, that it hurts us to be denounced as Dr. Parkhurst, for example, is denouncing us—from the pulpit and in the newspapers. I hope and trust that the *Evening Post,* a Wall Street paper, an organ of good business and all decent property interests, will give us aid and comfort—"

I wanted to protest; I probably gave some sign of a wish to correct him, as I did, early; he saw that and changed his note a little.

"Yes, yes, I know," he said, "the *Evening Post* will not take sides. A fair paper, it will be just and true to the facts. Right; I know that. None better. You will seek the truth, and the truth

you will report, as you find it. Right. But, my dear Mr.—Mr."—
he couldn't find the card—"you cannot get the truth from Dr.
Parkhurst nor from any other enemy of the police."

Again he saw me shy.

"Yes, yes, you must see Dr. Parkhurst, listen to him, but you
will listen to us, too, to me. You will want the news. Well, sir, I
control the news from the police department, and I can—I can
give and I can withhold the news. No, no, keep your seat. I am

THE CHIEF INSPECTOR
Tom Byrnes

only endeavoring to say to you that I am going to put you on the
same basis here as the old reporters who have been with us for
years, most of them, and in return I ask you, in all fairness, not to
print the stuff you get from the enemies of the police without
submitting it to me for correction or—at any rate—comment."

It was worse, it was plainer, than I had expected it to be. I could
see through this doughty chief of police; he was not the awe-
inspiring figure I had imagined. For Tom Byrnes was a famous
police chief; few people ever saw him; he was only a name, but
there were stories told about him, of his cunning, as a detective,
as a master of men, as a manhandler of criminals, and as a retriever
of stolen properties—stories that filled the upper world with respect and the lower with terror. He struck me as simple, no
complications at all—a man who would buy you or beat you, as
you might choose, but get you he would.

Not me. So I thought, and I think he felt as I meant him to:

that I was going to be a free lance at police headquarters. His eyes narrowed into two slits as he read me. To meet his covert threat to keep news from me I said that I had no use for his ordinary police news; I was sent there only to see what I might see, hear what might be said, and print what I could prove—of politics. That was all. I was willing to tell him in advance whatever of importance I meant to report—if he would always see me promptly: I could not allow any delays in news, of course.

Byrnes looked at me, listening and drumming with his fingers on the desk. When I had finished he rose, walked to his window, and drummed on the glass with his nails till, turning suddenly, he dismissed me.

"All right," he said, and he pressed a button which summoned Mangin, who came darting in as I went out through the swinging doors into and through the silent, staring crowd in the outer office into the hall. A reporter followed me, an elderly man, who turned out to be the day man of a morning newspaper.

"You have made a bad start," he said as he joined me. "You have made an enemy of the first inspector. I hope you made a friend of the chief. You'll need him, with Williams against you."

I believed this; I was depressed, but I am sure I did not show it.

"What do I need friends for?" I said. "They would only embarrass me in what I am here to do."

He did not ask me what it was that I meant to do. Like Williams, he, everybody, seemed to know what I was there for; maybe Williams had told the crowd while I was with Byrnes. But how did Williams know? I was awed by their detective sagacity; it was frightening. I did not learn till much later that the police are professional guessers, and not good ones, except in obvious cases.

"I know your city editor, Harry Wright," the reporter was saying, "and I know that he will expect you to get some news. And I can help you, if you will work with me for a while and take my advice till you know the ropes yourself."

This did not attract, it repelled me, this proposition, and I wanted to get away from this friend. He was talking about how to find an office. The best place for a police reporter was in the buildings across the street; there one could watch police headquarters, see who came and went, and run across in a moment for any news that might turn up. But all the rooms were taken; I would better have a desk in his office and pay him for half the telephone, heat, and light rates. I hardly heard. My attention was caught by a shaggy-looking fellow coming down the street and yelling, "M-m-ma-a-x. M-m-a-x."

"Who is that?" I asked.

"Oh, that! That's Jake Riis, the *Evening Sun* man."

So! That was Jacob A. Riis, the author of *How the Other Half Lives*, and not only a famous police reporter, but a well-known character in one half of the life of New York. I liked his looks.

"But what's he bawling for?" I asked.

"For his boy, Max, who gets his news for him. There he is."

And there was Max Fischel, a little old round, happy Jewish boy, coming out of the basement door of headquarters, his hand full of pieces of paper: notes. He ran across the street to Riis, who was just coming to work, and the two—geniuses—that's what they were, both of them—went into the building opposite, where on the first floor Riis reappeared to throw up his window, through which you could see him and Max settle down to work. Every morning for two or three years I saw this scene, and it came to have a meaning to me; I was soon imitating it as nearly as I could.

Jake Riis was a Danish American who "covered" police headquarters, the Health Department, which was then in the same building, and "the East Side," which was a short name for the poor and the foreign quarters of the city. And he not only got the news; he cared about the news. He hated passionately all tyrannies, abuses, miseries, and he fought them. He was a "terror" to the officials and landlords responsible, as he saw it, for the desperate condition of the tenements where the poor lived. He had "exposed" them in articles, books, and public speeches, and with results. All the philanthropists in town knew and backed Riis, who was able then, as a reformer and a reporter, too, to force the appointment of a Tenement House Commission that he gently led and fiercely drove to an investigation and a report which—followed up by this terrible reporter—resulted in the wiping out of whole blocks of rookeries, the making of small parks, and the regulation of the tenements. He had discovered these evils as a reporter, reporting, say, a suicide, a fire, or a murder. These were the news, which all the reporters got; only Riis wrote them as stories, with heart, humor, and understanding. And having "seen" the human side of the crime or the disaster, he had taken note also of the house or the block or the street where it happened. He went back and he described that, too; he called on the officers and landlords who permitted the conditions, and "blackmailed" them into reforms.

This had been going on for years when I came to police headquarters. Riis was growing old, but he had found and trained his boy, Max, to see and to understand as Riis did; and Max could see. It seemed to me that Max was born and not made. He did the early morning work, which was the key to the day. The police, stationed all over the city, reported all happenings in their precincts to headquarters—fires, accidents, crimes, and arrests—which were posted briefly in the basement telegraph office, where the reporters could see them. The morning newspaper men watched these bulletins, weighed them, and went out to investigate those that seemed likely to have a story back of them. They stayed up till their papers went to press, at two or three o'clock in the morning. When Riis first came to police headquarters as a young man, the evening newspaper men appeared at about eight or nine o'clock and began their work by conning the accumulation of bulletins dated from three o'clock on down to eight. These they divided up among themselves, each reporter going out on one. When they returned with their several stories, they exchanged the news, wrote each one all the stories, and then could settle down for the day to a poker game, which only big news could interrupt. Riis did not play poker; he joined in no "combine"; he worked alone, sometimes giving but never asking help. He began to beat the combine, which had to quit poker and work all day, still together, to keep up with and, if possible, beat Riis. They, all veterans, had the advantage of knowing the town and the police, who did not like Riis, but he carried the war into their camp by coming to work at seven o'clock, which gave him time to take two or three of the early morning bulletins, cover and write them all, and since most of the sensational incidents of a city are reported in those late night hours, the *Evening Sun* had such a lead on police news as the *Post* had had on Wall Street. And when the beaten editors drove their police reporters to work at seven o'clock, Riis, the scab, began to come at six, then five, then four. Nobody else started that early: no editor could demand it, and Riis himself could not stand it long. But each reporter had a copy boy, a messenger, to carry his stories downtown. Riis hit upon the idea of a boy who, besides carrying copy, could "cover" the city from three till seven, eight, nine, when Riis turned up to write the news. Max, who began with the facts, soon learned to see and form and deliver to Riis the stories of the night for which the *Evening Sun* was noted. Beautiful stories they were, too, sometimes, for Riis could write.

This, then, was what I was seeing, my first morning at police headquarters: Max furnishing Riis the night's stories, all ready made. I must know Riis. Waiting out in the street till he was through writing—when I saw Max take the copy and set off for his office downtown, I crossed over and called on Riis. In a loud, cheerful, hearty voice, he greeted me.

"Glad you've come," he said. "The *Post* can help a lot up here, and you've begun well."

"Begun well!" I exclaimed. "I haven't begun yet."

Riis roared his great laugh. "Oh, yes, you have. Max says you banged Alec Williams one and disappointed the old man himself."

He meant that I had failed with Superintendent Byrnes! I was about to protest, but Riis was shouting through that open window.

"That's the way to handle them! Knock 'em down, then you can pick them up and be the good Samaritan. It's their own way with us reporters. They put the fear of God into us, then they are kind to us—if we'll let them. Not to me. They are afraid of me, not I of them, and so with you. You have started off on top. Stay there."

He bade me keep out of the combine. "Play alone," he said. "The combine will beat you for a while; so will I, of course. The whole police force will help beat you. Sure. But you'll soon learn the game and hold your own."

He said, still embarrassingly aloud, that he had seen me talking with the other reporter.

"I know what he wanted," he laughed. "He proposed that you share his office, pay him—not his office, him—half the rent costs, be his Max, and—"

"How did you know that?"

"I didn't," Riis shouted, as the reporter we were talking about walked across the street and up the stairs to headquarters. "But —— tries to get every new reporter to fag for him; and most of them do. No. Don't you do it. I can't show you around much; too busy; but Max will," and he called "M-a-a-x" out of the window; then remembered: "Oh, yes, Max is gone downtown. Come on. I'll show you around."

He broke into all the offices, police and health, walked right in upon everybody he thought I should know, laughed, made them

"CLUBBER" WILLIAMS IN HIS PRIME

all laugh, and introduced me, not by name, but as the new *Evening Post* man. When we were coming back out of the building, at the front end of the hall, we saw two policemen half forcing, half carrying, a poor, broken, bandaged East Side Jew into the office opposite that of the Superintendent of Police. There were officers and citizens all about us, but Riis grasped my arm, and pointing to the prisoner as he stumbled in through the open door, he shouted —not, I think, for me alone to hear: "There you have a daily scene in Inspector Williams' office! That's a prisoner. Maybe he's done something wrong, that miserable Russian Jew; anyway he's done something the police don't like. But they haven't only arrested him, as you see; they have beaten him up. And look—"

The door opened, showed a row of bandaged Jews sitting against the wall in the inspector's office, and at his desk, Clubber Williams.

"See the others. There's a strike on the East Side, and there are always clubbed strikers here in this office. I'll tell you what to do while you are learning our ways up here; you hang around this office every morning, watch the broken heads brought in, and as the prisoners are discharged, ask them for their stories. No paper will print them, but you yourself might as well see and hear how strikes are broken by the police."

Inspector Williams had heard. He rose from his desk, pointed at the door, shouted something, and the doorman closed the door with a bang. And Jake Riis laughed. But there was no merriment in that loud laugh of Jake Riis; there was bold rage in his face, as he left me, banging out of the building. I stayed, as he suggested, and watched the scene. Many a morning when I had nothing else to do I stood and saw the police bring in and kick out their bandaged, bloody prisoners, not only strikers and foreigners, but thieves, too, and others of the miserable, friendless, troublesome poor.

CLUBS, CLUBBERS, AND CLUBBED

POLICE clubbing is an art, and few policemen master it. This
I learned while I was spending my first idle mornings at
police headquarters, watching the victims of the stick brought
in to be inspected by the inspector, Clubber Williams. Nobody
else seemed to be interested. Riis went straight to his office, and
calling M-m-a-x, took the boy's stories of the night and wrote
them. He would not, could not, look at the bruised and bleeding
strikers; it made him "mad." The other reporters, seeing me
standing at the front door, fascinated by the sight, advised me that
it was "nothing; happens every day during a strike." An old
policeman was a little more understanding.

Coming in with papers from his precinct, he halted beside me to
look at a specially wretched case: an old Jew, who plainly had
been hit many times with the long night sticks: across the nose
and eyes, on the side of the head, on his right hand, left arm or
shoulder, and his back. He was crying and shrank from the
slightest touch. It was pitiful, and I must have uttered some sign
of my disapproval. For the old cop spoke.

"You're right," he said. "It's rotten work. Makes a man sick to
see it."

I was relieved to find that there was some one that felt as
I did, and a policeman, too; but he went on to say that what I was
seeing was the bad work of young policemen. "They don't understand, they aren't taught as we were how to swing the stick. It's a
formidable weapon, but there's a trick to it. One lick is always
enough, if it is placed right."

So, I gathered, it was not an emotional but an esthetic criticism
I was hearing, and I asked for more. "How do you place it right,
this stick?"

"You a reporter?" he asked, and when I nodded yes, he said, "Well, then, you ought to know that a club, especially a night stick, is meant to knock a man unconscious. You can kill with it, you know, and you can batter a man all to pieces, like that striker just gone in there. That's not necessary. All you got to do is to tap the extremities, head or feet, so as to send a current through the spine. If you land on the peak of the head your prisoner lays down; if you hit both feet exactly right—"

The old chap stopped to laugh, and to my inquisitive surprise, he offered an explanation.

"It's the funniest sight in the world to see the effect of a proper lick with a stick on a man's two feet. You don't get the chance to try it often. In my day we old cops used to practice it, very easy, on one another, and when you could do it you'd go out and find your bum. I remember the first time I got one just right. He was asleep on his back on a park bench, his two feet stuck out clear and even. Gosh, I was glad, and careful. I sneaked up on him from behind, knelt down, spit on my hand, and aimed. I was so nervous that I dropped my raised arm twice before I felt steady and ready. Then—say, but then I let her go, I whacked level and straight, hitting the bottoms of both boots at the same instant, and, well, it happened—what they always said would happen. That bum rose, stiff like a stick; he didn't bend a knee or move an arm. I think he didn't wake up. He just rose up, running—I mean that he was running by the time he came erect, and with never a holler or a look behind, he was running hell-bent across that park and—I watched him; I walked over in the direction he disappeared and—he's running yet. Yep! I bet that when he woke up, he was surprised to find himself running; it was so unusual for him to run that it woke him, but he couldn't stop, of course. His spine—"

He stopped, seemed to see it all over again, and he laughed till he remembered his errand. Then he said seriously, "It was beautiful; nothing like this"—and walked off down the long hall to the detective bureau with his papers.

His view interested and held me for a moment; I had heard of art for art's sake, but it was not satisfying, as applied to police clubbing. I had feelings about the clubbers. I would like to have had them clubbed, and by young policemen who had never heard of the art. I can see now that I had the very emotion that those rough clubbers had. I passionately desired action, and so feeling, I dashed into the office of the Superintendent and told him about this daily procession of wounded.

"Yes, I know," said Byrnes. "They should not be brought in at the front. It looks bad, and I have given orders repeatedly that prisoners, especially damaged prisoners, be brought in at the rear. I'll see now that it's done. Thank you for calling my attention to the matter."

But why, I asked, why must prisoners be so terribly beaten up? —and I must have put some feeling into my question. Byrnes changed his style. He had two styles or manners of speech, one formal, affected, and English; the other informal and native Irish. "Oh, I get you," he said, his eyes closing down small and hard. "You want to know why we give strikers the stick! Well, I'll tell you. You go over on the East Side some night or morning; you watch the blankety-blanks picketing a shop. Just stand around and look, and say, you listen, too. And then you come back here and you tell me why you would land on 'em with a night stick if you had one in your hand."

A good idea. I asked where to go; he gave me some addresses, and the next morning early I was on hand at my first strike. I neither knew nor cared anything about labor troubles. I believed, or I would have said, that the workers should work and the bosses boss. Of socialism I had heard. We had been told all about Marx and his theories, briefly and sufficiently, in college, when we were studying the more serious, scientific economists. Again in Paris I had listened at the cafés to the artists in revolt talking about socialism and anarchism, and they seemed to regard them as theories which would give art a place in life and young artists a living—considerations which had nothing to do with ethics, my specialty, or me. When I turned up, cold and a bit late, on a dirty East Side street corner to watch a shop where the sensible workers wished to return to work and the union pickets were to try to keep them "out," I had no interest in the strike, in Labor and Capital, or any of that troublesome nonsense. I wanted to see why the police clubbed people. And I saw.

I saw, first, a small group of three policemen on the corner where the sweat-shop was. The policemen pointed it out to me, on the second floor of a tenement. They recognized me as a reporter. How? "By your clothes," said one. "Say," said another, "you washed your face when you got up, didn't you? Well." There was also a small group of East Side spectators near the cops, "out to see the fun." For the rest there seemed to be only people, Jewish men, women, and children—all in their queer, black old clothes—going about their business. But one of the officers taught me to distinguish a procession of young men and women marching slowly at wide intervals along the street and turning around the corner. These were the pickets, the cop said, "laying for scabs."

"And there," he added sharply, "there comes a scab—with his father and mother to protect him." He pointed and started toward a young man with an old Jewish couple a block away. How he knew it was a worker returning to work I could not tell until, as we approached, I saw the scared white face of the fellow and the anxious looks he and his parents cast all about them. But I observed that everybody else recognized him, as the police did; the crowd stopped to look his way, and the pickets began to concentrate upon the trio, the pickets and the police, slowly racing. Several pickets reached him first. Shouting, gesticulating, they grabbed him, and just as the three policemen and I ran up, one of the pickets yanked away the old people and another struck the scab, who dropped. My policeman's night stick whizzed through the air, hit and knocked out the picket who had struck the blow, and the other pickets ran away. There were shrieks, calls, and a whistle. The parents of the scab were lying moaning and crying upon him; the police had to peel them off to lift him to his feet. He was bleeding from a cut on the cheek, and he was bawling as I had never heard a man bawl. With his father, mother, and a policeman to escort him, he staggered to the shop, where he washed up and went to work. I stayed with my cop, who kicked up the picket; his wound was a great bump on the back of the head, and as he gathered his senses, he protested.

"What for did you—"

"Ah, shut up," the policeman answered. "Look a' here." He seized the fellow's arm, held it up for him and me to see—a brass knuckle on his right fist. "The emblem of the organization," the policeman called it with a grin.

Then I learned my first lesson in the conflict between Labor and Capital: the workers are, as Capital alleges, forced into the unions;

they do not all voluntarily seek to unite; some of them, most of them, have to be driven to it by the brass knuckle and forceful persuasion.

I did not draw this generalization then and there that morning. All that I gathered on the spot was that the police used the club against the brass knuckle; and, also, against the law. For the strikers, Labor generally, are sticklers for the law.

The prisoner was led away by my policeman, who, to my question, "Police headquarters?" answered scornfully, "Oh, no, we only take prisoners we club bad to the inspector; this one goes to court." I remained with the other policemen to wait for a case of "bad clubbing," as I told them. I saw none. They had had one earlier, they said, but why was I interested? I told them I had been watching the bad cases brought in to headquarters and that Byrnes had advised me to come over and find out for myself the explanation of such violence.

"All right," one of them said, "we'll show you." He explained that picketing was not allowed within a block of a shop, and pointing to the procession of pickets passing the very door, said, "Now you watch." He stepped in front of a big, black-bearded Jew, who stopped short, and demanded, "Vell, vat you vant?"

"I want you to cut out your picketing in front of this shop."

"Picketing!" the man exclaimed. "Vat you call it, picketing?"

"You know damned well what picketing is."

"Me? Nit. I ain't no picketer, I am law-abiding citizen peaceably going to my work. I got the right to walk in the street, maybe."

"Yea," the cop sneered, "you got th' right to walk in th' street to your work, sure, but why don't you go? I been watching you for an hour walking around and around this block."

"Me? No, sir. This is the first time I been passing here."

"Come off," the policeman hissed, angry, and he threatened with his stick.

"And besides," the picket said coolly, "it is too early yet for to be in the shop. My shop—"

"Your shop, nothing. All the shops at work have been working for an hour or two."

"Not mine, Mister. No, my shop—"

J. PIERPONT MORGAN, SR.

"All right," the cop broke in. "Where is your shop? Lead me to it."

The picket was startled. He had been lying, but he recovered his self-possession and accepted the challenge. "All right, ve vill go to my shop. Come on."

The policemen looked at each other, one nodded, and the other, with a wink at me, said, "Come on," and the three of us started off. I heard, as we walked around the corner down toward the East River, a debate on the law, the rights of man and especially of strikers, which was as irritating to me as later the debates in the U.S. Senate were on the constitutionality of some bill proposed—and for the same reason. The argument had nothing to do with the subject before the house. It was just a case of lawyers, disputing not the right, wisdom, or justice of the matter in hand, but precedents and decisions; and the policeman and the picket knew, disputed, and strained the law to their appointed uses. They irritated me, and they so irritated each other that I could see and understand why the policeman kept feeling of, weighing, and finally whirling nervously his long night stick, like a lion waving its tail. And just as he seemed about to haul off and belt the anarchist, as he called the picket—and, I'll confess, just when I wished he would crack him one—the picket shouted, "Here's my shop," and he broke away, dashed into a café, and as we followed, disappeared through the rear while we stood, defeated and foolish, under the eyes of the smiling, chuckling, sneering crowd in the crowded room; "a crowd of bums," the cop called them.

"They drive you crazy," the policeman said, as we walked back. "You and the public, you wonder why we fan these damned bums, crooks, and strikers with the stick. I'll tell you that if you had to deal with them and their lies and their rights you would hit 'em too."

"Well?" asked the other policeman when we got back.

"Oh," said my companion, "I let him go, the blankety-blank. He would have walked me to Harlem looking for his shop, and then it would have been closed and I would have been off post, for fair. Anything doing here?"

"No, nothing except that the boss of that shop there, he's been out here to give me a song and dance about letting his workers be beaten up in broad daylight under our very eyes. Said he was going to make a complaint to headquarters."

"The —— —— ——!"

"Why," I said, "what's the matter with the boss?"

"Oh, nothing much," my cop answered, whirling his stick in rage, "only I remember this boss when he was a union organizer. I beat him up once myself for picketing, and now he's got a shop himself he's still a-fighting the police for the law and his rights."

"Just like the workers!" I exclaimed.

"Oh, hell. They're all alike, workers and bosses, the same breed, the same rights to all th' law on their side and against all the law on th' other side."

"The law is just a club then," I remarked; "the police are a weapon to be used or denounced."

"You have said it," one cop said heartily, and the other nodded, "Sure."

I went back to headquarters, cleared up on some subjects: the psychology if not the ethics of the night stick, for example; and confused and interested in, among other subjects, strikers. Passing policemen on their posts and observing that they kept twirling their clubs, long or short, on their strings—some of them gracefully—I felt the ache they conveyed to rap some head with the handy little billy, a working-man, a boss, anybody. And realizing that it did not matter which, that these employers were ex-employees, that they were the same human beings, first on one side, then on the other—it made me want to study and, if I could persuade my editor to let me, report some East Side strikes. My experiences as a labor reporter were beginning.

V I

DR. PARKHURST'S VICE CRUSADE

LEARNING as I was that the newspapers, literature, and public opinion did not picture men and life as they are, it was nevertheless a weekly amazement to me to read in the Monday morning newspapers descriptive reports and caricatures of the Rev. Dr. Charles H. Parkhurst that represented him as a wild man, ridiculous, sensational, unscrupulous, or plain crazy; then to call on him and find a tall, slim, smiling gentleman, quiet, determined, fearless, and humorous; and then, finally, go on down to police headquarters and hear groups of policemen, politicians, and reporters talking in earnest about this fiend. I don't know how he is remembered; Dr. Parkhurst may be not remembered at all. He carried on his vice crusade all through the nineties, charging police and political corruption and forcing the State Legislature to appoint the Lexow Committee which investigated, proved, and exposed the police and Tammany corruption, caused the election of a reform administration, and led up to the whole period of muckraking and the development of the Progressive party. Such a service is not the kind that is appreciated by public opinion and history, and whenever I speak with old New Yorkers now of Dr. Parkhurst they are puzzled to hear of him as I see him: a man of strength, who was "wise" in the slangy sense and otherwise wise. He never told or preached half of what he knew. His method was simple. He received individuals, sometimes honest victims of police outrage, sometimes disgruntled politicians, policemen, or criminals with axes to grind, and he heard their stories, which multiplied as he went on his steady way of exposure and attack. The facts and hints he collected then had to be investigated by his Society for the Prevention of Crime, with attorneys and detectives who followed up these leads, proved or disproved them, discovered others by the way, and delivered the information with the evidence to the Doctor, who used them—wisely. All he gave in a sermon or a lecture was enough to startle his hearers and to frighten the police world with the suggestion that he knew all. He didn't. As it turned out he did not know "the half of it." But he knew enough, and he understood so well what he knew that by sticking within the provable facts, by selecting those that were the most typical and significant, and using these boldly, he carried his charges every time.

"The police are paid bribe money regularly by the saloons," he would charge. "That is why they do not close them. If they care to show that I am wrong, let them enforce the law and close the saloons. They will not. They cannot. They don't dare."

That is what he would say clearly, even fiercely, of a Sunday. On Monday morning, when I called and asked him how he knew that, he would give me prices, dates, and names, and, smiling, say, "Now you ask Byrnes what he is going to do."

At police headquarters I would call on the Superintendent, who knew, of course, my routine; I soon learned to "spot" detectives watching me. Byrnes was ready for me.

"Well, and what does the reverend gentleman say this morning?"

"He says that you won't close the saloons this week either."

"I'll show you," he shouted in a rage one morning. He pressed a button, and to his Sergeant Mangin, who responded, he commanded: "Summon all the inspectors to report here at eleven o'clock. And"—to me—"you too."

At eleven o'clock all the inspectors in full uniform and all the reporters were in the chief's office. He rose from his desk and said: "Inspectors of police, I have bidden you, again and again, to enforce the law requiring the closing of saloons at certain hours, especially at night and on Sundays. Once more I command you to order your captains to obey and enforce upon others obedience to the laws."

We report the news, describing the scene, and the next morning I call on Dr. Parkhurst, who says, "Good. We'll see," and smiling he adds: "You will see—if you keep your eyes open—you will see the saloon-keepers and district leaders running to police headquarters to ask Byrnes if he means it; if he does, to protest and to threaten him. And as for me, I'll wait till Sunday to say what I see."

I saw the procession of saloon-keepers, politicians, and others, many other people, calling on Byrnes. One day Tim Sullivan, the famous East Side ward boss, came up to me, straight in his direct way, and asked me what th' hell I was trying to do.

"I?" I exclaimed. "I'm not trying to do anything but get the news."

"The hell you ain't," he protested. "You are backing up that damned preacher. Before you came to headquarters the reporters paid no attention to what the blankety-blank said. But now you interview Byrnes, ask him what he's going to do about it, and the other reporters have to report what he says too. You're making it hard for the old man; he says so himself; and you're making it hard for us, too. Why? What's th' game? What do you get out of it all?"

"News," I laughed.

"News!" he echoed. "Say, if that's all you want I'll give you news; we'll all give you news. I can tip Byrnes to put you 'way inside on th' news."

"Go ahead," I answered, jesting, and to my consternation he darted back into Byrnes' office, and coming out, reported, "I've fixed that all right. Now you be good. See?"

This had consequences which I was not "wise" enough to foresee or detect. I did not understand that I was being bribed; nothing happened immediately. Riis joined me in pressing Byrnes to heed Dr. Parkhurst or at least to answer his tirades. The other reporters merely laughed at me and my naïveté, but police officers were polite and obliging. Byrnes offered me a beat on a burglary several days later and looked mystified when I declined it, saying priggishly that the *Post* did not care for that sort of news. What interested me was that the police court cases showed and the reporters reported that the liquor laws were not enforced, as Dr. Parkhurst knew. He said so in his next Sunday sermon; he said it furiously, with scathing sarcasm and jubilant triumph.

"Now," he said amiably Monday morning, "now see what Byrnes does by way of his next bluff."

I think that at that time Dr. Parkhurst was really driving at the closing of the saloons. The appeals of wives and children to him for relief from the week-end drunkenness of their husbands and fathers were worrying the clergyman and making him hope for the enforcement of the early closing laws so as to save some of the workers' wages. My interest was in the glimpses I was catching of the Tammany government, and, by the way, of political morals. The police were protecting from the law and from public opinion the law-breakers they were appointed and paid to protect the public from. That was an apparent fact about the New York government. And by way of morals there was the faithful keeping of the alleged contract of the police with the saloon-keepers. Anyway, I went from Dr. Parkhurst, not to Byrnes, but to Riis. After a talk with him, about the situation as I saw it, he went with me to interview Byrnes.

"What about it, Inspector?" Riis asked for us both.

"What about what?" Byrnes retorted, his Irish showing in his angry eyes and hanging jaw.

"Parkhurst says you were bluffing when you had us in here last Monday to hear you instruct the inspectors to shut up the town. Anyway they didn't do it. What next?"

The chief paced the floor a few times, then halted before Riis and challenged him.

"Is the *Sun* backing Parkhurst? I know the *Post* is, but as I read the *Sun*—"

He was referring to the attacks by the *Sun* upon both Parkhurst and the *Post* for their hypocritical policy of law-enforcement, but Riis, who was not only a reporter, cut him short.

"Never you mind the *Sun*," he said. "Say what you are going to do. That's the news of the day, and the *Sun* prints the news."

"Two o'clock," said Byrnes, pointing us to the door and going to his desk.

"The" inspector, as I have said, had a funny way of affecting the dignity which he thought belonged to his position as the head of the uniformed police force; he would speak English as English as he could, using the broad "a." But under the strain of a sudden temper, he would fall back into his native Irish. This happened that day.

At two o'clock, when the inspectors filed into his office with Riis and me, the Superintendent in full uniform was pretending to write at his desk. He was very busy, too busy to see us till we had stood there silent and waiting and winking at one another for a minute or two. It seemed long before Byrnes looked up, saw us, rose solemnly, and strode slowly around in front of his inspectors, who watched him come. He never looked at Riis and me. He stood glaring at his inspectors.

"Gentlemen," he began, "did not I command you last Monday on this very spot in this same office to enforce to the letter the laws regulating the saloons in this city, and—and to close them one and all at the legally fixed hours for closing?"

No answer of course, only silence and attention, while the chief, crouching low at them and balling his fists, cried, "Well, and what I want to know now is: did youse did it?"

I snorted, couldn't help it; and Byrnes whirled upon me, and his arm lifted at the door, he yelled, "Get out of here!" I ran; Riis stood, but the angry man added, "Both of you." Then Riis came out laughing too.

How Byrnes finished his broken scene, what he said further to his inspectors, we did not learn. The inspectors avoided us, slipping back into their offices with sobered faces and mute lips. But the next Saturday night and Sunday many saloons closed. Not all. There seemed to have been some request sent out from headquarters for a voluntary compliance with the law; the liquor dealers must have decided among them which were to close and which to remain open. Anyway, for the next few weeks different saloons seemed systematically to obey and disobey the law, and there were few raids, though there were some places, the most notorious, which never did close. They had "thrown away their keys" the day they opened up for business, and it was not till Theodore Roosevelt became Commissioner that these powerful men were brought to heel.

Why were these law-breakers so strong? And why was there such an opposition to the simple, superficial reforms of Dr. Parkhurst? I used to wonder at what I was seeing, and the reporters, policemen, politicians, who explained it all to me, wondered at my stupidity. I could understand the bribery and the contributions to political parties; that accounted for the police and Tammany Hall, and that satisfied the minds of my informants. But it did not explain to me the opposition to reform that was most bitter: that of good, prominent citizens who had no apparent connection with the underworld. As Dr. Parkhurst forced such results as the voluntary closing of some saloons, he was hated more and more openly by people whom one might expect to see approving his course: bankers, business men, and even other clergymen. There was something to find out about the organization of society, as it occurred in New York, something the "wise guys" of the under-world did not know or would not tell. I asked my friends in Wall Street to justify their indignation at Parkhurst, but all they would say was that his crusade "hurt business." That was the first time I heard that expression. "How can the closing of saloons hurt business in Wall Street?" I asked James B. Dill, who knew everything. He kicked my shin, hard, and when I exclaimed, he answered my question, "Why does your mouth cry out when only your shin is hurt?" That was the answer, but I could never be satisfied with a fact or a phrase; it was a picture I needed, a diagram of the connection between the saloon business and the banks, just as I had one of the nervous system that linked up my lower and upper extremities.

VII

THE UNDERWORLD

THE inspector, Byrnes, was cultivating my friendship, and he did it by letting me in to a view of his relations with thieves and the underworld generally. It may have been Tim Sullivan's hint that I could be won with "news"; it may have been that, wishing to impress me, he talked, and talking, naturally turned to the field where he was most impressive, his detective work. Before he was promoted to be Superintendent of Police, he had been for years the inspector in charge of the detective bureau. He had enjoyed that work, evidently, and his many miraculous services to prominent people who had been robbed had made him loom in their imagination as the man of mystery and of marvelous effects. They all knew him in Wall Street; big men down there envied me the privilege of knowing personally "the inspector," as they still called him.

"You see him? Every day? And he talked to you, man to man, like that?"

Few of them had seen him. Even those he had helped out of trouble had rarely met him personally. It was his pose to remain in the background, receiving communications through others—detectives or attorneys—and working in the dark, suddenly hand out his results. You saw only the hand and the restored property. Bankers told me tales of how somebody's house had been robbed; the inspector had been told about it, and having listened in silence a moment, had said, "Enough. Your diamonds will be delivered at your house within three days." And on the third day—not on the second or the fourth, but exactly when this amazing man had promised—your diamonds were handed in by two startling men "with the compliments of the inspector." Another banker had had his pocket picked of money and valuable papers; he did not mind the money, but the papers . . . Byrnes had got back the papers, all intact.

One of the most famous of our millionaire families had consulted Byrnes about a foreign nobleman who had won the love of a daughter of the house; what could be done to get rid of the fellow? "I'll see," Byrnes had answered, and a few days later he promised that the family would see no more of the foreigner. "You might let me have enough money for him to pay his passage home and perhaps a little more." Gladly they paid whatever Byrnes thought would "do," and no more was ever seen or heard of that trouble. Byrnes was the man to deal with blackmailers. Wall Street and "Society" had suffered from the possession by unscrupulous scoundrels of personal and more or less scandalous facts against its leaders; true stories. Byrnes could deal with them. You told him "all about it"; perhaps you made one more payment, and—that ended it. Byrnes established Fulton Street as the dead line beyond which no thief could go downtown. It was understood that, in return for these services, Byrnes was tipped on stocks, let in on "good things," and otherwise helped to make money, quite properly; and no doubt the gratitude to Byrnes was an element in the ingratitude to Parkhurst. But that did not explain the connection between the saloon nerves and the big-business brains. There was something else back of all these surface signs. What was it? And how did Byrnes perform his miracles?

While I was pondering these questions he did one for me. Drawing my salary one Saturday afternoon, I went home and took my wife out for dinner. As I was about to pay the waiter, I discovered that my pay envelope with the money was gone. My pocket had been picked. I complained to Byrnes by 'phone; he asked how much was in the envelope, how the envelope was addressed, and what lines of cars I had used to go home and to dinner. When I had answered all his questions, he said, "All right. I'll have it for you Monday morning." And on Monday morning Byrnes handed me the envelope with the money just as I had received it from my paper.

"How did he do it?" I asked the other reporters. They were playing their poker in a basement office and had not much time for me, a greenhorn. I had to repeat my question several times before one of them looked up and answered briefly.

"Huh," he said. "He knew what pickpockets were working the car lines you rode and he told the detectives who were watching them to tell them that they had robbed a friend of the chief's of so much money in such and such an envelope."

"But how—"

"Ah, say, you don't know enough to cover Wall Street, to say nothing of police headquarters. Byrnes passed the word that he wanted that dip back by Monday morning, and so, of course, it came back Monday morning."

What reporters know and don't report is news—not from the newspapers' point of view, but from the sociologists' and the novelists'. It enabled me, when I learned a little of it, to write my *Shame of the Cities*. But it took time and sharp listening to get that little. Though I had nothing to do, professionally, with criminal news, I used to go out with the other reporters on cases that were useless to my paper but interesting to me. Crime, as tragedy and as a part of the police system, fascinated me. I liked to go for lunch to the old Lyons restaurant on the Bowery with Max Fischel or some other of the "wise" reporters. They would point out to me the famous pickpockets, second-story men and sneaks that met and ate there; sometimes with equally famous detectives or police officials and politicians. Crime was a business, and criminals had "position" in the world, a place that was revealing itself to me. I soon knew more about it than Riis did, who had been a police reporter for years; I knew more than Max could tell Riis, who hated and would not believe or even hear some of the "awful things" he was told. Riis was interested not at all in vice and crime, only in the stories of people and the conditions in which they lived. I remember one morning hearing Riis roaring, as he could roar, at Max, who was reporting a police raid on a resort of fairies.

"Fairies!" Riis shouted, suspicious. "What are fairies?" And when Max began to define the word Riis rose up in a rage. "Not so," he cried. "There are no such creatures in this world." He threw down his pencil and rushed out of the office. He would not report that raid, and Max had to telephone enough to his paper to protect his chief.

There were fairies; there were all sorts of perverts; and they had a recognized standing in the demi-world; they had their saloons, where they were "protected" by the police for a price. That raid Riis would not report was due to a failure of some one to come through with the regular bit of blackmail overdue. And so with prostitution, so with beggars, so with thieves, as I gradually learned, first from the reporters, then from police officers I came to know well, then from the crooks themselves who learned to trust me, and all the while from Byrnes. When he discovered that, while and because I did not write criminal news, he could interest and trust me with it, he used to call me in and tell me detective stories of which he was the hero. He was bragging, and he was inventing, too. This I knew because I had found out where he hid the detective story-books he was reading, and borrowing them when he was not looking, I read and recognized in them the source of some of his best narratives. Thus I discovered that instead of detectives' posing for and inspiring the writers of detective fiction, it was the authors who inspired the detectives. For example:

One day a young policeman who had just been appointed a plain-clothes man appeared at headquarters so exultant that I asked him what he had done. He hesitated a moment; detectives are forbidden to tell of their feats; that must be left to the inspector; but he knew that I did not report crimes, and he did want to talk; so he told me that he had "got the dope" on a certain big robbery of a rich man's house up Fifth Avenue.

"You remember the case," he began. "Jewelry and silverware taken on a grand scale, and the owner hollered. That made the old man mad; with the public in on it, he had to make a showing; so we were all instructed to do our damnedest."

The police all over the world caution citizens who are robbed to report to headquarters and never to the press. They explain that detectives can work better if the thieves are not warned by the newspapers that the police are after them. This is absurd, of course. Thieves always know when the police are looking for them after a crime. The true reason of the police for privacy is that they don't like to have the public know how many unsolved crimes are committed, and they do like to deal privately and freely with the criminals. My detective assumed that I understood this; he assumed that I knew everything. His next assumption was that I knew that detectives specialized, as criminals do, in one class of crime, and that the detective's trade consists not in pursuing but in forming friendships with criminals.

"It wasn't any of my business," he said. "My assignment, of course, is to the dips [pickpockets]; I was promoted because I had cultivated them and their girls and was known to be in with 'em. The case was either a burglary or a plain robbery, a good job, too, and the burglars and such that ought to know about it were as mystified as the chief himself. They said that they hadn't any of 'em done it. The old man put some of them through the mill till he was convinced that no crook that is allowed either to operate or to live in New York was in on it in any way. He thought, and I remember I guessed, that it was an inside job: servants. But the servants had all been kept, and the old man couldn't get a word out of them; not to the point. He said that they seemed really as mystified as anybody. A pretty case, eh?

"Well, we heard no more of it for a couple of months. I had about forgotten it and the burglar gang had dropped it, when one night I saw a dip who had been on the bum all dressed up with lots of money. He used to work the Bridge cars [the old Brooklyn Bridge surface lines] but had a row with his pal and got fired. Unable to work, he was down and out. Here he was, all of a sudden, flush and sassy. I naturally asked what t'ell. 'Got a new girl,' they told me in the barroom where the dips hang out. I thought they meant that she was a young, pretty piece that earned him a lot of money, but when she was pointed out to me one night later she turned out to be a homely foreigner; couldn't pick up a dollar a night on the streets. I smelled a rat. 'She must work,' I thinks. 'A servant perhaps. But how, then, did she get the money?' I followed her home, and what do you think? She went to that house on Fifth Avenue. Say, I had something, and I knew it. I got hold of her pickpocket and asked him if he'd like to get back on the cars. He sure would; what would it cost? I said he knew what the price would be, and he said he knew, too. He'd think it over. And the next night he paid the price to the old man himself, me being there.

"The story was simple. The butler was the boy. He was a Frenchman, a regular at home, who got in wrong with his French police. He came over here to work his old game, which was to take a job and 'get' a maid, usually a homely one who would appreciate a little love. She did the actual lifting of the stuff; he sent it to pals in Paris, giving her a fair divvy. He was square with the money; square enough. She got more money than she ever saw before. But he wasn't square on the love end. He took her to dances, and there took up with other girls; neglected her, and she got mad and took up with my dip, who picked up all her money and all her story, which Byrnes has. The arrests were made last night."

This, then, was a true detective story. Two days later Byrnes called in the reporters, and announcing the arrests, related a detective yarn which was so full of clews, thought, night reflections, and acute reasoning—it was, in brief, so perfectly modeled upon the forms of the conventional detective story, that the cynical police reporters would not write it. They reported the news, the arrests, and left the story to the court. Byrnes often asked me if I knew why my colleagues did not use all his stories; I think now that he liked to tell them to me because I seemed to swallow them. We used to discuss criminals philosophically, and he then talked straight; at least he dropped remarks which confirmed the reporters' gossip about his methods.

Tapping on his window one afternoon, he beckoned me into his office, saying: "Here, now, I've got a case that puzzles me. There's a pickpocket downstairs [in the basement, he meant, where the cells were] who has always been straight with me. He operates all the big cities that I have no arrangement with; St. Paul, Seattle, 'Frisco, Los Angeles, back via New Orleans to the middle west and the east. He never works in New York. He keeps his woman here, and when he has made a pile he comes to town, every year, to go to the theaters, gamble a little, dine here and there, and, generally, live. He calls on me to report and get permission; he promises not to do a thing here, and I always have let him have his vacation. Never has he broken faith. He has never given me any information; he's no use to me; but he has been on the level till here the other day he was caught in a crowded surface car with a fine gold watch in his hand and a crowd on his neck. Why? He knew who was working that car; he knew they would kick at his butting in on their beat; he's a 'wise guy,' and yet he made his dip and, worst of all, got caught."

"Well?" I questioned. "Why don't you ask him about it?"

"Oh, I have, several times," said Byrnes. "But he gives me a rigmarole about having lifted the watch to see if he could and meaning to put it back. I can't get it; and I kind o' like the fellow. Now I'm going to send for him and leave you alone with him to see if you can get the answer."

Two detectives brought up the prisoner, and at a sign from Byrnes, left him standing just within the door.

"That's the man," said Byrnes to me for him to hear. "He can talk to you or not, as he pleases. If he does you may get his story; I can't. When you are through, press the first button."

As Byrnes went out, the thief looked curiously at me; he looked all around the room, at the windows, the doors, the desk, and back at me. Cool and silent, he looked me up and down, as I did him. He was a tall, slender, self-contained man of about thirty, with sharp, quick eyes, a sharp, thin nose, and long, beautiful hands which hung quiet but gave one a sense of life.

"The inspector," I began, "was telling me about you." I repeated exactly what Byrnes had said. "He likes you," I added. "I can see that; he wants to trust you, and he asked me, a reporter, to see if I could get your reason for operating that car-line when you had promised not to work in New York."

He walked swiftly over past me to the window, where he turned so that he could have the light on me, not himself.

"It's simple enough," he answered in a high-pitched little voice. "I did not operate that line, only that one car for that once; and that was not a dip. I didn't mean to steal the watch; I got caught putting it back."

I did not understand, and he must have seen my mystification. He sighed and said, "Some people think money is all there is to it." And when he saw that this added nothing to my understanding, he went on rapidly: "It was this way: I was riding that crowded car to get up to my hotel. Didn't need money. But I spotted a fellow standing up in the aisle with a thief-guard on his watch and as I studied the thing I saw it was a new trick—a new one on me. I would have liked to beat it; I didn't intend to, because of Byrnes, who has been square to me, pretty square; as square as a cop can be. You're not a bull, you say?"

"No, a reporter."

"A writer. Well, then, you ought to believe me," he answered.

"I moved up close to the smart Aleck with his wonderful watch-guard only to study it, and I couldn't see it all; only the bit of it that stuck out. It was fastened somehow in the vest pocket; I wanted to see how. My hands did, I mean. That's what you ought to get that the old man can't; that my fingers asked me to let them feel out that guard and—and—they bet they could break it, get the watch—and—and they promised they would put the watch back into the pocket on to the guard."

He looked distressed, even as he told me. "I oughtn't to have done it—in my position. Risking everything. I do like to come to New York and feel safe while I loaf. And I had no pal, you see, nobody to bump the fellow and draw off his attention. I think that it was that maybe, added to the new guard, which made me want to see if I could. Anyway I let my hands go, and they went in, felt and understood the guard; they got it, opened it, and I had the watch and all. And, honest, it was the best guard I ever went up against. I held it in my hands, looking it over, and was just about to put it back when the two dips that work that line jumped on the car front and back!"

He looked his exclamation; he was frightened.

"Now," he said proudly, "I ain't afraid of no bulls, see? But dips, and New York dips with a monopoly on that line, they hate us Westerners anyhow— I had to hurry."

His quiet hands began to work, his quick eyes darted here, there, about the room. He was seeing his emergency again, and as he saw it, his hands reached out to me.

"I saw those two pick me out; I saw them look at each other, then at the fellow I was dipping, then at what I had in my hands. We can see in my business, you know. So they saw me slip back the watch and—leave it. No time to replace the guard as it was. I just dropped it, and they were on me. They came from both ends of the car, banged on to the man as they wedged me, and 'Feel for your watch,' one of 'em called to the sucker.

"'Humph!' he said, throwing up his hands. Of course, they had me. The sucker, other passengers, and my two—two competitors, my two monopolists, they all jumped me and yelled, till the two plain-clothes men at Fourteenth Street came aboard and pinched me."

He paced nervously across the room, returned, and stopped before me.

"Do you understand?" he asked, and he very much wanted me to.

"We'll see," I answered. I pressed the button, and Byrnes came slowly back.

"Well," he said most casually. "What are we up against?"

"An artist," I said.

"What!"

"A poor helpless artist," I repeated, and I explained to the inspector that when a man is a master of his craft, he does sometimes practice his art when he should not; he cannot help it. I went into some detail, talking about the follies of painters and the weaknesses of writers, while Byrnes frowned and the pickpocket's face shone like a saint's with happiness. When Byrnes' frown cleared I knew I had put over my theory, and stopped. The thief seized my hand in both his and wrung it. Byrnes watched him a moment, then said to the prisoner, "All right. You can go. Only remember, New York is no place for artists. Get me?"

He rang the bell, the two plain-clothes men reappeared, and their chief commanded, "Turn him out."

I met that thief a few years later on a train going from Chicago to St. Louis, where I was muckraking. He came up to me in the dining-car, handed me my pocketbook, and as I recognized it and him, he said: "Never carry your wallet in your coat pocket. I know you don't care for money; an artist has his mind on other, more important matters than money—sometimes. But I find that, besides money, you carry your railroad tickets and other valuable or private papers, all in the same wad."

"Where did you lift it?" I asked.

"I saw you come to the train," he answered, "saw where you put the book when the conductor handed you back your slips, and —you really ought to know better—I thought I would teach you a lesson in the fine art of traveling. So I went to wash up when you did; I hung my coat up beside yours and at the same time transferred your pocketbook to my pocket."

I invited him to sit down and dine with me, and we had a long and to me at that time a very helpful talk about how the police do business with criminals in other cities than New York, the cities I was then working in and writing about, as he knew. That grateful thief paid me in full for what he called my "pull for him with Byrnes," who, by the way, never had any further cause to complain of his artist guest in New York.

"He used to call me in and tell me when some city was asking him to pick me up for them," the man said that night. "He tipped me, but he never gave me up. He was as square after that, almost as square, as one of us."

VIII

BOSSES: POLITICAL AND FINANCIAL

REPORTING at police headquarters was like a college education in this, that one had to take several courses all together. There was the police news, police policies and politics; the Ghetto, with its synagogues, theaters, and moral struggles; the strikes; and, on the side, Wall Street. It differed from college in this, that I was interested in each of these courses and could see that they belonged together. They all contributed to the learning of life as it is lived. The difficulty was to dovetail them into my time.

My daily routine began at breakfast with the reading of the morning newspapers for a general sense of the general news, for a definite idea of financial developments to see if there was anything in my (constructive) line, and a careful sifting of the police and political reports for leads to follow up. My wife and her mother used to help in this pleasant work; they learned to notice "uncovered ends" of stories; to raise questions which remained to be answered. We were acquiring the habitual attitude of the editorial mind: to look not only for information but for the lack of needed knowledge. I rose from breakfast with questions to go out and seek answers to.

My first call was on Dr. Parkhurst, who also had read the papers and was ready with his informed comments on the news in his field, explanations of raids and other police activities, which he had from his Society. He often had new experiences to report, his and his agents'. If he had attacks to refute or fresh charges to make, if some orator, politician, police officer, or newspaper accused him and his agents of, say, cruelty in causing the arrest of street walkers, he would dictate a statement, quiet, quick, that it was not worse to drive these women off the streets than it was to take away from them, as the police did, a share of their hard-earned money. If the police had raided a gambling-house he had designated as "running full-blast" and found "nothing doing," "nobody at home"; if, in other words, the papers said that the alleged gambling-joint was closed or vacant the night of the raid, Dr. Parkhurst would smile and say, "Advise Byrnes to call again and not to have the gamblers tipped off next time."

Sometimes he would warn me of the business that was to come up that day for action by the Board or by the Superintendent of Police, give me the bearing and background of it and the probable decision. At other times he would point his remarks at Richard Croker as the guilty head of Tammany just as Byrnes was the responsible head of the system of police graft. I usually left Parkhurst with an improved picture of the invisible government of New York and fresh lines of inquiry to follow up.

Arriving at my office across Mulberry Street from police headquarters, I looked over the night reports from the precincts in the basement, and if there was anything interesting, like a big fire, a murder, or a street row, I asked Max Fischel about it. He was loyal to Riis; he would not give me a "beat," but my point of view was so different from Riis's that Max could tell me enough for me to decide whether to go out myself and get the story or let it go. It was seldom that I had to write any of the "early morning news" for the *Post*. When Riis turned up, bawled for "M-a-a-x," and sat down to write, I went through the police offices, saw and talked with Byrnes about "what that crazy Parkhurst had said or done," with the inspectors and the Health Department. Then, if there was a meeting of the bi-partisan Board of (four) Police Commissioners, I attended and reported it. On tense days when the Parkhurst attacks were pressing, the meetings of these helpless politicians were dramatic and absurd. Two of them were Republican machine men; two were Tammany officials. They had full power under the law, but actually they had nothing to do with anything but routine expenditures and details of policy. The uniformed police governed themselves in cahoots with certain politicians and associations of liquor dealers, gamblers, and other law-breakers. The poor, weak, conspicuous Commissioners were nothing but a "front" to take the punishment. My professional job was, by their acts and sayings, to show this, and I did it gradually. Many a time I have sat with that Board with them all glaring at me and making, as I reported, speeches for me to hear and report, me and the other reporters. When in desperation they met behind closed doors, we reported that they were up to some chicanery which the public was not to know. They held no more private meetings for a while. When they had promotions to make, we used to find out and print in advance the names of the men the politicians and grafters had chosen for them to name, tell the political and scandalous reasons for the choice, and then watch and report their unhappy, humiliating obedience to "orders." It was an amazing example of professional political morality to me that these politicians were true to their backers and to one another. I offered the two Republicans many chances to serve their (theoretical) party interests and fight their (theoretical) enemy, Democratic Tammany, by turning against the system and joining the reform forces to put the rascals out. They were loyal to the graft, of which, so far as I could ever discover, they got no share. They were not good men, but there was honor among them. They suffered in silence like heroes for a cause; a bad cause and not their fault.

When there was no board meeting or other important police business, I reported by 'phone to the city editor, and he gave me other work, usually in or about Wall Street. I liked to keep in touch there. New corporations and combinations were forming, and when a great, rich company was announced in Wall Street as born in Jersey City and I had to run down the unknown directors only to find out that they were obscure clerks and bookkeepers in some bank or lawyer's office, James B. Dill would explain to me that they were "dummy directors."

"Dummy directors?"

"Yes, don't you know that all directors are dummies? Most presidents too. Chairmen of Boards, managers, and heads of departments are real enough, but the bosses of business are the bankers and financial operators; they have no office at all in the company, but they run it through—dummies."

"Well, but these directors are clerks, no use as a front."

"Yes, yes," Dill would laugh. "We're in a hurry now. We'll pick out some prominent, rich—gentlemen to go on the boards by and by when we get around to this detail. But perfectly tame dummies with good names of able fathers are not so easy to find. Wall Street is young. England has her nobility and old families and decaying rich houses to choose her 'guinea pigs' from; we have to wait for the sons of our rich old families to grow up and be college-bred to take orders, punishment, and ask no questions."

It was police and political parallels that enabled me to see Wall Street clearly. And by and by, as my wonder about politics outgrew my Wall Street interest, the financial practice began to light up the police and political government. In brief, as my dummy police commissioners were the key to Dill's dummy directors, so his dummy directors opened up my feeling for the dummy police board, dummy aldermen, mayors, governors. I remember, for example, how one day when I was bragging to my wife that, after all, though I was only a reporter, I had had chances to be something else, something respectable, she showed me a truth.

"I was offered the presidency of that book trust," I reminded her.

"Yes," she reminded me, "dummy president."

My wife was often a help to me. I saw in a flash, when she said that, how much less "position" meant than I had thought, how unflattering the offer was that I had boasted about. Would I take orders, as the head of a company, from the banker who appointed me, a banker who knew and cared nothing about books? What did he care about, that banker boss?

"Banker boss." I recall the day when that phrase occurred to me. I was on my way back from Wall Street to my office at police headquarters, with instructions to arrange for an interview with Richard Croker. Both Dr. Parkhurst and the editor of the *Post* asked me to question him about the police graft, some of which was supposed to be passed on up to him. He had no public office; "Dick" Croker was the boss, who nominated candidates for office, both elected and appointed, and so was being denounced as the actual, responsible ruler of the city. An absurd, illegal, disgraceful arrangement, my paper and my friends said. And it was, in my opinion too. I had accepted also, unthinkingly, the reformers' proposed remedy:

"Down with the boss. Away with politics and the politicians. Elect to office good business men who would give us a business government."

As I reviewed all this that day, for the purpose of questioning Croker about his boss-ship, I asked myself suddenly what was the difference between a political boss and a banker boss. None that I could see, except that one was a political, the other a financial, boss. Both political government and business government were run on the same lines, both had unofficial, unresponsible, invisible, actual governments back of the legal, constitutional "fronts." A keen personal interest inspired me, not to telephone, but to go on up to Croker's office, where he rarely appeared, in Tammany Hall on Fourteenth Street. He was there. He had his overcoat and hat on, ready to go out, and he invited me to walk along with him.

A sweet-faced man he was, all iron gray; his hair, his hat, his neat suit of clothes were of one tone of dark gray. His eyes were kind, and at my announcement that "the *Post* wanted to know—" a winning smile spread from his lips up to his eyes.

"Yes, I know that the *Post* wants to know; the *Post* needs to know, but 'Larry' Godkin would not learn anything from 'Dick' Croker. He sends you up here to get me to say something to quote and roast."

He strolled along slowly, watching his step; then he glanced amiably around at me and said: "Isn't that so? If I said something —no matter what—wouldn't he jump on it and me? He would not be content to print it as I would say it and as you would write it, letting his readers judge, and take or forget it. He would pick it up and pound me with it. Sure, boy, you know he would. And so you know that it would be foolish for me to say a word for publication."

I did not answer, but I could see the sense of his remarks, and I think he could see that I saw. "Sure," he said, as the smile disappeared. "You see that. A man in my position has got to keep his mouth shut. Let 'em talk, let 'em roast, and no matter how hot and fast and hard they throw it into you, stand up and take it. I will not talk to you—" He stopped, faced me down, and his eyes bored into me with a steady, unsmiling stare. Suddenly he relented. The sweet smile came back into his kind old face, and he added, "As a reporter.

"But," after a short pause, "I will talk to you, man to man. On the understanding that not a word of what I say is to be printed or even repeated to your editor, I will tell you anything you want to know, always, straight, unless it is about some one else. See?"

I knew perfectly well that a reporter should not accept confidences; it is unprofessional to let his personal curiosity cross his paper's interest in "news." The New York *World* of my day had a rule forbidding a correspondent, even at Washington, even with the President, to take any statement except for publication. But I was young. I was eager to know; knowledge was my price; and Mr. Richard Croker, as I always called him, had something in

MR. RICHARD CROKER

him that appealed to something in me. I respected, I came to like, that man. Anyway, I nodded my agreement, and often as I "saw" and interviewed him after that, I kept faith with him.

"Now, then," he said that day as we crossed Union Square, "what do you want to ask me?"

"Well, about this boss-ship," I began. "Why must there be a boss, when we've got a mayor and—a council and—"

"That's why," he broke in. "It's because there's a mayor *and* a council *and* judges *and*—a hundred other men to deal with. A government is nothing but a business, and you can't do business with a lot of officials, who check and cross one another and who come and go, there this year, out the next. A business man wants to do business with one man, and one who is always there to remember and carry out the—business."

"Business? Business?" I repeated. "I thought government was all politics."

He smiled, turning to look into my face.

"Ever heard that business is business?" he teased. "Well, so is politics business, and reporting—journalism, doctoring—all professions, arts, sports—everything is business."

"But business hasn't any bosses," I said.

He stopped, serious, and as I stopped with him to face him, he protested.

"Now, now, you ain't talking for publication either, and you tell me you have been a Wall Street reporter. If that is true, then you know as well as I do that Wall Street has its bosses just like Tammany and just like the Republican machine."

My blundering answer was the confession, first, that I did know that, and second, that I did not know it till that very day. Recounting to him the thoughts I had had on my way uptown about the parallel of dummy directors and dummy police commissioners, and banker bosses and political bosses, I felt ashamed of the fact that I had not seen those things while I was in Wall Street. My humiliation was wasted. Perhaps my chatter was naïve. Anyway it seemed to please Mr. Croker. He put his arm through mine, saying, "I guess you are on the square all right."

The change of subject embarrassed me; so I blurted out another question.

"But they don't have graft in business. They don't take bribes from saloons, and they don't take away the earnings of the women of the street. How can you stand for that in politics?"

We were walking again, slowly up Broadway, and he strode along in silence for so long that I was about to repeat my question, when he answered.

"There is graft in Wall Street, of course. You don't mean what you say about that. You mean that there isn't any dirty graft, like the police graft, don't you?"

"Yes, that was what I meant."

"Police graft is dirty graft," he said as if to himself. "We have to stand for it. If we get big graft, and the cops and small fry politicians know it, we can't decently kick at their petty stuff. Can we now?" He was looking at me again as he added with sharp emphasis, "We can't be hypocrites, like the reformers who some-- times seem to me not to know that they live on graft."

Again he stopped, and again he wanted to be believed. "This I tell you, boy, and don't you ever forget it: I never have touched a cent of the dirty police graft myself."

I believed it; I never forgot it. It turned out to be true. Richard Croker never said anything to me that was not true unless it was a statement for publication, and then, if it was a lie, he had a way of letting you know it. He had morality. He was true to his pro- fessional ethics. And he said things that could be used against him; that day, for example.

"But you do make money out of politics," I said as we paused to part at Madison Square.

"Like a business man in business," he answered, hard as nails, "I work for my own pocket all the time."

He faced me down with it, waiting to hear what I would answer, and when I did not answer, when he saw that I was thinking in a whirl, he turned warm and sweet again, held out his soft, small, white hand, and bade me good-by.

"Come and see me again," he invited, holding my hand. "Morn- ings are best, after breakfast, at the Club, but come whenever you like, and if I have time we'll talk it all over."

My days ended as that day did. I went home, told my little family all that I had seen and heard, and tried to find out what I thought about what I had learned. A bore? My wife may have felt it so, but her mother understood.

"Go on. Talk yourself clear," she would say. Sometimes I did, but most often I talked myself unclear. I seem to have had a conception, a diagram, of life which every new discovery wrecked or, if it held, had no place for new facts. Facts. It seems to me now that facts have had to beat their way into my head, banging on my brain like the bullets from a machine gun to get in; and it was only by being hit over and over again that I could let my old ideal and college-made picture of life be blown up and let the new, truer picture be blown in. No wonder some men cannot learn; they are subject only to a few shots, not riddled with volleys, daily, all their lives.

IX

THE GHETTO

Dew is a shower of jewels—in the country, and as it melts in the morning sun it sweetens the air. Not in a city. Police headquarters was in a tenement neighborhood, which seemed to steam on warm nights and sweat by day. I can remember still the damp, smelly chill of the asphalt pavement that greeted me when I came to my office in the early mornings. The tenements stank, the alleys puffed forth the stenches of the night. Slatternly women hung out of the windows to breathe and to gossip or quarrel across the courts; idle men and boys hung, half dressed, over the old iron fences or sat recovering from the night on the stoops of the houses which once had been the fine homes of the old families long since moved uptown. There was a business man in a new building next door to headquarters. He was a handsome, well-dressed wholesale dealer in brass fixtures and plumbers' supplies, and he may have thought he was waiting for buyers, but he was looking for something to happen, like the other neighbors. When a Black Maria drove up and discharged a load of thieves, prostitutes, broken strikers, or gambling-implements, he joined the crowd of loafers, men, women, and children, who gathered to enjoy the sight.

I looked for him, I looked for all the bums, when I turned into Mulberry Street; they were signs of expectancy from which I could guess whether there was news to write. If they were idle I might have time to breathe. I could not be sure, however, till I saw and spoke to the patrolman who acted as doorman of police headquarters. He was always on the stoop, idle, humorous, and Irish. He could not be surprised; he was always expectant and aware. I had to ask him, "Anything doing, Pat?"

"Not yet," he would say, and nodding his wise old head up

and down the street at the reporters, bums, business man, and women at their doors and windows, "They're all out, you see."

If these were not on post, if the reporters were in their offices and the neighbors stood in groups, Pat would answer my question with "Well, as you see, they're all telling—something." And slowly, with proper dignity and police mystery, he would tell me enough to judge whether it was a story I had to write. If I was in doubt, Riis's boy, Max, would settle it.

"What's up, Max?"

"Oh, nothing for you. A slum murder." Or "a roof chase after a thief," or "a baby fell off a fire-escape," or "a gang of toughs broke fences, door-bells, windows all along East Thirty-fifth Street."

The last was a common event. It was as unimportant as similar student pranks are in a college town. Reporters wrote it up only when they had nothing else to report and had to send in something to justify a day of poker. I wrote it once—twice. I had begun to break through my instructions to stick to police politics and Parkhurst exposures and ignore criminal news. I wrote crimes now and then, and the eagerness with which my city editor received them and the cautious way he slipped them into obscure parts of the paper encouraged me to believe that he wanted me gradually to get and so report regular police news that he could broaden the narrow scope of *Evening Post* news. He had been himself a police reporter; he knew the many kinds of stories that came out at headquarters, and he thought that Mr. Godkin would not mind if it was "written right"—not sensationally. Also he knew that I could not help trying it—somehow.

I took from Max that day the exact, outrageous details of the destructive raid of a gang of toughs in East Thirty-fifth Street and I described cheerfully, almost joyously, the breakages those drunks wreaked; I wrote it as nearly as I could in the jolly spirit of the night out. Max was a born seer; he had it all, and I must have reported it with his inspiration and his smile, for it was printed, and a few days later Wright called me down to the office and said that "the editor" had been receiving a stream of indignant letters asking how a paper like the *Post* could report such an outrage against order and property without a single syllable of indignation. I was so flattered that Wright was puzzled and rather angry. I had to remind him that there were two ways to report an incident like that: to express "our" indignation or to arouse the readers' rage; and that I thought the readers' emotion was more literary and more effective than ours.

"Such outrages happen frequently," I said. "The next time one occurs I will write it as an outrage instead of a descriptive narrative, and you will see that no reader will write to us; they will all be satisfied." And I did that. I began my next story, "An outrageous series of depredations was committed by a gang of drunken young hoodlums—" and all through the narrative I sprinkled denunciation. Not a letter, no protest; Wright was convinced, and he convinced Godkin that the editor did not always know the difference between a report and an editorial and that a description is often more editorial in effect than a Godkin editorial. Best of all, "we" let me report more.

Wright's wish and my ambition was to "do" a murder. One day as I was standing beside the doorman waiting for something to happen, we saw a reporter come running out of the basement and dart across into his office. The doorman winked at me and I stepped down to the telegraph bureau. A woman had been killed in Mulberry Bend. I came out and called, "Max!" Out he ran from his office, and we hurried down to the address in Little Italy. There was a crowd standing watching some children dancing beautifully around an organ-grinder who was playing a waltz.

"There's your story," said Max, pointing at the street scene. "Mine is inside."

Max understood. I went inside with him. We saw the dead woman, the blood, the wretched tenement apartment, and we talked to the neighbors, who told us how the murderer came into the court with the organ-grinder, and while the organ played and the children danced, he had seen the woman's face at the window, recognized her, rushed up, and cut her all to pieces; the crowd gathered and were about to beat the man to death when the police came, saved and arrested him. The poker-playing reporters came tearing up, asked for names, ages, and—details. Theirs was the sensational story of the day, all blood and no dancing. Riis wrote it as a melodrama with a moral, an old cry of his: "Mulberry Bend must go." And, by the way, it went. Such was the power of Riis! There's a small park now where Mulberry Bend was.

I wrote the murder as a descriptive sketch of Italian character, beginning with the dance music, bringing the murder in among the children whose cries called the mob; the excitement, the sudden rage, the saving arrest; and ending with the peaceful after-scene of the children dancing in the street, with the mob smiling and forgetting out in the street.

I saw and heard just such a story in Naples long afterward. Lying abed in the front room of the Hotel Santa Lucia, I was listening to the singers and players entertaining the late diners at the fish restaurants on the quay. One tenor sang high and clear above the rest; a pure, sweet voice, it rose over all the scene and seemed to abash all the other music. The whole dock grew quiet to listen. A victory; and the victor profited by, he seemed to abuse, his power. I could hear, I could feel, him swagger and strut, till a baritone in a boat lifted the same aria, took it away from the tenor, who tried to carry on, but hesitated, halted. The baritone laughed, a musical, a gleeful, provoking laugh. The challenge in it roused the tenor, who sang again, the "Santa Lucia," and we listened; I mean that the whole bay turned to him to hear, and the baritone too. A few thrilling bars and the tenor slipped, a false and over-drawn high note, and the baritone mocked it, laughed, and joining the tenor, sang with him, supporting him to the end. The tenor sang another, and another, the baritone playing him, now in unison, now the second; the two made glorious music, but it was a clinch. The baritone—a fisherman putting his boat in order; I got up, looked out, and saw him—the unprofessional singer corrected, helped, and—he spoiled parts of *Pagliacci* beautifully. His was the purer voice, his the more perfect mastery of the music. He yielded only when he liked, when he had to attend to his nets, to his boat. Sometimes the tenor had it alone for a whole song. I tired, I must have slept. Shouts wakened me, the excited cries and curses of a scuffle. Leaping to the window, I saw a writhing crowd on the wide stone stairway down into the water. It was a fight; I could see blows struck, hands flashing, up and down. The police came. . . . There was silence. The diners moved on, the boatmen went back into their boats, the crowd melted. They had seen a stabbing; an arrest, an ambulance call; they had taken sides, judged, and gone about their own businesses. In the dead quiet outside I went back to bed, but before I could sleep I heard a voice pipe up, a few notes of song, which, after a moment, another voice picked up and finished. By dawn the Bay of Naples was singing again, the dock was passing a bar from one opera, and laughing, matching it with a run from another, which made harmony. At sunrise when I glanced out, the sparkling waters and the villainous Neapolitans were shining as innocently as the sun himself.

The *Post* printed a murder, a mere mean murder, as news, and there was no news in it; only life. "We" published crime after that, all sorts of sensational stuff. Why not? Nobody noticed it, as crime. I soon found out that by going with the reporters to a fire or the scene of an accident was a way to see the town and the life of the town.

A synagogue that burned down during a service introduced me to the service; I attended another synagogue, asked questions, and realized that it was a bit of the Old Testament repeated after thousands of years, unchanged. And so I described that service and other services. They fascinated me, those old practices, and the picturesque customs and laws of the old orthodox Jews from Russia and Poland. Max, an East Side Jew himself, told me about them; I read up and talked to funny old, fine rabbis about them, and about their conflicts with their Americanized children. The *Post* observed all the holy days of the Ghetto. There were advance notices of their coming, with descriptions of the preparations and explanations of their sacred, ancient, biblical meaning, and then an account of them as I saw these days and nights observed in the homes and the churches of the poor. A queer mixture of comedy, tragedy, orthodoxy, and revelation, they interested our Christian readers. The uptown Jews complained now and then. Mr. Godkin himself required me once to call personally upon a socially prominent Jewish lady who had written to the editor asking why so much space was given to the ridiculous performances of the ignorant, foreign East Side Jews and none to the uptown Hebrews. I told her. I had the satisfaction of telling her about the comparative beauty, significance, and character of the uptown and downtown Jews. I must have talked well, for she threatened and tried to have me fired, as she put it. Fortunately, the editorial writers were under pressure also from prominent Jews to back up their side of a public controversy over the blackballing of a rich Jew by an uptown social club. "We" were fair to the Jews, editorially, but personally irritated. I was not "fired"; I was sent out to interview the proprietor of a hotel which excluded Jews, and he put his case in a very few words.

"I won't have one," he said. "I have had my experience and so learned that if you let one in because he is exceptional and fine, he will bring in others who are not exceptional, etc. By and by they will occupy the whole house, when the Christians leave. And then, when the Christians don't come any more, the Jews quit you to go where the Christians have gone, and there you are with an empty or a second-class house."

It would have been absurd to discharge me since I at that time was almost a Jew. I had become as infatuated with the Ghetto as eastern boys were with the wild west, and nailed a mazuza on my office door; I went to the synagogue on all the great Jewish holy days; on Yom Kippur I spent the whole twenty-four hours fasting and going from one synagogue to another. The music moved me most, but I knew and could follow with the awful feelings of a Jew the beautiful old ceremonies of the ancient orthodox services. My friends laughed at me; especially the Jews among them scoffed. "You are more Jewish than us Jews," they said, and since I have traveled I realize the absurdity of the American who is more French than the French, more German than the Kaiser. But there were some respecters of my respect. When Israel Zangwill, the author of *Tales of the Ghetto*, came from London to visit New York, he heard about me from Jews and asked me to be his guide for a survey of the East Side; and he saw and he went home and wrote *The Melting Pot*.

The tales of the New York Ghetto were heart-breaking comedies of the tragic conflict between the old and the new, the very old and the very new; in many matters, all at once: religion, class, clothes, manners, customs, language, culture. We all know the difference between youth and age, but our experience is between two generations. Among the Russian and other eastern Jewish families in New York it was an abyss of many generations; it was between parents out of the Middle Ages, sometimes out of the Old Testament days hundreds of years B.C., and the children of the streets of New York today. We saw it everywhere all the time. Responding to a reported suicide, we would pass a synagogue where a score or more of boys were sitting hatless in their old clothes, smoking cigarettes on the steps outside, and their fathers,

UPPER: CHIEF OF POLICE MAX SCHMITTBERGER (N.Y. WORLD NEWS SERVICE). LOWER LEFT: JACOB A. RIIS (FRANCES B. JOHNSTON). LOWER RIGHT: THE REV. CHARLES H. PARKHURST (N.Y. WORLD NEWS SERVICE).

all dressed in black, with their high hats, uncut beards, and temple curls, were going into the synagogues, tearing their hair and rending their garments. The reporters stopped to laugh; and it was comic; the old men, in their thrift, tore the lapels of their coats very carefully, a very little, but they wept tears, real tears. It was a revolution. Their sons were rebels against the law of Moses; they were lost souls, lost to God, the family, and to Israel of old. The police did not understand or sympathize. If there was a fight—and sometimes the fathers did lay hands on their sons, and the tough boys did biff their fathers in the eye; which brought out all the horrified elders of the whole neighborhood and all the sullen youth—when there was a "riot call," the police would rush in and club now the boys, now the parents, and now, in their Irish exasperation, both sides, bloodily and in vain. I used to feel that the blood did not hurt, but the tears did, the weeping and gnashing of teeth of the old Jews who were doomed and knew it. Two, three, thousand years of continuous devotion, courage, and suffering for a cause lost in a generation.

"Oh, Meester Report!" an old woman wailed one evening. "Come into my house and see my childer, my little girls." She seized and pulled me in (me and, I think, Max) up the stairs, weeping, into her clean, dark room, one room, where her three little girls were huddled at the one rear window, from which they—and we—could see a prostitute serving a customer. "*Da, se'en Sie,* there they are watching, always they watch." As the children rose at sight of us and ran away, the old woman told us how her children had always to see that beastly sight. "They count the men who come of a night," she said. "Ninety-three one night." (I shall never forget that number.) "My oldest girl says she will go into that business when she grows up; she says it's a good business, easy, and you can dress and eat and live."

"Why don't you pull down your curtain?" I asked.

"We have no curtain," she wept. "I hang up my dress across, but the childer when I sleep or go out, they crowd under it to see."

"Ask the woman to pull her blind."

"I have," she shrieked. "Oh, I have begged her on my knees, and she won't."

I went over and asked the girl to draw her curtain.

"I won't," she cried in a sudden rage. "That old woman had me raided, and the police—you know it—you know how they hound us now for Parkhurst. They drove me from where I was and I hid in here. That old woman, she sent for the police, and now I have to pay—big—to stay here."

"All right, all right," I shouted to down her mad shrieks of rage. "But her children look—"

"I don't care," the girl yelled back. "It serves her right, that old devil. I will get even. I will ruin her nasty children, as she says."

I threatened to "make" the police close her up, and down she came, all in tears.

"Don't, please don't, Mr. Reporter," she cried. "They'll run me out, the cops will, for you; I know; and I'll have a hell of a time to get found again by my customers. I'm doing well here now again; I can soon open a house maybe and get some girls and be respectable myself if—"

So we compromised. She pinned up a blanket on her window, and I promised not to have her driven out. When I came out into the street there was a patrolman at the door.

"What's the kick?" he asked.

I told him briefly all about it; he knew, nodded. "What's to be done?" he asked.

"Nothing," I answered hastily. "I have fixed it. Don't do anything. It's all all right now."

It wasn't, of course. Nothing was all right. Neither in this case, nor in prostitution generally, nor in the strikes—is there any right —or wrong; not that the police could do, nor I, nor the *Post*, nor Dr. Parkhurst. It was, it is, all a struggle between conflicting interests, between two blind opposite sides, neither of which is right or wrong.

X

THE LEXOW POLICE INVESTIGATION

NEW YORK in the nineties was about what Tennessee is now-adays, a provincial, moral community with a conscience, to which Dr. Parkhurst and the reformers could appeal, as they did, with fine blind faith. His mind represented our mind. He and we, the people, took a moral view of politics, government, business—everything. I do not mean that we were all good men and women. Some of us did some pretty bad things ourselves now and then, but we all meant well and so, on the whole, we felt that we were a pretty good people who wished for, voted for, and deserved a good government. We did not define "good" or "good government"; we did not have to. Everybody knew what was bad; our city government was bad. We knew that in a general way, and Dr. Parkhurst was making our vague sense of evil acutely definite by the simplest sort of moral revelation and reasoning.

He pointed out that there was a gambling-house running in the Tenderloin. Gambling is bad. No doubt about that; even gamblers admitted that gambling was wrong. There was a law against it. The law was all right; nobody doubted the righteousness of such a law. All that was necessary was to enforce that law, and we had a police force to do it. But when Dr. Parkhurst called upon the police to close the said gambling-house they would not do it, or if they made a raid, it was only to find the place all ready for them: with no business doing. Dr. Parkhurst said and we believed that the police had warned the gamblers. Why? Huh, we could guess the answer, and Dr. Parkhurst said it right out: bribery.

So it was with prostitution, which likewise is bad and against the law. There was some doubt, I remember, about the wisdom of this law. "Prostitution always has been, is everywhere, and always will be." This we heard, and it did seem cruel to hound these wretched women to distress. But Dr. Parkhurst was an able general, a clever strategist; he changed the question. Prostitution was in itself bad enough, but why should the police, who are there to enforce the law, permit these bad women to walk the streets and run their bad houses? And the answer was again: bribery.

The saloons, too. Drinking is bad. True, some of us drink; the best clubs of the best people have bars; and the saloon is the poor man's club. But the law allowed for all that. The law only regulated the liquor business; it designated reasonable opening and closing hours. If it was wrong in any particular, the remedy was to change the law. But why should the police, appointed and well paid to enforce the law, assume to amend it and protect the saloons? Bribery.

Bribery was the answer to all our questions, and bribery was wrong. Wasn't it? I never heard but one man in all those days defend bribery, and that one was an Englishman in the City Club. "If," he said to a group of us reformers, "if you are promoting a business and you encounter in the state an obstacle, you will bribe it out of your way just as you would blast a rock." I remember this because it was so "un-American" to our way of thinking. Americans did that, but even the blasters themselves did not say or think it. Our bribers in New York declared that they were "held up" by the police and the politicians; the gamblers, prostitutes, and liquor dealers were blackmailed. Whichever it was, however, whether blackmail or bribery, we were learning—Dr. Parkhurst and the investigators, I as a reporter, the people as newspaper readers—we were learning with astonishment that it was these corrupt practices that were making our good government bad.

"Well, and what are you going to do about it?"

Richard Croker asked that question. He asked it often, and I knew the spirit in which he put it to me, to us reporters. The old man, overwhelmed by the evidence produced and knowing how old and established the complicated system of bribery was, really wondered what could be done about it. He felt it was bad; our corruptest men were not cynical like that good Englishman. Croker was intellectually and morally a citizen of the civilization of New York. He had been as a youth a gang leader, the tough chief of the famous Tunnel Gang, had killed his man, and was the very type

THE LEXOW POLICE INVESTIGATION

that comes up now out of the depths of our cities as bandits, or politicians, or go-getters in business. But, like a modern gunman, he had the same moral ideas as the rest of us. A bandit acknowledges our laws against robbery, and Croker never did and never could have defended bribery. When some reporter betrayed his confidence and reported his puzzled questioning it was presented and taken as a defiant challenge. But as he used to say it to me, it was an awed, a moral, question; and it served a moral purpose.

Dr. Parkhurst and the rest of us exposers and reformers were merely destructive. We were showing up the evils of our police and our Tammany politics and government. Richard Croker's exclamation, the sensation of a day, was a call upon us to do something constructive. What? We did not know. I mean that I did not find anybody with any intelligent plan for the reform of a city. There may have been, there must have been, some individuals among the million or so of people in New York who knew what to do, and it was my job as a reporter to seek them out and report them, but within the limit of my search I found not one. I could not interview radicals, of course; there were not many of them anyhow; they were only faddists: coöperators, socialists (a few), anarchists, whom nobody would listen to. The *Post* asked me to go to the meetings and the offices of the educated leaders of law and the other professions, business, and—in brief—the leaders of thought and culture in New York, and I remember jotting down a note, long since lost, to the effect that there was no more science in society than there was in the universities; there was no political science, no science of economics and no understanding of the psychology of "bribery and corruption"; no thought-out plan for municipal reform. Facts we had, but no generalizations and no capacity to generalize. I felt the need, my old need, of a picture of the government as corrupted, but nobody could help me to paint one.

Dr. Parkhurst's constructive ideas were as simple and moral as his charges, which he continued to deliver with force and effect. His analysis of his facts was that, since only bad men would take bribes and since the Tammany police and political officers not only accepted but exacted them, our government was bad because there were bad men in office. And the cure was to discharge the bad men and elect good men. That expressed our popular mind; our educated men knew no better; so that was becoming the issue. The problem was to find good men to nominate and elect. Our old habit of turning out the party in power and electing the other party, which was good enough in national elections, would not do in our exceptionally bad city of New York. Our Republicans were almost as bad as our Democrats. We knew this by experience. In past crises of this moral kind, we had let the Republican State government interfere in the city government—without any relief. We had bi-partisan boards, like our police commissioners, and they had either winked at the corrupt practices of the Democrats or divided the graft. We were now for non-partisan boards, mayors, and a "civil service reform," modeled upon the British permanent officials. Mr. Godkin and the *Post* were leaders in the civil service reform movement, as Theodore Roosevelt was. But the great idea that grew out of our disgust with the politicians of both parties was to elect as mayor not a politician but a business man who would give us a good business government.

The first step taken, however, was to demand of the State Legislature the appointment of a commission to investigate the charges of Dr. Parkhurst and the reformers against the city police. I was sent to Albany on this issue, and my first sight of that capital brought back vividly to my memory the California Legislature when I played around Sacramento with my boy chum, Charlie Marple, the page. It was the same picture. The two deliberative bodies looked alike, they sounded alike, they acted alike; and, as I worked in with the other reporters to inquire about the likelihood and the probable personnel of the police inquiry, I realized that they were organized and run alike. I heard the same honest, cynical comments. The two parties, Republican and Democratic, were both tempted to send down the investigating committee, the Republicans because there was a chance to win the city away from the Democrats, the Democrats because a controlled commission might whitewash Tammany and shut up Dr. Parkhurst. And a whitewash was what was planned and expected. But the Democrats were afraid that the inquiry might escape control and really show up what everybody in Albany seemed to know existed, and they threatened and the Republican leaders dreaded a revelation of the Republicans involved. It was "playing with fire," as the leaders of both parties said, and not only to one another; they said it to us reporters. They assumed that we knew how things were, and no doubt the other reporters did know. I did not. I was learning about the city police, of course, but I was far from taking them as a matter of course as the Albany correspondents took them. I could hardly believe what I knew of New York, and as to Albany—I was willing, I pretended, to accept all I heard, but I simply was not able to. I went home in a state of mind that is now familiar to me: trying to digest what I could neither doubt nor believe.

I believed and I reported to my paper that the Legislature would appoint an investigating commission, which would be stacked to find everything as near all right as one can expect it to be in a great city. And a commission was appointed, the famous Lexow bi-partisan committee. Whether Senator Lexow, the chairman, had instructions to go easy or hard I do not know, but the expectation of a whitewash had aroused a sneering, laughing public opinion which Dr. Parkhurst, the reformers, and the press whipped up to indignation. The committee had to do something; some show of earnestness became politically essential, and they chose as their attorney William Travers Jerome, who could not be pulled off. He was a young man of good old New York antecedents, great dash, vigor, and courage, and he knew conditions like an insider. He knew, for example, what he was up against, the pulls, the threats, the dangers he must fight through, but also he believed that if he succeeded he would have a career in law and in politics. He set out to succeed. He chose assistants, detectives, friends he could trust. He called for evidence from Dr. Parkhurst and his society, from the public, from the police and the underworld. As soon as he had a few witnesses he began his public hearings, which were the news of the day, for Jerome himself was a picturesque figure, the solemn commissioners were a study, and the witnesses and their facts and their language were curious and sensational. Back of the hearings too there were goings-on which leaked. Jerome used police methods, the practices of prosecuting attorneys. With power, not only to hear, but to indict and try, he bargained with his witnesses; he could send them to prison, he could let them go, he could compromise, according as they told the truth and gave away the system and their colleagues, which was called squealing, or preserved their "honor among thieves." So he threatened, he traded—he "fought," as I afterward saw other investigators "fight the devil with fire." Evidently he had to fight both the enemy before him and his friends behind. There were delays —no sittings for days—and we heard rumors of "differences" among the commissioners and their attorneys; the power of the guilty police officers was very great. They had behind them the most powerful politicians in both parties, whom they could threaten, in their turn, to involve in their testimony; and the politicians could with threats call upon statesmen and business men high up. Once started, no one could foretell where the exposure would stop; it was indeed like a fire. A sensation for the public, that investigation was a worry, a tragedy, for the underworld and indeed for the upper world. Jerome must have had to compromise. The pressure upon him and the commission was irresistible, and my guess was that he had to agree to keep the revelations within the bounds of the police and their dealings with vice and small business. Anyway he did not go beyond that limit, which was set by the resolution under which the committee was appointed; he may have let some individuals escape, but Jerome showed enough.

I was not at many of the hearings; my post was at police head-quarters, and my job was to furnish the background and the con-nections and meaning of the evidence as it came out. Only on great days did I go to sit and watch and hear with staring eyes and staring mind. For it was news to me, as it must have been even to the crooks themselves, to see that what we had heard was true, to be forced to imagine what we knew, to be enabled to generalize our facts and fill out our imperfect picture of police corruption. The witnesses were policemen, police victims, small business men, saloon-keepers, crooks, at first, and each one told something you had known of others' doing or suffering. To Jerome this early testimony was meant only to involve and so force other, higher officials to testify; and sending for them, he would "put them through the third degree" to compel them to "come through." Many did. Clubber Williams, the first inspector, had to account for his riches—he had more money, more property, than he could have saved out of his salary. He had to admit that, but he said that he had earned it by speculation in some "lots [of land] in Japan." Most of the guilty witnesses dodged in some such way as that, but so many of them admitted so much and sketched out so many different angles of the truth that the newspaper readers,

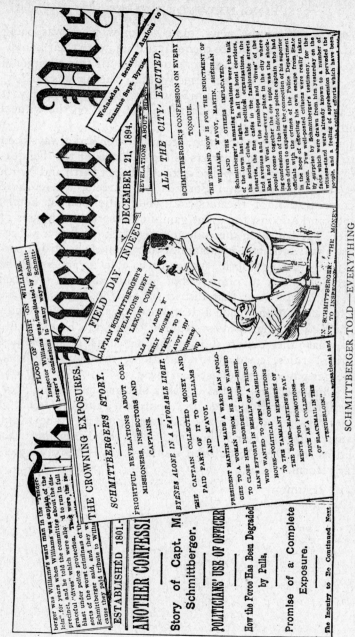

SCHMITTBERGER TOLD—EVERYTHING

From the New York *Evening Post* and the New York *Tribune*, December 22, 1894

reading every line of the news, came to know what was being concealed. And as for the police themselves, they, with their knowledge and their imaginations at work to clothe all this testimony, they felt, as I knew from them directly, that "the jig was up."

"They've got us," said Captain Schmittberger one dark day at police headquarters. And a few days later he went on the witness stand and told—everything.

A tall, powerful, handsome man, Schmittberger had always been known to us at police headquarters as the collector of the Tenderloin precinct, which was the police district between Fifth and Ninth Avenues, Twenty-eighth and Forty-eighth Streets, where there was a concentration of theaters and vaudeville houses, hotels, restaurants, and saloons, the great gambling-resorts and houses of prostitution. He had been the collector of "blackmail" as a policeman, ward man, and now, as captain of the precinct, he still superintended the gathering of bribe moneys, which, by arrangement, he distributed—so much to himself and his subordinates, so much more to the inspector of that district. When he went upon the stand in full uniform he made a clean breast of all his own doings, and the king-pin in the whole system of police graft, he knew and described what other officers did in other precincts, giving names, dates, prices, rules, customs, conversations, manners. In brief, Schmittberger gave the whole system away.

After Schmittberger's "squeal," other officers "laid down," too. Byrnes resigned; other "higher-ups" confessed; and the defeat of Tammany was assured. Even the bad people, the poor and mean, who always followed their leaders and voted the Tammany ticket —as solid as the Democratic solid south—even Tammany voters voted for reform.

XI

ROOSEVELT AND REFORM

Tᴴᴇ man the reformers united upon for mayor was William L. Strong. He was a merchant; he knew nothing of politics, and the politicians knew nothing of him. He was an ideal candidate, therefore. He was the good business man who would throw out the rascally politicians and give us a good business administration. For him were the "honest Republicans," the fine old aristocratic Democrats, the reformers called goo-goos after their Good Government Clubs, the "decent" newspapers, and the good people generally. Richard Croker, who managed the fight against us, had his own machine, parts of the Republican machine, the saloons, gambling-houses, all vice interests, sportsmen generally, and to my curious surprise many business men—the ablest, biggest, richest business men in local business: gas, transportation, banks, and the great financiers.

"Sure," said Croker one night to me, "your reformer friends talk about business, but the business men who have business with the city government and so know about the Tammany administration—they are with us."

That was during the campaign. Croker had plenty of money from his rich backers and assurance from himself. "You won't get a look-in," he declared. He talked, he looked, he behaved in a way that convinced me, for one, that our ticket would be defeated and Tammany and the crooked police vindicated. I did not report the reform side of the fight; the political reporters covered that and indeed the whole campaign, but I used to go out of personal curiosity to reform headquarters, and the managers there tried to, but could not, radiate confidence as Croker did. They could say that we were sure to win, but they looked anxious and spoke dubiously; their willing lies did not ring true. The first time I was persuaded that we would win was after the polls closed on Election Day, when, as the counting of the ballots began, Croker received us, as his habit was on Election Day, and calmly told us, not only that Tammany was beaten, but by how large a majority.

I was so astonished, so disappointed in Croker, whom I had believed, that I hung back as the other reporters ran off—not to quote the boss; it was understood that Croker's figures were not for publication, but—to whisper the "truth" to their chiefs. Croker saw me, came over, and laid his hand on my shoulder.

"You look flabbergasted," he said. "Why? You knew all along that it was a reform wave, didn't you?"

"How should I know that?" I protested.

"A political reporter, like a politician, has to know politics," he smiled. "The betting showed; the gamblers have our figures. But one trip of inquiry into any Tammany ward would have told you that Tammany voters were going to vote against us this year, and one ward is all wards in a city. Our people could not stand the rotten police corruption. They'll be back at the next election; they can't stand reform either. But this year they—as you see—" and, giving me a gentle shove, he added, smiling kindly, "as you ought to have known, boy."

The other reporters did, they said. "What do you do, read the papers or work for them?" one of them asked me, when I had sounded him.

Police headquarters was the proper background for my humiliation the day after the election. Everybody there was humble, too, and I sympathized with them. But they did not sympathize with me. Byrnes had nothing to say; Clubber Williams, hate in his eyes, stood with some papers in his hand to watch me come into the hall.

"Well, are you satisfied now?" he sneered at me.

"Not yet," I answered boldly, but I did not feel bold. I felt ashamed. Would I never see through the appearance of things to the facts? Never get past the lie to the truth? Victory was defeat for me. Dr. Parkhurst was calmly pleased. His attention, however, was fixed on the next step, the appointments to the police board. The fight was not over, he said; Mayor Strong was making "deals." Everybody was pulling and hauling upon him to do this or not do that, to name this man and not to name the other; the police board he had to appoint was the bone of contention among the groups who thought and said that they had "made him mayor." A business man, he did not know the ethics or the ways of politics. He gave promises that could not be kept because they were contradictory. I saw enough of it to realize that reform politics was still politics, only worse; reformers were not so smooth as the professional politicians, and it seemed to me they were not so honest—which was a very confusing theory to me. I remember having a talk with Jake Riis about it. His mind was single and simple. He declared that God was running it.

"Theodore Roosevelt is the man for president of the police board, and God will attend to his appointment. That's all I want to know. I don't care who the other commissioners are. T.R. is enough."

My academic interest in the difference between reformers and politicians did not interest him; my suggestion that maybe the ethics of politics and the ethics of business were different and that, therefore, a man like Croker was better in politics than a merchant like Strong, whereas a business man in business would be better than Croker—that bored Riis. He let me express my thoughts, but after all, I could think aloud more clearly with my mother-in-law than with Riis and other reporters. She was neither religious nor cynical. But Riis was right, in a way.

Roosevelt was appointed police commissioner. We got the news from our offices one day; Riis came shouting it out in the street, and within an hour up walked T.R. and three other gentlemen: Frederick Dent Grant, the son of General Grant; Avery D. Andrews, an ex-army officer, and Andrew D. Parker. I said that they walked. I mean that they came on foot; and three of them did walk, but T.R. ran. He came ahead down the street; he yelled, "Hello, Jake," to Riis, and running up the stairs to the front door of police headquarters, he waved us reporters to follow. We did. With the police officials standing around watching, the new board went up to the second story, where the old commissioners were waiting in their offices. T.R. seized Riis, who introduced me, and still running, he asked questions: "Where are our offices? Where is the board room? What do we do first?" Out of the half-heard answers he gathered the way to the board room, where the old commissioners waited, like three of the new commissioners, stiff, formal, and dignified. Not T.R. He introduced himself, his colleagues, with hand-shakes and then called a meeting of the new board; had himself elected president—this had been prearranged —and then adjourned to pull Riis and me with him into his office.

"Now, then, what'll we do?"

It was all breathless and sudden, but Riis and I were soon describing the situation to him, telling him which higher officers to consult, which to ignore and punish; what the forms were, the customs, rules, methods. It was just as if we three were the police board, T.R., Riis, and I, and as we got T.R. calmed down we made him promise to go a bit slow, to consult with his colleagues also. Then we went out into the hall, and there stood the three other commissioners together, waiting for us to go so that they could see T.R.

They did not like it a bit, as Parker told me afterward. "Thinks he's the whole board," he said; and the subsequent split of the commission was started right then and there. We warned T.R., and he tried to make it up to his colleagues. He consulted them when he thought of it, but Grant and Andrews did not know anything about the police, and Parker, a New Yorker, familiar with the conditions, had it in for T.R., who, he said, was stepping up on the police job as a ladder to something higher.

"Of course," Riis answered, when I told him Parker's opinion. "Teddy is bound for the presidency."

My theory of T.R. was that he merely forgot the courtesies due the board. He had been asked to take the police job, he had been urged to clean out the department, and considering it with his friends, had been thinking of it as his job, his alone, forgetting that it was a board; and so, when the others were appointed, he kept forgetting them. He was so intent upon the task that he did not think of his associates or anything else.

"Except the presidency," Riis would roar, and he was so happy in his certainty that God and T.R. were working toward that end that I challenged him one day.

"Let's ask him," I said.

Riis sprang up, and with a "come on" to me, dashed across the street up to T.R.'s office. And bursting in, Riis did ask him to settle our dispute. Was he working toward the presidency? The effect was frightening.

T.R. leaped to his feet, ran around his desk, and fists clenched,

OUR BOYS.

JACOB.

ONE of the nicest little boys we know is Jacob. He is very fond of another little boy named Teddy, and likes nothing better than to be with him. Teddy is a scrapper, and breaks loose every once in a while, whereas Jacob is very mild. But they get along beautifully

Jacob does not care much for toys, but likes to play with Teddy's silk hat Also any other thing that Teddy has that has been consecrated by use.

Jacob writes nice compositions and makes them into books. Once he wrote a piece about himself and then he wrote a piece about Teddy. The first was called an autobiography and the second a campaign document. Jacob is a very frank little boy and tells all he knows and feels, which sometimes makes you sorry for him. But, then again, you can't help but like him, because he loves Teddy so. Not because Teddy ought to be loved like this, but just because Jacob loves him.

Life

T.R. HAD FEW FRIENDS AS DEVOTED AS JAKE RIIS

teeth bared, he seemed about to strike or throttle Riis, who cowered away, amazed.

"Don't you dare ask me that," T.R. yelled at Riis. "Don't you put such ideas into my head. No friend of mine would ever say a thing like that, you—you—"

Riis's shocked face or T.R.'s recollection that he had few friends as devoted as Jake Riis halted him. He backed away, came up again to Riis, and put his arm over his shoulder. Then he beckoned me close and in an awed tone of voice explained.

"Never, never, you must never either of you ever remind a man at work on a political job that he may be president. It almost always kills him politically. He loses his nerve; he can't do his work; he gives up the very traits that are making him a possibility. I, for instance, am going to do great things here, hard things that require all the courage, ability, work that I am capable of, and I can do them if I think of them alone. But if I get to thinking of what it might lead to—"

He stopped, held us off, and looked into our faces with his face screwed up into a knot, as with lowered voice he said slowly: "I must be wanting to be president. Every young man does. But I won't let myself think of it; I must not, because if I do, I will begin to work for it, I'll be careful, calculating, cautious in word and act, and so—I'll beat myself. See?"

Again he looked at us as if we were enemies; then he threw us away from him and went back to his desk.

"Go on away, now," he said, "and don't you ever mention the— don't you ever mention that to me again."

As Riis and I were going, crestfallen, thoughtful, down the stairs, I said, "Well, you win, Riis."

"I do not," he answered, hot; so loyal was Jake Riis; but he was honest, too. He hurried on ahead, and we never mentioned the matter again even to each other.

The first thing the new police board did was to order the police to enforce the law, and when they did not obey, the second step was taken: the removal of the bad police officers. Byrnes had retired voluntarily, unprompted, and the day of his going is memorable to me. There were rumors of his retirement, and many business men and politicians called quietly, saw him, and as quietly slipped away. "What will happen to us now I dread to think," said a banker, who really looked frightened. I believe there were people who felt that all that stood between them and crime was this mysterious master of the police force. But thieves came too, and they were more frightened than the honest men. They did not call on Byrnes; they simply walked along the streets around police headquarters, and one man sat on the steps going up to the high stoop of the building. He sat with his head in his hands, his elbows on his knees, and seemed to heed nothing. I asked Tom the door-man who he was.

"Oh, just an old dip that the old man was good to sometimes. Thinks the world is coming to an end."

The crooks and the business men, and for that matter many of the police and police reporters (including myself), did not under-stand that it was not Byrnes but a well-nigh universal system that they were living and working under, a system of compromise and privilege for crooks and detectives that "the inspector" inherited and left intact. When Superintendent Byrnes retired that day and walked without good-by to any of us out of his office forever, men stopped and stood to watch him go, silent, respectful, sad, and the next day the world went on as usual.

Roosevelt had to decide whether to let the other higher officers retire on a pension or be tried. Some of the commissioners and public opinion were for punishment. "Discipline," they said; "re-venge," they meant. Riis and I were against trials. With Riis, the veteran police reporter, it was sentiment, I think. He was fond even of some of the worst men. My attitude was instinctive: against punishment; but it was not clear and straight. There were excep-tions. I wanted satisfaction from the clubber, Williams, and I told T.R. I wanted to be present when he fired him, and why. My argu-ment, however, was that trials were long, the law technical and unsure, and T.R., who was swift, stood in the main for retirement. And he was strengthened by his experience. As he began to send for officers and tell them they must go; either reluctantly resign, retire, or be put on trial, "pull" interfered, and not political pull alone.

"Hey, there," he yelled to me from his window one day, "come up here." I ran upstairs to his outer office, which was filled with all sorts of respectable people, evidently business men, lawyers, doctors, women, and two priests. Waving his hand around the circle of them, he squeezed through his teeth aloud: "I just want you to see the kind of people that are coming here to intercede for proven crooks. Come on, come into my office and listen to the reasons they give for letting bribers, clubbers, and crime-protectors stay on the police force and go on grafting on the public."

Of course he spoiled the sport for that day and that crowd. I sat with him awhile, but the callers who had heard what he said could not make their pleas very well. They were too embarrassed. But on other days when I saw a "string of pulls" calling on him, I went up and listened. They were amusing; they did not know what they were talking about. Most of them merely liked personally some officer who had asked them to intercede to keep him on the force. What I got out of it was that so-called "political influence" is really a common, human plea which politicians use best. The average good citizen tried to tell T.R. that the man he was pulling for was a good officer lied about. Since the officers T.R. was firing were all men fully exposed by the Lexow Committee—the worst of them—the good citizens' appeals only angered him. But when a politician came breezing in and said: "Sure, Mr. President, Captain Bill's a crook; most of 'em are crooks; most of all of us is so crooked we get cramps in our beds at night, but, hell, why pick on Bill? He knows you're straight, and if you ask him to go straight he will. Sure he will. I know Bill since he was a kid. All I ask you is to call him up, look into his face, and tell him what to do. You'll see: he'll do it."

That sort of song and dance would tempt us; and I mean us. "What'll we do?" T.R. would say after a plea like that from some regular Tammany leader, and I could not help laughing. I knew just how the commissioner felt. I wanted to see Captain Bill and ask him to stay and help reform, as T.R. did; and sometimes we did send for Bill, and, well, sometimes T.R. kept a proved crook for a crooked politician. The reporters observed and reported it, too.

Looking back at it now, I can see it better than I could then. I can see that the police assumed that T.R., being a reformer, might respond to a clergyman's appeal or "a word" from a business man or any other "good man" and be affronted by the plea of a politician, especially a Tammany opponent of reform. They did not know what false and offensive reasonings good people make. It was long before they learned that—for some reason, which they never did discover—the reform commission was, like the old board, subject to political pull. When they did learn it the character of the callers at police headquarters changed. Politicians came after that, prominent leaders of all parties—and failed often; they gave political reasons for mercy. The police never learned what it was that "got" T.R.

"What gets me," said an old police sergeant (the wisest rank on the police force), "what I can't unpuzzle is why he'll listen to Tim Sullivan and throw down the reform Mayor himself and laugh a Platt Republican leader out of his office; and then turn right around and tell Charlie Murphy [a Tammany leader] to go sing his song to the high marines in the harbor, and do a favor for Lem Quigg [a Platt machine leader] up the river."

Nor could I solve the riddle, any more than T.R. could. He thought he was carrying out the reform policy of "throwing out" the crooks and enforcing the law. He was having a hard time of it. He could not make the policemen on their beats close up the saloons at the closing hour. He told them to. He issued formal orders, he made personal appeals, and nothing happened. Talking it over, we guessed that the rank and file would not obey the board because the higher officers, like Inspector Williams, who gave T.R.'s instructions to their men, did so with a wink. By way of experiment I suggested that he force Williams out and then see what happened in his district. He agreed. He knew what had been disclosed of Williams's share in the blackmail fund; everybody remembered the rich inspector's "lots in Japan." I told about my experiences with this man and his brutal clubbings of East Side strikers.

"I said I'd be here at police headquarters till he was fired," I concluded.

"Did you?" T.R. asked. "Well, you will. You'll be right here in this room."

A few days later T.R. threw up his second-story window, leaned out, and yelled his famous cowboy call, "Hi yi yi." He often summoned Riis and me thus. When we poked our heads out of my window across the street this time, he called me alone.

"Not you, Jake. Steffens, come up here."

I hurried over up to his office, and there in the hall stood Williams, who glared as usual at me with eyes that looked like clubs. I passed on in to T.R., who bade me sit down on a certain chair at the back of the room. Then he summoned Williams and fired him; that is to say, he forced him to retire. It was done almost without words. Williams had been warned; the papers were all ready. He "signed there," rose, turned and looked at me, and disappeared.

He did, this one clubber; he went, but not the clubs. Skulls are still cracked—literally—in New York. My triumph was personal, mean, and incomplete.

T.R.'s was a little better. With Williams out and an acting inspector in command of that district, a young, inexperienced patrolman "took a chance," as he said. One night this young cop walked into Pat Callighan's saloon, laid his hand on Pat, and told him he was under arrest. Now Pat was a man of strength as well as power, and his gang was all there. He fought, the gang fought, there was a boozy, bloody battle, but the young cop with his night stick laid out enough men to hold off the rest. He arrested Pat Callighan. I saw this in the morning papers, and when T.R. arrived at his office I showed him his chance.

"Promote that cop," I said, "and you will show all the young policemen that you mean business. Pat Callighan is a sacred person in the underworld, a symbol. The key to his saloon was thrown in the river when he opened, and his door has never been locked since. If a patrolman dare arrest Pat and can get away with it, then all saloons can be closed."

T.R. did it. This young policeman was too newly appointed to be eligible for promotion, and there was strong opposition in the name of the law, but T.R. had announced that he would make a roundsman of this, the first policeman to believe him, and the board consented.

And sure enough, other policemen of all ranks began to obey the orders of the board. Some saloons and some gamblers were raided—not many; not all laws were enforced. T.R. went about at night with Riis as his guide to see the police at work. He had some bizarre experiences. He caught men off post, talking together; he caught them in all sorts of misconduct and had funny, picturesque adventures, which Riis described to all of us (so fair was he as a reporter) and which we all wrote to the amusement of newspaper readers. But what T.R. was really doing—the idea of Riis in proposing it—was to talk personally with the individual policemen and ask them to believe in him, in the law, which they were to enforce. T.R. knew, he said, the power they were up against, the tremendous, enduring power of organized evil, but he promised he would take care of them.

"It worked—a little," he used to say. "I told them that we

would back up and not only defend but promote those that served on our side, and I threatened we would pursue and punish those that served on the other side."

This he said, and while he was saying it, he was planning to "fire" Schmittberger, the captain, the key to the old system.

XII

SCHMITTBERGER: AN HONEST POLICEMAN

THE next summer after the Lexow investigation and Tammany defeat, I lived as a commuter at Riverside-on-Hudson. Those were bicycle days, and one morning as my wife and I were wheeling we met and passed Captain Schmittberger, the police Samson who had pulled down the whole structure of police graft and still lived. He had been sent to Goatville, as the cops called a remote country precinct like this where there was "nothing doing." He did not greet me. I saw him look, recognize me, and turn away. He had not forgotten that all through the investigation I had sung one monotonous song, day in and day out. "Get Schmittberger." If he would squeal he would deliver everybody and everything. Therefore, "Get Schmittberger."

"What a handsome man he is on his fine horse!" my wife said, and indeed he was a handsome big fellow, whether afoot or ahorseback. His beauty had made him what he was, won him his appointment to the police force, won him favors and promotions —his beauty and his honesty.

We saw him often after that. No matter how far we rode or into what lanes and by-ways we explored, we met Schmittberger always out somewhere on his mounted patrol, and I reported to Roosevelt and Parker that Schmittberger seemed to be always on the job. T.R. made no answer. Parker, a great walker, said he knew it. "Every time I go up that way," he mused, "I meet the captain; he is all over the shop, and there isn't a thing doing up there, not a saloon open, not a law broken."

One night a big river launch that belonged to a man who lived in our boarding-house was robbed at its moorings. I reported to police headquarters in the morning, and that evening Schmittberger rode up, tied his horse, and looked over the launch. When he came back I was sitting in a hammock near by, and I asked him what he could do about it.

"Not much," he answered mechanically as he remounted. "I've sent down an old ward man of mine to find out what they know about the gangs that are working the waters, but, you know, we can't do what we used to do. No connections any more. I don't believe any of us knows now who the river thieves are."

"Do you regret the old days, Captain?" I asked.

"I do not," he replied quick and straight from deep inside. "I wouldn't go through what I have gone through for—for a million times what there was in it for me. Never again. Not on your life."

There was something in the ring of this that tempted me to go on; not what he said, but his vehemence struck me as genuine.

"Get down, Captain," I said. "Let's have a talk."

He hesitated, gave me a look of surprise, inquiry—I could not quite read it, but he got down, tied his horse, and dropping into a big wicker chair, lighted a huge cigar.

"You don't believe me," he began. "And it is tough. We had bought that big house we live in, the Missus and me, and I had been paying off the mortgage till there was only a few thousands left. I'd 'a' paid it in a year more. Now it will never be cleared."

There was something conclusive about that "never," as if his mind was made up to no more graft.

"Can't save enough on your salary alone to settle it, slowly, sometime?"

"Salary!" he exclaimed. The police were well paid; a captain's pay was pretty good. But he said it wasn't good enough to cover more than living-expenses and interest in such a big house as he had chosen. Couldn't he sell that house and buy a simpler one?

"The Missus likes this one," he said, with finality again. "It's our home."

It was my turn to hesitate, but I decided to drive in the probe and see.

"But, Captain, we get it pretty straight that some of the cops are taking it again, a little, here and there, carefully—"

"Not me," he declared with a lifting in horror of his two hands. "Never again, never again." He even looked frightened, and as I stared back at him wondering, he sat up, and astonished, he said: "Say, you don't know what I've been through. You never had your kids sit silent at dinner, nudge one another on, and so pass the buck to the big boy you always kind of—wanted the respect of, and then had him swallow a lump and blurt out, 'I say, Pop, is it true this stuff they are saying? It's all lies, ain't it!'"

He couldn't go on, and I didn't want him to. I had forgotten, when I wrote my hounding facts and suspicions, that there were families back of these crooks, and children at home who sat silent, wondering at table whether their fathers were what the newspapers said.

"The other kids ask them at school," the captain blubbered, "and so they ask you." And when he got no help from me, no belief, he explained. "And you ask me if I'll do it again!"

"How did you ever get into it, Captain?" I asked to ease him. He told me.

He was a German boy, born, if I remember aright, in Hoboken, and apprenticed to a pastry cook in New York. Tall, rosy, frank, he must have been a pleasant sight in his white cap and jacket. "Customers liked me," he said; so he was sent out to deliver his fresh cookies at houses and restaurants near by. One day a couple of Tammany leaders admired him to his face, joked him on his height and good looks. "Like to see you in a police uniform," one of them jested, and Max, the German pastry cook, was so pleased, so surprised and eager, that the two "good fellows" agreed there and then to get him on the force.

"Won't cost you a cent either," one of them said. Max did not know then that there was a fixed price for an appointment on the force, a fee paid for pull. He had to study for an examination; he could hardly believe that he would ever be called, but he prepared under a man who made it his business to cram Tammany candidates, and to his joy and amazement, he was called, passed, and appointed. He was put through an unusually long, severe initiation at the hands of the older policemen in his station barracks. His account of it showed that they regarded him as an innocent, liked him, but were amused at his simplicity. He took it good-naturedly and so became popular with the men, and he was so naïve and obedient that his officers preferred him, especially for decorative posts, street corners where he showed off well.

"There was no traffic squad in those days," he explained, "but I was set up in the middle of Broadway and Thirty-fourth Street, where I got to know lots of people, who used to say, 'Hello, Max.' They laughed, but they were for me. They used to put in good words for me with my captain. Gosh, but I did like being a policeman. Do yet."

His night beat was on a side street where there were many houses of prostitution. He had no instructions, and he knew nothing of any laws against such places. He did nothing; he saw nothing for a policeman to do. On the next post, farther west, where the colored quarter began, there was always activity, and Schmittberger used to hang around that end of his beat to watch and envy the old policeman there his tussles with the niggers, who drank, sang songs, danced, and cut one another up with razors. One evening as he was pacing his own quiet tour a colored girl ran down the steps and with a "Here, officer," pressed a ten-dollar bill into his hand and darted back into the house. Not understanding it, Schmittberger went on down to the old cop, showed him the money, and described how he got it.

"Sure," said the veteran, "that's what the Cap put you on that fat job for: to make a little on the side." And he explained how, though the ward man collected the regular pay monthly from houses of prostitution, the patrolman on all such streets "got his" now and then.

"So the captain knows about it?"

"Sure thing. He knows everything like that, knows what every post in the precinct is worth, and his putting you where you are shows he likes you and wants to feed you up."

"But why?" Schmittberger asked, who did not understand what the money was for, and he laughed when he told how the old cop misunderstood his question.

"What for!" he exclaimed. "Oh, it's because you're so thin. He wants to fatten you up."

"But," Schmittberger related, "I had plenty to eat, so I turned in the money to the captain. That is, I started to. I laid it down on his desk and was beginning to tell him about it when he jumped down my throat. What did I take him for? And where did I get my nerve? I was scared; I thought the old cop had put up a joke on me to get me in bad with the captain, till all of a sudden he cooled down and said that he didn't take chicken-feed. I and the likes of me might take it and keep it."

A look of bewilderment—the original expression that he showed the captain, I guess—recurred on Schmittberger's face as he drew for me the conclusion he evidently drew then: "It was the tip, the size of it, that made him mad."

His captain seemed to have drawn a conclusion, too. He used Schmittberger more and more, and the story showed me—I'm not sure that Schmittberger saw it even as he told it—that he was being tried out in all sorts of delicate services: to carry money, to collect money, to do detective work. It was plain to me that that old captain was convincing himself that he had an honest, extraordinarily innocent policeman whom he could trust.

"He had me cultivate the fly-by-night-hawks; you know [I didn't], the drivers of old hacks, so old they're ashamed to come out by day. The drivers patrol the Tenderloin, pick up rich drunks coming out of the houses of prostitution, and drive 'em home by way of Central Park. There a pal jumps out, opens the door, and if the drunk is 'dead,' yanks him out and robs him. That's bad, because the sucker, left there on the ground, catches cold. But it wasn't done in our precinct: 'None of our business,' the captain said. And those fly hackmen were awfully useful to us. They knew all the crooks, gamblers, and girls in the world; they were called in on all sorts of phony business, all the way from making a get-away for somebody to driving a dead body to the river after a murder. They knew all the gossip of the ward, white, black, and yellow.

"Well, I got to know all these drivers, and pretty soon they were reporting to me. If the old man wanted the stuff back from a robbery, whether it was in one of our houses or in the Park, all I had to do was to take a walk down along their stand of an evening before they got busy and tell them. They'd deliver the next day. If they didn't I harried them; you know, kept them moving. 'Can't stand here,' I'd say. Or we'd put a couple of men on bicycles out to watch them pick up a fare and then shadow them till they took him home. They had to stool-pigeon for us, but usually they did it willing, and we, on our part, didn't bother them if we could help it."

This was the ABC of detective work, getting into relationships with a kind of criminal which enabled the police to feel sure that, in an emergency, if they must, they could solve a mystery, catch a criminal, or restore stolen property. When Schmittberger had "the night-hawks on his string," his captain switched him to niggers, beginning with the panel-houses. These are houses of prostitution in which there are sliding panels in the walls of a room. When a man goes into the room with a woman, he puts his clothes on a chair, the only chair there, which is close to the panel, and the pimp or some other woman can reach in and pick the pockets. White women practice the panel game; it is permitted in some high-priced houses that keep the stealings within reason; i.e., take some, but not so much of a man's money that he comes complaining to the police. Schmittberger's first and chief business was with the colored houses. A white man seldom squeals when he is robbed in them; he doesn't want even the police to know he has crossed the color line. The colored folk grow careless, there-fore; their pimps slip the panel and they can hardly restrain their temptation to take everything they find, from hundred-dollar bills to carfare and stamps. Schmittberger had to restrain them by making the acquaintance of both the women and their lovers, watching to see who was spending too much money, and organiz-ing a system of squealing on one another. He soon knew all about all their relations, methods, peculiarities, and controlled them as well as the colored temperament can be governed by friendship and fear.

In my later days at police headquarters, Schmittberger was be-loved by the colored people, but in the beginning he was so feared that mothers used to quiet their children by threatening that "Cap'n Max'll come and ketch you." I asked him once to take me to a notorious colored dance dive. "Better go alone," he said; "I'll spoil it." Upon my insistence he went, and sure enough, when he appeared there was first a hush, then a rush; negroes dived out of windows, doors, and down the stairs and up and down fire-escapes. "You see, every nigger that has been doing anything wrong has skipped. They think I know everything." Only innocent negroes remaining, the crowd was small, and since even an innocent nigger has a conscience, there was no spring in their dancing, no joy in their songs, no abandon in their drinking. They came up and petted and flattered the captain, but there was no fun in it for me. We left, and Schmittberger held me at the corner to watch the guilty blacks sneak back up to the dive. "They'll soon be happy again," he said.

After Schmittberger had been assigned to various sorts of special detective work and so obviously trained for the job, he was made a ward man. He told it with surprise. "All of a sudden, without any warning," he said, "the old Cap called me in and told me to 'shed that uniform, Max; you're going to be my ward man.'" Schmittberger shyly repeated to me the high praises the captain bestowed upon him by way of expressing his faith in his honesty. "I've watched you, young feller, tried you out, and I believe you will make straight collections and deliver the goods on the level." Schmittberger paused, embarrassed, then he boasted like a boy. "I did," he said, and I believed him.

The collections he was to make for his captain were the regular monthly payments by gamblers, prostitutes, saloons—all law-breakers—for the privilege of breaking the law, rightly called police protection. He had to go to the barrooms, gambling-houses, and houses of prostitution, take and sometimes force the payment, which amounted to some twenty plus thousand dollars a month, bring the money to the police station, count it with the captain, who split it—so much for the Superintendent, so much for the inspector, so much for himself, and a small percentage for the ward men, of whom there were two. Other ranks and men, who got none of this regular graft, were allowed to pick up tips and "goods" as they could. Sergeants at the desk received tips from prisoners, shared in the business of feeding them, and enjoyed other privileges; they earned "good money" on bail bonds. Patrolmen on "good posts" received tips, as Schmittberger did when he was a young cop. This chicken-feed mounted up in a "fat precinct" like the Tenderloin, but was beneath the dignity of a self-respecting captain. The big business was the regular graft that Schmittberger handled for years, all in the day's work, without losing either his honesty or, it seemed to me, all his innocence. I often afterward reviewed this part of his experience; it bore upon my old interest in moral and ethical psychology. My note was that the process of corruption had begun so quietly with that first tip and proceeded so gradually in an environment where it was all a matter of course that this man never realized what he was doing till the Lexow

Committee's exposure, with the public (and private) horror and the press comment on it, exposed him to himself.

"I didn't know how it looked," he said that evening by the river. "I never saw it as you saw it till I saw the other Lexow witnesses telling things. And then I had to ask the Missus if I'd look like that if I squealed. 'Ah, no,' she answered. 'You couldn't look like that.' I wasn't like them, she said, and then when I did holler I looked the worst of all."

It was true. His testimony was the completest, most appalling of all; his confession summed up the whole rotten business, and yet as he spoke of it to me he looked like a nice big boy caught stealing apples. He seemed to want me to tell him he wasn't so bad after all. When I didn't, he gave it up.

"I guess I was, but, do you know, I don't feel bad; not inside."

My wife came out to join us. I introduced him to the "Missus," as he called her.

"Can you catch the robbers that damaged the boat?" she asked him, to make conversation.

"I'm afraid not," he answered; "we're on the level now, as I've just been explaining."

She didn't know what he meant and was so puzzled that she did not try to make more conversation. The captain rose, untied and mounted his horse. He ran his hand down into the animal's mane, turned his bent head to face my wife, and said, "I wish you'd help me make your husband believe that I'm on the square —now."

"I will," she responded completely. "You come again, and we'll work together on him."

He rode off without a good-by or a look back.

"Why didn't you say something?" she reproached me.

I told her what I meant to do. "Oh, that's better," she said. "But what did he mean by saying he couldn't catch the thieves that so damaged that boat because he was honest now?"

XIII

SAVING SCHMITTBERGER

IT WAS understandable that public opinion should have expected to see Captain Schmittberger, the confessed collector of the police graft system, punished or at least discharged. The belief in the existence of good men and bad men and that the guilty should suffer is deeply implanted in all men, and the star Lexow witness was a villain in two ways, in two worlds. The good were against him for his grafting, the underworld for squealing. Both counts counted with me. But I thought I saw a chance to make an experiment in morals.

Cannot an honest man do dishonest things and remain honest?

Isn't a strong man, however bad, socially better than a weak man, however good?

Schmittberger had been strong as a crook. He was bold in the collection of blackmail, honest in the distribution of the graft. His public confession was complete, detailed, and picturesque, and as I have shown, his private story indicated that he had not realized what he was doing. He was still honest, a good man doing bad things. He struck me as a type that would serve as well on the reform as on the graft side if he were given a chance. I wanted him tried out on that theory, the theory that society can safely use some men whom we foolishly punished and outlawed. I did not say all this to those whom I appealed to. To Dr. Parkhurst I argued that we, the reformers, could not afford to penalize a policeman for coming over to our side, exposing organized evil and, in brief, for confessing his sins and reforming. The clergyman hesitated, shook his head, but partly for me, I think, and partly for my moral argument, he consented to back me up. This was his state of mind till the fight over Schmittberger began. Then he, a fighter, fought, and also a strong man, he fought to the end, which came years later when we had Schmittberger made chief of police.

Roosevelt was harder to win. He listened to my rather full report of the interview with the captain till I wound up with the suggestion that he keep and use the man. "No, no, no," he revolted. He was deep in his struggle with the police, however, trying to command or persuade them to believe in him and in reform. They would not. Here and there a young policeman made an arrest, and T.R. praised publicly and promoted such men as examples. This policy had some effect. The police gradually were convinced that T.R. personally was on the level.

"But, hell, what does he know about the police business or politics?" they would say to Riis and me. "And he and reform won't last. Look at 'em, getting all mixed up, fighting among themselves. Reform and T.R. will soon be over and out, and Tammany will be back. Then what do we get, us cops that have played the reform game? We'll get nothin' in the neck."

Many an analyzing talk we, the kitchen police board, T.R., Riis, and I, had over this problem; so when I spoke for Schmittberger I presented his as a case in point. If he would move the captain down from Goatville to a bad, fat, grafty precinct, Schmittberger would clean it up, make the police under him enforce the law, and best of all, the board would show that it knew and would favor the police officers on "our side." "The police and Tammany and the vice men and women know that Schmittberger is against them now and for us," I said. "That's why they want him out. But as Dr. Parkhurst asks, why do we want him out?"

He yielded at last. "Go to Parker," he said. "I am not cunning enough to deal with that sort of—espionage. Parker loves it. Let him try out your honest crook. I'll abide by his decision." The sneer was a spark from the waxing conflict between the president of the board and Commissioner Parker and for my interest in Parker, a new type to me. I had met in literature, in history and court memoirs, but never before in life, the man that liked to sit back and pull wires just to see the puppets jump. That was Parker. He was a Democrat, and T.R. was a Republican; but Parker won Grant, the second Republican, to his heel, and T.R. got Andrews, the second Democrat. The split, which finally broke up the board and spoiled the work, was not along party lines, and it had nothing to do with policy. They called each other names: "politicians," "fakers," even "crooks," but I listened to both sides all the time, and my conviction is that the trouble was due solely to the character of the two leaders, T.R. and Parker. T.R. liked to lead cavalry charges with a whoop out in the open, Parker to direct his troops mysteriously from the rear unseen. He hated the way T.R. took command of the police from the first day and kept saying "I" and "my policy." So did the other commissioners, and Parker enjoyed turning up at a meeting one day with Grant to block some proposition of the president. He tried to get Andrews, too, but the young West Pointer did not like the crafty conspirator; he did not approve of T.R.'s cowboy style either, but he stared Parker down and joined and stood by the president. Also he warned him to look out for Grant; too late. Grant was with Parker, and T.R. could not win him back. His efforts delighted Parker, who described them to me.

"T.R. jumped on Grant," he smiled wickedly. "The personification of obstinacy, the son of his father naturally turned into an army mule. T.R. can never get him now."

"But what are you doing it for?" I asked.

"Oh, just for ducks," he answered, "just to see the big bomb splutter, the boss leader of men blow up."

"How did you get Grant?"

"I didn't have him, except on one very reasonable proposition, till T.R. nailed him to me, as I counted upon his doing. My theory was that when Grant voted once, unexpectedly, with me, T.R. would land on him, as he did. And Grant—well, Grant has one trait at least of his father's genius. He will fight it out on this line if it takes all summer, and if he falters T.R. will kick him back to me."

T.R. tried in every way, morally, politically, and socially, to take Grant from Parker, but always spoiled his successes by some burst of impatience which caused Grant to balk, smile, and vote with Parker. Grant was always good-natured. I compared him once to the daily report of the Chicago hog market: "dull but firm."

"Mrs. Grant did not like that," he drawled to me the next morning, "but I did. It was hard on the hogs, but I don't care for hogs except as pork."

Parker knew all about T.R.'s efforts to get Grant. "They had a dinner in the swell set last night," he would say. "All the wives are against me, you know, all for T.R. Mrs. Grant, too. I have nobody to help me hold Grant but T.R. The Mayor is to talk to Grant today again, at 11:45."

Parker knew everything, exactly. When I told him about Schmittberger, that he was doing his duty as a policeman, he knew it. "He's on patrol all the time," he said. "There isn't a place open in his precinct. Not much there, but what there is is obeying the law."

I told him I had urged T.R. to use him, but—to spur Parker on, I said, "He won't. I wish you would try him out."

He looked at me, smiling. "You know how to get me, don't you? Well, we'll see."

A few days later Schmittberger was transferred to the precinct next below his, and within a week Parker said that the "new broom had swept away" two poolrooms that were running there. Very soon after that the commissioner had a severer test for "my" captain. He had the evidence on some wire-tappers in the Hundredth Street precinct. These were criminals who picked off the wires the results of horse races, held up the news till their confederates could put down some bets and then, in a few minutes, win on certainties. Parker's plan was to have the wire-tappers arrested, show them that he could convict them, and then offer to let them go if they would buy with marked money from Schmittberger the privilege of working in that precinct. When all was ready Schmittberger was transferred to that command, and a few days later Parker sent for me.

"Remember those wire-tappers that were going to bribe Schmittberger? Well, they're in the hospital. They tell me that they had hardly got started talking business when the captain leaped on them, knocked them down, and kicked them bodily out of the police station across the sidewalk into the street."

"And Schmittberger, what does he say?"

"Not a word. He hasn't reported the case. He called an ambulance and forgot it. I think that, if you'll warn him to wear gloves on his fists, we can use him to clean up all the bad precincts in town. He seems to be down on bribers, and after this gets around the underworld he is not likely to be tempted very much."

T.R. was dee-lighted with this story. "Atta boy," he shouted. He did not ask me to caution "my captain."

Thereafter Schmittberger was called "the broom," and not only the Roosevelt board, all police commissioners used him as a sweep. "Well, send Schmittberger," they would say when things got too bad anywhere, and he certainly did clean up. He was indeed terrible. He knew the crooks, knew the crooked game, and cared nothing for the technicalities of the law. Like all converts, he was worse than the accustomed righteous.

"To hell with the Constitution," he shouted once at some Reds who cited that sacred instrument as a guaranty of their rights. He was still a policeman, in this and in other ways. I saw him attacked by a mob of strikers at the Fourth Avenue car barns. He was alone for a few minutes; he stood head high above the waves of fists that broke on him, and when some policemen arrived they could not get in to him.

"Throw me a billy," he called to them, and a club was tossed hurtling over his head. He caught it in the air, brought it down on a head, and so, cracking skulls all the way, he waded out of the mess over the fallen strikers, turned with the squad that had come out, and cleared the street. He was an artist with a police club, "tapping 'em" always on the top of the skull so that they closed up like a knife. He was a trained, an expert, policeman; he could plan a parade, a march, or a traffic arrangement better than any man of his day; he understood how to creep in behind the draft at a fire and make a rescue.

His reliability, once established, was a comfort to the reform board, but his ferocity when in action, especially in strikes, troubled me, and I undertook to tame it. He had learned of my part in his restoration to favor and was so grateful that he would take any advice from me. To cure him of his police hate of strikers I had him shifted to an East Side precinct where he had never served.

"What'll I do over there?" he asked me. He had come to my house to find out why I had him sent there. "Niggers I know, but Jews—?"

I reminded him that the poor, immigrant East Side Jews were a new and friendless people who never got a square deal. They were difficult, quarreling among themselves, aggressive, acquisitive, and sharp in their dealings with other people; and they were insistent upon their rights. No matter. They had to fight, not only for their life, but for a living wage. He might be patient, considerate, and fair with them, giving them plenty of leeway for their peculiarities, no matter how offensive they were.

"When they come to you," I said, "listen to them and try to settle their quarrels without a fight or an arrest."

"I'll do it," he said, and he did it. He allotted his first morning hours to his friendly court, hearing not only of ecclesiastical, financial, and art disputes, but taking complaints of husbands against wives, wives against husbands, parents against children, children against parents, employers against workers, and workers against bosses. Letting both sides argue themselves tired, he decided cases unofficially and with such common sense that the arrests in that precinct lessened perceptibly. He cautioned his men against the use of the night stick and learned himself to spare heads. "My fists are good enough," he said. With these he cleared the vice resorts, to the tearful joy of the old Jewish families who were relieved thus of one menace to their boys and girls. He became a non-partisan in strikes, seeing what I had seen: that employers were as grasping and unreasonable as the men. He tolerated the Reds, letting the socialists and anarchists hold meetings, demonstrations, and parades, and he came to be so respected by those agitators that one socialist parade cheered him when he appeared with a squad of policemen to lead and protect the marchers.

My ex-collector of bribes was a success. He could learn; he had learned as much from us reformers as he had from the old grafters. I was proud of him, Dr. Parkhurst was astonished and pleased, Parker called him "my broom," and Roosevelt called him "my big stick." There were other "reformed cops," not many, but enough to put most of the gamblers out of business, keep prostitutes within bounds, and enforce, a little, the laws regulating saloons. The police commissioners were changing the environment and the spirit of the police gradually, and they might have succeeded as well as later boards if they had not quarreled among themselves. Divided two against two, they became deadlocked and could go only as far as T.R. could drive by himself. The board would not always support him, but it could not keep him from breaking through and giving orders and examples on his own.

"I'll do that," he would say; "I'll do it first and fight it out with Parker afterward."

The public and the press watched and were disgusted; the politicians waited and laughed; the police sneered. The tide of political approval that had elected the reform administration was ebbing, and Mayor Strong and his advisers could do nothing. The mayor, a good merchant, was a bad politician. He could not stay on either side of the police board war, nor could he hold the two parties together, and he had not the strength to call for resignations.

"Say," said Schmittberger, "we'll be beaten and Tammany'll come back." Often he said it, and there was alarm in his tone and eyes. He was afraid of what would happen to him when his old crowd came into power.

"You go right on," I advised him. "Dr. Parkhurst and I will be here all the time, and we'll take care of you."

I could tell him that, and some few others, but I could not reassure all the police officers and men that came over to our side, and most of them slowed up. T.R. could not hold them. Other heads of departments failed likewise to get bold, steady service from their men. The explanation is simple.

Policemen and the rank and file of government officials are either born or brought up in an environment of unbelief. They know facts; they know how things are really done; they don't develop illusions as I did in my protected youth, and their surprises are at unexpected good, not, like mine, at unexpected evil. They know that good is rare and short-lived. The New York police force did not vote for, they voted pretty generally against, reform; and they forced votes for Tammany. When the reformers won the police were astonished, and since the victory had been won at the cost of police exposures they were prejudiced and afraid. Of course. But what counted with them was their belief that reformers are no better than others, that they lack the knowledge, efficiency, and machinery to establish permanent reforms.

"Reforms, yes," said a cautious reform chief of police whom Parker got T.R. to choose. "They can find a Colonel Waring in the army to clean streets; they can appoint a man that can clean tenements; they can do a lot of little things, but they cannot make any real change in conditions. I am willing to play up with T.R.

but I cannot help keeping one eye on the signs of the failure of reform and the return to Tammany. Tammany is not a wave; it's the sea itself; and I am not going to fall out altogether with what stays to follow a bunch of climbers who pass on to Albany and Washington. I have a career to make, too, only mine is right here in New York."

Like Schmittberger, this shrewd, street-schooled policeman, whom T.R. called "bad," had the strength to be of as much service to good government as bad. There were many such; there are many such. There are outlawed criminals whom I would like to have in office under me if I were a responsible mayor or governor; as a voter I would prefer certain bold, intelligent bandits to a "good man" like Mayor Strong or a "good-natured" general like Commissioner Grant. T.R. himself and Parker were all right, each in his own way; but they should not be asked to work together on the same job, especially if the job be police reform. The public knew that Roosevelt was confused, when his announced policy of enforcing the law because it was the law was challenged by the citation of hundreds of statutes too ridiculous to be enforced. Parker would have enforced some laws, ignored others, keeping in his own mind his private aim, first to train the police to habits of obedience, and second to reform the town, gradually. Either would work; both have worked temporarily, but separately.

Reform was beaten. Tammany did come back. The police and other cynics were right. And as they predicted, the reformers passed on up, T.R. to the navy and the army, the governorship at Albany, and the presidency at Washington. But the reform policemen had to stay and face Tammany Hall, their friends the saloon men, gamblers, and all the rest of the people who had felt the clubs on their heads or the business losses caused by—reform, yes; but at the hands of—traitors on the police force.

I passed on up, too. My city editor, Wright, and Seymour, the publisher of the *Evening Post*, went over to the old *Commercial-Advertiser*, a paper with some two or three thousand circulation—nothing in a city like New York. They proposed to carry out there the news policy they had not been able to work out on the *Post*: to print all sorts of news. The assistant city editor, Milholen, was made city editor of the *Post*, and he called me to be his assistant. I left police headquarters, therefore, but I was too interested in the police story and the predicament of my friends there to forget them. When Tammany came in and I heard the underworld saying, "Now we'll get the cops that soaked us, and first Schmittberger," I wrote and printed their intention, suggested editorials, and prompted Dr. Parkhurst to warn Tammany.

"Now we'll see who are the honest men on the force. Tammany will point them out to us by firing them."

I saw Croker, too, and I appealed to his political sense. "Don't give yourself away." He said it was none of his business; the new administration had to deal with such details. But he wondered what they could do with Schmittberger if they kept him. "Doesn't Tammany ever have use for a broom?" I asked.

He reflected a moment, smiled as if he had an idea; and, "We'll see," he said.

I don't know what his idea was, but Schmittberger was kept, and the use made of him was the same as the reformers': to clean up. Wherever there was a precinct backward in payments or subject to some recalcitrant political leader, Democratic or Republican, the Tammany administration sent Schmittberger there, and he shut off the graft, closed up the vice business, till the disobedient came to terms. Then the terrible captain was transferred to the next precinct that had to be brought into line.

"I'm playing their game," said Schmittberger to me, and he did not like it, but his face cleared when I bade him never mind. I think he consulted Dr. Parkhurst also and was similarly reassured. Thus he became an institution under Tammany and had no more troubles until another reform administration came in, with the police job to do all over again.

The effect of the exposure and reorganization by the Roosevelt board of police was to reform the methods of corruption and graft. The reformers did not learn much, but Tammany and the vice interests did; they saw that it was foolish and dangerous to let so many in on the graft. Patrolmen, sergeants, captains, inspectors, chief—everybody had his rake-off. With so many knowing so much about what was going on, it was inevitable that the facts should become public property and that, under pressure, some individuals would be caught, weaken, and expose the system, dragging down Tammany Hall and hurting business. Tammany, therefore, centralized the graft, cut off all subordinates (leaving them nothing but tips or "pickings"), and arranged to have protection granted and payments made and received by a few men chosen for their nerve and reliability. These men were never identified except by rumor; the whole business of police protection for law-breakers was resumed, and the results, a wide-open town and a corrupt police force, were all the public saw. But these were enough. The next reform administration elected, that of Mayor Seth Low, found the police the most urgent and obvious problem. The mayor chose General Francis V. Greene, a military man, who had been the head or front of the infamous asphalt trust of Philadelphia. By that time I was muckraking for a magazine, was working in Pittsburgh, knew something of Pennsylvania politics, and so believed that Greene was—what the asphalt trust was. When I received telegrams from Dr. Parkhurst and, through my wife, from Schmittberger that the captain was in danger, I was not surprised. I hastened to New York, prepared to fight. My wife and Schmittberger, awaiting me at my home, showed me a newspaper clipping: a list of police officers to be promoted as act-ing inspectors and chief of police. Schmittberger was not among them; few "honest men" were on that list; most of them were shrewd crooks. Schmittberger came in and broke down: "Now they'll get me, all right; might as well quit." I asked him to wait and see. I went straight over to General Greene's pretty little old house and was received at once.

Too excited and indignant to be even polite, I threw the clipping down on the general's desk before him, exclaiming, "Do you mean to appoint that list?"

"Yes, I did," he said coolly. "I threw it out to draw comment. If you have any to make, I'll be glad to hear what you know against those men."

"Well, they're mostly crooks," I said hotly. "Your first task is to win the belief of the police force that you are 'wise,' that you know who is who and mean to promote honest men. You will be judged by the cops you appoint, and the police know, as we police reporters know, that this is a list of crooks that has been put over on you."

I was standing, he was sitting; I was angry, he was quiet, atten-tive, thoughtful.

"What do you know against these men?"

"Know!" I flamed, and I told him some things, but I cut myself short with the savage inquiry, "But what's the use? What I know is what you know when, in command of troops, you advance some men and keep others where they can do no harm."

He was watching as well as listening, and he was slow. After a long pause he asked me whom I would promote in his present state of inexperience of the force and the urgent emergency. I named a list, including Schmittberger.

"Schmittberger?" he inquired. "Do you think that a man who is guilty of the crimes he has confessed—"

He did not finish. I walked up to his desk, leaned over it, and said in his face, "Do you, who have been the head of the asphalt trust, ask me that?"

I afterward heard in Philadelphia that General Greene had been put at the head of the trust as a front, to lend it credit with his undoubted honesty and ability, and that when he learned what he was representing he resigned. Anyway, I was wrong in my estimate of him; the Philadelphians convinced me that General Greene had a perfect record. And his police performance was proof of it. His deportment that evening in his house when I insulted him might have shown what he was.

"I will try Schmittberger," he said.

I almost collapsed with astonishment and relief.

"Yes," I said, "put him in the worst district you have and have him watched. Let his enemies, let some of those crooks on your list, shadow Schmittberger and report to you. You ought to have a squad of detectives anyway, to furnish you information."

He nodded, reflecting.

"Let me have your list, by the way," he said.

I gave it him, he rose, and—in a few days most of my list was appointed, including Schmittberger. When it was published in an evening paper the new acting inspector came running with it to my house, crying, "We're made, we're made."

He was tried, permanently promoted, and finally became chief of police, where he served honestly till he died. And among his proudest possessions were written letters of high praise from all his reform commissioners from Roosevelt to Colonel Arthur Woods, and none was so explicit and complete as that of General S. V. R. Greene.

XIV

I MAKE A CRIME WAVE

EVERY now and then there occurs the phenomenon called a
crime wave. New York has such waves periodically; other
cities have them; and they sweep over the public and
nearly drown the lawyers, judges, preachers, and other leading
citizens who feel that they must explain and cure these extraordinary outbreaks of lawlessness. Their diagnoses and their remedies
are always the same: the disease is lawlessness; the cure is more
law, more arrests, swifter trials, and harsher penalties. The sociologists and other scientists go deeper into the wave; the trouble with
them is they do not come up.

I enjoy crime waves. I made one once; Jake Riis helped; many
reporters joined in the uplift of the rising tide of crime; and T.R.
stopped it. I feel that I know something the wise men do not
know about crime waves and so get a certain sense of happy
superiority out of reading editorials, sermons, speeches, and
learned theses on my specialty. It was this way.

The basement of the old police headquarters was a cool place
in summer and detectives, prisoners, and we reporters used to sit
together down there and gossip or doze or play cards. Good stories
of the underworld were told there, better than are ever printed
as news. They were true stories, and true detective stories are more
fascinating than the fiction even of the masters. Sometimes a prisoner would give his version of his crime and his capture after the
detective who had caught him told his. Sometimes the stories
were dull, technical, so to speak, and therefore interesting enough
to the participants, like ex-soldiers comparing notes of a battle
after the war.

One day I was dozing away, bored by a long dispute as to
whether it had happened on a Thursday or a Friday night, when

a fresh voice broke into the debate. The speaker was evidently bored too.

"Ah, say, cut that," he said. "I'll tell you a good one on two cops up on Murray Hill. They were talking at the corner of Fortieth Street and Madison when a wagon drove up to a house, a swell residence closed for the summer. The family was away and a caretaker was in charge. The caretaker was Billy Bones, that Chicago house-buster who has no business to be in New York anyhow, and the driver of the wagon was our own well-known sneak, Mr. Busy-Bee. They had planned a clean-out of that house; Billy had got the job for that super-purpose, not to take care of the house, but, as I say, to clean it. It was dusk, the hour they had agreed upon for the job, and they were a bit troubled at the sight of the cops on the corner. Busy-Bee pointed 'em out when Billy Bones answered his ring and came to the door. Billy felt of his face to feel if his chin was clean-shaved equal on both sides; it was; so he says, 'Oh, well, they're not Chicago bulls; they're only New Yorkers. If they come up we'll ask 'em to help us. See?'

"The Bee has no local pride, no loyalty. The traitor says, 'All right, Billy. We'll try it; I don't want to hire the wagon twice for nothin'. Let's get some heavy things down on the sidewalk so as to give them something to do.' They did that. They brought out more and some bigger things than they ought to have taken. The sidewalk was a mess when the cops parted at the corner and one of 'em comes down to see who was cluttering up his beat so that honest citizens could hardly pass. He came up to the Bee, who was sweating more than he would have if he wasn't scared.

" 'Why don't you get some of those things into the wagon,' the cop ast him, 'instead of cluttering up th' right o' way this away?'

"Because the Bee had to swallow before he could speak, Bones comes down the steps with a trunk and explains that, as th' caretaker, he wants to get the things out and close the house as soon as possible; that they meant to load up afterward, but everything was out now, and if the cop would lend 'em a hand they'd clean the sidewalk in two shakes. The cop didn't like the work.

"What did he join the force for? he asked Bones, and Bones didn't answer that. 'Couldn't of,' he told me. 'I couldn't no more of explained that than I could of told why the force joined th' cop.' All he says was, 'Ah, come on, be a sport an' give me a boost with this trunk.' The cop boosted that trunk; he boosted other trunks; he put the parlor clock in himself. Say, that cop did more of that crime than the Bee did. The Bee apologized afterward to Bones for layin' off. He wasn't malingerin', he said. He simply wasn't used to workin' on housecleanin' with policemen. And Bones adds to me—to me, mind you, a plain-clothes detective sergeant—Bones adds as a postscript to the Bee's reflection on policemen, 'He means policemen in uniform.'

"Well, anyway, that burglary was done with police aid and protection. When the wagon was loaded Bones got his coat, locked the front door inside, came out by the service entrance with his coat and hat on, and thanking the cop, got up on the seat with Busy-Bee, the driver, and drove off with a selected load of pictures, furniture, clothes, and odds and ends, which amounted, the owner says, to about ten thousand dollars! Why, Bones and the Bee alone got eight hundred for it from Barny Levy, the fence."

There was some laughter, a little comment, and the conversation passed on to idle gossip again. Pretending to wake up, I stretched, rose, and idly walked out. In my office across the street I wrote a news story of that robbery, but only because the victim was the well-known family of a popular Wall Street broker. I could not give away the source of my information; it might exclude me from the basement. I did not repeat the joke on the cop who helped the thieves. The *Post* having it alone, however, the morning newspapers printed the "beat," and Riis was asked by his editor the next day why he did not have it. In the course of his irritated reply he said that he could get all he wanted of that sort of stuff, and his editor answered, "All right, get it, then."

That afternoon Riis reported a burglary which I knew nothing about, and it was my turn to be called down. My editor wanted to know why I was beaten.

"I thought you didn't want crimes in the *Post*."

"No, but a big burglary like that—"

All right. I called on my assistant, Robert, and told him we must get some crimes. We spent the day buttonholing detectives; I sat an hour asleep in the basement in vain. Nothing but old stories. Robert saved the day. He learned, and I wrote, of the robbery of a Fifth Avenue club. That was a beat, but Riis had two robberies that were beats on me. By that time the other evening papers were having some thefts of their own. The poker club reporters were loafers only by choice. They could get the news when they had to, and being awakened by the scrap between Riis and me, they broke up their game and went to work, a combine, and they were soon beating me, as Riis was. I was sorry I had started it. Robert or I had to sleep in turns in the basement, and we picked up some crimes, but Riis had two or three a day, and the combine had at least one a day. The morning newspapers not only rewrote ours; they had crimes of their own, which they grouped to show that there was a crime wave.

It was indeed one of the worst crime waves I ever witnessed, and the explanations were embarrassing to the reform police board, which my paper and my friends were supporting, in their difficult reform work. The opposition papers, Tammany, and the unreformed police officers rejoiced in the outbreak of crime, which showed that the reformed police and especially the new detective service could not deal with criminals in a city like New York. This criticism had a point which pricked the conscience even of Roosevelt himself. He had got rid of Superintendent Byrnes, the most famous of New York's detectives, removed Byrnes's self-trained inspector, and put in a captain who would have no dealings with professional criminals. The old system was built upon the understood relations of the crooks and the detective bureau. Certain selected criminals in each class, pickpockets, sneak thieves, burglars, etc., were allowed to operate within reason; the field was divided among them by groups, each of which had a monopoly. In return for the paid-for privilege the groups were to defend their monopoly from outsiders, report the arrival in town of strangers from other cities, and upon demand furnish information (not evidence) to the detectives and return stolen goods. This was called regulation and control, and it worked pretty well; more to the glory of the police, who could perform "miracles of efficiency" when the victim of a robbery was worth serving, but of course it did not stop stealing; it protected only citizens with pull, power, or privilege. There were many crimes done within and without the system, which depended for public sufferance on the suppression of the news, as any detective system does. But Byrnes had taught New Yorkers to report their losses to the police, never to the press.

"If you tell us your troubles we have a chance to detect the criminal," he said over and over again. "If you tell your friends or the press the thieves are warned and run away, and we can do nothing."

If citizens would reverse this method and report both to the press and the police they would learn something; they would soon find out how many crimes are committed in a day, how few are "detected," and force the police to detect many more. And as for warning the criminals, these wise men know that the police always are told of a crime and that detectives work hardest on a case that is in the papers.

Roosevelt's chief of detectives was appointed because he hated the old system, held it to be useless, and declared that he had a better way of dealing with the crooks. He asked leave to run the old crooks out of town, to watch for and arrest at the railroad stations new and known arrivals and to drive them away by threats of holding them as fugitives from justice until he could obtain evidence against them from the cities where they had been working. This method was succeeding so well that Commissioner Parker, who was watching it, was satisfied with the progress made, and T.R. believed all was well till the crime wave rose and frightened him. He suspected Parker anyhow; the detective chief was Parker's choice, and the outbreak of crimes all over the city so alarmed him that he was almost persuaded that the opposition was right in its criticism: that the police reformers, knowing nothing of crime, criminals, and police work, technically, had blundered in changing the system, the good old Byrnes method of handling this, the real business of the police; not to interfere with business and sport, but to catch and punish house-breakers and other law-breakers. He called a secret meeting of the police board and was making one of his picturesque harangues when Commissioner Parker interrupted him.

"Mr. President, you can stop this crime wave whenever you want to."

"I! How?"

"Call off your friends Riis and Steffens. They started it, and—they're sick of it. They'll be glad to quit if you'll ask them to."

Roosevelt was perplexed, as Parker meant him to be.

"I don't understand," he said.

Parker, who was "wise" and liked to mystify, explained that when the crime wave was running high he inquired into it, not as the editorial writers did, and the jurists and the scientists; he asked for the police records of crimes and arrests. These showed no increase at all; on the contrary the totals of crimes showed a diminution and the arrests an increase. It was only the newspaper reports of crimes that had increased; there was a wave of publicity only. He turned therefore to the newspaper boys and asked them about it—"not your friends Riis and Steffens, but the regular fellows, the poker combine. They explained it. They said that the morning newspapers got their crimes from the courts where only arrested prisoners are tried or held for trial, and that their own, the evening papers, got their stories by hard detective work, which they hate to have to do. But they must continue as long as your friends, Mr. President, keep up their fight. They started it; the other reporters didn't know where they got the dope from; they thought some inside office detectives were squealing."

T.R. adjourned the meeting, sent for Riis and me, and bang! "What's this I hear? You two and this crime wave? Getting us into trouble? You? I'd never have believed it. You?" Up and down his room he strode. Betrayed he was, and by us whom he had trusted? Who, then, could be trusted? And for what? Why had we done it? Why?

"And you laugh!" he blazed at me. I couldn't help it. But Riis saved us. He was contrite; he looked ashamed, and T.R. saw it.

"You, Jake," he said, "you tell me about it."

Riis told him about it, how I got him called down by printing a beat, and he had to get even. And did. "I beat the pot out of you," he boasted to me, his pride reviving. "And I can go right on doing it. I can get not one or two crimes a day; if I must I can get half a dozen, a dozen. I can get all there are every day.

"But"—he turned to T.R.—"I don't want to. So I'll tell you where my leak is, and you can close it up. I have had it for years, seldom used it, but—you can stop it for ever."

And Riis, the honest, told us how the reports of all crimes of high degree against property were sent in by the precincts to the heads of inspection districts and then were all compiled in a completed list which was filed in a certain pigeon-hole in the outer office of the chief inspector. Not he, but his boy, Max, had observed the making and filing of this list one day long ago; he had reported it to Riis, who resisted temptation to some extent.

"I told Max never to pry into that pigeon-hole—except in emergencies. And we never did, except in emergencies. But when you"—he blazed at me—"when you got so smart, I got so mad that I told Max to go to it, and, well—" He turned back to "Mr. President, that file is in the extreme left of the third row of pigeon-holes from the bottom. It should be kept in the inside office."

"And you?" T.R. whirled upon me.

I had to tell him about my naps in the basement among the gossiping detectives. I did not want to give up hearing the gossip, and I asked, and T.R. and Riis agreed to grant me, leave to go there on condition that I would use it only to collect local color for fiction or data for the scientific purposes of my studies in sociology and ethics.

Thus the crime wave was ended to the satisfaction of all. T.R. took pleasure in telling Parker that he had deleted, not only the cause, but the source of the wave, which was in Parker's department. He would not say what it was; sufficed that it was closed for ever. Parker had to resolve that mystery by learning from the chief of detectives that the president had ordered the daily crime file removed from the public to his inner office—for ever. Both commissioners, separately, promised that the wave would soon recede; and it did. When Riis and I ceased reporting robberies the poker combine resumed their game, and the morning newspapers discovered that the fickle public were "sick of crime" and wanted something else. The monthly magazines and the scientific quarterlies had some belated, heavy, incorrect analyses of the periodicity of lawlessness; they had no way to account for it then. The criminals could work o' nights, honest citizens could sleep, and judges could afford to be more just.

XV

I INHERIT A FORTUNE

AMONG the foreign news cables to the *Evening Post* one day was a personal message for me from the German Consulate at Naples: Johann Friedrich Krudewolf had died there, leaving instructions immediately to inform me, the residuary heir and the sole executor of his will. I felt as a bird must feel when it is shot on the wing. I remembered my promise to Johann to stop whatever I was doing to go to Germany and carry out his wishes when he died, but I did not want to be stopped then when I was in full career. Remorse, too, I felt, not only sorrow. I had long known that my old university chum had to die young, but I had almost forgotten it, and him, too. I had answered his letters, but not promptly and with not much interest in his painful labor to keep alive and carry on his researches in art history. So far as I could recall them my letters were full of my own selfish, healthy interest in my vivid, purposeless life. Ashamed and depressed, I went home early that afternoon, got out some of Johann's recent letters, and they also were full of me and my doings; they were answers to mine and, therefore, about me. Always me: as my mother had always said.

My wife, to turn my thoughts, suggested that maybe some of the money left me was really for me; and I had been wanting money to use in Wall Street. That made it worse, and my mother-in-law, Mrs. Bontecou, remarked that Johann must have loved me.

"More than you loved him," my wife added.

"That was his gain," said Mrs. Bontecou.

"And my loss," I answered.

"You will always be loved more than you love," said Josephine. I felt that to be true, but I thought she was thinking of herself.

She may have read my mind, for she said, "Look at your parents—"

This was an old grievance of hers. I had not reported our marriage till I had made good in New York, was earning my living, and, with my wife's novel published, we were independent. I had accepted financial aid from my mother-in-law and would not heed my wife's plea that my family ought to have shared the burden. And then, when my father and mother did come to New York to attend our wedding, they were hurt to hear that we had been married several years.

My mother wept, and my father asked, "Why?" Josephine answered out of her anger at me that when I received my father's letter advising me not to come home but to stay in New York, go to work there, and learn the practical side of life, I had declared that I would not only do that; I would never again ask him for money or other help.

"But," he protested, "if I had known you were married—"

"There," Josephine triumphed. "I told you," she said to me.

She had told me always when fear seized me—whenever I felt that the circumstances of life and the conditions of journalism would make of me what I saw it make of old reporters and editorial writers, a Greek slave in Rome, a writer of the master's opinions—then my wife had reminded me that there was my father to lend me the money to buy my liberty. And he would have done it. He said at our mournful wedding funeral in New York that he had cast me off only to try me out, and he offered then again to buy me an interest in a San Francisco evening newspaper. Josephine besought me to accept, and when I refused she declared I was selfish both as to them and as to her. And she punished us all for my obstinacy, me, my parents, and my sisters, who soon after came home by way of New York from three years at Göttingen. I think she thought I would refuse to take Johann's money, too.

Johann's money was different. It was probably a small sum; Johann was through with it, and, as Mrs. Bontecou and I recalled, he had bound me when I last saw him to do something with it for him. He had spoken of founding a scholarship. One of the shots that wounded me and my selfishness was the obligation I was under to interrupt my work to go to Europe to do this something with Johann's money. My wife liked that, and she had us ready to sail when the letter came from Johann's attorney, W. Lorenz, giving details.

W. Lorenz wrote that the estate would be valued at somewhere around 100,000 marks or $25,000. There were many bequests, both to persons and to institutions. The attorney had ordered the body of the deceased to be shipped home and would direct the funeral and burial, but I must come to choose a family plot, where I had to gather from many places the bones of other members of his family. When all was done, W. Lorenz estimated that my inheritance, the residuary estate, would amount to some $12,000. Nothing about a scholarship, no special duty such as Johann's solemn pledge had implied. Why, then, had he left the money to me? What was I to do with it for him?

Now the seat of this modest estate, the home of the Krudewolf family, was Lehe-bei-Bremerhaven, and Bremerhaven was the harbor for Bremen. We took a North German Lloyd ship, therefore, and on the way up the narrow channel to Bremerhaven, passed and looked with a curious personal wonder at the small village, Lehe, which only the captain and members of the crew knew or had ever heard of. Some of the crew lived there; it was indeed a seaman's village, and my steward, whose wife and children waved to him from the shore, wondered what in the world we two foreigners were bound there for. And so at the dock in Bremerhaven porters, officials, ticket-takers could not believe that we wanted to "go back to Lehe." There, straight ahead, was the way to the train to Bremen; everybody else always went from the boat to the train and so on to Bremen and Berlin. It was something of a fight to get ourselves and our baggage out of the stream to Bremen, and then, when we did escape to the street in Bremerhaven, it called forth all our German and some rage to convince the porter and the carriage driver that we were to go through Bremerhaven back to Lehe. "Nobody goes to Lehe"—"there is nothing to see in Lehe"—"it is nothing, Lehe"—"even Bremerhaveners never go to Lehe." Our final release came from a bystander who explained it all in a muttered sentence of which I caught but one word, "*verrückt*." I knew the rest; so did the porter and the driver. We were crazy Americans and so were allowed to drive out through Bremerhaven on one long street which became, at a wave of the driver's whip, the main street of Lehe also. My house was No. 32.

My house! It was a neat, white shop, tight up against and exactly like the shops on both sides, which, in turn, were of a solid block of similar business houses running a mile or so both ways. It did not look like mine, and I did not think of it as mine till our carriage stopped and three women and a man rushed out of it at us, crying joyously, *"Wilkommen, Herr Hausherr,"* to me, and a more formal, less joyous greeting to "my gracious lady."

They were Frau Hamel, the mother, two daughters, and a son, who leased the ground floor of the house and ran the shops, the two shops, one on each side of the main entrance to the three-story house. The driver was so astonished that he could only sit up on his seat and exclaim, "So, they *live* here. *You* live here!" The family had to take our baggage, and they did it merrily, laughing and talking, greeting and explaining. They swept us and our baggage into the hall, up the clean stairs to our *Wohnung*, the family residence for many years of the Krudewolfs, Johann's, his father's, his father's father's, and so on. It was ready for us, neat and white, polished, dusted, furnished—just as it had always been kept—as homelike a place as I have ever seen.

"We'll serve you supper here in half an hour," said these amazing tenants, leaving us to clean up after our journey. We looked into the closets, bureaus, chests in all the rooms, and my wife exclaimed. Space had been cleared for our clothes, but there were drawers and chests filled with fine old linen for beds and tables, stuff enough for several such houses, and some of the chests were beautiful old carved, rare boxes.

"All yours," said the three tenants when they came up with the supper, and "Look here!" They unlocked a great box in a back room; it was full of funny old heavy silver sets. "Three complete services," they said, "most of it, like the linen, never used."

"But why? Whence?" we asked.

"Every bride brought something rich, silver or linen or both, and such things are kept; not used. You use ordinary things."

That was the custom; that was the tragedy of our inheritance. As we looked over the items of the property left to me, a foreigner, by the last of the Krudewolfs, houses, lands, stocks and bonds, furniture, clothes, and miscellany of all sorts, we heard, and we saw in the accounts, the story of slow growth and thrift—the savings of sacrifice—for generations—all for us, strangers, who had had no part, little sympathy, and nothing but pity for the lives that had given up so much for us.

"Why did Johann leave this all to me?" I asked these kindly women, who seemed always to have been tenants and servitors, too, of the family.

They did not know. They looked at one another as if the question had never occurred to them, and the mother cast it aside. "All we know is that he did." That was enough for them.

"And why do you serve us supper?" my wife asked.

"Oh, we always served Johann when he was home, and his father before that."

Was it included in the lease? No. Yes. Maybe. They would let me see the lease if I wished, but it really didn't matter. They would buy our food for us, anything we liked, and present the bill, but we could not cook and prepare the table or clean the rooms. That was their part; it had always been so. The *Mandatar*, W. Lorenz, would explain everything, but—with looks of amiability—they hoped there would be no changes.

But, why, by the way, had the attorney not called that first evening?

Oh, they answered, he said that he would save the cost of a useless visit. He charged for each and every service, and if he came that night when we were tired we could do no business; so he was coming in the morning, when he not only could greet us but would have time to show us the accounts and make it worth our while.

He came in the morning after our breakfast in the pretty garden back of the house. He was a tall, dried-up professional man in an old professional long black coat—with flat red hair, a kind old smiling face, and a lame left arm, like the Kaiser's. He often mentioned that, "like the Kaiser's"; it turned the defect into a decoration. He used it to hold his brief-case tight against his ribs. He greeted us, as the tenants had, with a "Welcome, Mr. Landlord and *gnädige Frau*," but he swept the table clear, laid out his papers, and wanted to go to work.

I wanted to ask some questions: why had Johann left me his property? But W. Lorenz was reporting, while piling his papers in order, what he had done since Johann's death and my succession to the estate, how he had got the news, opened the will in court before witnesses, and begun at once to obey its directions, ordering the body shipped, preparing for the funeral, which he described in business details. He would show me the grave, unmarked, which I was to put a stone on. His report was completed, with prices paid, for which he showed me the bills.

My difficulty was to realize that this was my business, that I was the master he regarded me as.

"But, *Herr Mandatar,* why did Johann make me his heir? What does he ask of me?"

"I am coming to that," said W. Lorenz, and he drew out the will, read it with all its many small bequests and requests—nothing for me to do; nothing, I mean, that this, his old family attorney and agent, could not do. I said so.

"But you have to see to all these things," he answered. "I will do them if you bid me do them, but you are responsible for me and for my correct performance of them." He read the figures of the added-up column of bequests, but the sum was only about half the value of the whole estate. What was the rest for?

"The rest is for you," the matter-of-fact old man answered. "I read you the clause—" He was going to re-read it.

"No," I interrupted. "What I want to know is why Johann left the rest to me, a foreigner? What did he ever write or say to you to indicate why he gave it to me?"

"Ah, that! He never said anything—he would not write anything like that to me. I am his agent; I may say that I am a friend of the family, though that might be presumptuous. I would not ask, I would not permit myself to ask, that question. Only an enemy or—or an indignant relative or a malicious neighbor would question a will."

Were there indignant relatives and malicious neighbors?

W. Lorenz fingered his papers, looked up and away, before he answered.

"The will has been filed for probate," he said, "and no one has entered a protest. If they do the will gives all to you."

It was no use pumping the *Mandatar.* He talked business, not gossip; he took account of laws, documents, and legal acts, not grumblings and emotions. We went on to arrange in order the steps to be taken to execute the will, item by item, and to settle the estate, which he assumed I proposed to turn into money. It was not dull, any of it, as W. Lorenz discussed and did it. It was all so actual; my appearances in court and at public offices were insights into a Germany I did not know; an orderly, smoothly running machine, which worked as well for me, a foreigner, as for any one else—hard, precise, but impersonal and efficient.

Josephine had a still more interesting side to attend to. She had to see the relatives remembered in the will, mostly children, and their parents let her feel that there was some resentment. They did not say much, and Josephine thought to placate them by gifts of clothes, silverware, and furniture. The Hamils approved this "generosity," but W. Lorenz shook his just red head.

"You should be careful about that," he cautioned me. "The will of the deceased gave, but also it withheld, and what is withheld is of the very essence of the document. Johann may have made you his heir partly because he wished to deprive his relatives of the inheritance."

Did the kind old man know more than he would tell? Was there a story back of this strange will? No, he said, he was only studying the document to interpret the will of the deceased.

"But these are properties that I do not want and will not sell," I said, pointing to the bridal linens and other family heirlooms.

"Give them, then, to the children that are named in the will," the old man advised. "Them our dead friend had no feeling against, but all others whom he overlooked you should not give to."

To try him out, I offered him some little things. He refused them. "I am not named, except as an attorney," he said. "If he had meant me to be a beneficiary he would have given me something himself."

So just and so loyal was this impersonal professional friend of my friend. All I could persuade him to take was a lot of old German guidebooks to Europe. He saw them, evidently coveted them, and when he felt my disappointment at his refusal of more valuable things he said one day that he would take *one* of two guidebooks to Switzerland.

"I have always wanted to travel in the Schweitz," he explained.

"Good," I answered quick. "Take the Baedeker's Schweitz and

take also the Germanies which you will have to use to get to Switzerland." And he did. He hesitated; he seemed to be resisting a temptation; it was too much for him; he suddenly reached for the books, gathered them under his lame arm, and hurried away with what turned out to be a prize—to him, a treasure that became an occupation for the rest of his life and, by the way, the key that unlocked his professional character and let me into his human being.

W. Lorenz became a traveler. His sisters told me about it; they "consulted" me about it, for they were alarmed. They said that that night when he came home with the guidebooks, he sat right down with them and a sheet of legal cap paper to plan a trip to Switzerland. He worked late on it, and the next night he took it up again, this journey which he was making. The two old maiden ladies, who adored their brother and lived his regular life, were mystified and frightened by the change wrought in him by those guidebooks.

"He plans tours all the time," they whispered, "expensive tours which will ruin him. He has always been so saving, hardly enough to eat, and now—he wants us to go with him. Yes. He asked us the other day if we would go. We refused, of course, absolutely, indignantly. We said we could not afford any such extravagance, and we meant that he could not afford it either. But he said—do you know what he said? He said, 'Oh, *then* I can do it.'"

They were thrifty, too. They were too thrifty to waste their slow-growing, neat little substance on riotous travel, and the brother profited by their refusal to accompany him. This he revealed to me one night when I went up to his house to see him about some business that had turned up unexpectedly. His sisters purposely slipped me in upon him as he was at work on one of a pile of sheets of paper on the dining-room table under a center light. He looked guilty. He kept his hands down on his maps as he stood to receive me, and his parchment face seemed to blush. He answered my question and waited for me to go—no invitation to sit down.

"What are you doing?" I pried, nodding at the papers.

"Oh, nothing," he answered, "just planning a journey."

"Fine. Where to? Anywhere I've been? Show me."

Reluctantly he lifted his hands, and shyly he said he was revising a tour of Switzerland. I pulled his neatly written sheet of paper around to me and saw that it was an itemized plan from Lehe-bei-Bremerhaven to and through Switzerland and back. It was complete. There was the carfare to the Bremerhaven station for a train at 6:50 A.M., the cost of a third-class ticket to Bremen, carfare to the hotel there, which was named, with the prices for lunch, supper and bed, light, service, and tips. There were fees to museums and sights, all listed in order with the time of entrance and exit. He started from Bremen the next morning early, after coffee, fifty pfennigs, and carfare to the station, with the price of a third-class ticket—and so on and on across Germany to Switzerland, day by day, hours, prices, meals, hotels, fees, all blocked out by stops, with the costs listed and summed up each day, each week, and a grand total at the bottom of the right-hand side of the sheet. There were several sights and side-trips canceled.

"Why?" I asked. I had made them, one with Johann, I said, and they were worth while.

"Too expensive," he swallowed.

"And this plan?" I pointed to another sheet with a complete plan for the same general tour with more stops.

"That was too much too. I can't afford it."

"And this?" I drew out another, a smaller one.

"Well," said Lorenz, with a slight cough, "that was an itinerary I drew when I thought my sisters were going along; it left out many places I wanted to see, but I could not work them in; I felt pretty bad till it occurred to me that maybe my sisters would not care to suffer the fatigue of travel at all. So I asked them, and sure enough, they did not want to go, not anywhere."

His relief shone out of his face, it had to break through a cloud of shame or shyness or something, but—he was glad.

"When they refused to leave home to travel—anywhere," he said, "why, then I was free to make this big plan that was too big; but now this last one, this is possible." He stopped, hung his head, fussed with the papers. "I don't suppose I'll ever go; it costs an awful lot, but—well, I can. It's within my means. I can do it— if I'm careful; if the books are correct."

I understood. All of a sudden I knew that W. Lorenz would never make a tour of Switzerland, never meant to travel at all except on paper. And I understood that the same thrift which would keep him home would keep him traveling on paper with precise care for each item of expense, and all within his means. I remembered my boyhood when I used to play I was Napoleon or a trapper or an explorer and played out my make-believe secretly, in detail, and practically, well within the possibilities. And I remembered, too, the grown-ups who caught me making believe and did not laugh at me, but confessed that they also were really something else than what they appeared to be and so entered into my game and took me into theirs. Their behavior and mine—the shyness, shame, and sneaking persistence—it was all just like the embarrassed manner of W. Lorenz. So I gave him one long, understanding look, which he returned—the look, not of man to man, but of kid to kid, and I broke in.

"Sit down," I said quietly, "and I'll show you something."

He sat down, relieved, happy, eager, and I showed him how he could make his Swiss tour and include all the places he had left out and more. He did not know that he could save money by buying at Bremerhaven a round-trip ticket (*Rundreise*). He was amazed, he was thrilled, as I read from the general hints in the guide-book about the system which cut the whole cost of train travel by just about one-third. We worked his itinerary over together, and when I rose to go I had promised to bring up, and he was impatient to accept, other guidebooks—Austria and Italy, France and Spain, and Norway and Sweden.

"Why, we can travel all over Europe!" he exclaimed as he saw me out of the front door. He said it so loud that he looked back into the house to see if his sisters had heard. "They would never understand," he whispered, and then he said aloud again, "I can go anywhere, almost."

"Why not?" said I. "If you take your time, learn all the tricks of travel, and look out for the smaller items, like food, carfare, and tips, you can see one by one all the countries of Europe, and right, too."

"Yes, and within my means," he rejoiced with a joyous clasp of my hand.

XVI

I BECOME A CAPITALIST

WHEN W. Lorenz let me into his scheme for the secret satisfaction of his two great, apparently conflicting passions, first to save all his savings, and second to travel all over the world, he was bound to let me in also on the true story of his client, our friend Johann. He might conceal some of his own secrets; he did, in fact. I discovered one day that he proposed to do some traveling fourth-class, "only on long dull day stretches," and only to save enough money to visit places off his general itinerary, places double-starred in the guidebook. I opposed that economy. He was too old and frail to stand the discomfort of a box car without seats, among soldiers and tramps. He gave it up finally. At any rate he laid that plan aside and took up another, which he went to work on, cutting hotels and meals to save the equivalent of the difference between third and fourth class.

Meanwhile my wife, sorting over the heirlooms of the Krudewolf family with Frau Hamil and her two daughters and consulting with them as to the disposition of the things we did not want, had crept into the confidence of these good women and so heard their version of the Krudewolf saga. These two stories unlocked my memory till I could recall and understand remarks Johann had made to me when we were students at Heidelberg and Leipzig—remarks which, pieced together in the light of the gossip of Lehe, gave me his own story and some inkling of the purpose of his strange will.

A pretty little basket held all the elements of the tale. My wife discovered it in the attic one afternoon. W. Lorenz and I had been selling bonds and stocks, odd pieces of land, and when we had some money on hand, we went to Bremen and other places in between Lehe and Bremen to gather up the bones of certain ancestors whom Johann required in his will that I bring and bury together somewhere. I was making a plot in the Lehe cemetery and had ordered a fine bust of Johann, by a sculptor he had spoken well of, to crown the graves. I had left the inventory of the house to her, and she had worked her way slowly, conscientiously, up to the attic, which was the most fascinating of all. She and the Frau Hamil and the Fräulein Hamil spent days there over the old dresses, hats, toys, schoolbooks—everything that an old family attic should contain. But the Hamils had house and shops to attend to; they could not be always there, and my wife was alone when she called me up and showed me the pretty little flat basket. As I stared at it, wondering why she was so interested, she lifted the lid and disclosed two crowns of artificial flowers, some trinkets and cheap jewelry, a long, thin book in brown paper, which looked like a butcher's book, and, on top of all, two yellow third-class tickets to Bremen *und zurück* that had never been used. What did these mean?

My wife called Frau Hamil, who, at sight of the basket, called her daughters, who closed the shops and came and stared. They all looked into the basket, at one another, back into the basket, and at us, and they seemed to communicate and decide something.

"Those two wreaths," Frau Hamil said, "were the bridal crowns of the two sisters who married Herr Krudewolf; the jewelry was theirs. The book I don't know. But the tickets I know. They were found clutched in the hand of the second wife when I came up and saw her lying there dead."

I had been fluttering the pages of the butcher book. It was the roughly kept accounts of the growth of the family fortune for some seven generations. It began in an illiterate hand with the evaluation of a small farm, worth a few hundred thalers, and the dower of a bride. Another such hand added a few bits of land and a bridal dower. Another and another added dowers, a few hundred thalers and then a few thousand marks. Then there was the sale of the farm, all but a few pieces of land, and a record of the price, over 50,000 marks. This, I reckoned, was in the hand of Johann's grandfather. The next hand was more modern, and it added a large sum in money, 20,000 marks, and two bridal dowers, 10,000 each. It was a record of thrift; there were no losses or big expenditures; there were small profits. The increases came with the wives.

"This book," I said, "is the history of the sacrifices and savings of the Krudewolf family."

"Ah," Frau Hamil answered, "of their success."

"Yes, over seven generations. But those return tickets to Bremen, what are they?"

"Sit down and I'll tell you," said Frau Hamil, and we sat down on the boxes and old chests.

"Herr Krudewolf, Johann's father," she began, "was a good man, but hard. He was a sea-captain; he went to sea as a lad, studied, and worked up till he commanded ships that sailed all around the world. He sailed to America, often, and he learned something there that made him give up the sea; or maybe it was when his wife, Johann's own mother, died in giving birth to her baby that the father retired from the sea. Anyway he bought the house with the shops, which he meant Johann to have a big business in. Everything was for Johann, who was to be a great merchant, like they are in America. He was too old to become a business man himself, but Johann—the baby could learn.

"But the father could not bring up the baby; he asked the mother's sister to do it, and he married her. He loved her, too. Ah, yes, he loved his wife. He could not help loving his wife. She was an angel; we all loved her, and Johann adored her. She was his mother, the only mother he knew, and she adored Johann. And *der Herr Kapitän*, he loved his wife and his child, too; he lived only for them. But—"

Frau Hamil looked at her daughters, who looked at her till she looked away to continue.

"We think that Herr Krudewolf was made hard by the sea and the seamen he had to command. It is said that he was terrible on board ship; sailors who lived here in Lehe and sailed under him tell how he ruled them without mercy. They, too, these sailors, were hard men, strong and terrible; they feared nothing and nobody, neither at sea nor ashore—nobody but the *Herr Kapitän*, and him they feared always, even at home here, even on the street. They cursed him behind his back, but to his face, when they met him, they were afraid. Johann's father was a hard, hard man. He loved his wife; he loved his son; and he was good; he was honest and just; but he was strict; and he commanded his wife and his son, his relatives, and—us, his tenants, as he ruled his crews at sea."

Frau Hamil rested a moment; she looked at no one. She looked into the basket, touched the crowns, the tickets.

"Frau Krudewolf became ill. She was not strong, to begin with; she had the weakness in the chest that her sister had, and she was frail. And she was gentle, so gentle. Her voice was low and very sweet; when she bade you do something she seemed only to plead with you to do it. And when she answered her husband you could hardly hear her. She respected her husband, of course; she was a good wife, but her happiness was in the baby, the little boy who grew and was quiet. He talked to his mother. He couldn't talk much to his father, because he was a dreamy boy with wild ideas and wishes, and his father would not listen to his prattle about traveling and studying and learning and writing. But the mother did. She would sit and listen, or later, she lay on her bed and let Johann talk and imagine things; she loved it. I think that she wanted what Johann wanted, not what her husband wanted. There was some trouble; I think it was over Johann's being apprenticed to the merchant. Johann cried and cried and cried, and his mother, too, but he did what his father said. He was a good boy, an obedient son.

"And then the tickets. I must tell you about them. As Johann grew up and became a young man, when he went to work in the business to learn, the mother became worse. Captain Krudewolf did not believe she was very ill. She had always lain a good deal on her bed, but by and by she stayed in bed; she did not get up any more, and finally, one day, she was very ill, a hemorrhage. Even then the captain was not concerned, but he called a doctor. It was the doctor who made him believe. He came downstairs and, drawing the captain aside, whispered something to him. I heard only what the captain said. He said, 'Die!' He shouted it, and that was the only time I ever saw him weak. He ran upstairs; I followed, and I heard. He went to his wife's room; he went in, and he knelt down by her bed, and he asked her if she felt bad. She said she didn't. He asked her if what the doctor said was true; she said she thought it was. And he cried. It was awful to see that strong, terrible, good man cry; just like Johann. He wanted to know if he had not been a good husband to her; she put her hand on his bent head and said something. I could not hear.

" 'Haven't I given you everything you wanted or could want?' he asked her, and before she could answer, he asked her if there was anything in the world that she wanted that she did not have, and she said, 'Yes, there is. *Ich möcht' a 'mal die Welt anseh'n.'* She wanted to see the world.

"He sprang up, that broken, weeping man; he came out, ran downstairs and out of the house. When he came back he had those two tickets, and he took them upstairs and he showed them to her —to Bremen—and back; he put them into her hand, and she clutched them, she clung to them, till she died. We, Herr Krudewolf and I, we found them; we could hardly get them out of her hand."

"Did Johann himself put these things in that basket?" I asked the women. They said that he did; when his father died Johann had gone over everything, put all in order, and must himself have made up that little basketful of keepsakes. "I did the gathering and packing," Mrs. Hamil said, "and I never saw that basket."

So Johann had seen the relation of the bridal trinkets, the butcher-book, and two return tickets to—the world. I carried off the book; I showed it to W. Lorenz, who was interested enough to cast up the figures, making corrections, and to draw a moral from it. "So are family fortunes saved up, bit by bit."

"Bride by bride," I commented bitterly.

"Not only," he corrected. "There was careful saving in all that."

"What for? For me?"

He nodded. "Yes, as it turned out. But to the men who saved it the fortune was capital for a business."

"Which Johann did not want. Why did the father insist on his boy's doing something he didn't want to do?"

"Johann's father," said Lorenz, "was a stern, strong man. He learned in America—he said that there was money in shops, there was money in trade, but there was no money in sailing ships. He learned that there was more money in trade ashore; so he came ashore. He was too old; he was too impatient with people; he was spoiled by the sea for business ashore. But he had a son. He brought up Johann to be what he could not be. He bought the house with the shops for him; he apprenticed him to a merchant; he would put his money into his son's business. It was a good plan; it is too bad Johann did not follow it. He had queer ideas of traveling and studying, and his mother listened to him, and I think she encouraged him. Anyway she listened as a mother will to the dreams that a boy will have."

To my direct questions Lorenz answered that he thought she interceded with the father for the boy, but without effect.

"Even after her death?" I asked, thinking of the father's remorse and the two yellow tickets. Lorenz was silent a long moment.

"Johann did not give up his place in the shop till his father died," he said, and as I sat there taking in the meaning of this, the *Mandatar* added gently, "Johann's father was a very determined man."

We were in the *Mandatar's* dark little overloaded office, he at his desk, I in the one client's chair. Our easy labors over the estate that were coming to a close had been suspended, and I knew Lorenz wished to get on with the settlement. I had proposed to pay all the bequests, free of taxes paid. He approved. I could do whatever I pleased for the schools, the city, the city park, and the relatives named. But when I suggested giving money or goods to any other relative he objected. There was something back of his resistance. I must know what that was. I recalled aloud things Johann had said long ago to me. He had loathed business in any form. He resented the power of parents over children. He had asked me if my father had any fixed idea of my education, future, and general welfare. When I said, "No, not fixed," he declared me fortunate. "My father," he said, "knew what was good for his son. My whole family did, all except my mother."

"Did Johann's relatives," I asked, "back up his father?"

"Yes, they did," said Lorenz that day.

"Hard?"

The *Mandatar* squirmed, but he let out his professional secret to the full.

"After the old man was buried and Johann took over the estate, he quit his position in the business. He announced his plan to go away to study, and there was a row. The relatives held that he had no right to squander in study, travels, and pleasure the family savings of generations."

"Then that is the reason why he has cast them all off, all but the children," I said, relieved.

Lorenz nodded. "That," he said, "is why I think you should not give anything to them."

"Why haven't you said so before?"

"It is not so stated in the will," he answered, "and he never said it to me or you. I go, and I think you should go, by the will."

"I will," I said.

"By his will," he said, "not his ill-will, not his hate."

Then the just, wise old attorney told me of some kindnesses I could do. The Hamils wanted to buy the house. "You can get more for it in the open market," he said, "but they were good to Johann; they served the family always; they are sweet people. They have a little money, and they can add a sum which they can borrow from the institutions Johann has given money to: the exact amount of those bequests." I agreed to that. "Good," he said; then he told me that a relative Johann used to find amusement in, a man who had lived long in Brooklyn and come back home well-to-do but full of America and American superiority—this old uncle wanted to buy at a low but sufficient price a piece of land between two separated pieces of his land. "The other relatives hate this man," said Lorenz, "but Johann rather liked him." I agreed to that. I agreed to several such arrangements, and he went out, and I sold the land. I saw why the relatives hated the buyer, but I saw, too, why Johann found him fun. He did "rub in" Brooklyn, where he had lived unhappily; he had hated it, been homesick, but as something to talk about that would make Lehe and Bremerhaven and even Bremen look small, he found Brooklyn, to say nothing of New York, very useful.

The Hamils had the happiest day of their lives, I think, buying their house from me. They set the table in the garden for the bargaining, which Lorenz drove hard for me and the estate, only to be glad every time I took the buyers' side and went against him.

The business was settled with smiles; the daughters literally danced with glee. The only day to compare with that day was the day of the payment, the actual transfer of the money. And that was a day I shall never forget. Everybody dressed in his best for it, and I soon saw why.

The moneys we had collected from sales and settlements were all deposited in cash in the savings bank. Lorenz, in his Sunday best, called for me, with some money to deposit—gold. We turned it in at the bank, drew out some 42,000 marks in gold coins, which we carried in bags to the three institutions which got it in three sums, counted out on large tables. The recipients, accepting these sums, came with us to the Hamils' house, where, in the parlor, they counted out the money, which was united in a loan to Frau Hamil. She gathered it up, held it a moment, and then counted it out with her additional cash, also in gold coins. We counted it again, and Lorenz swept it into his bags and back we went, alone now, to the bank, where we redeposited the same coins we had drawn out a few hours earlier.

"Why not use checks?" I asked, and the answer was that that system had been tried and found unsafe. I had to make a very slow, elaborate deal with a Bremen bank to get what was coming to me into the form of a draft on New York. However, that was done, and all was settled except the bill for professional services of W. Lorenz. He was slow about rendering it. It was a long, detailed, complicated bill, he said, and I could well believe that. He had been doing practically nothing else than my business for three or four months, and I expected a big bill; I had kept in cash a large amount to meet it, and as he worked on it nights, I began to fear I had under-estimated the amount. He himself was embarrassed when he ushered me into his office to present it, and I was shocked by the length of it, many foolscap sheets. But the items: carfare downtown, 10 pfennigs (he walked back); appearance in court, 1 mark; argument in court, 1.50. So it went; every single service done was entered, but at such rates as these; and the total? One hundred and sixty-four marks, twenty-five pfennigs! About forty dollars.

I counted out exactly that amount, down to the pfennigs; he gave me some small change to make it exact. Then I handed him a few hundred marks.

"What's that for?" he asked.

"Oh, for a trip to Venice."

"From Switzerland!" he exclaimed, receiving it, delighted.

"But"—he clouded—"I can go on to Rome with all that," he said.

"Yes," I answered, "but you can't get back."

"Let's see." He hoped, and he rose to go to the dining-room where the guidebooks were kept.

"No, no, Lorenz, not now," I protested. "There's something else I want you to do for me. Tell me why Johann left his money to me. He said once that there was something he wanted me to do with it. What was it? What did he want me to use it for?"

Lorenz dropped back in his chair. He trifled with his papers. "There is nothing on record to bind you at all," he said. "But I think that he wanted you to be free."

"Free?"

"Yes, free of your father, free of your family, free to do what you might want to do, study or go into business or—travel—"

"To Rome."

"Yes," he mumbled. "I think so."

"Yes, and I think so too," I said. "I think that's it." For I remembered once when we were making a foot-tour of the Saxische Schweitz that Johann had said that money was liberty. We were discussing whether to go on and see Prague or to return to Leipzig.

"Money is not money," he said; "it is liberty."

And that's what Johann's money has been for me. It was only some $12,000, but I knew how to make it more. I had not been a reporter in Wall Street for nothing. When I got back to New York my father wrote, asking me what I proposed to do with the money. "Speculate," I answered, and he, frightened, straightway wanted to borrow it all from me. He said he needed it just then; I suspected that he wished to save it for me, but I lent him one half of it, and with the rest, to his amazement, I slowly, surely, easily made enough money to make me free for life, as my friend Johann Friedrich Krudewolf willed, free even of Wall Street.

XVII

REMAKING A NEWSPAPER

NEWSPAPER is indeed like a woman or a politician. When
it is young, honest, and full of ideals, it is attractive, trusted,
and full of the possibilities of power. Powerful men see
this, see its uses, and so seek to possess it. And some of them do
get and keep it, and they use, abuse, and finally ruin it. The
Commercial Advertiser, the oldest newspaper in New York,
looked like a wretched old street-walker or a used-up, ex-"good"
governor, when "we" got hold of it in 1897. It had a circulation of
some 2500, no influence, and it must have cost its keeper the income
on a small fortune to make up its losses. But there is a difference
between a fallen human being and a painted prostitute. A newspaper can be saved—to sell again, as we discovered.

"We" were Henry J. Wright, the city editor of the *Evening
Post*, who became the editor-in-chief of the old *Commercial*;
J. S. Seymour, the publisher of the *Post*, who took the same position on the wreck; Norman Hapgood and myself, whom they
brought with them from the reportorial staff; and later, Joseph B.
Bishop, an editorial writer. Hapgood had the theaters, I the city
department, and he and I went to work without any instructions
except to be careful about spending money. Editorially we were
free, and I think Wright and Seymour were free, from any re-
quirement beyond that of making the bankrupt a profitable property, which meant, at that stage, a good newspaper. Anyhow that
was the spirit in which we went to work in the news department,
and the result was a busy, happy, progressively successful period
of four or five years.

My inspiration was a love of New York, just as it was, and my
ambition was to have it reported so that New Yorkers might see,
not merely read of it, as it was: rich and poor, wicked and good,

ugly but beautiful, growing, great. I had no policy that went very deep. "We" inherited from the *Post* an opposition to Tammany and corruption, but I really liked Croker and the "bad men" I knew more than I realized, much more than I liked the reformers "we" consulted and supported.

"He's a crook," I would tell a reporter, "but he's a great crook," and I think now that I meant he was a New York crook and

BEFORE "WE" TOOK IT OVER

therefore a character for us and all other New Yorkers to know intimately and be proud of.

My reporters liked our attitude. They were picked men and women, picked for their unusual, literary pose. I hated the professional newspaper man; I had seen him going down, down, down, and I dreaded his fate. I remember once how one of them came to me for a job at the beginning of our enterprise when I needed reporters. I recognized the type; I smelled it on his alcoholic breath, read it on his cynical lips. To stall him, I asked him what experience he had had.

"Experience!" he echoed. "I have been Washington correspondent of the *Herald,* city editor of the *Tribune,* London man for the *Times.* I"—he waved his arm contemptuously out over our long, big city room and concluded—"I have been the editor of this shebang."

"Then there is no place here for you now," I cried at him, my hands up in horror.

"What am I to do then?" he asked bitterly.

"Go out of this office," I answered, "turn to the left till you come to the corner, then turn right and go—go till you come to the dock."

"And then?" he questioned. "What then?"

"Go on," I finished. "Don't stop. Keep right on."

It was astonishing, my outburst, and I must have shouted it at the poor wretch, for some one asked me as I came back to my desk why I had been so loud and fierce. My answer surprised me. I said that to have that man on my staff would have been like seeing the ghost of my future constantly before my eyes. I had not realized till that moment the subconscious fear in which I was working, the depth of my dread of becoming a professional newspaper man. I wanted none on my staff. I wanted fresh, young, enthusiastic writers who would see and make others see the life of the city. This meant individual styles, and old newspaper men wrote in the style of their paper, the *Sun* men in the *Sun* style, *Post* men in the Godkin manner.

There were professionals on the staff I inherited, of course; there were no others at first. I discharged some at once, and I was discharging the rest so fast that Mr. Wright remonstrated. Shouldn't I wait till I had found substitutes? I did not want to; it was only Wright's insistence that made me keep the few men that stayed, luckily. There was a Wall Street man, who was no expert, and a political reporter who was an expert but so bored that he wrote dead stuff. He was of use only for tips; other men wrote the stories he thought he had covered. There was Miss Josephine Meagan, who did the woman's department; she was a young woman but an old trained professional who soon proved indispensable. The most useful to the staff was John Weier, a young man but a newspaper man who saved our amateur lives many a time by his quick, knowing skill and amiable willingness to help any one out of a hole. The most useful to me personally was the assistant city editor, Charles Lachaussee. I did not know it, but I was not an editor nor any other kind of executive. Lachaussee was. He carried on the routine and filled in wherever I was neglectful, forgetful, and incapable. This he did so tactfully, so quietly that I think nobody remarked at the time and I myself came only later to recognize that whatever of completeness and steadiness there was in our city news service was due to this modest, experienced wheel-horse. I kept, I clung to, Lachaussee by instinct, and I can see in memory reporters going also instinctively to him for the needed instructions I did not give them.

The rest of the old staff were dismissed suddenly—and their places were filled by utterly inexperienced writers. Hutchins Hapgood, a brother of Norman, was one of the first. He, too, loved, if not New York, then life and people and ideas. Soon after him came Neith Boyce, an unsentimental, pretty girl, who ran a romance through the city room by editing Hutch and his copy till he fell in love with and married her. Another New Yorker taken early was Abraham Cahan, an East Side Russian socialist, later to become editor of the Jewish *Daily Forward,* who made incessant propaganda among us for the Marxian program and for Russian realism; but he had published a novel and in the paper wrote fact stories direct from the news, just as Hutch Hapgood picked up philosophy from artists, bums, and thieves. In the main, however, the *Commercial* reporters were sought out of the graduating classes of the universities, Harvard, Yale, Princeton, and Columbia, where we let it be known that writers were wanted— not newspaper men, but writers.

My verbal advertisement and my announced rules drew the right kind of young men. I would take fellows, I said, whose professor of English believed they were going to be able to write and who themselves wanted to be writers, provided, however, that they did not intend to be journalists. "We" had use for any one who, openly or secretly, hoped to be a poet, a novelist, or an essayist. I could not pay them much in money, but as an offset I promised to give them opportunities to see life as it happened in all the news varieties. No one would be kept long in any department; as soon as a reporter became expert in one branch of work, he would be turned into another. This was not only for their sakes, but for ours also. When a reporter no longer saw red at a fire, when he was so used to police news that a murder was not a human tragedy but only a crime, he could not write police news for us. We preferred the fresh staring eyes to the informed mind and the blunted pencil. To express if not to enforce this, I used to warn my staff that whenever a reporter became a good all-round newspaper man he would be fired. And to encourage each man to form and write in his own style, I declared that if any two reporters came to write alike, one of them would have to go. There was to be no *Commercial Advertiser* style, no *Commercial* men. So also there were no rules about promptitude, sobriety, accuracy; no lists of friends or enemies of the paper; no editorial policy; no "beats"; and best of all, there was no insistence even upon these rules, which were broken at any one's convenience.

My practice was to take as many university graduates as came each year after their Commencement, and trying them out in the summer when the older men were on vacation, select in the fall those that we liked, "we" being myself, Lachaussee, and the other reporters, who were harder judges than I was. Most of the men who made good were from Harvard. Other colleges sent us candidates who were elected. Walter S. Edwards, from Columbia, was one of the most sensitive reporters I ever knew. He "covered" Dick Croker, the Tammany boss, with an affection which this lovable man deserved and returned—Edwards covered him with love and with (unintended) ridicule. But music was Edwards's gift, not literature. Mr. Wright got from Columbia a young man, George Wharton, who created a school news department which was a model. From Yale came Larkin G. Mead, a nephew of William Dean Howells, who couldn't spell, punctuate, or keep to the rules of primary grammar, but had a sensitive eye, red hair, and freckles, and drove words like nails. There was the copy desk downstairs and the typesetters upstairs to make his living English correct. "Red" Mead of Yale was one of our stars. On the desk, besides Neith Boyce, was Pitts Duffield, who had taste and a gift for the appreciation and ordering of other writers' writings. He became a publisher.

Eugene Walter, who became a playwright, worked for us for some time and suffered all the time. He was one of those men who wanted to write, was sure he could, but had not yet found his form. He was not a success as a reporter, but when he turned to the stage he did brilliant things. Harvey J. O'Higgins came to us for a job, but, as Carl Hovey put it recently in a letter, "We didn't think he was any good; so we allowed him to work on the telegraph desk, but he practiced writing on our Saturday supplement." Edwin Lefevre reported Wall Street for us, but he had the newspaper man's sense of news. He wrote the bald, important facts for the publication and then, after the paper went to press, told us the stories which, under the drive of our scorn, he afterward wrote and published under the title *Wall Street Stories*.

The Harvard men who stayed and gave character to the city news were Hutchins Hapgood, Carl Hovey (afterward editor of the *Metropolitan Magazine*, now a Hollywood editor and writer), Guy H. Scull (who has since died), Robert S. Dunn, a novelist—all writers; and there were others, like Humphrey T. Nicholls, who were not naturally gifted but could report, because Harvard somehow taught her students that there is such a thing as the beautiful in this world and that there is an art in writing. I think now that one member of the Cambridge faculty, Professor Copeland, had a great deal to do with our success with Harvard men. He understood what kind of students we were looking for, and he was wise enough to send me that sort and no others. I say "wise," and I might say "extraordinary," for most men and most of the professors of English I was in touch with thought only of getting some young friend "a job," any job. Professor Copeland knew that that was worse than useless; it was harmful to put a young man in a position he was not fitted for and so start him off with a failure. Nor is it a service to the employer. Mr. Copeland considered both his students and me; he sent me only the fellows he was sure could see and express the beauty in the mean streets of a hard, beautiful city. Every one of his men made good. But I have always given credit for that to Harvard in general. That university gave, and I think gives, something of what is called culture and made its students aware not only, like other American colleges, of what men know, but of that also which men do not know and have to discover of "the True and the Beautiful."

We talked of such things on our paper. We dared to use such words as "literature," "art," "journalism," not only in the city room itself, but at a fire or in the barrooms where the Press drank. The old hacks hated it and ridiculed us; we were the freshmen of Park Row, and our tittle-tattle was sophomoric. But we did not care what the old bums said, and as for the star men of the other papers, we could see in their printed stuff that they likewise were laboring at the art of telling stories. Cynicism was a pose in the journalism of those days, and my staff did not take it. They meant to be writers, and they did not pretend to be working only for money. How could they on the miserable wages I paid, $12, $15, $20 a week? My contract with them was to pay them in opportunities, to see actual tragedies and comedies and to report them. They were not held accountable for news beats; Lachaussee and I with the city news service of the Associated Press could take care that we were not beaten; my young writers were expected to beat the other papers only in the way they presented the news. The flash of a murder would come in. I did not rush a man out to get the news first; Lachaussee would write a short bulletin for the next edition while I would call up, say, Cahan; I would ask him to sit down and then, without any urge, tell him quietly what to do.

"Here, Cahan, is a report that a man has murdered his wife, a rather bloody, hacked-up crime. We don't care about that. But there's a story in it. That man loved that woman well enough once to marry her, and now he has hated her enough to cut her all to pieces. If you can find out just what happened between that wedding and this murder, you will have a novel for yourself and a short story for me. Go on now, take your time, and get this tragedy, as a tragedy."

Our stated ideal for a murder story was that it should be so understood and told that the murderer would not be hanged, not by our readers. We never achieved our ideal, but there it was; and it is scientifically and artistically the true ideal for an artist and for a newspaper: to get the news so completely and to report it so humanly that the reader will see himself in the other fellow's place.

Our theory was not generally accepted even in our own office. No ideal was unchallenged there. It was a place of constant debate. Any answer ever offered to the question, "What is art?" was disputed, and hotly, too. This may have been Cahan's influence. He brought the spirit of the East Side into our shop. The Ghetto and the Russian Jews, a disputatious lot, were splitting just then into two parties over the question of realism in the arts. Cahan took

us, as he could get us, one by one or in groups, to the cafés where
the debate was on at every table and to the theaters where the
audience divided: the realist party hissing a romantic play, the
romanticists fighting for it with clapping hands and sometimes
with fists or nails. A remarkable phenomenon it was, a community
of thousands of people fighting over an art question as savagely as
other people had fought over political or religious questions, dividing families, setting brother against brother, breaking up business
firms, and finally, actually forcing the organization of a rival
theater with a company pledged to realism against the old theater,
which would play any good piece.

I rejoiced when this East Side controversy flowed over into my
newspaper. I had enjoyed and profited by my police reporter's
interest in the picturesque Ghetto, and I knew it was good—good
journalism and good business—for my reporters to follow and report the happenings over there. It increased our circulation; the
Jews read the *Commercial,* and it broadened the minds of the
staff and of our readers. Norman Hapgood reviewed the Yiddish
theaters or let Cahan and other reporters write criticisms of their
shows; he often put their plays and performances at the head of
his column, where they often belonged. The Yiddish stage was
about the best in New York at that time both in stuff and in acting;
some of their players went on to the English-speaking stage afterward.

Whatever it was that did it, whether it was Cahan and the
Ghetto or my encouragement, the *Commercial* city room had ideals
and flaunted them openly. There were clashing notes. Neith Boyce
used to smother the sentimentality of Hutch Hapgood when he
became too soft. He brought in one day an interview he had had
with a broken-down tramp on a park bench. Hutch saw in it
philosophy and pathos, and he wrote it so. I sensed in the tender
way in which he handed it to me that he felt it to be a sensitive
manuscript, which meant that he would fight against any editing.
I turned it over to Miss Boyce, who edited it as freely as if it had
been an advertising write-up, and sent it up to the composing room.
When it appeared in the paper it was under her heading, "He
Lost His Grip," a title which changed the whole meaning of the
story. I saw Hutch hold it up like a wounded bird, almost with
tears in his eyes. He said not a word, however, and I (alone, I

think now) did not understand why he stood such treatment from Miss Boyce till one day when he came in late and unhurried with an important bit of news. I jumped on him only to have him hold me and, pointing to a sun-ray lighting upon the girl's red hair, ask me if it was not beautiful to have such a touch of color in our dingy old city room. Then I understood all that had happened and foresaw what was going to happen. For Neith Boyce was as romantic in her way as Hutch Hapgood was in his way, and as idealistic and ambitious as any one on the staff, as her novels and other writings have proven since.

XVIII

A HAPPY NEWSPAPER STAFF

IT is fun to make or remake a newspaper. It is work, too, hard work, and the sport of it appears best as one looks back at it, but we of the *Commercial Advertiser* saw the humor of it at the time. Neith Boyce helped us there, she and Harry Thurston Peck. They were irresponsible enough to see it objectively as a game and to play the useful part of fans. Peck was a professor at Columbia University and the editor of *The Bookman*, but he was one of those tireless geniuses who never have enough to do. He had accepted also the editorship of our book department. With a stenographer and an assistant editor he carried on pages and pages of book reviews, literary notes and news; he had his *Bookman* and his lectures to attend to, but he used to sit in his stovepipe hat and white spats in "the culprit's chair" beside my city desk and watch us collect the news of the city, watch and wonder and ask questions.

"But how do you know there's a fire there?" or "Will the mayor answer such question? Won't he throw the reporter out?" And later, as he learned the business of news-gathering, he would raise the order of his questions: "So they really do such things? Take bribes and steal?"

Neith Boyce sat directly behind me at the copy desk, quiet, golden, sharp, quick, and whimsical. She saved my nerves from explosions. I sent Guy Scull, a yachtsman himself, to the dry dock in Brooklyn to get and telephone the official handicap measurements of the two yachts about to race off Sandy Hook for the international cup. The figures came in, but not from Scull, and another man, who was reporting another angle of the race preliminaries, was asked to find the lost reporter. He came back to the office after the paper had gone to press with Scull humbly in tow and reported, "I found him on a pile of lumber in the Navy Yard writing poetry."

Neith Boyce laughed just in time to make me see my ridiculous staff of writers as I see them now, all gathered around Guy Scull and debating whether his lines were merely verse or really poetry. The measurement of the yachts was editorial business, not literature. And Peck, the literary editor, sympathized with me, and said so to the staff, who only stared at him, and went on talking "over my head," as he put it when he came back beaten to me. But the editor of *The Bookman* was reconciled to my staff and to my policy of using inexperienced writers when he saw the results of some of the general assignments "we" gave: to look for one instance of gayety in New York, with the promise to report it in the paper as conspicuously as a murder. All the reporters joined in that search, and though none of them brought in an account of pure gayety, we did have, and we put on the first page with stud heads, two or three instances of merriment. Peck agreed that "mere gayety" does not occur in America. He was most enthusiastic, however, over a joint report by the whole staff of "How Grief Is Expressed." Reporters often see tragedies, deaths at fires, injuries in the streets and in falling buildings; they see the relatives find their injured and killed, and they carry the first news of disaster. I had asked everybody to observe directly the actual expression of sorrow, and the reports did not bear out the stage and the novels; there is more blowing of the nose in real life. Peck suggested other such studies: manifestations of indignation, real and pretended, of rage, surprise, cunning, etc., and I soon had my writers reporting in their daily news stories such close and correct observation of the details of demeanor that artists and professional men began to take notice. William Dean Howells, the novelist, once said that no writer or artist could afford not to read the *Commercial Advertiser*, and Professor Peck was as pleased as if Howells had recommended his columns of book reviews. There was nothing narrow about Harry Thurston Peck, and that's why he made *The Bookman* what it was, the authority on the literature of his day.

He and other editors entered into some of our games. One of my test assignments for a new reporter was to go and see and write the difference between Fifth Avenue and Broadway or Thirty-sixth and Thirty-seventh Streets. Norman Hapgood tried one of these, and everybody on the paper "did" the parade at Easter; we printed them all, a whole page which probably no one read through except the men and women on the paper. What of it? The readers got the results. The concentration of the staff on the technique of writing made them better reporters; yes, and got us "beats."

Carl Hovey outwrote all the reporters in New York one day when Archbishop Ireland came into the harbor from Rome with some news. The wise old prelate would not tell his news—"not a word," he said to the reporters, "not a single word." They were all balked but Hovey, who told us how the archbishop refused to talk. He reported how he looked, how he waved his long, canny finger, smiling, as he warned the reporters not to make up a fake; and how he came upon the crowd lying on the deck, their heads together, trying to fake up something—the fine old priest came up, cast his shadow over them, and startled them with his "Now, now, now, what are you all up to?" Our readers *saw* that happen, and they saw the archbishop and the kind of dignified, humorous, fine human being he was; and that was half the news of that day.

Carl Hovey, after he made the *Metropolitan Magazine*, became an editor on one of the most successful of the big movie lots, where I saw him recently. Just for the fun of it I asked him what the art was of making photo-plays. He answered quite seriously: "It's just what we learned on the old *Commercial;* you go and see something interesting and then you show it interestingly, that's all."

Yes, we used to talk art, and we tried openly, shamelessly, to practice it on that good old newspaper, all of us, even Robert Dunn, who would not himself recognize literature and broke up every conversation he could butt into about it. He began with his first day, when he came to us fresh from Harvard. The moment he was accepted on the staff, he turned and by his sarcasm damped a group of art talkers. "Bah!" he said. "There is no such thing."

One by one those reporters stepped up to me, and with Neith Boyce laughing, they begged me not to keep Dunn. "He'll spoil the spirit of the paper," they said. "We'll see," I answered, and the next morning I sent him off to a near-by one-alarm fire. He saw and he described it; Miss Boyce and I read, and without a change, sent it up to be set. It was in our first edition, and as the other reporters came in with their stories to write, they glanced at the paper and they read Dunn's short sketch of that fire. The first was Cahan, who was most against Dunn; he came up to me with his finger on the story.

"Who wrote that?" he asked.

"Dunn," I answered.

"Oh-h-h," he groaned. "We'll have to keep him, won't we!"

Dunn could write and Dunn could bite, and he bit and wrote his way through with us for months. He had no respect for anybody or anything. Some friend of his family told me that his method of conversation was to draw people out till he discovered what they held most sacred and then to "spit on the emblem thereof." He certainly spat upon us, all of us, and all our emblems. He would have split up the staff if he could have let any one follow or take sides with him. But no, he scoffed at those who agreed with him and soon had no one to speak to. I did not want to discharge him; I explained the situation and besought him to make it up with the other reporters.

"You mean that you want me to speak"—he looked around for an example, and seeing Cahan, he continued—"actually talk with Cahan?"

"Yes," I said.

"All right, I will, just for you," he said, and he walked up to Cahan and asked him, "Say, Cahan, why is it you East Side Jews never bathe?"

No use. I had to fire Dunn, and the staff hung around and regretfully watched it done. The boy came up, handsome, defiant, and stood there eying me as I told him how sorry I was to lose him.

"You can write, Dunn," I said. "The gift is in you, and you are sincere in the exercise of it. Your scorn of literature is affected; your contempt for seriousness and for the rest of us is—"

"Contempt for talk and talkers," he broke in. "Writing is all right, but talking about writing is—talk."

"A pose," I said.

"Every Harvard man has a pose," he sneered the circle of Harvard men around, "except me. And that's mine: to have no pose."

No use. I repeated that he could write, and I erred by remarking that he could be made a great reporter. I could train him myself if I were willing to abuse him, but I did not care to spoil my disposition, cuss him out, and discipline him; so I had decided to let him go, with a bit of advice. He laughed.

My advice was that he go out and find out who was the worst city editor in town, the meanest, the most first-mate-like martinet in the business. "Let him treat you rough for a while," I said; "take his medicine and learn to report; then, when you think you can be decent, come back to me, and I'll give you a job again."

"And finish making me a newspaper man!" he added. "Fine," he said. "But how do you know that I want to be a newspaper man? I've seen him; I've seen you all. Suppose I became one, suppose I should do what you advise and succeeded, suppose I rose and rose and rose beyond the utmost possibilities of the reporter's dreams and became—let me say—became finally and triumphantly a—say—a city editor—"

His handsome, honest, fearless face was twisted into hateful contempt as he paused, looked around at the listening staff, and so back to me.

"I'd rather clean streets," he finished.

And I admired and liked him more than ever. "Never mind, Dunn," I said, "I was not thinking of making you or anybody else a newspaper man; you know I prefer writers and ask you all only to report, to write what you see and hear, as you, for instance, can't help doing. You go on and do what I say, and I repeat my promise. If you will then come back to me I'll take you on again."

"Never," he said, and he marched proudly down the long room out and away. Proudly, I say; Dunn was pride in person. He went away and did exactly what I advised. He found the most terrible city editor in town and asked him for a job. And the most terrible started right in on him.

"Dunn," this fierce man said. "Experience: Harvard and the *Commercial Advertiser*. That means you can't write anything but literature. No matter. I have desk men that can write newspaper stuff. I'll take you on. You can do Harlem on the dead watch, midnight till daylight, and you needn't ever come to the office. Telephone your dope, and I'll have a reporter write it for you."

Dunn accepted, did Harlem all one winter, telephoning his news and letting it be written for him by the hack desk men. He went to the office once. The city editor called him up on the 'phone one night and called him down; he roasted Dunn so outrageously, with such insults to him, Harvard, and his family, that Dunn hung up, saying, "Wait. I'm coming down to lick you."

He didn't have to. That city editor, like me, really admired and liked Dunn. He also respected the unbroken spirit of the boy, and—there was no fight. There was no relaxation of the discipline, either.

One afternoon in the spring Dunn appeared, badly dressed in dirty old clothes, but head high, at the entrance to my office. I saw him sweep the office boy aside and come on slowly toward me. He seemed to me to be kicking himself up that long aisle, forcing himself to trample on his pride, and sensing the struggle, I jumped up and went to meet him.

"Have you come back to work, Dunn?" I asked, and he stopped and looked wondering at me.

"Say," he said, "will you take me back after—after what I said?"

"You bet I will."

Well, he did not want just then to come actually on the city staff. He had spent his vacations from Harvard exploring in the north, Canada and Alaska, hard, dangerous traveling, with little equipment and few companions. He knew the books and the technique of exploration, and he had an aunt who financed all such "follies," as his family called them. A great woman, she must have been; I never saw her, but I have somehow a picture in my head of Dunn's aunt, who taught me something about young men.

"My aunt," Dunn said that day, "my aunt is putting up enough money to start me on a trip into an unexplored area of Alaska, and I'd like to write about it for you, to make enough to get back."

I said I'd pay him double space-rates for all he would send me, and when he got back, give him a job if he wanted one. This he agreed to; he made his trip; he nearly lost his life, but he wrote us many perfect prose reports; and in the fall he rejoined the staff, who were as glad as I was to have him and his stuff on the paper. It was all so true; Dunn simply could not lie. I used to assign him to report reform meetings; most of my men so disliked reformers that they could not write fairly about anything they said or did. Dunn was the most prejudiced and always threatened to ridicule such a meeting; he meant it, too, but, pencil in hand, this born artist had to report things as they were.

It was this observation about him that prompted me to have him taken along on Dr. Frederick Cook's first attempt to climb Mt. McKinley. I had seen a good deal of arctic explorers, read their books, and heard their gossip, which revealed to me that no book in that field had told it all; they all left out the worst of the wranglings and depressions which were an essential part of the truth about human nature in such tests. Dunn went with Cook on this expedition; he wrote what I regard as a classic on exploration, *The Shameless Diary of an Explorer;* and I think now that it was his presence that caused the failure to top the mountain, and the second expedition. I mean that Cook too must have seen that he could not trust Dunn to stand for a lie and so went and reported the "top" later without this shameless explorer. But the odd thing about Dunn is that he was the most literary of the writers he affected to despise, the most idealistic. Dunn has written novels, or rather he has overwritten—book after book of beautiful truth. He and he alone of them all was an artist for art's sake.

XIX

GETTING OLD BILL DEVERY

THEODORE SCHROEDER, a well-known New Yorker who was spending his life and his livelihood fighting for liberty, halted me on the street one day to tell me with the glee of a collector that he had "come upon the most beautiful tyranny you ever heard of." He related the story, but I hardly listened. I was enjoying his esthetic joy in his discovery of a wrong to set right. We of the *Commercial* were like Schroeder.

A newspaper, to advertise itself and build up circulation and power, has, now and then, to do something besides print the news: help elect or defeat a party, force a public improvement through or stop an outrage, bring to justice some public enemy or rescue a popular hero from the machinery of the law. The *Commercial* rejoiced in the most beautiful opportunities to increase our growing circulation. There was the Cuban war, the Boer war, and best of all—Tammany was back in power.

The reform administration, which some of us on the *Evening Post* had helped to elect with the ammunition supplied by the Lexow police exposures, had failed somehow. William L. Strong, the good business man chosen as mayor to cast out the devil of politics and give us a good business government, had appointed Colonel Waring, an army officer, to clean our streets, and T. Roosevelt's bi-partisan board of non-partisan police commissioners to clean out the police department. These men did clean both the streets and the police force as they were never cleaned before, never. Many other departments likewise were scrubbed till they shone with polish and businesslike order and efficiency. "We" (meaning chiefly myself now) were shocked almost into thought when this good government was beaten and the old gang turned back into power. The only considerable failure I noticed was one that revived for a moment my old student interest in ethics.

Mayor Strong, the good man in business, was a bad man in politics. Some critics put it that the good business man was a bad politician, and that, too, was true. Mr. Strong tried to play the political game; he was pledged not to, but he found that he had to, and—he could not. His moves were technically wrong. But what struck me was that this business man and his business ethics were immoral in politics; his word was not good; his resistance to pull was so weak that he sought by compromise to satisfy everybody; and his ideas of integrity, ethical perhaps in a merchant, were downright dishonest in government.

This observation in the reform mayor, confirmed by the conduct of other business men in his administration and contrasted with the queer and attractive candor of the "honest crooks" I knew in politics, led me to a tentative theory which I noted in my old notebook on morals: "Ethics are professional; they differ in different occupations; and an ethical practitioner, formed and fitted in one profession, trade, or business, is apt to be disqualified thereby for another occupation morally as well as technically."

This I noted and passed on. There was no time to think. Newsmongering calls for action, not reflection, and Tammany, hungry and irritated, was providing us with a world of public enemies to hate and unconcealed schemes to expose, all in the familiar field of our experience on the *Post*. The only obstacle that troubled us was that we did not hate, we rather loved, our enemies, who rather liked us.

For instance: the Tammany mayor appointed as director of the Aquarium a man who knew nothing about fishes. The experts, proud of their famous collection, asked us to interview this ignoramus and show up his ignorance out of his own mouth. Fine. I sent down, fully instructed, a reporter, one of our best college graduates, who came back, not with the incompetent director's hide, but with the glad news that he had discovered "a character." The interview which he wrote and we ran did indeed expose the character's ignorance; out of his own mouth came the cheerful confession that he had never before met a fish face to face except cooked upon a plate or hooked upon a line. But he had taken the reporter out to the tanks, talked about the fishes there as if they were human beings, read into and out of their facial expressions and behavior such motives, sentiments, and thoughts that you felt that the new Tammany director, however scientifically unknowing he was about fishes, was an expert on men and life, reporters, newspapers, and the public. Now this was all very well as literature, but the unscrupulous writer who was supposed to be a reporter on an anti-Tammany newspaper wrote the wise things this bad man said as if his genial wisdom were a fair substitute for technical ignorance, and "we" went right on making this bad appointment seem good in the eyes of the world by printing other interviews with him on the fishes' views of politics, art, and—whatever came up in the news. We used him as he should have been used, not as Tammany used him. We used him as a commentator on the news of the day, as what the Greeks would have called a comic voice in the chorus, what the newspapers now dub a columnist. But the effect upon the unthinking readers must have been to welcome his appointment as a fish man.

We were clearer on William S. Devery, who was made chief of police to reform, not the department, but the system of police graft, as he understood and told me when I called to congratulate him on his appointment, renew our old acquaintance, and warn him that I meant to "get" him.

"Good," he said. "We both been appreciated and promoted, you to city editor, me to chief of police; you to be a head for headless reporters, me to be the same for a lot of flat feet and glad hands. We'll have a fight, and I hope you'll enjoy it as I will. I'll win, you know, and it'll be a credit to you and the rest of the reformers. For you learned me the business. Honest. I never knew it was so good till you showed it all up in black and white. All the matter with the police business was that it was mismanaged, too democratic, every cop in on it, somehow. I'm a-goin' to fix that. Concentrate it. I'm a-goin' to fix this police graft so as you squealers won't get nothin' to squeal at."

"Nothing but you," I interjected.

"Oh, say," he said, "there is me. Sure. I forgot that. You can make a holler about me. But it's all right. That's what I'm here for: to be shot at. I'm the hero, see? You can bring your guns up here, station 'em out there in front of police headquarters, and shoot 'em off every day at me. I'll just shut the windows to keep th' noise out and go right along doing business just th' same. Better.

So long's you keep on making friends for me I won't mind bein' enemies with you."

It was easy for Dr. Parkhurst and the other Christian ministers to hate Devery and reproach us for loving our enemy; they never met him. I acknowledged and "we" reported, yes, and proved that he was no more fit to be a chief of police than the fish man was to be director of the Aquarium, but as a character, as a work of art, he was a masterpiece. Not only I myself—every reporter I ever assigned to roast the man came back smiling and put the smile in his report. Their excuse was the excuse Shakespeare would have offered if some contemporary critic had reproved him for creating such a lovely villain as Iago. The poet's eye in a fine frenzy rolling would have said, "Yes, but isn't Iago the most villainous villain you ever saw?" Or Schroeder, with his "most beautiful tyranny." It's the divine point of view: "Yes, Devery is—as you say—no proper chief of police, but speaking as one artist to another, wouldn't you be proud if you had created old Bill?"

I tried to prejudice my police reporter against the chief. His name was Robert E. Moran. He was an office boy, the most impudent, daring, get-there kid on the *Evening Post* when I, as a police reporter, asked for a "boy" like Jake Riis's Max. Robert was not like Max when he was first sent to me; he was not a seer of the heart of things; but Max, I, and the police soon made of him a police reporter. He knew what news was, understood and could tell (not write) it, and as for the police business, he became a master of that, inside and out. By the time I went over to the *Commercial*, "Bobby," as the police called him, was as "wise" as a bright, disrespectful Irish boy educated in the police school could be; so I took him with me to be my police man. His only fault was that he was, as he said, "dead on to Devery"; he liked him; they liked each other. I recalled seeing them once, the big policeman and the small boy, sitting hip to haunch on the headquarters steps, quarreling, to be sure, but quarreling as the Irish quarrel only when they love each other. To break up this unprofessional friendship, I told the chief that Robert was to be my eyes, and then I told Robert what the chief said.

"Huh, Moran! I ain't afraid o' him. He's Irish himself, as Irish as me."

Robert called on the chief to ask him if he had said that and what he meant by it.

"No," Devery answered. "I did not say that, not exactly. What I said was that you were an Irish bum, which I ain't, and that I could beat you at any game, crooked or straight, underground, overhead, or on the level. Get me? I said back of your back and I'll repeat it in front of your face—I says that I might 'a' been afraid of your boss, but of you—bah! Bah, I'm saying to you."

CAPTAIN "BILL" DEVERY

When he saw that the boy was firing up into a flame he laughed and added the truth. "Say, Bobby boy, honest now, just between us two crooks, I ain't afraid of your boss neither. Do you want to know who I'm askeered of? It's me, Bill Devery himself. Get me?"

Robert nodded; he really did see the menace Devery's honesty was to his crookedness, and that irritated the chief, too.

"Well, then," he said, "if you get me so easy as that, you can run along out of here, and say, don't you never forget that you and me's enemies—to the death."

The boy came out smiling, blown from behind by a huge laugh which followed him into the street, the laugh of the chief chorused by the laughter of the chief's police staff, aides, secretaries, and doormen.

Thus the fight began, and so it continued, the graft, the scandal, and the laughter all growing together. The chief was building up his system so boldly that the police understood and laughed about it. "Bad" men were advanced or transferred to "fat" precincts, "good" men were demoted or sent "up among the goats," to lean precincts. Robert telephoned, laughing, the reasons gossip gave for these moves. I could not use half that the boy reported—too libelous; but I could write enough to show that "we" knew, and Devery saw that and did not care because he read the smile in what I wrote.

One day Robert telephoned that the chief had decided to sit himself as judge at the police trials. The police commissioners had always heard, in turn, these cases which were complaints, by citizens or officers, of infractions of the police regulations by policemen of all grades. The newspapers paid little heed to these petty cases. Roosevelt had shone at them in his day, and Devery must have seen the chance they offered to teach the force his wishes, his policy. He was sitting in judgment the day Robert called me up to say that "it was a picnic; the chief was giving himself away in every case he tried.

"He tells a cop accused of kissing a girl in a dark hallway that he is fined, not for being off post, but for getting caught. Any man good enough to be a policeman would help a nice girl to a kiss, the chief says. 'I would kiss a girl myself; there's lots of things I'd do and do do,' he says, 'but I'll never get caught. And so I can and I do herewith fine you good and plenty for getting caught. Two days' pay.'"

So Robert reported, and his half-angry, half-laughing comment was that two days' pay was not good and plenty; it was nothing at all. And it was the same in all cases. The chief justice blustered and thundered, pretending to be a fierce disciplinarian, whereas he was "easy" and really encouraged misconduct.

"Red" Mead was assigned to cover the next week's police trials and show up this bad judge. I felt that I had erred in my choice of a Yale man while I was telling him what Robert had reported. Mead's rosy face lighted up; he grinned and hurried off to his task before I had finished my instructions, and sure enough, he

came back that day with a humorous story. He did show up
Devery; you could see the big fellow tight in his uncomfortable
uniform sitting formally up there on the bench and handing out
justice with a hard mouth and a laughing, sometimes a winking eye,
to the cops who feigned fear and obviously rejoiced in the police
Solomon come to judgment. You could hear—as well as read—
the mocking chief imitating like a nigger the mouth-filling mind-
emptying technical phrases of the law. You could feel—you did not
have to read—that this jolly judge was teaching the bad cops to
do, undetected, whatever they jolly well liked, so long as they
did not butt into anything "touchin' on an' appertainin' to" police
business. And—worst of all or best of all—although the whole
scene made plain that there was police business and that police
business was business and came first, therefore, with pleasure
only second, the effect was to make our readers not indignant but
happy; the Harvard reporters applauded the Yale man, and I,
the one responsible reporter, after trying out other writers, sent
Mead again and again to make a comedy of Bill Devery's tragic
lynching of police discipline. Other papers followed us, sent their
most humorous writers to get the chief's "wise cracks" in his blend
of formal law language and the slang of the underworld.
"Touchin' on an' appertainin' to" became a cliché in the language
of New Yorkers. And meanwhile the evil grew.

"Say, boss," the chief said to me one day when we met on the
street, "there's a question I got to ast you. Honest now, all jokin'
aside. You know so much more than I do, specially crooked knowledge about crooked men and things, I got to ast you a question
that's been botherin' me some of late."

He was holding me by both shoulders till, seeing he had my
undivided attention, he put his troublesome question.

"What I want to know is, have you noticed any stray grafts
runnin' around loose that I have overlooked?"

And then, without waiting for me to say "No," he laughed his
good laugh, gave me a rude shove, and strode away.

"I don't like to ride," he said one day as he stepped out of his
carriage to enter his office. "I'm more used to walking, and I feel
better on my two nice big police feet, but it's the fashion in my set,
when you're getting rich, to show it forth and not be hiding your
light under no bushels, whatever in th' hell they are."

"We" did get him finally. In and about the chief's office were a couple of police officers whom I had served in my day. They would have gone to jail for me, as they said; and they did risk their rank and their living and their lives. For after all—all jokes aside— police business is business and there were men in it then, as there are men in it now, capable of doing murder or hiring it done. My friends were guilty of acts which would justify murder. They "tipped me off" on any of the chief's plans or deeds that they learned of, and they heard and saw quite enough. Unlike my reporter's gossip, these informers' stories I could print; if it came to a libel suit, they would testify. They didn't want to have to testify. They begged me to be careful, and I was. I wrote, usually without names, accounts of Devery's most intimate and secret agreements with gamblers, wire-tappers, and other law-breakers, with his instructions to captains and inspectors.

Devery knew I was getting it "straight." He laughed, but he worried. If I got something so dangerous that "we" could not "spread it," I would cut out the hidden paragraph and ask Robert to call on the chief, show it to him, and say that I "presented my compliments and begged very respectfully to ask what t'hell." Devery loved the mockery of form and always responded in kind. Robert would come away to telephone me something like this: "The Chief read your most interesting clipping and asked me to present his compliments and tell you kindly to go to hell."

One forenoon Devery had in his office a famous "reform" police captain, who said he was "tired of being out of it" and would like to get back in on the game. Devery, who took delight in the down- fall of reformers, told the captain that if he would return to his precinct, let certain men open poolrooms, and play fair with them and him for a month or so, he, the chief, would bring him downtown to a fat precinct. I had that agreement in the noon edition of the paper. A month or two later when the captain called again in the morning, reported, and was accepted into the fold, the chief ordered him transferred to the promised precinct. I had the transfer in the paper at noon, before the order was published. That afternoon, when Devery got back from lunch with the *Commercial Advertiser* in his hands, he sent for all the reporters and complained that he had no privacy.

"Look," he said, "I do something honest and fair at eleven

o'clock, and it's all in the papers at twelve as a piece of crooked corruption. What am I to do about it? What do you advise, Moran?"

Robert said he didn't know anything about it.

"Oh," the chief sneered, "I know you didn't know about it. You! Huh, the man that did that, the man that's doing it to me every day, is—well, he's the kind of a guy I'd like to make a policeman of, which I'd never make one of you. No, sir, I'm not looking for an innocent dub; I'm out for the guilty party that's got a leak in my office that I can't stop up."

"Well," said Moran, who knew that the chief despised plainclothes men, "why don't you put a detective on the job?"

The chief exploded. "Detective! Detective!! Hell! What I need is a plumber."

Such sayings, though not all published, were passed around from mouth to mouth, from the under to the upper world, till the scandal of Devery grew with his popularity. Many newspapers found fault with him, the editorial writers criticizing him seriously. All righteous men deplored his happy, honest wickedness; he must be punished. The wicked deplored his shamelessness, which frightened them; they did not care to punish him, of course; he served them boldly, and it would have been all right if he had talked humorously with them in the clubs and barrooms, but to tell the world what he was doing was a violation of their code, and bad politics. Not only the righteous, crooked men also are hypocrites. My impression, and I think Devery's, was that Tammany and a large body of his customers and the wisest of his police agents quietly turned against Devery. Anyway he had to go, and it was the system that "fired" him. The unofficial excuse of the firing officials was that Devery had made himself a scandal.

Devery had beaten himself as he feared he would, as he told Robert Moran he might. But he resented the disloyalty of his own kind. And by the same token he respected us of the *Commercial*, who had consistently distinguished between him as a person and as a chief of police. I think that we never printed a paragraph against this crook that did not betray our involuntary liking for his honesty, courage, and character.

When the order for his retirement was published, Mr. Wright, the editor of the paper, came down to my desk and remarked that we ought to have a photograph of the chief to print the day of his departure. I reminded him that Devery never gave out his picture, and Wright knew that, but he thought that "somehow we ought to be able to get one for such an occasion." The smiling manner of his hint gave me an idea.

"I'll get one," I said, and he crossed to the other side. "How?" he asked.

"I'll get it from the chief himself."

"I'd like to hear your conversation with him."

"You can," I answered, and I told him to go to his 'phone and listen in while I talked to Devery. He did.

"Hello, Chief," I called affectionately. "This is the city editor of the *Commercial*."

"The hell it is," he replied amiably. "What can I do for the city editor of the foremost paper in New York?"

"Lend me your photograph for publication."

"What!" And I could hear heavy, indignant breathing. I hurried.

"Yes, Chief. Listen. I know that you never give out your face for publication, and I can guess the reason. But also you are enough of a politician to understand that when a paper like the *Commercial* has spent years trying to get an official fired from his job, it likes to hang up his picture with a boast, 'William S. Devery, the unspeakable chief of police, whom the *Commercial Advertiser* has finally succeeded in ousting from—'"

The heavy breathing grew to gasps. I changed my tune.

"No, Chief, but honest, now, we have given you more space than we have given to any other public man, and I really think that we ought to have your picture and have it alone."

He burst. "Well, Jesus Christ! Of all the good God-damned gall. Send up your man."

And then, when he was all packed up ready to leave his office, he called in all the reporters at police headquarters, and Robert reported that his farewell was as follows:

"Gentlemen, I have summoned you to bid you good-by and to ask you politely to tell your editors to go to hell; all except you, Moran. Give my compliments to the city editor of the *Commercial Advertiser*."

We were, and we remained, friends as long as Devery lived.

He retired to his own home ward a rich man and set out to be the political boss, the Tammany leader, of that district. When Tammany opposed and beat him he was amazed, and he used to talk with me about it. His theory, his experience, of life had taught him that all you had to do to succeed was to get money, and that then, when you had "the stuff," you could buy with it anything you wanted. This he believed; that was his philosophy and his religion. His last chapter in life proved to him that it wasn't so, and Devery tried to think it out, change his mind, and the effort was in vain. It broke his heart; that and the queer mix-up of disloyal friends and loyal enemies.

"You, f'rinstance," he said one night on his favorite corner, "you been a good friend o' mine, and you ain't my friend at all. I mean —oh, hell, I don't know what I mean; do you?"

THE CUBAN WAR AND T.R.

Glancing back over the last few chapters, I see that I have presented fairly well the conceit of myself and of my staff of local reporters. "We" knew it all; we knew how to tell it; we were "making" the paper, which was, indeed, growing in circulation. H. J. Wright, the editor, let us think that we were doing it. There were other departments, on which he worked hard, but we rarely noticed them and nobody asked us to. Even the business office did not bother us much. Now and then the publisher, Seymour, hoping to bring in a new advertiser, would 'phone me to send one of my "best reporters" to some shop to write up some advertisement.

"What!" I would answer. "Let one of my writers write a reading notice? No, sir. We do news, not dirty work."

He would come frowning upstairs to see Wright. No doubt he complained, but I never heard a word of it from the editor. The write-up appeared in the paper, written, and well written, too, by Josephine Meagen. We of the city room came to admire this quiet little trained reporter of fashion news, even though she was not in our department; she was almost in our class.

Sometimes an advertiser who thought he owned the paper would telephone direct to me. He had a piece of news which he wanted a good man to report. "Oh," I would answer, "you are a business man. Well, you have the wrong number. This is the news department. We have a business department that attends to business. Call up the publisher."

In a few minutes Seymour came running upstairs, and giving me a look of indignation, disappeared into Wright's office, whence I heard the angry noises of his resentment and the soft purring of the editor. The matter was smoothed out somehow; they hired a Russian named Mendeloff, who was charged to my salary list but took orders mainly from Wright and Seymour. He did the commercial journalism for the business department after that. The city department heard no more of the advertisers' influence on the local news policy of the paper.

There was other news than city news. There was state, national, and foreign news, but we ignored it. It may have been important in the world's history, but it was not well written, and, you understand, we were writers; I was a newspaper man, temporarily, but my staff were writers, getting the news as material for poetry, plays, or fiction, and writing it as news for practice. The reporters on the other papers sneered at us, and the profession would have cut us; only we cut first, and being the youngest journalists, we could outdo their contempt with our pity. Those were times when a *Commercial* reporter met and praised some fellow like Richard Harding Davis for some story which we had analyzed and found pretty well written. Our applause did not improve our standing on Park Row, but we did not see that until later, too late. By that time we were old enough to realize that neither our talents nor our egotism were extraordinary and that an affectation of modesty was better than honesty as a policy.

Among the news of our day were a presidential election and the Cuban and the Boer wars. We used the presidential election to further our interest and purposes in the city election that occurred with it. The Cuban war served as a smoke-screen under which we played around in the city news, developing our cubs into reporters. We reported the local preparations for the war and the formation of the Rough Riders and other units of the army. We saw just enough of the commercialism of the business of supplies to agree that the place for a war correspondent to go was not the front, but the rear of a fighting army. There was a good deal besides canned beef to show up and protect the troops from. About the only reporting we did of the front was a long series of letters from Captain Theodore H. Low, a Marine officer on the battleship *Iowa*. He must have spent all his spare time writing those volunteer letters which pictured in detail everything that happened on a fighting ship just as it happened, the bombardment of San Juan, Porto Rico, in much the same tone as a frolic of the idle sailors. There was no more order than there was emphasis in this correspondence, but Pitts Duffield gave the letters form. Duffield had his work to do editing local copy, but his love was Captain Low's stuff. He kept it in a drawer, and whenever he had time he pulled it out and worked on it, cutting and piecing, weaving and connecting it up into copy that looked like embroidery. Day after day it ran, and "we" were proud of it as about the simplest, truest reporting done in that war. Other papers copied it enough to confirm our superiority in and to the Cuban war.

When the Boer war came we had an opportunity to appear at the front with a full-fledged war correspondent. Guy H. Scull wanted to go. He said he would pay his own expenses if we would give him credentials that would enable him to pass the British War Office. Scull arranged in London to write also for the London *Telegraph*, and his correspondence was a success in London. To us in New York it proved only that any of us could go anywhere in the world and write beautifully about anything. Any of us. True, Guy Scull was a gifted writer, but we did not then regard him as any better than the rest of us, and Carl Hovey recalled recently that upon Scull's return, covered with credit for battles pictured and soldiers characterized, he sat down and wrote a weather report like any ordinary reporter.

But the Cuban war ended in the city department. The army—all that was worth while of it, Colonel Roosevelt and the Rough Riders and some other regiments that had stood out in the war news—landed at Montauk. We all took turns going down there to report the scenes, types, and incidents of that camp. This was in accordance with the contract with my reporters that, in lieu of fair salaries, they were all to have equal chances to see and report —life. Also it was in accordance with our theory of journalism that anything that interested any of us would interest our readers and, therefore, would be news if reported interestingly. Unprofessional, this; the current theory which has prevailed on both newspapers and magazines is that the reader is a dub and that the editor must guess what the dub likes or will stand, give him that and nothing else. We knew nothing of the law of demand and supply; so we had a column from Montauk on a trooper treating two guests to fly-decked pie and eating all three portions himself.

This trooper, Edwin Emerson, was the bane of Colonel Roose-

Photo by Brown Brothers

THEODORE ROOSEVELT

"The gift of the gods to Theodore Roosevelt was joy . . . joy in life."

velt's short Army life. He had been a colleague of mine on the *Evening Post* and was fired for guessing wrong the verdict of a jury in a criminal case. When I became a city editor he offered to report for me, and needing a friend, I took him on. He came to my house for dinner one night when he should have been working and told me he had the news I expected; he got it by telephoning to the mounted police station. The next day, when he handed in his report and I told him it was wrong, that that new police station had no telephone, he laughed heartily. Edwin Emerson was a happy chap; he asked me to get him another job. The *Evening Sun* took him and fired him, as he said himself, "because, you see, they had three lists: names never to be mentioned; names never to be mentioned without praise; and names never to be mentioned without a roast. I couldn't help it. I specialized in mentioning the unmentionables, in roasting those to be praised, and in praising those to be roasted. So—can you help me to another job?"

I couldn't, but Seth Low, the ex-president of Columbia University, persuaded the secretary of the Woman's College to take Emerson as his secretary. When he turned up to ask for another job, he explained—happily, of course—"Well, you see, it was this way. The secretary of the Woman's College had a theory of education which I think is bad. I discovered it by accident. He was away on a vacation, and his children, coming home from school with my children, called for me and I began telling them (and my children) fairy tales. The children had never heard any fairy tales; they were hungry for them. Well, as you know, I know all the fairy tales of all the nations of the earth, and I make up more. So when the secretary of the Woman's College came back he found that his children could tell him all the fairy tales of all languages and were able themselves to make up more. Since his theory was that children should be taught nothing but facts, and principally scientific facts, he felt that his experiment on his own children had been interfered with and his children's minds ruined. He dismissed me. I don't mind that; I can see those hungry little children eating up my unscientific but lovely literature of childhood, and—well, say, can you give me a letter of introduction to T.R.? Judging by the kind of men he is choosing for his Rough Riders, I feel I am born for his regiment."

I gave Emerson a letter in those terms, saying that the bearer was peculiarly fitted to be a Rough Rider; and when the regiment came back to Montauk with Emerson (happily) in irons and T.R. roared at me his remonstrance, I bade him read my letter and see that I had told him the truth. The Colonel yelped with rage and laughter and let Emerson escape for an hour to show me the camp (and the Rough Riders' pie stand). He really liked Emerson, too; all Emerson's friends and victims liked this soldier of fortune and professional correspondent, all except the secretary of the Woman's College and another correspondent who alleges that Emerson once undertook to sell a horse for him and forgot (and was sorry for and never ceased to apologize to) the horse, which must have starved to death in the gulch where Emerson hid him.

T.R. gives some space to Emerson in his work on the Rough Riders or, as Mr. Dooley named it, *Alone in Cubiia*. He said that he put him under arrest for writing "a description of the personnel of his regiment," and when I objected that that should not have been a crime, the Colonel changed the subject.

"Say," he said, "they are talking me for governor of New York. Should I run?"

Now Roosevelt did not ask one such questions as that for the sake of an answer. They were merely questions he was asking himself out loud, but it was fun to reply as if he were putting them to you. I answered this question promptly and firmly.

"Yes, sure."

Astonished and diverted, he whirled upon me with another question: "Why?"

"Oh," I said, "it will make Platt and his machine so mad."

He lost his temper, but we were standing just inside the flaps of his tent and two ex-cowboys of his regiment came racing and yelling down through the crowded camp, and T.R. ran out to wave his hat and give the cowboy yelp. That eased him till I asked if it wasn't against orders to tear through camp like that.

"Yes, it is," he said, and he sneaked into his tent out of sight.

"Don't you enforce the law any more?" I asked.

"Yes; no. Oh, well, the war's all over. But honest, now, what is your real reason for my running for governor?"

"So that I can have the inside track on the political news and get a beat a day."

He turned his back on me, declaring he could never draw any

serious advice from me. But I asked him to observe that my answer implied that I believed he would be elected. "And you will," I said, reasoning that the reluctant willingness of Senator Platt, the Republican State boss, to support Roosevelt, suggested that this knowing politician knew that election was sure to follow the nomination of the war hero. There were obstacles, however. T.R. as police president and as a reformer had always opposed the boss, and it would be embarrassing for him now to deal with and accept his indispensable aid. T.R. sat on a box in his tent, wagging his head.

"We'll see," he said at last. "Meanwhile I'll get on with my book." And he resumed the dictation to the waiting stenographer. I knew T.R. well enough to feel sure that he would run for governor; which was news, even to T.R.

COLONEL ROOSEVELT AS GOVERNOR

THE colonel of the Rough Riders wriggled out of the army at Montauk as he had wriggled into it, fast. He said he had to get to New York to consult his friends and others about running for governor.

"I don't know whether I can get the nomination," he said, "and I don't know whether to take it—if I can get it."

"You don't think with your brains, do you?" I answered, and to meet the look of astonishment on his over-expressive countenance, I added that he had decided in his hips or somewhere not only to take the nomination but to go and get it, if he must, and to be elected.

His outthrust jaw drew slowly back, and he laughed. "That's so," he said. "How did you know it before I did?"

"You don't know it yet," I answered.

I didn't know how I read his mind. Having to watch him for news all those years at police headquarters, I had learned to guess what he meant while I listened to his answers to our questions, as a sailor looks for the weather in the sky and the sea. All reporters look as well as listen when their news sources are talking; how else do the newspapers report so correctly the news gathered out of lies! Roosevelt's lies were unconscious. He was an honest man; he could not tell a lie until he had made himself believe it. He did not know that day at Montauk, even when he acknowledged that I did, that he meant to be governor of New York. He did not deny my assertion that he "didn't know it yet." He turned away, then turned back, and named out loud to himself the men (and women; his sister Mrs. Robinson was one of them) whom he had to consult.

"And Platt?" I asked.

344

"No, never," he answered.

Senator Thomas C. Platt, the Republican State boss, was the counter villain of Richard Croker; he was the anti-Tammany city boss. The reformers hated them both, and Roosevelt was a reformer. He did not really hate bosses; the make-up of his regiment—dudes and athletes from the east and gunmen from the west—showed what his hips preferred. Only his mind ran with

Life

"LIFE'S SUNDAY SCHOOL CLASS"

Present: Teddy Roosevelt, Willie Bryan, Tommy Platt, Jacob Riis, Booker T. Washington

the reformers, who were already asking, under the lead of Godkin in the *Evening Post*, whether Teddy would surrender to Platt, call on and make a trade with him. And Roosevelt did not have to yield to the boss. He returned from Cuba as Lindbergh later came back from Paris: a hero. When he lighted on Montauk Point, the colonel of the Rough Riders could have been elected to anything; Platt sincerely hated him, but the Senator was a politician, and he knew that his best chance of carrying the State was to have Teddy lead his ticket. My information, from the political reporters, was that Platt would not ask Roosevelt for any pledge; all he wanted was a formal acknowledgment of his leadership and some outward sign of the "united front" so dear to machines. This I reported to the colonel, who did not understand himself.

"You don't have to see Platt," I said, "but you will."

"Will I?" he snapped, and though he was standing inside his tent his lower jaw seemed to protrude beyond the flap. But it soon went indoors.

"Why will I?" he asked, and his curiosity about himself was as sincere as his rage at my presumptuous prophecy.

"You're a practical man," I answered, and I used the phrase as we reformers used it, contemptuously, and T.R. seized it straight.

"I am, you know," he said. "I'm a practical man." And he repeated it several times then; he repeated it again and again during his very practical political career. "We are practical men," he wrote once to a railroad president, and the newspapers played it up as news. Roosevelt was a natural politician.

He called in New York on Senator Platt. After consulting with all his friends, after many meetings of the family, with advice for and against the step, the colonel sneaked over and called on the boss of the Republican State machine. There was no bargaining; Platt exacted no pledges. T.R. came back with his pride up, his jaw out, and his fist clenched. He had not yielded one iota of his independence.

"None was asked, was there?" I questioned.

He was pacing, like a fighting man, up and down the dining-room of his sister Mrs. Robinson's house, and my question seemed to hit him like a blow. He stopped, stared angrily at me, and then answered meekly, "No."

"But"—he advanced upon me furiously—"they are accusing me of surrendering to Platt."

"Oh, it is the reformers you mean; it is their bodies you are, walking on, their eyes you are pummeling."

He laughed. "Yes. Nobody saw me call on Platt, but the news of it has leaked out. How? How? How?"

"Platt," I suggested. "That's all he got out of it: your recognition of his bad eminence. He must have that known."

T.R. stood rocking a moment. "Of course," he said. "Of course. He didn't care to see me; he wanted others to see me see him. Of course. So he— Come with me."

He darted for the hall, grabbed his hat, and with me after him, he tore over to a room, a sort of office, where he was making his headquarters. There was no one there.

"Now," he said, "you've got to help me. I have to deny that I 'saw' Platt. The reformers are making bonfires of my call, and I must put them out. I must write a denial. You do it. Sit down there at that desk and write a correction."

"But," I protested, "it's true. You did see Platt."

"Yes, yes, I know, but there must be some way to make a statement that will—cover the case."

"That is a job for a statesman, not for a reporter."

He lost his temper, accused me of joking all the time, even in emergencies; I was no use, not in a charge. This was no joking business. As his wont was, he satisfied his rage completely in words and came out quiet and reasonable.

"I'll tell you what to do," I grinned. "You sit down at that desk, write out your statement like a reporter, and I like an editor will read copy, pass or reject it as plausible, and maybe edit it a bit."

He did that. He sat down, wrote painfully a short statement, and handed it to me. I read it and must have smiled.

"I know," he said. "That won't do, but it can be done, and I'll do it." He wrote another denial, offered it hopefully, and as I read the copy and he read my grin, he knew again. "I know, I know, but wait—we'll get it."

He wrote and wrote, one statement after another, till the desk was strewn with rejected sheets. It was late. I had to go home to dinner; he had other things to do.

"Look here, Colonel," I suggested. "We can't go on all night at this one job, and it isn't necessary. There is no known literary form for denying a fact without lying, and that you don't want to do. Why not pick out one of those statements, destroying all the others, set the selected one up on your desk, and read it before and after meals, till, in a day or two, you'll come to believe it yourself? Then give it out. It will be true then."

He looked up at me; I suppressed all signs of joking, and he muttered, "I *can* do that; I can *do* it. Which one shall I keep?"

I picked up at random one copy; he shook his head. "No, this is the best," and he held up his choice. I agreed. We destroyed the others, and I stood the chosen one on the lid of his desk, saying, "Now then. Read it twice before breakfast, once after; once before luncheon, twice after; and so on till bedtime. Read it on going to bed till you fall asleep. That's the principle of prayer. Some morning you will find that it's true."

"Good night," he said abruptly, and he hurried me away.

The demand from the press for a statement from T.R. was becoming irresistible. Knowing that one existed, I wanted it first. I had told my office about the written statement, and they wanted it first. After waiting two days I asked our candidate for it. I put my question wrong.

"Well, Colonel," I said, "have you got that lie so that you believe it yourself?"

He was furious. He leaped up from his desk where the statement stood and yelled at me that I "would spoil anything"; he was just getting so that he could have given out the statement, and I, by my insulting question, I had set him back, probably a day or two.

"And it ought to come out," he complained. "Everybody's after it, and there it is. Why should I hold it back?" But he would not give it to me. "Not on your life," he said.

The next day I read it, not in my paper, but in the morning newspapers, and my office was disgusted with me. Some of them suggested that it might be better for me to stay at my desk, mind my own business, and let reporters do the reporting. But I liked reporting better than editing; so I went on reporting. When I had the assignments all given out I sent myself up to see the Republican candidate for governor.

"Well," I said that morning, "I see that you did finally get where you could believe and publish that—statement."

"It's true, that statement," he exclaimed. "That statement is absolutely and literally true."

"Sure," I said. "I told you you'd come to believe it yourself."

He stood there at his desk, looking as he often looked: as if he had half a mind to beat me up. He never did; never got more than half a mind. I was lucky.

"Say," he said one day during that campaign, "things aren't going well up the state. I must try a new tactic. What'll it be?"

"Why not an old one?"

"Which?"

"Oh," I said, "go up there and eat dirt. Confess you're wrong on something, made a mistake, committed a sin, or were about to."

"But I'm not," he answered grimly.

"I'm talking politics," I said, "not facts."

He charged across the room, charged back, and stopped in front of me. Boring his eyes defiantly into mine, he said, "You think that's a joke, don't you? Well, it isn't. That is politics, good politics, and—"

"What's the difference?"

"There you go again. Think you're funny. But I tell you that trick will work, and I'm going to work it. It'll make the people see that I'm just like them; one of them."

He did it; it worked; and all through his career he showed that he knew when to make or confess a blunder. Yes, T.R. was a very practical politician, and it was partly from watching him sympathetically that I lost some of my contempt for politicians and practical men generally.

And I did watch T.R. Doubleday, Page and Company contracted with me to write his life, and I contracted with T.R. to tell me his story and give me the documents. Not a line of it was ever written; it was too hard a job for me to do while I was city-editing. We started it, however. T.R. was finishing his book on the Rough Riders and running for governor; he could do a lot of things at once.

"Come on," he would call after some political conference. "Let's walk and talk."

Darting out of his house at Oyster Bay, he would jump a fence and crash into the woods, telling me, who came running breathlessly after him, how, when he was a child, his father—

"My really great father—a gentleman and a sport—he was the first American to drive four horses handsomely through New York—in style, in the good old English style, with everything that belonged—he worked for, he saved, my life. I was a weak-lunged, asthmatic child, and I remember—I think I remember—him carrying me in my distress, in my battles for breath, up and down a room all night. Handsome dandy that he was, the thought of him now and always has been a sense of comfort. I could breathe, I could sleep, when he had me in his arms. My father— he got me breath, he got me lungs, strength—life."

I remember this because I was all out of breath when I heard it; I was chasing along behind the once asthmatic athlete who was taking a rest from his politics by tearing through the brush of those Long Island woods for fun.

"I wish," I remember saying to him, "I do wish, Colonel, that you would be a father to me as your father was to you."

"How?" he stopped to demand.

"By carrying me in your arms till I can get my breath."

"Oh," he said. "Don't you love to run like a deer through the timber?"

"Maybe," I answered, "but not like a bull moose, not like a hound after a bull moose."

The pretense of taking his *Life* was kept up for a few years; it was a good excuse to be near him when he was a source of news, as governor and as president. Many a good story came out thus, and I did write some magazine articles about him. I could stand well the stuff he poured out of his memory and his reflections, but I could not stand the cross-country walks which were runs to me, running and jumping over plowed fields and high fences.

When he was governor he let me in on his most private political plannings, conferences, hesitations, and decisions. They were all news to me. I mean that I heard and saw what the governor said and did from the merely professional point of view of a newspaper reporter. A few years later I would have had a more philosophic attitude; I would have had theories and opinions and purposes of my own, and I might have tried to influence the man in power that I was so close to. At that time I had no theories beyond those of the ordinary reformer. Roosevelt's governorship, his Legislature, and the situation in the State and city of New York were a mere spectacle to me, interesting, dramatic, comic, but taken all in the day's work, as a matter of course. The meaning of it came out later, when I was seeing other governors at work in other States.

I could see that the bosses and the business interests were willing to use up Governor Roosevelt as they are wont to destroy the political possibilities of the presidents, governors, mayors, and legislators they find they can use for their purposes. Roosevelt used to tell how they came to him with their extravagant demands for privileges, holding out offers of contributions and backing for the U.S. senatorship and even for the presidency. And he did some things for the interests. But T.R. was a practical politician; he saw that he must stand in with the powers that govern our government, but that he could not, for his sake and for theirs, give them all that they asked.

"They want the earth," he blurted one day, "and they would destroy me and themselves and the earth itself to get it."

His habit was to spend the middle of the week, while the Legislature was in session, at Albany, and on Friday, when it adjourned, he would come to New York to stay till Monday afternoon or Tuesday morning. I met him at the station when he arrived in New York, kept in close touch all the time he was there, and saw him off when he took train for the capital. We had an understanding that I was to know all the political acts that he was contemplating, with his reasons for them. At Albany we had a man, Larry Graham, a charming, handsome fellow whom the governor liked, who acted as Albany correspondent. Graham did not know New York politics very well; he had had no experience in that field as a reporter. He was not a "wise" old newspaper man; he was, like the rest of our staff, a fresh, young, open-eyed observer; he differed from the others in that he was not a writer. He rested while I worked week-ends, and he returned with the Governor to Albany with instructions, not to write and wire, but to telephone me, when the news we both expected and understood was released by T.R. I wrote it, and I wrote it as one having authority. This was most unprofessional, but it was amusing, and as T.R. said, "It worked." T.R. was rarely quoted; no other authority was cited. As we were sure of our news, it was stated briefly, firmly, positively, upon our own authority. The result was that when we had a beat, other papers had to say that "the *Commercial Advertiser* said," which had the effect of making people think the paper was an authority, on the inside, especially as our news was so regularly confirmed by executive and legislative acts. When we were beaten, when some other newspaper reported something that we had overlooked, we used to say, "The *Sun* reports so and so.

This is correct." It was impudence; it was an annoyance to the *Sun* men, and other newspaper people made disagreeable remarks about us in Park Row. But we of the conceited *Commercial* enjoyed it all, and we made the whole street laugh with us before we were through.

One week-end when Larry Graham was in town he reported to me with some embarrassment that Franklin Clarkin, the city editor of the *Evening Post*, had made him an offer of $75 a week to quit us and cover Albany for him. "What shall I do?" asked Graham.

"Take it, of course," I answered. "We're paying you only $35; you have a family behind you and a career ahead. Go to the *Post*, sure."

"But—" Graham did not want to go. He liked our crowd, and he realized that Clarkin did not know that he, Graham, was not writing all his dispatches. But he consulted with the staff, and they all saw the humor of the situation; they made me promise to take Graham back any time he wished to come, and then they—"we"— all pushed our Albany correspondent over upon the *Post*. A few weeks later I met Clarkin on the street.

"Say," he said, "what sort of a gold brick is this that you have sold me?"

"Graham is no gold brick," I answered. "No man on the *Commercial* is a gold brick; they are all bricks and pure gold, but they are not gold bricks."

He backed up. He liked Graham, felt his charm, and got the results of his popularity with the governor and the legislators; Graham got the news all right, "but," said Clarkin, "he does not write it; he wires it in bulletin form, like notes, and there is no force in it." I explained that that was the way we had taught Graham to report—short bulletins which I took and rewrote *ex cathedra* in the tone and style of the All-Wise.

Clarkin walked along, silent a moment; then he smiled. "What shall I do?" he asked.

"Oh," I said, "keep Graham and hire a good city editor, me, for instance."

But this was bluff on my part. I was not so superior as I pretended. It was just about that time that my wife was having me examined by a physician who wagged his head and told her—not me—that I "could not keep it up." I was on the "verge of nervous prostration." And I happened just about that time to overhear one man in the business department say to Wright, the editor-in-chief, that I was all in. "We've got out of that man just about all there ever was in him."

T.R., approaching the end of his term as governor, was saying what he saw ahead—and among these was, to use his own winking word, "Washington."

"There'll be something for you and Graham, too," he hinted. But I was not interested. I remember that I answered that all I wanted was a sinecure, "a well-paid job with no work to do."

"Find one and you shall have it," he promised, but the very energy of his promise depressed me. I was emptied of energy— done, for once. If I had been told I was to have "seen" sixteen other cities as I had seen New York, and eleven States, I would probably have died.

PART III
MUCKRAKING

FROM NEWSPAPER TO MAGAZINE

"THE muckrakers dominated a period of the history of the United States. Muckraking was a movement the origin of which will some day be a subject of historical inquiry. You were the first of the muckrakers. If you will tell now how you happened to start muckraking not only will you contribute to our knowledge of an important chapter of American history; you may throw light upon the rise and the run of social movements."

A professor of history thus addressed me recently, and I had to answer first that I was not the original muckraker; the prophets of the Old Testament were ahead of me, and—to make a big jump in time—so were the writers, editors, and reporters (including myself) of the 1890's who were finding fault with "things as they are" in the pre-muckraking period. But my second and more salient answer to the university professor was that my contribution to history would be, not a letter, not a philosophical dissertation, but a story, a confession of innocence. I did not intend to be a muckraker; I did not know that I was one till President Roosevelt picked the name out of Bunyan's *Pilgrim's Progress* and pinned it on us; and even then he said that he did not mean me. Those were innocent days; we were all innocent folk; but no doubt all movements, whether for good or for evil, are as innocent of intention as ours.

One day toward the end of my newspaper service, John S. Phillips, an associate editor of *McClure's Magazine*, called on me in the city room of the *Commercial Advertiser*. He took me out to lunch, and gradually, cautiously—characteristically—he revealed his purpose: to find a managing editor for the magazine. John Finley held the post at the moment, but he was about to be called elsewhere to more academic work, and S. S. McClure, Phillips, and the other editors wanted a trained young newspaper editor to manage the editorial office and carry on the policy of the magazine. August F. Jaccaci, the art editor of *McClure's,* had been watching the *Commercial Advertiser* grow; he had asked our dramatic editor Norman Hapgood who it was that had made that paper, and evidently Hapgood had given me the credit, or part of it. Anyway they had decided to ask me to come over and help make *McClure's* what they meant it to be. Phillips was sounding me to see if he thought I could do it. My recollection is that I was not eager; I liked the *Commercial,* disliked the idea of leaving my staff and all the fun we were having. And I was tired out. I think that Phillips went back and reported that I was not enthusiastic. But they had no one else in sight, and I discovered that my newspaper chief was nonresistant; he rather encouraged me to go. It was then that I learned that my employers thought that I was "all in," exhausted, "used up." Phillips came back another day, and I was more willing to listen to him.

"What will be your policy on the magazine?" he asked.

"Put news into it," I answered. I had been "thinking it over," and it had occurred to me that there were some news stories which ran so long and meant so much that the newspaper readers lost track of them. A weekly might comment upon such stories, but a monthly could come along, tell the whole, completed story all over again, and bring out the meaning of it all with comment.

Phillips seemed to see that and to approve. He took me up to his office. S. S. McClure was absent, but John Finley was there, and Jaccaci and Albert C. Boyden. Jaccaci probed me hard, took me to his home, talked with and drew me out. That was his way. He could not be a friend; he had to be a lover, and he worked wonders with the artists who illustrated for him. No employer of employees he, but a fellow worker, an intimate friend; he was what was called an inspiration. He was really an editor, only he did not edit copy; he edited the men, and his influence was all the more powerful because it was so personal. His department was art, but writing—everything was art to him, and he made love to and won and got results from the writers as well as the illustrators.

It was Jaccaci who clinched my contract. He saw that I was indeed tired by my newspaper work and backed my insistence that

I have the summer for a rest. I was to come to the magazine in the fall. That disappointed the others; the magazine needed a managing editor then, in the spring. Phillips wagged his head; he was thinking of the office; but "Jac," as we called Jaccacci, was thinking of me as he always thought of the artist or the writer, the editor and all the employees, as persons.

"Boyden can manage the office temporarily," Jac said.

I went up into the Adirondacks to a cabin on Fourth Lake that my wife had made ready. I don't remember going there; the thought of rest had so relaxed me that I fell into a daze which turned, when I arrived at that cabin, into a sleep. Twenty hours I slept that first day and night; nineteen the second. One, or at most two, meals a day I ate, and the rest of the time I slept on a pine-bough bed on the porch of that little house for weeks. I swam in the lake; by and by I began to paddle in a canoe or row. One Sunday morning we awoke late to find all our provisions gone and Edwin Emerson sitting by our store, finishing the crumbs. He laughed, went to a near-by hotel for a hearty breakfast with us, and then tramped on. I don't know where he came from or where he was going. Another day my wife's father came to visit us, Dr. R. B. Bontecou. He paddled me around the lake and told stories of his youthful explorations on the Amazon. There were no other visitors, no books, no news, nothing but dreamless nights and dreamy days in the woods and on the waters of that beautiful natural park. It was so lovely that I have never cared to go back, lest the Adirondacks should prove real or active or thoughtful. I never woke up till three of my agreed-upon four months of vacation were gone. Then I telegraphed *McClure's* to ask if I might not come at once; they answered, "Come," and I went to work, to another long period of concentration. It was just like springing up from a bed and diving into the lake—and life. The water was cold.

There was a desk for me at *McClure's;* no doubt there was an opportunity, too: the editorial department needed organization, but I was not an organizer. Nor an executive. There was executive work to do; Bert Boyden was doing it, temporarily. He was, temporarily, in the place of John Finley; he remained, temporarily, in the place when I came to take it. Boyden was acting-managing editor all through my term as managing editor, and after I left he still remained, temporarily, as acting-managing editor. The situation was just like that which saved me when I became city editor of the newspaper; only I understood it better now. I simply was not an editor. As I wandered around that magazine office looking for work, I realized that I was a false alarm. Lachaussee, my assistant on the *Commercial Advertiser*, had done the managing there; here on *McClure's* Boyden did it. I did more directing on the newspaper; I really led or drove the staff of reporters. On the magazine there was no staff for me to direct. Miss Ida M. Tarbell and Ray Stannard Baker were regularly employed as writers, but they had already been assigned to subjects. Miss Tarbell was writing *The History of Standard Oil*, and Baker was doing semi-scientific articles and a series on Germany. S. S. McClure, the editor, was directing their work. For me were left only the authors, who, for the most part, did not come to the office but sent in their manuscripts; and other contributors, like explorers, who had to be seen and persuaded to write for us. A fair field for work, and pleasant, but that was pretty well covered by McClure himself, and by the other editors. I did some of that, but I did not do it well. I was too much on the side of the writer; preferred what an author wanted to do to what we wanted him to do; paid him his price instead of ours.

James Hopper exposed this fault of mine. He sent in from the Philippines two or three powerfully written short stories. Viola Roseboro, our reader, recognized their promise of a new great talent. She rarely missed a good piece of work. She discovered Hopper toward the end of a long, hard day of manuscript reading. She sprang up, put on her hat, and came down to the office from her Harlem flat just as we were closing.

"Here," she said to me, secretively, "here is a new writer. His stories are brutal, and there'll be opposition to them. You read them tonight, and we'll make a fight for them together."

I read these manuscripts, I felt what she felt, and sure enough, the other editors recognized their power but would not accept them. Miss Roseboro pleaded, in vain. Everybody was for returning these stories with a good letter asking for a look at anything else Hopper might do; the author, not his works, was what interested the office. I fell in with that. "Either we take these stories," I insisted, "or we take the author." They agreed to send for the author. Hopper came, we gave him a job—reading proofs, I think

—and set about trying to make him write more popular short stories. I took him home with me, to Cos Cob, to tell him what to write and how. "You gave me some very bad advice," he said afterward. He must have taken some of it, for he did write several stories which we printed. He was making a name for himself when S. S. McClure came home from Europe and took charge. He liked Hopper's gift.

"That's one good thing you have done," he said of my editorship. A puzzling remark that worried me. The only other thing he approved was my correspondence with authors. "You treat them as if you knew that we live on them and had to have them and their work." This sounded like a disapproval of others.

One day Hopper came up to my desk, laid down a new story, and said he wished he could get better pay for his fiction. I read into his manuscript, saw that it was one of his best pieces of work, and handed it back to him. "Send it somewhere else," I said. "It will be taken. That will show us that you are appreciated and—you can raise your price on us."

When this story appeared, "S.S.," as we called McClure, raised a rumpus. He could raise a rumpus. He clamored for Hopper, jumped on him for daring to send his stuff out when he was on our salary list, and Hopper wilted and told him he had acted on my advice.

"Steffens told me to offer it outside."

McClure left Hopper, came running in to me, and he raised a rumpus for me. I was turning authors away, sending good stories to other editors—why, why, why? I told him: to force us by competition to pay our authors more, and to meet his look of astonishment, I reminded him that he had bidden me remember that we lived on the authors, that we must treat them well, and that meant, I reasoned, that we must remember that they had to live on us. He looked around to see that no one was listening; then he bent down and, like a conspirator, whispered: "That's right. Raise their pay, but don't tell anybody else what you are doing. And"—this he spoke aloud and erect—"don't ever send away another such good tale as this of Hopper's."

That was Sam McClure, the wild editor of *McClure's Magazine*. Blond, smiling, enthusiastic, unreliable, he was the receiver of the ideas of his day. He was a flower that did not sit and wait for the bees to come and take his honey and leave their seeds. He flew forth to find and rob the bees. He was rarely in the office. "I can't sit still," he shouted. "That's your job. I don't see how you can do it." One reason he could not stay in the office was that we checked him. That, too, was my job, the job of all of us, to hold down S.S. But his nerves drove him, too; his curiosity, his love of being in it, his need to wonder and to be wondered about. He followed the news, especially big, personal news. If a new author rose on the horizon, or an explorer started for it, or a statesman blew in over it, S.S. went forth to meet him and "get him into *McClure's*." To Africa he traveled, to Europe often, to the west, south, east, and the north of the United States to see things and men, to listen and to talk. Field work was his work. Ideas were his meat, and he never knew where he got them. He told an explorer once what the explorer had seen in the Antarctic; he picked out a few suggestive remarks from the dull man's short account and, taking the story away from him, described the man's own trip to him so vividly that S.S. was fascinated. He wired us that he had ordered, not an article, but a series. We all hated serial articles; they tied us up, and S.S. knew that. When he came home he would not stay; he ran right off to Europe. We didn't know why till the explorer himself came in and handed me his hopeless serial.

"Mr. McClure ordered this," he said confidently, and he named the high price he had been promised.

"Mr. McClure did not order these articles," I answered. "He ordered his own vision of your experience. You have written what you saw; you should have written what McClure saw in the Antarctic."

Realizing that S.S. had gone abroad to get out of the mess he had left us, we had an editorial council. We simply could not use this stuff; couldn't even get it re-written for the author who knew or told mainly that he "rose at 5:55 A.M. and marched four hours." I solved that problem. The man happened to be going to Europe. I gave him the address of Mr. McClure, and that was the last we heard of that explorer. S.S. either put him off or settled with him out of his own pocket.

Another time, when S.S. had been away and left us wondering at his haste to catch a ship, two young men turned up in the office. I saw them wandering about as I had when I arrived. Mr. Phillips seemed to know them; no one else; and when I asked him who they were, he said: "Oh, don't you know them? They are just a couple of boys S.S. found making a success of a newspaper out west. He got interested in their story, persuaded them to sell out and come to us, one to take your place, the other mine."

"Well, but what'll we do with them?"

"Nothing. Let them play around at any work they can find till— It will solve itself."

Those two young men hung around a short time; then they went out and found positions elsewhere. They became very successful men in the publishing and advertising business, and they never showed any resentment of McClure's mistaken interference in their careers. They wondered about but they could not understand what had happened.

It was always so when S.S. went away; there was always some act of his enthusiasm for us to counteract. And it was always so when he came back from a trip. He would come straight from the ship to the office, call us together, and tell us what he had seen and heard, said and done. With his valise full of clippings, papers, books, and letters, to prove it, he showed us that he had the greatest features any publisher had ever had, the most marvelous, really world-stunning ideas or stories. Sometimes he had good things. He brought back Kipling's *Kim* from one trip to England. Usually, too, he had some great discovery in science or a subject for inquiry and report at home here. And we accepted, calmly, but appreciatively also, some of his suggestions. But we had to unite and fight against, say, five out of seven of his new, world-thrilling, history-making schemes. He could fight as well as we. He had the magazines we had made in his absence as weapons to attack us with. We were failures; we were dead weights; he was the inspiration, the creative spirit, on the magazine, and we served only to hold him back, McClure and *McClure's*. I used at first to take his side; he was "the man" among us, and he ought to be given his head. But that was impossible and expensive. Most of his great ideas were foolish, and I joined with the rest finally and served as one of the four-wheel brakes upon the madness of McClure's genius. Phillips was hard, patient, but immovable; Jaccacci was like S.S. himself, temperamental and explosive; I was variable—now for, now against the chief, but not very serious. It was Miss Tarbell, a devoted friend of S.S., a devoted friend of all of us, who with her tact softened these battles or found a way to compromise and peace. I could laugh because "we," the office editors, had the control; we simply did not carry out the impossible or the mad schemes of the chief even when, for peace, we affected to agree to them. And S.S. soon forgot; he had other greatest ideas or authors in the world.

The result of my course was that S.S. often told the other editors that I was the only great editor of them all—all but himself. And this he contradicted privately. He wanted me to be his editor, his first mate, and he watched me with hope, and he helped me with encouragement. He was often with me, both in the office and in his home or mine. We became pals. His brother, Robert McClure, objected. He said I was not an editor, but he blundered with his evidence. I was writing stories and essays for the magazine, and I wrote under another name an article, "Masters of Their Craft." Robert McClure wrote to "The Editor" a letter, evidently for me to open and read, saying that I should be dismissed and the man that wrote that article be put in my place. I passed that letter on to S.S., who enjoyed the situation but said that his brother did not. One day S.S. sat down by my side, and he told me very impressively that his brother was right just the same.

"You may have been an editor," he said very sincerely, very kindly. "You may be an editor. But you don't know how to edit a magazine. You must learn to."

"How can I learn?" I asked him, angrily.

He laid his hand on my knee. "Not here," he said. "You can't learn to edit a magazine here in this office."

"Where then can I learn? Where shall I go to learn to be an editor?"

He sprang up and waved his hand around a wide circle.

"Anywhere," he said. "Anywhere else. Get out of here, travel, go—somewhere. Go out in the advertising department. Ask them where they have transportation credit. Buy a railroad ticket, get on a train, and there, where it lands you, there you will learn to edit a magazine."

I did that. We had a bill against the Lackawanna Railroad for advertising. I took an order for a ticket to Chicago, and there, sure enough, I learned—not exactly how to edit a magazine, but I started something which did "make" not one but several magazines. I started our political muckraking.

I I

ST. LOUIS, A CITY INSIDE OUT

MY BUSINESS as a New York editor in Chicago was to call upon and draw out writers, editors, and leading citizens, to see what they were interested in, and invite some of them to write for *McClure's*. I had a list of such men. Bert Boyden, who was managing me as well as my work, gave it me, and at the end he added the name of his "brother Bill," a member of the law firm, Matz, Fisher, and Boyden. It was only as a matter of courtesy that I called finally upon William C. Boyden, and as a matter of courtesy this genial man turned his chair, his body, and his whole mind around upon my business. Had the men I had seen suggested anything for the magazine? No.

"Well, then, let's see," he said, and he went to work. "To begin here at home, there's my partner, Walter Fisher; he's undertaking to reform the city government of Chicago—"

"Reform? Chicago?" I laughed, and I must have expressed the idea that that might be news, if true, but—impossible.

"No?" said Boyden, who never argued or urged. "Well, then—let's see now. Oh, I'll tell you. Up in St. Paul there's a very quiet little old German gentleman named Weyerhäuser, who has gathered into his possession much of the timberlands of the United States. He owns wide areas of the west and northwest, and now he is acquiring the forests of the southern States. I know about him because of a law case. He wanted to log lumber down streams so small that boats could not float on them, and he couldn't legally, because they were not 'navigable streams.' So he had the courts decide that logs were boats; a stream that navigated logs was a navigable stream; so—"

"What about him?" I asked.

"Nothing," said Boyden, "except that there is a great, effective
365

human power of whom nothing is known, nothing is ever printed. He's one of the richest men in America, richer than some of your famous New York millionaires, and the public has never heard of him."

I went to St. Paul, found Weyerhäuser's modest, orderly office, and learned from his clerks that he always refused to be interviewed. They told me a little about him, how precise he was, how quiet, methodical, prompt. "Gets down here to the office every day at exactly 7:30." I think that was the minute; maybe it was 7:15. Anyway I was there five minutes before the hour named the next morning, and when the round, gray, smiling German arrived I asked him for an interview.

"I am never interviewed," he said. "I don't care for write-ups." He was about to go on through the swinging gate.

"I don't propose to write you up," I said. "I want to write you down."

He stopped, looked. "Come in," he invited, holding the gate open.

He led on into his private office, sat us both down, and then, without glancing at his mail, he said, "Now, then, what can I do for you?"

I told him I had learned that he had started with nothing and acquired a fortune and half the forests of America. "What did it cost you?" I asked.

He started to shake his head as if to say, "Nothing," but he was staring at me, and his intelligent, wide-open eyes saw something of my meaning. His smile vanished; his face grew serious. "You mean—"

"Yes, I mean that there are lots of able men in this country who have set out with no capital, made millions, and then tell us it cost them nothing but work, hard work. I think it cost them— something else. I think it cost them as much or more than they made. How rich are you?"

He sat still a moment, then rose and closed his office door. When he came back—all very slowly, deliberately—and sat down, he said seriously: "I don't know how rich I am. I'll ask the bank downstairs later to make an estimate for us. And I don't know what it has cost me—either. I have often wondered. You mean the things I have had to do to—to do business? Yes. I thought so. Well, that has bothered me a great deal. I have often wanted to talk it over with somebody. There was nobody—"

"Why not your pastor?"

"Oh, the clergy—they don't understand."

"They just tell you to stop it?"

"Yes, and you can't."

"Well, there's your banker, other successful business men," I suggested.

He saw my smile, but he wouldn't join in the jest. "Some of them worry, too," he protested, "but—"

He stopped, shaking his head.

"They just say to go on?"

He nodded, abstractedly. We were silent a moment; he was thinking; he wanted to talk.

"What do you have to do—?" I asked softly, and there was an immediate response. He had been looking down; his face turned up to me, and he said: "I'd like to tell you. Can I? In confidence? You can't print it, of course."

I hesitated; it wasn't fair to the magazine to take this for myself, but what could I do?

"I promise; sure," I promised.

He told me what he did to get hold of the timber, how he did it, how he got and used power in politics. And he told me, questioningly, how he justified it. He began with the ordinary practices of a business man, contributions to campaign funds. He was testing me. Did I judge? Did I show shock? I didn't. I saw the compulsion upon him, said so, and he, encouraged, opened up more and more of the picture. We were shut in there all the forenoon, three or four hours. I did not try to help or hurt him, just listened, and he talked himself out. Toward noon he got back to his balance of profits on money and his loss in—something, and he remembered his promise. He called up the bank downstairs on the 'phone.

"There's a man here," he said, "who has asked me how rich I am. Can you make a rough estimate? No? Too long a job? All right." He hung up. "He doesn't know either, can't say offhand."

"It doesn't matter now," I said. "Does it?"

"No. That isn't the point. We've got the cost; the profits don't matter."

This he said absentmindedly, and absentmindedly he saw me to the door. I went away and back to Chicago, like Weyerhäuser, absentmindedly, thinking how much better a man can be than he thinks he is.

"Well, then," said Boyden, "if you didn't get an article out of Weyerhäuser, here's another chance. There's a man down in St. Louis; his name is Folk; he is raising the deuce of a row about bribery in the board of aldermen. We get the dust of it in the papers but no clear idea of just what it's all about. Why not go down there, see this man Folk, and have him and his findings written up plain for us who don't know St. Louis?"

That was in the line of the policy I had proposed for the magazine, a national publication: to take confused, local, serial news of the newspapers and report it all together in one long short story for the whole country. I went that night to St. Louis, and by noon the next day I was sitting with Joseph W. Folk in a quiet corner of the old Planters Hotel lobby. He had "dropped everything" to come there. He needed help, publicity.

"The local newspapers are backing me up, now, some heartily; all are printing the news. But they don't know yet what I know." He looked around as if pursued. "The ramifications of this thing, the directions the trails of evidence are taking, the character of the opposition I encounter—I'm afraid I'll soon be losing all local support. You publish in New York. You are not subject to the pulls and the threats of St. Louis. You might see me through and so set the pace for the papers published here. But I warn you that what is coming is beyond belief; I can hardly credit my own eyes and ears."

The man was dazed. Having shown thus for one little moment his inner disturbance, he smiled, put up a cool, courageous front, which he rarely lowered thereafter. He was a small man, small-boned, with a white face sharpened by thin black hair and dark eyes. A southerner from Tennessee, he came of the race of southern Puritans who have the hard, righteous traits of their New England cousins, and chivalry besides, and the pride they had put on to cover their conscience against slave-holding. Folk's hardest virtue was duty. He had had the world all pictured for him in the schools of Tennessee and in his law studies. The Bible, the English common law, the Constitution of the United States, and

the charter of the City of St. Louis described things as they were—
so he had believed when he came up from Tennessee to start his
career as a corporation attorney. He went into politics, a bit, for
the practice in public speaking, to make friends (and clients), and
to prepare the way for the eloquent statesmanship which southern
boys dream of. He became circuit attorney, the prosecuting officer
of the St. Louis district, by chance, almost against his will. He had
no interest in, he had the common horror among law students
of "criminal law" (where the finest opportunities are). But the
political bosses were in a tangle with their own several aspirants
for the office, and there was that harmless, respectable young man
Joe Folk, who was president of the harmless, respectable Democratic Club. Ed Butler, the big Democratic boss, bade Folk stand
for the election as circuit attorney.

"I'll have to do my duty," Folk warned him softly.

"Oh, sure," Butler answered; the boss had had experience of
what "duty" meant to rising young men.

Now the office of the public prosecutor is a high mountain upside
down, from the top of which a man with eyes to see can see all
the world, the flesh, and the devil, and most observers adjust their
glasses to the glare of it. Folk couldn't. Sitting there in that lobby,
telling his story that day, I felt the pain he felt. His Tennessee
schoolboy's picture was painted deep in fast colors. He had to believe that an American city was a government by law, and when
the boss or his heelers came to the circuit attorney and told him
whom to appoint as his assistants, what to do; when Ed Butler—
not a judge in court, nor an officer of the law, but a one-time horse-
shoer and now a representative of law-breakers—when this crook
walked into Folk's office as if it were his office and said: "Joe, you
will name So-and-so your first assistant, this and that man second
and third, and—you will let our ballot-stuffers go and give the
other bosses' repeaters the limit—"

When Folk described it thus, with startled eyes, you could see
that his picture of the world was being all slashed to pieces.

"I and my office, the criminal law, was to be run by—criminals!"

He put it like that. He had imagination. He must have had,
because, piecing together the fragments of his torn picture, he
startled my imagination and made me make a picture, too. I was

taking the single, separate facts of political corruption and joining them into a new view of a city as it is. He interrupted me.

"But that's all nothing," he said. "That's only the start of it. That's what set me inquiring into other, into all, cases."

Folk had begun to prosecute the men who had gone about stuffing the ballot boxes for him and his party as well as for the enemy. "But they elected you, Joe," Butler remonstrated. "Without them and us you wouldn't have been where you are."

"I am doing my sworn duty," answered Folk, the Puritan.

"Well, then, we'll get you," Butler threatened.

"Not till I have first got you," the Southerner said proudly.

He discovered, however, that he had to have witnesses and evidence to win convictions; and he discovered that when a prisoner was in sight of the penitentiary he would, to save himself, peach on others. This was the practice of prosecutors—to indict and trade with peachers. Like Jerome in New York, Folk generalized; he realized that this was power. By offering leniency, he, the circuit attorney, could learn what was back of crimes; and so Folk bargained for confessions first from his ballot-stuffers whose stories were descriptions of politics; and then—

One afternoon, late in January, 1902, a newspaper reporter, known as "Red" Galvin, called Mr. Folk's attention to a ten-line newspaper item to the effect that a large sum of money had been placed in a bank for the purpose of bribing certain assemblymen to secure the passage of a street railroad ordinance. No names were mentioned, but Mr. Galvin surmised that the bill referred to was one introduced in behalf of the Suburban Railway Company. An hour later Mr. Folk sent the names of nearly one hundred persons to the sheriff, with instructions to subpoena them before the grand jury at once. The list included councilmen, members of the House of Delegates, officers and directors of the Suburban Railway, bank presidents and cashiers. Folk knew nothing, and he was not able to learn much.

Rumors he heard, but political gossip is often correct, and he had also his own judgment of the relative strength and weakness of the many men he suspected. He picked on Charles H. Turner, president of the Suburban Railway, and Philip Stock, a lobbyist for the brewers, who, he had heard, was the legislative agent in the railway deal. He thought they would peach. He summoned them before the grand jury, and he began to bluff.

"Gentlemen," he said to them in that presence, "I have secured enough evidence to warrant the return of indictments against you for bribery, and I shall prosecute you to the full extent of the law and send you to the penitentiary unless you tell the grand jury the complete history of the corruptionist methods employed by you to secure the passage of Ordinance No. 44."

He gave them three days to decide, three days of pulls, protests, threats, tears, from them and their friends; and who were not their friends? Folk was astonished as Police Commissioner Roosevelt had been at "the prominence and respectability of the men and women who intercede for crooks." Roosevelt had yielded to some prayers, a little. Folk did his duty; he was hard, quiet, patient. Messrs. Turner and Stock broke down and confessed. They told all about this deal: names, prices, dates. They told, or they involved other men who told all about other deals by which business men, high and low, big and little, had been systematically obtaining franchises, grants, licenses, exemptions, and public properties for years and were planning to get other such privileges in the future.

As Folk told briefly, sharply, swiftly these stories of the confessions of boodling, he seemed to sink whiter and quieter into the darkness of that corner of the hotel lobby; his pinpoint eyes watched me to see (as he told me afterward) if I saw what he saw, and when I was silent, expressionless, he could not stand it. He shot forward and shouted—no, he whispered, but the way he whispered and blazed made it sound like a shout:

"It is good business men that are corrupting our bad politicians; it is good business that causes bad government—in St. Louis."

A moment he waited, then: "It is the leading citizens that are battening on our city—in St. Louis."

He waited, watching again, and when I made no response, he lay, he fell back, in his chair and said very simply: "Just as the public prosecutor and the criminal courts represent criminals, so the legislative bodies, the representative government, represents bribery and business, not the people—in St. Louis."

What Folk's mind was doing was simple, but unusual. He was sweeping all his cases of bribery together to form a truth out of his facts. He was generalizing. Instead of minding his own business and prosecuting each set of boodlers for each of the many felonies he had uncovered, he was thinking about them all together and seeing what they meant all together.

"Bribery is no mere felony," he exclaimed. "It's treason." And again, as he was rehearsing how all the confessing bribers and bribe-takers wound up by saying, "That's the way it's done, Mr. Folk; you can't do business any other way," the startled prosecutor said: "It's systematic. That *is* the way it is done. Bribery and corruption is a process of revolution, to make a democratic government represent, not the people, but a part, the worse part, of the people."

"Or—the best," I muttered, and he sprang up, echoing, "Yes, the best, the leading business men of St. Louis."

I wrote to *McClure's* that I had an article for them and that as soon as I could find a man to write it I would return to New York. Folk named over all the reporters who had been writing his revelations and suggested Claude H. Wetmore, whom I saw and instructed. He was to write an article on Folk and St. Louis.

St. Louis, mind you. Wetmore, not I, was to describe the extraordinary conditions disclosed by this extraordinary circuit attorney in St. Louis. I was not yet a muckraker. I was an editor, and it never occurred to me to write this myself. On my way home, my mind began doing what Folk's had done. I was generalizing. I thought of New York. The extraordinary conditions of St. Louis were like the extraordinary conditions of New York. The corruption I had seen in New York was of the police; that of St. Louis was of the board of aldermen, but I had read of the aldermanic corruption of New York in the Tweed days. I had heard of Philadelphia, and in the newspapers there were scrappy reports of something in Minneapolis similar to New York police corruption.

Were not the extraordinary conditions of St. Louis and New York the ordinary conditions of city government in the United States? No, not yet. I couldn't say that yet.

When Wetmore's article came in to the office, I made some changes in it. He had left out some salient facts; he had spared some very conspicuous characters; he had "gone easy" on the boss, Ed Butler, for example. I put in what I remembered of what he had omitted. He remonstrated; he could not live and work in

MUCKRAKERS

LEFT: IDA M. TARBELL (PURDY). UPPER: RAY STANNARD BAKER (PACH BROS.).
LOWER: LINCOLN STEFFENS (E. CHICKERING, BOSTON).

St. Louis if the article was printed as I had edited it. When I insisted, he compromised. I must sign it with him and take the blame
for my insertions. Good. Done. And so I appeared as a muckraker.
But I made my bow also as a graft philosopher. I wrote the title
of that article, "Tweed Days in St. Louis," and inserted a few
comparisons, just enough to suggest the idea that was taking a

---

TWEED DAYS IN ST LOUIS

Joseph W Folk's Single-handed Exposure of Corruption, High and Low

BY CLAUDE H. WETMORE AND LINCOLN STEFFENS

ST. LOUIS, the fourth city in size in the United States, is making two announce-ments to the world : one that it is the worst governed city in the land ; the other that it wishes all men to come and see it. It isn't our worst governed city ; Philadelphia is that. But St. Louis is worth examining while we have it inside out.

There is a man at work there, one man, work-ing all alone, but he is the Circuit (district or might have won. But a change occurred. Pub-lic spirit became private spirit, public enter-prise became private greed.

Along about 1890, public franchises and privileges were sought not only for legitimate profit and common convenience, but for loot. Taking but slight and always selfish interest in the public councils, the big men misused politics. The riff-raff, catching the smell of corruption, rushed into the Municipal As-

---

THE FIRST MUCKRAKING ARTICLE

McClure's Magazine, October, 1902

hard hold on me, the idea that Folk had expressed: that bribery
is not a mere felony, but a revolutionary process which was going
on in all our cities and that, if I could trace it to its source, I might
find the cause of political corruption and—the cure.

But first, to make sure that the process was identical everywhere,
I must go and make a study of the police corruption of Minneapolis, to compare it with that of New York. St. Louis would
not do for such an inquiry. Folk said there was no such systematic
corruption of the police in St. Louis as I had described to him in
New York.

THE SHAME OF MINNEAPOLIS

M R. MC CLURE dictated the title and the thesis of the article
I was going to write on Minneapolis before I left New
York. This was not so preposterous as it sounds. The
exposure of Minneapolis was all over; the main facts had been
running scrappily as news in the papers for a year. My job was
to collect and combine the news serial into one digested, complete
review.

"We'll call it 'The Shame of Minneapolis,'" Mr. McClure
said, "and we'll point out that democracy is at fault; that one man
has to run a city just as one man has to run a business to make it a
success."

Mr. McClure thought he knew what was the cause of political
corruption and inefficiency, and he had the cure all ready. Almost
everybody had. The article on St. Louis brought forth letters,
editorials, and all sorts of comment, explaining the extraordinary
conditions described. Republicans blamed the Democrats; they
overlooked the fact that the worst period in St. Louis had been
under a Republican mayor. Eastern interpreters said St. Louis
was a western city. New England remarked upon the large foreign
population in St. Louis, a German town. European newspapers
and men like James Bryce talked about youth; America was a
young country, and the political scandals were growing-pains. The
English spoke of democracy with a complacent side-glance at the
aristocracy of their governing class. Business men indicted the
politicians and politics as the cause and offered business men and
business as the cure. They did not note that it was business men
who bribed the politicians in St. Louis and that prominent business
men who had been elected to the city council to clean up the city
were among the confessing boodlers. I myself had held some of

these beliefs; I thought vaguely that there was something in them. And I had never for a moment questioned the great moral assumption which underlay all this thinking: that political evils were due to bad men of some sort and curable by the substitution of good men. I was on the level with my time, my contemporaries, and our readers.

Indeed I think now that my writings of that period were effective because I set out on my search with all the taught ignorance of my day. It was this that put the astonishment, shame, and patriotic indignation into my reports. The Reds of all classes and nations knew of old what to me were discoveries, but I had studied in college their theories: socialism, anarchism, single tax, etc.; I had read and recited their absurdities to the professor of political economy who gave me high marks and—immunity against heresy. In a word, I was an example of the American college education which fixes the mind of youth so that it knows all about everything and cannot learn, "cannot be carried away, like the mob, by every new, wild idea it comes across."

But the German universities had corrected my American culture to some extent: the laboratory work in psychology there had hammered into me that explanations of natural phenomena— quick, superficial, common-sense convictions—were apt to be nothing but protective guards set up by the poor, weak human mind to save itself from the temptation and effort to think; that, if you know too surely, you cannot learn; and that, for the purposes of research, you may have theories, but never, never knowledge. I wanted to study cities scientifically, and I argued with Mr. McClure that it would heighten the interest in the articles we were planning to start out with blank minds and search like detectives for the keys to the mystery, the clews to the truth. He would not have it so. Science did not interest the readers, except as a source of wonders; and besides he was sure of that which he had learned by experience on *McClure's Magazine* and by observation in all other business—that the dictatorship of one strong, wise man (like Sam McClure or Judge Gary) would abolish our political evils and give us a strong, wise administrator of cities.

We had a pretty hot fight, and McClure won. What I went to Minneapolis to write was that democracy was a failure and that a good dictator was what is needed.

What I went to this western Republican city of Scandinavian people led by New Englanders to find out for myself was, whether the police corruption there was not like that of New York, and whether Minneapolis did not have, like St. Louis and New York, some systematic corruption of its board of aldermen.

Minneapolis bore out Mr. McClure's certainty, even as St. Louis had, and New York. One man, the mayor, Dr. A. A. Ames, had been the boss of the politics, the government, and the grafting of Minneapolis, performing the same functions there that first Tweed, then Croker, had performed in New York and Ed Butler had performed in St. Louis. And one man, Hovey C. Clarke, the foreman of a grand jury, had forced through the exposure and reform of Minneapolis as Joseph W. Folk was doing in St. Louis. Moreover the system of the police graft uncovered was like that of New York. There were differences. The mayor himself, not (as in New York) the chief of police, was the head of the graft organization; Dr. Ames had made his brother, Col. Fred. W. Ames, chief of police. The boss-mayor organized and tried, through his brother, to direct the police graft. But this police graft was, like New York's, a deliberate, detailed management of the police force, not to prevent, detect, or arrest crime, but to protect, share with, and direct the criminals. The so-called moral element of the people played into the hands of the police criminals, as in New York, by requiring strict laws against vice and crime. The liquor business was to be regulated, prostitution and gambling were forbidden, and, of course, murder, stealing, and all felonies were heavily punishable. Mayor Ames and the police force, with professional criminals to advise them, made a schedule of prices for the privilege of breaking the laws. Saloons paid so much a month to ignore the closing-hours, the laws against slot-machines and gambling, and the limitations upon the age of drinkers and gamblers. Houses of prostitution, which were a necessity in this center for lumberjacks, had been regulated by a system of formal, regular arrests and small fines once a month. Ames cut the fines and, for the regular payment of bribes, let these houses run, increased the number of them, and encouraged panel games and other forms of robbery. Gambling on a large scale was allowed, with the mayor and police as partners in the profits, and the profits were increased by making the games "crooked." The dealer's percentage was lifted; wheels were "fixed." But petty gambling was introduced, literally, and so was stealing. Confidence men, porch climbers, burglars, and all sorts of thieves were not only permitted to operate, with the police to watch them work, to protect them from interruption and prevent them from holding out on the mayor and his cabinet; word was also passed out into the underworld outside that clever crooks would be welcomed in Minneapolis if they would play fair with the police. Thieves and swindlers came to town and looked over the situation from their point of view. Some saw the police and made terms; others were seen by the police and invited to go to work.

All of this in great detail, with names, prices, places, dates, and actual conversations, was told over and over again by the confessing officers and crooks before the grand jury; it is a matter of record there, and some of it was repeated at trials in court. A few cases will illustrate. "Billy" Edwards was a "big mitt man," an expert at cards, who swindled "suckers" by playing stud poker and stacking the hands. Norbeck, a detective, knew him of old and offered to set up a "joint" for him and one Charlie Howard, to bring in suckers, and, standing himself at the door, to throw a scare into the "trimmed squealers," who wanted to appeal to the police.

"I had been out to the Coast," Edwards related; "I hadn't seen Norbeck for some time. After I returned I boarded a Minneapolis car one evening. Norbeck and Detective De Laittre were on the same car. When Norbeck saw me he came up, shook hands, and said, 'Hello, Billy, how goes it?' I said, 'Not very well.'

"Then he says, 'Things have changed here since you went away. Me and Gardner [the mayor's collector and graft manager] are the whole thing. They thought I didn't know a thing, but I turned a few tricks and now I'm It.'

" 'I'm glad of that, Chris,' I said. He says, 'I've got great things for you. I'm going to fix up a joint for you.' 'That's good,' I said, 'but I don't believe you can do it.' 'Oh, yes, I can,' he replied; 'I'm It now, Gardner and me.' 'Well, if you can do it,' says I, 'there's money in it.' 'How much can you pay?' he asked. 'Oh, $150 to $200 a week,' says I. 'That settles it,' he said. 'I'll take you down to see Gardner, and we'll fix it up.' "

The next evening the detective and the big mitt man called

on Gardner, who talked business in a general way, showed them a drawerful of money collected from the women on his list to be paid over to the old man (the mayor) when he returned from his hunting trip. "Afterward," said Edwards, "he told me the Mayor was well pleased with our $500, said everything was all right and for us to go ahead."

Link Crossman, another confidence man associated with Edwards, said that Gardner demanded $1000 a week at first and compromised on $500 for the mayor, $50 for Gardner, and $50 for Norbeck. To the chief of police, Fred Ames, they paid only tips. "The first week we ran," said Crossman, "I gave Fred $15. Norbeck took me down there. We shook hands, and I handed him an envelope with $15. He pulled out a list of steerers we had sent him and said he wanted to go over them with me. Another time I slipped $25 into his hand as he was standing in the hallway of City Hall."

There were many big and petty gambling-joints, all served by the police in the same way. "Steerers" or "boosters" met "suckers" in the streets, hotels, railway stations, won their confidence, and steered them to the joint. The suckers were known by the sums they were cheated (or, in thieves' jargon, trimmed) of: "the one-hundred-and-two-dollar man," "the thirty-five-dollar man." One man, Roman Meix, was called by his own name; he lost $775 and was distinguished by the persistence of his complaints. They all "kicked" some, and that is how the police force earned their "cut" (share) of the profits. Detective Norbeck, stationed at the street door of the joint for that purpose, heard the first "squeals" and tried to frighten the victims away. "Oh," he would say, "so you have been gambling, eh? Got a license? No! Well, then, you better get right out of this town, quick." Sometimes he accompanied the grumbler to the station and saw him off. If he was not thus to be put off, the detective directed him to the chief of police. Fred Ames "stalled," trying to wear out the fellow's patience in his waiting-room, and if that did not work he threatened an arrest or trouble.

Burglaries were common, many of them planned by the police. One case established on the court records was the robbery of the Pabst Brewing Company office. The officers persuaded an employee to learn the combination of the safe and, with a regular burglar, to clean it out one night, while the police captain and the detectives stood guard outside.

The ever-increasing number and boldness of the crimes committed, the joyous effrontery of the police criminals, the width of the openness of this wide-open town, shocked the rather Puritan citizens of Minneapolis. As it went on year after year, the police and other city officials quarreled over the spoils, formed groups or gangs which competed for the business, and intrigued for the favor and authority of the mayor, who grew careless and weak. And they arrested and otherwise interfered with one another's burglars, thieves, gamblers, and women. It was this double-crossing that laid them open to exposure and the indictments which followed. A graft system has to be controlled and regulated like any other business.

But the fact that stuck out of all the revelations of the police graft system of Minneapolis was that it was just like the police graft system which the equally "extraordinary" evidence of the Lexow investigation had disclosed in New York.

Nor was that the extent of it. The police graft system of Minneapolis was like the police graft system of its so-called Twin City, St. Paul, across the river. It was the same as in Seattle, Portland, San Francisco, Chicago, New Orleans, and of most of the cities in between.

This I learned from the inside. Hovey C. Clarke, the foreman of the grand jury, who had forced through the investigation which had driven the mayor and his administration out of the city, had in hiding the two big mitt men mentioned above, Billy Edwards and Charlie Howard. They had been double-crossed by the Ames gang and lay angry in jail when Clarke found them. He asked them to tell their story. That was the sin of sins in their profession; it was "squealing," and they were not stool-pigeons. But they were "mad," and their old police partners were both double-crossers and crooks—"crooked crooks," they said—and Clarke was not.

"I know men," Edwards said to me, "and I knew that Clarke was a square man with guts."

He and Howard told their whole story to Clarke, and they handed to him as evidence a small butcher book, a rough, well-kept ledger of stealings and divisions week by week. Thieves rarely keep books; they had done it in Minneapolis to play fair with the police and avoid the disputes that were causing so much trouble. Since it itemized the sums taken from victims, all expenses, the percentage and amounts paid for rent, cards, all costs, and the share in dollars of the mayor, chief of police, and each detective, this, the Big Mitt Ledger, was a clinching piece of evidence. Mr. Clarke had taken and was keeping it and the big mitt men for the trial of the mayor. The newspapers knew about and had been looking for it. Mr. Clarke let the grand jury man who had it lend it to me, and I photographed and printed it in my article. But I wanted to see these men to ask them about "the system of police graft in other cities," and I appealed to Clarke to tell me where they were hiding. My excuse was that I had to have them interpret for me the slang in the Big Mitt Ledger.

"But all those men are waiting for," he objected, "is to get and destroy the Big Mitt Ledger. They are not prisoners; they are bound only by their word to stay where they are and by my promise to return the book. If they once get their hands on that they'll skip."

"No, they won't," I declared, and my certainty, which I could not myself have accounted for, convinced him. He gave me the address of a vacant house in a remote part of town, and I was knocking at the door at eight o'clock the next morning. Men are normal in the morning, and at home.

There was one thump of bare feet on a floor, then silence. They were startled, wondering, dressing. I waited, knocked again quietly, and heard a board creak in the hall, near the door. Drawing back so that an eye at the keyhole could see me plainly, I held the Big Mitt Ledger in plain sight. That tempted the peeping eye, no doubt. The key turned softly. I stepped up and knocked again, impatiently, and the door opened a crack, an unshaven face peeked out, a very suspicious eye.

"Only a reporter," I said, "from New York. I've got the Big Mitt Ledger, and I want you to explain some of the items to me."

The door closed; there were whisperings, and then the door opened. Billy Edwards, in shirt and trousers, with Howard staring close behind—at the book in my hand—made way for me to enter; and Howard, whose book it was, who had kept the account, took it from me as absentmindedly as I surrendered it. We went in to

McClure's Magazine

VOL. XX   JANUARY, 1903   NO. 3

THE SHAME OF MINNEAPOLIS

The Rescue and Redemption of a City that was Sold Out

BY LINCOLN STEFFENS

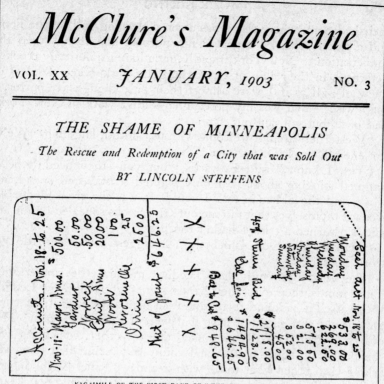

FAC-SIMILE OF THE FIRST PAGE OF "THE BIG MITT LEDGER"

An account kept by a swindler of the dealings of his "Joint" with City Officials, showing first payments made to Mayor Ames, his brother, the Chief of Police and Detectives. This book figured in trials and newspaper reports of the exposure, but was "lost"; and its whereabouts was the mystery of the proceedings. This is the first glimpse that any one, except "Cheerful Charlie" Howard, who kept it, and members of the grand jury, has had of the book

WHENEVER anything extraordinary is done in American municipal politics, whether for good or for evil, you can trace it almost invariably to one man. The people do not do it. Neither do the "gangs," "combines," or political parties. These are but instruments by which bosses (not leaders; we Americans are not led, but driven) rule the people, and commonly sell them out. But there are at least two forms of the autocracy which has supplanted the democracy here as it has everywhere it has been tried. One is that of the organized majority by which, as in Tammany Hall in New York and the Republican machine in Philadelphia, the boss has normal control of more than half the voters. The other is that of the adroitly managed minority. The "good people" are herded into parties and stupefied with convictions and a name, Republican or Democrat; while the "bad people" are so organized or interested by the boss that he can wield their votes to enforce terms with party managers and decide elections. St. Louis is a conspicuous example of this form. Minneapolis is another. Colonel Ed. Butler is the unscrupulous opportunist who handled the non-partisan minority which turned St. Louis into a "boodle town." In Minneapolis "Doc" Ames was the man.

THE BIG MITT LEDGER WAS A CLINCHING PIECE OF EVIDENCE

their bedroom, where there was a cot, a sleeping-roll on the floor, and a rickety chair. I repeated my purpose and then turned the conversation to New York, rapidly, mentioning familiarly crooked detectives in their line of crime, burglars, pickpockets I knew or knew of—all as if I were almost their pal; though a reporter, I was "wise"—that was my pose. They didn't work in New York; had once, but got run out.

"Westerners are not welcome with us," I said, laughing. "We've got enough crooks of our own."

"Yes, I know," said Edwards, "but you—they needn't be so damned stinking about it. I only wanted to stay and spend, not work, and the old man said I could. It was the crooked double-crossers themselves that ran me out; the crooks squealed on me and said I'd turned a trick I hadn't touched."

"Had to pin it on somebody," I suggested. "Where do you work regular?"

They had been only half heeding me and the conversation. Their minds, their eyes, their hands, were on the Big Mitt Ledger; they passed it back and forth, and each man as he took it, affectionately, held and gazed at it as if it were a baby, their baby. They did want that book. They looked at each other, consulting with their eyes so plainly that even I could understand that they were asking each other what to do with it and with me. Never looking at it myself, pretending to have forgotten it, I mentioned Clarke familiarly, other grand jurors, friends in power, in the upper world and in the underworld in Minneapolis, New York, St. Louis, Chicago—to remind them that I was no rank outsider to be trifled with; but I spoke as if I were not thinking either of myself or the book. And they eased. They entered into our talk completely. They had not decided what to do; they only put off the decision, I felt, but they talked with concentration on the subject.

They had been working the Coast—Seattle, Portland, San Francisco, and Los Angeles—when they were sent for to come to Minneapolis. As "good men" (in their line) they were known and needed by Norbeck and the other "wise bulls" in Minneapolis. It looked good, but it wasn't. Seattle was better; Frisco was best. They described how business was done there, just as in Minneapolis, only the system was older, safer, more tried and expert. "These Minneapolis pols are bums," they said, and they meant, they explained, that Ames and his "crowd" of politicians had not grown up in the system; they had seen it working and thought it was easy. "And it ain't. You ought to see the discipline in Frisco, and as for Chicago and New York—" They were not in it in Chicago and New York, and they were sore at their exclusion; but they took their hats off to the efficiency of the system there.

"But it's the same system as out west here," I suggested.

"Sure, it's the same everywhere, but—with a difference. It takes time to work it out right, time and ability and lots and lots of square dealing. Petty crooks can't make it, not amateurs like this bunch of bums here."

"St. Louis?" I asked.

They didn't know St. Louis. They knew fellows that worked there; they had heard—of course—but no, they knew nothing of St. Louis, except by hearsay.

I had what I came for; enough; but I must play out my game. I took the Big Mitt Ledger; I felt Howard's shock when I picked it out of his hand, and both of the men put their hands on it as I held it, opening the pages and asking for explanations of items. When I was satisfied and rose to go, Howard had the precious book. The conversation on the way to the front door was all decentralized again. I carried it on; they responded absentmindedly; their real conversation was between themselves, with their eyes. I had not the least fear that they would keep that book; they could not but have felt my confidence. Not by a glance did I show that I was even thinking of the prize. I was talking, telling anecdotes about Inspector Byrnes at police headquarters in New York, when they had worked me out of the hall upon the front porch; I had pretended to forget the book till, suddenly, I pretended to remember.

"Oh, yes, the book," I said. "I must not forget that. Hovey Clarke would be—"

I was shaking hands, first with Howard, who had the book, then with Edwards; my left hand was out for the book, which to my relief, touched it, drew back, slipped in and back, and then all the way in. I closed slowly on it and put it into my pocket. And I returned it to Hovey Clarke. And when I slipped that book, carelessly, of course—quite by the way—into Mr. Clarke's hand, it seemed to me that, while he received it likewise intent upon our irrelevant conversation, he was suppressing a relief as great and as insulting as mine when I got it back from my crooks.

However that may be, when I told him that according to these, his own star witnesses, the system of police protection of crime and vice as he knew it in his town was typical of that in other cities, he bade me "go and see the new, the acting mayor, D. Percy Jones, about that." I went and I heard from this educated, aristocratic gentleman, another phase of the situation, another story, another question.

"*Can* a city government deal with vice and crime without some compromising arrangement with the criminals?"

Mayor Jones asked me that. I had meant to ask him, but he spoke first.

I ACHIEVE FAME AND SOMETHING
BETTER

A LEARNING mind makes a good teacher. The new acting Mayor Jones, whom the grand jury appointed to hold its gains, was a novice. He was young, rich, college-bred, an idealist, but he was honest-minded. He had intellectual integrity. He was one of a group of the sons of successful citizens who had heard that bad men made our good American municipal government bad and, therefore, decided that they, good men, would go into politics and make the bad government good. Percy Jones was an alderman when Hovey C. Clarke, an older business man, had happened to be chosen foreman of the grand jury, had happened to be annoyed by the blatancy of the vice-grafting administration of Mayor Ames, and so, opposed and threatened, had set his hard jaw and gone after the bad men.

The captain of industry type, Clarke found that he could, by will-power and brain-power, clean up a city as well as he could do any other business. He did it, and he did it fast and well; he became a dictator, a ruthless, good tyrant who ruled by fear. But he did not want to be a ruler in politics. He had not made his fortune yet and he was impatient to return to private business. He chose Percy Jones to carry on, partly because he knew that the young man was honest and fearless, but partly because Jones had been out of town during the fight and therefore was clear of all the factions, hates, and jealousies of a reform war.

There was a twinkle in Hovey Clarke's eye when, toward the end of my stay in Minneapolis, he bade me go and see Mayor Jones. We were sitting in the lobby of the hotel where Clarke lived; we were summing up his experience; trying to turn into wisdom the knowledge he had picked up out of his grand jury findings. He had been appalled at the discovery that vice and crime were protected. I had told him what his "big mitt" men, Billy Edwards and Charlie Howard, had said to me in the vacant house out in the suburbs: that all the other western cities had the same system, that that was the way crime was regulated, that it was by permitting some thieves to work in a town that the police were able to keep visiting crooks out and to control those who were admitted.

"If that is the police system," I said, "how can you here in Minneapolis check crime with no police alliance with the criminals?"

Mr. Clarke sat up sharp, and I was sure he had an impulse to make a fighting answer, but his face and his pose relaxed. He smiled and he said, "You go and ask Mayor Jones that."

I went to Mayor Jones, but I didn't have to ask him the question. After a few polite preliminaries in his office, a very few, the mayor said, suddenly, in eager earnest: "But listen now, I'm going to tell you what I have done and what has been done to me during the short time I have been here. And then I'm going to ask you what I should do."

All through those muckraking days I was mistaken for an expert who knew all about graft and politics and government and could tell anybody just what to do about them. Thieves, politicians, business men, reformers, and our magazine readers, they all assumed that I had what I was trying to get: knowledge. In one way this was fortunate. The "wise guys" would tell me their secrets. Thinking I knew anyhow, they felt that they might as well talk, the big mitt men, for example; and I encouraged their self-deception. In another way my reputation for omniscience was embarrassing, as it was that morning when young Mayor Jones turned upon me for advice. He so needed it; he was so sure that I could give it—

This honest young mind that believed integrity and courage were all that a good mayor required, had taken office with the police problem pressing for solution. It looked simple. He would appoint as chief of police an honest man with no criminal or vice connections and let him organize a police force to drive out the law-breakers—all of them, of course. You don't traffic with crime. You simply enforce the law. His first discovery was that the police job is a specialty, calling for some technical experience. There were no men in his town with police experience enough to organize and direct a police force not tainted in some degree by the recent exposures and plottings. He finally chose for chief a church deacon and a personal friend, on the theory that he must have in that post a man whom he could trust. As policemen he and the deacon chose, cunningly, men whom the ex-mayor and his brother, the ex-chief, had discharged. There must have been something good in them, and so far as there was evil, it would be against the old gang and the old practices.

His next discovery was that he, the mayor, and his new police force could not enforce the law against prostitution. That vice had to be permitted to run. So the women were restricted to a certain patrol district and there allowed to do business free of blackmail and fines.

His third discovery was that good citizens, property owners, whose houses were cleaned of prostitution, rose up in wrath against this arrangement, which lost them their high rent. More astonishing to the good mayor, these landlords were able to set the clergy and other good citizens after him for compromising with sin and not only not enforcing but officially permitting the breaking of the law. He stood fast, Jones did. He might not have been able to if he had been a politician and sought reëlection. Mayor Jones could see that a "bad" man in his place would feel forced by the good people to be less honest with the bad. His strict, temporary, but well-intentioned regulation of other habits and vices brought up against him the power of the saloon-keepers, brewers, other property owners, and allied businesses.

But Mayor Jones's most educative discovery was in the field of crime: felonies, robberies. There had been a decrease in crime while Hovey Clarke was at work, and the mayor had no trouble for a week or two. Then the criminals resumed their business, houses were robbed, and the deacon chief of police could not detect or prevent them. The crimes leaked, too. In some way the news of them got into the papers. The victims were indignant; their neighbors were alarmed; Mayor Jones and his police were humiliated and a bit frightened. They were ready to listen when one day some gamblers called and offered the mayor a way out.

If the mayor would let them, a syndicate, open four gambling-houses downtown, they would see that no other games ran in any part of the city. Mr. Jones listened, pondered, shook his head, and drew them on. He would allow six weeks for negotiations, and he observed that there were no crimes in that time. By and by the gamblers mentioned that fact, and they raised their bid. They were not criminals, the gamblers said, nor were they the associates of criminals, but they knew that class and their ways and their plans. No honest police force, unaided, could deal with crime. Thieves would soon be at work again in Minneapolis, and what could Mr. Jones do against them with a police force headed by a church deacon?

The gamblers offered to control the criminals of the city.

The mayor, deeply interested, declared that he did not believe there was any danger of a fresh outbreak of crime. The gamblers smiled and went away. By an odd coincidence there happened just after that what the papers called "an epidemic of crime." They were petty thefts, but they occupied the mayor. He wondered at their opportuneness. His chief wondered how the news of them got out.

The gamblers reappeared. Hadn't they said so? Hadn't they warned the mayor that crimes would break out again? They had, but the mayor said that mere "porch climbers" could not frighten him. The gamblers answered that the porch climbers were only the beginning; bigger crimes would come next. And sure enough, one, two, three burglaries occurred in houses of prominent people whom Jones knew; then there was a fourth, and the fourth was in the house of a relative of Mayor Jones.

The gamblers called again. If they could have the monopoly of gambling in Minneapolis, they would do all that they had promised before, and if any large burglaries did occur, they would recover the "swag" and sometimes catch the thief. Mr. Jones expressed doubt as to their ability to do so much. The gamblers offered to prove it; they would get back for the mayor the jewelry stolen from the last four houses robbed. The mayor was curious to see this done, and the gamblers went away. After a few days the stolen goods came back, parcel by parcel. With all the usual police-criminal mystery, it was delivered to the chief of police.

When the gamblers called again, they found the mayor ready with his decision on their proposition. It was this: There should be no gambling with police connivance in his city during his term of office. He must have appeared very bold, strong, and sure when he said this to the gamblers, but when he repeated it to me he was not sure.

"Can we do it?" he asked me, and it was an anxious inquiry. He explained that he had decided so straight and short because his term in office was to be so short. If he had had before him a long term as mayor, he said, he would certainly have reconsidered or considered longer his answer to the underworld. He believed he would still have decided as he did, but knowing what he knew, he would have given studious reflection to the question: Can a city be governed without any alliance with crime and vice? It was an open question, and when he put it to me I was thinking of St. Louis. Wasn't there a police-graft-criminal system there also, as in Minneapolis, as in the other western cities, as in New York? I did not ask that of Mr. Jones. I asked him a seemingly irrelevant, very relevant question. When he was talking about the solid business-church-good-people's opposition to his policy, I asked him why he did not investigate the board of aldermen. His answer gave me a thrill.

"Oh," he said, "we had one. Several years back we had a scandal about the corruption of the council. That's what started my group out as reformers."

So the system, both ends of it, had occurred in Minneapolis, as in St. Louis, as—everywhere? I was on the track of a truth, a scientific basis for a science of politics. The first step toward confirmation was to return to St. Louis. I hurried to Chicago. There were delays: other things to do, authors to see. I was, after all, an editor, not primarily a writer, and certainly not a scientist. The magazine with the Minneapolis article had appeared when I took the train for St. Louis, and I remember hearing men in the washroom talking about it and me. They named my name, correctly, approvingly. Again in the dining-car I heard it from others. Evidently my first article was being read; it was a success.

Maybe I was a success, and—yes, this was notoriety, a little like fame. It was pleasant, but it was not nearly so wonderful as I had imagined it would be. I looked at the men who were giving me my taste of fame, and, business men, I thought that if their town were investigated they might be caught bribing or backing the bribers. But suppose they were honest men, what of it? What did such men know? Fame wasn't what it was cracked up to be. That I thought, with a feeling of shame which grew month by month as my disappointment grew—the feeling that there was something positively offensive about public approval, that it liked the wrong part of your work, made you out to be other than you were, and then tried to keep you up or down to expectations.

· The real reason for my distaste, however, was that I was exalted by the belief that I had a theory of graft which I was about to put to a test that was scientific: that political corruption was everywhere the same. Since Minneapolis and New York had both business and police corruption, then St. Louis, whose business corruption Folk was showing, must have also the police-vice-criminal corruption—which Folk had not found, which he denied. And that's the way I went at the circuit attorney when I met him—positively.

"Folk," I said, "there must be a police graft system here in St. Louis." He shook his head, no; but I told him why I was so sure: "Minneapolis, New York—"

"No, no," he rebelled, and his reluctance suggested that he was merely shying off from more work. To meet this I proposed that he inquire, not with a view to prosecute, but only for my information, whether there was not—what I suspected.

"It won't take you an hour," I said. "You have boodlers in jail who are already confessing their own crimes; they will tell you how prostitution, gambling, crime, and vice are handled. Send for one of them and ask him; make him describe the methods; meanwhile I will go down into the underworld and find out what I can."

We parted to meet at dinner that evening, I to go my way, he his, and when we met again in the hotel lobby, Folk with bulging eyes exclaimed: "It's here. And it is like Minneapolis; it is exactly like New York. Exactly. Methods, divisions, prices—all the same."

At dinner we exchanged facts, going into detail. Folk, with his conscientious sense of duty, was unhappy, thinking that he ought to break up this horrible system of police graft. He did not want to; he had about all he could do with the business boodling. I advised him not to tackle the underworld. The good citizens of St. Louis already were turning against him; if he attacked the bad people also he would lose all support; he might not be able to find twelve men for a jury.

"And besides," I said, "it is enough that we know that three cities are alike; we don't have to prove it here. I'll go on to other cities and show that they are the same."

I remember how Folk sat and wrestled with his thoughts, alone, silent, till by and by he looked up and said exactly what was on his mind.

"I am beaten already in St. Louis," he sighed. "I have to try Boss Butler in some other town; I couldn't convict him in St. Louis. The people are against me."

A pause, then: "I can't be reëlected here either. I ought to finish this job—I am bound to run for circuit attorney again. The voters of St. Louis will beat me and—what I stand for."

"Why don't you go for yourself where you are going for Boss Butler?" I asked.

"Where's that?" he asked.

"To Missouri," I answered. "You are appealing the case of Butler to the people of the State. Good. Appeal to Missouri against St. Louis for yourself."

He still did not catch the idea. "How?" he asked, puzzled.

"Don't run in St. Louis for circuit attorney. Run for governor of Missouri."

He threw down his napkin. "Of course," he said. "But of course. All the boodle trails lead up to the State Legislature. I'll go there, and I'll follow them back from there to St. Louis. The voters of Missouri still are on the side of Right."

"The voters of Missouri still *think* they are on the side of Right," I corrected.

THE SHAMELESSNESS OF ST. LOUIS

WHEN Circuit Attorney Folk confirmed my theory that there was organized police corruption in St. Louis as well as boodling business, I was eager to go on to another city to see if the same system of graft existed there—Chicago, for example. Enough was known of Chicago and Philadelphia to indicate that they would come up to standard, but it would not be scientific, sportsmanlike, or convincing to choose such sure things.

"Did I hear you say you were going to walk to the station?" a downtown hotel clerk asked me in Chicago one night. "Don't do it. It isn't safe. Take a cab."

Chicago was very tempting. Mr. McClure urged me to do it next, for editorial reasons. My article on Minneapolis had succeeded beyond all expectations. The newsstand sales had exhausted the printed supply; subscriptions were coming in; and the mail was bringing letters of praise, appreciation, and suggestion. "Come here to this place," they wrote from many cities, towns, and even villages; "you will find scandals that will make Minneapolis and St. Louis look like models of good government."

"Evidently," I argued with the editor-in-chief, "you could shoot me out of a gun fired at random and, wherever I lighted, there would be a story, the same way."

My mind was on my theory, but Mr. McClure's was on our business; we must increase the sensationalism of our articles if we were to hold and reap our advantage. We must find some city, like Chicago or Philadelphia, that was worse than St. Louis and Minneapolis. The disagreement became acute; it divided the office and might have caused trouble had not Miss Ida M. Tarbell made peace, as she so often did thereafter. Sensible, capable, and very affectionate, she knew each one of us and all our idiosyncrasies and troubles. She had none of her own so far as we ever heard. When we were deadlocked we might each of us send for her, and down she would come to the office, smiling, like a tall, good-looking young mother, to say, "Hush, children." She would pick out the sense in each of our contentions, and putting them together with her own good sense, give me a victory over S.S., him a triumph over Phillips, and take away from all of us only the privilege of gloating. The interest of the magazine was pointed out, and we and she went back to work. In this case she saw and reminded us that there was plenty of time to decide on the next place to choose. Meanwhile St. Louis was to be done again and more thoroughly. I wanted to trace and comprehend for myself the ramifications of this typical, invisible government of the American city; the magazine wanted to publish the further revelations of Mr. Folk's later inquiries and, by the way, to help elect this man governor of Missouri. We made a vague compromise, therefore. I was to write little or nothing of my theory, stick to facts, and then, St. Louis done, we would choose almost any place I liked for our fourth city.

This was good journalism. S. S. McClure was a good journalist, one of the best I ever knew, and he knew it, and he knew why. One day when I returned to him a manuscript he had asked me to read and pass upon, he picked up, glanced at, and dropped unread into the waste-basket a long memorandum I had written. "What's this?" he demanded. "A review? I don't want your literary criticism of a manuscript. All I ask of you is whether you like it or not." Seeing that I was miffed, he explained.

"Look," he said. "I want to know if you enjoy a story, because, if you do, then I know that, say, ten thousand readers will like it. If Miss Tarbell likes a thing, it means that fifty thousand will like it. That's something to go by. But I go most by myself. For if I like a thing, then I know that millions will like it. My mind and my taste are so common that I'm the best editor." He paused, smiled, and slowly, reluctantly added, "There's only one better editor than I am, and that's Frank Munsey. If he likes a thing, then everybody will like it."

Mr. McClure was interested in facts, startling facts, not in philosophical generalizations. He hated, he feared, my dawning theory. He had his own theories, like his readers. They differed among themselves, but they were sure, every one of them. I alone did not know. I alone was not to give my theory. That was our agreement. When I entered into it, however, I made a mental reservation that while I would indeed load my new article on St. Louis with the libelous, dangerous, explosive facts in Folk's possession, I would aim them and the whole story, like a gun, at the current popular theories (including Mr. McClure's); and, I hoped, blow them out of the way for a statement later of my own diagnosis, when I was ready to frame one. I was a good shot in those days. I could write to the understanding and hit the convictions of the public because I shared or had so recently shared them.

I have told how, as the boy chum of a page in the Legislature of California, I had seen from below the machinery and bribery of politics; as a New York reporter I had seen police, political, legislative, and judicial corruption; but I did with these observations what other people do with such disturbing knowledge: I put them off in a separate compartment of the brain. I did not let them alter my conception of life. My picture of the world as it seemed to be was much the same as my readers'. It was this that made me a pretty good journalist; it is this that makes good journalism. The reporter and the editor must sincerely share the cultural ignorance, the superstitions, the beliefs, of their readers, and keep no more than one edition ahead of them. You may beat the public to the news, not to the truth.

The leading question raised in my second article on St. Louis was, "Is democracy a failure?" A trick, a political trick! I had no doubt that the people could and would govern themselves, and Folk had none. The question was put only to appeal to the pride and the loyalty of the voters. Folk had shown, and I wrote, how they were herded into parties—the majority of them; how they were led to transfer to the party machines the loyalty they owed to their city, State, and the United States; how they were fooled thus, into voting straight for the nominees of a bi-partisan or a non-partisan gang of known grafters, who controlled both machines and won elections by swinging the purchasable votes of the minority of worst citizens to the worst ticket; and how these leading grafters used their power to sell out franchises, permissions, and other valuable grants and public properties to the highest bidders, sometimes "good" local business men, sometimes "bad" New York and other "foreign" financiers. Folk had learned, and I reported, that these crooked politicians had intended to sell the Union Market, the old Court House, and the water works. Nor had they given up these plans. The water works—the water supply of the city—was estimated to be worth forty millions by the boodlers, who proposed to let it go for fifteen millions and so make a million each for the fifteen members of the ring.

THE SHAMELESSNESS OF ST. LOUIS

Something New in the History of American Municipal Democracy

BY LINCOLN STEFFENS

Author of "The Shame of Minneapolis"

TWEED'S classic question, "What are you going to do about it?" is the most humiliating challenge ever delivered by the One Man to the Many. But it was pertinent. It was the question then; it is the question now. Will the people rule? That is what it means. Is democracy possible? The recent accounts in this magazine, of financial corruption in St. Louis and of police corruption in Minneapolis raised the same question. They were inquiries into American municipal democracy, and, so far as they went, they were pretty complete

have organized to keep it safe, and make the memory of "Doc" Ames a civic treasure, and Minneapolis a city without reproach.

What St. Louis "Did About It"

Minneapolis may fail, as New York has failed; but at least these two cities could be moved by shame. Not so St. Louis. Joseph W. Folk, the circuit attorney, who began alone, is going right on alone, indicting, trying, convicting boodlers, high and low, following the workings of the combine through all of its startling

McClure's Magazine, March, 1903

"The scheme was to do it and skip," said one of the gang to me, "and if you could mix it all up with some filtering scheme, it could be done. . . . It will be done some day."

This we printed, and the facts that these very men, confessing, indicted, some of them on trial, still sat in the municipal council; that they were going on with their grafting there and fighting Folk step by step; that they were organizing the next political campaign to beat him and keep their places, their power, and carry out their piratical plans. *McClure's Magazine* "told the world" all this that St. Louis knew better and in more detail than "we" did, in the hope and in the faith that the citizens of St. Louis would rise up and vindicate the democracy which the American people, Folk, and I believed in. Yes, I too believed in political democracy even while I was observing that all political signs indicated that the boodle gang would defeat Folk if he ran for re-election as circuit attorney in St. Louis, and therefore was advising him to appeal over the heads of the people of St. Louis to the people of Missouri by running for governor! What about the mind of man that can see and think that way? My mind, for example. My brain is at least human. What sort of organ is it that can face all the facts against a belief and still stick to its belief?

Folk had his case against Ed Butler, the boss, transferred from the courts of St. Louis to Columbia, the university town of Missouri. I went there to see that trial, and I felt the sentiment for Folk. It was expressed in chiseled words over the old court house: "Oh, Justice, when driven from other habitations, make this thy dwelling-place." Folk did not attack Butler; he handled his case as if democracy and Missouri were on trial, not the boss, and his final plea, almost whispered, was for "Missouri, Missouri." The boss was convicted. The people were all right—in Missouri. But back in St. Louis they were not right. The first comment I heard there when we all returned was the obstinate declaration, everywhere repeated, that "Butler would never wear the stripes." The boss himself behaved wisely. He stayed indoors for a few weeks—till a committee of citizens from the best residence section called upon him to come out and put through the House of Delegates a bill for the improvement of a street in their neighborhood. And Butler had this done. One of the first greetings to Folk was a warning from a high source that now at length he had gone far enough. He paid no heed to this. He proceeded to the trial of other cases. One of them was of Henry Nicolaus, a rich brewer, for bribery. Mr. Nicolaus pleaded that he did not know what was to be the use of a note for $140,000 which he had endorsed. Pretty bad? The judge immediately took the case from the jury and directed a verdict of not guilty. This was the first case Folk had lost; he won the next eight, making his record fourteen won to one lost. But the Supreme Court took up the fight. Slowly, one by one, then by wholesale, this highest court of appeal reversed the boodle cases. The machinery of justice broke down under the strain of boodle pull. And the political machinery did not break down.

The bi-partisan gang, with reformers and business men for backers, united on a boodle ticket, elected it, and—Boss Butler reorganized the "new" House of Delegates with his man for speaker and the superintendent of his garbage plant (in the interest of which he offered the bribe for which he was convicted) for chairman of the Sanitary Committee!

What was the matter? Folk and I asked that question many a time, without finding or framing an answer to it. And all that time we were acting upon the answer, which we must have had in our nervous system somewhere; it simply did not take the form of words in our brains. Our talks were all in the course of making up speeches for his campaign in Missouri for governor of the State, things for him to say to the people of Missouri to persuade them to save him from defeat at the hands of the people of St. Louis. We knew in our bones, and those addresses of Joe Folk to Missouri will show that we knew, that the voters of the State were in that stage of mental innocence which the voters of St. Louis were in when the disclosures of corruption began there. They thought they were innocent; they thought that bad men were deceiving and misleading them; they did not know that they themselves were involved and interested in the corruption. St. Louis found out. Missouri would find out some day, too. When that day came, as it did, then the people of the State would unite with the citizens of St. Louis to stop Folk and his interference with their business.

The people of St. Louis, like the people of Minneapolis and New York, were against bribery in the abstract and against the corruption that involved the police, vice, and petty politicians. They backed reformers who attacked these petty evils. When Folk went on to discover that not only Ed Butler's garbage business but the franchises of public service corporations were linked up with garbage and gambling and prostitution, some of the people turned against Folk. They had stock or friends who held stock in these companies and so could see that they did not belong with what they called the honest citizenry. Therefore Folk had to appeal to the people of Missouri. And they elected him governor before he had gone so far that they saw that they were in it. Then Folk had the people of the United States behind him. He was a possibility for president at one time after he was governor of Missouri, when he could not have been reëlected governor of Missouri.

What did this all mean? What was this system? Folk and I could not answer this question either. Like the other question, we knew the answer, but we didn't want to face it—not clearly. I'm sure Folk didn't. One day I saw a book on his living-room table, *Social Problems* by Henry George. He saw me see it; we had just been wondering together about the nature and the cure of political corruption.

"That book explains the whole thing," Folk said.

"Have you read it?" I asked.

"No," he said. "I read into it enough to see that that man has it all sized up, and—I dropped it, as I did another book a socialist brought me."

"Why?" I demanded, astonished.

"Oh," said Folk, "if I once got socialism or any other cut-and-dried solution into my head, I'd be ruined—politically. Couldn't get anywhere. But you are not in politics. Why don't you read them?"

I gave him my reason, which was different from his, much better, I thought. My reason was that I had not only read, I had studied those books under a regular professor of political economy at college, and so knew that there was nothing in them. As Folk was to go on blundering to a career, so I was to go on "scientifically" to trace the system and see if it was the same in other cities as in St. Louis, Minneapolis, and New York.

V I

PITTSBURGH: HELL WITH THE
LID LIFTED

BEFORE I had finished my work in St. Louis, while "we" were still undecided what city to do next, a high official of the Gould railroad system invited me to his office there and nominated Pittsburgh. He said it was utterly corrupt, worse than St. Louis, as bad as Philadelphia. He knew because the Goulds were seeking a terminal there, and though the chamber of commerce and business men generally saw the advantage of another road to compete with "the Penn," they could do nothing. The political business ring which ran the city and linked up with the Matt Quay ring which ran the State belonged to and protected the monopoly of the Pennsylvania Railway. He and the Gould agents had long been negotiating; they still were, but there was no hope of success. They had seen deep into the methods and the power of the corrupt rulers of Pittsburgh, Pa. He was personally indignant at this state of things. If I would go there and show it up as I had St. Louis, the Gould people would quietly furnish me their facts, the evidence to prove the worst and free the city from its hateful tyranny.

This invitation attracted me and my associates on *McClure's*. It might be that the Goulds' plan was to talk business diplomatically to the faces of the Pittsburgh bosses while I was kicking them from behind, but I didn't care. When thieves fall out honest men get their due, and I was still an honest man. It was a great chance for me. I personally dreaded to undertake all by myself the exploration of a strange city. I had never done that. My editors and readers had been thinking of me as an investigator and exposer of evil; even this Gould official spoke as if I had exposed St. Louis. I had indeed done some original research as a reporter of

police and political corruption in New York, but I was not an
investigator; I had simply gone where some one else, Joe Folk
or Hovey Clarke, had been doing the work, and picking up the
fruits of their labor and risk, described and interpreted their
evidence.

I was afraid that a lone-handed attack upon a city might expose
me more than it would the grafters.

On the other hand it would set me up in professional and public
esteem to walk into a city like Pittsburgh, and with the secret aid
of such a group of attorneys, lobbyists, and detectives as the
Wabash Railroad had there, lift the lid and show what was boiling
under it. And that was the Gould proposition. I had to promise
never to divulge the sources of my information; he might hint to
the Pittsburgh and Pennsylvania ring about me, but I must never
tell anybody about him.

Pittsburgh fitted into my theoretical purposes. It was not
notorious like Philadelphia and Chicago; its exposure would come
as a surprise. Again, having seen in other cities that political corruption was not political, but business, I was myself keen to look
through business eyes into a city which, governed by politicians
for big business, was in a fight of one railroad against another and
hurting little business. A third advantage was that Pittsburgh
was a Scotch-Irish-American city. Some apologists for American
municipal government met my use of St. Louis, New York, and
Minneapolis as typical cities by pointing out that St. Louis was
German, Minneapolis Scandinavian, and New York—Irish. Pittsburgh would be in the way of an answer to that rubbish. But there
was another bit of propaganda to consider.

In those days educated citizens of cities said, and I think they
believed—they certainly acted upon the theory—that it was the
ignorant foreign riff-raff of the big congested towns that made
municipal politics so bad. The reformers of New York, St. Louis,
Minneapolis, etc., were forever asking their State Legislatures to
take away from the municipalities the police and other local powers
which were most obviously abused. According to my dawning
theory, just as one city must be like another, so a State must be
like its cities. Folk was finding out the truth of this. He had not
yet begun to act upon it, but his gathering evidence went to show
that Missouri was corrupted by the same men and methods as

St. Louis. I had agreed to go back there some day and report what he discovered and proved on the State he was to be governor of. Meanwhile I needed to know and be prepared to make comparisons with some other State. Pennsylvania would do very well, and Pittsburgh first, then Philadelphia, would take me into the State of Pennsylvania.

I have never lost my first picture of Pittsburgh when I went there to write about it. It looked like hell, literally. Arriving of an evening, I walked out aimlessly into the smoky gloom of its deep-dug streets and somehow got across a bridge up on a hill that overlooked the city, with its fiery furnaces and the two rivers which pinched it in. The blast ovens opened periodically and threw their volcanic light upon the cloud of mist and smoke above the town and gilded the silver rivers, which were high and threatening floods. I wrote that night to Jaccacci, the art editor, to send me an artist—not an illustrator, but a painter—to paint that scene. Jules Guérin came, and he saw and he did paint a picture, which I possess and enjoy to this day, of "Pittsburgh as Hell with the Lid Off." It is my picture. I contributed as much to it as Guérin did. I contributed to it the sense of dread which was in me; I was afraid of the mystery and the might of that city which was rolling out steel and millionaires. I was afraid of it because I had to "do" it—alone.

The Goulds had gone back on me. I don't recall whether I told Guérin, but the day he came to Pittsburgh I had called at the office where the Gould official in St. Louis had directed me to go for the facts on Pittsburgh, and they did not know me. The man I was to see received me, but he had never heard either of me or of the promise to help me. So he said. His embarrassed manner and his quick understanding glance at his secretary belied his assertion, but he said that they were not trying to force their way into Pittsburgh; they were willing to come there if the city and the business men generally wanted another road, but the Pennsylvania handled the traffic so far, and the Goulds had a satisfactory arrangement with the Penn. I understood. The negotiations were proceeding better than the St. Louis man had expected; there was no need of blackmail from behind while the Gould agents bargained diplomatically in front; the Goulds were to be taken into the group of big business interests that controlled the government;

so no other savior was required. I understood right away what later insiders and, indeed, events confirmed, but I was lost and lonely just the same.

As I wandered, a stranger, through that vast mystery of a city, looking for a place or a person to begin my inquiries, I wanted to run away. I could not. I had to stay. "We" had announced that I was to investigate and expose the corruption of that invisible government which looked so big and strong, so menacing and—so invisible. No Folk this time, no Hovey Clarke, no friends at all, not even an acquaintance. Even the hotel clerks were cold; they knew; the newspapers had reported my arrival and my purpose. Everybody concerned must have been watching and laughing at me; I spotted the detectives set upon me to observe and report my movements. I seemed to read in the faces of whispering, smiling groups in the lobbies, on the exchanges, on the streets, the amused wonder at my bewilderment.

I have traveled since in many foreign countries; I have never been in any place where I felt so like a foreigner, so lonely, unwelcome, and ridiculous, as during those first dreadful days in Pittsburgh.

But I remembered—sitting in my dreary hotel room—I bethought me of my profession, and how always on the newspapers there are men who know more than their papers print; who know everything. And the people of a city, they too know something; they know at least what everybody knows. I tried it. I asked men who happened to sit next to me on street cars or at a restaurant: "Who is your political boss?" And they could tell me. There had been two—Chris Magee and William Flynn, but Chris died. So Flynn was left alone. Yes, there were big business men back of him; and they knew what their names were—well-known names, Andrew W. Mellon, for example. They knew, too, these ordinary citizens, "how the game was worked" and some of the big grafts. They could tell me the great scandals, with the rumored prices, dates, and division of profits. Similar rumors had turned out to be right in New York, and I remembered that they were right in St. Louis.

I went to the newspaper offices, one by one, all of them, and I hit upon an approach which I have since used on all subjects—business, politics, reform. There are honest men in all walks of life, honestly ignorant; they sincerely believe things are as they seem and truthfully repeat to you the current lies that make everything look all right. They don't know what is what, but they do know who is who in their own business, just as they know who is the boss of their city. The question I framed for the newspaper offices, as for the city, was directed to find the boss of the paper. Calling with my card at the editorial office, I would ask the office boy: "Say, kid, who is 'it' here?"

"Why," he would answer, "Mr. So-and-so is the editor."

"No, no," I protested. "I don't mean the front, I mean—really."

"Oh, you mean the owner. That's Mr. Blank."

Feigning disgust and disappointment, I would say, "The owner, he's only the rear as the editor is the front. What I mean is, who's running the shebang? Who knows what's what and—who decides?"

"Oh," he would exclaim—whether he was the office boy, a reporter, or an editorial writer—his face lighting up with the intelligence faces habitually conceal— "Oh, the man you are looking for is—Nut Brown."

Nut Brown is a name similar to that of the man who helped me first in Pittsburgh. He was a reporter on one of the Pittsburgh papers, a reporter who did not and could not write—not English— on a paper that was in the Pittsburgh-Pennsylvania political business ring. Nut Brown really ran that paper, editors, publishers, and the owner, and seldom appeared in the office.

"He's hardly ever here," his office boy said. "That's his desk"— pointing—"but he's too busy to use it. And he has no office. He's all over town all the time. But you'll find him—let's see now—you go to the office of the stock brokers, White and Black, at the close. He'll be there."

And there he was, looking what he was: a "wise guy" who had started as a newsboy, missed school, and learned life as it happened to him. He never wondered about "really," never suffered ideals. He was a success as a politician, as a reporter, as a business man. He played the game, beat it, and was not cynical.

"Sure," he said, when I presented myself and my purpose to him, "I'll give you the dope."

He did. He verified the rumors I had heard from the men on the street, elaborated them, and when I stopped him to ask about evidence to back up his facts and avoid or meet suits for libel, he had his answer ready.

"Oliver McClintock has the proofs."

Oliver McClintock! I had heard of him: nothing good. Nobody had spoken well of this merchant reformer who was the spoil-sport of Pittsburgh. He "nosed into" everything, was "forever kicking," and "never got anywhere." The arch, the only, lonely fighter for the right in Pittsburgh, he was impotent yet unsuppress-ible. He was the one man I was to avoid; so I had been warned, and so I believed. The first respectful word I heard of this man came thus suddenly from Nut Brown, a grafter, and he under-stood and enjoyed my exclamatory astonishment: "Oliver Mc-Clintock!"

"Yes," said Nut, "Oliver McClintock has the goods on us. He's a ———— ———— ————. That's what we say to the mob, but to ourselves in private, we stand hats off to little Mr. Oliver McClintock. He's a fighter. If he had an army, if he had a minority, if he had ten men—I mean *men*—he would whip the whole crooked bunch of us."

With this introduction I called on Mr. Oliver McClintock in his place of business, and he, the moment he caught my name and purpose, put his finger to his lips, looked all around him and led the way to his inner office. There behind closed doors I heard fully, for the first time, the American reformer's story, a modern tragedy of defeat, humiliation, martyrdom. He was an astute business man who, somehow, had kept apart the child's picture of a noble world of brave men and good women, the picture of romance and the school histories. And, off by itself, life as he had lived and learned it in Pittsburgh had drawn for him another picture. As he told, whispering, how he had discovered bit by bit what really went on in government and business, he had been first incredulous, then convinced, inspired like the heroes of old to go forth and fight, humbly, as a soldier under some great leader, the Monster of Cor-ruption, Fraud, Lies. He had spoken to some of his friends, other business men, prominent, leading citizens, and had them try to put him off; and when he insisted that it was all wrong and that some-thing must be done he was warned. He could not believe his own ears. He was "wrong on his facts," but even if he were right he must keep hands off or—his business would be hurt, and his family, and himself.

This quiet, white-haired merchant set out to prove his facts. He watched the letting of city contracts, kept accounts, and soon had little paper piles of evidence to show the regular, outrageous grafting of the ring in all public business. He offered it for publication; he showed it privately to friends; and he became a center to which all knowledge of graft naturally flowed. He knew and could prove what was going on in little business and big business, but no one wanted his demonstrations. He was shunned; even in his shop and in the bosom of his own family he was silenced. Mr. McClintock never ceased his investigations, but he had no use for his data till I came along. I took it. I didn't print much of it. It was too detailed and dull; the public won't read figures. And that is not what evidence is for. I learned not to print but to store away in a safe place the evidence I gathered, keeping it against the always possible libel suit that might be brought. I had to show it to the attorney of the magazine (who always said my evidence was not sufficient and that my articles should not be published). But my best use of Oliver McClintock's (and all other) piles of facts was to read them through to trace the methods and the practices of the grafters, see in them the outline of the invisible government, and, meanest of all, to let the political members of the ring and their business backers know that I had and could bring into court the ammunition of this fighting man, who only asked a chance to testify and so tell his story. Blackmail!

Mr. McClintock was my Folk for Pittsburgh. He did my work and stood for what I wrote—stood ready to back up what I said. And on the other hand, we of *McClure's* were a comfort, a release, and a backer for McClintock as we had been for Folk. We were their only friends; we made their labors of some effect. There are in all American cities today McClintocks if not Folks who know and can prove what is going on, but there are no muckrakers to write, and no muckraking publications to print, their facts.

I didn't write one-tenth of the truth that Oliver McClintock offered me. All I wrote was enough to show that, both in petty police graft and in big business corruption, Pittsburgh was like New York, St. Louis, and Minneapolis. My own interest was in what I was seeing from Pittsburgh of the condition of Pennsylvania—so like Missouri, and like the State of New York. I would do Philadelphia next; Pittsburgh was an introduction to the other, bigger city. McClintock's trails of evidence often ran off by way of Harrisburg, the capital city of Pennsylvania, to Philadelphia, the metropolis. I felt ready for that city; I felt ready, however, largely because I was sure that there would be a McClintock there, some beaten reformer who had knowledge with proofs which he would

> # PITTSBURG: A CITY ASHAMED
> ### THE STORY OF A CITIZENS' PARTY THAT BROKE THROUGH ONE RING INTO ANOTHER

HELL WITH THE LID LIFTED
McClure's Magazine, May, 1903

be glad to give me and which now, after four similar cities, I would be able and bold enough to use to the full. And I remember, as I left Pittsburgh, calling upon and thanking Oliver McClintock for his service to me. And I remember the glint in his unsentimental eye when I told him and tried to make him realize the meaning of the fact that, even though the people of Pittsburgh, high, middle, and low, shunned him on the streets, the rulers of his city, who knew what he knew and knew also what a he man was, privately, very secretly, held him to be the First Citizen of Pittsburgh—as he was.

VII

PHILADELPHIA: A DEFEATED PEOPLE

S o sure was I now of the family resemblance of American cities that I went at Philadelphia with as much confidence as I had felt fear and doubt before Pittsburgh. I knew just what to look for. In my mind was a map of the actual government, a diagram of a city, which I sketched for S. S. McClure. He was frightened.

"Your theory is getting you," he protested. "You think you know so much that you won't be able to see and report the news."

My teasing answer was that one of the methods of scientific research was to form an hypothesis and test it with the facts, and one of the tests of truth was to base a prediction upon your theory and watch the outcome of the event. And as for news, I reminded him that my theory meant that we were approaching a foundation for a science of politics and government.

If the graft and corruption of politics, which he looked upon as exceptional, local, and criminal, occurred everywhere in the same form, then this universal evil must be, not an accidental consequence of the wickedness of bad men, but the impersonal effect of natural causes, which it might be possible to identify and deal with without hating or punishing anybody.

Mr. McClure would not laugh, nor would he see the "good news" in my theory. He pretended to hate the idea, but I felt that his concern was for our journalism. He feared that, as a doctrinaire, I would degenerate from a reporter into a propagandist; and there was danger there. I was not afraid myself. I liked to change my mind. There was a risk in theorizing. I had witnessed, close up, the fatal, comic effect upon professors and students of hypotheses which had become unconscious convictions. And thus warned, I had thrown overboard, as a reporter facing facts, many of my college-bred notions in my specialty, morals. It was hard to do; ideas harden like arteries; indeed, one theory of mine is that convictions are identical with hardened arteries. But the facts I had to report professionally, over and over again, forced me to drop my academic theories one by one; and my reward was the discovery that it was as pleasant to change one's mind as it was to change one's clothes. The practice led one to other, more fascinating—theories.

For example: no general ethical principle known to me held in practice; or could hold. Only special, professional ethics limited the conduct of men, and these differed so fundamentally that a "good merchant," like Mayor Strong of New York, might be a "bad politician." One reason for this was that, while a business man is trained to meet and deal with the temptations of business, he is a novice and weak before those of politics. Another reason is that what is right in business may be wrong in politics. Richard Croker, the Tammany boss, was not so "bad" in business as Mayor Strong was "bad" in politics. Nay, Croker was not so "bad" in business as he was as a politician. When he confessed under public cross-examination that he "worked for his own pocket all the time" he was denounced and politically doomed. But W. L. Strong, as a merchant, had done that all his life, and he was not condemned for making a profit. That was a matter of course in commerce. As a successful profiteer, the rich merchant was promoted to be mayor of New York and failed as a reform official because his business ethics and training did not fit him for the job. Revising my ethical teachings, therefore, I drew another, more interesting, tentative moral theory, viz.: that the ethics and the morals of politics are higher than those of business.

As a matter of fact, however, hardly any of my old academic theories held in practice, and so now my new theories of government began to be blown up or altered. Philadelphia, for instance, changed my hypothesis of the identity of American municipal governments.

The system stood. There was the same old arrangement of a mayor, councilmen, and the usual elected officials, all described in the new Bullitt Charter, which had been drawn by an expert of experience, intelligence, and integrity, to meet and to defeat the typical evils of the corrupt politics of old. And yet, back of this charter and working with and through it, there were the same old boss, ring, and machine, governing Philadelphia as St. Louis, Minneapolis, New York, and Pittsburgh were governed. What shocked me most, however, was to learn right away that the famous Bullitt Charter had adopted a principle which I had formulated as a theory of reform and offered urgently to Dr. Parkhurst and other New York reformers for their new Greater New York Charter. The Bullitt Charter centered power in the mayor, put him in a position to do either good or evil, but made him by the same token responsible, so that the voters might know whom to praise or blame, promote or throw out of office. I had to note a (to me) new and startling theory, viz.: that the form of government did not matter; that constitutions and charters did not affect essentially the actual government.

I put this in the place of the old American theory of checks and balances, and to anticipate a bit, I never myself thereafter read the charter of any city or State that I studied. The paper government did not count. And I found in Pennsylvania that the bosses there knew this. Some of them helped the reformers put over their new, anti-graft charter. Their purpose was not reform. The State boss, Senator Matthew S. Quay, had had difficulties with a city boss, and it was to beat him that he made his State Legislature pass the Bullitt Charter, as an ouster. He said that he would deal with the difficulties of that instrument when he came to them, and he did. The old city boss knocked out by Quay and the new charter, the Senator appointed Israel W. Durham, a ward politician, to be boss of Philadelphia. This was new to me; no State boss could have named the boss of any city I had seen. A boss is a natural growth, not a legal device like a mayor. And even Quay had had to choose a ward boss and help him to master the party machinery. There was something to study in all this. The present point, however, is that in spite of the new, wise charter and the all-powerful mayor, the system prevailed. Quay and his city lieutenant ruled, as before reform, the two machines of the two old parties and, therefore, the mayor and elected officers; and they made the government represent, not the people as a whole, but the business, the same old businesses which contributed to the corruption of—all the cities I knew.

All was regular, and, as usual, all was known to everybody. I asked the manager of the hotel where I registered for the names of the bosses and reformers. He was not interested in politics, not in the least; but he knew. "Iz" Durham was the Dick Croker, the "Doc" Ames, the Ed Butler, of Philadelphia. The Oliver Mc-Clintock of Pittsburgh was named Rudolph Blankenburg in Philadelphia; the Joseph W. Folk was Rotherwell; the Charles H. Parkhurst was the Watch and Ward Society. The parallel of Philadelphia with other cities was so perfect that it was comic. And yet—there were differences, the differences I have mentioned, and other variations, not only such unimportant differences, but one subtle, very significant great difference.

My hotel man, for example, said that at the last election, when he went to the polls, he was challenged; he had "voted already." He answered that he had not voted; there was a dispute, and it developed that his name and his brother's name had been voted on by machine repeaters. "Lots of my friends had the same experience," he told me. "I kicked so hard that they let me vote, but they called in a couple of gangsters to offset my ballot by voting the other way—in the names of George Washington and Benjamin Franklin."

This humorous impudence was characteristic of Philadelphia; the gang voted "for fun" all the names of the signers of the sacred Constitution of the United States, of the new charter and the membership lists of the swell clubs. This joyous defiance of the holies of holies was only a sign of the novelty I saw in this fine old city. The novelty was the attitude of this hotel man and of other good citizens of Philadelphia toward their notorious, insulting, cynical political and business crooks.

He and his kind did nothing about it. "There is nothing to be done," the hotel man said. "We have tried reforms over and over again; we have striven to beat this game; and we never got anywhere." The reformers I saw took much the same view. They were still working, but only on details, not for a thoroughgoing reform of the government. They had facts. There was no difficulty at all about getting all the evidence one wanted of any of the many, many scandals that had been and still were disgracing the city. And the reformers were able, courageous men. One of the most persistent of these fighters was E. A. Von Valkenburg, the editor-in-chief of the Philadelphia *North American*, a great newspaper owned by Thomas B., the son of John Wanamaker. Von Valkenburg was a smiling, experienced newspaper man, who had reported or edited in other towns in Pennsylvania. He knew everybody and everything. He printed everything, too. Threatened with assassination, he simply moved his desk out of range of his window and went right on getting and publishing the evidence, the libelous, uncontradicted facts. The gang tried to blackmail the owner of the paper with an exposure of something personal; John Wanamaker answered with a public offer of $2,500,000 for a street railway franchise which the mayor was about to give away. The *North American* was not to be intimidated, but neither was the gang. Mayor Ashbridge met Wanamaker's cash offer by signing away the franchise, quick. And Von Valkenburg wanted to know from me how in the deuce the reformers got so far as they did in St. Louis and Minneapolis. He and he alone in his city seemed to have some hope of beating the system there. I could not tell him how to do it; he pumped and pumped, and he was "wise" in his questionings. But I did not know the answer he needed; I was full of questionings myself, not of answers. I must ask for answers myself, answers which none of the reformers could give.

In desperation one day I called at the office of the boss, Israel W. Durham. His secretary shook his head. "Don't think Mr. Durham will see you; too busy." He would ask. He came out with his eyes and mouth open in surprise. "Go in," he said, and I went in, and saw a man well worth knowing. He was sitting, a slight figure, relaxed at his desk. "Not well," I thought. Only his eyes were quick; they were kind, inquiring. He did not rise. As I halted on his threshold, he nodded a smiling welcome.

"Close the door," he said quietly. "I want to ask you a couple of questions."

"Oh, no, you don't," I protested. "I came to this town for information, and everybody is asking me questions, like you. I draw the line. You've got to answer me first."

He smiled. "All right," he said. "Your turn first, then mine. What do you want to know?"

There had been a burst, a volcanic eruption, of "steals" and "jobs," all in the administration of Mayor Ashbridge. I asked Durham how they dared do such a wild, wholesale business in such a short time. He did not mind the assumption, in my question, that the franchise grants were steals and that he knew it. He waited a moment; then asked me quietly if I meant to quote him.

No, I said. I was really puzzled and wanted only to understand the politics of the Ashbridge administration; technically it looked like bad politics, "bad bad politics," I remember saying. He shook his head slowly, thoughtfully, no.

"In the first place," he said, "Ashbridge wished it so. He wanted but one term in office, and having no further ambition, he wanted to crowd as much business as we would let him into that one term. And we—we talked it all over. With the mayor known to be for one term only we would have to stay here and take the permanent blame. The responsibility fell upon me. But we reasoned—"

"Well," I urged, when he halted there, "you could put over one of those steals in New York or anywhere else, but one would be enough to strain any machine I know of. And five or—more!" He smiled.

"We reasoned," he resumed, "we agreed among ourselves that it was exactly the five or—more that would save us."

He let me express my bewilderment; then he cleared it as by a lightning flash.

"If we did any one of these things alone the papers and the public could concentrate on it, get the facts, and fight. But we reasoned that if we poured them all out fast and furious, one, two, three—one after the other—the papers couldn't handle them all and the public would be stunned and—give up. Too much."

We sat there, he amused, I as stunned as his public.

"Well, you Pennsylvania politicians know something even Tammany doesn't know."

He nodded. "Yes," he said. "We know a lot they don't know. We know that public despair is possible and that that is good politics."

So that was why my hotel host, and the reformers, and the professors at the university, and the good citizens generally, said there was nothing to be done.

"Yes," Iz Durham answered. "The Bullitt Charter was a great thing for us. It was the best, last throw of the reformers, and when we took that charter and went right on with our business, we took the heart out of our reform forever."

"Then," I summed it up, "then Philadelphia is a city where reform is over."

He nodded, watching me humorously, while I went on theorizing out loud. Here was the difference I had felt in this city: that Philadelphia was in the condition St. Louis would be in after the graft system had recovered from Folk and his attacks. The people of a city would accommodate themselves to the revealed conditions and practices and rearrange their ideas and fit their minds to things as they are. The boss listened; he stopped smiling, but he nodded.

"Political corruption," I went on, "is, then, a process. It is not a temporary evil, not an accidental wickedness, not a passing symptom of the youth of a people. It is a natural process by which a democracy is made gradually over into a plutocracy. Treason, in brief, is not a bad act; it is an inevitable, successful policy, and the

PHILADELPHIA: CORRUPT AND CONTENTED

A TITLE WHICH STUCK

From *McClure's Magazine*, July, 1903

cities differ one from another according to age. Philadelphia is worse than St. Louis because it is older—in experience."

I soon had the boss bewildered and as puzzled and serious and shocked as I had been.

"If this process goes on," I said, "then this American republic of ours will be a government that represents the organized evils of a privileged class." I had forgotten Durham; I wasn't accusing him of wrong-doing. But I remember the awed tone in which he broke into my soliloquy to ask how it could be stopped. I saw that he cared. I said I didn't know, and I rose to go to think over the ideas I had got into my head. He protested.

"But I had some questions to ask you," he said, "and you promised to answer mine if I answered yours."

"Sure, I did. What's your question?"

"In your articles on St. Louis," he began, "you said that the boss there, Ed Butler, governed the city with a minority of both parties. Here we have to have a majority of both parties. How does Butler do it his way?"

I explained in general that by controlling the shifting, the purchasable, and the organized voters, he could influence the nominations of both parties and then, at the polls, pick the winners, either all of one party or the best crooks from both tickets. That did not satisfy Durham. He saw that, but he wanted to know how it was worked out in detail, in the wards, for example, and then in the conventions and Legislature. I became enthusiastic. I had been interested in those details myself and had inquired into them; I had not written the results, and no one else had ever asked for them. To Durham, a politician, they were fascinating, and forgetting his use for them, I talked on like an enthusiast to a willing listener, as one artist to another. And I satisfied him on two points.

"Yes," he said thoughtfully when I had finished my exposition of the technique of grafting politics with a minority of each party. "Yes," he reflected again. "That's all right. That would work, I can see. And"—slapping his knee, he exclaimed—"it's cheap, too, cheaper than our way."

And, then, as he moved with me to the door, he said quite seriously, "I think that I get you now."

The sudden personal turn stalled me. "What do you mean, get me?"

"Well," he said, "we've been looking you over since you came to town, reading your other stuff and wondering how you, a reformer, get on to the game the way you do; you know the way it's done."

"Yes?" I said. "And what is the explanation you say you've got?"

"Oh, I can see that you are a born crook that's gone straight."

A few astonished questions from me brought the admission from him that he thought that I had all the instincts of a politician who had, somehow, gone into reform instead of into the machine. But when I laughed over this and offered him jests, he wouldn't have it.

"There was another question that I had to ask," he said.

I had to press him to ask it; he wanted to, and he didn't want to. And when at last he blurted it out, he would not let me answer.

"What I was going to ask you was just what it is that I do that's so rotten wrong. It seems to me I am pretty square with my friends and—with everybody. But the other side, they say I'm a crook, and I don't deny it. I am as sure as they are that I go wrong somewhere. But where? What they charge me with is not so bad, not as I see it. I'm loyal to my ward and to my—own, and yet— Well, there's something wrong with me, and I'd like to know: what is it?"

I started to answer, somehow, not to answer his question, but to speak, when he stopped me. He raised his hand.

"Not now," he said. "Don't tell me now."

"Why not?" I asked, curious.

"Because I believe that you can tell me, and I don't want to know now. It might make me want to quit, and I can't. But I'm a sick man. I'll soon have to quit, and when I can and not hurt my friends, I'm going to ask you to come over and tell me what I do that's so rotten wrong. Will you?"

I promised, and he opened the door for me to go, and sharply he closed it after me.

VIII

THE DYING BOSS

ISRAEL W. DURHAM, the boss of Philadelphia, returned my call upon him often. He used to sneak up to my hotel room, "just to chew the rag," he said. So did others come: reformers, business men, politicians, teachers and professors, newspaper men with tips, and ordinary citizens with grievances. These gave me information; facts poured in upon me till I was surfeited with and hated them—and some of the people who brought them. I liked Mr. Durham's visits; he never offered me information. It was against the rules of his game to "peach," and though he sometimes confirmed or corrected information I was in doubt about, though he never denied any facts, he did not give anybody or anything away. His service to me was in explaining apparently inconsistent facts and helping me form a picture of them. In a word: the boss was an aid to my digestion.

What did I do for him? I think that I gave him a philosophic view of politics, an objective look at himself and his business. Helping me to make a diagram of his city government out of my comparatively few facts, he with his mass of experience obviously was seeing for himself what he and his corrupt politics meant fundamentally. When I said that one business man's bribe was nothing but a crime, but a succession of business briberies over the years was a corruption of government to make it represent business, he said thoughtfully, "Then contributions to campaign funds are more regular and, therefore, worse than bribes!" He had imagination. He always went me one better. I repeated the ideas that I had expressed as they occurred so startlingly to me in our first interview, ideas his remarks had suggested. I repeated again and again that political corruption was a process, and I repeated because I could not accept it myself. If that were so, then Nature, God, was on the side of the bribers. In a country where business is dominant, business men must and will corrupt a government which can pass laws to hinder or help business. But there must be something wrong— unsocial—at the bottom of the organization of businesses which have to control government. I doubted my thesis. But the boss who was the chief of the agency that was illustrating this theory— Mr. Durham saw it.

He accepted the thesis I broached and doubted. "We ought to stop the process," he ejaculated with feeling, and he kept saying, "It ought to be stopped; it mustn't go on." And when I answered that he could stop it, he and his kind, that the men who did the wrong had the power, imagination, and courage to undo it, he agreed with me. "The reformers can't," I added; "they lack the knowledge, the tools, and the honesty." He hesitated, then understood and nodded, "Yes, they ain't straight, and they haven't got the nerve." And once after a long silence the boss sighed and said, "I wish I was young again or had my health—"

He saw the job, and it tempted him, as the same prospect attracted many such political and business leaders. I have had many similar experiences since with big, bad men and I find that, if they are big enough and bad enough, they seem to be as eager to do great good as great evil. They simply are not asked to do good; the drift of things, the rewards, the applause and education, are all the other way. "Iz" Durham, whom the reformers and the good people of Philadelphia despised, was, man for man, better than they were; he was the best man I met in that town, the best for mental grasp, for the knowledge of life and facts in his line, and—he had one other advantage which is something akin to honesty but must be described in other terms. The New Testament puts it the most clearly and briefly. Jesus said that He could save sinners; the righteous He could not save.

Mr. Israel W. Durham and other political bosses and some big business men and some plain thieves, like Jack Black, for example —they know that they are sinners and they don't deny it (except under oath), and they don't try to justify themselves. That is why it is such a comfort to sit down and talk with them. They accept, and you can start with, the facts, as you can in a conversation with scientists. They can be saved, and some day, when they are asked to. they may help us to save society. They are our best men, those convinced sinners who do not deny facts to excuse themselves. But the petty honest men who do not know that or when or how they sin, they will not face and so they cannot deal with things as they are. In St. Louis they thought that they were for reform, and discovering that they had stock or friends in the graft, turned cowards and persecutors of Joe Folk just as their kind forced the Romans to crucify the Jewish Messiah. In Philadelphia these same citizens had begun to change their ethics, their political philosophy, and their (sure) theories of economics to justify their surrender to business graft and political corruption. The corruption of Philadelphia had reached up to the very minds of men. The only man there who saw the enormity of the evil he and they all were doing, the size and the probable cost of the job of rectification, was the honest crook, Durham, whose chief inquiry was, "Just what do I do that's so rotten wrong?"

Perhaps he came to see me in the hope of gathering my answer to this question. All approaches to it interested him, but he was afraid of a direct statement. His reason recalled the attitude of the lumber king, Weyerhäuser, who said he couldn't ask the clergy, because they would tell him to quit, and he couldn't quit; and it was no use asking his bankers, because they would sincerely justify what he had to do. Durham did not evade the direct question because he doubted that he did "something rotten wrong"; he was sure of his wickedness, surer than I was, but he didn't want it defined because he was already tempted to—save himself and his city. He only postponed the answer, however. When I was about to leave Philadelphia he said that he had a fatal disease, and when he knew that the end was near, he would send for me, and I had to promise to come to him. And sure enough, some time later when I was busy at other things I received Durham's wire to "Come; you promised to," and I went.

That interview—Durham's story, pieced out with pertinent parts of other bosses' stories, the boyhood of Charlie Murphy, the Tammany boss, and President Roosevelt's description of Senator Matt Quay on his death-bed—I wrote all this as fiction under the title The Dying Boss. The plain facts are that Durham, weak and stricken, told me that he was ready, at last, to hear what his "real sin" was, and I said that it was disloyalty. He was shocked and incredulous. Since he held that loyalty was his chief and perhaps his one virtue, since he had never gone back on his friends, and—whatever else he had done, which was a-plenty—since he had been always a true, square friend, my charge was totally unexpected and hardly believable. And my argument, as it gradually convinced him, was devastating. He was a born leader of the common people, I reasoned; he had taught them to like and to trust him, even with their votes; he had gathered up and organized the power which lay in their ballots, their trust and their loyalty to him; and he, the good fellow, had taken his neighbors' faith and sovereignty and turned it into franchises and other grants of the common wealth, which he and his gang had sold to rich business men and other enemies of the people. He was a traitor to his own. He had asked for it straight, I gave it him—straight, and he got it. Not one word of evasion or excuse. He took it lying down, and all he said after a long, wan silence was: "Say, I sure ought to go to hell for that, and what'll they do to me? Do you think they'll set me on fire for—for what you said—disloyalty?"

I had to repair the damage I had done. I had to say something to reassure him; he looked as if he would faint. So I asked him what he did to fellows in his gang that went back on him. He said that he didn't do much; he let 'em go. Well, I answered, as brutally as I could put it, didn't he believe that his God was as merciful and forgiving as he, "Iz" Durham, was? He got that, too. He looked better, and he lingered longer than the doctors had predicted.

The Quay incident might as well come in here while I am writing about Pennsylvania and the character of bad bosses. I did not do that State, as I meant to, after Pittsburgh and Philadelphia; it was a waste of work, but I never did write Pennsylvania and therefore never met the State boss in his State, where alone one could know him. My meetings with the Senator were all in Washington, and always rather formal. The glimpse into his character that reminded me of his lieutenant, Durham, was a free gift from T.R. One day when I was loafing at the White House door, the president appeared, coming from outside.

"Come on in," he said, as he jerked my arm and carried me with him into his office.

"I have just done an unusual thing and had a most unusual experience. I have made a call on a senator. The president does not make calls, you know, but I got word from Quay that he was dying; so I rushed right over and—I saw him."

T.R. had thrown off his hat and he did not sit down. He was excited. He walked up and down the office while I waited, standing. By and by he came up to me and told his story, which I made a note of immediately afterward.

"I was admitted into the senator's sick room, and there he lay, long and still in his bed, eying me. I—well, you know how when somebody is sick or dying—you know how you feel you've got to say something cheerful, something banal. So I chirped up, all jolly and—and silly, and said, 'Why, Senator, how well you look! You'll soon be up and out and with us again.' It sounded bad enough to me. It must have made Quay sick. He didn't say a word for a minute; just looked at me and picked at the counterpane with his long, thin fingers. Gee, I felt cheap. Then he shook his head slowly, very slowly, and said: 'No, Mr. President, I'll not be with you again. I am dying. And'—as I started to remonstrate, he lifted a hand to stop my—politeness—'that's all right, dying; only I hate to be dying here on a bed like this. What I would like would be to crawl off on a rock in the sun and die like a wolf.'"

The president was evidently seeing the scene he described and was moved by it. He hurried on to say, briskly, choppily, that Quay explained that he had sent for him with a purpose. He had been all his life the titular chief and protector of the Indians of the old Five Nations. "He was part Indian himself, you know," T.R. said. Now that he was going, Quay was worried about those Indians, and so he was going to ask the president to take his place as the chief and the protector of the Five Nations. "And you bet I was proud to be chosen. I promised Quay to take and fill his place, and I will. And Quay was satisfied. 'That's all,' he said. 'Now I can die in peace.' But," said T.R., "wasn't it just like Quay to wish he could crawl off like a wolf on a big, lone rock and die in the sun?"

And then the president became angry with me; he berated me for not appreciating men like Quay. He became almost violent as he recited my "roasts" of the bosses and other "really great men." I said that I made a distinction between such men and their crimes; it was the crimes I denounced, not them. No use. He waxed more and more furious, and I saw that he was abusing me only to relieve his feelings. And he did find relief; he quieted down, told the story of the day over again, and ended by wishing that he might himself, finally, crawl off in the sun and die like a wolf on a rock. He changed the order of the phrases in Quay's swan song every time he repeated it.

But the curious thing was that T.R., who knew me and my changing ideas, was at that time hatching his denunciation of muck-rakers for denouncing men like Quay and Durham, whom I was learning to appreciate more and better, I think, than he did. It goes to show how slow I was to broach even in conversation my dawning sense of their value; I could hardly believe I was right. It upset too many of my theories of morals and politics, as Philadelphia did.

CHICAGO: AN EXAMPLE OF REFORM

MY REPORT on "Philadelphia, Corrupt and Contented," seemed to give the impression, which lasts to this day, that that beautiful old American city was the worst in the land. Not true, of course. It was only older than St. Louis and Minneapolis, and I might have shown that and put Philadelphia in its relative position, if I had gone from there to Boston or some other old town in New England; Boston was the logical next step. But my editorial associates on *McClure's* opposed my choice as they did my theory. They were for Chicago next.

My colleagues harbored, unconsciously perhaps, the theory then general among critics of government: that our political corruption was the worst in the world because we were the youngest nation. Our cities were suffering from what they called growing-pains, and as they grew older they would grow better. James Bryce, the English muckraker (of other countries), and E. L. Godkin, the Irish-English editor of my old paper, the New York *Evening Post,* taught this theory of youth, and I think they put over on Americans (and Europeans, too) the belief that England and English ideas and political practices were higher than ours; British liberalism was the ideal toward which we should strive.

Boston, Mass., and the rest of New England were a fair first test for my theory that England was our fate, not our hope. Boston, New England, was older than Philadelphia, Pa.; it was as proud as Philadelphia was contented; New England was almost as quiet, busy, rich, and aristocratic as old England. But that was the trouble. Boston and New England looked so good and sounded so quiet that we feared an investigation there might prove an anti-climax. I, too, was in doubt; indeed the respectability of Boston made me doubt my theory. I agreed, finally, that we should find something worse than Philadelphia, and Chicago would certainly be that. No doubt about it. I was sure Chicago would provide the sensationally wicked story we were looking for. And I went there with my mind made up: to expose the rough, anarchistic criminality of a wild, young western city. No one could have told me that I was to find there an example of reform, a sensible, aristocratic-democratic reform experiment.

William C. Boyden tried to. I called first on the amiable brother of my assistant managing editor. I told him I was going to "do" Chicago at last.

"Then you'd better meet my partner, Walter L. Fisher," he said.

"Why?" I asked. "Isn't he the reformer you wanted me to write up the last time I was here?"

"Yes," Boyden answered, and he said no more. He didn't even smile. He seemed to fall in with my plan to go straight to the machine bosses and "get the low-down on Chicago." So I started, and right away I discovered that there was something awry. I called on Hinkey Dink and Bathhouse John. They looked their parts; they were ward leaders all right; but they would not, they could not, talk politics. They launched into tirades against the reformers who were messing up everything in Chicago. Reformers! Patiently I pressed my inquiries into the system. Who was the boss of Chicago? Nobody, they said. Who owned the mayor? Nobody. Who controlled the city council? The Voters League, a reform organization! Absurd. I could not take it from these politicians that reformers had such power anywhere, to say nothing of in Chicago. There was something the matter; that I could believe. The machine existed; the system was there. My mental diagram of "the" American city fitted Chicago, but it was out of joint. The machine didn't work; the bosses were in trouble.

Turning to my own profession for guidance, I called on James N. Keeley, the managing editor of the *Tribune*. He proved to be, like me, an editor in a chair that could not hold him. A reporter at bottom, he was interested only in the news and often went out himself to get a story. He had gone as far away as Egypt once to get one. Keeley was a genius; he knew politics, his city, everything; he fascinated me, but he was no use to me. I appealed to Charles Montrose Faye, the city editor of the *Daily News*, who was reported to be "about the wisest guy" in the business. He stuttered, but he was able to express his contempt for me and a refusal to help me in any way.

"Y-you," he blazed, "you N-N-New York n-n-newspaper men, you c-come here knowing j-j-just what y-y-you'll f-f-find and nobody c-c-can tell you anything. I-I-I won't t-t-try. Go on—g-g-get it all all wrong and be damned."

Apparently he thought I was prejudiced. But I wasn't; was I? Like most men, I regarded myself as open-minded and honest at the least. In doubt of myself and in despair of Chicago, I decided to call on and consult Clarence S. Darrow, the philosopher and attorney who defended criminals and must therefore know his city from the underworld up. He might set me right. Having sent in my card, I waited in his outer office, watching his door as anxiously, as hopefully, as any client ever watched and waited. He came out, tall, hulking, absorbed; he held my card in his hand and studied it as if trying to recall where he had seen my name. He kept coming toward me till, close up, he threw back his head, looked into my face, and exclaimed: "Oh, I know. You are the man that believes in honesty!" And he laughed, and laughed, and laughed. He took and he shook my hand, but he laughed till tears came into his eyes. And he did not invite me into his office; he did not answer my questions. They only amused him the more, and I—well, I ran away. It was a year or two before I understood what Darrow meant by my belief in honesty; all I gathered at the time was that he, too, despised me as a person prejudiced by a fool conviction of some sort and not worth a moment even of his loafing time.

Humiliated and angry, I went straight to the supreme political boss of Illinois, Billy Lorimer, afterward U.S. senator. Bosses don't laugh at, they help, a fellow who is down and out, and by the time I reached his office I had whipped myself into a state of mind which expressed itself in my first question.

"What's the matter with your machine here?"

"Nothing," he answered quickly. "Why?"

"Well, it doesn't seem to run," I said. "It's the bummest political organization I have ever seen."

He defended the organization. I cited Tammany, St. Louis, Philadelphia—there were machines that worked; there were bosses that bossed. Here? Bah! He flared up and said something about the people of Chicago. "People!" I laughed at him the way Darrow had just laughed at me. He was a boss that believed in the people. He mentioned "the reformers." Reformers! I said I had seen reformers, some even of his, and they were all alike. No real boss ever suffered anything more than temporary inconvenience from reformers. He thought I'd find that Chicago reformers were different. I thought it was the Chicago politicians that were different: weak, incompetent—

"You," he charged, "with your sneers at reformers and Chicago and—all. How long have you been here? What do you know about us? What reformers have you seen?"

I laughed, and he: "Say, have you seen that son of a bitch, Fisher?"

I wilted. I feel even now that I owe it to myself to say that it was upon the authority of the big boss himself that I turned to look at Chicago as an example of reform. Chicago! The stuff was there for the other, the original story; it still is: the police graft, the traffic of authority with criminals, gamblers, prostitutes, liquor dealers, all sorts of thieves, and some sorts of murderers. The evil of Chicago was obvious, general, bold. I was warned again and again against my wanderings around in the Loop at night; the wide-openness of protected vice and crime fascinated my bulging eyes. Hinkey Dink himself said I ought not to walk home alone from his place. But I lived in a downtown club, and as a newspaper man I could not keep away from the scenes that were evidences of a great news story. How our readers would have liked the stuff I was seeing! The New York Tenderloin was a model of order and virtue compared with the badly regulated, police-paid criminal lawlessness of the Chicago Loop and its spokes. Just the same, all this was not what in newspaper parlance is called the feature of a news story of Chicago; evidently. Was it? With reluctance and doubt I acted upon the advice of the head and front of this system. I returned to Boyden's office and saw that— partner of his, Walter Fisher.

Fisher punished me with scorn for my scorn of him. Boyden must have described my attitude to him. Boyden had too much humor not to report my sure belief that Fisher and Chicago reformers in general were not worth my attention. So, though he received me politely, Fisher was short with his answers. No doubt my hangover of skepticism annoyed him. I had to acknowledge that he had some power, he and his Voters League, but how did he get it? How did he hold it? What was he doing with it?

"You are not making a very good government," I remarked sarcastically, citing the sinful scenes I had seen.

No, Fisher answered coldly. They were not out for good government, not yet. That might come later. For the present the League was fighting for representative government. The city council had been bought and owned by Yerkes, the street railway magnate, and other business men who wanted franchises, extensions, and privileges generally. Fisher and the Chicago reformers were forcing the aldermen to stand for the city, and in dealing with business men, to represent the public interest in making bargains. They were fighting first the corruption of their own class, letting the police evils of the lawless wait; they were reforming the good, not the bad, people. That might explain the popular support they had won for their movement. But just how did they manage it?

Fisher offered to this question no answer that meant anything to me. He would not generalize. He showed me files of information about candidates and politicians, such as I had seen in New York and Philadelphia. Ammunition. How was it used? He outlined in a bored tone of voice the scheme of the Municipal Voters League. No light in that. It was all incomprehensible, politically, till we happened to speak of the Seventeenth Ward, which the League carried one year for a Republican, the next year for a Democrat, the third for a Republican again. How did they do that?

Fisher came to life. His face lighted up; a keen shrewd look came into it, a twinkle in his eyes, and he told me the story. It was a story of politics. Another ward was another, different story, but it was politics. Fisher was a politician. The methods of these League reformers were the methods of politics: they dealt with each ward according to the actual situation there. They got the facts, knew the candidates, politicians, parties, grafts, and the people in a ward, and then, with this information, by publicity and by trading they swung the anonymous minority that followed the League all together to one side and one ultimate purpose.

Very practical politics, this, but was it wisdom? It was not. It was a sort of instinct, the Chicago instinct. It just happened. Walter L. Fisher was the third of the leaders of the League, which itself evolved by—accident, or instinct. Some young fellows, William Kent, the son of a millionaire; John Maynard Harlan, the son of a justice of the Supreme Court; and others of that ilk, ran for and were elected aldermen. With reporters like Finley Peter Dunne to report them, they made scenes in that "bear garden," the board of aldermen. They made informed but challenging speeches, charging their crooked colleagues with the facts, risking murder.

"Couldn't accomplish anything," said Billy Kent, whom Fisher called in to tell me the early history of the movement. "We were voted down, but we did make the meetings of the board as interesting as loud noises and bad smells could make them; we furnished the humorous reporters with 'news,' which soon got the people watching. Antics, farce, melodrama! Harlan was our orator, and he was some orator. He'd walk down in front of a boodler and call him a crook. With the details we raked up and the bad names the rest of us invented, Harlan would sock him—for Peter Dunne to hear, see, quote, describe. Some fun."

With such scenes in the limelight the people were aroused, and two hundred leading citizens met, with Lyman J. Gage, a leading banker, at their head, to do something. The two hundred appointed a committee of fifteen to find something to do. One of the fifteen drew a plan for a new municipal party—the old, old scheme. Chicago set out like any other city on the beaten path that has been proven an *impasse* over and over again. But Chicago had men who knew or felt that this was all wrong. They blocked this move. They blocked a motion to investigate conditions. "We know enough," they said; "a committee of investigation is a stall." They blocked a proposal to go to the corrupt State Legislature for a new charter, and they would not wait for the next mayoralty election to elect a good business man as mayor to give them good government. They maneuvered the big committee to seek a man, one man, to organize a league of voters to fight every fight that came up. He was not to run for office; he was to be a leader, a boss, with a minority to swing.

George E. Cole was the man they chose. He was a "second-class business man" (he said to me), about five feet tall and be-

tween two and three feet across the shoulders—a fighter. He
looked like a sea captain, and he worked and he talked like one.
He picked a crew of nine—chosen for what they could do, not for
what they represented—got rid of the big committees, and without
plans, began to "let people know we were there." With his short
legs apart, his weak eyes blinking, he stood on the bridge in the
limelight and shouted that he was going to beat the crooks up for
reëlection. Chicago likes audacity and is always willing to have
anybody try anything once; no matter who you are, where you
come from, or what you set out to do, Chicago will give you a
chance. The sporting spirit is the spirit of Chicago. When, therefore, George Cole stood up and said that he and a small, unknown
committee were out to clean up the Board of Aldermen, the town
looked, laughed, and asked how. "We're going to publish the
records of the thieves that want to get back at the trough," said
Cole, and he produced the facts, acts, votes that Kent, Harlan, and
the other decent aldermen had on their indecent colleagues. Cole
said that of the thirty-four retiring aldermen twenty-six were
rogues; some of the rogues quit; others were beaten in their wards,
each ward being handled by itself. "Old King Cole," "Boss Cole,"
was charged with politics, blackmail, deals—he did not care. He
was as terrible with respectable candidates as he was with rough-
necks; he defied the pull of leading citizens, even if they were
(as they were, some of them) on the old Committee of Twenty
that gave the League birth. No respecter of persons, parties, or
liberal principles, he carried the League to victories and a power
that amazed and amused Chicago. When his health failed he was
succeeded by Billy Kent, and when Kent was exhausted he gave
way to Fisher, who carried on the methods of the League, except
that, having power now, he did not have to be noisy. He printed
the facts quietly, made deals in the wards, got his majority of
aldermen, and then organized, instructed, and pledged them right
in his private office. I saw that done one night. In Fisher's office
I saw him, a reform boss, perform exactly like a regular political
boss, browbeat and control a various lot of (honest and dishonest)
politicians, and then send them out, watched and controlled, to
represent what they all knew or agreed was the best interest of the
whole people of Chicago. And as boss and secretary, Walter L.
Fisher dealt with the big financial interests that sought riches out

of the commonwealth of Chicago and made them give some service. It was a long, slow, hard task; it lasted years, ten or twelve, and when I wrote it I described this as an example of a reform that was working. And of course, from a journalistic point of view, the exhibition of Chicago as something for other cities to imitate was a sensation; it was more astonishing "news" than the graft article which I had meant to write could possibly have been. Here was a way to do it, and other cities did follow Chicago's lead. That is to say, they set up Municipal Voters Leagues, and sure enough, some of them got results; not good government, not normal representative government, but—a temporary betterment.

Chicago failed finally; it is ripe now for either a sensational political story or a new reform movement. And I was seeing, and I noted in my report, the beginnings of the end, without realizing that those beginnings were to be the end. Walter L. Fisher, afterward in the Cabinet of President Taft and a man now with an international reputation for ability and acumen, was not and never has been a radical. He did not see or touch sources of privilege. All he used his great power in Chicago for was to persuade, or, if need be, force the business interests that had to come to him to get their privileges, to make open terms with and render some service to his city. It was just what big business said it wanted, a government that understands and is just to business. And they, those business men and their fellow business men, in Chicago, in New York, everywhere—they hated and fought and clamored and wriggled and bribed out of their contracts with the practical, honest, fair "reform" government of Chicago. And finally they killed it as literally as the gunmen of Chicago now kill one another, and as safely. Why? They said (to me) that what they wanted was, not this so-called representative, but good government.

X

NEW YORK: GOOD GOVERNMENT

CHICAGO led not down to Boston, as we had expected, but up
to New York. The reception of the article on Chicago as
an example of reform indicated that our readers were interested in reform quite as much as they were in graft, that they
wanted to know what to do to get good government. That was the
idea or the phrase: "good government." I had been hit hard by
the distinction the Chicago reformers drew between good government and representative government. It would be good journalism
to find and report immediately an experiment in good government
to parallel the Chicago experiment in representative government.
And there was one: New York.

Yes, New York. Having set out from there with the New
Yorker's provincial conceit that our city was the worst in the land,
it was a bit of a shock to go back home to see it as good. What had
made the change? Comparison with other worst cities? Not only
that. Relativity is a principle of political criticism, and the fourth
dimension of time corrects one's calculations. Age makes a difference in cities as in citizens, and it was to see how much and which
way that I had meant to go to old Boston after old Philadelphia
and young Chicago. But New York was as old in years as Boston,
and yet all the while I was watching the Chicago reformers trying
to force their aldermen, good and bad, to represent the common
interest of the city, I was contrasting them with the Goo-Goos of
New York who were organizing to put good men, preferably good
business men, into office to give them good government. They had
won, those good government reformers; they were in power.
That very year (1903) they were preparing for an election which
was to let the voting New Yorkers decide whether to keep the
good reformers in office or oust them and go back to Tammany

430

Hall. There, then, at home—where reform should begin—was the opportunity to boost my old reform friends and to see an experiment in good government.

Returning to New York and revisiting my old haunts and my old friends, I gathered quickly two impressions which turned out to be right: first, that New York did have good government, or a good administration; second, that good government was doomed to defeat in the fall.

The mayor, Seth Low, was a business man and the son of a business man, rich, educated, honest, and trained to his political job. He had been the mayor of Brooklyn, before its merger into Greater New York, and president of Columbia University, to which he had given money. He was a man who always gave more than he took. To prepare himself for the mayoralty he had made six months' intensive study of the finances of New York. He had appointed under him men who were not only good men and not always business men; he chose some experts; and he and they together made plans for the betterment of the government, which they were carrying out with conspicuous efficiency. Some of their achievements were permanent. Just as Mayor Strong's Street Cleaning Department, having shown the way and faced down the public shock at its cost, having taught the New Yorkers what clean streets are—just as this achievement was never lost, so Seth Low's finance department, his tenement house administration, his applied principles of taxation—charging the land values rather than improvements—these stand to this day as monuments to the greatness of Mayor Low's administration. And he was planning more. He and his cabinet were students of municipal government throughout their term in office; they were all becoming, like the professional municipal managers in some German cities, masters of their craft. In a word, Mr. Low and his cabinet were just about ready to make New York what a city might be under our economic system, when that 1903 election threw them out.

Why? What was the matter? Didn't the voters know that this government was good? My old reformed police chief, Schmittberger, knew that the police department was good. He chuckled over its goodness: laws were pretty well enforced, graft was cut to a minimum, good policemen were recognized, promoted, or supported. And he bade me, if I doubted, go around and listen to the kicks of the criminals, liquor men, prostitutes, and gamblers, and to the grumbling of the cops. I did, and it was precisely this goodness that the underworld did not like. Of course. But Trinity Church, the old and rich establishment that faces Wall Street, had no good words for the good administration; Trinity owns acres of tenements and is governed by high financiers and other leading laymen. The police courts were just. The reporters said so, and the people who had to go to them, either to make or to answer complaints, did not deny it. Mr. Low had appointed as magistrates upright gentlemen and lawyers, who read the law to the people and did not often yield to "pull," like the Tammany heelers whom they displaced. But apparently, the poor, like the rich, preferred a human element in their judges. It was precisely the righteousness

NEW YORK: GOOD GOVERNMENT IN DANGER

McClure's Magazine, November, 1903

of the reform magistrates that was unpopular. In the tenements the tenants felt about the new and really good tenement house laws and regulations as Trinity and the other landlords felt. The two parties complained of different evils, but the new laws hit them both, and—it was the even justice that was so detestable. So with the real estate men and the tax-payers. And so with business men generally and with the reformers.

The City Club was the Tammany Hall of the reformers of New York in those days. It was a sort of exchange where we came together to share our hopes and our fears, our gossip and our truth. The Good Government Clubs' leaders, the men who had picked and elected Seth Low, were not enthusiastic about him and his record in the early summer of 1903. Yes, they would probably renominate him; they weren't sure, but—who else was there? It was astonishing. Their answers to questions indicated no doubt of the goodness of the mayor or of his appointments, policy, and performances, but— But what? They didn't say what; they didn't seem to know what. I had to guess, and my guesses were disconcerting. Didn't they, didn't anybody, really like good government? Not even the good government men? Were reformers also selfish?

No, they did not all want offices for themselves. It was something else.

And the business men—they said in Chicago that they did not like "representative government"; they preferred good government, and they thought they did. But here in New York, where they had it, they were down on good government. They also were not very clear as to the reasons; they did not, they could not, talk much. They contributed to the Tammany campaign fund and let their money talk for them. All one could gather from all that they all said was that good government hurt business in New York somehow, as representative government somehow hurt business in Chicago. Both cities were alike in that their governments, their laws, customs, practices, represented business generally and big or privileged businesses especially. The system stood. My mental diagram of an American city fitted New York and Chicago as it did Philadelphia, Pittsburgh, Minneapolis, and St. Louis. The only difference that threw light on the business opposition to the good government achieved in New York was that, whereas the Chicago reformers were openly fighting the special representation of certain bribing businesses there, in New York there was no thought of this.

Seth Low and his party in power and his Good Government Club backers were not radicals in any sense. Mr. Low himself was hardly a liberal; he was what would be called in England a conservative. He accepted the system; he took over the government as generations of corrupters had made it, and he was trying, without any fundamental change, to make it an efficient, orderly business-like organization for the protection and furtherance of all business, private and public. The special interests of the usual corrupters of politics, the light, transportation, and contracting businesses, were respected; even the vice interests were disturbed, not purposely, but by way of forcing the police to be "good."

When the money of business and the votes of the people threw out the Seth Low administration in the fall, it seemed rational to conclude that business men do not want good government much more than they want a representative democracy, that the people do not like good men and good government, or, let us say, professionally good men in office and unyielding good government. They both prefer "bad" government. Anyhow, with the issue as clear as that, they voted Tammany back into power in New York. In Chicago the business men opposed the representative reform in vain; the people supported it.

The experiment in good government failed, politically; the experiment in representative government was succeeding—so far.

All up in the air myself, I went to my home in Cos Cob, Connecticut, and made a book of my seven articles on the cities I had reported. The McClure, Phillips Company published it as *The Shame of the Cities*. It offered very few conclusions. I could not interpret my own observations; so in the introduction I said that the book was printed as the articles were written, as journalism with a purpose: "to sound for the civic pride of an apparently shameless citizenship." And blaming the people, the American people, I pointed out that "no one class is at fault, nor any breed, nor any particular interest or group or party. The misgovernment of the American people is misgovernment by the American people." The typical American citizen is the business man, a bad citizen. If he is a big business man, he does not neglect, he is busy with, politics, and very businesslike. But I did not blame even the big business men, only the people, who, I showed, were corrupt in small ways as their leaders were in big ways, and I appealed to them in patriotic and moral terms to cease from following their bad leaders. I besought them to follow good leaders, like President Roosevelt and Joseph W. Folk—I!

One day Upton Sinclair called on me at the office of *McClure's* and remonstrated.

"What you report," he said, "is enough to make a complete picture of the system, but you seem not to see it. Don't you see it? Don't you see what you are showing?"

My answer was a description of what I saw, and it was all that he saw, apparently, for he went out and said that "that man sees it all right." What Sinclair did not realize was that I could hardly believe what I was seeing, and that I could not, in so short a time, change my mind to fit the new picture. I was not yet over my education; so I had my two pictures, one on top of the other, on the canvas of my mind. I needed time to adjust my imagination to the facts as they were, not more experience, but time; so I loafed around home in the old New England town of Greenwich, Conn., sailing a boat and talking to the Cos Cob artists, to the fishermen and the townspeople. I stood on Election Day in the undertaker's in Greenwich and saw the voters file through, getting their three

"DON'T YOU SEE IT?"
Drawing by Art Young

dollars each to support the machine, but my occupation was dull digestion, understanding the mass, the mess, of observations I had in my head and getting ready to go out to muckrake some States.

COS COB: AN ART COLONY

Cos cob, Conn., is a little old fishing-village strung along one side of one long street facing Cos Cob harbor in the town of Greenwich, which is the first New England community the New York, New Haven and Hartford Railroad passes on the way east. Within commuting distance of New York, many people who could not lose touch with the great city went there for their country homes or board, the rich to parklike Greenwich, the others to picturesque Cos Cob. My small family had been going to Cos Cob for several years, and I went there whenever I became so loaded with facts that I had to run away to "think it out" and put it down. Cos Cob was a good place to think, as I thought; for thinking, as I know it, is an unconscious or a subconscious process. Dropping the subject I have to think out, I sail a boat, work in the garden or at anything that takes my attention and keeps me employed physically, while the facts, say, of Chicago or New York, arrange themselves in the order of an article. There was a good deal to do in Cos Cob.

Quiet, almost dead, it was a paintable spot frequented by artists who worked, painters who actually painted: Twachtman and the Murphys, Childe Hassam and Elmer MacRae; by writers who wrote: Bert Leston Taylor, Wallace Irwin, Thompson Seton; by editors and publishers: Gilman Hall of *Ainslee's* and *Everybody's,* Don Seitz of the *World,* Moody of the *Evening Sun.* Even the arty people, who always follow artists as flies follow cattle, did not only talk and yearn for expression, but labored at their own chosen crafts which did not choose them. It was an "art colony"; the painters there were sometimes called "the Cos Cob school"; we talked art, and we had a contempt for people who talked business and politics. The townspeople and fishermen were all right; they fitted into the land- and seascapes, but toward the rest of the world, toward the successful New Yorkers who were buying up Greenwich and modernizing that lovely old town, we were such snobs that after cutting us and then discovering that we were cutting them, they used to try to get in with us. And they couldn't.

One rich woman whose husband had taken, cleared, gardened, and illuminated with electric light the side of a hill our painters used to paint, drove up to the Holly House, where most of us lived, to ask for rooms. The daughter of the house, recognizing her and her equipage, told her that "we did not take in rich people."

The Holly House was a great, rambling, beautiful old accident —so old that it had its slave quarters up under the roof; and it looked out from under elms as high as oaks upon the inner harbor and an abandoned boat-building house with sail lofts. There was a long veranda where the breezes blew down from the river, up from the Sound, and cooled the debaters and settled the dinner debates that Twachtman started. We dined all together at one long table in a fine, dark, beflowered dining-room. The game was always the same. Twachtman would whisper to me as he passed on to his place, "I'll say there can be no art except under a monarchy." Waiting for a lull in the conversation, he would declare aloud his assertion, which was my cue to declare the opposite. "You are wrong, Twachtman. Art is a flower of liberty and blossoms only in republics." Others would break in on his side or mine, and marking our followers, he and I led the debate, heating it up, arousing anger—any passion, till, having everybody pledged and bitter on a side, we would gradually change around till he was arguing for the republic, I for the monarchy. Our goal was to carry, each of us, all our party around the circle without losing a partisan. The next night Twachtman would whisper and later declare that "foreign women are not beautiful; only American women have real beauty," and again we would try to lead our heelers around to the opposite view. It was amazing how often we could do it. We had difficulty with only one man, Mr. Frederick Dow, a lawyer, not merely an attorney, but a trained mind. He did not take part in the argument; he only listened and suffered. "How illogical!" he would exclaim. "You are arguing yourselves around! You are changing sides. Can't you see it?

Don't you know it?" Even his exposure did not halt many of our followers; they were more loyal or more combative than they were reasonable. But the game hurt Dow so much that he got up from the table once to run away, with his hands holding his head. "I can't stand it," he cried. Twachtman took mercy on him and told me to tell him what we were up to. After that the only logical mind there used to sit amused at the table and join us afterward on the veranda, where, abandoned and betrayed by their leaders, the artists, writers, and their wives fought it out alone till the night air calmed them or somebody saw or said something else.

One of the questions we used to debate was whether artists had any use for their minds. Twachtman asserted that they painted with their nerves and muscles and that, if they thought, they—or their pictures—were lost. This argument lasted through the season; it came up again and again, and I became identified with Twachtman's thesis that artists were and should be headless; he for their intelligence. One spring we found the railroad building a new bridge over the neck of the harbor. Everybody was disgusted. It was a busy scene of noisy, steaming, smoking activity, and it spoiled the view and the peace of the place. I defended the railroad on the theory that activity also was a theme for painters; not a dead village only, but a busy harbor was worth painting, and I prophesied that in a month or two all the painters would be painting that bridge-building, with the girders a-swinging and the smoke a-blowing in the wind. I had to go west that summer, and when I got back one forenoon in the fall I passed all the Cos Cob school with their easels set and painting the noisy, dirty bridge improvement. None of them greeted me; they wouldn't look up at me, trudging by with my bag and my smile of happiness at being home with them again. Twachtman alone spoke to me, and all he said was, "Ah, go to hell."

A Chinese captain of industry kept my mind off my work. He had a method. He had worked his way up along the shore of the Sound, setting up a laundry in each place. When he had it going he appointed an agent, another Chinaman, to carry on the local business while he went on to the next place. This trust-building business was known to the natives of Cos Cob, and when Ah Sing opened a place on the inner harbor right opposite the post office we all sided with the villagers and said: "Well, let him try it. He might have conquered other, New York State sea villages; but he can't get us. No outsider can break into a good old New England community like Cos Cob. Mrs. Marshall does our washing, and no Chink shall get us away from her." Mrs. Marshall came, on both sides, from old, old families that came over on that certain ship which carried more passengers than any bottom ever floated by man except possibly the ark. Distinguished men had borne her names, and all the old New Englanders and all the visitors who stood for justice boycotted that Chinaman, who did nothing but fish. Day after day for weeks Ah Sing fished in front of his workless laundry; day after day the villagers watched him fish and asked one another how long he could hold out. He smiled, spoke pleasantly to people who would not speak to him. One day when I was getting into my boat and nobody was looking I asked him how he expected to succeed there.

"Oh," he said, "allee time just the same. Allee place no come till bymeby." And he went right on fishing.

But he fished in a curious way, and he caught lots of fish; the fish he caught were of a variety white folks didn't take, but he dried and he ate them. Everybody, especially the fishermen, were curious about it all. They laughed at first when they saw him sink a small open net on his pole, leave it, and go back later to take up a panful of fish. You'd see the fishermen walk past him to look into his catch and study his net. But they didn't report satisfactorily after such a betrayal of interest. Others tried it. One day an oysterman drew up the net; there were fishes in it, and he, looking around, saw that Ah Sing had left his pan there ready for this event. The oysterman dumped the fish out of the net into the pan and then lowered the net again into the water. Others who had seen this repeated the act of curiosity, sport, or decency, and pretty soon we saw the villagers on their way to the post office and back habitually lift the funny net and empty the funny fish into the pan. A week or so of this, and Ah Sing was seen talking to the talkative villagers. The Chink was a pleasant-spoken, genial good fellow, and his talk about fishing in China was curious. Others talked to him; everybody talked to Ah Sing; and finally, when I came back from a long trip, I found the laundry going full time and everybody having their washing done by the Chink, who was cheap, by the way. I don't know how it went with Mrs. Marshall, but Ah Sing was gone; his cousin ran his laundry, and he said that the boss was carrying on his string of chain laundries up

Boston way. A fisher for men was Ah Sing, and a prophet of industry.

Ernest Thompson Seton, the writer of animal stories, came along one year looking at the landscape as real estate. He was after a piece of land to make a park of, a home and a headquarters for the Boy Scouts he was organizing in his fertile mind. He didn't himself have much business sense, but his wife, Grace, a California girl, had. When she married him in Paris she saw with the eyes of her father, Albert Gallatin, that Seton Thompson (as he then was) had possibilities, and she undertook his management. She raised his prices, widened his market, and set him talking and lecturing as well as writing. His search for land—to buy, not to paint—led him on long walks, and I, going with him, learned to see a new interest in nature. I talked real estate to the Cos Cob artists, who sneered and resisted, but I made a game of it, and some of us played it. The game was called "real estating," and you played it by going around or letting the real estate men drive you around to see houses, plots, or farms of land for sale. It gave you an excuse to go into houses, good old New England houses, and see antique fireplaces and furniture; some of the more un-scrupulous people degraded the game to a free hunt for furniture, and, I was sorry to observe, they found real bargains in chairs, tables, beds, etc. The best sportsmen among us really looked at the land and the houses, and the score was the number of places you saw and the number of temptations you resisted. There was a risk in it. You might come upon something so irresistibly lovely and cheap that you did actually buy. That counted as a defeat and put you out of the game. I fell for a seventy-acre tract when Seton bought his estate; my seventy acres was his second choice. I sold it afterward for twice what I paid for it, but I was jeered at for losing the game. Others lost out, too. August F. Jaccacci, the art editor of *McClure's*, fell when I fell. He bought the largest tract of all.

Bert Leston Taylor liked this game; he introduced it into Chicago later when he went to the *Tribune* to write his "Line o' Type a Day." He beat the game, never bought anything. But it was not wisdom that saved him. B.L.T. was helpless, dependent on his family at Cos Cob; so was his wife, a pianist. Their house-hold was managed by their daughter, then a child of ten or twelve.

B.L.T. worked on *Puck*, and we, his humorous neighbors, wondered what use a comic weekly could have for such a sober-headed serious thinker. He went sailing with me. Neither of us knew anything about a boat. One day our sloop stopped softly in a light breeze, and we could not make it move. We consulted, and Taylor was the son of a sea captain; we laid out all our knowledge of ships, smoked and thought, but no thought of ours would budge that boat or shade us from the hot sun. We must have lain out there for an hour when I noted that we were drifting down upon the bridge. Startled but happy, we steered for the shore. When we landed, an oysterman who had seen our distress said quietly to us, "When you get stuck in the mud that-a way all you got to do is raise your centerboard a minute or so."

As we walked modestly home, B.L.T. said, "That seafaring man seems to think that we were stuck in the mud. Did you know that?"

"No," I said, "but I know what set us free. Do you?"

"No," he said, and proudly I told him my guess: "The rising tide."

Taylor looked at me in admiration, then turned and left me. He consulted me frequently after that, and not only on navigation. When he received an offer of ten thousand a year to leave *Puck* to go to the Chicago *Tribune*, he and his wife called on me and mine to consider whether to go at once or take the summer off for the fishing-trip he had planned in the Canadian woods. He loved fishing, and he showed me his reckoning of costs for the trip. It was to be very cheap; he gloried in the prospect of such an inexpensive summer of sport; and he grew more and more firm in his decision to disregard the *Tribune's* telegrams to "please come at once." They could whistle; he was going to fish.

Just for deviltry I figured out on a piece of paper that ten thousand dollars was about $200 a week, which, added to his other expenses, raised the cost of his summer vacation of three months something like $2,500. He looked at his wife, who looked at him, and sadly he said, "Too expensive," and he went home, packed up, and hurried to Chicago and his "Line o' Type."

Sailing was my favorite form of digestion. The fact that I didn't know how intensified the concentration upon the boat and my avoidance of conscious thought. And my crew was a sailor,

Gilman Hall. He took a certain interest in me because he had discovered me; me and O. Henry. As an editor of *Ainslee's Magazine*, he had printed our first "works." O. Henry had always made
"Gim," as we called Hall, pay for his discovery by turning him
into his private banker. I repaid our easiest editor by letting him
edit my navigation—as crew. And he worked faithfully, obeyed
my (amended) commands, and no matter how far out on the
Sound I sailed, could be trusted always to get us back. He paid
half the cost of our first boat, called *Molasses*, which we bought for
ten dollars, for the boat only—without the name. The seller kept
the name. Unfortunately we took over the *Molasses* just before a
storm which sank her at her anchorage. After that for a year or
two we sailed in hired or borrowed boats, but principally we talked
of buying boats. I used to talk about boat-buying and sailing in
the office of the magazine, in Wall Street, everywhere.

One day the business manager of *McClure's* came grumbling
up to my desk and asked me impatiently, "What kind of a boat do
you want? I got to know. I can't just go and buy a boat."

Astonished and irritated, I asked him what business it was of
his, and he explained that it wasn't his but S. S. McClure's.

"S.S. came to me just now and said that you wanted a boat and
to buy you one. But how can I go out and buy you a boat, like
that, unless I know what sort of boat you want." He went on
talking indignantly, about how he had never bought a boat, didn't
know a sloop from a steam launch or where to go for them. He
agreed with S.S. that my work was profitable to the magazine and
I ought to be paid more and it was cheaper to make me a present
than to raise my salary, but it did make a difference whether the
gift was a steam yacht or a catboat.

I named the boat I wanted, and the builder (an advertiser) to
go to, and in a few weeks Gilman Hall was handling the sails of
a new twenty-foot sloop while I was holding the tiller and, quite
unawares, rearranging my two pictures of the American city, as
it is imagined and as it is, and wondering about the States of the
United States.

Harry Leon Wilson expressed our neighbors and the world one
day when I was taking B.L.T. out for a sail in my new boat.

"Well," he said, with penetrating sincerity, "I hope you both
drown."

XII

THE SHAME OF THE STATES: MISSOURI

THE voluntary return of New York City to Tammany after a trial of "good government," followed by the news that the Chicago reformers were forced to carry their fight for a "representative city government" back up into the Legislature and out into the State of Illinois, convinced me that "we" must stop talking so much about cities and show that municipalities were parts of States; which were as bad or as good as their cities, and that municipal reform without State reform was impossible. The State machine, whether of the same or a different party, would back the city machine; a corrupted State would defend the graft of a corrupted city. My theory now was that the State was the unit of action for good or for evil. Turning definitely, as I thought, to the States, we decided to take Missouri first. I knew enough to start with about any one of five States: Pennsylvania, Missouri, New York, Illinois, Connecticut. But Folk, the St. Louis prosecutor, running for governor of Missouri, was a living example of a city reformer driven back to State reform, and he was calling upon us for help. He was pretty sure of election; it would be a credit to "us" to appear to carry a State and make a governor. And then, Folk had all the facts that I would need. I went to St. Louis.

I went there in fear and trembling, and I learned right away the cowardice of courage. Harry Hawes, one of the politicians who felt themselves injured by my articles on St. Louis, had said (I heard) that he was going to shoot me on sight. Hawes became U.S. senator afterward; he may have said nothing of the sort; but I was told in New York and again after I got to St. Louis that he had repeatedly threatened publicly and privately to bump me off, and I believed it. My fear was sharp; my dread grew until it became unbearable. I did not know what to do; I was astonished at what I did do. Late one afternoon I saw him board a street car, and without any thought or plan or gun I ran out into the street, caught that moving car as it was passing, and swinging on, edged my way through the packed passengers right up beside my would-be murderer. In fear I did it; it might have looked like heroism or preparedness; the experience has made me always suspicious of bravery. Hawes turned casually, saw me, and to my joyous relief, put out his hand.

The Boss Busters' Club Listens to Remedies for Graftitis and Bossism

From left to right: Tom L. Johnson, District-Attorney Jerome, Austen G. Fox, Mayor Weaver, Ernest Colby, George L. Record. On opposite page, Norman Hapgood, Richard Gilder.

"Hel-lo!" he exclaimed. "You back here again?"

Yes. I was back.

"And what are you going to do this time?"

"The same thing," I said. "Only I want to get the State now, tie it up with the city, and make it clearer."

"So?" he answered, and we chatted along until I had gone blocks out of my way. Then I bade him good-by and jumped off the car. I felt better. I felt brave, and I liked the thrill of courage. I must see more of the enemy.

Folk had the facts at his finger ends, on the tip of his tongue. Of course. He had been handling them over and over in his court trials, and he was rehearsing them now for his campaign speeches, which we worked on together. Our purpose was the same: to arrange the overwhelming mass of evidence, confessions, and underworld gossip so as to paint a picture of the government as it actually was on the canvas of the old picture of Missouri as the Missourians thought it was: the paper government drawn in the constitution, charters, histories, and schoolbooks. And Folk was a painter. I heard some of his speeches, and they were masterly statements; they were good pictures. He was a cool, appealing, rather gentle orator, very moving, but his imagination was the force that carried his audiences, his ability to choose out of the mass of his material all that he needed and no more than he needed to draw his outline of the corrupted government. And that was my task, a writer's, not a detective's job: to select a few of the multitudinous facts to show the truth about—any State in the United Sates.

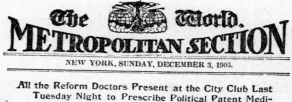

NEW YORK, SUNDAY, DECEMBER 3, 1905.

All the Reform Doctors Present at the City Club Last Tuesday Night to Prescribe Political Patent Medicines Guaranteed to Cure All Civic Ills—Dr. Johnson, of Cleveland, Highly Recommends His Old Reliable Cure, While Mayor Weaver Gives a Splendid Testimonial to the Weaver Wonder Worker—Dr. Colby, the Jersey Miracle Performer, Among Those Present, While Our Own Dr. Jerome Presided at His Laboratory. ✸ ✸ ✸ ✸ ✸ ✸ ✸

My report was published under the journalistic title "Folk's Fight for Missouri," first in *McClure's Magazine*, later in the book of State articles entitled *The Struggle for Self-Government*, published by McClure, Phillips and Company in 1906. This book, all the books of muckraking articles, are out of print, but I am not going to rewrite the Missouri article here. In brief it showed that the business corruption of politics and government in Missouri was the same as in the city of St. Louis—the same methods, the same motives, purposes, and men, all to the same end: to make the State officials, the Legislature, the courts, part of a system representing the special interest of bribers, corruptionists, and criminals; that acts of bribery and corruption done as a series of felonies form a continuous process which transforms the theoretically democratic government of the State and its cities into a plutocratic system which disserves the people and serves the seekers of privileges. It explained why the courts reversed Folk's cases; the judges were nominated by the machines from among the attorneys of corporations and criminals. But besides the St. Louis bribers and contributors to campaign funds, there appeared in Missouri inter-State railroads and national trusts: public service corporations, schoolbook publishers, a baking-powder company, and many others that I found later at work in other States. These were buying laws and law interpretations, sometimes against the interest of special Missouri industries and the common Missouri interest. It was indeed a system as well as a process, a city, State, and, apparently, an inter-State business system, not a political and certainly not a democratic government.

To me this was appalling; it was almost incredible; and I was asking myself, as Folk was, who was doing it? "Who" was our question still, not yet "what," and most people today do not ask what causes crime, corruption, and war, but *who* is the guilty man or men. I had had to talk with the guilty politicians and had been balked by the discovery that they were not "bad"; they were certainly good fellows, if not good men. They had indeed taken bribes, but they said that business men paid the bribes. It was the business men, then, who were the corrupters of politics and the bad men. I must see more of them. I did in Missouri. I had to call on the chief attorney for the big boodlers; he had a collection in his office of the typewritten court records which I wanted to look through. The editor of one of the local St. Louis newspapers knew him well personally. When I told him what I wanted from the enemy he remarked, "You have your nerve with you; he'll never see you; why should he help you expose him and his clients?" But he 'phoned my request, listened to the answer, and, "Well, I'll be damned," he exclaimed. "He will see you right away. Says he wants to." I went over to the attorney's office. There were other callers waiting. When my card went in a client came out immediately, and the attorney was at the door, holding it open for me. "Come in," he said. I walked in, crossed the room to a window, then turned, and my host was still standing at the door, holding it open and staring at me, apparently astonished.

"What's the matter?" I asked, astonished in turn.

"Oh, hell," he answered, "I thought you were six feet tall."

He was measuring with his eye my shrinking five feet six and three quarters, but he suddenly closed the door and came up to me.

"I understand that you want certain court records," he said. "You can have them. I wish I could do what you are doing, you and Joe Folk. You are right. We are wrong; I never realized how wrong we were. You understand, we thought we were after only this law or that franchise. We never stopped to think that other men also wanted a this or a that, and that all of us together were doing something rotten. We never saw it whole the way you see it. It's fierce when you take it all in at one gulp like this."

He walked away; he walked back.

"I can't do anything myself, not now any more. I'm on the other side. I and my clients are fighting, with our backs to the prison bars, and fight we will and fight we must. I can't appear on your side. Not now, not ever, I guess. But I am for what you are doing; lots of us are now, but we can't change. Too late. We must fight for our very lives. And we will, I will. But, privately, here— well, if there's anything I have that you want—you shall have it."

Not so bad, this man, and there were others, William Ziegler, for example. This millionaire captain of industry, who started with nothing, founded and personally drove to success the national baking-powder trust, was caught and indicted for bribery in Missouri. He and his inter-State lobbyist, Daniel J. Kelly, had been active in twenty-four States, which they found, Kelly said (to me), all ripe and ready for them, so corrupted by their own business men that a national visitor with money was more than welcome. There was nothing inherently bad in Kelly, and Ziegler was in some ways an ideal citizen. Ziegler was the man who at that time was spending millions to back arctic explorers in their expeditions to plant the American flag on the North Pole. I found him a generous, able, courageous, and rather humble-minded man who was not only willing, but eager to tell me his story, and in telling it, he made it worse even than Folk had described it in his complaints, more ruthless, more universal. He had "got" not only Legislatures and governors but chemical experts and newspapers to serve his dubious purposes for pay. The strange thing about Ziegler was that he had imagination. When the meaning and the effect of his policy of bribery and corruption, his and his fellow business men's, was generalized for him, he was shocked. He saw the picture and he revolted, as Iz Durham had.

"I didn't want to do that," he said over and over again. "I simply did not see it so. I fought each fight as it came up."

"Yes," I said, "you business men say, as if you were wise, that you cross bridges when you come to them."

"I certainly did not mean to change the government."

When I returned to New York and wrote and submitted the Missouri article with pages on Ziegler, the business department of the magazine remarked dryly that the baking-powder company's standing back page advertisement would probably go out. I said that it would stay more surely than ever, and just as a test, I called again on Ziegler about it. He said, and he told the magazine, that his company's advertisement would stand as long as he lived. This was after he read the proofs of that article which showed, I think, better than anything I ever wrote what political corruption is and what it means morally. He read it as a citizen, as a patriotic, somewhat sentimental man, and he laid it down several times to let his imagination work on it. At the end he said, "It's hell, isn't it? And I am playing the very devil!"

Ex-President Grover Cleveland took it similarly. Albert Boyden, our managing editor, was a friend of Mr. Cleveland, who was then at Princeton. Boyden asked me to go down there to see him.

"He is all broken up over that Missouri exposé and would like to ask you some questions about it."

I went, of course. I assumed that Cleveland, as a Democrat, was disturbed by the reflection upon his party. As an ex-mayor of Buffalo and an ex-governor of New York, who had begun his career as an exposer of fraud and corruption in his own city and State, he must know all that Folk knew. But when I called he said nothing about his party; he spoke of democracy as an ideal. He asked no questions, either. All he said was: "I have read that article, and I can't believe it. How can you believe all that with"— he pointed out of the window—"with the sun shining like that?"

He monologued along about how he recognized the facts I gave, and he believed them. "I am not doubting your report on Folk's evidence. It is the picture as a whole that I cannot accept. No, no, I don't doubt that either. It is true. I have seen it myself in office.

I simply cannot make my imagination look at it as it is. It is too terrible. You will have to repeat and repeat that story, in other States, to get it through our heads."

I told him I was going to repeat it in Illinois next, and he wished me well. But as we went to the door and stood there in the sun he shook his head. "I suppose I'll never be able to see that bribery and corruption can be done by good men and that it is a process changing the very nature of our government. No. I cannot see that."

I left the fine old strong man feeling that it was his imagination that balked, and recalling the other men I had seen moved, the villains of my piece, I wondered if it were not merely a failure of imagination that was at fault in America, the inability of the minds of powerful men who knew the facts, who make the facts, to form them into a picture.

XIII

ILLINOIS: THE PROGRESSIVE MOVEMENT

SEVERAL movements, so called, were developing out of the muckraking or rather out of the discontent which the muckraking was feeding with facts. The Progressive Party was one of these; another was the commission form of government, which caught Mr. McClure's fancy. He wanted me to break off from the States to write it up. I refused; didn't I know that the form of government did not matter? Washington, D.C., had long had a commission form. In order to get rid of the near majority of colored voters there, that city had abandoned all pretense of democracy; it had disfranchised all voters, white, brown, yellow, and black, and turned the municipal government over to a commission consisting of a committee of Congress and leading local citizens named by the president. And the president then was Theodore Roosevelt! What a chance to find out how a select committee of statesmen and business men governed a city unhampered by politicians, parties, and the mob! What a chance to show the city experimenters how that experiment with commissions had worked out in the long run! What a lead up into Congress and the Federal government! I had been in Washington enough to know that that municipality was a scandalously corrupt government, and being the national capital, its exposure would be a sensational news story. But I was through with cities, I thought. States now, and I had seen some of the big, national grafting businesses, escaping out of Missouri over into Republican Ohio. One of these offered me some incitement to follow its trail.

The representative of a great schoolbook publishing trust called on me at the office of the magazine in New York, and pointing to the reference to his concern in the list I had printed of national corruptionists uncovered by Folk in Missouri, said he understood that I meant to follow up and expose the whole textbook business in politics. I had not thought of it.

"Well," he said with all the authority of an advertiser, "don't do it. I warn you. We will fight."

I told him he had given me a good idea. The facts I had heard everywhere, in cities, in Legislatures, on trains, about the activities of the schoolbook publishers, would, if collected, verified, and printed, make a lovely scandal. They would illustrate the use, not only of money, but of women to "get" principals of schools, trustees, and teachers. They would show also how professors in universities were made careful as to what they taught their students and what they wrote.

Professors can, and some of them do, make two or three times as much money out of their textbooks as they do in salary as teachers, and of course a professor suspected of "radicalism" would not be asked to write a textbook for youth, and "radicalism" in the textbook publishing business means "original" or "suggestive" of thought.

After that warning, which was delivered in the presence of our advertising man, I ached to dig into the schoolbook business; it would explain so much of the evil in America. I told that blackmailer that I certainly would act upon his fecund suggestion, and I am sorry I did not keep my word. The Hearst newspapers have done it since, but in scattered, serial form, not so as to make a picture.

Resisting all these leads, I went from Missouri next door to Illinois. The obvious parallel offered by those two States would confirm or correct my theory about State governments as part of city government and the unit for reform efforts. The city reformers, balked by the State machine and threatened with State legislation by big business, had rallied behind Charles S. Deneen, like Folk in St. Louis, a Cook County, Chicago prosecuting attorney who had convicted so many rich men that there was a Bankers' Row of cells in the jail. The reformers were backing Deneen for governor, and George E. Cole, the founder of the Chicago Voters League, was organizing a State Voters League to apply the same methods to the Legislature that had worked in the board of aldermen. He was keeping a record of the votes on measures which would show whether the legislator represented the people or the political business machine. That Illinois was Republican, Missouri Democratic, helped to make clear that the editors of the magazine saw no difference between the parties and that big business and big politics did not see any either. The very businesses that were caught corrupting the Democratic government of Missouri appeared as Republicans in Illinois.

"What businesses?" A railroad president asked me that question. He had been pointing out that it was Yerkes and the public service corporations whom the Chicago reformers were fighting at Springfield and Chicago, and he was protesting my "sweeping generalization" in charging political corruption to business. He had me there, I admitted. Not all business was active in politics; I had found only some businesses, those that I called Big Businesses. A closer analysis came later, in Ohio. But in Illinois I had got down only to the distinction between Big and Small Business and admitted to my railroad friend that it was the Big Business Men who led and the little fellows only followed. When he objected that it was only some big businesses that played politics and added, "The railroads are big and they don't"—I told him that the big politicians said that the railroads had started it, and having got about all they wanted, let the public service corporations who wanted things carry on their dirty work. He denied that and I went back to the politicians, older men who knew some Illinois history. They declared that the railroads of that State had always been and still were the basic business in politics, that they let the Illinois Central attend to their common political affairs, contributing to the cost, and that they still were able to go to Chicago or Illinois and get anything they wanted. Going back and forth between these two debaters, I dug up information enough to silence my railroad man, who had only been trying to mislead me. He was "wise" himself, as western corruptionists usually are; they are not like the typical eastern magnates; out west they know, but they won't own up till they see that you know. Driven to the last ditch, this railroad president said that "the roads kept their hand in politics now only to defend themselves against demagoguery." And by way of illustration he said, "Like that we are suffering from in Wisconsin."

"Wisconsin? LaFollette?" I asked.

"Yes, that blankety-blank-blank demagogue, Bob LaFollette,"

he answered. "Why don't you ever show up such fellows as LaFollette and Tom Johnson? Why always jump on us?"

That seemed a just complaint. We had exposed the bribers and the bribe-takers; we had backed reformers like Folk and Fisher. I meant to write up some other reformers. It would be fair, and good journalism, to expose a demagogue like LaFollette. My railroad president, seeing me intrigued by his idea, followed up his advantage. If I would go next to Wisconsin and tackle LaFollette, he would write to his business friends in Milwaukee to furnish me with the evidence, plenty of it. He knew and recited some. I wrote to Mr. McClure, and he agreed to the plan. So I finished up the Illinois article, which was a repetition of the Missouri article, a perfect parallel. Then I called on my railroad president, took from him his introductions to "wise men" in Milwaukee, who were to give me the material to show up—an example of a State reform that went far to prove my State thesis.

Meanwhile Illinois and Missouri demonstrated the same thesis. Folk, the prosecuting attorney of St. Louis, and Deneen, the prosecuting attorney of Chicago, were elected governors, the one of Missouri, the other of Illinois. The city reformers, having appealed to the citizens of their States, had won a response and a victory.

XIV

WISCONSIN AND BOB LA FOLLETTE

WHEN, toward the end of my survey of Illinois, I sneaked up to Milwaukee to call on the men who were to display "the goods on that demagogue, Governor Bob LaFollette," I had no doubt that the man was a charlatan and a crook. And my colleagues on the magazine had none, and the reformers and the public nationally. The reverberations of the noise this trouble-maker had been making in his own State had been heard all over the country, and the comment on it had painted a portrait of LaFollette which was fixed on the public mind as it was on mine. It made him look like two other notorious "demagogues" of the day, William Jennings Bryan and Tom L. Johnson. My task was to get and prove the specific charges against him and give the ready-made type a likeness to LaFollette.

The banker, whom I called on first, was suspicious of me; he had read something of mine. As he read over the letter I handed him and as I talked, showing my earnest preconception, he opened up, and—LaFollette was a crooked hypocrite who stirred up the people with socialist-anarchist ideas and hurt business. "Good," I said, "let's begin with the evidence of his crookedness." The banker had none, but he said the corporation attorney to whom also I had a letter could prove the dishonesty. We telephoned to him to come over. Meanwhile the banker set out to demonstrate the other charges: hypocrisy, socialism-anarchism, etc., and he was going fast and hot till I realized that my witness had more feeling than facts; or if he had facts, he could not handle them. He would start with some act of LaFollette and blow up in a rage. He certainly hated the man, but I could not write rage. My ready-made story of a crooked demagogue was fading when, to the banker's relief and mine, the railroad attorney arrived with papers: evidence?

This attorney took charge at once. He said he had had full instructions from Chicago to lay the case fully before me; I was all right. When I told him how far we had got, the banker and I, and how I wanted first the proofs of the dishonesty alleged, he said: "Oh, no, no. You are getting off wrong. LaFollette isn't dishonest. On the contrary, the man is dangerous precisely because he is so sincere. He's a fanatic."

"But he's a hypocrite," I appealed, fearing the loss of my great story.

"He is that," said the attorney. "He kicks about bosses and is himself a boss. He talked against the political machine and then built up an organization that is a perfect machine."

"And an agitator?"

"That's the worst of him. He's not only an orator, he's a born actor; and the way that man goes around spreading discontent is a menace to law, property, business, and all American institutions. If we don't stop him here he will go out and agitate all over the United States. We're getting him now; you'll get him next. That man must be blocked."

"Yes," said the banker, "LaFollette will spread socialism all over the world."

"But," I asked, "Milwaukee is full of socialists; are they following LaFollette?"

"No, no," the attorney corrected. "LaFollette isn't a socialist. He has nearly busted the socialists here, taken the votes right away from them. The socialists are reasonable men compared with this agitator, who is more of a Populist."

"Well, then, what does he teach and what does he do?" I asked.

The attorney, with the banker sitting by frowning, impatient, presented in good order the charges against LaFollette, the measures he had furthered, the legislation passed and proposed, his political methods. Horrified himself at the items on his list and alarmed over the policy and the power of this demagogue, he delivered the indictment with emotion, force, eloquence. The only hitch was that Bob LaFollette's measures seemed fair to me, his methods democratic, his purposes right but moderate, and his fighting strength and spirit hopeful and heroic.

A day, a night, and another day of this condemnation by those men and others they introduced me to, and I was converted. Governor LaFollette's enemies convinced me that I was on the track of the best story yet, the story of a straight, able, fearless individual who was trying to achieve not merely good but representative government, and this in a State, not in a city. It was not what I came here for, but it was just what I wanted: an experience in State reform.

Returning to Chicago, I communicated with my colleagues on *McClure's*. It must have been a surprise to them, my change of

"THE LITTLE GIANT"
Cartoon by Art Young

attitude, but they consented. I finished up in Chicago, then called on Governor LaFollette at Madison. I saw him before he saw me, and what I saw was a powerful man who, short but solid, swift and willful in motion, in speech, in decision, gave the impression of a tall, a big, man. He had meant to be an actor; he was one always. His lines were his own, but he consciously, artfully recited them well and for effect which, like an artist, he calculated. But what I saw at my first sight of him was a sincere, ardent man who, whether standing, sitting, or in motion, had the grace of trained strength, both physical and mental. When my name was whispered to him he came at me, running. LaFollette received me eagerly as a friend, as a partisan of his, a life-saver. He had read my articles on other cities and States and assumed, of course, that I would be on his side. I did not like this. I was coming over, but it takes time to change your mind, and I was not yet over on his side. He was not aware of my troubles, had not heard of my secret visit to Milwaukee; and he was in trouble himself. He was at a crisis in his career. Elected governor and in power, he had failed to do all that he had promised. The old machinery, by bribery, blackmail, threats, and women, had taken away from LaFollette enough of "his" legislators to defeat or amend his bills, and they were getting ready to beat him at the polls by accusing him of radicalism for proposing such measures, and of inefficiency and fraud for failing to pass them. He had no sufficient newspaper support. He feared that he could not explain it all to his own people, and he felt that the hostile opinion of the country outside his State, which the old Wisconsin machine was representing, was hurting him at home. He needed a friend; he needed just what I could give him, national, non-partisan support. He took me home for supper with his family, who all greeted me warmly, even intimately, on the assumption that I was their ally. I stood it for a while, then I repelled Mrs. LaFollette with a rebuke that was rude and ridiculous, so offensive indeed that I find that I cannot confess it even now. Fola LaFollette, who was there, said afterward that she never has felt so sorry for any two people as for her mother and me. My excuse was, and it is, that I had a vague plan to work up my article on LaFollette out of nothing but what his enemies were giving me; any friendly intimacy between me and the LaFollettes might spoil the effect I wished to get. And I did draw my clinching facts from the old machine men. I saw more of the opposition in Wisconsin than I did in any other similar situation. But shame for my gross discourtesy and my sense of the anxious search the governor was making of the horizon for rescue made me compromise. I closed in on him with a proposition that he take the time to tell me his whole story from boyhood on, both the good and the bad of it, his mistakes and his crimes as well as his intentions, ideals, and high purposes, leaving it to me to write it as I pleased. He agreed; he thought it over for a few days and decided, "Yes. I'll do it— at the St. Louis Exposition, where I have to visit the Wisconsin exhibition and building. I have to be there anyway. I'll have only formal duties to perform. Most of the time I am there I can spend with you. I'll tell you everything, everything, and leave it to you to deal with as you see fit."

Bob LaFollette was called the little giant. Rather short in stature, but broad and strong, he had the gift of muscled, nervous power, and he kept himself in training all his life. Every speech he made was an exercise in calisthenics. His hands and his face were expressive; they had to be to make his balled fighting fists appeal for peace and his proud, defiant countenance ask for the reasonableness he always looked for even in an audience he was attacking. His sincerity, his integrity, his complete devotion to his ideal, were indubitable; no one who heard could suspect his singleness of purpose or his courage. The strange contradictions in him were that he was a fighter—for peace; he battered his fist so terribly in one great speech for peace during the World War that he had to have it treated and then carried it in bandages for weeks. Art Young drew a caricature of it as a pacifist's hand across the seas. He was a dictator dictating democracy, a proud man begging for the blessing of justice upon the meek, whom he organized and inspired to take it—any way. Impatient, he was slow and thorough. He prepared for a speech like a man writing a book.

When he met me in his room at the St. Louis Fair, he had on the table before him a stack of books, documents, bills, and newspapers. And he used them. He certainly kept his word to tell me everything. We were closeted there for a week of hard-working days. It must have hurt his pride, but he stripped, politically; I know, because his opponents in Wisconsin, later, told me nothing against him that LaFollette had not told me in St. Louis, and there were some faults in his career that they did not mention. Perhaps they had forgotten them; I think that they did not know about some of them. I know that there were two or three acts of his that he brought up out of the depths because he wasn't sure himself whether they were right or wrong. He had not tackled all the evils he saw, for instance; his reason was that, like Folk, he had his hands full already. He had stood by some of his partisans who had gone wrong; hoped they would come back and go right. Meaning to be just and fair, he didn't know always what was justice. Intending to do right, he wasn't sure enough of what is right to satisfy himself in some cases. He put to me the questions that troubled him, and he left it to me to answer them in my narrative. His part was to lay it all out before me, himself, his acts, the circumstances, his reasons, excuses, purposes, and he did that conscientiously, in order and with ability, giving as well as his enemies did afterward their interpretations and their charges and their joy in his faults and failures.

As he went on with his story, I took notes—enough for a book— the open book of an ambitious young man who, fitted in the schools and University of Wisconsin with the common, patriotic conception of his country and his government, discovered bit by bit what the facts were, and, shocked, set out to fight for democracy, justice, honesty. He set out ambitiously on a public career, encountered a local boss in a Federal office, and appealed over his head to the people of his home county to be nominated and elected district attorney. This was his first offense; he was irregular; he defied the machine of his (Republican) party. The politicians said that Bob LaFollette worked on the delegates and the voters at night, under cover of darkness. True. And when he felt the power and suffered the methods and the lying attacks of the party and its backing higher up, he continued to work under cover and constantly, like the politicians; but also he worked in the open, day and night. His method, in brief, was to go around to towns and cross-roads, make long, carefully stated speeches of fact, and appealing to the idealism of patriotism, watch the audience for faces, mostly young faces which he thought showed inspiration. These he invited to come to him afterward; he showed them what the job was, asked them if they would do their part in their district; and so he built up an organized following so responsive to him that it was called a machine. As it was—a powerful political machine which came to control the Republican Party in Wisconsin. The Stalwarts, as the old machine men and their business backers were called, became irregulars; they voted against and fought their party. They united with the old machine Democrats to beat their party. But LaFollette drew into it democratic Democrats and independents enough to make a majority for the Republicans, who came thus in Wisconsin to represent the people.

That was Bob LaFollette's crime. When Governor LaFollette returned to his State one way and I by another route, I called on the Stalwarts for facts, provable charges, and on LaFollette only for his specific answers or admissions. As in Milwaukee, so in

Madison, the indictments withered. They fell back to his one real
sin: that he had taken the Republican party away from the corrupters of it and led it to stand for—what? I said above that it
represented the people, but it did that only in the sense that it
labored for and gradually achieved the very moderate aims of
LaFollette, a liberal, and the liberals. When I pointed this out to
such men as Old Boss Keyes and Philip Spooner they were
stumped. They bade me go to Milwaukee again and see the men
there who knew things, especially a certain attorney who had
written a book against LaFollette's railroad legislation. Since they
did not know that I had been to Milwaukee and I could not go
away to write without having it known that I had seen Milwaukee,
I went there as openly as I could. Stalwarts called on me, offered
me—rage, indignation, allegations I had investigated. As I received their stuff credulously at first, then began to ask questions,
they spread the report that I was "no fool" and, apparently, "put
up a job on me." Anyway, against my wish, several of them invited, urged, me to go with them to see that certain attorney who
knew so much. I refused. One day I was invited to luncheon in the
Hotel Pfister. My hosts, smiling at and nudging one another, led
me through the barroom and stopped suddenly to present me to
the attorney whom they regarded as so clever and well up on the
facts. There was a crowd in the barroom, and the crowd closed in
on us to see the fun.

"Why haven't you come to see me?" the attorney asked, smiling
around the circle of listeners.

"Oh," I answered, "I have read your book. I see that you know,
but I feel that I should know something for certain before I
trouble a witness like you."

"Don't be afraid of me," he laughed. "Ask me anything you
like. I'll answer you, now."

I was up against it. The crowd snickered, and I saw that I had
to meet the challenge and ask a question. The underworld have to
think you are "wise," or your writings won't "go." I thought a
moment, eyeing my man, and I remembered that there was one
alleged scandal which I had learned all about and which everybody there knew all about. I asked my opponent to tell me the
truth of that matter. He began, as I had expected, to tell me the
scandalous story as it first appeared, before the investigation, and I

encouraged him by my exclamations to give it me all wrong, as he did.

"Oh, so that's the way of it!" I said. "I didn't know that! Nobody ever told me that!" And all the time the crowd was laughing, winking, and driving him to "fill me up" more and more. I waited till he was all through; then I said: "I am amazed at your story. It's so much worse than I had any idea. If that's so, LaFollette is a damned rascal. But listen now, this is the way I have got it after a rather careful investigation." And I told it as it was and as that crowd and that witness knew it was, with references to the records and proofs.

Before I had finished, the audience was still and cold, they were looking at the attorney as if he were caught stealing, and he, angry, turned on me and demanded: "If you know all about it, why the hell do you ask me?"

"Because," I answered, "I have heard that you have the evidence on LaFollette, that I must see and listen to and believe you; so, when you stalled me for the amusement of this crowd, I decided to take the chance to test the reliability of the witness."

The laugh was on him, and there was a laugh. It swept him out of his anger.

"Come on and have a drink," he called and so saved his face —a little. I never saw him again. I had read his book and that was quite enough; it was a propaganda volume on what the Stalwarts wanted the world to believe, not on the facts. The incident, told and retold, helped me greatly: it discouraged lying to me and spread the impression that I knew what I pretended to inquire about and that I was leaning toward LaFollette, not the Stalwarts.

Back in Madison, Philip L. Spooner, a brother of John C. Spooner, the very distinguished U.S. senator from Wisconsin and a leading Stalwart, reproached me for my partisanship. I reminded him that I had come there against LaFollette and that I was going over because he and his crowd had failed to furnish any proofs of their charges. "Get me a list of Bob's crimes, with the names of witnesses to testify, and I'll investigate them," I challenged. He said he would, and in a week he brought me such a list. There were some thirty offenses on it, with the names and addresses of men who had witnessed or suffered them. They were scattered all over the State. I asked Spooner if it would be fair if I visited all the men on the list who lived on the railroads and neglected the rest. He agreed to that; he helped me check them off, and I saw—Wisconsin; one of the most beautiful States I had or have seen in all my travels. I had never heard that fat land of small lakes and rivers, green meadows, and dark forests praised as lovely; it isn't grand enough to be celebrated like the scenic Hudson River or Niagara Falls, the Rockies, the Sierras, New England. It is more like the lake country of old England, quietly, modestly, contentedly, almost universally beautiful.

And I saw, by the way, the men Phil Spooner checked for me to visit, men who knew actual instances of LaFollette's corruption, trickery, and boss-ship. Full of the beauties of their country, my wife and I found them full of it too. Scandinavians, Germans, old Americans, these ex-legislators or business men or farmers in their habitat were, each of them, honest men who, like the big, bad crooks in the cities, meant well and had ideals. When I told them what I was doing and how I had to depend upon them for the truth, they responded. They did not tell their stories as they may have told them in the lobby and in the barrooms of Madison; they told them as they happened. At any rate they explained away all the evil there was in the gang's account of those cases; every single one of those witnesses dropped the indictment out of their testimony, and, though some of them had been hurt by LaFollette, they—all—said that Bob was straight; he was hard; he was a driver, yes, even a boss, but he did all that he did for his public purposes.

Bob LaFollette was restoring representative government in Wisconsin, and by his oratory and his fierce dictatorship and his relentless conspicuous persistence he was making his people understand—all of them, apparently, not only the common people whom he preferred, but the best people too; they also knew. They might denounce him, they might lie to the stranger, but in their heart of hearts they knew. It was a great experiment, LaFollette's: State reform that began in the capital of the State and spread out close to the soil. It was opposed by the cities, just as city reform was opposed by the States, but the startling thing—even though I expected it—was how this State reform encountered also the resistance of the Federal government. And just as Folk and the Chicago reformers had been forced to carry their fight up out of the cities into the States whence the trail of the serpent led, so Governor LaFollette, having carried his State several times, found that he had to go on up to the Senate. The trail of corruption is the road to success for the reformer as well as for other men. He won the next election for governor and then ran for and was elected to the U.S. Senate. He did not rush off to the Senate right away. It was characteristic of him that he remained as governor months after he was promoted to the Senate. He stuck to his post till he finished and forced the Legislature to pass all his pending measures. Then and not till then did he go on, where I saw I had to go, to the head of the system of the American government in —Washington. His career there, as in his own State, is the story of the heroism it takes to fight in America for American ideals.

RHODE ISLAND: THE GOOD OLD
AMERICAN STOCK

I T IS dangerous to reason about politics and government; it is
safer to go and see. While the city reformers of St. Louis and
Chicago were appealing to the people of Missouri and Illinois
and getting results, and LaFollette was leading the people of
Wisconsin into a State reform movement and winning, year after
year; just as I was drawing conclusions about the superiority of
the honest masses out in the country and of the State over the city
as a unit for political action, two eastern newspapers came out with
exposures of Rhode Island. They showed that the people there
were bought with cash at the polls, first by the old aristocracy, then
by the modern business leaders who were selling their stealings to
Wall Street and sending the head of the Rhode Island system,
Nelson W. Aldrich, to the U.S. Senate, where he was known as
"the political boss of the United States." Missouri, Illinois, and
Wisconsin were middle western, comparatively young States;
Rhode Island was an old New England State, one of the original
thirteen colonies that united for the Revolutionary War. It was
almost as old, as pure American, and as "good" as Massachusetts,
and there was no trouble with the cities in Rhode Island; the
State dominated the cities; the system was a State system founded
upon the corruption of the American voters out in the country.

Here was a chance to check up on democracy; to look into New
England, whence came our ideals and our culture; to test my theory
that old governments are as much corrupter than new governments
as they are older; to compare the city and the State systems, and
to strike the trail up to the very tiptop of the (then supposedly better) Federal government. I went to Rhode Island to see.

The system, as I had found it everywhere, was there; it was

the actual government of Rhode Island, and you could see it at a glance. There was an elected governor, for example; at that time, he was Dr. Lucius F. C. Garvin, a fine old New England gentleman, the kind of man most New England gentlemen think they are. Governor Garvin sat helpless, neglected, alone in his office, with plenty of time to tell me all about the conditions which distressed him and to confess his utter lack of power. He was not the actual governor. A blind man, General Charles R. Brayton, the political boss, was the actual, permanent governor or dictator of Rhode Island. The architect of the State House in Providence had built no room for the boss. General Brayton received in the sheriff's office the lines of visitors who had business with the State, openly. And openly he did that business. He ran the Legislature across the hall. He said so; everybody knew it; and he ran it for business men. He said that he used to represent (and make the Legislature and the State government represent) the New York, New Haven and Hartford Railroad. That was in the days of steam, when the road was after franchises, grants, exemptions, and properties. He still received, he said, $10,000 a year and was "of attorney" for the road. But electricity and the public service corporations came, and these, combining all the city and country street and trolley roads into the Rhode Island Company, were the new business bosses of this political boss. They came first. After them came the manufacturers and the employers of labor, and all businesses that wanted something. He could and he did do for comparatively small "fees" all sorts of things that were not antagonistic to the railroad and the Rhode Island Company. He had had himself admitted to the bar so that he could take fees instead of bribes. But the fact is that he sold out franchises, privileges, properties, protection, and licenses to business contributors and bribers who, in the case of the well-named Rhode Island Company, sold out to Philadelphia and New York financiers. It was the best-established, most accepted, most shameless system that I had seen, and it was a State thing, of State, not of city, origin. Rhode Island was a State for sale, and cheap. Why?

Because it is a small State? That was General Brayton's explanation. "Bad, but not a bit worse than many other States. Because Rhode Island is small you can see things better." The blind boss was blind only physically. Living in Connecticut, I knew he was right about that neighbor. New Hampshire was being exposed as in the same condition of meanness, corrupt and cheap. And there was Massachusetts, which was unexposed. I could see enough of New England in the blazing light of Rhode Island to strengthen my theory that time is a factor in the process of corruption, that the older the State the worse—not the better, as so many authorities thought. But there were some other differences besides age to be noted in Rhode Island.

The Legislature was not the scene of the corruption, and the cities were not the origin or the foundation of it. The reformers of Rhode Island, a licked lot, were city men. The legislators came from the country, and they came bought. They had no power, low salaries; they took orders absolutely. The boss in his blindness sent in for a senator one morning to "lead me out to (let us say) drink." One explanation of this was that submissive legislators who learned to take orders from the boss were advanced in their careers; he appointed them to judgeships and other political jobs, threw them law business and, if they were not lawyers, contracts and other business. He had pull enough to get men jobs with his client corporations. But the reason that bore upon the question in my mind was that these legislators came bought.

It was the people, the voters, who were bribed. The local explanation of this was the explanation of other conditions, the small part the cities played in corruption and reform. Rhode Island started out as an aristocracy; this was in its colonial days. "Freeholders" and their oldest sons alone participated in the colonial government under the charter of Charles II (1663), and after the Revolution, when other States adopted constitutions, Rhode Island carried on under the royal charter till 1842. It is sufficient to remark that this form of government aristocracy, which so many thinkers think is good, blew up in the Dorr Rebellion. It was too intolerable even to Americans. The next step in Rhode Island was a "commercial aristocracy." The constitution of 1842 extended the suffrage from holders of real to those possessed also of personal property—if they were native-born. The "foreign vote" was restricted as before to real estate holders till 1888, when personal property qualified a foreign-born as well as a native voter. The "mob" who owned nothing and paid no taxes (in person) were allowed to vote only upon registering four months before election and then not "upon any proposition to impose a tax or the expenditure of money." Registered voters, for example, could not vote for members of city councils.

The most effective restriction of the suffrage, however, was the constitutional scheme of disproportionate representation. The governor, elected by a majority (not by a plurality) of the voters of all classes, was a "part executive," a presiding officer with no power and no veto. All legislative powers were lodged in the General Assembly of two houses. The lower house was limited to seventy-two members, regardless of the population, and while each town had at least one member, no city could have more than one-sixth of the membership. This was undemocratic enough, but the Senate, says the constitution, shall consist of one senator from each town and city in the State.

A town in New England is what is known in other States as a township. There were thirty-eight towns and cities in Rhode Island. Their population in 1900 was 428,551. Of this total, 36,027 lived in twenty towns. Thus less than one-eleventh of the people elected more than one-half—a majority—of the Senate. Providence, the metropolis, with 29,030 voters, had one senator; Little Compton elected one, one year, by a unanimous vote of seventy-eight. There were fourteen such "towns" with less than 500 voters each, twenty with less than 2000 each. The corrupt or corruptible cities were put where many reformers would have them: out of power. The foreign population and labor, the irresponsible propertyless voters, were disfranchised. The sovereignty of the State was lodged in the hands of the "good old American stock out in the country." What happened?

The good old American stock sold out. And their price was low. There was an excuse for it, of course. It is "an ancient custom of the country," and "everybody does it." As Governor Garvin stated in a message: "That bribery exists to a great extent in the elections in the State is a matter of common knowledge. No general election passes without the purchase of votes by one or both parties. . . . Many assemblymen occupy their seats by means of purchased votes. . . . Bribery is so common and has existed for so many years that the awful nature of the crime ceases to impress. In some towns the bribery takes place openly; it is not called bribery. The money paid the voter, whether *two, five, or twenty dollars, is spoken of as 'payment for his time.'*"

The details of the popular bribery of Rhode Island, showing the extent of the custom, the number and the character of the voters who took money for their votes, the age and the standing of the practice, how the churches did not dare attack it and the university professors had to keep still—all this is in the article on Rhode Island in my book entitled *The Struggle for Self-Government*. I shall summarize here only a bit of what I carried away with me when I went home to Greenwich, Conn., to write my report.

The people, whom Governor LaFollette was deifying in Wisconsin, are corruptible. They were bought and they sold out in Rhode Island, precisely because they had the power, and limited in number and in their charge for votes, they and not their representatives were the market for corruption. In Wisconsin, Illinois, Missouri, it was cheaper to fix the nominations or wait and buy the representatives of the people. In New England it was cheaper to buy the people, and therefore they were tempted and fell. And I say New England because in my own town, Greenwich, I saw the voters, "respectable men" who did not need the money, fall in line and take their three or five dollars; and I knew from friends that this occurred in New Hampshire, Vermont, Maine, and in some towns in Massachusetts.

About this time a politician from Sacramento, California, caught up with me. He had written me, followed me around; he must see me. When we met he said he was a friend of my father, who would vouch for his word.

"I'm a crook," he said. "And I run with crooks, high and low, but say, the lowest, meanest crooks in politics are these here good American farmers. They'll sell, sure, but they won't stay bought. They're a bunch of double-crossers who'll take five dollars from you, then go and get three dollars from the other side and vote against you. You have shown up my pals, and you are showing up the business men. If you'll come out our way and show up the farmers, I'll give you the dope and I'll confess myself."

I meant to look into the farmer, the country vote out in some of the newer States; I never did. I think my California politician was prejudiced by some of his experiences, but after New England I did go this far in private generalization.

Wherever the farmers, wherever the common people are tempted to sell out, they are found to be as corruptible as the better people, whether politicians, business men, aristocrats, or church men.

Political corruption is not a matter of men or classes or education or character of any sort; it is a matter of pressure. Wherever the pressure is brought to bear, society and government cave in. The problem, then, is one of dealing with the pressure, of discovering and dealing with the cause or the source of the pressure to buy and corrupt.

But I did not, I could not, write that yet. I still believed, and my readers still believed, that there were some kinds of men that would neither buy nor sell and that the job was to get such men into power.

XVI

OHIO: A TALE OF TWO CITIES

WHEN "Fighting Bob" LaFollette of Wisconsin failed me as a demagogue and turned under investigation from a villain into a hero, I meant to expose Tom L. Johnson, the loud, laughing mayor of Cleveland. There was nothing heroic about him. There was no doubt that he, a big business man in politics, was a demagogue and a dangerous man. But I was through with cities, I thought. It would have been good journalism to "show up" a bad reformer, but Tom Johnson was a city reformer. One of his lieutenants, Dr. Frederic C. Howe, had published a book, expressing in the title the belief of the Cleveland group, *The City the Hope of Democracy*. However bad Tom Johnson was, however false his hope and Howe's, to write about them was to go back from the States and do another city. The way out for me was to tackle the State of Ohio.

Traveling back and forth between the east and the west, I had been crossing that State frequently. It tempted me. Ohio had succeeded Virginia as the source of presidents, cabinet men, judges, great statesmen; it was the State of Mark Hanna and his President McKinley, of the good Governor Herrick, Boss Cox of Cincinnati, Golden Rule Jones of Toledo, as well as of Tom Johnson of Cleveland. Ohio was on the great broad way to Washington, but it was not an open road. It was a labyrinthine mix-up of cross roads and tunnels. I knew something of it. I had stopped off in Toledo, and Brand Whitlock, who was my sort of a reformer, took me to Sam Jones, who took me home, sat me down, and humorously, wonderingly, for hours read aloud to me Walt Whitman and the New Testament. Never a word about the State or the nation, nothing about the city, even, or politics. The poet and the prophet were his political leaders. He was practicing what they preached: literally, religiously, gleefully; and Brand Whitlock smiled, and Ned Cochran, a Scripps editor, jeered, at the confusion applied Christianity caused in the minds of a Christian community, and they wondered at the way the sinners understood and respected the Golden Rule. The churches, the chambers of commerce, the best clubs, hated Golden Rule Jones, who was repeatedly elected mayor; professional criminals visited but did not operate in Toledo. Jones's story was a good one, odd and significant, but it had nothing to do with Ohio and the U.S.A.—not then; not to me.

And Tom Johnson—I had stopped off in Cleveland, called on Fred Howe, who spoke my language; he introduced me to the rest of "the Johnson gang." They were sincere, able, thinking men, all of them, a well-chosen staff, and they were happy in their work. The Cleveland reformers were the happiest reformers I had ever met. But they followed and believed in, they almost adored, Tom Johnson. How easily misled reformers are! Not I. They took me to the mayor, and I watched him do business an hour or so before I met him. It was like seeing a captain of industry on the stage: he received his callers one by one, swiftly, without haste; he listened, all attention, till he understood; then he would smile or laugh, give a decision, and—"Next!" No asking for time to "think it over" or to "consult his colleagues," no talk of "commissions to investigate," no "come again next week." It was no or yes, genial, jolly, but final. Tom Johnson was the big business man, the very type. But I was not to be taken in; no big business man could fool me. When my turn came I went, businesslike, straight to the heart of my business. Waving aside all politeness, all appearances, and the bunk, I asked my leading question.

"What are you up to, Mr. Mayor? What are you after?"

"That I cannot tell you," he answered just as straight. "You wouldn't understand if I did."

His contempt struck me, as Darrow's had, with a troubled wonder which carried the sense that I was missing something. I answered Tom Johnson's challenge with a threat. I would look around his town and see for myself what he was doing, and he agreed to that heartily.

"That's the way to do it," he said. "The town is open to you. We'll give you the freedom of the city. You may go where you like, ask anything you want to know, and if anybody refuses to open a door or answer your questions, you come back to me and I'll tell you. And then, when you know something, we can talk."

Fred Howe told me afterward that the mayor forbade them to try to influence me; they were to give me any information I might ask for, but otherwise I was to be let alone. Tom Johnson's orders were obeyed. I was as alone as I was in Pittsburgh, and I proceeded in Cleveland as I did there: talked to newspaper men, saw the politicians on the other side, and invited facts or even rumors from the enemy. I could not get anything against Tom Johnson and his administration except complaints so trivial that they only confirmed the impression I was suffering that there was nothing very bad about this city government; it was almost "good." I went away with a sense of defeat to carry on in Illinois and Wisconsin, for, you understand, I knew about big, bad business men; knew what a business government was; and knew that Tom Johnson, the street railway magnate, was not giving his time and his service to Cleveland for the city's sake. I would wait; he would soon be showing what he was after. He would be running for governor or the U.S. Senate, or his honest young associates would be passing innocently some franchise for his guilty uses. It was a year or more before I came back to Cleveland. I finished my Illinois, Wisconsin, and Rhode Island, and then, sure enough, Tom Johnson was running for governor. By that time, however, I had seen and I had grasped the nature of the compulsion which drove city reformers to the State and governors like LaFollette to the Senate at Washington. It was not necessarily ambition; it was a search for the seat of American sovereignty, and probably the bad business men and the bad politicians followed that same pursuit. They were all feeling for the throne whence they could wield power and do what they wanted to do.

But the immediate inquiry that directed me to Ohio was an explanation I heard often in Rhode Island of the corruption of the voters there and in New England. Historically-minded men said that the people in these old States were more or less degenerate; they had been picked over, and the best of them for several generations had gone west. What I had seen in the Rhode Island villages was the leavings of a great race. This explanation was a sharp contradiction of the English and aristocratic Irish and American liberal theory that American corruption was a matter of our youth, the shriek of our growing-pains. It was a confirmation of my old idea that corruption grew with time. In the meanwhile, however, I had been coming to another idea: that corruption, like a disease, attacked the weakest spot in the system, which, in Rhode Island, was the people, and that, since the best (the ablest, most powerful and the richest) people bought the good people, and the better people profited by and condoned the practice and the result, there was something wrong with our ideals, with the so-called New England ideals which came over from England to us with the Puritan, Pilgrim, and other fathers when they had moved west in search of land and liberty. Wasn't it likely that their sons would carry west with them the same ideals and set up the same conditions in the wilderness? Maybe that accounted for the state of Missouri, Illinois, and Wisconsin. And maybe it was the youth of those States that explained the reform revolt there or (or *and*) the large mixture of other races and ideas, southerners in Missouri, Germans in Illinois, Scandinavians and Germans in Wisconsin.

Ohio was settled and made what it is by the picked young men and women who went from New England to this Western Reserve (as regions of public land were called when they were opened for emigrants from eastern States). By following Tom Johnson from Cleveland out into the State of Ohio I could see a new, young, all-American-made society.

But I must first be clear and sure about Tom Johnson. Not easy. I still carried the well-nigh universal picture of him, as a demagogue, as a quack like his friend Bryan; the only correction I had made of this popular sketch was to add that he was unusually able, a successful captain of industry who, having collected a fortune, had turned to politics for some business purpose and to ranting radicalism as a political method. Knowingly. He was none of your unconscious crooks. Tom Johnson was an intelligent man. And yet even he could be fooled by propaganda, by the very propaganda that was hurting him.

While I was working on the LaFollette story I met Johnson by chance one day in St. Louis. He knew what I was doing, and he may have heard that I had expected to find LaFollette a demagogue. Anyway, when we had exchanged greetings he asked about

LaFollette the question I was asking about him: whether he wasn't a damned demagogue.

"What!" I exclaimed. "You ask that? You?"

And I told him that I had begun to suspect that, whenever a man in public life was called a demagogue, there was something good about him, something dangerous to the system. And that since the plutogogues could not fasten any crime on him they fell back on the all-sufficient charge that he was a demagogue. "You, for example," I whizzed, for I was convinced then about LaFollette, and I was indignant at Johnson. "You attract me because you are called a demagogue. Can't they say anything else against you? That's pretty good. But here you are, the man who wouldn't talk to me once because I would not be able to understand you—you —you can't understand the propaganda you swallow; you—you ask me if LaFollette is a demagogue and a crook."

He apologized, and I bade him go and apologize to LaFollette. He did. He accepted him completely. But also he saw what was troubling me about Tom Johnson—the question of his sincerity— and he helped me answer it. When I arrived in Cleveland to study Ohio, Johnson told me his personal story. He was a poor boy, the son of southern parents ruined by the war. To help out the family he sold newspapers from the city in his small home town. Fat, jolly, and bright, he made friends, and one of them, the conductor on the train that brought in the papers, said to him one day: "See here, Tom, I like you and I'm going to boost your business. Hereafter I'll bring papers only for you. You'll have a monopoly and can charge what you like, twenty-five cents apiece for them."

Tom Johnson not only made some money, he learned the principle of monopoly; and when he grew older and the other boys in his gang used to talk about going to work at a trade or in the grocery or some other store, he wondered at their folly in choosing a competitive line. He meant to start in some monopoly, and he did; he went into the street railway business, and he applied the monopoly principle to it. The street railways were monopolies, each of its route, but they competed with one another for power, control, domination. He discovered an idea that would bring him control. Most street car lines in his day in all cities started from the center of the town and ran out to some city limit and back. Each got thus the heavy traffic, downtown in the morning to work, back home in the evening. If he could unite two such lines and run them clear through a town, his one consolidated road would get, in addition to the up and down business, the lighter but good midday traffic across town and so have an advantage that would enable him to beat the other companies and force them into one consolidated monopoly. He worked these principles to a triumph in several cities and was applying them in Cleveland; he had already got the Big Consolidated there and was driving out Mark Hanna, with his "Little Con," when something happened. Tom Johnson read a book.

The peanut butcher on a train one day was trying to sell him Henry George's *Social Problems* when the conductor passing down the aisle said, "That's a book you ought to read, Mr. Johnson." The street railway man had a soft spot for conductors; he took this one's advice, and after buying and reading the book, went to his attorney and said: "I want you to answer that book for me. I can't. And I must. For if that book is right I am all wrong and I'll have to get out of my business." The lawyer answered Henry George, but only as a lawyer, not to his client's satisfaction. Tom Johnson went to New York, called together a group of his rich friends, and put it up to them. They all read Henry George, met one night, and discussed it till daylight. Johnson defended the book; he didn't want to accept its doctrines; he begged his friends to upset them, and they tried; they were able men, too, but Tom Johnson had seen the light, and his friends not only failed to clear his mind of the single-tax theories; they were themselves convinced. They all saw what Henry George pointed out: that excessive riches came unearned to individuals and companies owning land, natural resources, like water, coal, oil, etc., and franchises, such as steam and street railways, which, being common wealth to start with, became more and more valuable as the growing population increased the need and the value of these natural monopolies. The increased value of them was created by the mere growth of the population, who should have it, and George proposed that government should take it back by taxing nothing but the values of land, natural resources, and monopolies.

Tom Johnson returned to Cleveland, sold out his monopoly business, gradually, and went into politics as a successful business man with a vision, a plan. He ran for Congress, was elected, and there, in Washington, worked and voted against his own interests for the public interest. He did it genially, jovially, with humor, but with all the force of his good mind and powerful will. He could not accomplish much. A large representative body is no place for an executive, he discovered, and the House of Representatives, filled with men nominated by the State machines, had long ago been organized into a stronghold of the system. Tom Johnson consulted with Henry George, and they decided that the thing for Johnson to do was to go to a city, run for mayor, and try for the control so that he could apply the George principles and set an example in policy and in achievement, for all cities, all States.

That, then, was what Tom Johnson was up to in Cleveland, that was what he was after, to make there what he called the City on a Hill.

XVII

THE CITY ON A HILL

TOM JOHNSON's ambition was big enough to account for him. To take one city and solve there the social, economic, political problems and so set an example to other super-business men of a job worth doing and to the world of a government as it should be—that was as understandable as the wish to make a million dollars. Especially since this business man already had his million plus. My petty suspicions of Tom Johnson vanished. He belonged in the class with Folk and LaFollette, Roosevelt, Seth Low, and Walter Fisher. He was on "our side," the people's; that was why the other side, the plutogogues, called him a demagogue. But I heard some of Tom Johnson's campaign speeches in the infamous tent he moved about for meetings in parts of the town where there were no halls or where opponents closed halls against him. His "circus" speeches were indeed entertaining; he encouraged questions from the floor, and he answered them with quick wit and barbed facts; but those political meetings were more like classes in economics and current (local) history than harangues. The only just complaint of his enemies was that he "had gone back on his class." This was said by men who almost in the same breath would declare that reform was not a class struggle, that there was no such thing as class consciousness, no classes, in America; and they meant it, too. The charge against Tom Johnson, Folk, La-Follette and, later, Rudolph Spreckels, of treason to their class, is an expression of our unconscious class consciousness, and an example of our appalling sincerity, miscalled hypocrisy.

Tom Johnson had gone back on his class and on himself as well. He was a convert from plutocracy to democracy, and that made a great difference. He was not merely a good rich man, like Seth Low, out to "give" us good government; he was not merely able and efficient like Fisher, forceful and energetic like Roosevelt, honest and persistent like Joe Folk. Tom Johnson had not always been a good, honest man; he had been a street railway magnate in politics and had done some—not all, but all that he had found necessary to his business—of the corrupting things a street railway man typically does. In his home town, Cleveland, in his own company, the Big Con, there was a man, Horace Andrews, who was more scrupulous than Johnson. Johnson himself said that, and he illustrated it with inside stories of the days when he was in business. And his stories, his business, and his political career showed him that the ethics and the morals of politics are higher than those of business. He had to be more honest in public than in private business; honesty, he found, is the best policy for reform politics. And Horace Andrews did not find it good business. It was my acquaintance with these two men that helped me to understand what Clarence Darrow meant when he laughed at me as "the man that believed in honesty."

Honesty is not enough; it takes intelligence, some knowledge or theory of economics, courage, strength, will power, humor, leadership—it takes intellectual integrity to solve our political problems. And these Tom Johnson had above all the politicians of my day. His courage was the laughing sort; his humor was the kind that saved him tears. He had the instinct and the habit of experimentation, and he had the training of a big, successful man of business on the other side of politics. A practical business man, he was a practical politician, too. He knew the game. He could pick and lead a team; men loved to follow him; he made it fun. Resourceful and understanding of the economics of a fight, he could make clear to others what they were up against and what they had to do about it. At a time when his whole administration was in an angry struggle with the street railway, he granted publicly an extension of the line a few blocks to a new baseball park. It looked like a surrender, even treason, to his own crowd as well as to the people. But he took the opportunity of the attention upon that issue to explain that it was the street railway franchise they were fighting, not the street railway nor the service.

"We want the street railway to carry people where they want to go, right up to the ball park. I would force them to deliver passengers at the park if they wouldn't do it voluntarily. So I give them a license to extend the line, not a franchise, not a property."

He cleared my head of a lot of rubbish, left there from my academic education and reform associations. I asked him one day why he had thought I would not understand him if he told me what he was up to in Cleveland.

"Oh, I could see," he said, "that you did not know what it was that corrupted politics. First you thought it was bad politicians, who turned out to be pretty good fellows. Then you blamed the bad business men who bribed the good fellows, till you discovered that not all business men bribed and that those who did were pretty good business men. The little business men didn't bribe; so you settled upon, you invented, the phrase 'big business,' and that's as far as you and your kind have got: that it is big business that does all the harm. Hell! Can't you see that it's privileged business that does it? Whether it's a big steam railroad that wants a franchise or a little gambling-house that wants not to be raided, a temperance society that wants a law passed, a poor little prostitute, or a big merchant occupying an alley for storage—it's those who seek privileges who corrupt, it's those who possess privileges that defend our corrupt politics. Can't you see that?"

This was more like a flash of light than a speech, and as I took it in and shed it around in my head, he added: "It is privilege that causes evil in the world, not wickedness; and not men."

And I remembered then something I heard him say one day to a group of the business men he was fighting, something neither they nor I understood at the time. To a remonstrance of theirs that I do not recall, he blurted out: "It's fun, running the business of the city of Cleveland; it's the biggest, most complicated, most difficult, and most satisfying business in Cleveland. A street railway is child's play, compared with it; a coal mine is a snap; a bank?— Bah. There's something that blinds you fellows, and I know what it is. It's what fooled me so long when I was running public service corporations. And I'll tell you something you want to know: how to beat me.

"If I could take away from you the things you have, the franchises, the privileges, that make you enemies of your city, you would see what I see and run for my job yourselves, and you'd beat me for mayor and manage the city of Cleveland better than I do."

I recalled another incident that occurred soon after Tom Johnson was first elected mayor. A committee of clergymen called on him to protest his policy on vice. He did not enforce the law. He had sent for the saloon men and told them that if they would keep order, refuse to sell to children, permit no gambling-machines, and not pay blackmail to his police, he would give them, free of cost, the privilege of running over the exact limits of the law. He had summoned all the women who keep bawdy houses and told them that if they would be reasonably quiet, rob no customers, and pay nothing to policemen or any other men, he would let them do business. The clergymen had heard of this, and they were indignant. The city was conniving at vice. He told them that he did not understand vice, but he did know that it stood in with business and political corruption because it sought also the privilege of breaking the law. He gave vice that privilege for the price of quiet and non-interference with his police force, to get rid of them in order that he, a business man, might as mayor deal with the corruption which he did understand. And he warned them that if they, the clergy, added to his difficulties by their cries for good government, he would turn upon them and explain why they were keen on the sins of the bad people who did not go to church and defenders of the crimes of the good people who supported the churches. He had very little trouble from the churches, but that was partly because the Rev. Mr. Williams of Cleveland, later the Episcopal bishop of Michigan, was a single-taxer and understood what Johnson was up to, that he was "trying, not to enforce Christianity, but to make it possible."

Wise, then, and "wise," Mayor Tom Johnson and his administration seemed to me the best possible experiment we could have for the testing of several theories: First, that what we needed was a good business man to head a business administration; business men hated and opposed the Johnson administration as they did Seth Low's and the Municipal Voters League. Second, that the city was the hope of democracy. Tom Johnson struck at the sources of the evils, not at the individuals and classes usually blamed, with all his fine intelligence and all the powers of an unusually powerful mayor. He explained his acts with patience, care, and eloquence to the whole town; he held the votes of the common people; he was elected again and again. But he uncovered the system under Mark

Hanna; the system became conscious, and the city system, which Johnson beat in Cleveland, appealed to the State system, which so blocked Johnson in the town that he and his group had to make a State campaign for the governorship and the Legislature. In that they discovered that the State was corrupt, the voters purchasable as in Rhode Island or subjected to corrupt party organization as in Missouri. The Johnson crowd did not win the governorship; they won only a strong minority in the Legislature, which Frederic C. Howe was the very able and effective floor leader of in the State Senate. The Cleveland reformers had Toledo with them, but the bad business men of Cleveland were able, under the leadership of Mark Hanna, to abolish the charters of all the cities in Ohio and force upon them all a new charter, with scattered powers and responsibilities and, therefore, license to evil. This in the State created by the picked, vigorous, young, idealistic immigrants from degenerate old New England!

Nor is this all. The charter good young Ohio chose for all its cities was that of Cincinnati; so I went to Cincinnati to see what selected, undegenerate Americans like so much.

XVIII

CINCINNATI AND BOSS COX

I N WASHINGTON, D.C., a year or so after all this, President
Roosevelt one day invited me, with suspicious urgency, to
luncheon in the White House. When I got there, early, I had
to wait a few minutes with some other guests, all strangers to me,
till T.R. came bouncing in and, with a laugh, introduced me to
Mayor Fleishman of Cincinnati.

"The amusing thing is that I can," he said to the other guests,
and he went on to say that I had made a study of Cincinnati and
a report on conditions there. "And he never called on, he never
saw, the mayor!"

It was a challenge, a reproach; it was meant for a humorous
rebuke, and Mr. Fleishman joined in the laughter and the challenge. "Yes," he said, "I expected you to call, and you never
did."

So this was why T.R. had so insisted upon my coming to
luncheon that day. I kept a polite silence for a moment; then,
when the laughter died down, I admitted that I had not seen the
mayor of Cincinnati when I was there, adding that I did not have
to. Mr. Fleishman was elected to the office, but he wasn't the
mayor; he was the front, not the head, of the city government.
George Cox was the head of that city; he was the whole government; and on him I had called punctiliously, frequently, and
profitably.

It was the president's turn, and Mr. Fleishman's, to be—politely
silent, and they were till T.R. said "Come on" and led us out to
the table. There he started another subject of conversation, on the
Supreme Court and his disappointment with a decision of a justice
whom he had just named. The new justice had voted against the
known expectations of the president on a certain big case.

482

"I suppose," T.R. said sharply, "I infer that you would be willing to call on that justice."

"After that decision I would," I answered. "Before it I'd have called on you, Mr. President."

"Then your presence here is an honor to me," he said; he could be a pretty rough rider.

"It's an acknowledgment that you are the president, and my very good friend. If Mr. McKinley were in the White House I'd probably have been lunching with Mark Hanna or Boss Cox."

And just to keep the president from slugging me, I offered to retell the story of my first call on Mr. George Cox in Cincinnati. The president had read it; with a glance at Mr. Fleishman, who also had read it, he stopped me. "We know that story," he said, and he took up the Supreme Court again. He characterized the chief justice; he was sailing down the list of them, one ripping sentence to each, till he caught Mrs. Roosevelt's eye. There was a young army officer at the table, several women, and I was a reporter. T.R. stopped short, started something else, and carried on like the rushing river he was, then suddenly got back to the Supreme Court justices and finished them off in style. But let's get back to Cincinnati.

When I went to Cincinnati from Cleveland I knew the conditions there, what was what and who was who, and early in my first morning, before eight o'clock, I sought out Boss Cox. His office was over his "Mecca" saloon, in a mean little front hall room one flight up. The door was open. I saw a great hulk of a man, sitting there alone, his back to the door, his feet up on the window sill; he was reading a newspaper. I knocked; no response. I walked in; he did not look up.

"Mr. Cox?" I said.

An affirmative grunt.

"Mr. Cox, I understand that you are the boss of Cincinnati."

Slowly his feet came down, one by one. They slowly walked his chair around, and a stolid face turned to let two dark, sharp eyes study me. While they measured, I gave my name and explained that I was "a student of politics, corrupt politics, and bosses." I repeated that I had heard he was the boss of Cincinnati. "Are you?" I asked.

"I am," he grumbled in his hoarse, throaty voice.

"Of course you have a mayor, and a council, and judges?"

"I have," he admitted, "but"—he pointed with his thumb back over his shoulder to the desk—"I have a telephone, too."

"And you have citizens, too, in your city? American men and women?"

He stared a long moment, silent, then turned heavily around back to his paper. That short interview was a summary of the truth about Cincinnati, a rather cultivated city of kindly people, descendants of pioneers, New Englanders, southerners, and Germans, dominated by a dictatorship, which they actually feared and which did not fear them—and which did sell them out—to their knowledge. Everybody had tales to tell of this literal tyranny and of shameful graft, both of politics and business, of the schools and of the courts; but there were only a few individuals who dared tell you their stories: Elliot H. Pendleton, ex-Judge Rufus B. Smith, one newspaper editor, and a dozen other men. And excepting only Pendleton, these did not like to be seen with me and instinctively whispered when they told their facts. Cox's Republican machine, which was in open partnership with the Democratic machine, kept lists of voters, watched them, "had things on them"; and it punished—actually; it hurt your business. But also it could and it did help your business if you "went along."

I had to depend on Cox for the protection of what I had to write. There was no counting on witnesses to defend a case of libel; they would not testify. I went back, therefore, to the boss, and I made a deal with him. He had had me watched; detectives followed me, and they let me and everybody else see them. That was one of the reasons why men would not talk. I like myself to be shadowed. I soon learned to lead my detectives up to the office of some man who, they knew, could give me evidence. Once inside, even if the witness would not give me anything, I would manage to entertain him long enough to make the detectives report, with their professional suspicion, that I had been "closeted with" a possible informer for an hour or two or three. And I found that Cox knew this and swallowed the suspicion.

After the first few days in his town I went back to him one early morning. He was more polite the second visit than he was the first. He whirled around in his chair to receive me.

"Well, what you getting?"

I told him some stories, well-known incidents. "Lies," he blurted, "all damn lies."

"Are they?" I asked naïvely. "I'll go over the ground again." The next morning I called again, early, and I said: "Those stories are true, Mr. Cox. There are some inaccuracies," and I named and corrected them. "The rest is true." When he did not deny that, I made my proposition.

"Look here, Mr. Cox, you have detectives on me. You must be curious about whom I see and what I learn. Keep the dicks on; they will give you a check on me, and I'll come in every day or two and tell you what I get. You can correct my information, but you must be square with me. I'm a stranger, I can be misled, but you mustn't mislead me; not you. You need not tell me anything, of course; it's up to me to find my own facts; but I'll give you a chance to nail the lies people tell me, and you, the party of the second part—since I am depending on you—you mustn't deceive me."

He blinked; he turned to the window and looked out. He turned back, stared, without a flicker of his eyelids, without a word. I had to close the bargain.

"All right," I said. "That's a go then."

"Make it always early," he answered and turned away.

My chief source of information in Cincinnati was the editor of the *Post*, a Scripps paper. That man could tell, in complete and precise detail, a connected story of his city, which he illustrated from his files and the files of other papers, and he gave time to my job. I had to see other men, of course, to verify and add to his facts, but he had what we call the "dope." His "dope" was much more than I could write, but I had a use for it.

I have often been asked why it was that with all the libelous matter I printed, I never had a suit for libel. My relations with Cox may answer that question in part. In the course of the weeks I worked in Cincinnati I learned many facts about the boss and his gang; I don't know how many, but let us say that I had stuff for twenty-five charges against him. I told them all to him. I made my calls early and often; I gave him always all I had. He would balk at each new one.

"Say, who filled you up with that?"

"Not true?" I would say.

"Not the way you've got it."

All right, I would check it, "a lie"; he watched me write that, and I would go away to come back the next day to say, usually, "That's true, Mr. Cox," or "I have that judgeship story corrected, Mr. Cox." This I would say and look him in the eye. My theory was that Cox was "square" and that I had made him feel that I was trusting him. And I did, and he rose to it.

"What's the next dose you are swallowing?"

So he would pass on indictments, till there were, say, the twenty-five which he knew I knew. And then when the article appeared he read it, and there were only, say, eight or ten, those that sufficed in a brief space to make my picture, all I could handle. But Cox saw, and he said to me (at a political convention): "Say, boy, you didn't use half the dope you had in that swipe you gave me."

My readers thought that I had been hard on Cox, but Cox thought that I had gone easy to spare him. He may have feared that in a libel suit I would bring out the rest of my evidence, but I think that he thought that I had spared him all I could, as one honest crook to another. And that was the point of view from which we talked.

What kind of machine did he have? That was the question I kept before us. There was graft, of course; every city had graft; and there was politics, and business, but how was the graft, politics, and business done, from the graft point of view, from the esthetic point of view? Was it smoothly, cleverly done, or was it rough, blundering, and loud? He was fascinated by descriptions of other machines; he hated comparisons with his, but just the same he admired my admiration for them when they were "good," as in Philadelphia. What he wanted from me was a judgment with praise of his "system," and I withheld that till the day I was quitting Cincinnati and had called to take leave of Mr. Cox.

"Well, and what do you think of it?" he asked, referring of course to his machine.

"Pretty good," I said.

"Pretty—" He was too disgusted to finish. "Best you ever saw!" he retorted finally.

"Well, I can't tell," I said. "My criterion for a graft organization is how few divide the graft. How many divide it here?"

"Ain't no graft," he grumbled.

"Then it's a mighty poor thing."

He pondered a moment; then: "How many do you say divides up here?"

"Three at least," I said. "You and Garry Herman and Rud Hynicke."

"Ugh!" he grunted scornfully, and wagging one finger slowly before my face, he said, "There's only one divides up here."

Not true, this, not exactly. Cox wasn't lying. He was getting old and vain and was boasting a bit. He meant, as I meant, that he, or he and his two lieutenants, controlled and cut the political graft, which others received shares of as he directed. Cox probably did decide how much each participant received; his statement made me believe that he had the final say even over Herman and Hynicke. And Cox was going into the banking and other business, too. He was rich, and he was very powerful in business as well as politics. And he was right about his machine and its methods; they had been, it seemed to me, about the most perfect organization of the sort that I had seen or heard of. But as I moved about the town, questioned politicians and citizens who knew, I had learned that Cox and his ward leaders were living on their reputation. They were neglecting the detailed work they used to do, did not keep up their voting lists and the blackmail data on citizens. The fear of them and their diligence remained, but not the ground for it. I sounded Cox on this observation, and his fierce resistance to it convinced me that that was his tender spot.

I reported to the reformers that Cox's machine was a myth and could be beaten. They did not, they could not, believe it. They agreed to nominate a ticket and work for it, using my article when it appeared to stir the voters to prove I was all wrong on the citizenship of Cincinnati. I promised to take back what I said about the voters there, if they overthrew Cox. This deal was carried out, but the reformers would not run themselves; they nominated a young man, almost a boy, for mayor, and when to their amazement he was elected, he could not do much, and Cox and his machine came back into power.

Of course I can see now that the Cox machine was founded upon the solid ground of privileges; it was built up into the very structure of society. Reform is an abnormal thing, and when the reformers fail, as they do and must, the city or the State falls back to the norm, the corrupt norm. Even Cox did not understand this. He blamed the reformers for their failures. He despised good citizens; he sneered at the business men who shunned him in public and sought his services in private. He did not pretend to be what he was not; he submitted to my assumption always, that he was a grafter. Like Richard Croker, all he insisted on was that he was "better than them," and he waved his hand around him down-town and uptown.

When he read my article his sole criticism was that I had made him say, in that first interview, that he dictated to judges. My question was, "You have a mayor, a council, judges?" and I said he answered that he had a telephone, too. He declared that I did not say "judges." He may not have heard or heeded it, but I did. I had a special reason for including the bench: Judge Smith had told me his story. My own opinion is that Cox had been persuaded by some lawyers that "we must respect the courts"; however bad they are, we must not criticize them; and that is being accepted as the limit. I wrote once that a certain captain of industry "controlled governors, legislators, judges, churches, schools, and news-papers," and when I showed him the manuscript he penciled out the word "judges." The rest could stand, and that's what Cox thought, no doubt—that the "courts" should have been "respected." The rest was all right.

The rest, in Cincinnati, was the mayor, the council, the city departments, the public property, the schools, newspapers, public opinion, and voters; and the city's influence and power in the State; and a share of the State's share in the Federal government. And a big majority—"everybody"—was back of all this. And Mark Hanna and the business men of Cleveland preferred the condition of Cincinnati. And the State of Ohio, the creation anew of the new New Englanders, was in such a state of mind that it helped put over upon all the cities there the charter and the condition of Cincinnati. Hanna, the native Republican boss, led the Democratic party to beat Tom Johnson, but the initial mover and the final approver of this business man's anarchism were acts of the courts.

XIX

SOME THEORIES: BIG BUSINESS AND PRIVILEGED BUSINESS

MY *Ohio: a Tale of Two Cities* must have struck some readers as valuable. Soon after it was published, Tom Johnson met on a train a stranger who said he had seen the check the mayor sent me to pay for it, and the amount was large, as large as the witness. Mr. Johnson embarrassed him by remarking that "that was funny. I'll ask Steffens if he ever saw the check," he said. "For I'm Tom Johnson, and I never saw it."

The stranger choked and gradually moved away, but before he went he insisted that he had seen the check. His banker had shown it to him, and it was indorsed as received by me and as paid by the bank. Johnson may have been half persuaded, for he asked me if I had "ever seen anything like it."

By way of answer I related how I had discovered that when I wanted to get at the springs of thought and action in a man I was to write about, I should ask him about other men, and usually the witness would attribute to all others the motives and purposes which guided him. A vain man thought everybody was "after publicity," an ambitious man that his neighbors were "after office," a money-maker that we all are "after money." And just for fun, I reminded Tom Johnson that he had asked me once if Bob La-Follette wasn't a demagogue. While Tom Johnson was fumbling with this half-truth, I offered him another; I rattled on about the need men felt to explain away a disturbing fact or idea to save themselves from the labor of thinking it out. Mayor Johnson, for example, had been disturbed by the appearance of Governor La-Follette on the right side, and having no time to investigate, had accepted thoughtlessly of the governor the enemies' explanation of both of them. And the man who had seen the mayor's check to me

489

had probably seen only a banker who was probably answering all the facts I put into my Ohio article by saying that probably I had been well paid by the rich mayor for reporting them. That would answer, not only those facts, but all doubts about Tom Johnson, too, and me. As the mayor knew, many people go to their bankers for advice, and not only on money matters; and they get it, too. Bankers, who have no more wisdom than they have money of their own, pay out opinions as they pay out credit, with the awe-inspiring manner of one who could pay more, much more, out of his reserves, if he liked.

Boss Cox, who was most injured by the article, did not openly deny or privately resent it. He was out of power for a term, which he spent in repairing his neglected machine.

The practical politicians profited by exposure and defeat; not the reformers.

In the interval between Cox's defeat and his restoration to power I met him at a national convention of the Republican party. He greeted me warmly, but briefly; he made no reference to my article; he said nothing at all then. A couple of days later there was a secret session of the dominating bosses of the convention, and a group of correspondents waited outside the decisive door for hours. When Cox came out first, alone, he waved us aside. "Not a word," he said roughly, but his eye fell upon me and he added, "except to you." He drew me aside, told me "what was doing," and left me without any injunction to wait with the news till it reached the convention. I did hold it; I was not filing spot news. I took Cox's confidence as I felt he meant it, as a sign of his good will, of his appreciation of the fact that I had not made the most or the worst of the goods he knew I had on him.

The bosses and bad men generally "stood for the truth" and recognized my impersonal restraint in what I reported. It was the good men who resented the facts, partly, no doubt, because they don't know and won't recognize the truth.

Governor Myron T. Herrick of Ohio, for example, showed his indignation years later when I met him in Paris as the U.S. ambassador to France. He said I had walked into his office at Columbus and told him to his face that he was not the governor, and that he had had to put me out. Inexact. When I called on him the ex-banker was very hospitable, even confidential. He assumed that he and I were both good citizens on the same side in politics, anti-graft, for reform, but not for men who went too far, like Tom Johnson. To stop the eloquence and get down to business, I asked him who was the actual governor of his State.

"I am," he snapped.

"Good," I said; "then you can tell me the inside story of ———" and I mentioned a couple of scandalous deals of his administration, acts upon which he had said one thing and done another. He

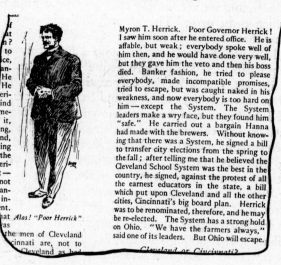

Myron T. Herrick. Poor Governor Herrick! I saw him soon after he entered office. He is affable, but weak; everybody spoke well of him then, and he would have done very well, but they gave him the veto and then his boss died. Banker fashion, he tried to please everybody, made incompatible promises, tried to escape, but was caught naked in his weakness, and now everybody is too hard on him — except the System. The System leaders make a wry face, but they found him "safe." He carried out a bargain Hanna had made with the brewers. Without knowing that there was a System, he signed a bill to transfer city elections from the spring to the fall; after telling me that he believed the Cleveland School System was the best in the country, he signed, against the protest of all the earnest educators in the state, a bill which put upon Cleveland and all the other cities, Cincinnati's big board plan. Herrick was to be renominated, therefore, and he may be re-elected. The System has a strong hold on Ohio. "We have the farmers always," said one of its leaders. But Ohio will escape.

Alas! "Poor Herrick"

OHIO: A TALE OF TWO CITIES
McClure's Magazine, July, 1905

couldn't, he said, and he convinced me that he really did not himself understand what had happened. He had listened to advice, and being a reasonable man, had taken it. So I said I must find the actual governor, "your governor," I put it, "who gives you the advice you act on." He was indignant, but when I admitted his innocence and besought him to name the man who, having more power than the governor, put over those deals which I had to know about, he was placated. He soon was smiling again; we had a pleasant walk in the dusk to his residence and a talk which revealed the sweet reasonableness, the consideration for others, the wish to serve—as well as the amiable willingness to take and convey diplomatically an order from above—which made Mr. Herrick the charming, successful war- and peace-time ambassador he became. What he bore so long against me was that after our nice talk I went off and wrote that he was only the titular head of the State, who was lost and bewildered when his boss, Mark Hanna, died.

"Big business" was, and it still is, the current name of the devil, the root of all evil, political and economic. It is a blind phrase, useless; it leads nowhere. We can't abolish business, we cannot regulate big business, and we are finding that we cannot limit bigness in business, which must grow. The phrase does not cover what we mean. I know that; I must have known it, else Tom Johnson could not have told it me. As early as St. Louis I had seen and written that the big businesses which were active in political corruption were the railroads, public service corporations, banks, etc., which are "big," but also saloons, gambling and bawdy houses, which are small. And I had seen and written that what these big and little businesses all had in common was not size but the need of privileges: franchises and special legislation, which required legislative corruption; protective tariffs, interpretations of laws in their special interest or leniency or "protection" in the enforcement of laws, calling for "pulls" with judges, prosecutors, and the police. As Tom Johnson said, then, it was "privilege" that was the source of the evil; it was "privileged business" that was the devil, and I had been describing and meaning this all the time I had been writing "big business." Why? My old German professor of psychology had taught us to distinguish between perception and apperception, between seeing things with the eyes and reaching out with the mind to grasp them, what the new school of *Gestalt* psychology now calls "insight." Tom Johnson was tempting me to apperceive the perception that it was privilege that hurt us. Not easy, this; it was consequential; it went to the bottom of all our moral culture of right and wrong.

If it was privilege that caused what we called evil, it was privilege that had to be dealt with, not men. Not big men, not bad men, not crooks, and not capitalists—not even the capitalist class! Punishment of individuals, the class struggle and strikes, wars—all hatred, vengeance, force, were unscientific. To put in prison a man who bought government to get a street railway franchise was wrong; we should put the franchise where men can't get it. To shift our votes from one to another of two political parties, both of which are organized to serve the privileged or the privilege-seekers, was folly. To throw out the rascals and put into office honest men without removing that which makes good men do bad things was as irrational as our experience had taught us it was "unpractical." The international wars of corrupted governments for trade routes, foreign markets, "empire" and the natural resources of backward countries, strikes and the class war for the conquest of economic power and advantages—these were as senseless as passing laws for reform and for peace. It's all upside down. What society does is to teach the ideal of success, set up the temptation of power and riches to men and nations—if they are brave enough to risk and able enough to escape the threats of penalties for getting caught. These warnings keep off all but the best men, biologically best. Then when these best men succeed we honor them, and if they slip we hate and punish them. What we ought to do is to let the losers of the race go, and take down the prizes we offer to the winners.

Tom Johnson was proposing in Cleveland to take down the prizes by wiping out privileges and all hope of privileges. His theory was that the big business men there would then come over on the city's side and be for, instead of against, good government. That was what he meant when he told his old colleagues in the street railway and other public service corporations that if he could take away their franchises they would soon be running for office in order still to have big business to do. It was his own personal experience. When he rid himself of his incentives to contribute to the political machine he quit that, became a reformer and the mayor and manager of the biggest business in Cleveland, the city's business.

His proposed method of taking over the prizes for anti-social conduct was public ownership and operation of all public service corporations and the taxation of land values, not socialism, but the Henry George plan for the closing up of all the sources of unearned wealth. His public ownership was in the interest, not only of efficiency and economy in the management of street railways, etc., but to get those businesses and those able private operators out of politics. As to his new incentive: he lost money; it cost him much more than his salary to be mayor and carry on his policy. The incentive of profit was lacking entirely, but it was obvious that his ambition to set an example in Cleveland of a solution of the universal political-economic problem of government was a stronger motive than profit in a man with imagination. I have often wondered why more men don't see that, and the answer that occurred to me came also from Tom Johnson. He thought that by removing the cause of his anti-social conduct, he changed, but he had his purpose, too, his ideal, the vision he developed out of a book. Few men have such ideals. The ideals of America, for example, the ideals that came to Ohio probably from New England and from Old England, are antiquated, dried up, contradictory; honesty and wealth, morality and success, individual achievement and respectability, privileges and democracy—these won't take us very far.

There was something wrong in our ends as well as in our beginnings, in what we are after as well as in what is after us, in American ideals as well as in American conduct and its causes.

XX

NEW JERSEY: A TRUST FACTORY

L ooking back over a life, one can trace a certain logic which is rather deceptive. From Ohio I went to New Jersey, and that was right. Jersey was the head waters of the main stream of corruption against which the reformers everywhere were trying to swim back—back to Jeffersonian democracy. If a converted captain of industry like Tom Johnson and his organized party could not, with all their courage, ability, and understanding, make a stand in Ohio and set up in Cleveland their City on a Hill, then the way of New Jersey was the way for Ohio and the rest of us, the way of Alexander Hamilton. For Hamilton first saw the uses of a State like New Jersey, a State in between other, more active States like New York and Pennsylvania. He began there to do the things one could not quite do in New York; he went to New Jersey for the charters and grabs impossible in New York. He founded companies which took over from the State water fronts and water powers which he foresaw would be invaluable in the future as gangways for national traffic. One of his companies seized the Jersey shores of the Hudson River available for ferry landings, and he did not attempt to take the New York shores. Another company of his asked for and received from this backyard State, where nobody lived and watched, powers to operate in other States, powers not yet to be had from those other States to build up privileged groups and exploit the people. For a century after Hamilton railroad companies and financiers of Philadelphia and New York had followed their great leader in to Jersey to get leave to break the laws of other States, and they came to rule that State absolutely, these "foreigners," as the Jerseyites called them. And I had learned in my Wall Street days from James B. Dill himself how he and his associates, after trying their

495

own State, New York, with no knowledge of the history of New Jersey, had availed themselves of its ancient weakness to start there that system of selling cheap to big trusts and smaller corporations, charters that enabled them to do those things which the anti-trust laws and the anti-trust opinions of that anti-monopoly period forbade.

Jersey was one of the gates through which the flood of privilege broke over this country, and I could have sensed there the irresistible force of that mighty current. I could have seen how, once started, nobody and nothing but a revolution could stop it; I could have seen, too, that it was deliberately, knowingly, purposely started; for certainly Alexander Hamilton understood and formulated his political theories and policies on the principle of a government by a privileged, superior class. He distrusted the people, and he was right in this; the American people have in the long run followed him and not Jefferson, who trusted them. And wasn't Hamilton fundamentally right? Are there not natural forces that make in his direction? Jersey was the place to answer these questions, but I had not yet raised these questions in my own mind. I did not see the significance of Jersey till after the war and the revolution in Europe.

The reason I went to New Jersey after Wisconsin and Ohio was logical, not economically, but professionally. We felt on the magazine that we had overdrawn our credit with our readers. They might have followed us in our support of one or two reformers, like Folk of St. Louis and Fisher of Chicago; they might have stood for one "demagogue," but two like LaFollette and Tom Johnson in succession—that was too much, as the letters to the editor indicated. "Can't you find anything good in this country?" they asked. We understood. They wanted something good in the main stream. And Mr. McClure had long been wisely urging me to write up some such good. To humor him I consented once about this time. I would rake out some men and movements, not reform, but practical, to report. "Where will you begin," he asked eagerly; "in New York?" I said no, I would begin at home in my own town, Greenwich, Conn. And I did look there, and I found three good stories. One of them was a tale of a barber in Greenwich who heard some of his politician customers talking contemptuously of a new department created in that State to fight the pests that were attacking the trees of New England and to take care generally of all vegetation. The barber gathered that the appointment of a

·LIFE·

Beef, Iron and Whine.

WE have come to regard the magazine guns of literature with terror. We have been paying ten cents for ten pages of trusts, turbulence and twaddle, and ten times ten pages of soap, auto and lithia ads.; we have seen the Pharaoh of Kerosene embalmed in Ida Tarballs; we have gasped over Tom Lossing's Field Book of American Swindlers; we have watched the Steffens knocked out of the civic grafter; and have endured lynchings, strikes and other features of a strenuous civilization by the Baker's dozen; and yet the end is not in sight. A new vista of atrocities opens upon our affrighted vision; a new set of swindles and outrages awaits us at the ten-cent, literary, quick-lunch counter.

In the coming months the woes of town-trodden railroads oppressed and

tortured by conscienceless capital will call for our tears; the high-handed tyranny of a government seeking to cur-

tail the gains of bashful beef boodlers and guileless grub grafters will demand our indignation; the clamorous cattle raiser, the indignant egg incubator, the howling hen breeder, the hapless hog herder, the shouting steer fattener, the passionate cold-storage vaulter, and all the pragmatic primary plunderers of pot and pantry, will demand that we will rise in our majesty with a stuffed club and soak the Beef Banditti of Chicago. And we will rise, like trout to a bait, and wrathfully swat the wholesale swindlers who swindle the retail swindlers who swindle us, the American asses, who carry all the swindlers on our backs.

Meantime the hot and heavy hand of the Strenuous One has landed on the Beef Banditti, who are sternly advised that while they may loot the cupboard of the American ass individually, they do so at their peril when they do it as a bunch. Solo swindling is honored and protected by the law; quartette swindling stirs the liver and spleen of even the frappé Supreme Court.

A great American principle has been enunciated; the Armour of the Pig and Plunder Association has been pierced; and the quills upon the fretful Pork Combine are spilling ink and invective with violence and verbosity. The Beef Banditti with poignant pathos point to the purity of their motives; they admit trimming impartially the parlous producer and clamorous consumer; but they allege the assaults upon their patriotism and philanthropy come from the artful commission merchants, who heretofore did all the skinning themselves. With fearless dignity they state there has been too much competi-

tion in the business of looting; it was degenerating from high art to petty larceny; the common people were irritated at its vulgarity and lack of system; and for the comfort and safety of the nation, it was felt that swindling should be organized and done on business principles. Naturally the railroads and middlemen objected and called the police; no self-respecting looter, remembering the sacrifices of his fathers for freedom, will submit to monopoly; it was immoral and unconstitutional; and the honest grafter indignantly demanded that he be protected in the collection of the rake-off guaranteed him under the laws of the Republic. It was a call to freemen, which, if unheeded, would condemn many a noble looter to go to work, to be grafted like an ordinary American ass.

A crisis had arrived. The American ass waked up and brayed in strident tones for something to be done; and the continent trembled.

The American, as we know, is a law-

Life

"CAN'T YOU FIND ANYTHING GOOD IN THIS COUNTRY?"

head of this bureau had been given to the Greenwich bosses as their share of the spoils for that year, and the politicians despised it. The barber asked for the job; he begged for it so earnestly that partly as a joke, partly to show their contempt for the new-fangled bureau, they appointed him, and he, gifted by chance for that sort of work, took the job, studied up, and in brief had become one of the leading expert authorities in his field.

I forget now what the two other "good stories" were, but I cited these and enough such subjects that I had come across else-where to show my colleagues that it would take several very diligent reporters to begin to get and report all the "good works" and workers outside of my line in the United States. Mr. Mc-Clure threw up his hands, and I urged him to let me stick to my line; and I revealed two good stories I had had up my sleeve all the while for just this emergency, Mark Fagan and Everett Colby of New Jersey.

Mark Fagan was a young Irish Catholic undertaker who had been elected mayor of Jersey City and was trying to "serve the people." He was religious about it, prayed to God for help every morning when he climbed the steps of his city hall, and so simple, so worshiped by the common folk, and best of all, so seeing, that his story was sure, I thought, to restore us in the eyes of our readers. And it did. I let go in it all the sentiment Mark Fagan felt for his service; I did not fail to show what he was up against: the solid system of Jersey City, the national railroad terminal, the water front of which Hamilton had taken for ferries. One of Fagan's fights was to get his sewer pipes through to the river. It was a long, hard, losing fight that this honest, uneducated, human baby was making, and it took him to Trenton, where I described, often in his language, what he saw of the State system, and the captains of industry, the leaders of society, politics, and finance. It was muckraking, but of a new, a sentimental sort.

And while I was following Mark, the humble, Christian soldier, I came upon Everett Colby, "the Gentleman from Essex." Why do fiction writers invent stories and characters when they can find them ready-made, and made, so to speak, by God, who outdoes all the poets, playwrights, and novelists in plot, in characters, in detail, and in significant truth? Everett Colby was a rich man's son; his father was one of the builders of the Wisconsin Central Railroad and a man of imagination, force, ability, and courage— a type, that father, a pioneer captain of industry, one of the hun-dreds of great producers whom this country produced. Their children must, some of them, inherit some of their genius. Everett Colby had some of his father's gifts, but he inherited also some of his father's riches. There is a large and growing class of the rich sons and daughters of great, rich men, and if we are ever to have an aristocracy it might be expected to derive from this class. One of the excuses the rich offer for the combined accumulation of easy money is that they must have enough for their families, their children. But their children . . .

Young Colby was brought up only to play. Like other rich children he could throw as much strength, nerve, and concentrated intelligence into sport as their fathers put into the game of life; but having been brought up only to play, they can't work— "can't," not won't. They don't know how; they don't know anything but games, and they cannot learn. Everett Colby was headed straight for this fate when a man got hold of him, J. A. Browning, a teacher who taught. This teacher had a small class of rich boys who had busy fathers and loving mothers: Harold and Stanley McCormick, Percy and John D. Rockefeller, Jr., and Everett Colby. Colby was in the worst condition. He could only play. "He played hard," said Mr. Browning, "but it was sport, not work. He couldn't read till he was fifteen; he couldn't fix his attention. I got into his mind through his hands, and—" Finally this teacher tempted the boy to work, to finish something, and so entered him with young John D. into Brown University, where again he played, hard. He became captain of the best football team Brown had had up to that time. But he did some work, too; he was graduated in 1897. A tour of the world, law, marriage, polo, a home in New Jersey, and a broker's office in Wall Street. Nothing, no job, till he remembered a boyhood ambition to go into politics; that was why he had gone in for debating at college and studied law.

He wanted to go into politics—not to do anything in particular, not to accomplish any special purpose. His aim, like a young English aristocrat's, was to make a political career. His friends advised him to see the political boss of his county and his party; so he called on Major Lenz, the German-American Republican boss of Essex, who saw at once what use he could have for the rich, handsome son of a railroad magnate, who thought politics was speechmaking. He started Colby by letting him speak and holding out a future. The boy began, therefore, on the inside, in the machine service, and his discoveries, one by one, of the organization and purposes, crimes, humiliations, and effect of the political career were from the inside. He went to the Legislature, and he served the machine there, but with his staring, unbelieving eyes he saw— more and more. He met Mark Fagan, the Christian mayor of Jersey City; and with Mark he met George L. Record, a veteran reformer who, as a single taxer, understood economics, politics, and political economy. Just as there are business bosses back of political bosses, so there occur economic navigators behind reform sailors. Record was the master mind back of all the reforms and reformers of New Jersey for years. He, through Mark Fagan, lit up the perceptions of Everett Colby, but as they talked to him, young Colby had only to gather together what these outsiders suspected and explained the economics of to form a rounded picture of government as it is. As assemblyman for Essex, leader of the House, and as senator, the young Gentleman from Essex saw the whole thing, saw it and felt it; and finally he fought it. He combined all the various local reform fights into a movement and was leading it with large majority backings when I knew and wrote about him. It was a clear story, a pictured exposition of the system everywhere in America.

But nothing came of it. Colby disappeared. Record stayed; but Mark Fagan was beaten, finally. I never saw Colby again, never heard of him afterward. Fagan I met one Sunday as he was coming out of the Metropolitan Museum of Art. He liked pictures. He had been at one time a gilder and a cleaner of paintings, "which got me to like paintings," he said. He had been enjoying the masterpieces he knew best in the Museum, and he talked of them simply and right; he really "got" painting. We drifted from art to politics, and he said quite as simply that he was out; he was in business again. And when I asked him what it was that finally beat him he stopped and said, not expecting to be believed: "Why, it was my Church that finally beat me. They sent the Church after me, and the Church beat me with the people."

The stories of Mark Fagan and Everett Colby served a double purpose for me: they set me back up in the mind of our readers, and they introduced me well into the history of the State of New Jersey, which in two articles I traced through a long century of the process of corruption, from the time "foreign" interest began to buy it from its people to the time when its complete subservience to Philadelphia and New York was turned to the grave uses of the trusts against the other States of the Union. It was time to go to the capital of the United States and see the national system. And Theodore Roosevelt, my friend and a reformer, was president. I could "get a look in."

T.R. AS PRESIDENT

THE gift of the gods to Theodore Roosevelt was joy, joy in life. He took joy in everything he did, in hunting, camping, and ranching, in politics, in reforming the police or the civil service, in organizing and commanding the Rough Riders.

One exception was his disappointment in William H. Taft, his secretary of war, whom he chose to succeed him as president. That was bitter, but he could laugh at it and himself for mistaking his affection for judgment. Another tragedy in his life was President Wilson's refusal to give him and General Wood commands in France, and I think that he enjoyed his hate of Wilson; he expressed it so well; he indulged it so completely. Yes, I think that he took joy in his utterly uncurbed loathing for the Great War president.

But the greatest joy in T.R.'s life was at his succession to the presidency. I went to Washington to see him; many reformers went there to see the first reformer president take charge. We were like the bankers T.R. described to me, later, much later, when his administration suddenly announced a bond issue.

"It was just as if we had shot some big animal and the carcass lay there exposed for a feast. The bankers all over the country rose like buzzards, took their bearings, and then flew in a flock straight here to—the carrion."

So we reformers went up in the air when President McKinley was shot, took our bearings, and flew straight to our first president, T.R. And he understood, he shared, our joy. He was not yet living in the White House. He used the offices, which were then in the main building, upstairs on the second floor; he worked there by day, but he had to go home at night to his own residence till the McKinleys were moved out and the White House was made ready for Mrs. Roosevelt. His offices were crowded with people, mostly reformers, all day long, and the president did his work among them with little privacy and much rejoicing. He strode triumphant around among us, talking and shaking hands, dictating and signing letters, and laughing. Washington, the whole country, was in mourning, and no doubt the president felt that he should hold himself down; he didn't; he tried to, but his joy showed in every word and movement. I think that he thought he was suppressing his feelings and yearned for release, which he seized when he could. One evening after dusk, when it was time for him to go home, he grabbed William Allen White with one hand, me with the other, and saying, "Let's get out of this," he propelled us out of the White House into the streets, where, for an hour or more, he allowed his gladness to explode. With his feet, his fists, his face and with free words he laughed at his luck. He laughed at the rage of Boss Platt and at the tragic disappointment of Mark Hanna; these two had not only lost their President McKinley but had been given as a substitute the man they had thought to bury in the vice-presidency. T.R. yelped at their downfall. And he laughed with glee at the power and place that had come to him. The assassination of McKinley had affected him, true, but in a romantic way. He described what he would do if an assassin attacked him. He looked about him in the shadows of the trees we were passing under—he looked for the dastardly coward that might pounce upon him, and, it seemed to me, he hoped the would-be murderer would appear then and there—say at the next dark corner—as he described, as he enacted, what he, the president, would do to him, with his fists, with his feet, with those big, clean teeth. It would have frightened the assassin to see and hear what it was T.R. would have done to him; it may have filled Bill White with terror; what I sensed was the passionate thrill the president was actually finding in the assassination of his assassin.

I had come to Washington to find out whether the fighting reformer president, who used to see things as I saw them, saw them now as I saw them now, and what he meant to do with them. I spent my afternoons in the press gallery of the Senate and the House, watching the senators and representatives I knew about in their States at work representing—what? There was Aldrich of Rhode Island, moving about, chatting with individual senators, rarely making a speech, but busy just the same. I knew what he represented in Rhode Island. He was chairman of the finance committee of the Senate. What was he doing? Well, I knew what he was doing. And I knew what the senators he was talking to were there to do. The Senate was the chamber of the bosses. Two senators from each State, one represented the political machine that betrayed the people of his State, the other represented the leading business men of his State whom the boss worked for there. The U.S. Senate represented corruption, business, as I saw it in those days; it was a chamber of traitors, and we used to talk about the treason of the Senate. And they did not know what we meant.

Aldrich sent a page to invite me down to the Marble Room one day. I went, expecting to be asked what I meant by writing something like that about him in my article on Rhode Island. Not at all. He was very gentle, almost meek, in his friendly greeting, and all he remonstrated with me for was that I wrote that he started out as a boy in a butcher shop or a grocery.

"It was a wholesale grocery business," he said, and when I promised to correct that in my book he was satisfied. "And then," he said, "what did you mean by saying that we business men don't understand business, even our own business?"

"Well," I answered, "when you consolidated all the trolleys in Providence, you promised to give universal transfers, and you didn't. For years you fought those who tried to force you to. It was a long, corrupt, corrupting fight. And, then at last, when you were beaten and you had to give the transfers, what happened?"

"It was funny, what happened," he said. "Our earnings increased."

"I knew that would happen," I said. "I had seen it happen in other cities, and so, though I am not a street railway business man, I knew that much about your business. And you didn't. You don't. You business men don't know your own business."

He stared, crestfallen, then gently bade me good day and went back to the management of the Senate of business men, business lawyers, and business politicians who filled that chamber then.

I told the president the incident and put to him my question.

"The representatives and the senators," I said, "those that I know, those who come from States that I have investigated are picked men, chosen for their tried service to the system in their

States. They stand for all you are against; they are against all you are for. They have the departments filled with men they have had sent here to be rewarded for anti-social service, and as vacancies occur, they will want you to appoint rascals of similar records." He nodded. He knew that. T.R. saw the machine; he did not see the system. He saw the party organizations of the politicians; he saw some "bad" trusts back of the bad politics, but he did not see the good trusts back of the bad trusts that were back of the bad machines. He did not see that the corruption he resisted was a process to make the government represent business rather than politics and the people.

"I am on to the crooked machines," he said, "and the machinists, too. Yes, even in the Congress."

"What are you going to do about them and their demands for jobs for their heelers?"

"Deal with them," he snapped. "If they'll vote for my measures I'll appoint their nominees to Federal jobs. And I'm going to tell them so. They think I won't, you know. I'm going to call in a couple of machine senators and a few key congressmen and tell them I'll trade."

I protested, not at his dealing with them; that might be a way to get results. I doubted it; I would have liked then to see T.R. fight the whole system. But I protested at the time only the waste of the political strength that lay in the politicians' opinion of him. His reputation among them as a reformer who would not play the crooked game of buying votes in Congress with Federal appointments was, I argued, an asset. So long as Congressmen believed he would not do it they would ask less, prize more what they got, and serve him better for his few, reluctant concessions.

"No, no," he came back with his whole body. "I'm going at it my own way. I want service out of the men I appoint, too. So I'm going to pass the word that I'll play the game, appoint their men for their support of my bills, but"—this with his teeth showing and his fists balled—"their men that I appoint have got to take my orders and obey them up to the hilt."

That was his policy with the bosses, the political and the business agents in and out of the Senate and the House. He played the game with them; he did business with them; and he told them he would, from the very start. He did not fight, he helped build up, the political machine—and he made it partly his. I think that that was one of his purposes: to build up the party organization with enough of his appointees and to lead it with such an expectation of reward and punishment that it would nominate and help elect him to the presidency. T.R. was a politician much more than he was a reformer; in the phraseology of the radicals, he was a careerist, an opportunist with no deep insight into issues, but he was interesting, picturesque.

I accused him of this superficiality once during his first term, when he was keeping his promise to carry out McKinley's policies. That was his excuse for doing "nothing much." He was "being good" so as to be available for a second term.

"You don't stand for anything fundamental," I said, and he laughed. He was sitting behind his desk; I was standing before it. He loved to quarrel amiably with his friends, and it was hard to hit him. So now, to get in under his guard and land on his equanimity, I said with all the scorn I could put into it, "All you represent is the square deal."

"That's it," he shouted, and rising to his feet, he banged the desk with his hands. "That's my slogan: the square deal. I'll throw that out in my next statement. The square deal." And he did.

What did he care how I meant and used it? He knew how it would be taken; he felt in his political sense how all kinds of people would take it as an ideal, as a sufficient ideal, and out he threw it; and he was right. "A square deal," a phrase shot at him in reproach and criticism, he seized upon and published as his war cry; and a good one, as it proved.

Again, when I accused him of dealing with Aldrich, he met the charge with a story.

"Aldrich?" he said. "Aldrich is a great man to me; not personally, but as the leader of the Senate. He is a king pin in my game. Sure. I bow to Aldrich; I talk to Aldrich; I respect him, as he does not respect me. I'm just a president, and he has seen lots of presidents. He, Aldrich, bows to J. P. Morgan. Morgan's a banker. The other day J. P. Morgan came to Washington, and he and I and Aldrich had a—a—a conference. That's the word"—this with a laugh and a leer—"conference. And I noticed how he, Morgan, addressed himself to me, not to Aldrich. Aldrich was a senator, and bankers know, they meet, lots of senators. Senators are all in their day's work. But presidents—Morgan talked to me, while I talked to Aldrich, who talked to Morgan. And there we sat—I can see us there; I saw it at the time, and I could hardly help laughing out loud—I, a president, half turned to and ad-

NELSON W. ALDRICH: "POLITICAL BOSS OF THE UNITED STATES"
The San Francisco Bulletin, March 17, 1906

dressing the senator, the senator turned to and addressing the banker, and the banker facing and speaking to me, the president of the United States."

He laughed hilariously, slapped his knee, and saw it again, with joy, without any regard for my remonstrance with his dickering and dealing with the boss of the U.S. And when I repeated my objections to Aldrich, he pushed me away: "Ah, go on. Don't I dicker and deal with you, too, and you are a reporter, the press. To play up to you is to play the demagogue, to get the people you write pieces to."

My dickering and dealing against Aldrich was to draw the president into an alliance with the other reform leaders who were gradually coming to the Senate to replace the Aldriches, Spooners, Platts. What became the Progressive party was a movement already, and we muckrakers were expressing it and making votes for the future. Roosevelt saw that; he acknowledged its force and vitality, but he knew also where the power was, and the power was still in the old "gang," in the old machines. LaFollette of Wisconsin was one of the first of the new leaders to reach the Senate. I got a promise, very reluctant, from him to meet the president when he came to Washington to be sworn in, and I wangled a promise—equally reluctant—from the president to receive LaFollette. I was happy over the prospect of an open leadership for the national progressive movement; I knew how hard this was to achieve, because I had noticed that local or State leaders of reform were characteristically lone leaders, who could not work with other men, especially with their equals; they had subordinates about them. But T.R. was not afraid of his equals or even of superiors. When he appointed Elihu Root in his cabinet, I objected that Root represented the trusts and high finance and was so able that he would run his president. T.R. made that fierce face of his, and with his hands and his teeth, said, "I'm not afraid of Root, and you'll see. When he is here under me I'll 'run' him, as you call it. He will serve my policies."

So I had no fear that T.R. would rebuff LaFollette. They did not like each other, but my only doubt was of LaFollette. When they met at the White House, the president and the senator, it was comic. They began to back off from each other before they met; their hands touched, but their eyes, their bodies, their feet walked away. I don't recall a word that either of them said; they probably said nothing but "glad to meet you." It was all over in a second, and I was outside with LaFollette, who hurried away.

The progressive movement went on with leaders, but no leader —as it must, I guess. Bosses are possible, not leaders, in politics; and issues—except the square deal—are born, not made.

XXII

THE PRESIDENT IS SHAVED

A GREAT political ambition was taking hold of me, and the presidency of my old friend Roosevelt was my opportunity to achieve my high purpose. I told him about it; or I tried to. It was hard to tell him anything; it was easy to make him talk, even about a State secret, but to reverse the process and make him listen was well-nigh impossible. John Morley, who tried to converse, likened the president's monologue to Niagara Falls, but T.R. was more like a mighty dam which would break and drown you at your first word. So now, when I mentioned my ambition, he burst.

"Ambition! You? I thought you disapproved of ambition. You used to when we were policemen together in New York. I told you then that you were wrong, and I'll tell you now that you are right. And I'll give you a chance to prove it to yourself. You can have any office you like, in my gift—almost."

The last word, "almost," was a thought; the rest was only a flood of generous impulse, and more was coming; an essay on ambition was rising to overwhelm me. But I had him. When I had asked him to fix an hour when I could see him any day, he had looked at his schedule and said he had no time left, but, seeing my disappointment, he looked again and pounced upon a time.

"I'll tell you," he said. "You can have the barber's hour. He comes in to shave me every day at 12.40, and you can come in with him."

Lucky arrangement it turned out to be. It gave me two shots at a purpose. Since he would pour forth at your first suggestion, I always came into the room primed with a question that I fired quick; and he went off. All the time the barber worked the president would talk till—the second shot—the razor was working upon T.R.'s lower lip. Then I had a second chance to get in a word to hold or turn the flood of his monologue.

The eulogy of ambition flowed with the razor over his cheeks, chin, neck, but when the barber bent over the presidential head and began to shave the lower lip, I explained.

My high ambition was not to hold or even to fill and do the work of a political office, but to change the criterion of political criticism. I would investigate the Federal government as I had municipal and State government and so do it as to raise the question—not necessarily to answer, but to ask and make everybody ask—what our representative government represented.

The president wriggled, twisted; he was ready already to break out over me, but I had begged the barber to shave the lip close and slow, and he was holding on. "Steady, Mr. President."

"Why keep on asking whether a senator is honest when what we want to know is whether he represents us, the people, or some special interest? Or a president," I tossed in, partly to heighten the agony. "Are you honest? And what if you are? You might be honest and honestly represent the railroads or Wall Street. Honesty is a matter of intelligence, really; or the opposite. There's some conflict between honesty and intelligence. But here we all are asking all the time whether this man or that Congressman is a crook or an honest man, and only a crook is honest enough and intelligent enough to know what we all should want to know, namely, whether he stands for the tariff grafters or the consumers—"

"One moment, Mr. President," the barber said to the writhing honest president; "one moment, please."

"Now what I want to do," I said, "is to go around Washington here asking you and the Congress and the departments, what you represent, you representatives, and leave your immortal souls to—the clergy."

The barber jumped back, his razor high in the air, and I backed off a little, as the president sprang upright in the chair and was off.

"You can't do that," he shouted. "You can ask the question, but you can't make others ask it. They'll all go back to honesty—and want to know if we are good men and sincere. And it is a moral question, politics, and—" so on. The barber bathed his face in cool water, combed his hair, and did all he could to soothe the man, but the monologue on morality flowed. "Even if you find a senator misrepresenting us," he said, "you will have to discover why, and if the reason isn't a bribe it's no use. That senator is honest and all right."

"Not with me," I interjected.

"Nor with me," he closed. "But we are talking about getting the voters to take your point of view."

"And the leaders—"

"And you're too sweeping," he continued. "An honest man can be for a protective tariff—"

"If he's not intelligent," I helped, but it did not help. That caused a crash. He got off on the tariff and used my "narrowness" to prove how dangerous my question was; and from that to good intentions; and from that— He was called to luncheon, and he hunched into his coat, and talking all the time, he banged out, slammed the door, talking, I am sure, on the other side. I'll bet his luncheon guests got it that day. For he was thinking, and his form of thinking was talking, talking aloud. Which was encouraging to me. He might talk himself into thinking my way—enough to let me write my experimental articles.

And speaking of his talking: I was listening to him think aloud in his office one cabinet day, and as the members of his cabinet came in one by one and took their seats at the great table—all in full view—in the cabinet room, T.R. did not look at them. He was talking about Wall Street and the opposition growing against him down there. After a while, when the cabinet was all seated, the president rose slowly, thinking aloud, and said, "I must go now"; and he saw me to the door next to the wide-open double doors of the cabinet room. I stepped into the hall, and meeting Loeb, the secretary to the president, halted to talk with him, but as we stood there I could see through another door into the cabinet room. The president was standing back of his chair and looking, not at the cabinet, but at Loeb and me absentmindedly till, his eyes fixed, he beckoned to me, and himself darted to the side door.

"Say," he said, still to himself, "they are passing around some wild stories about me in Wall Street, that I drink to excess, actually get drunk, and even that I take dope. Now what should I do about that? Should I take it up and fight it or should I ignore it?"

Obviously he did not expect an answer; he was asking himself the question. But just for fun I answered him. In the same absent-minded, unemphatic way that he had spoken, I said: "Ah, Mr. President, if I were you, I would in that case follow your good old rule in all such matters."

"Old rule?" he repeated in a daze. "My old rule? What old rule?"

"Never to deny anything unless it is true," I said quietly.

"Never—deny—anything—unless it's—" He was saying it quietly, as I had, but he woke up suddenly. "Ah, go on," he exclaimed, and he thrust me away down the hall and laughed and closed the door. And I heard him laughing in the cabinet room as if he were telling it to his advisers—whom I did not hear laughing.

He did eventually nail that lie. He brought a suit. T.R.'s vice was not drink; he tasted wine at meals, as people in wine countries learn to do; and he had no need for more. He was himself strong drink. His vice was eating; it was not bad enough to be called gluttony, but he was a fast and an enormous eater. A good, big dinner and a lively company would make him almost drunk. I remember one evening when, after such a dinner, he came out into a reception room to keep an appointment with me. He closed the door behind him, and as I rose, he commanded "Sit down" and himself sank into a big chair. He was excited; talked; got up, walked about, sat again. A bucket of iced Apollinaris was served, and he drank that, glass after glass. He had eaten too much. Up and down he got, and, as I stood up and sat down with him as inconspicuously as I could, he roared: "Sit down, and stay down. That's why I asked you to come at this hour; I couldn't have stayed in there where they all—men and women, too—rise when I rise, sit when the president sits. It's awful. It's unbearable. I want, after dinner, to move about and— Well, I won't have you bobbing up and down as I do. You sit and stay seated."

He hated forms; everybody knew that, but I had never seen him so fierce about it as that night. He usually laughed, as he did when he told some of us how he had entertained two distinguished English army officers who called on him with letters.

"They were sportsmen," he said, "riders, hunters, walkers, but they were stiff before me. I was the president, you see, the representative of American sovereignty, and they knew how to behave in the presence of the king. Bah. I said: 'Let's take a walk. No. Just as we are. I'll not change.' So they couldn't. In our best afternoon clothes, therefore, we set out and—I know the worst way—we crossed roads and fields, jumped fences, and— Oh, they kept up. They'd have died rather than fail the king. They tore along after me, kept close up, and I felt they were beating me at my own game. But I had an idea. I made a big swing around to come home and struck the middle of a duck pond. You know. Not deep, up to my waist, but covered with duck oil. You know. There they hesitated. Not I. I marched right in, keeping the conversation going, and—well, they gasped, but in they waded, and so, conversing politely, as two gentlemen and the king, we crossed, up to our bellies, and came out, dripping, but polite and unnoticing; we came up to the White House and—we bowed, formally, and like three courtly rats, we shook hands and parted."

I thought and I remarked that those British officers had a story to tell.

"Yes!" he said. "But they'll never tell it. They are gentlemen, and"—this with a wry face—"you do not repeat what you hear or tell what you see in the presence of the king."

I kept before him my purpose to write up Washington, he resisting, I urging, for months. His consent was necessary because I proposed to use his experiences, his story, his conflict with the system there, as my material, and he naturally did not care to take the risk of my possible indiscretions and his.

"We are both lacking in discretion," he said. "You go and do other cities and other—"

"Heroes," I offered, "who don't matter."

He didn't laugh at that sally. He said simply: "That's funny. That is just exactly what I mean: that my case is important and that others are not. Sounds pretty selfish, doesn't it?"

This was T.R.'s head trying to understand his own thoughts, which occurred somewhere else in his nervous system. He was not an "intellectual"; he was a man of action. He read everything, he knew a lot, and he had what he knew always handy. He could talk well on many subjects. But he often did not know why he did what he did, gave reasons instead of his actual motives for conduct.

The point about his unwillingness to tell me his experiences with the system, with the machines in the Senate and the House, with the courts, with the local District government of the city of Washington, and with Wall Street, was that he was not fighting these but trying to work with them. He was not a reformer in the

White House; he was a careerist on the people's side, but working
to wangle some concessions from the powers that be and make them
do some things for the country at large. He had come to see that
it did not matter so much what the reason or the bribe was that
made a senator go "wrong"; he acknowledged privately that the
essential thing was what the man represented, how he voted on roll
call on bills that expressed the issue between democracy and plutocracy. And he did finally consent to my scheme. But for a long
while he would not let me do it, with his collaboration, because in
his hips, in his bones, he knew that he was not a hero fighting for
a representative democracy. I went off therefore on trips to other
men, like Ben Lindsey and W. S. U'ren, who were openly in conflict with the system. I kept coming back to Washington to follow
Roosevelt's course, and I used to tell him, for a purpose, what I
was seeing; and he understood all this; he reacted like a democrat
and like an historian to it all, but he was slow to move himself.

"I am fighting, too," he would say, and once he gave as an
example: "My bills to regulate and to control railroads and trusts
—they make the issue. They bring me into a straight, open fight
with the special interests."

"Yes," I said. "They might do it if you fought hard and
straight, but you compromise. You let the railroads amend your
railroad bill. It's only 'a' railroad law you want; not to cut the
railroads out of the government."

"A law?" he repeated.

"Yes, a law—the best bill which you can get the railroads to consent to."

And characteristically, he proved my argument. He dug out
and showed me a letter signed by A. J. Cassatt, the president of
the Pennsylvania Railroad, analyzing and pleading for altera-
tions in the railroad bill then up in Congress. He showed it to me
and pointed out the concessions asked for, which he thought he
might make, to get it through.

T.R. was an honest mind. He stood for the square deal even in
an argument, even in a discussion of his own faith. But he had no
economics, he never understood the political issue between the
common and the special interests; neither as a police commissioner
nor as a president did he grasp the difference between morality and
representation.

"Whom did you fire from the police force?" I asked him once in the White House when we were talking about good and bad senators.

"Crooks," he answered.

"No, you didn't," I contradicted. "You fired crooks who would not stand with you, you kept the crooks who helped you enforce the law because it was the law."

He grinned, thinking of some good police crooks that we both liked.

"You like honest crooks, just as we all do," I hammered, "and you hate some honest men, like the rest of us. All you ask, really, is that, crooked or honest, they shall be on your side and represent you."

"But I represent the common good," he declared.

"Fine. Then why not see what you and all of us should see and ask: that representatives shall represent us, the people?"

"The people won't understand that," he objected, and that objection was a hip thought, a hunch. "You can't make the voters see that the police force represents criminals, only that the Tammany policemen are crooks."

So we left it till the president of the people could see—what the people couldn't.

"CARTE BLANCHE" FROM THE PRESIDENT

XXIII

BEN LINDSEY: THE KIDS' JUDGE

WHILE President Roosevelt did not seek to unite and lead
the reform movements round about him, he was willing
to be followed by the local and State reformers. If LaFollette had met him with any hint of lieutenancy, the president would
have welcomed him as he did other reformers who were not out-
and-out against the system as a whole. But T.R. sensed the dangerous fact that the Wisconsin leader, having beaten the machine
in his State and restored constitutional democratic government
there, meant to fight the business organization of the Senate and
everywhere else. And LaFollette saw that Roosevelt as president
was working with the Senate, the party machine, with the system.
LaFollette would have made the Federal government govern, as
he had made his State government sovereign over railroads, public
service corporations, business as well as the people. T.R. was
broaching and even forcing some measures to regulate business,
which brought him up against certain businesses and which might
have raised into plain sight the actual issue of that day: special vs.
the common interests; plutocracy vs. democracy. But, when the
lines were drawn, T.R. sent, not for the reform leaders, but for
Aldrich and Lodge, Cassatt or Morgan.

"We are both practical men," he wrote to Cassatt.

He compromised to get his bill through; he let the railroads
amend his railroad bill in order to win them and their senators to
pass it. President Roosevelt governed with the consent of the
governors. LaFollette would have governed them with the consent only of the people they misgoverned.

Hamilton and Jefferson again, and it remains to be seen which
is the better way. Jefferson's ideals of political democracy prevailed then. Even the Hamiltonians, the very corrupters of gov-

ernment, had been brought up with democratic ideals. Whatever men did, they thought pretty much our way; there was conflict inside the heads of individuals as well as outside in society. It would have been easy to make the democratic issue an actual political division. For, with all the variety of purposes of the many reform movements scattered over the United States, the leaders always came finally to a fight with the system. I used to tell reformers who asked me what to do to start out with any reform that their people understood, to fight for it and watch for the opposition; then to turn and fight the interest back of that till other, greater interests appeared behind that; to turn then and fight these. They would soon find and be forced to fight the united organization of all the grafts which, together, governed their city, State, and nation.

Ben Lindsey's story showed me this apparent truth. He started with the children and ended with organized society against him. A county judge in Denver, he was grinding out legal justice honestly, blindly, till one day a mother's cry in the back of his court room startled him into consciousness. He had just tried and sentenced to imprisonment the woman's son, and he looked at the boy. I mean that he looked as a human being at the bad boy, and he saw that the boy wasn't so bad. He had done a bad thing, but he was just a boy. The judge came down off the bench. He retried the frightened defendant with the mother as a witness, and brushing aside the law, he let the prisoner go, him and his mother. He suspended sentence, and he went off himself to see the jail where he had been sending such boys. He saw. That jail, like most jails, was a school of crime. It was a lousy place where filthy bums and hard criminals practiced vice, and talked, and taught the tricks and the ideals of the criminal life.

Judge Ben B. Lindsey came thus to represent the children, not the law and not yet democracy and the people, but only the children of the people. He tried the young criminals as he had the first mother's boy; he had to fight the police. When they brought in "really bad boys," kids that had committed bold crimes, the kind that become big criminals and bandits, and the judge came down from the bench to talk with them understandingly, the police protested. "You can't mollycoddle this boy, Judge. He's stolen bicycles [or whatever], and we got to get back the property." "Yes,

I know. You're thinking of the property, but I'm thinking of the boy. I'll recover the bicycles for you; won't I, kid? And I'll save the boy, too."

Ben Lindsey discovered about children what I was discovering about men: that there are no bad boys and girls, and no good ones either. There are only strong boys and girls and weak boys and girls. The bad ones whom the police were really afraid of, the boys and girls who did very bad things, who committed robberies and hold-ups, rode the brakes of trains, and dared to do bold criminal acts—they were so strong that, when Lindsey put it up to them to control themselves and do what he called "good things," they were able to respond and deliver the goods. They could take their fares and their commitment papers and go alone, with no cop to guard them, to the reform school. The good boys and girls could not do that. They were either little prigs or weaklings who were led into crime by their leaders, the bad boys, but they wished "the kids' judge" could make them try to master themselves. In a word, there was so much good will among them that Judge Lindsey began to ask what made all these good boys and girls say and do such vicious things.

When an especially bad child came or was brought before him and he talked with and won the confidence of the criminal, he would ask to be taken "home" and shown the neighborhood where bad kids lived and played. The judge found that the bad kids spoke the language, expressed the ideas, and had the ideals of the adults they were brought up with. His child guides led him to bad parents, bad homes, bad neighborhoods, to slums, mostly, and to the Tenderloin, where the police and society were the enemies, vice and crime and ward politics the business or the adventures, of life. Lindsey proposed to wipe out the Tenderloin and improve the slums. Not much bigger than a boy and as naïvely logical as a child, his idea was to abolish the conditions which made strong boys and girls do bad things.

He started to clean up, and at first there was no opposition. Who would not help save the kids? A politician then, Lindsey went to the other politicians, and they did some of the things he wanted done—quietly but well. He forgets this. The kids' judge has never been able to learn about grown-ups what he discovered about the children, that it is conditions or some *thing* that makes strong men and women do bad things. He had not gone very far when he encountered opposition from bad men, he said. Gamblers, the keepers and owners of brothels, brewery and liquor interests, rose and united to stop him. They also were living under conditions that had to be changed. But Lindsey's purpose was so sensible that sensible men and women rallied to his support. Some reformers appeared to lead, and there was a fight, and the reformers won it. Most people were for the Juvenile Court and its judge, who was becoming famous and making Denver famous.

But this fight and the others that followed disturbed things as they were in Denver; the party machines and bosses felt threatened. Lindsey and his group had no ambition for political or business power or even for offices, but the votes they won, the secret ballots cast for them, altered the balance of power. The cleaning up of the slums and the Tenderloin would take away from the political bosses the shifting vote which, as they bought and placed it, gave them the decision as between the nearly equally balanced votes of the good citizens who were loyal to their parties. As in my other cities, it was not the good citizens; it was the purchasable minority that swung from one party to the other and so decided elections. Lindsey's reform of the low-down wards where children were made bad was a menace to the power of the machines which were contending for the privilege of serving the public utility and other business interests. The political bosses explained this to the business bosses, who passed the word to their fellow captains of industry, to their directors, stockholders and customers, and to their wives and their ministers—to all the good people of the better classes, that Lindsey's work for children might be very good in itself, but it was hurting business; and so he must be taught or forced to keep out of politics. He could deal with the children after they had done evil, but he must not interfere with the conditions which led them into evil. Those conditions were a part of the conditions that made business good and paid dividends.

Lindsey and his friends saw this, too, and they began to fight the public utilities and other corrupting businesses which depended upon poverty, vice, and bad politics. They and the whole town learned to see the connection. A new business was started in Colorado; cotton mills were built, and the chamber of commerce was enthusiastic over the development of a new enterprise. But

Lindsey heard and saw that, to compete with the south, Colorado would have to furnish children to work in those mills. He beat the new cotton industry. He came upon graft in the Board of County Commissioners; he exposed that. He came to care about the welfare of labor, which had so many children, and that brought him into a clash with Colorado Fuel and Iron, and employers generally. In brief, Lindsey was soon at war with the whole system which was the government of his State and of its colleges, churches, and of society. He has told the whole story in his book, *The Beast and the Jungle*. He carried on for years. He lobbied bills for his Juvenile Court through the Legislature; he had parents and adults generally made answerable to the court for their fault in the offenses of children. He had influence with the bad politicians, who understood what he was up to and were willing to slip over a decent law. It was the top of society that was against the judge, the lawyers who were not needed in children's cases as Lindsey conducted them, clergymen and teachers; and these, the professional, business, and social leaders, were weakened by the secret services Lindsey had rendered them by saving their own children from jail and public disgrace. It was the lower classes, honest labor and the growing children themselves, who voted *en bloc* and carried voters for Ben Lindsey.

There have been other juvenile courts modeled upon Lindsey's since his proved so useful. They have not had to fight so hard, but they did not follow through as their prophet did. They established institutions, as the followers of Christ founded churches, and they minded their own business as the Christians kept out of politics. They save the children; the juvenile courts of some cities are as efficient as Denver's, but they did not try to remove the social and economic causes of the evil-doing of children.

In the sunny days when I was sitting in the parks of Denver hearing Ben Lindsey's story, I was struck by the logic of his course from effect back to causes—as a method; by his daring, triumphant experiments with the strength he felt and appealed to in bad boys (he would not then talk for publication about his bad girls); and most of all I was influenced by the observation that this man was applying Christianity to a very practical problem.

XXIV

MUCKRAKING MYSELF—A LITTLE

A s a journalist, I was keen to deal with certain sayings which men used to express their unformed thoughts and save themselves from the labor of thinking out what they meant. "Don't knock; boost," was one of these thought-savers. It was the grafters' answer to all muckraking, and, passed on to the absentminded citizens, we heard it everywhere. To meet it halfway, I persuaded one of the writers on *Life* to print a cartoon of a burglar, caught climbing into a window by a policeman with a club, looking down and saying, "Don't knock, boost."

Another universal saying of those days was that "capital and labor should get together," as if the interminable struggle of these conflicting interests could be settled by a conference. While working in Chicago, I came across a local newspaper scandal over the corruption by the big employers of the labor unions in the building trades, and I recalled that in New York a similar exposure was brewing. The leading builders had recognized the unions, bought the labor leaders, and used their power to call strikes on the smaller, independent contractors and so drive out competition. I wrote to the editors of *McClure's* to send out some one to describe, first, the Chicago facts and then to follow up with the New York parallel, to show that capital and labor had got together and that the result was conspiracies to establish monopolies in the business of building.

Ray Stannard Baker came to Chicago, and with my references for a start and my idea for a title, wrote a stirring article, "Capital and Labor Get Together." His article overshadowed mine on Illinois, and when I got home, my wife remonstrated with me for "giving away my ideas." I had not thought of that. My answer to her was that it didn't matter who wrote the article; the important thing was to get the idea out. I was not only an article-writer; I was an editor, and—and, besides, Baker and my colleagues knew it was my idea. "Nonsense," she said; "Baker will never remember from whom he got the subject," and she invited him to dinner and asked him how he came to write that article. He told her the genesis of it, with no mention of me! She won, smiled, and I felt —yellow; whether with jealousy of Baker or humiliation at the

LINCOLN STEFFENS   R. S. BAKER

"THESE, LADIES AND GENTLEMEN, ARE MAGA-
ZINE REFORMERS . . ."
The World, December 3, 1905

defeat by my wife, I don't know. It was an old cause of friction between her and me: my habit of "telling all I knew" and her insistence upon my "career." The incident made me feel mean.

The reason my professional jealousy made me feel so bad was that I was righteous. With all my growing contempt for good people, I was one of them. Unconsciously I wanted to be one of them. How could that be? I saw those law-abiding backbones of society, in city after city, start out for a moral reform—of course; they were for anything good; and they backed the reformers quietly but solidly till they were told (by their banker or their paper) or until they felt that the reform was affecting them socially or economically; then I saw them halt, turn back, and say that reform was "going too far." That was another of the thought-savers of the educated who think that they think. No reform could get anywhere without going too far; any reform that is to accomplish anything worth while must go on and on until it catches and hurts these men and women; I was preferring the conscious crooks; and yet I was one of the righteous.

I learned this of myself by trying to write a fiction story in the course of which I had to describe the inner thoughts of a bribe-taker. And I could not. I never took a bribe; so I thought I did not know and could not divine the psychology of bribery. A murder, yes; I had been angry enough to contemplate killing; but bribery—no. I had not ever been tempted by money. Had I?

Hadn't I? I put off thinking this out and facing my yellow streak till my next long, lone railroad journey. That was on one of those fine trains which nobody traveled in on the Lackawanna road. I had a Pullman car all to myself and a clear day ahead. The porter was ordered to be attentive; so I put him off by telling him that he must leave me alone all day. I told him why, too.

"I have to find and face my yellow streak," I said, "and convince myself that I'm a crook."

It was a hard day's work. The yellow was easy. I did have the streak. My professional jealousy may not have been dominant; absentmindedness covered it pretty well. But my wife, who had presence of mind, knew me better than I knew myself; and all she had to do was to scratch the surface and there it was: envy, jealousy, and all the rest. The only trouble I had was to face the yellow and call it yellow and say to myself that I was—what I was. It's odd that I hate to say it even now when I know that we all have some yellow and that it's only a matter of degree. But I did face myself down that day, and the porter saw it in my behavior or my face. He had been watching me on and off, and now when I arrived at a satisfactory conclusion he came up the aisle.

"Did ya catch the crook, boss?" he asked.

"No," I said. "I saw the yellow, and now I've got to see the crook."

That was more strenuous. I took the stream of my wishing to be intelligent, rather than good; I was conscious of whatever I did that was crooked. But I did not take bribes; I didn't want money, no, nor honors. Hadn't I refused a doctor's degree? Hadn't I declined to be put short of a stock I was writing down? Then I was—not as other men; I was, in brief, not only honest, I was righteous. I backed off. I didn't want to go where I was arriving. I didn't want to be righteous, and there I was, exactly like the righteous who were corrupted by their own ignorance of their own graft. How did I differ from them? They also thought they were not bribed; and they didn't do anything felonious. But they were slowed up as reformers and voters by—what? By their business interest. They were not bought by the briber's money; they were bribed by their own money. And—so was I. Nobody could, by an offer of money, make me suppress a fact or color a truth, but—yes, I did go a bit slow—sometimes—in something I wrote. Why? To keep my job, to keep my credit, to hold my readers and "get by" my editors. Well, that was it. I was cheap, like any other good man; I did not come high, like an honest crook; I could be "got" with my own salary. And the psychology of that was the psychology of the bribe-taker, whether the bribe-taker knew he was a bribe-taker or thought that he was an honest man.

What a relief! What a humiliation and what an advantage! Now I could be as good as I liked and not be a righteous man any more. I could be intelligent; I could do a crooked thing and not be either a cynic or a fool. I would be able to face the men I admired—the men who did bribery and corruption, and knew it—and talk about it with them—honestly.

Now all this is relevant here in this narrative because of a very curious and probably significant result. I was never again mistaken for an honest man by a crook. Good people have often erred; they take me sometimes as one of them, too radical, but—honest. But the politicians, the big, bad ones and the little, intelligent ones, they and the consciously corrupting business leaders have ever since acted with me upon the understanding that I was one of them. It facilitated my work; it explains much of my success in getting at the facts of a situation. The porter that day, as he was brushing me off, said that I acted more's if I'd escaped than's if I'd got caught.

"I did," I said, "I caught myself and then I let myself go."

But my generalization about good people was too sweeping. There were exceptions that troubled me, and I soon struck a lead that cleared me somewhat. There was an investigation in Wisconsin of the repurchase by a lumber senator of his seat in the Senate. He had "opened a barrel at both ends," and his agent who handled the money was snitching on the stand. He told how he had bought up ward after ward in Milwaukee, all sorts of wards, poor and rich, disreputable and highly respectable, but there were exceptions. He couldn't buy certain wards, "didn't even try." Why? "Oh, I knew it was no use." What was the matter with them? "They were bum wards," he said. Pressed for an explanation, he said that they were "all socialists."

The socialists were jubilant, of course, but it could not mean that socialists were different from other men. Socialists were not particularly honest. There must be some other reason, some objective difference, and knowing Milwaukee and the socialists there and their activity, enthusiasm, and their power (they were approaching election to office, since achieved and held), I concluded that it was their vision, their imminent hope, of a better world that made them unpurchasable. They were as honest as any fanatics are; they were believers in some hopeful vision. And then I asked myself a question. If it was vision that made such a difference in men, vision is what we need in the world. What vision, what belief in the future, could be introduced among men? And suddenly it occurred to me that Christianity conveyed such a faith, hope, and—vision. And the good people that went so wrong, in politics, had that belief. What did the Christians believe, exactly? I decided then and there to read the New Testament the next time I was at home and had time, not myself to believe, but to see what the good, church-going Christians believed.

The experience was an adventure so startling that I wanted everybody else to have it; I still recommend people to re-read the New Testament as I read it, without reverence, with feet up on a desk and a pipe in the mouth, as news. It is news. It made the stuff I was writing in the magazine, old stuff. All my stories of all the cities and States were one story; they had different names, dates, and locations, but the essential facts were the same in them all; and these were all in that old story of Christ in the New Testament. Jesus had discovered and declared, for example, the worthlessness of the good people. He said that he could not save the righteous, only sinners. The righteous believed that! There was more, much more.

This child of the people, Jesus, born and brought up in a humble carpenter's family in a little village in Palestine, was unusually intelligent, far-seeing, and thoughtful. He saw a way out; he set forth to save the world, and the people heard him gladly. Just like Folk, Lindsey, LaFollette, Tom Johnson, Mark Fagan. He said things and he did things; he was pretty clear, but he went too far, and the better people turned against him; they plotted with the priests and the leading citizens until they won the mob to rise against him. Then they bribed one of his disciples to betray him to the police and the judge of the system. And the judge, a man of the world, gave the people the choice between the prophet of love and peace and a robber leader who practiced force; and the mob, led by the best people, preferred Barabbas and let Jesus go hang. He was crucified, just as my leaders of the people were crucified.

Did the Christians know this? Did the churches preach it, and the rest of his teachings, the economic changes he must have taught his followers? The Acts of the Apostles showed them practicing communists!—as if he knew that they could not practice Christianity under the system; they could not love one another under our intense competition. He had evidently tried not only to preach Christianity, but proposed also a scheme to make it possible! The Christian churches seem to have overlooked that detail. They overlooked the vision, too.

For several years after that reading I visited the churches. Wherever I was on a Sunday—and I was in many, many places—I went to church—to many, many churches of many denominations; and I never heard this preached. I have never heard Christianity, as Jesus taught it in the New Testament, preached to the Christians. But I did see it practiced, in politics. It was an element in every reform movement that won the support of the people. I saw it applied by individuals to bad men, women, and children. I began to try it myself; and it worked. Christianity, unpreached and untaught and unlearned among the righteous, works wonders still among the sinners. I would put it to a public test some day and see how it worked on a grand scale and see also who saw it.

XXV

LIFE INSURANCE

WHILE I had been reporting political corruption, Ray Stannard Baker had been describing the corruption of labor unions by contractors in the building business, and Miss Ida M. Tarbell had been writing the history of the Standard Oil Company, which was a story of a group of business men committing crimes such as arson, corrupting politics and railroads, seeking legal and economic advantages, such as rebates, over their competitors, and fiercely abusing their ill-gotten power to form a monopoly. Baker and I were finding that business was back of labor and political evils; Miss Tarbell, that business itself was "bad." Naturally. The source of so much evil must be itself evil. But Miss Tarbell's exposure of the Standard Oil was met with the excuse that that company was exceptionally bad and new; we had had in a previous generation similar stories of Gould, Vanderbilt, Jim Fisk, and of their railroads. These, however, were also new businesses at that time. It might well be that it was new businesses that were bad, chartered or privileged business, not business as such. The public service corporations, which succeeded the railroads, took over from them the burden of keeping politics and government for business. But the railroads stayed in politics after they had all they wanted and were through. And so did the public utilities after they were through.

Why? I asked the manager of the Street Railway in Cincinnati that question when I was in his town. I reminded him that his company had got in its Foraker law all that it asked for, all that any other such company had ever been granted, more than it could ever use. He nodded; true. "And yet," I said, "the politicians all agree that you are the first and biggest contributor to the corruption of politics here. Now why?"

"Did you ever notice what our capitalization is?"

"Yes," I said. "Fifty-five millions."

"Well," he drawled, "I think—I'm not sure, but I reckon that I could rebuild and reëquip these roads for eight or nine—say, eleven millions."

"Well?"

"JOHN THE BAPTIST: HIGH FINANCE IS NOW GETTING SO HIGH THAT SOME PEOPLE EXPECT TO GET TO HEAVEN FROM THE TOP OF IT."—*Life*

Ida M. Tarbell had been writing the history of the Standard Oil Company

"Well," he smiled, "the difference between eleven millions and fifty-five millions is the measure of our—our vulnerability."

No honest government would let a public utility charge the people of a city fares to cover the interest or dividends on forty-four millions of watered stock. So the street railway, like the other watered railways, like other businesses that were doing something unsocial, "had to" get into politics and stay there to protect their —vulnerability. "Business is business," they said in those days; and my theory was not only that politics and government were business, but that business too was business, corrupt like the politics it corrupted.

But no, the answer of business and of the public mind was that business itself was good—honest, efficient, faithful. "And"—this was the enraging saying that saved so much thought, stirred so much feeling and misled so many voters and writers and speakers —"the cure for our bad politics and our inefficient government is the election to office of good business men who would give us a good, businesslike government." No. Not men like Rockefeller or Gould, but, you know, good business men from good, old businesses, not railroads, not the Standard Oil, but old, established, respectable businesses.

Then came the exposure of the life insurance companies, a revelation of graft to an extent that made my cities look restrained. "Say," said a Chicago politician, "if we did anything like that— you'd call us—"

"Be careful," I warned him.

"Well, then," he moderated, "let's say you'd call us—gentlemen."

And I recalled how Richard Croker and Ed Butler had declared when caught and shamed that "anyhow we're better'n them."

There was petty graft in life insurance and big stealings, "pulls" and "jobs" and high finance. There was collusion, and outrageous prices in stationery bills and all supplies were a graft, an old, grown graft. There were building scandals, with the officers of the companies making fortunes out of the construction of the conspicuous buildings they erected in different cities, just as in municipal politics there were scandalous conspiracies for the building at double cost of city halls, court houses, jails. And, to be brief, it was the likeness of the business graft in a business to the so-called political graft in our cities and States that fascinated me. For here was the government of business by business men I had been hearing about so long. And by good business men, too, governing an old, respectable business. These life insurance companies were not profit-making concerns; only one of them was a stock company, and that, the Equitable, had put out but a small issue of shares, for the declared purpose of keeping the business in the control of good, safe, honest men. Otherwise they were as like in their charters as our cities are. They were founded, conducted, and advertised as the "sacred trusts of widows and orphans"; on that theory they lobbied at Legislatures for special privileges, and with that slogan they appealed to all the world; and fathers, mothers, guardians, and children furnished all the money the companies had for life insurance policies of various sorts to provide for the needy when the need came.

As managers of big national trust funds the officers chosen were likely to be, and they were regarded as, especially unselfish, able, trustworthy men, such, let us say, as the business world would choose to be mayors, governors, presidents; and the great boards of directors (very large bodies of very honorable men, picked for distinction in all lines of business, with financiers predominating) must have been the kind of men business would have sent to our political Legislatures, Congress. Some of them were in the U.S. Senate. Well, these executives were exposed as corrupt or inefficient; they either knew what was going on under them or they should have known; some of them did know; some of them were the leading conspirators in the jobs put over. And as for those solemn, pretentious boards of directors who legislated for those trust funds and for the widows and orphans who depended on them —it was revealed that they were known as "dummy directors" for the same reason that our legislators are in fact dummy representatives. Together these picked officers and directors gave a government of this picked business so rotten that it would not have survived in politics. When I had seen it all, as it came out, I said to business men in Wall Street that they should turn the insurance business over to some picked politicians; I could pick crooks who would do better than those highly respectable business men. But the questions I asked were: What about other businesses? Weren't they as badly run? Is not the business government of business generally worse than the political government of and for business? If a public, non-profit, trust business is as bad as the life insurance, what must be the condition of some of the private businesses that are run only for profits?

This line of inquiry seemed to frighten business men, and they were most emphatic in their denial of my aspersion. But I had a rejoinder. The life insurance exposures began with one company, and remembering that as one city was, so were the others, I called upon prominent gentlemen I knew personally in the other companies and asked them if their company was not in the same condition. They all said no; of course they would; but I noticed that some of them denied me calmly as if they really were sure, while others became excited and acted as if they knew better (or worse).

As if they knew what turned out to be true—that as one life insurance was, so were the others, exactly. And I remember that, toward the end, when we knew all about the sacred business of life insurance, I besought the investigators to poke into fire insurance and see what they found. They wouldn't, not then; but a few years later there was a suspicious fire in a big warehouse. There was an investigation, and—fire insurance was just like life insurance. There are other lines of insurance, marine, for instance; but why stop at insurance? Most of the men in those insurance businesses are in other lines of business; most of them had other main lines of their own; and it was notorious that we had in the business world a system of interlocking directorates under which the same men appeared over and over again on many, many boards. Weren't they professional dummy directors? Didn't they cover and represent the same sort of business corruption for the same purposes and for the same bosses, wherever they were?

Yes, bosses. There are bosses in business as there are in politics. The life insurance companies, uncovered, showed this so clearly that one could look back at other business scandals, the Erie and the N.Y. Central, the old Central Pacific Railroad, and see that there was system in the rude, sensational facts. Power without responsibility is the purpose of the boss system in politics; the political boss wants to nominate and control mayors and governors, aldermen and legislators, judges, and departments and commissions, so as to be able to command those dummies to do things that he rarely would be willing to do himself. A story of Boss Odell and Governor Roosevelt will illustrate. Odell was the acting Republican State boss when T.R. was in Albany, and as such he tried to force the governor to do his part toward delivering over to a private corporation the water supply of New York City. I knew some of the Wall Street men in this scheme; T.R. told me his end of it. He refused to stand for it, and the Wall Street men were disappointed. But Odell, who only represented the true political boss, Platt, became governor after T.R., and the high financiers were elated.

"Now we'll get our water bills through," they said. But they didn't, and when the failure was evident I called on one of them to ask why.

"Odell won't do it," my friend said, crestfallen.

"But why not?" I asked. "He wanted Governor Roosevelt to do it. Why won't he do it himself now that he is in power? What does he say?"

"Oh, he says, 'Not on your life. I might ask another man to go up against a proposition like that, but I won't, not I. It would kill the man who was responsible for it, politically.'"

One of the little things reformers might do to check the worst of our abuses would be to elect the big political and business bosses to office, where, being responsible and being, not honest, but intelligent, they will not do half the things they ask their good, honest, usually unintelligent dummies to do. They would give better government than righteous men. I have often said that I could give any city good government with only crooks in office under me, with not a single honest man to help or hinder. And that is only a slight exaggeration of a very practical, significant truth.

And so in business. The dummy directors and the dummy executives of all those life insurance companies were appointed, and the petty and the big inside grafts were permitted, carelessly or knowingly, by the big business bosses who kept out of the companies themselves in order that they, bankers mostly, might have great blocks of the bonds, etc., of their flotations taken by the life insurance trust funds. Let's be fair and clear now. The bankers believed in the investments they offered the insurance companies; the law and policy required that those companies buy only certain first-class securities. But the many bankers were in competition for the good, first-class business of the insurance companies, and the biggest bankers sought only an inside preference for their goods by controlling the dummies and playing in with the principals in the life insurance companies. These preferred bankers were, then, the business bosses who "stood for" the graft and so controlled —not only the life insurance companies, but other big borrowers of credit, like the railroads and other major corporations. They did not go into these companies; they stayed outside and controlled them for their purposes. J. P. Morgan, Senior, for example, was a boss of many railroads, banks, corporations, and life insurance companies; he was an officer in very few.

The political-business parallel was almost perfect. It brought political and business government together under one head. For I had been seeing that back of the political boss was the business boss whose agent he was, and now I was seeing that the business boss was back also of the politics of business and business graft. I could at that time have named the one actual business dictator of the business, politics, and—everything else, of many cities which had charters describing a republican, democratic form of government, charters like those of life insurance companies. For corporations have all the elements of a constitutional government. There are the consumers who correspond with the people in a city, State, or nation; they have no votes in a corporation. The ballot is limited in business, as business men would have it limited in politics, to property-holders; only stockholders vote in a corporation. And stockholders are led by their leaders (bankers, brokers, and attorneys) to turn over their ballots, called proxies, to the party in power, which nominates and elects the officers and the directors, who, as we have seen, are controlled and made to obey, like legislators and executives in politics, the wishes of the outside bosses. If stockholders and business directors are an example of what property-holders in politics would do to government, it would be more sensible to take the political ballot away from them; stockholders rarely go to a stockholders' meeting, and in my day the newspapers had to whip property-holders and taxpayers to the polls.

Rudolph Spreckels, the San Francisco banker, told me once how he, a large minority stockholder, got control of the gas company in his city. He discovered graft and inefficiency in the business and set out to throw the rascals out. Knowing that the rascals would call for proxies in the usual way, without stamps, he, Spreckels, issued his appeal for proxies, inclosing an addressed envelope— with a two-cent stamp on it. Spreckels was not popular, but he got the majority. So cheap were those shareholders, those property-owners! The voters, the common, ordinary riff-raff of New England towns, in Connecticut where I lived, for example—they charged and got all the way from $2.50 to $3.00 a vote; they would have spurned two cents.

There is one more point in my parallel of business and politics. The life insurance exposure was followed by a reform. Charles E. Hughes was this business reformer. He was the investigator, and an able one. He worked; he fought, but he worked. The mass of details, the piles of accounts and correspondence he had to wade through, were literally immense. It was said at the time that when he kept calling for more and more data, the crooks in the companies had a meeting and decided to "fix Hughes." They would send him everything, and they did send him truck-loads of stuff. But Hughes, undaunted, employed a great staff of experts, who really went through those loads of papers and dug up and digested everything and displayed it on the stand in the cross-examination of witnesses. Mr. Hughes must have learned all there was to learn of both big graft and petty graft. He certainly revealed enough to enable anybody with any imagination to see plainly the stark lines of the system, and that it was all for the sake of bankers' control. What did he do about it?

He handed over the control legally and openly to the bankers who had had it politically. If he had done the same thing in a political upheaval he would have delivered over the corrupt city or State to the business bosses back of the political bosses and so have removed the inducement to bad politics. The bankers bought or otherwise accepted the great trust, and they are running those insurance companies today, no doubt, as they are running their own business. Hughes, the business reformer of business, was not denounced and cast out as political reformers are. No crucifixion for him. He was elected governor of the State of New York; he was made a Supreme Court justice, a secretary of state; and he was nominated for president of the United States.

XXVI

MAKING THE "AMERICAN MAGAZINE"

OTHING fails like success. The saying used to be, and probably still is, the other way. But *McClure's Magazine* was
a success; we had circulation, revenue, power. In the building up of that triumph we had been happy, all of us; it was fun,
the struggle. There had been troubles, money difficulties, and some
personal rows. Out in the field, far from New York, I did not
know much about them as they occurred. I heard about them after
they were over, and they were amusing; other people's tragedies
are our comedies. As my colleagues related the outrageous things
S. S. McClure said or did, I compared his dictatorship with those
of my cities and States; and they were indeed funny, except when
they affected me.

Once when I was in Cleveland, Bert Boyden telephoned to me
that an article I had written had been held out of the magazine
by S.S. That was different; he might do such things to others, but
to me— I took a train, and I got S.S. in a room, and—the article
appeared in the next number. I had no trouble with the boss, I
said. But now, when I was in New York for the life insurance
investigation, I realized that those who had to live and work every
day with him were learning to hate him. I got more of his varia-
bility, temperament and extravagance, both in ideas and in expenditures. Wild with enthusiasm one day for the greatest scheme
ever born in the mind of man, he would throw it out the next
day for another greatest editorial idea ever conceived. The editor
had to be edited. One day he wanted me to flay the business men
involved in the insurance scandals; the next he had met the president of one of the companies and seen and heard from his family
that he was being literally killed by the shame of his exposure.
I must spare him. Pull! Political influence right in my own office!

I resisted. I would not be pulled off like a heeler by my boss. I was still righteous; I would report the facts, no matter how much anybody suffered; and the staff was with me.

And then that life insurance man did die! It took very little inquiry to learn that he died of grief and shame; he had tortured himself to death. And we had wanted to punish him; I had. My intellectual conviction of myself for righteousness had not gone far; all my observations of the truth that not men but conditions are to blame had left my impulse, my feelings, my habits of action, untouched. This experience, coming on top of my relations with so many bad men who did their bad deeds reluctantly, drove my understanding deeper. And I saw that S.S. was right with his pull; I saw again that pull was the quality of mercy which must enter into justice. My article (never finished) on the life insurance company was held down strictly to the system, with very little about individuals.

But the office politics at *McClure's* went on, more and more bitterly, until the proposition came up to leave *McClure's*, all of us, and make a magazine of our own. I was in and out of New York, didn't have part in all the plans, and so don't know all that was said and done. When John S. Phillips, of McClure, Phillips and Company, came to my house one night and laid before me a plan to buy the *American Magazine*, I agreed to go into it. And a goodly company it was: Phillips and Miss Tarbell, Baker, Boyden, and myself, just as on *McClure's*, William Allen White and Finley Peter ("Dooley") Dunne from outside. Later came that finished scholar, Albert Jay Nock, to put in mastered English for us editorials which expressed with his grave smile and chuckling tolerance "our" interpretations of things human. "We" all were to edit a writers' magazine. August F. Jaccacci was retiring altogether. There were some difficulties among the owners of McClure stock, but they were soon settled. There was nothing mean about S. S. McClure.

We began the making of the *American*, and we met to assign one another subjects. I was to do William Randolph Hearst; Dunne was to write some "Dooley" articles, Phillips editorials, and so on. It was a feast of fun, at first, and my subject kept me in New York where I could enjoy it. We all knew one another pretty well, excepting only Peter Dunne, who was new as an office companion. He provided most of the entertainment, and not only by his wit and his wisdom; he had wisdom, but could not apply it to Peter Dunne. He could not master himself. He could not make himself write. I never knew a writer who made such a labor of writing; he seemed to hate it; he certainly ran away from it whenever he could. We have heard that Joseph Conrad, called to his writing of a morning by his wife, would throw himself on the floor like a child and kick and groan—it was so hard to write. Dunne was like that.

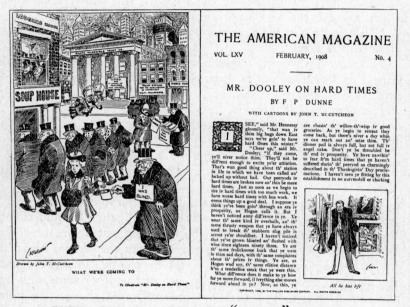

DUNNE WAS TO WRITE SOME "DOOLEY" ARTICLES

Coming into the office one day, I started to go down the hall to my room, when Boyden, the office editor, hissed to me. "Say," he said, "hurry past Dunne's door. He is working. He will call to you; he is looking for any excuse to stop writing; so don't halt and talk. Go on to your own desk." And sure enough, Dunne called me as I went by his door and cussed me when I did not hear or heed. And his cusses were enough to halt me, too; they were so explicit. But we left him alone for an hour or two, when I heard him moving about. I went in.

"Hello, Dunne."

"Ah, go to hell."

"No, but tell me, what's the matter?"

"You wouldn't understand if I did, none of you. You're only a lot of business men that don't understand anything but circulation and advertising and—"

He ranted on in bitter earnestness awhile; there was something the matter. What was it? I kept asking every time he paused for breath, and at last he told me.

"They have been papering these rooms, you know; improving them. Look at the new paper on mine."

I looked. It was plain, tinted paper, a neat, quiet tone. "What about it?" I asked.

"I knew you wouldn't understand. Do you remember the old paper? It was lined out in squares, with a flower at all the intersections."

I remembered it, horrid.

"Oh, sure," he said. "You'd never see the beauty of it. That's what I say."

"But you, Dunne, what did you see in it?"

He paused, and for the first time he smiled; but he expressed himself.

"That old paper had its charm, its uses. I could come in here, get out my pad and my pen, and then—well, then I could count the flowers from the ceiling to the floor and put down the sum. Then I'd count the flowers crossways and put that down. And I'd multiply the perpendicular sum by the horizontal. Then I'd count the diagonal and multiply that by each of the other sums, and by the sum of them. And that was one wall, and there were four walls. . . . Now, doggone it, now I come in here and I've got to write. There's nothing to count, no sums to multiply; I've just got to sit here doing nothing or—write."

He laughed, but he was sore; he was ridiculous, but he was in earnest. Humorists are like that. Dunne told us one day how he and several other humorists had gone to call on Mark Twain, who was, as usual, sick abed. "And," said Dunne, "we all sat there in that room and talked about things till we were all crying over life and man, actually weeping." There was nobody so boring as Dunne himself when he was thinking out a Dooley article. He would talk about it from this view and the other and still another angle for days, at dinner, at lunch; and you could hardly stand it or stop him. His habit was to go for luncheon with Bob Collier, Norman Hapgood, Charles Dana Gibson, and some others of that ilk. I was there one day when he was, as Hapgood whispered to me, working up a Dooley dialogue on the unfair treatment of the Irish in politics.

"We divide you into parties," he was mumbling, "and we run your parties. We get you out to the polls; we tell you whom to vote for, and then we vote you. And what do we get for all the dirty work? District leaderships, perhaps; appointments as police-men." He went on tracing the political labors of the Irish out into State politics and up into national politics: all the dirty, hard work they did, the Irish, and all they got were mean, local jobs. Never a president or a governor, never in a cabinet or the Supreme Court. . . .

We were all silent; he was spoiling our day; the luncheon was a dull failure; and at last when Dunne said, "I'm going to Teddy and ask him to pick out somewhere some one decent Irishman that may be fit for a high office and appoint him," Charles Dana Gibson kicked back his chair, rose, and remonstrated.

"But, Peter, it would look better, I think, if you would let some one else than yourself speak to the president for you."

Dunne was interested in what I was writing about Hearst; they all were. I soon realized that they expected me to expose Hearst and the Hearst papers as I had the worst bosses and the worst cities. And I had no such intention. Hearst, in journalism, was like a reformer in politics; he was an innovator who was crashing into the business, upsetting the settled order of things, and he was not doing it as we would have had it done. He was doing it his way. Journalists and all newspaper readers who were dissatisfied with newspapers as they were thought, like good citizens in cities, that they wanted a change, something new, but they did not want what Hearst was giving them. It was an old story. The Jews of old were looking for a Messiah, but they pictured him as a king coming on a throne to do what they wanted done. The good citizens of Jersey City had been looking for a leader, but they did not expect him to be an Irish Catholic undertaker like Mark Fagan; and the best people of Cleveland hoped to be saved, but not by a jolly captain of industry such as Tom Johnson. Well, it was so with my fellow craftsmen; they wished that some one would come along with money and brains enough to make a newspaper which they could all read, and perhaps write for, happily. But Hearst—he, with his millions, was making a paper that nobody liked; "everybody" loathed his sheets in every city where he had one. We forbade it in our clubs; we wouldn't be seen with it, except here and there one of us would "fall for the money" and write for it. And some of these "hirelings" had the decency to be ashamed and to betray the Hearst papers. It was true that his papers began to win a circulation. Of course. He had discovered that there was room at the bottom, and with sensational news sensationally written and pictured, he did reach for and get the people. He was a demagogue; he was pro-labor. I cannot describe the hate of those days for Hearst except to say that it was worse than it is now. And I was to express this; I was to show him up, him and his views and his methods. "We" did not say that, at the start; I was not supposed to be in any need of instruction; I was all right. But just the same I was to submit my article to my colleagues, not when it was all done, but as I wrote it, paragraph by paragraph. I began very cautiously.

I began with an axiom, that Hearst was Hearst; and there was a row on the board of editors. The prevalent theory was that Hearst had money but no brains and that he hired the brains that made his papers for him. In New York it was Brisbane; in Chicago it was Andy Lawrence; in San Francisco it was some one else. I showed that all those three papers, with very different editors, were all alike, and I implied that some one other than the trio was the dominating spirit in all those similar papers. And I suggested that it was Hearst, and I evidently meant to go on to the conclusion that Hearst had brains.

"Brisbane!" Dunne exclaimed. I had fallen under the spell of Brisbane, and he had bred in my brain the ridiculous idea. I answered that if we were to show up Hearst and blame him for his papers, we must show him to be responsible for them. No use. I ought to show that, first, Hearst did not exist; and second, that he was—what they thought. It was a comedy. It was a fight, paragraph by paragraph; and it became pretty serious. We might have split over it. My good friends could not see why I should listen so much to Brisbane when I might have listened to them.

"But Brisbane knows more about Hearst than you do," I protested, and that was probable; but I added, "And he is fairer." As he was. Brisbane was clear on Hearst, both his strength and his weaknesses, and he gave me and he illustrated a fine, balanced analysis of the man without any prejudice that he cared to put over on me. But my colleagues were so outraged at the discovery that I was really taken in by Brisbane that it looked as if the break had come. Miss Tarbell saved the day, as she used to on *McClure's*.

"Never mind now," she said. "What shall we call the article?" as if it were to be accepted after all.

John Phillips said, "Oh, we'll take a simple title, say: William Randolph Hearst by Lincoln Steffens—"

"Out of Arthur Brisbane," Dunne added in his rage, and we broke up laughing, all but Dunne.

Now, I was influenced by all this pressure; and I knew it. I was not a righteous man in this matter. My article, having built up a curiosity about "Hearst, the Man of Mystery" (as it was finally called), led to an interview which I had with him, as arranged, on a train from Chicago to New York. He was slow to talk, put off the interview from hour to hour; and when we did meet he was not interested till we got well into it. Even then he seemed to be more interested in the technique of my probing, in how I went after Hearst, than in Hearst; and his comment to Brisbane afterward bore out that impression. He said that I was the best interviewer he had ever encountered. And he did answer my questions, quietly, sufficiently, and I landed in New York with a clear sense of the man.

He respected his father and his father's ideas and ideals, which he, the son, alone may have heard. In a larger way, it was some of his father's ends that the son was pursuing. But William Randolph Hearst would have done what he has done without the inspiration or the riches of George Hearst. He had strength, too; there was breed there; the mother, Mrs. Phoebe Hearst, was somebody, and she backed her son as the father had led him. In my article I quoted the interview, and I made some comment, but I did not say what I really thought. I thought that Hearst was a great man, able, self-dependent, self-educated (though he had been to Harvard) and clear-headed; he had no moral illusions; he saw straight as far as he saw, and he saw pretty far, further than

THE AMERICAN MAGAZINE

VOL. LXIII   NOVEMBER 1906   No 1

HEARST, THE MAN OF MYSTERY

BY LINCOLN STEFFENS

AUTHOR OF "THE SHAME OF THE CITIES," ETC

ILLUSTRATED WITH PORTRAITS AND PHOTOGRAPHS

*This article is an examination of the fitness of Mr. Hearst for office, based on funda-
mental grounds It considers him seriously as a remarkable phenomenon in public affairs,
whom it is our duty to try to understand. His political and journalistic ideas are
given as they are presented by himself and his followers, with all credit for sincerity.
Even then our conclusions are that Mr Hearst does not typify the movement he
represents or give reasons for hoping that he will be able to accomplish what he
thinks he can.*—THE EDITOR.

ALL over the country all
sorts and conditions of
men are asking "What
about Hearst?" and, if
they think you should be
able to answer, they put
the question with an eagerness—or an anxiety—which denotes a
very real desire to know. And nobody
seems to know. They have read his
"yellow" newspapers, heard some yellow
gossip about him, and "that's enough."

Some of those who say that Hearst's
newspapers are enough to judge the man by,
say also that Hearst's newspapers are not
Hearst's; that he did not make them. A
rich young man, Hearst was able to buy
brains, and the talented men he hired,
having put themselves into his newspapers,
are putting him into politics. Almost his
very existence is denied. The *New York
Evening Post* declared last August that
"William Randolph Hearst" was a myth, a
syndicate, a trade-mark, an empty name

What the Mystery Means

Is there such a man? Somebody must be
back of the papers and the politics that bear

his name If it isn't Hearst himself, who is
it? And whether "Hearst" is Hearst or
somebody else, what manner of man is it
that moved in silence behind all the noise
he was making, arousing in some people
dread, in others hope, but compelling
in all an interest which of itself is significant? For, suppose the worst of Hearst:
suppose him to be a yellow millionaire,
without a mind of his own or the morals
of other people; suppose his inherited
millions have fallen under the control
of an unscrupulous group of able men
who, by pandering in journalism to the
love of the vices, and by playing in politics
with the hatred of the riches of the rich,
propose to bring on a class war and destroy
the U. S. Government—what does it mean
of the American people that so many of
them read the Hearst newspapers and look
to such a political leadership with at least
half a mind to follow it? Why should a
myth be a "menace" in this land of prosperity and liberty? We approach, in more
senses than one, a national question when
we ask who, what, where is the reality behind the mystery of William Randolph
Hearst, the unknown?

Now the way to solve a riddle like this is,

A TITLE "WE" COULDN'T AGREE ON

I did then; and, studious of the methods which he adopted after experimentation, he was driving toward his unannounced purpose: to establish some measure of democracy, with patient but ruthless— force. He had ambition, not to sit in the offices he ran for, but to do something in them, to do himself things which his candidates never did satisfactorily. In my article I said that he proposed, like a rich man, to give the people democracy, as others of his sort give charity or an art museum. I did not understand myself then what a part dictatorship has to play in democracy. And I found, as his chief fault, that he was not moral; I was just getting over my own righteousness, but I had not yet arrived where Hearst was born, apparently, at the point of view whence one sees that it is economic, rather than moral, forces that count, as with me in this very article. I compromised in it with my colleagues to keep my job. The only criticism I think now, since I have watched his career, to be worth writing is that Hearst, with his patience, his superb tolerance, does not require his own editors to understand his policies. He is so far ahead of his staffs that they can hardly see him; and so, of course, they cannot make either this remarkable man or his perfectly rational ideas comprehensible to his readers, the people Hearst would like to see served.

But I did write an article on Hearst which the *American Magazine,* self-governed by the writer's themselves, would and did publish. I was a success.

XXVII

TIMBER FRAUDS IN OREGON

AFTER Hearst, the exposure, just beginning, of the Labor government of San Francisco. I had been looking toward my old curiosities, Boston and the Federal government at Washington. But these subjects would interest my fellow craftsmen on the *American Magazine;* they would want to have a hand in the writing of articles on an eastern city and on the national government, whereas San Francisco was far away; they did not know anybody there, I thought, and I could follow my own interest. And my interest was to show the inside of a Labor government.

Having recently seen, in the life insurance exposures, an example of government by business men, I might take San Francisco as a practical experiment in the theory so widely held by liberals, semi-radicals, and working-men, that a government by labor would be better than a government by capitalists, employers, business men, or their agents.

Another, a more personal, reason moved me westward, however. I had long been wishing, secretly, to go home to live in California. I did not say anything about it to my wife or my colleagues. My wife was absorbed in making Little Point, a place I had bought in Riverside, Connecticut, across the river and down the harbor from Cos Cob. She liked that home, and she did not like California or Californians. She had never been to California, but she had heard Californians talk about California! That was enough for her. "Why don't you all go there if it is so wonderful?" she said. I reminded her that I had never praised the State, hardly ever mentioned it to her; she certainly could not suspect me of hankering for my own, my native State. My California theory was that if I could ever take her there, the State would win her; I could leave it to California to speak for itself—California and the west. To "do" San Francisco, I had to go back and follow the career of the chief prosecutor, Francis J. Heney. He had got into some sort of scandal in Arizona and shot a man in Tucson. This was being recalled to his damage in San Francisco, and I must know all about it. That meant that I had to know something about the State of Arizona. And then this wild western reformer, this cowboy and gunman from California and Arizona, had been the chief prosecutor of the timber frauds of the northwest, especially in Oregon. I must know about that and the States up there and the Federal government in two departments, the Interior Department and the attorney general's. And then California. I persuaded my wife to go with me on this slow tour of the far west, with never a word of any but my professional interest, nothing about my secret design to win her for the west.

We stopped first in Denver just to see Ben Lindsey and James H. Causey, Edward P. Costigan, and Mrs. Costigan—all my reformer friends there, not the sky-high city with its light, its clean air, and its distant horizon of Rocky Mountains. I never spoke of the charm either of that city or of my friends, and when she did, I was surprised out of my absorption in the ugly, professional fact that Ben Lindsey and his gang of men, women, and children had to fight hard and constantly for their very simple reforms.

Tucson, Arizona, was to me merely the scene of Frank Heney's adventures. She had to see for herself that pictorially it was a great black-and-white, an arrangement of cool, black shadows and hot, white lights. And she did remark that out there in Arizona and in the desert you could see the rotundity of the earth. I pretended to be blind to all this beauty. I talked only of the fresh view I was getting of the first stage of civilized corruption of a new community, the raw, rude bribery and force of a young community, and of the fact that it was the shooting political boss of Tucson that Heney had shot—to save his own life. For the undenied local story was that this boss, who ran everything and everybody, was preventing his wife from getting a divorce by his open threat to shoot any attorney who would dare to take her case. Heney, a cowboy, had moved in from the ranches to practice law; he took the woman's case. "Couldn't refuse to take any case in a town where I'd hung up my shingle," they said he said. The husband used to

ride in a buggy, with a driver, all the way home with Heney
every day, insulting him to make him "draw." And Heney, who
was a fighting man, would not draw; "not till I'd won that case,"
he said. Then, one midday, after the divorce was granted, Heney
saw the boss husband coming at him across the city square with
his gun out and a crowd to see; he came like a bull till Heney, having no gun, sprang at the charging boss and seized the weapon.
They wrestled for it, all their four hands on it, and as it gradually

FRANCIS J. HENEY   DR. J. C. HANDY

SHOOTER AND SHOT

moved around to point at his opponent's body, Heney fired. The
boss dropped and died, and a grand jury agreed with a mob of witnesses that it was justifiable homicide.

My interest was in the rise of the man, Heney, through his
haphazard fighting all over the State, against every evil he saw, to
be secretary of state, and then, on the inside, in what he saw of the
coming corruption of a new State, and his forced compromise with
some of it. He could not fight it all; many of his partisans turned
out as bad as their enemies. Heney did not understand, and so he
was defeated politically, but never personally, in Arizona. I think
that this picturesque career against that picturesque background

fascinated my wife. I know that she kept talking about the winter weather, the sun booming up every day; we had never a drop of rain in Colorado, Arizona, and New Mexico, where we dallied.

New Mexico is the strangest, most exaggerated, most obvious, but also most incredible beauty in these United States. I saw my wife gasp at its purple mountains, as I have seen eastern people gasp at paintings of them and of the desert. And faithful painters who have dared to indicate—not to copy, but just to suggest—the colors and the shapes of the southwest, John O'Shea, for example, will tell you of the anger of art lovers at the "lies" they put in their canvases. My good wife, as we traveled slowly down through those scenes of floating mountains on to the simple sand-seas of the speechless desert, looked and surrendered. It was beautiful. She spoke mostly of the weather, the daily sun-filled weather. But I knew she bowed to the southwest, for one day she said, "California can't be more beautiful than this, can it?" Wait, I thought; we were coming to the border.

The day we crossed the State line into California it began to rain. It began as a soft, quiet relief, which cooled the air and laid the dust, but it gathered strength, that rain; it poured down. You could not see the orange groves; all you could see was the rising rivers, the running floods, the washouts. Los Angeles had no streets, only muddy rivers, and we had to stay there awhile. It rained all the time; in San Diego where I slyly "had to go" it poured. On the way up to San Francisco the train was delayed by washouts, and as it continued to rain, she saw some workmen, she said, hold up one side of the track for our train to pass slowly by!

It rained in San Francisco. I had to stay there to see what was called the graft prosecution: Fremont Older, Rudolph Spreckels, Frank Heney, William J. Burns. They took me in, and I was getting the lay of things when I fell ill. It was the rain. My wife wanted to go on—somewhere. Well, I had to do a lot of work in Oregon; so we took a train to Portland. The railroad through northern California passes some beautiful and some magnificent scenery. We saw none. We saw only the rain, which poured all the time we were in California, forty days and forty nights, and ceased, in California, when we crossed over into Oregon. But it rained in Oregon. My wife became ill in Portland; she was poisoned by fish, but she blamed the rain. And then, as she was lying ill, a telegram warned her to come home; her father was dangerously ill. She got up, took a train for the east, and the day after she left I had to forward a wire that her father had died. We never spoke of California and the west in my family after that; and when Californians mentioned their State in their terms we were silent. "We know California; we were there once; nobody could tell us about sunny California." We were going to live all the rest of our days in the east, where you did see the sun sometimes.

When I was left alone in Portland the sun came out, and I could see that Oregon was in that early stage of civilization where the people are considered enough to let the leaders of public opinion in on the graft. Like Arizona. The governor of Arizona with whom Heney was secretary of state was an editor; in Oregon the editor of the leading paper was caught making a financial agreement to be elected U.S. senator. And W. S. U'ren, "the lawgiver, father of the initiative and referendum," a Populist leader, was a powerful lobbyist, who played the game, like Roosevelt, with the system. He had all the big, bad politicians voting for and finally enacting what he called the tools for self-government by the people. This he did by trading; he traded Pop votes on senatorships, etc., for machine votes for his democratic measures. Otherwise the system in Oregon and its cities was just like the system elsewhere.

Timber was the new source of corruption. The railroads, public service corporations, vice and crime, were the chief villains, of course, but public-land stealing and the timber grants were close up in the front rank of vested interests, and that was what the prosecutions of Francis J. Heney and the detective work of William J. Burns had exposed. That was my special subject, and as a newspaper man to newspaper men, I would like to point out that there is easy news-getting in an old exposure. Witnesses with valuable information and documents, who held tight when the fight was on, are relaxed when it is all over. They are surprised and sometimes grieved at the sudden loss of interest in their facts. I have found always when I came along late that there were those who would seek me out to tell me things they had not told before and regretted having suppressed. Good stories hate to be wasted. It was so in Oregon. The records of the cases worked up by Burns and tried by Heney were enough, but the witnesses they could not get opened up to me, and I soon had a complete picture of the crimes committed, the methods used, all over the forested west, and the rise of society against the interference with this rich but destructive graft.

The interference came, in this case, from outside. The famous timber fraud prosecutions were by President Roosevelt's attorney general's department of corrupt acts and policies by the Federal Department of the Interior. Individuals and companies involved were some of them residents of Oregon, Washington, California, and other western States, and the State officials and local political parties played a part. Senators, representatives, and appointees to Federal office from these States had built up, protected, and used the Federal departments to further the frauds, so that this whole story was a clear sight of the interlocking of the local, State, and Federal machine as all of one system. One old truth came out badly. Just as we had observed that a railroad commission, whether State or national, established to regulate railroads, came finally to represent the railroads; as a public utility commission came to act for the companies, against the consumers; and as the police appointed to arrest crime were corrupted to license criminals—so a Federal department created to execute land, timber, and mineral laws in the public interest was organized (by political appointments) and bought by systematic bribery to take the part of the land grafters, timber thieves, and big mine-jumpers.

When the smoldering allegations of timber grant frauds burst into a roaring fire, the secretary of the interior, a very distinguished lawyer and statesman from the middle west, decided to do something about it. It was hard for him to believe that such crookedness could happen, especially in such a decorous department as this that he had inherited and inspected. He had looked into the faces of the permanent officials; he could see that they were good men and true; but he had to act. He asked the Treasury Department for an able, honest, trustworthy detective from the Secret Service. William J. Burns came and said he would investigate and report. And in a short time, within a few days, Burns came back, said it was true; there were timber grants on a whole-sale scale, and he named the guilty men in the department, some of them very close to the secretary.

The secretary started back astonished, gripped his desk, and stared at Burns in his professional pride, and he did not admire the detective. When he recovered he took the telephone and asked the Treasury to call off their man Burns and send him what he had requested, a trustworthy detective.

Now, what Burns had done was to find out, first, if there was much graft in the Department. Any crook who knows will tell that to any equal, any "wise guy" who is capable of understanding. Burns heard that there was very much, very old, and very settled graft, and how in general it was handled. Then Burns inquired which officials, from top to bottom, would have to be in on the graft, if there was graft. That is to say, what men were in positions where they had to know what was going on and, by acts, permit it. That, too, is easy to find out. Any one with imagination could see that this must be the system, and Burns has imagination. He would call it common sense; he is not, I found, aware that he has the gift of insight that is common only among artists. The secretary did not have it. If attorneys-at-law have it, they seem to train it out of their minds by the substitution for it of what they call evidence. And Burns understands evidence. He pleaded with the secretary that he did not pretend to have proof of his judgment; he had only suspicion, and that was *a priori*, but it was reasonable; and it might take a year or more, but he knew where to look for the evidence, and he would get it.

The secretary would not give such a man a year. He was frightened, and he frightened Burns, whose opportunity this was to rise out of the ruck of Treasury operators and become a great detective. He was desperate, and he was not without resources. He said that if the secretary would give him a few days, he would convince him. He would obtain from some one of the higher permanent officials near the secretary a complete confession.

That, or Burns's vigor or his will, must have caught the unimaginative secretary's mind. He consented and Burns rushed out into the Department, had pointed out to him the men he had accused, and looking them over, picked out one, a southern gentleman, with great dignity, but a weak mouth and timid eyes. He called on him at his house, I think it was, and said, "You're a crook, and we've got you."

Burns made his charge with his finger in the man's face, with all the certainty in his own face and attitude of the man with imagination. I've seen him do this. It is acting, but no actor on the stage has the incentive or the art to act as Burns can act—to break a man down and "get" him. And in this case Burns was acting for his life, as the other man was, who had to play the part of an inno-cent "southern gentleman of family," as he said. But Burns was the stronger man, the better actor, and he described to the accused what he must have done if he was guilty. In a word, Burns de-scribed his imaginings as facts, and—the man broke down, con-fessed all his misdeeds, and peached on the others. Within the period of his promise the detective presented to the secretary a serial scene of troubled, confessing officials, some of the very men Burns had accused so lightly, so promptly, so alarmingly.

The secretary had to let Burns go on with his investigation, and it did take more than a year to gather, present in court, and, get-ting convictions, by the way, set forth the whole system of timber grants in Oregon and near-by States. Heney prosecuted. A stranger in the State, he soon discovered that the timber thieves, the land and lumber companies, had not only the Department—all that they wanted of it—and the senators and representatives, but Fed-eral judges and U.S. marshals. He had to go to Washington and ask President Roosevelt to transfer judges, remove U.S. district attorneys, and appoint U.S. marshals, before he could summon un-fixed jurors, trust the courts, and have an even chance to convict. And even then . . . But Burns, the detective, saw to it that the juries were fair, Burns and U.S. Marshal Charles Reed—Jack Reed's father, whom Heney had asked Roosevelt for.

Reformers "have to" use pull, politics, and the tricks of the game, the system itself, when they are fighting it.

When I left Oregon to follow the trail to San Francisco I felt that I knew the persons in my story, their records, methods, faults, and strength. And I was asking myself whether men are not well-nigh blameless, and only "the system" at fault. An oft-repeated idea, this, but it was vivid in my mind as I rode over the high, wooded mountains into California again.

XXVIII

SAN FRANCISCO: A LABOR GOVERNMENT

O N A peak of Russian Hill, San Francisco, in a neat, becoming little house, lived a gentleman, Mr. Joseph Worster, an exquisite, very shy old bachelor gentleman who loved the city, which, somehow, understood him. A hard-boiled labor leader, meeting him walking during the street-car strike, remonstrated.

"You ought to ride, Mr. Worster. Oh, sure, we ask everybody to help us by walking, but that don't mean you. You take a car; we'll understand your riding."

Mr. Worster thanked the strike leader and walked on. He walked till the strike was over.

This gentle man became my spiritual guide through the mazes of the graft prosecution. A New Englander and a Swedenborgian minister, he thought that he was moral and the town thought he was, but he was really an esthete who saw and practiced and personified the Beautiful rather than the Good and the True. His tiny church was a work of art, a temple to taste, set in a large, cool, formal garden. The conflict of his culture and his instinct confused him. Standing on his hill one night, dressed as always in his well-cut, perfectly brushed and pressed long black clerical garb, he looked away from the bay down upon the red lights of Chinatown, Little Italy, and the Barbary Coast, and whispered, "Beautiful."

"But wicked," he added to me, after a long moment of silence. "It is very wicked. And, do you know, I think that that is why I love it so, this wicked, beautiful city."

He said that and he looked ashamed of himself. As he did when he confessed one day that he "loved" the big, brutal street-car strike that was tearing along with the brutal, daily graft exposures.

But he did not look ashamed, he looked very just, when I asked him another day what had become of two ex-convicts whom he had taken into his house upon their discharge from the penitentiary.

"Oh, they are gone," he flashed. "I caught them looking over some writings of mine on my desk."

"So!" I said. "You forgive their burglary, but not—"

"Ah, but they must be gentlemen," he answered. "Even burglars. Like the strike, like the graft and the prosecution of grafters, like the wicked city itself—everybody and everything must be—understandable, beautiful; not ugly."

And, having spoken thus as one having authority, this delicate arbiter of taste shrank back, down into his habitual mien of humility; which confused me till one afternoon as we came together out of court where we had heard the evidence and seen the double-crossing witnesses of some utter human depravity, he stopped on the sidewalk to say, with downcast eyes, "That, then, is the way we are!"

"You, Mr. Worster?"

He glanced up at me, turned away and down again.

"I—I am like those poor creatures in that court room. Secretly. And my secret sin is worse than any of theirs. It is conscious; it is conscious superiority. Do you know what I was saying to myself as I sat there listening to those witnesses? I kept saying, 'Well, I wouldn't do that; not that.'"

"But you wouldn't, would you?"

He looked astonished at me. He started to walk on, halted, and reddening a bit, he said: "I have never done any of the things that they did. I have never been tempted to. But I have done similar things; I have done and I have left undone things that made those men in there do what they did. And I keep forgetting it."

He walked on, I with him for a block or two, when he lifted his face again to—almost moan, "I cannot—ever—get over my New England sense of superiority."

There was no smile. His face had gone white, whiter than his hair, against his fine black hat and coat. He meant it deeply. Mr. Worster was one of the few men not convicted but convinced and reformed by the graft prosecution of San Francisco. Another was Fremont Older.

Older was the man who started it all. A big, tall, willful, very temperamental editor, he was aroused first as a journalist by the crude joyousness of the new set of grafters who got hold of the city. He had seen a good deal of politics and exposed some of it. San Francisco and California had always been a graft, but the old order was comparatively methodical and decent, the product of a slow, natural growth. The new labor administration of the city, which was bossed by a young college graduate, Abe Ruef, and personified by the musicians' union, Mayor Schmitz and a board of labor supervisors—this new "crowd" was not used to the license and the easy money of politics. They had more power and more money than they had ever dreamed of having, and the effect was not to give them that "sense of responsibility" which is supposed to turn radicals into conservatives. They did forget most of their red Labor purposes, but that was because they became interested in the graft. Which, by the way, is the true psychology of the conservatism of power and possession. This Labor government went off, like a lot of college students, on a joy ride, a grafting drunk, and the watching newspaper man saw the opening their careless conduct gave him for—news.

Fremont Older called for help on Rudolph Spreckels, a smiling, young, personally powerful millionaire, who had made and won some smiling, very revealing fights against graft and corruption in corporations, practices like those disclosed in the life insurance companies, and others. He had seen in Pennsylvania, before he was of age, machinery destroyed by the sabotage of his father's employees—bribed by a competitor's agents. He had discovered that his night superintendent was corrupted by the trust to let goods spoil and his head bookkeeper to deliver information daily to the enemy. This was his education. He had not gone much to school, never to college. He had not learned any illusions to lose, as I had, for example. He did not think that business was good and politics bad. This young man had learned at first hand that capital also "throws bricks," "destroys property," "hurts business," practices pulls, pads payrolls, and bribes men not only in politics but in business, and that as for unions, Organized Business can close banks to a scab borrower. His father, Claus Spreckels, had had this last done to him in a fight, which, by the way, Rudolph won and made his first million on. But he had won all his fights. He was the surest fighter I had ever met, and I think the reason was that he knew both the game and himself by experience. Never having been taught the lies we call idealism, he was not taken by surprise; he was not disappointed that men behaved unexpectedly, basely; in the formative period of his youth he measured himself against older men as he found them, and he beat them and their crookedness, straight. He had come out an idealist, but his idealism was founded upon the facts of life and his own measured strength.

Spreckels smiled when Older called upon him to suggest the graft prosecution. He had determined already himself to investigate, expose, and break up the Labor graft, and not because it was Labor. He knew that the Labor party was no more Labor than the Republican party is republican or the Democratic party democratic —by experiences with all of them. They were all alike to him, but Labor was new, and, as Older saw, "raw." Abe Ruef had twice come to Spreckels with businesslike propositions. The first one was to serve Spreckels and his corporations as an attorney; the Labor boss said he was an able lawyer and "otherwise useful." The second time Ruef offered to use Organized Labor to throw a bond issue, regardless of his low bid, to Spreckels, the banker, by calling a short railway strike to frighten off all other bidders, who would not know that the trouble was temporary. Aware thus of what Labor was willing to do for a capitalist, he knew also that other business men had accepted what he had declined. In brief, Spreckels knew, from all sides, from Capital and from Labor, from the inside and from the outside, that the Labor administration was representing the same business, vice, and criminal interests that every other party represented in every city and State where he had done business. And he had made up his mind and told a few of his friends that he meant to do what Older proposed.

They clicked therefore. Older was thinking more of the labor grafters, Spreckels of the capitalist grafters, but they agreed to proceed. They had been watching the hard but persistent and winning fight of Francis J. Heney and William J. Burns in Oregon, and Heney was a Californian, born in San Francisco. Older went east, asked President Roosevelt to let them have "next on" Heney and Burns, and T.R. consented. The earthquake and fire intervened, but these four finally went to work as the famous graft prosecution of San Francisco.

When I came down the Oregon trail of Heney and Burns, they

took me into their councils as a sort of prophet and jester; and I began to prophesy. I could; I had hindsight. They had some, too, of course, but they were, as I told them, 'way behind me. They were honest men, for example. They were about where I was when Clarence Darrow accused me in Chicago of believing in honesty. They believed that the world was divided into honest men and crooks. Burns had another phrase for the crooks. To him they were sons of bitches. Whatever they called them, however, all four of these men, with the backing of all good citizens, set out to catch and punish the dishonest men and elect to office honest men whom Spreckels proposed to watch forever. There was a place in and out of that prosecution for a jester and a prophet.

"Ruef and I and Mr. Worster are the only men, not crooks, who are not honest men," I jested. "Wait," I prophesied.

At that early stage of the man-hunt, the crooks who were being caught were petty politicians, the bribe-takers, whom honest Republicans and honest Democrats, honest business men and honest men and women generally, regarded as Labor politicians. "And what can you expect of a Labor government?" they said, and the only reply to that came from the working-men, who, sensing class prejudice, were inclined to defend Labor. The class line was drawing. But, as Spreckels predicted, as soon as the evidence began to show that these Labor representatives had been selling out to Capital, the workers were shocked into a demand for the punishment of these miserable bribe-takers.

My prophecy or jest was hind-sighted back upon the experience of other towns that where there were bribe-takers there were usually bribe-givers. The prosecution nodded. "Of course." But should they act upon that matter of course? To "get" the bribe-givers, they must have the testimony of the bribe-takers, and the price was to let the bribe-takers go. Well, they were going to do that. Sure. They were after Abe Ruef, the arch-bribe-giver. They and 'most everybody was for that, too. But I prophesied that the actual bribe-giver, the man who handled the money, did not take it out of his own pocket. He was an agent who obtained the money he paid from higher-ups. Ruef, for example, was merely the go-between; he acted for others, probably prominent business men and leading citizens who would not themselves commit a felony and had to have some one else do it, some one tested and true whom they could trust. The political boss, Ruef, would know who those men were in San Francisco.

They were fun, those meetings of that board of strategy. I was an expert councilor. I know how to have my advice taken up to a certain point. I first find out what the men in doubt really want to do, and then I advise them to do that. And so with propaganda. You can't tell anybody anything he does not know. But you can remind men of what they do know and sometimes bring their knowledge into action. These four willful, obstinate men knew what I was reminding them of: that there existed nothing exceptional in San Francisco. The policy of the graft prosecution should be, as it partly was, to catch the bribe-takers and let them go for the delivery of the bribe-givers; and then, having caught thus the bribe-givers, Rueff and the others let them go for the delivery of the big captains of industry they acted for. And then, for a straight, clear confession or explanation of just what it was that made these leaders of the city corrupt their city, let them go. All. No punishment. In short, I labored humorously, and I think pleasantly, for the exposure in San Francisco of the universal state of business corruption of politics to show What was hurting us, not Who.

Except for the last item this was and it became definitely the policy of the graft prosecution. To let everybody go was too much for them; there were some crooks who should suffer. Mr. Worster, up on Russian Hill, "loved" the idea of mercy, but he was a Christian, a sinner. He did not care to see other sinners punished. But the graft prosecution was, as I say, still righteous. They laughed at my philosophy and my illustrative stories, as they started up the line of that program, the world with them, almost the whole world.

The Bohemian Club gave a dinner where as guests Heney and I spoke, saying what all men thought they thought. Rudolph Spreckels took me often to his, the Pacific Union Club. I saw some very prominent business men avoid us, a few who knew; but generally we were received with cordial approval. Our university at Berkeley invited, first, me to speak—I was a graduate; then Heney, who was fired—as he said in his speech, "for the same reason I am recalled to address you"—for fighting. And Benjamin Ide Wheeler, the president, whispered to me that our alma mater was going to confer upon us both honorary degrees of doctor of philosophy. I whispered the news to Heney, but I whispered also the prophecy that if by Commencement the prosecution had gone beyond the bribe-takers and was reaching for the higher-ups, we would not be doctors; we would get no more bids to dine and speak, and I would be excluded from the clubs. The business leaders who give out the bribe money control honors, too. And this prophecy came true. By and by Spreckels was asked not to bring me to his club any more. It was bad enough to see him, a member, who could not be excluded; the two of us together, talking, probably, about who was who in the graft world, was too much. It was the same with other clubs. There were no more invitations anywhere higher up. And I recall, with the prophet's mean satisfaction, seeing Heney on Commencement Day reading in a newspaper the lists of graduates and of new honorary doctors. He was all agrin as he looked up, and handing me the paper, said: "Want to see why we didn't get our honorary degrees? Read that list of Regents."

Not one of those Regents, as I remember the list, had been named yet in any of Heney's cases or indictments; and none of them was ever a defendant or particularly accused. But they were higher-ups in business, law, society, of course; they were just the kind of men appointed to govern and adorn universities and life insurance companies, etc. The graft prosecution, however, had by that time gone far enough so that some of those Regents and Francis J. Heney knew that the trail of exposure led up to them or their friends and to their "vested interests." The class line was becoming felt, and these righteous men were finding out that they belonged on the side of "the bad," in this case Labor, government!

"Why, it would seem that my class," said Mr. Worster, "is not against a Labor government or a bad Labor government, but only against a good Labor government."

"No," I suggested, "our class is for any government that represents us and our business. The badness comes from making a Labor or a democratic government represent us."

And he agreed, after a pondering moment, this understanding man, and rather eagerly, because, he remarked, "San Franciscans never were very righteous, like us New Englanders; they are becoming respectable, but they are not yet hypocrites." Mr. Worster did want to go on loving his wicked city, and I encouraged him.

"Maybe the graft prosecution, by convincing the respectables of their wickedness, will make them conscious hypocrites," I said; and when he looked bewildered at me, I added, "Like you, Mr. Worster." And since he still stared, I finished: "Aware of their inferiority and conscious of its sinful unintelligence."

"Then you would put intelligence before goodness?" He interpreted.

"No, but first before righteousness."

"I—see."

But it was not alone the graft prosecution, with its practice of taking the confessions of the low-down politicians who betrayed the higher-ups, that was dividing the sheep from the goats and making the black sheep conscious of their goathood. The arrival from the east of a big business man helped. Patrick Calhoun of New York, Pittsburgh, St. Louis, and the Solid South, a street railway magnate, who was interested in the San Francisco street car company, saw from afar the menace to business in the progressive exposures of Rudolph Spreckels's graft prosecution. Calhoun was conscious, and therefore charming and graceful. He knew always what he was doing, and he knew Spreckels. Calhoun had twice tried to "get" Spreckels by what Spreckels regarded as bribes. His failure, remembered, reminded Calhoun that a prosecution with Spreckels back of it would go "too far." He collected the backing, financial and social, of the public utilities in the east and came out to San Francisco to fight Spreckels. He had a plan. His plan was to make it a class fight, Capital against Labor, and he was sure he could make his class conscious and passionate. Also he said, very intelligently, that Labor was not labor-class-conscious but upper-class-numbed, and that when he opened the war as he meant to wage it, he would have on his side not only the rich but the middle and most of the working and poor people, who never ceased from thinking that they would some day be of the rich. A majority.

And Calhoun's weapon was to be a strike, a violent street railway strike, which he, the president of the company, would deliberately force, with bribery and a wage dispute, and which he, a capitalist, would direct as if against himself. A war with one commander, himself, moving both armies. And this happened. We had evidence of it then; we know it now. And this event it was that nearly broke up the graft prosecution, changed the issue, and by making the righteous of all classes and groups angry fighters for their side, saved them from conviction and from intelligent hypocrisy.

XXIX

HOW HARD IT IS TO KEEP THINGS WRONG

WHEN Patrick Calhoun came to San Francisco to make his final fight against the graft prosecution he came prepared. He had his friends in the east apply all their pulls, financial, social, political, journalistic, to commanding individuals and companies in California. Everybody must help Mr. Calhoun. His friends were many. Of a fine old southern family, pedigreed back through the Calhouns to Patrick Henry, he had social position everywhere, here and abroad. In many financial deals he was an insider in high finance and industry. He was a backer and user of politics in several States. With the manners, the habits, and the culture of the old south, he had added to his inborn virtues of pride, courage, and superiority the practices of the more practical north. Mr. Calhoun was a man of the world; he was an expert in modern ways. He was a New Southerner. And he looked his part. He was a tall, straight, handsome man, with the eyes of a lion, the grace of a tiger-cat, and the strength of a serpent. He was, like Rudolph Spreckels, unbeaten and unbeatable.

"Look out for Pat Calhoun," wrote Tom Johnson to me. "They can't get him down. He won't go into a penitentiary. If he is convicted he will take you all along with him to—where he'd rather go; judge, attorneys—all."

Tom Johnson, an old associate of Calhoun's, had been asked to speak to me. And others were asked to "get" me for Calhoun; in such detail did this fighter prepare to fight. He came to San Francisco, rented a fine old house in a swell district, and began to entertain socially. His plan was, as I have said, to start a street railway strike, make it bitter and violent, till, the class line drawn with hate, he could save the city by appearing to lick labor and make a settlement on his own victorious terms. He knew he could do this. He knew by experience that organized labor was almost as corruptible as organized party politics; that the Labor administration of San Francisco was, like any Republican or Democratic city government, bought over and owned by big businesses, his own among them; and that Labor leaders and the Labor mayor, boss, and officials had been demoralized by the easy money they were getting in large sums. And the graft prosecution knew this and were showing it up, step by step, up toward Mr. Patrick Calhoun, who, therefore, decided to take and keep one step ahead of —Mr. Rudolph Spreckels. He would buy a strike as he had bought franchises. The public and the workers would never know; they would be so repelled by the outrages of the strikers and the strike-breakers that they would be utterly diverted from their wrath at political graft and cry for "law and order."

Bold, this was intelligent, too. I was admiring and I wanted to see this realist. But I also was a realist. I knew that until I had the facts, which the graft prosecution was only beginning to gather, I could not properly interview such a man. He would overwhelm me with his superior knowledge, and he might, with his charm, fool me. And he was after me; not only Tom Johnson, my own office wrote to me to be sure to see and give a fair hearing to Mr. Calhoun. The editors of the magazine had never done anything like that before. When I still waited I got a message, a perfectly proper, but very impatient message from Peter Dunne that I must see Calhoun—at once. I called up Calhoun, explained that of course I wanted to see him and have a talk, but that I had to know what I was talking about. He laughed and said that Dunne understood better than I did: that he wished me to hear his side of the case before Spreckels and his gang had had time to prejudice me. "All right," I said, "I'll call whenever you like, but you will have to do all the talking; I can't even ask questions."

"Come now," he said, "today, this afternoon, to my house, not here in the office. We'll be alone uptown there."

He received me in the great living-room of his house, a beautiful, very long room, and after a brief repetition of our telephone conversation, he seated me on a sofa at the near end of the room. He walked away thoughtfully, head down, halfway down the room, then whirled, head and one hand up, and began—a speech.

THE PRESS

UPPER LEFT: WILLIAM RANDOLPH HEARST (COPYRIGHT BY J. E. PURDY & CO.).
UPPER RIGHT: WILLIAM ALLEN WHITE (N.Y. WORLD NEWS SERVICE). LOWER
LEFT: S. S. MC CLURE (N.Y. WORLD NEWS SERVICE). LOWER RIGHT: ARTHUR
BRISBANE (COPYRIGHT BY MISHKIN).

"Mr. Steffens," he said, "I am a gentleman"—pause—"and a southern Democrat."

This would never do. I recalled my old rule for interviewing: never to let the interviewed get started on a speech; he will say only what he wants you to say, not what he himself thinks; and he will dominate.

So I threw up one of my hands as high as his, and called: "Wait, Mr. Calhoun. Wait just a moment. I have known gentlemen to corrupt legislatures, buy judges, and steal franchises till—well—I don't know any longer what the word gentleman means." He was listening attentively. His hand was slowly descending. He was looking at me questioningly. I went on in a lighter tone. "And as for a southern Democrat, Mr. Calhoun—if you are a southern Democrat, you ain't no democrat at all at all."

He rocked there a moment, smiled, threw up both hands, and came and sat down beside me.

"That's better," I said. "Let's talk, straight, man to man."

"Fine," he laughed. "What about?"

"Oh," I said, "since I don't know anything about San Francisco, let's get acquainted by talking a bit about St. Louis. We both know St. Louis."

We talked about St. Louis. He talked, I mean. I started him on Folk's graft prosecution, and he took the lead, told me some stories I had never heard, then went deep down into the workings of the machine there with the business system. He was trying to entertain me, politely, but honestly, frankly, and he did entertain me. For half an hour he described the inside of the olden days of Folk and Butler, described men and incidents and grafts, just as one crook to another. And it was intelligent talk, too, the talk of a man who played the game, as he found it, with a humorist's, not a moralist's, sense of the ridiculousness, not the evil, of it all. Evidently Patrick Calhoun was one of the kind of men I liked, the kind that kept their minds intact, no matter what they do, and did not habitually or sincerely justify himself. I got a much better impression of the man than that which his prepared speech would have given me. And I said so. It was only for mischief that, as we rose, I startled him by asking a reporter's question.

"Mr. Calhoun, do you realize what you have been doing this whole half hour?"

"No," he joked. "What have I been doing?"

"You have been telling me all about the grafting in St. Louis."

"Well, but what of that?"

"Oh, nothing," I said. "Only, you know that I am supposed to be an expert on graft. I made a long, close study of the graft in St. Louis at a time when the lid was off. I learned a lot about it, as much as an outsider can, and now you have been showing me that you know more about it than I do."

With a look of alarm he said, "You are not going to say that, are you?"

"No, no," I answered. "I am not going to write that now; I am only going to think it." And so, laughing, we walked to the door, where we arranged to meet again whenever either of us wished to communicate. We never did. He did not send for me any more, and I did not have to go to him. He was tried in court; it was a long, slow, tense fight, and Mr. Calhoun was acquitted. But he was hurt, within himself. His friends, society, San Francisco, were loyal to their leader, but he began to age, as any one could see, and he became less active and died a few years later, an old man, an old, American gentleman. Patrick Calhoun died of intelligence. He knew what he was about. His associates were saved by their cunning rationalization, which was able to find excuses for what they "had to do"—or by their cynicism.

Another man the graft prosecution did not "get" was William F. Herrin, the political boss of California. The chief attorney for the Southern Pacific Railroad, he was the prime minister of the actual sovereign of his own State and a power in Oregon and other States and territories through which the road ran. But he represented not only the railroad. California was one of those States where the railroad was the principal corruptionist, the central active sovereign. In Rhode Island the railroad, having got about all it wanted, slipped back and let the more needy corporations, the public utility companies, collect and handle the money and the men; the New Haven road was a mere contributor there and paid the local political boss a salary. And that is the stage California has progressed to now. The graft prosecution and their child (and Roosevelt's), the Progressive party under Governor Hiram Johnson, put the railroad out of politics as the chief corruptionist, and that is what Spreckels should have aimed at. But the graft prose-

cution, being still in the state of mind which sees only and blames individuals instead of "interests," desired ardently to "get" that bad man, the railroad's State boss, after they had convicted Ruef. It was the failure with Calhoun that saved Herrin from trial; the evidence against him was less than that "on Calhoun."

Now Herrin was "wise." The responsible attorney for a railroad and conscientious railroad men have told me—and convinced me, too—that you cannot run a railroad without corrupting and controlling government. All discussion of public ownership is foolish; either the State will own and operate the railroads and other public utilities or these public corporations will "own" and govern that State. C. P. Huntington, one of the Big Four who built the old Central Pacific Railroad which became the Southern Pacific, said it. He was William F. Herrin's predecessor in the political department and had generaled from the lobby of the Legislature himself the fight of the railroad against a railroad commission to regulate railroads.

The night he was beaten, as the Legislature was adjourning victoriously, he said: "So they are going to regulate the railroads, eh? Well, then, the railroads must regulate the regulators." And he went after, and he got finally, the railroad commission. But his word was "must"; he "had to" do it; a railroad must govern, somehow, the State or the commission that otherwise would govern the railroad.

Mr. Herrin "had to" govern in the interest of the railroad he represented. I admitted the compulsion; the graft prosecution did not. I had respect for the man. But then I saw and talked with and learned something from Mr. Herrin. My experience with this man illustrates the rightness of the policy I had suggested to the graft prosecution: to let all indicted individuals go unpunished in return for "confessions" or explanations of the wrongs that they had done.

Mr. Herrin sent for me. It was during a crisis at the height of the exposures and trials, and I assumed of course that he would speak to me about San Francisco. But no, it was about Oregon. In my report on the timber grafts I had said that the plunderers of public forests had stolen also, and in the same way, with the connivance of railroad officials who should have guarded them, the timber lands of the railroad as well. My example was a steal from the Southern Pacific, and in telling it I used, without quoting, the exact language of a long telegram from Mr. Herrin. I can see now that he must have been curious to know how I came to be speaking in the words of a private dispatch.

When, in response to his invitation, I called, I said that I was glad that he had sent for me; that I had a question for him.

"Yes?" he said amiably. "But so have I a question for you, and mine comes first."

"If mine can come second," I laughed.

"I promise," he smiled. "I mean that I promise to hear—I may not be able to answer it."

"Agreed," I said.

"Well, then, how did you get the assurance to write and publish such a charge as that which you made, without proof, in your account of the Oregon timber frauds—that charge of crime against the officers of the Southern Pacific Railroad?"

"Why, Mr. Herrin, I had and I can produce the Western Union copy of your long telegram. Didn't you notice that I used your own words?"

He sat silent, thinking a long while. Then he said: "No use asking you where you got it?"

"None," I grinned.

Another pause, ended by: "Well, and what is your question?"

"This is my question," I said. "You are the responsible political representative in California of the railroad, the banks, and the other big public utilities—you are really the representative of all privileged property in this State. I understand what you do and have to do in that capacity. But what I do not understand is why you ever came to let Ruef and all the petty city grafters carry on their gross grafts in a way that was sure to make a scandal and hurt business and endanger property."

He looked at me, amazed.

"Don't you understand that?" he asked. I felt that he suspected me of a merely rhetorical question, not of inquiring ignorance. But I did mean it, and I convinced him that I did.

"You have been looking into politics all over this country; you are supposed to know how things are done, and you don't know— you don't understand that?"

I confessed I didn't.

"You don't know what it costs in time, labor, and money to keep a State—safe and—and—"

"Corrupt," I offered.

He paid no heed. He went on in earnest. He said that he, the railroad, appropriated a political fund and received contributions to it from other businesses, and that this money was used to finance party conventions, pay the expenses of some delegates, and now and then to furnish campaign funds for candidates as well as for campaign committees. That was a lot of money. That was about all they ever did, he said. "That's about all we can do. But that is not enough. We have to let these little skates get theirs; we have to sit by and see them run riot and take risks that risk our interests, too. We can't help it."

And then he startled me into a perception that was new.

"The Southern Pacific Railroad and all the companies and interests associated with us are not rich enough to pay all that politics costs."

That moment was the first time I realized the effort required to make the world go wrong. Always on the reform side, fresh from the scene of the labor, the fighting, the anxieties, the expenditures, of the graft prosecution, I was prepared but astonished to hear that the other side also was having a hard battle. But what I got over and beyond that was this—that the organized society which we call the State is, like a ship at sea, forever straining to right itself and that it takes, and gets, as much force to keep it off the wind and wrong as we reformers think it takes, and does not get, to sail it straight.

This statement of this honest-minded man was the greatest discovery I made in California. The graft prosecution exposed San Francisco as thoroughly as any city or State had been exposed in my experience. But all it showed was only a little more completely the very same system that had been shown in all the other cities and States. The only difference was not a real difference: the labor element in it. It was not a Labor government. The Labor party, in power, became a business government.

The political problem is an economic, an engineering—it is not a moral problem. The graft prosecution, fortunately, did not convict many individuals. Abe Ruef was sent to the penitentiary for eleven years, and there were some other victims, lesser men, not higher-ups. Francis J. Heney, the fighting, thinking, working prosecutor, was shot in the courtroom by a talesman he had challenged as an ex-convict picked for the Ruef jury by the defense. Burns and Heney's other associates always insisted that this would-be assassin had been put up to fire the bullet that went through Heney's lower face, deafening an ear, just missing the tongue, and throwing him out of the case. Hiram Johnson, an attorney in the graft prosecution, took the case, and it was he, with his fire and force, who won the great final victory and so came to head the Progressive movement in California, became governor and U.S. senator.

But—a big but—the city and the State were not convicted. A prosecution and an exposure like that, with punishments for objectives, put people in their places, show them which side they are on, but, busy fighting, they do not accept the conviction that they are "bad people."

In San Francisco, only Mr. Worster and Fremont Older got self-conviction out of all that strain and stress. Older, kind, just, even sentimental, having put Ruef in jail, rose in his journalistic triumph to ask what it was that made this young, able college graduate act as the agent boss. And Older saw that Ruef was no more guilty than other men, including Older. So Older turned round and labored for years to get Ruef out of the penitentiary and finally won the boss a parole, such a parole as the editor now seeks for other convicts, any other strong men that played the game and got caught. But Older has made a study since of psychiatry and sees that our whole penal system is unscientific. We punish people who are sick as we used to punish the insane. We don't know what else to do. A negro convict put the case very well once, as Older sees it.

He, John D. Barry, and I were visiting the condemned men's cells in Folsom Prison one day, and we came upon this negro squatting on the floor, peering out through the bars. He was a very big, strong fellow with a good skin, a gentle animal-like look out of his clear eyes. I spoke to him.

"What you got to die for, Bill?"

"Murder," he answered quickly. "They say I killed a man."

"Did you? Tell us about it."

"Well, boss, I got into a race riot and something hit me on the head. And when I woke up they told me I had gone mad and killed somebody. I was put away for life, and one day I got a pain in the head, that old place, and when I came to they said I'd killed a guard. So I got to be killed now."

"That's hard," I said. "You didn't know what you did! They oughtn't to kill a man for that."

"Oh, I ain't so sure about it. You see, boss, if they don't kill me for it, I might get the pain again and go and kill somebody else. Can't tell. So it may be all right to kill me all right, but—only, you see, it don't seem to be my fault."

Older, I think, would have condemned that man to undergo a surgical operation; he might, like the simple negro, agree to a sentence to death; might, I say. "But," he would say, "why punish?"

XXX

LOS ANGELES AND THE APPLE

S AN FRANCISCO learned nothing from the graft prosecution, nothing but facts—no lessons that were applied either economically or politically. The fighting passion persisted. Francis J. Heney was hated and admired as a fighter and highly respected as a lawyer, but his practice was so damaged by the fear of the prejudice of the courts against him that he had to remove his office to Los Angeles. Fremont Older was punished by business men through his paper. The circulation had gone up and continued to grow as his change of policy from righteous wrath to mercy for the under dog became clear. Its advertising suffered, and his personal standing as an editor was attacked privately by the business men who finally drove the owners to get rid of him. Hearst called Older to his rival evening paper, the *Call*, which immediately began to rise till it passed and finally absorbed the *Bulletin*. William J. Burns had proved himself to the men he called sons of bitches so that when he organized a national detective bureau they joined it as subscribers. Hiram Johnson, as governor, put the railroad out of power for a while; he gave one of the most efficient administrations any State has ever had, was re-elected, and then went to the U.S. Senate as the political reform boss of California. But there was no fundamental reform in the city or the State.

Were exposures useless? I could not at that time believe this. I went back to my theory that it was the threat of punishment which, by forcing men to defend themselves, put them in a state of mind where they could not see straight and learn. I wrote an article entitled "An Apology for Graft," showing that our economic system, which held up riches, power and acclaim as prizes to men bold enough and able enough to buy corruptly timber, mines, oil fields, and franchises and "get away with it," was at fault, and that San Francisco's graft trials showed that; and showed that we should change the system and meanwhile let the crooks go, who would confess and tell us the truth. The only reaction I got from this article was the wonder of good citizens and liberals whether I had sold out and gone back on reform!

Then it occurred to me to go to Los Angeles to see if that city had learned anything from the sight of San Francisco exposed. No one down there had been threatened with punishment; they had only to look on and see themselves in the fix of the San Franciscans. I called on Dr. John R. Haynes, a rich, very kind veteran reformer, who understands economics and men pretty well. He took me into the swell Jonathan Club, introduced me to some public service corporation men; others that I knew came up, and soon there was a group of "knowing" Los Angeles business leaders deploring the conditions of politics and business in San Francisco. They were cheerful about it. There was a self-congratulatory note in their grief at the shame of San Francisco, poor San Francisco. Los Angeles was, fortunately, not like that. I thought they were joking.

"Wait a moment," I said. "You have been having your sport with me, a San Franciscan. It's my turn now. You know, don't you; I know that you know, and you know that I know, that Los Angeles is in the same condition as San Francisco. The only difference is that San Francisco has been, and Los Angeles has not been, shown up."

Silence. Uneasiness, but no denial. I waited for the street railway or gas men to think, and one of them did mutter something about "another difference, San Francisco had a Labor government."

"Labor government!" I exclaimed, and I reminded them that that Labor government had sold out to capital and represented business.

Again no denial, only silence. They knew. They had forgotten. They wished to forget, to ignore what they knew. They had no fear of punishment, but they had learned no more from the experience of San Francisco than the San Franciscans had.

"I'll tell you what I'll do," I said into their silence. "If you will call a closed meeting somewhere soon and invite only yourselves, and your wives, and your associates, fellow directors, man-

agers, attorneys, and—and your priests and their wives—no outsiders at all—I will show you that you yourselves should want, at
the least, the public ownership of all public utilities and natural
resources."

They laughed; it was partly the laugh of relief. The tension
of my accusations had been unclublike. They laughed and we
broke up, but they accepted my challenge. They would have a
little dinner and eat me up.

Dr. Haynes managed the affair very well. He had the right
kind of people there, some hundred or more. No outsiders. Nobody
to enjoy and spoil the debate by making us conscious of a contest.
It was a conversation. The arrangement was that I was to state my
thesis and argument in a short twenty minutes, after which any
one of the company might challenge any point of mine, preferably
in the form of a question. But I asked leave to answer each questioner before another spoke. No objections.

I restated my thesis. My argument was a narrative, my own
story. I had gone forth, thinking what they thought, that bad men
caused bad government, especially politicians. Having to see them
for information, I found politicians to be not bad men; they were
pretty good fellows. They blamed the bad business men who, they
said, bribed them.

Who, then, were those bad business men? They named them,
each in his city, and as I saw them they were not bad, but they
were always in the same businesses. Regardless of character, education, and station, the people in these businesses were in the corruption of politics and the resistance to reform. This suggested that
it was these businesses, not the men in them, that were the cause
of our evil. And that's what they told me. They did not like or
wish or mean, they said they "had to" do evil. I could not for a
long time believe this. It sounded like a weak excuse when a big,
powerful captain of industry declared that the bad politicians "held
him up" and struck him for a bribe or a contribution to a campaign
fund. It was only after going through many cities and States and
hearing always the same plea of compulsion that I was persuaded
at last that it is true.

"You cannot build or operate a railroad," I said, "or a street
railway, gas, water, or power company, develop and operate a
mine, or get forests and cut timber on a large scale, or run any

LOS ANGELES AND THE APPLE   573

privileged business, without corrupting or joining in the corruption of the government. You tell me privately that you must, and here I am telling you semi-publicly that you must. And that is so all over the country. And that means that we have an organization of society in which, for some reason, you and your kind, the ablest, most intelligent, most imaginative, daring, and resourceful leaders of society, are and must be against society and its laws and its all-around growth."

My conclusion was that we all of us, they as well as I—they more than I—should seek to rid all individuals of those things that make them work against the greater, common welfare.

The first question from that company, and the last, was, "Who started the evil?" I reminded them that the question should be what, not who, and that everything they believed would be brought together by the answer. If it was some Thing that hurt us we could be Christians and forgive sinners; we could cease from punishing men and develop an environment in which men would be tempted to be good. No use; those business men wanted me to admit that the politicians made the conditions that business men were subject to. I related how the San Francisco banker, William H. Crocker, had argued that he had to do business under conditions as he found them, and I had reminded him that his father and the rest of the Big Four who built the Central Pacific Railroad were blamed by the politicians for corrupting the State and making the conditions he, the son and successor, "had to" continue.

Somebody mentioned the fear that government operation was always inefficient. I cited Seattle, where a publicly owned power plant was breaking down so often that there was an investigation, and they learned that the private competitors had paid certain political employees to sabotage the city's plant.

Another voice asked if the public operation of utilities would not put them into politics. To answer that, I turned to William Mulholland, the popular, highly respected engineer, who was the manager of the city's water system. He had been the manager when the water company was a private corporation, and it was notorious that he was then a very active and efficient politician. Everybody in that room knew that Mr. Mulholland had said over and over again that the change from private to public operation had got him and the business out of politics. When I passed the question of politics to him he did not have to answer. The whole company burst into laughter.

There were other questions, other arguments against business in politics, which I learned in college. But the ever-recurring question that night was Who? Who started it? Who is to be blamed and—punished? And at last, the Episcopal bishop of that diocese stated it in a form that suggested an answer. I was emphasizing the point that society really offers a prize for evil-doing: money, position, power. "Let's take down the offer of a reward," I said. "Let's abolish—privileges."

The bishop rose and very kindly, very courteously said that he felt that I was not meeting the minds of my hearers. "What we want to know," he said, "is who founded this system, who started it, not only in San Francisco and Los Angeles, in this or the last generation, but back, 'way back, in the beginning."

"Oh, I think I see," I said. "You want to fix the fault at the very start of things. Maybe we can, Bishop. Most people, you know, say it was Adam. But Adam, you remember, he said that it was Eve, the woman; she did it. And Eve said no, no, it wasn't she; it was the serpent. And that's where you clergy have stuck ever since. You blame that serpent, Satan. Now I come and I am trying to show you that it was, it is, the apple."

The bishop sat down. You could hear him sit down. For there was silence, a long moment, and in that silence the meeting adjourned.

XXXI

FREE-LANCING IN WASHINGTON, D.C.

T HAT debate in Los Angeles served only to clear and convince me, not the audience of course, in what lay the cause of our political evils. I ought now to go to Boston and see how our moral culture was working out there. But I wanted also to do Washington, D.C., and the Federal government. And most of all I wanted to stop muckraking. I had come so definitely to the conclusion that man's ideas were determined by the teachings of his childhood, by his business interests, by his environment, and not by logic, that muckraking looked useless. Society moved like a glacier, slowly; if it progressed it grew like an oak tree—slowly. One might water and manure the soil about it, but it was no use shouting at it. I would like to go on and see and describe Boston and Washington, but not in a magazine.

A personal experience contributed to this conviction. The editing of the *American Magazine* by a group of fellow writers was a scattered control which was more cautious and interfering than S. S. McClure's dictatorship. We all had been a unit against S.S., and we could disobey him, the lone boss. I rarely let him influence me against my judgment. All the writers on the editorial board of our own magazine took an interest in what I was writing, and they had an appeal that *McClure's* lacked. I had, we all had, a financial interest in the *American*—stock. I was asked to "go easy" at first, because we were just starting and needed friends. This I defied; I fear that I wrote offensive letters to the office, for I felt that we were coming under the same economic control that I despised in others. I did not "go easy." By and by they ceased to caution me; all they did was to send me occasional "reports of progress"; we were gaining in circulation, in advertising, in profits. I needed no nudging to realize that we had a chance to make a success of the

American Magazine and perhaps a lot of money each. And I noticed, with some pain, shame, and lying denials to myself, that I was going easy. All by myself, without any outside influence, I was being bought off by my own money, by the prospect of earning money.

I resigned from the *American*. If my mind was to be made up by my environment, I would change my environment. I resigned, and I promised myself never again to work where my money was. To go to Washington, I had myself syndicated among the newspapers, which expected me to expose the Federal government as I had cities. That was not my own intention. I wanted to see what kind of government Washington had, a city with the people disfranchised and the administration in the hands of men picked by the president and by and from Congress. That was an ideal arrangement for those who blamed the voters for the evils of politics and thought that a few carefully chosen, expert, experienced men, free from demagogy, would give us good government. The District of Columbia and Washington had, I found, a long history of just such graft and corruption as other cities had, and it was not much better even under Roosevelt; it only tried to be. The public service corporations and banks, in the hands of experts from Cincinnati and other corrupt cities, controlled; Congressmen on the old boards had not only sold out to high finance, they had gone on graft drunks which were a scandal the helpless citizens knew all about. Evidently it was true that the form of a government makes little difference; there is no solution in an undemocratic arrangement; on the contrary, public opinion, with votes, is some slight check upon a plutocracy. It stops the noise of the grafting.

The other question I sought to answer was: What does our Federal government represent? Regardless of efficiency and honesty, I would find out whether the president, the Congress, and the Departments stood for the common interest of the people or for the special interests of parts of the people. I called on the president, reminded him of my old purpose, and he accepted it, he said. He was sure he represented the people, and he certainly meant to. When we got down to specific bills and acts of his, two facts were evident. One was that he did not always know what the common interest was; his education was not economic, it was moral. The other fact was that he had to make deals with the Senate and the House; he said so himself; and he said that this was often a complete check upon him, because the senators and representatives did not represent the common interest. He would say this, and then he would fly into a rage when I said it.

"You are going to write it," he explained, "and that will hurt many honest senators and representatives who sincerely serve special interests." The moral point of view: if two senators voted for Wall Street, one for a bribe, the other for nothing, T.R. held the "wise" senator all wrong and the foolish senator all right. Bribery was the crime, not misrepresentation, according to T.R.

I accused him of bribery. There was a scene; it was all comedy, this period of muckraking in the White House. He said I ought to be thrown out into the street, but I said that it was he who had told me of his bribery. How? When? "Well," I said, "didn't you tell me that you had to get along with the Senate as it was?"

"Yes."

"Didn't you say that to get certain senators you had to appoint their candidates to office?"

"Yes."

"Well, then, you gave them their price to vote your way."

"But," he argued, "that wasn't bribery." I said it was the worst form of bribery; it was getting the people's senators to vote for the people's bills by paying them not his money but the people's money, in the form of a public office salary. That was not only bribery and a sneaking sort of cheap bribery, but it was building up the system he and the people were fighting. He reared around his room in a heat, but his sense of fun and fact was always near.

"Come now, Mr. President," I said. "Be honest with yourself and me. What is the most outrageous appointment you have ever made to get a senator?"

He halted, reflected: "The most outrageous . . . the worst . . . Let's see, what is the worst appointment I ever made?" And with a laughing shout, he answered: "Oh, I know. I made the brother of Senator Blank's mistress the district attorney of Blank City. The senator hated me, personally and politically. He was bad enough himself, but he would vote against a bill just because I wanted it. I had to 'get' him, and—well, I did for him what no one else would ever have done, and—and he has voted my way, since, sometimes."

"Good," I said. "I mean bad. What's the next worst?"

He told me. We went down the line from next to next, and he enjoyed it. "But gee whiz!" he broke in on himself. "You're not going to print all this."

"No," I said. "I'll not be so indiscreet as you were. I'll not name names; I'll leave blanks, or I'll just omit details and say simply that you also, even you, find that you have to buy the votes in the Senate and the House to get the representatives of the people to vote for your people's measures."

He was appalled, almost speechless; his balled fists and wrenching arms wanted to express him. But I pointed out that the liberal papers were already saying something to the same effect, that the people were reading and seeing this, and that they did not understand that, since they elected to the Senate men who represented special interests, he, their president, had to bid high to buy them over to the people's side.

"It's always been your policy," I reminded him, "to meet true charges with confessions. Let me now confess for you, and I'll bet you will hear less of this in the future."

He did not exactly consent, but he cooled down and discussed the matter quietly till—well, anyway one of my weekly syndicated articles did say, very definitely, that the president of the United States "had to" bribe legislators in the Senate and the House to vote for the people against the interests represented by the machines that had corrupted them and that while it explained some Federal appointments Roosevelt had made, it showed how, to fight the system, he had to help build and maintain it. There was a row, of course. Some of his cabinet must have stirred up the president to the frightened heat I found him in when I responded to his summons to the White House. He had with him in his private office the lawyers in his cabinet. It seemed to me that they were much angrier than T.R., who ranted, but not as I knew he could rant when he was personally aroused. He accused me of misusing English, "to call that bribery and corruption." This enraged the lawyers, who exclaimed, "English! Bad English!" And Secretary Moody said, indignantly, solemnly, "It is libel, Mr. President; it is criminal libel against the president of the United States."

"Whew!" I said. "Is it as bad as that? You going to indict and try me for criminal libel against the president? Tell me, then, can I call the president as a witness to prove that he told me the facts upon which I based—"

"No, no, no," T.R. interrupted, and the mad way he spoke convinced me that he had not told the cabinet that he had given me his most outrageous appointment and the next worst and the next. He didn't want them to hear any more of that. "No," he said, "there is no thought of criminal charges. Absurd. This is a difference of opinion between two writers about the use of words." And he backed me off in a corner as if to dismiss those absurd lawyers, and he shouted, he almost hit me with his whirling fists, saying that his "approval of the candidates for Federal appointments" was not bribery and corruption, not "in English."

"Not in England," I corrected, "and it soon won't be here, when men like you do it and get us all used to it. But—"

"You don't know English, you don't understand the tools of your own trade, you mishandle words—"

"Mr. President, wait," I begged him. "These politicians have frightened you out of your candor. You wait a few weeks and you'll see that that article will have laid to rest the growing charge against you. It will have put over the necessity upon you to deal with the kind of men the machines send to Washington to work against you."

He quieted down. We, he and I, settled into a private talk, and I saw the indignant cabinet lawyers slink, disgusted, out of "our presence." As they went I laughed and pointed to their hunched backs.

"They don't understand you, Mr. President," I said.

"What don't they understand?" he demanded, suspicious.

"They don't understand that you are an honest man; you are almost as honest as an honest crook."

It was my turn to be thrown out. He literally pushed me through the door. I apologized. I called back, "Almost, I said; almost; not quite." But he slammed the door; he laughed, but he made a great noise.

What I said was true. If T.R. had acknowledged with his mind what he knew in his hips, if he could have done the little customary evils he did consciously, without justifying them, he would have been a much greater, wiser man. But he was educated; he would not, he could not, always let his head know what his hands were up to.

One day I went in to see him with another correspondent, who walked right up to him and asked him about running for a third term. That question was up; the president must have been thinking about it. But when that correspondent put it to him, direct—"Mr. President, what about this third term business? Are you going to run for it?"—I was astonished. I was so astounded at the correspondent that I looked at him, not at the president; at the questioner, not for the answer; and I must have shown my amazement.

For the president, instead of answering the other man, turned upon me and said: "Why are you so shocked at that question?"

"I wasn't shocked at the question," I said. "I was astonished at the way he asked it."

"Why? How?" the president pressed, and I was confused. I did not know exactly what I meant. My answer was blundering.

"Why," I said, "he addressed his question to—your—mind."

"And what should he have addressed it to, if not to my mind?"

"I—I don't know," I fumbled. "But I have known you a long time, and my impression is that you don't think things out in your mind but that you mull them over somewhere else in your nervous system and—and form your conclusion in, say, your hips. If I wanted to get the answer he is after I would talk around indirectly till I got you to thinking out loud about what you were unconsciously concluding in your—hips."

It was T.R. that was astonished now. He stood there, hands on his desk, thinking; and then he said to the other correspondent: "Do you know, that's true. I do think down—down there somewhere. I am thinking over this third term business down there, and I think I have come to a conclusion. But I don't know it yet. I don't know yet what to say to you."

The other correspondent expressed astonishment in his turn—and disgust, too. He was annoyed at me for "butting in," I guess. He went out in a huff, and the president started to think aloud, indirectly, about that third term business. All I remember of what he said was an illustration of what I mean. T.R. said that he had "been thinking that Bill Taft would carry on" his policies, that "Bill Taft understood—" Of course Taft never understood anything about T.R.'s policies, but it was evident, wasn't it, that T.R.'s hips were deciding not to run himself for a third term, but to let Taft run? And that correspondent missed "news" by not knowing that an honest man and an "intellectual" uses his dishonest brain to cover or to discover his honest thinking, which is, really, very like a lowbrow's.

I wrote about ten weekly articles for that syndicate, showing that both Houses of Congress and the executive departments I studied were not representative. Since my purpose was to set up that criterion, I said nothing about honesty or efficiency; I asked and answered only one question in various forms. "What do they represent?" It was no use, and I could not keep it up anyway. I was serving about one hundred papers all over the country. That meant one hundred editors, who complained that I showed up no graft, wrote nothing sensational. That was their criterion: dishonesty, stealing, graft. If an honest senator honestly served a trust that was no disservice to the people; that was not wrong. I tried to be plainer, clearer—simple enough for the editors to understand. But they called my articles essays, and since that was not what was expected of me, I was in the unhappy position of the illustrators I had known who, having started in the magazines with a sketch of a pretty girl or a cowboy, had to draw always "something like that"—nothing but pretty girls from the one, nothing but cowboys from the other. I must rake muck all my life.

T.R. had just given us that word. At the Gridiron Club of the Washington correspondents, he denounced as "muckrakers" the writers who raked the muck of society and never looked up. I called on him the next morning about something else, but I said, "Well, you have put an end to all these journalistic investigations that have made you." He answered that he had no such intention, that he didn't mean me, for example. He had been aroused to wrath by an article on "poor old Chauncey Depew" by David Graham Phillips. The senator, he said, was having a lot of personal troubles, and then to have himself painted as a traitor in a series called "The Treason of the Senate," "that was too much." T.R. said that he spoke "to comfort Depew." I think he may have thought that, but I think also that he was irritated and felt the satiety of the public with muckraking. Anyway, I was right in my immediate sense that T.R. had called the close of a chapter. I was through with it myself, in the old form. My editors were dissatisfied. I was making more money on the newspapers than I had ever made on the magazines, as much a week as I had made in months before. It was a temptation to go on, but I could not; I could not write an article a week. I have ever since wondered at the columnists who can do one a day—for years! I quit Washington and went back to New York to rest and to play.

XXXII

WALL STREET AGAIN

I T WAS pleasant to go home to stay. And I had a home. I
haven't said much about it, because I was not much there,
and home and wife were little in my thoughts—as my wife
told me, very effectively, after she died. We had been looking for
a place of our own all the time we were boarding at Cos Cob; we
had been "real-estating." Thompson Seton, as I have said, taught
us that game. He took me with him on his rambles to see property
for sale "back of Cos Cob." It was cheap there. Back of Greenwich, where the New York rich had settled, it was high in price,
as high as $1000 an acre, whereas only two or three miles east it
was $10, $25, $50 an acre. And wilder, more abandoned, more
beautiful. It was fun to take long walks or buggy-rides with Seton
to spy out this land.

Tall, handsome, poet-like, he was animal-like, too. I suppose
"childlike" is the word most people would use to describe the
animal sense he had for springs and water courses, trees, plants,
and shady nooks that we saw. Real estate men and the natives
could not understand what he saw in tangled swamps and hopeless
woods. They preferred land that had at least been cleared. There
was one small hill that attracted me. It was clothed in beautiful
old, big trees, and the old Yankee who owned it, seeing that I had
a half a mind to buy it, said, "You like it? Well, you wait till
spring, and I'll make you take it. I know why you hesitate now."
He spent the winter clearing it and when in the spring I came
back to see it and threw up my hands at the bare, wrecked hill, saying it was spoiled for my uses, he gave us all up.

Seton saw in land, not only what a painter looked for, but the
animals. He would say, "How deer would love that"—or squirrels
or owls. He could see, too, what—how little—he would do with

each piece that he found "available." He pictured his roads and his trails, located and built his house, as a child might. He was deliberate, as if he liked the search, till he had three or four to choose from. That, the choice, was the only difficulty. But he did choose one at last, and I took his second choice. Others came in for his third and fourth choices. Seton could have started a boom of the abandoned farms of Connecticut, if he had had any mind for it or if there had been a western realtor there to mislead him.

To my astonishment I was unhappy when I bought my land. I couldn't go real-estating any more; I liked the game, and I had played it and lost. I decided, however, that I would play once more. Seton went to work on his piece; I let mine lie and went looking for another place. Left alone and reluctant to walk, I began rowing a boat or sailing in search of seashore property. That heightened the sport. The only flaw in it was that as I sailed up and down the Sound, seeing points and nooks for a house, far and ever farther away from Cos Cob, I knew all the time that the place I liked best was right in the harbor, a tiny cape in Riverside that I called Little Point, about an acre and two-thirds, with a sandy beach, a bay, and an old house under trees on a hill.

"That's the place," I'd say, every time we passed it, and my wife would answer, "Why not buy it, then?"

There were two good reasons. One was that it was surrounded by the rich; I liked better the artists' side of the river. The other was that it was not for sale. One autumn, just as we were about to move to town, a fisherman who knew what I liked spoke to me.

"That Scutt place is for sale," he said. "Old man Scutt died, and his will directs a city man who used to fish off that point and talk Sundays to him, who fished off'n his wall, to sell his place."

I saw the city fisherman, who said yes, he had the sale to make, but he asked, "What do you want it for? You can fish just as well from a boat anchored off the place as from the land." I sold the seventy acres "back of Cos Cob" and bought Little Point, where, like Seton, I went to work. No more real-estating for me. I went on wistfully looking at "lovely places," but—I gradually sank into Little Point, not into Riverside. We saved ourselves from our rich neighbors by being what they called "stinkers," what we called snobs; we "associated" only with oystermen, fishermen, and the "bum" writers and painters of Cos Cob. Irving Bacheller, a

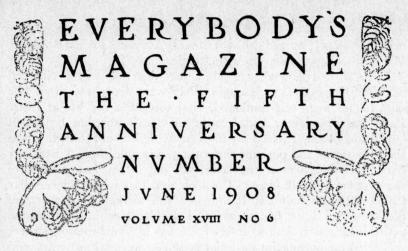

EVERYBODY'S MAGAZINE

THE · FIFTH ANNIVERSARY NVMBER

JVNE 1908
VOLVME XVIII   NO 6

Roosevelt—Taft—La Follette

on

What the Matter Is In America and What to Do About It

By LINCOLN STEFFENS

Author of "The Shame of the Cities," "The Struggle for Self-Government," etc

With Photographs specially taken by Éduard J. Steichen

EDITOR'S NOTE.—The men who are to make the race for the presidency of the United States are to be nominated during the next two months. With the candidates we are all familiar. But what do they really think about us and our problems and how, if elected, will they go about solving them? Tell us that and we will know what to do. Lincoln Steffens has undertaken in this article to put the Republican leaders on record. · The turn of the Democrats will come in July. Here President Roosevelt, Secretary Taft, and Senator La Follette explain what they believe to be the matter in the United States and how they would set about straightening out our national ills. Every one to whom the destinies of the United States are important should read this article.

I'M tired of exposure. I know something is wrong; something big. But what is it? Don't go on proving the evil over and over again. Tell us what to do about it. That's what we want to know. And let me tell you this: You show us what to do and—we'll do it."

A good, average American said that; he spoke as thousands upon thousands are speaking. And he and the thousands are right.

The time has come to discuss the causes of our American corruption and—cures. We have the facts. For years now investigators have been bringing forth the facts, and there should (and there shall) be no interruption of the inquiry. The command to "know thyself" is as good for a nation as for an individual, and the evidence is not all in. But we have enough to make out a case against ourselves. And the case

ONE OF LINCOLN STEFFENS' FIRST ARTICLES IN "EVERYBODY'S"

neighbor, had just published a novel, *Keeping up with Lizzie.*
We did not try to keep up with Lizzie.

Meanwhile I had taken a job, a part-time job on the editorial
board of *Everybody's Magazine.* My wife drove me to it. She
said, in her firm, self-contained, vital way, that my life at Little
Point was like dying. And I could see that it was, but I thought
—I would not have dared say it—that dying was not so bad. It was
the pleasantest and perhaps the most serviceable thing I had ever
done. I could go mow the lawn, sail out in my boat to talk to
the oystermen, walk over to Cos Cob, and loaf while laborers like
Childe Hassam painted. It annoyed the workers, but that was
pleasant, too. They had to work; I didn't; I could bum around
and think, or not. And so in town. It was like real-estating; there
was a risk of getting into a job, but if you were strong you could
go down into the editorial rooms of the magazines, peep into a
smoky cave, and say, cheerily, "Hello, Dunne. Working?"

And Peter Dunne would look up, glad of the interruption, to
say, "Hello. What are you doing?"

"Nothing," I would swagger, and watch envy spoil the good
looks of whatever poor slave I was visiting. If I overdid it at the
American Magazine I could go down to the newspaper offices,
where they really work, where they run and write or sit and hate
you. I imagine that the spirits of the dead don't visit the living
because they realize that even their loved ones will hate them for
their happy leisure. Well, there were other publications. I'd go to
Everybody's, see John O'Hara Cosgrave or Gilman Hall. This
was not so good. The other offices knew and said that I was down
and out; they had not heard that on *Everybody's;* so they were
always offering me work.

"Want to go out and get a good story on—"

"No," I said many times, but I made there a mistake which did
not matter on the *Globe* newspaper and the *American* and *Mc-
Clure's.* I kept telling the *Everybody's* editors how to edit a publication. The others knew that I did not know how and that they
did. *Everybody's* did not know how, and they did not know that
I did not know how. I told Cosgrave and Hall so many things
for them to do that finally they invited me to join their editorial
board and meet with them once or twice a week. I happened to
tell my wife about this; I was only bragging, but that's how I

happened to lose out in loafing as I had in real-estating. She made me take the job.

It was hard work again. E. J. Ridgway was the editor. He meant it to be hard work. He said he would pay me ten thousand a year for that part-time job, and I refused it, saying I did not want to feel that I had to earn that much; I would tell him at the end of the year how little I hoped to have earned. And I recall that at the end of the year I asked for five thousand, which he paid and then added a couple of thousand (I think it was; perhaps more) as a "Christmas present." He was that sort of man. He liked to share his prosperity, and he was prosperous.

Everybody's had been running the highly sensational exposures of high financiers called "Frenzied Finance" by Thomas W. Lawson, the Boston speculator, who knew the top men of Wall Street and their methods. Tom Lawson had been reading us muckrakers, and he said that he could make our exposures look like thirty cents if he told what he knew. Ridgway had offered him the space, and Cosgrave undertook to drive him to dictate his stories and then to edit them into shape. The result was such an exposure of high finance that the management of my cities looked like good government. Also, by the way, the circulation and the profits of *Everybody's Magazine* rose to a peak. The editors believed in Wall Street as a popular subject. I saw my chance to study and report the politics of business in the form of a series of articles on the control of credit. This took me back into Wall Street, which had changed as much as I had. I found men of my age, whom I had known as stock-brokers and subordinates, swelling around as presidents of banks and trust and other companies. Fine. They were proud, and I was congratulatory; but as I saw them often, I discovered that they still were subordinates. They were, like mayors of cities, only fronts for the old president or some owner of the bank who had retired to the quiet seclusion of boss. The boss system, shown in the exposures and in the reform of the life insurance companies, had become the regular thing in business. Banks had been consolidated, companies merged, young men promoted to the very highest old executive positions, and all under the control of unofficial, unresponsible older men, who played together and so merged their power. It was all done exactly as in politics, and one use of this concentrating power was to dominate politics. My conclusion was that there was indeed such a thing in America as sovereignty, a throne, which, as in Europe, had slipped from under the kings and the president and away from the people, too. It was the unidentified seat of actual power, which, in the final analysis, was the absolute control of credit;

THE CURB—MANHATTAN

Drawing by José C. Orozco. Courtesy of the
Delphic Studios

political power and business power and money were only phases of this business man's political control of the function of money-lending, of credit-lending. The bosses did not have to buy companies as they had to bribe political parties; like the political bosses, they had only to command the owners of property and the possessors of votes (whether ballots or proxies) to gain obedience. All but the few, very few, exceptional men wanted some one else

Everybody's Magazine

VOL. XXIII   SEPTEMBER 1910   NO. 3

IT

An Exposition
of the Sovereign Political Power
of Organized Business

By

LINCOLN STEFFENS

AUTHOR OF "THE STRUGGLE-FOR SELF-GOVERNMENT," "THE SHAME OF THE CITIES," "UPBUILDERS."

Editor's Note: This is the first of a series of articles in which Mr. Steffens is to do to business what he did to politics. He reported so that everybody saw it, the business in American government: city, state, national. He proposes now to describe, so that we can all comprehend it, the politics in business; all business, but especially big, corporate business.

As to Mr. Steffens' qualifications for this large task, all we need add here to what is known of him, is that his turn from machine politics to the mechanism of business is a return to his first love. Mr. Steffens began his career as a reporter in Wall Street

The BOSS of All The Bosses

IT is said in Wall Street that one man is supreme down there now If that is so, it is time to talk business. We have been neglecting business; we have been paying too much attention to politics; all of us have; the American people. And the cost of living is but a part of the price we shall have to pay for our absorption in our public affairs. It is true we have something to show for it; there's a balance to our credit: We are beginning to understand politics. Even our politicians are beginning to understand politics a little. And their lessons should not be interrupted. But our public business isn't our only business. We all have our private business also to attend to, and if one man dominates that, it means that the boss has developed in business as well as in politics. And if that is so, it is high time to understand business; it is time even for business men to understand business

For if Mr. J. P. Morgan is the boss of

IN ALL MY TIME J. P. MORGAN SAT ON THE AMERICAN THRONE

to decide and command. What this instinctive drift toward dictatorship meant I did not see; all I could see was that it was universal; it occurred in politics, business, society, journalism. While
men cried aloud for liberty they called secretly for a boss. And
what the boss was working with and for was privileges. In a bank
he wanted to say what loans should be made and who should have
them; in politics he wanted to say who is to have privileges, and
the political boss lets his business boss decide that. The business
boss, then, is the sovereign. In all my time J. P. Morgan sat on
the American throne as the boss of bosses, as the ultimate American sovereign.

One day soon after my article to this effect was published, I
was in the Morgan bank. A junior partner tapped on his glass cage
and beckoned me in. He said that he had laid on J.P.'s desk the
magazine, open at my article, saw him read it and read it again
and then shake his head. He didn't understand it. The junior
partner said that J.P. had no sense of "absolute power" and that
as a matter of fact his power was not absolute; it was very limited,
and he told me an incident to prove it. J.P. had discovered that
he could not make the New York, New Haven and Hartford
Railroad, which he controlled, buy its coal from a coal company
he controlled, without the consent of "Diamond Jim" Brady. He
was so enraged that he was going to fight Brady; "if he did nothing else the rest of his life, he would lick that man." But he didn't;
he accepted him, and the reason was that Brady represented a
company in which the officers of the New Haven and other railroads held shares; the company had the exclusive privilege of selling supplies to those railroads. It was a racket, of course, but the
ramifications of its business, influence, and power were so com-
plex that even Morgan dared not touch it. Therefore he was not a
sovereign.

It is a very common error to think of sovereignty as absolute.
Rasputin, a sovereign in Russia, made that mistake; many kings
have made it and so lost their power to premiers and ministers
who represented the "vested interests" of powerful classes, groups,
and individuals. A dictator is never absolute. Nothing is absolute.
A political boss concentrates in himself and personifies a very
"wise" adjustment of the grafts upon which his throne is established. He must know these, reckon their power, and bring them

all to the support of his power, which is, therefore, representative and limited. Mussolini, in our day, had to "deal with" the Church of Rome. A business boss has to yield to the powerful men who support him. The Southern Pacific Railroad had to "let the city grafters get theirs." The big bankers had to let the life insurance officers and employees get theirs. J. P. Morgan should have known what he soon found out, that he could not lick Diamond Jim Brady. Under a dictatorship nobody is free, not even the dictator; sovereign power is as representative as a democracy. It's all a matter of what is represented by His Majesty on the throne. In short, what I got out of my second period in Wall Street was this perception that everything I looked into in organized society was really a dictatorship, in this sense, that it was an organization of the privileged for the control of privileges, of the sources of privilege, and of the thoughts and acts of the unprivileged; and that neither the privileged nor the unprivileged, neither the bosses nor the bossed, understood this or meant it.

XXXIII

CUBS: WALTER LIPPMANN, FOR EXAMPLE

IN JOURNALISM as in other lines, it was not better men, it was more intelligent men, that we needed. So I urged the editorial board of *Everybody's* to seek better reporters, to find their own cubs and train them from the start as magazine writers. Their policy, the practice of all magazines, was to watch the newspapers and take over men who distinguished or offered themselves.

"Like us," I said, quick, lest the ex-newspaper men on the board should say or think, "But we are products of that system and —look at us." Since it is "looking at us" that proves the need of some reform, it is well to anticipate, as I did, by pointing out politely, that we, long and well-trained newspaper men, were hard to re-form. We did not make magazines; we made Sunday or weekly newspapers once a month. We limited the scope, the style, the interests, of the monthlies; we reported politics, exploration, crime, love, and business as the newspapers did, narrowly, superficially, because we could not get over our early training on the dailies. We did not branch out into the reporting of the sciences and the arts and go deeper into the daily news. The consequence was that the newspapers were growing over our field faster than we were getting into theirs.

"Let's find and form our own cubs," I pleaded.

Recalling my success as a city editor with cubs taken fresh from the graduating classes of colleges, I advised a systematic annual search of seniors for one or two of the best of them, from our point of view. Gilman Hall nodded approval; Cosgrave shook his head doubtfully; Ridgway was silent. The pretty girl who took notes scratched them out: no decision.

We passed on to other business till one day Ridgway, impatient of my persistence, said: "All right, Steffens. If you think you can walk into a bunch of undergraduates and pick a winner, try it. But don't wish your genius on us. You take him; take him as your secretary. We'll pay his salary. You train him as a magazine writer, and—well, if you can get anything your cub writes into the magazine within a year, I'll say your experiment will have proven your theory."

A challenge? A chance! I had long wondered that not only editors but other leaders of men who are forever seeking good human stuff for their staffs and for their successors did not make a business of searching the colleges, the cheapest labor market in the world, for men—gifted writers, born executives, instinctive organizers, natural chemists, physicists, schooled workers in all lines. Why let discovered talent escape into odd jobs where they don't fit, are unhappy and often ruined? Why wait till the few survivors of the wasteful practice find their own places, by chance, late? I suppose it is because employers, looking over a crowd of college boys, see a yelling, vain, hopeless mob of fools. They don't ask about, they don't hear of, the always existing few quiet students with concealed gifts in the rooters at a football game. They see, and they may take, a star player now and then for a popular bond salesman, not the boy who is only a brilliant planet in the chemical laboratory or the soul of the college paper.

It was late summer when I went to Cambridge. The graduated class of Harvard was scattered. There were a few of them left around Boston, and some professors. I described the man I was after, not the job I had to offer. If you mention a job, people think of a "friend who needs a job." I asked for the ablest mind that could express itself in writing. Three names were offered, only three, and after a little conversation everybody agreed on one— Walter Lippmann. I found Lippmann, saw right away what his classmates saw in him. He asked me intelligent, not practical, questions about my proposition and when they were answered, gave up the job he had and came home to New York to work with me on my Wall Street series of articles. It was reporting. I was writing in my house in Connecticut. He went to Wall Street for facts, which he reported to me. He "caught on" right away. Keen, quiet, industrious, he understood the meaning of all that he learned; and he asked the men he met for more than I asked him for. He searched them; I know it because he searched me, too, for my ideas and theories. My view that our work was scientific and that I should be able to predict the facts he went forth to find, he heard with canny doubt. To put it to a test we picked out a little, lively business community in south Jersey where there was a big business, a packing-house center. I had never been there, but I described the system of politics and business as it must exist there if our picture of Wall Street and government was right. He took a train, investigated the town, and brought back a report which met the prediction; it was printed, I think, later.

For I did not forget Mr. Ridgeway's challenge. Lippmann must

WALTER LIPPMANN

write something for the magazine. I suggested that he begin with a subject well within his own personal knowledge, do it by himself, and one day, very soon, he brought me a short essay on "William James—An Open Mind." It was well done, but he rewrote part of it, and since Professor James was dead and the newspaper tradition on a magazine forbade obituaries, I changed the title to "The Open Mind—William James" and, to make the test fair, omitted the author's name. I submitted the article, it went through the regular course, and it turned up in proof as mine, with my name under the title. Lippmann proof-read it, correcting all errors except that of the signature. That I left till the last, page proof, and it came out in the next number "By Walter Lippmann." The editors were surprised, but they took not only other writings of his but the magazine cub himself. Before the year was up he was one of the editors of *Everybody's*. They did not, however, follow up the search of colleges for men.

While Lippmann was with me we muckraked Greenwich, Connecticut, the town of which Riverside was a part. I had been lecturing, and one evening in a theater in an eastern Connecticut city I was interrupted by a man in a box. He rose and said that what I described of the corruption of cities might be true of New York, Philadelphia, and points west, but no such conditions prevailed in Connecticut. That city, for example, was not corrupt. I learned later that my heckler was a leading banker; all I could see at the moment was that he was a commanding, respected man. I replied that I did not know his town, but I did know some of Connecticut. "You may not know it, but I happen to be a resident of Greenwich, Connecticut, and I can tell you that that town is as corrupt as any city in the United States. Shall I describe Greenwich?" He sat down, didn't want me to speak of Greenwich, but there was a mischievous young editor in Greenwich, Norman Talcott, who reported what I had said of the town and challenged me to prove my libel. A town meeting was called and Lippmann investigated the town, he and my colored gardener. My wife was very ill at the time, and I could not leave the house. Lippmann gathered records; the colored boy "hung out around" the politicians and gathered the gossip. He said that there was betting on the result and that the bosses were giving odds that I'd win. I would myself have bet on my plan.

There was some interest in the event. The New York newspapers sent reporters to "see me get mine in my own home town." The hall was full. The colored boy carried to the platform a valise of the documents, which Lippmann piled neatly upon the table. The boy, all agrin, sat down on the edge of the stage, Lippmann on a stool near a great blackboard. When I came up on the platform I asked for a moderator, as the New Englanders call a chairman; a very respectable citizen was chosen. He asked me aloud what he was to say, and I told him, also aloud, to announce that I was to show the people of Greenwich that they were as corrupt as any city in the country, that there would be an opportunity for discussion, and that, finally, there would be a vote.

My plan was to make that town see and declare itself, without many local facts, to get it to do what Los Angeles could not do, recognize itself in descriptions of San Francisco, St. Louis, and other cities. I began with Greenwich, however. When I said that

Greenwich was corrupt I explained that I meant not the buildings and the streets but the people, "you, here, the citizens of the town, and I will start with the reminder that at the last election you saw me, lots of you saw me, standing in the undertaker's shop, watching you pass through there getting your $2.50 per voter. We both know that, but I know something you don't know. I know and you don't that while you were getting your $2.50, the Italians were getting $2.75 a vote."

This statement caused a sensation. The Yankee voters did not like to be outdone in a bargain, and they had heard as a rumor what I asserted as a fact. Men in the audience looked around at the bosses in the back of the room for a repetition of the denials that had been made to them. There were none. The bosses knew I knew. After a short pause for the correction that did not come, I proceeded from the bottom of Greenwich to the top of Connecticut; I quoted a governor who had defended the customary bribery at the polls by saying that he deemed it "right, for a man who knows what is right, to influence even with money the votes of voters who are ignorant." That they all knew, and I argued that these two instances went to show that Greenwich, Connecticut, was worse than cities and States outside of New England. But that was not my thesis; I was there only to prove that Greenwich, Conn., New England, was as bad as other parts of the country. And with Lippmann at the blackboard and the black boy shining on the edge of the stage, I described and Lippmann diagramed the corruption of government:

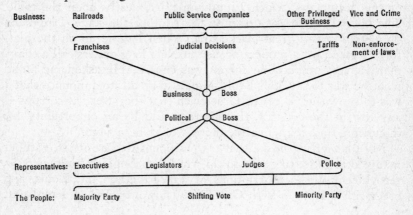

UPPER LEFT: EDWARD A. FILENE (BLANK & STOLLER). UPPER RIGHT: COLONEL ARTHUR WOODS (COPYRIGHT BY PIRIE MAC DONALD). LOWER LEFT: JUDGE BEN B. LINDSEY. LOWER RIGHT: MARTIN LOMASNY (NOTMAN'S).

Suddenly I stopped my long narrative and asked, "Have I made good?" The faces before me manifested surprise. Greenwich had not been mentioned for an hour; it had been forgotten, when I asked again, "Have I shown that Greenwich is as corrupt as the places I have named?" The meeting looked at me in wonder or disappointment or—something till I turned, pointed at the black-board, and said, "Well, but isn't that a perfect picture of the gov-ernment of Greenwich?" There was a moment of study of Lipp-mann's diagram; then there was a burst of applause and laughter. Seeing that they saw it, I asked the audience to call out the local names to fill in the diagram, and the crowd shouted them to Lipp-mann, who wrote them in their places.

There was no discussion until I offered my resolution that "we, the people of Greenwich, in town meeting assembled, admit that we are as corrupt as any community so far exposed in this coun-try." Then came protests, but that meeting carried that resolution over the protests with a shout, and the protestants, all typical leading citizens, property-holders, taxpayers (as they call them-selves), failed to hold the crowd, and one of them finally ap-pealed to me, as a property-holder, etc., to withdraw my motion. I said I would if they would have another meeting and join with me in a plan to beat the bosses and clean up the town. That was agreed to, the meeting adjourned, and we did have another meet-ing to start a movement which, eventually, ousted the old boss and put the reformers in power.. There was no reform, however. It was a change in personnel, from men who had been convinced that they were "bad" to good, respectable, educated gentlemen who did not know how bad they were or how to govern a town.

What I got out of this was the theory that political propaganda can accomplish something if, instead of appealing to malice and the love of scandal in "good men," it reached for the imagination of "bad men." Even voters who sell their votes can be made to see themselves as they see others. There is no salvation in "education," but education might help a little. This and some other experiences led Lippmann and me to try an experiment in education at Harvard, later.

XXXIV

A SUCCESSFUL FAILURE

WHILE I was half playing, half working, on *Everybody's Magazine* in New York and Riverside, Edward A. Filene, the Boston merchant, sought me out and invited me to muckrake Boston. Boston! He did not know, of course, that I had long wished to go there to study, at their source, the American ideals which did not "work" in the rest of the country. He evidently expected a regular "exposure" of the political corruption of his city, but he said I would be free to do and write whatever I liked. His proposition was that I go to Boston with my family, live there a year, investigate and report the conditions as I found them, and, if I saw one, draw a plan for a way out. He would raise a small but sufficient fund to pay my expenses. In return for the money, my report was to become not mine but the committee's, who would publish and receive any profits there were on the book.

I accepted this offer, closed my Riverside house, and moved, with my wife and her mother, to Boston and went to work first on this man, Filene. He interested me. A big business man, he seemed to be a democrat, a thinker, who said things like an intellectual, but who went and did them like a practical man of business. I have never got over some of Filene's sayings. "There are no miracles," for example. When he said that the first time, I passed it as commonplace. The second time he said it, it struck me that he believed it to such an extent that he acted upon it. He was telling how as a youth he had an eczema which was so bad that it set him apart at school and kept him from going to Harvard. "I wanted to be a statesman," he said; "so I had to go to college, but I couldn't. I was too offensive to look at; so I went into my father's business and decided there that I would be a business

statesman. For I saw that there was plenty to do in making business scientific. There were evils to correct, and I could see that
anybody could correct them if he realized that there were no
miracles of evil either, that it was only a matter of removing the
causes of evil. But first I must find and remove the cause of my
eczema."

He called on the Boston physicians who specialized in skin
diseases, but he asked them to explain, not to cure, his malady.
What was eczema? What caused it? He got from them the titles
of books which he read and the names of specialists anywhere in
the world whom he consulted with his growing knowledge of
eczema. He came to know all that all the experts knew about his
kind of eczema. And then he cured himself by treating not the
skin but the root causes of the condition of his skin. It was in this
sense that he meant that there are no miracles. It was in this literal
sense that his sayings, many of them the merest platitudes, were
so vivid in his mind that they came to me like discoveries really
fit to act upon as he acted upon them. Maybe I was discovering
only a difference between intellectuals and men of action. For I
noticed that when I said something to him he did not follow my
logic; reason was not convincing to him; he was imagining my
proposition in action, and he took or he rejected it according to
whether he could see it being done. But, if he did see it working,
he would try it on. He asked me once how he could overcome the
class, race, and religious differences which split up Boston so that
the city could not act as a unit on anything. There was the old,
lingering prejudice against the Catholics and the Irish, for and
against the "Brahmins," as the old families were called. I suggested, humorously, a City Club where all these varieties of
Bostonese would meet and learn to know one another. We talked
about it; he was serious; and I became interested. He was talking
about ways and means, all political, and he decided that it was a
good idea because it could be done. And he did it, politically. He
inquired around for a popular, able organizer; he offered him a
good salary and a life career; and he told him what to do. The
organizer was to make a list of all the going clubs in Boston, find
out who were the leading spirits in each club, gather each of these
sets of leaders at a meeting, and tell them, privately and separately, what he was up to. He and these men were to found a

downtown club, good, cheap, convenient, where they were to bring together all sorts of men just to meet one another and so overcome prejudices. The club was to be for the common good of Boston; it was to discuss and hear discussed all sorts of local problems, but was never to act, never to go into politics or do anything; only listen, talk, understand. This was to develop a Boston city spirit and give individual citizens a chance to become known. Filene himself made a search for a cook. He knew that good food, cheap, was essential; so he went to all sorts of restaurants in all the cities he visited, looking for good food. When he had a good meal he talked to the chef, and—well, he found an undiscovered genius in a third-class New York restaurant, and he engaged him to come to the Boston City Club when it was ready. He saw the list of members as it grew, made sure that, however prominent or obscure, they were the men who made their own clubs. Then, with all the forces going that must make a live club, he, Filene, went off on a trip around the world—to "really get it that the earth was round." When he came back the Boston City Club was the most successful club in Boston and going far beyond his control. Every one of the first members of that club knew that he and a few of his friends and the directors were in a conspiracy for the democratization of Boston, but none but the directors knew that Filene, a quiet director, was in on the plot.

Another time Filene thought that the Merchants Association, the Board of Trade, and the Chamber of Commerce of Boston should be merged into one and democratized. He was a member of none of them; they were all against his (and his friends') activities in the matter of the graft and political corruption of the public service corporations; and some of these old commercial institutions owned buildings and valuable properties and privileges. Filene, the rank outsider, analyzed the forces for and against his scheme; he set picked conspirators at work, and he, a reformer, "a troublemaker who hurt business" and a newcomer in business, did finally consolidate those dead old institutions into one powerful, active Chamber of Commerce with a big, broad, ever-increasing membership. And having done that in Boston, he similarly reformed the chambers of commerce in other cities, and then he united all of them into a national Chamber of Commerce, which, right after the war, he brought into an international Chamber of

Commerce made up of the representatives of reformed chambers of commerce in European and other countries.

A miracle? No. This was done by a tried method that set in motion certain known forces.

"Yes," said Louis D. Brandeis, who used to work with Filene in those early days and was his chief adviser, "Filene is forever making weapons for the enemy."

Those chambers of commerce all over the world are powerful reactionary influences. Filene is as helpless in them as he is in the Boston City Club, but he was a democrat, a liberal democrat; he was sure that democracy must be as good for business as for politics. Anyhow, believing in it, he was for democracy everywhere always, even in his own store.

He had a yacht at Marblehead when I first knew him, and like so many yachtsmen, was always on the lookout for guests to use his boat. He put me aboard that first summer in Boston and brought me books, papers, magazines, every evening to keep me entertained. One day I picked up the weekly paper published by his employees, and on the first page was an article by E. A. Filene himself. It was a reproachful account of how his ambition was to have his business taken away from him by his employees; he had given them constitutional powers which would, if used, enable the workers to govern themselves, manage the business, and finally get possession of the company. And, he wrote, all the employees ever used these powers for was to achieve a few minor privileges, such as shorter hours and a half holiday. He expressed his great disappointment.

"Do you mean that, E.A.?" I asked him at the evening meal.

He most certainly did, and he gave more details of the folly of his employees. Would he allow me to address his employees? He would. Would he attend the meeting himself? He promised. And within a week he brought me an invitation to speak at a regular shop meeting. He went with me to confront those hundreds of young men and women. I told them how, in cities and States, the people had votes with power to govern, but did not exercise their rights; they let their bosses rule them scandalously. My hearers laughed at the people of New York, Philadelphia, Missouri, etc. They did not laugh so much when I showed them that the citizens of Boston let slip their powers in the same way and to the same ridiculous effects. They tittered, however; they could see that the people of Boston were abused.

But when I paused and took up them and their store, there was silence. Pointing at Mr. Filene, I said that he said that they, his employees, were as weak and as ridiculous as the citizens of any city. I quoted from his article in their shop paper his complaint that he had given them power to take over the company and that they used it only for trivialities, not always in the interest of the business.

"There he sits," I said. "He will stop me if I say anything un-true. He asked me to come here and see if I could not lead you to see the chance you have to take and govern and own this great business. He says he can't make you believe it. He says that he, the boss, is a democrat and that you, the workers, are not; that you want to be bossed; that all you want is a little more pay and a little more time to play. I say that you here are a fair test of democracy and that if you don't want to take over this offered shop it means that the people don't want to govern their cities, States, and—themselves. Anyhow, you have no right to laugh at New Yorkers, Philadelphians, Missourians, and your Boston neighbors."

There was no answer, no sound. I asked Filene to withdraw a moment and then asked that hunk of "the people" to say some-thing. Not a word. It was the boss who afterward, on the way home, asked me how he could stir up a demand on the part of his employees for more power and, ultimately, possession. "I will leave them my stock if they will show any disposition to—use it." All I could suggest at the time was that he hire and encourage some "agitators."

"We have some now," he answered. "They do not agitate for power; it is they who start the demands for petty privileges."

E.A., as his friends call him, has built up one of the greatest big department stores in the United States. He has several thou-sand employees, a capitalization of millions, and he has made his shop a leader in the retail trade, all by the application, as a boss, of the principles of democracy to business. He invented a method, called everywhere the "basement store," to save and to distribute at a price lowered every week the surplus goods that once were de-stroyed. I remember the shock with which he pointed out to me one day a newspaper account of the burning by manufacturers of a lot of pianos that had been overproduced. He saw that waste, and he worked on the problem till he solved it in his line, and when he solved it, persuaded his competitors to adopt his method.

He calls his life a failure, "the failure of a successful millionaire," but that is because he did not do the two things he wanted most to do. His first ambition was his shop democracy. His second and greatest was to be to distribution what Ford afterward became to manufacturing.

"The cost of the distribution of manufactured goods now," he said to me way back in 1908-9, "is 55 per cent. of the price of those goods. This is disgraceful; this is bad management. I would like to lower that percentage."

And here the other day, twenty years later, he said, "The cost of distribution is higher than it was then, even in my store." He said this to justify his own view that he had been defeated and was a failure.

Anyhow, this was the man who invited me to Boston. There were others, he said, who contributed to the fund, but I was never told who they were. E. A. Filene was my sole boss in Boston.

XXXV

THE MUCK I RAKED IN BOSTON

I LIVED and worked a year in Boston, with two results or none. The first was a book which was never published; the second was a plan which was published but never carried out. The book was supposed to be destructive, a statement and an analysis of the conditions, a diagnosis of the disease; the Boston 1915 Plan was to have been constructive, a cure, a way out. The book took me several years to write, and when it was done, went to the committee, who tried to find a publisher, as I did, in vain. There was, in Boston, some suspicion that the committee suppressed it. The assumption was that I had muckraked the politics of the city, as I had other cities, and that my committee of anonymous leading citizens did not like the picture drawn, and owning it, hid it from the light.

Upton Sinclair probably thought that at the time. When, twenty years later, he was writing his novel on Boston and the Sacco-Vanzetti case, he asked for my old manuscript. Since he returned it promptly without a word of comment and no use made of it in his book, I infer that he exonerates the Boston committee. He would not have published it himself; it was not what he expected. That book was a disappointment to everybody, and my theory is that it had no relation to any kind of thinking that was being done at that time. It was an attempt to muckrake our American ideals (not our bad conduct but our virtues) as a sign and as a continuing cause of our evils. In a country and in an era in which good people believed that bad people caused the evil which good people, if elected to power, would cure, and the more scientific minds held that bad economics caused both the evils and the ideals, there was no public, there were no publishers, for my thesis that there were two sources of evil and that one of the two was our ideals. Upton Sinclair, like George Bernard Shaw, possesses, practices, and believes in the virtues I was finding fault with in Boston. Shaw and Sinclair represent the economic reformers, the Socialists, who really believe in morality. And my Boston committee men may not have been able to practice, but they still believed in, their individual ethics and their social ideals as a cure, not a cause, of evil. They represented moral reformers, numerous in Boston, who wanted me to show up the evils so that they could reform them by the applied force of their morality.

Their morality did not work elsewhere. It had gone west from New England, often with the New Englanders who settled, dominated, grafted and got rich on, and yet bewailed the conditions of places like Ohio, Minneapolis, and Oregon, where foreigners and other wicked people were blamed—blamed for the system the New Englanders instinctively established. Their ideals were such that they not only permitted and ultimately defended, they created, evil wherever they went. But it wasn't fair to judge this culture out west. The conditions of Ohio and California did not conform with the ideals of New England; the Yankee theory was that the west could still be saved by and should be schooled in the high ideals and the respectability of—not Rhode Island; that was exceptionally bad, like Connecticut and New Hampshire and Vermont; these were indeed New England States, but they had, for some reason, slipped; no, but these States and the western States, the whole country, could be cured by the culture of—Boston, Massachusetts. What were the conditions in old, cultured Boston, where our good, old, American ideals and virtues were started, worked out, and still lived, as ideals?

Boston was corrupt. So was Massachusetts, New England. The first impression I got was that Boston was worse than Philadelphia, that Boston and Massachusetts were the worst that I had ever seen and felt. But I recalled my old theory of progression in corruption. So it was truer to say that Boston was in a later, lower, worse stage of the same growing system which gripped all the other cities that I had studied. Massachusetts was deeper in the same organization of privilege and false or contradictory thinking that prevailed in the other States I had seen. It was not exceptional even in New England; it was typical of New England, which was darkest America. What seemed "better" in Boston was really worse. There was no one political boss of Boston, as there was of most cities. This fact suggests that the political boss will pass; he is a scandalous agent, who, like the boss of California quoted, "has to let the little grafters get theirs." The political boss has passed out in Boston; the business bosses have dispensed with him, and they have found that they can manage the corruption of politics themselves much better.

There was less scandal in Boston, fewer exposures, and those that were started were kept within bounds as in old England, where likewise there are no bosses, where likewise gentlemen attend to all the politics. This made Boston look better than Philadelphia; this made it harder to muckrake. There had been an exposure just before I arrived in the city. A grand jury had taken up some rumors, inquired into them, and was getting evidence of political corruption, especially in public contracts. But when the witnesses began to point the way up out of politics into business the investigation was stopped. And it was squelched before the scandal had reached men and interests important enough to make national news out of the mere local scandal. I had a chapter on this; Walter Lippmann wrote it for me. I could not write it myself. The facts and the meaning of it were so common; I had reported the like so often that my mind or my stomach revolted at the repetition. Boston was so like other cities that I could not—I did not—muckrake its politics, which were all business. What Boston suggested to me was the idea that business and politics must be one; that it was natural, inevitable, and—possibly—right that business should—by bribery, corruption, or—somehow get and be the government.

This theory of the unification of business management and political government was supported later by what I saw in Europe, but at the time, with my American ideals, I was stopped from thinking much about it because I had to think also of what that meant to labor and the farmers and us, the people, who were in business only as workers, consumers, and spectators. Democracy! I believed in democracy; so I could not, would not, see. For my democracy was a conviction, not a theory; so it excluded a new theory. In brief, I was, as I can see now, in the same state of mind as Boston, only more troubled, less adjusted, less sure. Boston was doing one thing and thinking another, moving on and looking back, preaching modern business and believing in the principles and the ideals of another era or eras. And that was what was the matter with Boston and me, not what we did, but what we thought.

You could see it, plain, in Boston, founded by a lot of earnest Puritans from England who had the "truth" and wished to be free to practice it, who came to the new country to set up liberty and the Right. How can one believe in both liberty and the Right? The Puritans took liberty for themselves, but they could not grant it to others who were wrong. They believed in the Christian ideals, but they founded a system of economics—the only one they knew —which rewarded, nay, which required, thrift, cunning, and possessions—the ownership of properties which would enable them to live without the necessity to do work, which they said they believed in and gradually learned to avoid. As they succeeded, some of them, and acquired wealth, they mistook their plutocracy for aristocracy and soothed their Christian ideals with a scholarly admixture of the ideals of the Greek aristocracy. But they always kept their religion and their culture out of politics and business. They formed, as we all do, watertight compartments of the mind, learned from the start to think one way and do another. As the Puritans went on from agriculture to industry they kept their principles as convictions in one lobe of their brains, which they did not let know what the other lobe was doing. They could corrupt their democratic, agricultural government and social organization to their business uses and still be honest men and democrats who believed and said what the Governor of Connecticut said: "It is right for us (the aristocrats) who know what is right to (buy votes and otherwise) influence the ignorant who do not know what is right." They could believe in the nobility and discipline of labor and yet justify the accumulation of riches to save their children from the discipline of labor. They could stand for free speech, a free press, and all that, and tyrannically suppress agitators and buy up or boycott papers that spread discontent. Boston has carried the practice of hypocrisy to the nth degree of refinement, grace, and failure. New England is dying of hypocrisy. That was what I wrote into my Boston book, and the remedy I offered was —more hypocrisy.

What I mean by this I can illustrate by reporting a conversation with President Eliot of Harvard. It was at the end of his term, just before he gave way to President Lawrence Lowell. Meeting him one day in the Yard, I joined him and proposed that he let me give a short course to seniors on "the forms in which the first steps to bribery and corruption come to young men in all walks of life." He was interested enough to let me give examples of what I would teach.

"A young lawyer is sent to court to ask for a postponement of a case. He fails to get it, and another, older young attorney goes and gets it. The failure asks the success how he did it, and the success says he tipped the clerk of the court. The failure learns thus a lesson which he applies thereafter so well that some day later you find him in the lobby at Hartford or Albany 'tipping' legislators and never knowing that he is a briber."

President Eliot liked this, an actual story; he stood and drew out more and more. He was moved almost to a consideration of my proposition till he happened to ask me what my course would lead up to.

"You would teach those things to stop the doing of them?" he asked.

"Oh, no," I blurted. "I don't mean to keep the boys from succeeding in their professions. All I want to do is to make it impossible for them to be crooks and not know it. Intelligence is what I am aiming at, not honesty. We have, we Americans, quite enough honesty now. What we need is integrity, intellectual honesty."

That ended me with Mr. Eliot. He gave me a piercing look, a polite bow, and walked on to his office. I would have liked to tell him how about that time President Mellon of the New York, New Haven and Hartford Railroad, a western man, who had acquired what I wished all young men to have, asked me in his office one day how he could get himself and his railroad out of politics. I asked him why he asked that, and the long answer was that he had "done politics" in the railroad business out west, realized what that meant to him and to society, and had made up his mind, when Morgan called him east, to cut it out. And he was finding that he could not cut it out; when he did not do what had always been done in Massachusetts, Rhode Island, Connecticut, and New York, his railroad was held up and his directors made it hot for him. He had tried, but he was finding that he "had to" do it.

"Well, that's the answer, Mr. Mellon," I said. "That's what I hear all over this country. You can't run a railroad without corrupting and running the government."

He was amazed that I, a reformer, should say that. "You tell me that? You!" he repeated.

"Yes," I said. "I tell you that; it's evidently a fact, a truth, a hateful truth, which most men who acknowledge it don't feel the hatefulness of, as you do. They excuse it; they ignore it; they are not intelligent."

"But what, then, shall I do?" he almost cried.

My suggestion was that since he knew and hated what he had to do, he should stay on the job and do it up brown. "If we can have all such positions filled with intelligent men who, knowingly, corrupt government, it would be a great step ahead of where we are now—betrayed by a lot of honest men who think they are the moral pillars of society."

Mr. Mellon did not seem satisfied with my advice, and a year or two later he resigned. I fictionized this incident in the story of "The Reluctant Briber," and I hope President Eliot read it. He wasn't satisfied with my advice to him either. And there was one other New Englander who was dumbfounded by the idea of, for the present, putting intelligence above morality.

On a train going from Boston to New Haven for a Harvard-Yale football game, Edward A. Filene told me he had just left in the smoking-room one of the steel men who had been indicted in the slight exposure I referred to above: the exposure of collusive bidding for city contracts. I went in and sat beside this young business man and drew from him his story. He was bitter about it, and inclined to be cynical, which is a symptom of defeat, of a failure to think through some emotional experience.

He had been one of those good citizens, he said, who had stood up boldly for the grand jury probe into political corruption, and then when it came he was, to his amazement, one of the first witnesses called. And, by Jove, he was called as an evil-doer, a felon, and—and, yes, he was guilty. Had he not gone into a pool of steel men to agree on bids so that each in turn would get contracts, at a "fair price"? He had. It was not exactly a pool, but there had been a lot of throat-cutting in the trade; the competitive bidding had cut prices down till no man could make any profit. Really. So the steel men met informally, and—it wasn't a pool; that is to say, they did not call or think of it as a pool, and certainly there was no criminal intent; but, yes, they did agree to agree on prices and on who was to get each contract. "And," he said bitterly, "that was absolutely necessary; it was a crime, but it is necessary. I was not punished, much; I was let off easy, but I was—I was a crook."

"And you still have to be a crook?" I asked, and he was shocked; so I added, "You still have to have some understanding with the other bidders? A pool? Collusive bids?"

He did; slowly he admitted it, and, an honest man, his only pose was—the cynic. That's what I hate, cynicism, and that's what I tried to break with my answer.

"Well," I said, "you are lucky. Your town, this country, is full up with honest men such as you were, who are crooks without ever knowing it. They are good, but they are not intelligent. You are intelligent. If you know that you are a crook and that you have to be a crook, you are, where all Bostoners would like to be and think they are, in the aristocracy of men who know that some of our laws run counter to the forces of nature, to the economic pressure of business."

"What, for example?" He was interested.

"Well, you know, for example, that there is something wrong with an anti-trust law that forbids the apparently inevitable formation of pools, which are the first step toward the organization of monopolies."

"But monopolies are wrong, aren't they?"

"There is something wrong about monopolies, I think, either in their origin or in their private control, but men like you, who see that they are necessary and evil somehow, are on the way to find out just what it is that is wrong and cure it. Good business men —like you, before you were caught and convicted—will never solve a problem that calls for knowledge, study, and insight."

Still in doubt, he looked at me to see if I was serious, and I was. I restated my theorem.

"You are one of the few Boston men who are what they all think they are, good and true. You are in the way of becoming an intelligent and therefore an unhappy crook."

One of the gentlemen on one of my first committees, an aristocrat, a Brahmin, confessed to me that he had inherited a lot of old houses that were let to prostitutes. He had always loathed the thought that he took his rent in dirty money thus obtained, but what could he do? He was willing to sell all this property if I thought he should get rid of it. I did not advise that. In the first place, I argued, it would put some other good man into that bad business; and in the second, it would deprive him, the present owner, of the value to him of the consciousness that he was what we all are unconsciously, in on the evils we abhor. If he held on to that property he would have the cultural advantage of knowing that he was in the business of prostitution and could not get out except by putting into it some one else who might not appreciate the moral advantage of self-knowledge.

XXXVI

"BOSTON 1915"

Having diagnosed the disease of Boston as unconscious guilt, due to the conflict between its intellectual culture in old ideals and its activities in a new (industrial) organization of society; and having tried out on a few individuals the healing effect of the sight of themselves as honest men doing dishonest things, as law-abiding citizens breaking the law, as good respectable gentlemen in partnership with prostitutes and politicians, I settled upon that as the cure for the city—to try to draw a plan for its reform that would lead the community as a whole to see that Something was making them all do what they did not want to do, and lead them to deal with that Thing or those Things. In a word: the Boston 1915 Plan was to produce a city of people on to themselves, and so uncomfortably "on" that they would either change the conditions or become a community of conscious crooks or, best of all, give up their old ideals and form new ideals which would fit modern life and save the United States from hypocrisy and the fate of nations.

Comic? Yes, but the alternative to comedy is tragedy. Evolution, being a fact, must be consciously, intelligently accepted by men, or they are likely to fall into revolution, as they have. And a revolution may be ridiculous, but it is not funny. I know a very wise economic reformer out west who works with and for evolution in politics steadily, though he believes that revolution is inevitable. He is a comedy character. Sober-faced, even solemn, he goes about his impossible business year in and year out with never a laugh or a smile in public. I could not understand it; I could never do it myself. I had to laugh at myself publicly or privately. And so with this man; I learned on dubious authority that this model reformer, when his day's work is done and he puts out the light to go to bed, kneels always as in prayer; he puts his hands over his face, buries his head in the bed clothes, and laughs, and laughs, and laughs. He shook the house the night of the day when he met me, but he was shocked with real alarm when I told him that I, too, laughed, but openly, in clubs and in my meetings. "I never noticed it," he said. "No," I answered, "and no one else has ever noticed what I alone have discovered: that I am the funniest humorist in the world, the most comic of persons, and my own most appreciative spectator, as you are yours." He seized my hand, soberly; it was like a mute compact; and then—well, then, we almost cried. It was so comic; we were comic, I mean, we and our good intentions.

And this touching scene occurred before I set out to make intellectual Boston intelligent, to make good people good for something. That would require economic reforms as well as education. How was it to be done without a revolution?

My sponsor, E. A. Filene, called together a group of earnest, representative men, some of them reformers, not all; and they asked me that question. I told them the story of the briber in Wisconsin who had handled the money to buy for a lumber king a seat in the U.S. Senate. He was confessing how he had spent it in Milwaukee, ward by ward, till he came to a "bum ward," which you could not buy, because the socialists in them had a plan to save the world. It was vision that made men honest, devoted (to a cause), courageous—heroes; like the early Christians, when Christianity was a vision of world salvation.

So, I said to the Boston group, we must have something for the men and women of the city to be devoted to, some vision of the future of Boston. As it stood, Boston was partly a place to live in, partly a place to live on. The city was accepted as all done. If we could sketch out a picture of the city as it might be made, or even as it was evidently going inevitably to be, the people of Boston, both good and bad, both respectable and common, might become so interested that they would neither rob it nor let it be robbed. This meant a plan, and I suggested that we put into our plan only projects—for buildings both private and public, for parks and roads, for reforms and social improvements, objectives already proposed by separate groups, companies, and individuals. We'd find out what everybody was planning to do, each by himself, in business, politics, religion, and social reform, and spread out all these plans as one unified Plan for Boston to show accomplished by, say, 1922. The date was a mistake. In 1908 it was impossible to contemplate 1922. It was visionary, they said, and when I answered that a vision should be a bit visionary, they agreed, but 1922 was too visionary, too far off. It was evident that the human mind is so used to thinking close to the present that fourteen years ahead is incomprehensible. Those men talked in 1908 as if 1922 would never come, and when we finally compromised on 1915 and made the Boston 1915 Plan, it was only with the lifting of practical eyebrows and the shrugging of businesslike shoulders.

However, we did get on to the execution of the plan. Who was to organize and carry out this visionary plan which was to be got so vividly into people's heads that they would resent a political or a business graft, not because it was a "steal," but because it delayed the program of the city, and that would lead to such a demand for revenue and a clearance of obstacles that public opinion would question certain franchises and the leading citizens who held or sought them? Who was to lead the movement against the leading grafters? My suggestion that the leading grafters themselves should be the leaders in this "reform movement" was a shock. These good citizens thought that we should have only good and, if possible, the best citizens on the Committee of the Boston 1915 Plan. It took a lot of debate to persuade them to see my point: that good people and the best men had been tried all through the world's history and especially in Boston; and they had failed. The clergy had governed Boston once, then the aristocracy, then the leading business men. All these forms of goodness had had their day. Let's give up the good men and try the strong men. It was true that the strong men were often bad men or busy with bad businesses, but, I argued, if we could start these natural leaders to working on our good plan, they might become interested in it. They would find it big and difficult, but they liked hard, large jobs. There would be obstacles and opposition, but they loved a fight. Indeed, it was the fighting which might convert these bad men to carry on where good men commonly lay down.

But would we be able to get them started? I was sure of it; I did not want to go out myself to enlist them. I was not an organizer; the committee should find a man of action to do the work. There was so much doubt about the possibility of winning the natural leaders to our side that finally I offered to prove that it could be done; I'd get one man, any one they named, for an example. Who was the worst, the most impossible, man in Boston?

"Martin Lomasny," they said, all in quick agreement. A politician he was. I had expected them to name a big business man, some hard-boiled captain of industry, but they were themselves all business and professional men. Of course they would think first of a politician. I accepted the nomination, and the next morning early I took my little dog, Mickey Sweeney, and went over in the bad wards where Martin Lomasny was the boss. Everybody I asked knew where to find "Martin"; one tough guided me to the open door and pointed up the stairs to the large pool-room on the second floor where the boss "hung out." He was there, alone.

As Martin Lomasny came toward me in the slow strength of his stride and I saw the heavy jaw and the hard face of the man, I wilted. No place for a vision in those eyes. And his speech!

"Who do you want?" he demanded.

"Martin Lomasny."

"That's me," he said. "Who are you?"

I told him. "Sure," he said. "I've read your stuff. What do you want?"

"I want to muckrake this town of Boston, find out what's wrong with it and a way to make it right."

He stood there, expressionless, looking at me a moment; then: "Well, and what do you want of me?"

"Help. I'm no detective. I can't go around in gumshoes getting the facts. My method is to find out the men who are running things all wrong and get them to tell me what they do and how they do it and why and for whom. Without that I can't do a thing."

He was still standing there, eying me. And he certainly did look bad, cold, hard. He wasn't afraid of silence. He took his time; then he said: "And how did you happen to come to me?"

"The reformers sent me to you," I answered. "They tried to tell me some things, but they didn't know much, and what they have got they don't get always right. Good men don't understand; only bad men."

"Well—"

"Well"—I had to say it—"well, I asked them who was the worst man in town, and they named you. So I've come to get the low-down on things, and—will you give it to me?"

"Go on talking," he said. "I'm sizin' you up."

This was a difficult setting for a speech, but I made one. I said that one of the ways of saying what was the matter with democracy was to see that the leaders of the people betrayed them. Instead of leading a city or a nation to a career, leaders who won the faith and the votes of the mob used them to make careers for themselves. "All leaders do it: captains of industry, doctors and attorneys, editors, priests—all the natural leaders of society are making successes of themselves and so—a failure of democracy. This isn't right. Our ideal is individual, not social, success, and that's what has to be changed, this ideal. We have got to get the leaders to have a more social ideal, and I have come to Boston to develop one in all your leaders here, and I want to begin with the political leaders, like you, who seem to me to be the first and worst traitors. I have to find out what they do, as I said, and how and why."

"That's enough," he snapped. "I'll help you. You're on the level. Come in here."

He led the way out of the big hall where his voters came to play pool and, in winter, to be warm; we went into his office, where he pointed to a safe.

"See that?" he said. "That's full of facts, documents, records, 'the goods' on everybody and everything, the evidence to prove what we all know, we politicians. You can have it all."

That morning and many a night thereafter I sat in one chair, Mickey Sweeney in another, Martin Lomasny in a third, and we talked about Boston and the leading men of Boston. The Ninth Ward boss told us everything I wanted to know. He kept his word. He did not—when it came right down to it, he would not—give me his evidence against individuals. His stuff was ammunition that he thought he would use if he was attacked. When I asked him how a certain banker put over a certain deal, Martin would start to tell me, and then halt, think, and say: "No. Look here. I can give you what you want best by telling you what I did in that matter." And that he would freely relate, and that showed how things were worked, laid bare the workings of the system. But the only individual he ever exposed was Martin Lomasny, who, believe it or not, was one of the best men I met in Boston. He was honest; he had intellectual integrity. He saw things straight and talked straight about them. He had the mind and the imagination to do that. And he had heart, both for daring and for kindness.

One day late in the winter, after I had seen the business end of politics, it occurred to me that I had neglected the police and the police graft. I didn't mean to write about it, but I felt that I should know it; and yet I hated the dirty job of visiting and inquiring into the houses of prostitution, vice, gambling, and professional crime.

"Why not go and get it all second-hand but right from Martin?" I had not seen him for weeks. Taking my dog again, I climbed up into his office, and there he was, alone as usual, his feet up on a desk. No greeting from him. I apologized for not having been around lately.

"No, but your dog has," he grumbled. "He comes to see me now and then. He's all right, that dog, a true friend."

And it was true. I learned from others I had seen much of that after I quit them Mickey Sweeney had kept up the connection by occasional calls. Martin said Mickey would come into his office, jump up on the chair he used to sit on, stay a few minutes, then smile, and run along around his social circle of personal calls.

"You must want something," Martin grumbled at me.

"I do," I said. "I want to know about the police graft here."

"Police graft?" he repeated. He did not like comprehensive questions. I made it more explicit.

"Yes," I said. "Police graft. What do you do about the petty crooks?"

He was cross, or he pretended to be.

"What do you mean by petty crooks?"

"Oh, you know, the dips, the burglars and thieves, the regular professional crooks that we honest grafters call criminals."

"And what do you mean by what I do about them?"

"Well, you go to the front for them, don't you? See the district attorney or a judge or the cops—you get them off, don't you?"

"Yes, I do," he said, dropping his feet and facing me with three fingers thrust under my nose. "Three times."

I laughed. "Ah, now, don't you sometimes do it four times?"

He was defying me. "Seven times? Martin, don't you even get 'em off seventy times seven times?"

"Yes, I do," he burst. "I never quit some of 'em, not the way you do."

"Of course," I said. "You stick, but tell me, how do you justify it to yourself, saving these hopeless crooks over and over and over again when you know they'll come back and do it over and over and over again!"

I did not expect him to answer this question. It was more of an exclamation on my part, but he did answer it; inarticulate people can sometimes express themselves.

"I think," said Martin Lomasny, "that there's got to be in every ward somebody that any bloke can come to—no matter what he's done—and get help. Help, you understand; none of your law and your justice, but help."

That hit me hard, and we got no further that day. I postponed police graft. I just sat there and took in what Martin had said, and as I took it in I saw that churches had been built upon that need and that sanctuary service, that it was fundamental, that the political boss and his so-called machine stood upon that rock. They provided help and counsel and a hiding-place in emergencies for friendless men, women, and children who were in dire need, who were in guilty need, with the mob of justice after them. And, as I sat there and thought I saw that if we were to build up in Boston an organization to replace the political machine and so win to the town the loyalty that now went to the boss and his party, we must provide for that service.

I went away, full of that idea, to consult with Filene and Brandeis and others about it. Mr. Brandeis saw it; so did E. A. Filene, who said: "Yes. There is something to do there. I have always felt that it was wrong to outlaw anybody. No one should ever be made to feel that he is beyond the pale." I concocted a plan for a committee to sit in a ward, to be composed of a physician to give medical help, an attorney to give legal counsel, a business man not only to give business advice but to find jobs for men in business as well as in politics, a clergyman to offer spiritual comfort, and one other, preferably some one who had done wrong enough himself to understand guilt. We found some men for the committee: Brandeis for the lawyer, Dr. L. R. G. Crandon for the doctor, the Rev. Mr. Samuel Eliot, a very exceptional clergyman, for the spiritual adviser; and Filene was to be or suggest the business man. I was stuck for a "bad man" till I thought of Martin himself.

"Will he help us undermine his own power?" E.A. asked. I said I'd see, and I called on him—to see.

"Hello, Martin," I greeted him one night at his headquarters. "I think I've got a scheme to beat you out in your own ward."

"Yea?"

"Yes. You remember what you said the other day about help for the helpless? Well, I been thinking about that, and I can see that by giving men aid in their troubles you get their gratitude and they pay you back with the only thing they've got, their votes and their loyalty, which you take to send yourself to the Legislature and your party to—other places of power. Now Boston has to get that loyalty and those ballots by rendering the service you render. See?"

"Yes?" He saw, quizzically. "How you going to do it?"

I told him about the committee and who they were and what they were to do. "Brandeis to give the law, E.A. to get the jobs—"

"Will they do it?" he asked, surprised.

"They have promised to." And he was impressed. I went on to name the rest of the committee, the clergyman, the doctor. "And, now," I said, "we need a human being; you know, a fellow who can understand a crook, even a repeater, to steer the rest of the committee and keep them away from Justice and Right and—and deservingness; as I say, a human being."

"Yes, and that's where you got stuck," he said.

"No, I've just the man, the very man, the only man I know of who can beat you at your own game in your own ward."

"Who?" he queried; he was really interested.

"Martin Lomasny," I answered, and I gave him a moment to recover. Then: "Will you do it?"

"Yes," he said very quietly, "I'll try it out."

"I knew you would," I said. "But I won't let you. Not like that. You have answered on the spur of the moment, and that won't go with me. You must think it over. And, say, you've got to talk it over with the gang. They'll kick, you know."

I saw the dictator harden against those prospective kicks, but I rose to go, saying that, anyway, I would not take his impulsive consent, only a deliberate conclusion after reflection. I hastened away, and a few days later he called me up on the telephone.

"You were right about the gang," he said. "They are kicking like steers. They went right up in the air, and they haven't come down. Won't speak to me, they're so hot."

"What do they say?" I asked.

"Oh, they say that I'm a sucker to be taken in by a reformer. They call you a reformer. And they say besides that it's all right for me to turn reformer if I want to, that I've got mine, but how about them? They haven't got theirs yet, and—all like that."

"Well," I said, "that's right, isn't it? It isn't square to take them in on a game that hasn't been explained to them, is it, now?"

"I can see that now," he said. "But I didn't think you'd see it and—and agree with them."

"I'll tell you what we'll do," I suggested. "You call them together tonight, and I'll be down there and talk to them."

"Oh, will you?" He was unusually expressive, and his expression was that of relief or gladness and some worry.

"Sure. Why not? Why you so anxious, Martin?"

"Oh, well, it's pretty strained down here. They are sore at me. I'd like to see you talk to them the way you did to me. I'll bet they fall for you, too; I want to see that so that they won't be able to high-hat me any more."

So we arranged for a meeting that night in Martin's office.

XXXVII

PRINCIPALS AND HEELERS

M Y MEETING with the Ninth Ward boss of Boston and his ring—and one other similar experience in that town— taught me something. They explained, in a way, why I failed with my Boston 1915 movement, but they showed also that my failure was partly personal, that an intellectual cannot do an executive and an organizing job and should not try to. No new lesson? No. I had learned it before; I was always falling into executive jobs, as you see, and so are other intellectuals. The world is full of unhappy people who are in places they don't fit. If we would accept, we human beings, the probability that we are divisible into as many varieties as dogs are, and horses and even birds, and if each of us would learn young whether he is, roughly speaking, an executive or a thinker, artist, talker, worker, scholar, or scientist, we would find our jobs sooner and be happier ever after.

I failed with my Boston Plan, and maybe such a plan for a city is impracticable; but my experience indicates, I think, that some such city planning might work under capable management. Anyway it had an appeal. When I reported to my committee that Martin Lomasny, whom they had nominated as the worst leading citizen in town, was willing to serve with us, the answer was that he was an exception, exceptionally sentimental or easy. My theory that "human nature" was all right and that all it needed was some inspiration, a plan, an objective, was not accepted. I could not "get" other politicians and bad men. Nor was I sure myself that I could. The meeting with Martin's gang was a fair test. He was an older man, ripe with experience, and "wise." That's why he was a boss. His gang were younger men whom he had picked for strength as they grew up in his ward. They would be hard-boiled, practical, typical. If I could win them it would prove that the young, natural leaders of men would like to respond to a decent social purpose, just as well as they did to a lesser call. An organizer who would do or find a staff to do on a mass scale what I did might lead a town or a State or a country—to a community service. (Russia and the Five-Year Plan proved this later.) But, to sense the humor of the situation that night when I went to the boss's meeting, please picture Lomasny himself sitting apart, with his feet up on a window sill and his back to the room—an outcast from the "gang" of his eight or ten lieutenants who faced me, the intruder, a reformer. There were no introductions, only silence, and enmity for me and their leader.

I grinned. I didn't feel like smiling. They were an able-looking lot of young men, most of them big and strong, and all of them clear-eyed and acute. It was I who suggested chairs. Silently we sat, and they waited, an attentive, if unfriendly, audience. I described to them the corrupt system of Boston and Massachusetts as I knew they knew it, pretty much as Martin had given it to me; only I did not speak of stealing and dishonesty. I called it a system of disloyalty, a typical arrangement which occurred everywhere. Natural leaders were born to lead the people, who really need loyal leaders. They could not solve their own social problems; they wanted their leaders to represent them and take care of their social interests. They gave those leaders their faith and their votes, all they had. They stuck. No outsider could swing them away from their leaders; no reformer or business man could shake the people's faith in the people's ward leaders. So the business men who wanted to get from the people part of their common wealth had to deal with the people's leaders, and the people's leaders sold out the people, betrayed the pitiful faith of the masses in their weakness, and—hence our American government is no longer a democracy, but a plutocracy.

For half an hour I elaborated and illustrated, citing cases they knew, summing up their knowledge to make them form the picture. Their faces relaxed, their eyes grew friendly. "Not reform, democracy is what we need. Not honesty; that does not pay; not education; the educated are the hardest to educate; it is loyalty and imagination and a social plan that we must develop, a scheme that will enlist the voluntary devotion of everybody, the good and the bad, the strong and the weak. But first we must get the leaders, the political traitors." They listened, they saw something, they consented. I could see that, but I could see that the boss with his big back to us could not see it, till when I had done and rested, after a perfect silence of a minute one of the lieutenants spoke up.

"And what's your scheme?" he said. Then I saw Martin take down his upper leg and put it under the lower and relax. He knew by that question that they had "fallen for" me. Now for the scheme, which I outlined as I had to Martin. There were some questions, a few; they were the sharp, critical questions that a practical politician would ask if he were thinking of carrying out the plan. "How would this work, and that? Would a committee like that be patient with a repeater? What would they do with a dope fiend who could not be cured?" I answered as best I could. "A committee like that," I said, for example, "would discover the need for a hospital for the incurables of vice and crime." They nodded. They all seemed to go along with me, with one exception. That man had not said a word. He had struck me from the first as the keenest, most antagonistic, but his face had cleared first, relaxed from opposition to perplexity. I felt that he was working on my problem from my point of view.

But when at last he spoke, he said: "Nope. It won't work, your scheme; not the way you think. If Martin is on that committee, he and he alone will understand the business; the others won't, and he'll be steering them all. And the guys that come up for help or favors, they'll damn soon see that. And so Martin will get all the gratitude and more power than ever out of it. No, you can see that, can't you?" He turned to me to ask that, and, sure, I saw his point. And I dropped the committee idea right then and there. But I did not drop the scheme. I appealed to him and to them all.

"All right, then. You say my scheme won't work. Give me one that will. It's your problem, not mine alone. I'm only a reformer, no politician. You and your pals, you care, I can see, for the people in the ward; you hate the system as much as I do. That, too, I can see. Well, it's your job more than mine, this political reform. Do you fellows, now, you, tell me how to work it."

They did. That group of regular politicians tackled the problem of reform. "Why don't you do this?" "No, but you could do that." They labored together for an hour or more, till Martin

Lomasny, rising suddenly with a frowning face that did not quite conceal a twinkling eye and a rude manner that expressed his delight, ordered us all off the premises.

"Get out of here, you reformers, all of you. Gwan now. It's midnight, and you don't any of you know anything about what you are talking about."

Which was the truth. A few days later one of those men, seeing me on Beacon Street near the City Club, ran across to stop me and say: "Say, I've been thinking it over, that scheme, and I've hit upon a way." And he described it with enthusiasm, a way to beat the politicians and start a reform in Boston. It was "no good," as I showed him; and he saw that it "wouldn't work." But I saw two truths, one for comfort of reformers, the other for scientists to experiment with.

Reformers will be pleased to observe that politicians on the reform side are as clumsy and as incapable as they, the reformers, are. And the political scientists, when they are born, will note well that regular politicians can be tempted to "work for the right," even against themselves.

When I was about to leave Boston, Martin Lomasny called on me to say good-by. He had promised to hold a secret meeting with his group, who spoke to him now, and decide together and tell me what they would do for "Boston 1915."

"We have considered it several times; at every meeting we talk about it, and the gang authorizes me to say to you that we won't join the plan; we don't believe it will work. And we won't vote for any of your respectable candidates for office; we know them, and they are no good. But this we'll do. If ever you see a chance for us to do something for fundamental democracy, you come personally and tell me—you yourself—no letters and no messengers; you come, and you say to me that you want us to help, and we'll give you the whole God-damn works."

"Fine," I said, "but that will be hard, you know. I'll come to you late, perhaps, and what I'll ask will be something that you may not see is democratic. You'll say you can't do that—"

He stopped me. "If you say to do it I'll deliver the machine to do it."

Now it became known that Martin would do things for me—objective, impersonal things—and once, a year or two later, when

I happened to be in Boston, several Progressives asked me in the City Club to intercede with the boss, who was blocking in the Legislature a bill to democratize the method of electing delegates to national political party conventions. It was a measure I was interested in at the time; so I went up on the hill and saw Lomasny in the lobby. As I told him what I wanted, his face fell.

"But you are late," he protested. "All of us [bosses] have settled on it to beat that bill. Why, it would keep me from going to a presidential convention! You can't—don't ask me that."

I reminded him of the warning I made when I took his promise, that I might be late and that he would say he could not do that. He looked sad, but as he turned away he said, "All right, but you go in and watch the Senate when I do it."

I went in, and I did not see Martin at all. What I saw was men I knew, members of Martin's crowd and other legislators, springing, one by one, to their feet, gathering in a huddle, and then looking over at me. And two or three of them rushed out into the lobby to demand of me, "Say, what you been doing to Martin?"

"Calling your old promise," I answered, and they walked back in on the floor, and when the bill came up, it was passed with ring votes for it.

Nor was that the end. The next morning I read in the newspapers a New York dispatch saying that Roosevelt had received a report from his Boston representatives to the effect that they had beaten the bosses in Massachusetts and passed their bill over the opposition of the machine. A few hours later the responsible reformers, the same who had asked me to speak to Lomasny, came in, crestfallen, ashamed.

"Well, what do you want now?" I asked them.

They stammered out that the bosses had seen their boast in the papers, a bit of brag that they had sent T.R. confidentially; and the machine was going to call up the bill again for reconsideration and beat it. Would I speak to Lomasny again?

No, I wouldn't. They were dejected; they accepted my refusal, but—but . . . "You may go see Lomasny," I said, "you yourselves. Tell him you are reformers and good men; tell him you lied to T.R., and being caught, came to me to ask me to use my pull again on him. Say I refused, and you may tell him that when I refused I said that I gave as my reasons that I would not have him think for one moment that I doubted him just because some honest men had told a lie about him."

They did call on Martin; they repeated what I had said, and when the bill was reconsidered, it was passed again. The bad boss, the worst man in Boston, had made good, of course.

Now for the good men of Boston. I could tell a bookful about them; I did; but here now one incident will have to do. A fine group of young, aristocratic Harvard graduates, who desired earnestly to be useful citizens, asked me to spend an evening with them, to explain and answer their questions about the Boston 1915 Plan, which tempted them. We met early and stayed late. I laid out the scheme, the reasons for it and the purpose, in detail. They expressed the usual doubts; I satisfied them, evidently. Anyhow they said they were persuaded, and I thought they were for us. They represented an element that could do the work almost alone. They were youth, the well-to-do or rich young men of the cultured class of the city. But I saw no more of them for a week or so; then I observed one avoiding me, then another. I caught a third and asked him why he was cutting me. He said that after thinking over our conversation, he had come to the conclusion that the plan was impracticable. "It is all right in theory, but it wouldn't work." I made a point of meeting and questioning the others, who all said the same thing in the same words: "Theoretically the plan looked good, but practically—" The old cliché, over and over again. Having a theory of my own about such thought-savers, I traced this one back from the mouths of those young gentlemen to a man who was an ex-mayor of Boston and a gentleman, too, and I learned that those young men, like many of their elders, had the habit, whenever they wanted to know what to think or do in politics, of going to this ex-mayor for advice. He told them what to think. He was a leader of thought, a man of experience and of theory, too. His theory of reform was to limit the suffrage to property-owners and college graduates. This was the opposite of mine. I also was a man of experience, and my experience was such that if I were to limit the suffrage, I would disfranchise property-owners and college graduates. But I bowed to this ex-mayor of Boston. He was a principal. He did his own thinking; however I disagreed with him, I respected him as an independent man and, therefore, a leader. But those others—the

young gentlemen and the old gentlemen—who could not think
for themselves and had to go to him—or somebody—to find out
their minds . . .

We understand that there are bosses and heelers in politics,
and we despise heelers, but we do not sufficiently recognize that
there are leaders and heelers in business, in reform, in society.
I have shown all through this book that instinctively always and
sometimes consciously, I sought out the bosses, the men who were
"it" on newspapers, in politics and business, everywhere. And yet
I had not quite drawn the conclusion that sprang out of this last
of an accumulation of experiences in muckraking, that:

In every city, as in every walk of life, there are principals and
there are heelers; the principals are few; the heelers are many.
You can always tell them. Go to a man, put a proposition to him,
and watch; if he decides for or against it on the spot for himself,
he is apt to be a principal and worth talking to. But if he can't
come to a decision, asks time and a chance to consult with his associates, he is a heeler, a "yes" man; he is not worth talking to. To
get anything done, one must find and win over the free principals,
and it is an utter waste of time to talk to or work with the heelers.
They will take your argument or your book to their principal, and
he can blast it with a phrase. So get the principals, and let them get
their sheep.

The Boston 1915 Plan fell into the hands of heelers; there
were some principals for it, like Martin Lomasny, who, be it observed, was always inclined to decide without consulting even his
gang, who, be it also observed, were not heelers, all of them, but
young principals whom he had chosen for that reason. There were
some independent, self-governing men in the Boston reform movement, but one of the causes of its failure was that I had not yet
learned, to the point of acting upon it, the very essential, practical
truth that heelers will actually kill, that only, *only* principals will
give life to—anything.

GREENWICH VILLAGE

UPPER LEFT: MAX̄ EASTMAN (ARNOLD GENTHE). UPPER RIGHT: BILL HAYWOOD (N.Y. WORLD NEWS SERVICE). LOWER LEFT: MABEL DODGE (N.Y. WORLD NEWS SERVICE). LOWER RIGHT: JACK REED (N.Y. WORLD NEWS SERVICE).

PART IV
REVOLUTION

I

PLAYING WITH REDS AND LIBERALS IN NEW YORK

WHEN I came home to New York from Boston, muckraking, for me, was over, and so was reform. Reform? Walking on Fifth Avenue one day, I met President Mellon of the New York, New Haven and Hartford Railroad, which was suffering just then from a series of accidents, chiefly rear-end collisions. Halting in front of me, he held me up.

"See here," he said aggressively; "you know so much more than I do about running a railroad, let me give you a problem. Ever since we've had these rear-end collisions all our trains are running with the last car empty. Nobody will ride in the last car. Now then, what would you do about that?"

"That's easy," I answered. "I'd cut off the last car."

I lifted my hat and passed on, quick, before he recovered, and when I turned and looked back at him from a distance he was standing there, staring after me. I touched my hat again and hurried on, but I guessed that he felt about my railroad reform the way I did about political reform. "Boston 1915" did not prove, but Boston and my experience with the reformers of other cities did convince me for the time, that the reformation of politics and business by propaganda and political action was impossible. Nothing but revolution could change the system, I thought.

I must see the revolutionists: the reds, the socialists, anarchists, the I.W.W.'s, and the single-taxers, who all seemed to seek the roots of the matter. I must see also the other muckrakers and liberals who had been in the way of having experiences like mine. There were several of these in New York. Some of the muckrakers had not been thinking at all; they had their profession or their principles to which they stuck throughout all their experiences. It was amazing to me to hear how little the muckrakers had learned from their muckraking. No wonder our readers got only our facts and the thrills of our sensations. Most of my old friends thought just what we all thought together in the beginning. They would utter the same old clichés: "The cure for the evils of democracy is more democracy." If I suggested that the cure for the evils of political democracy is economic democracy, they would look blank. They were thoughtless conservatives, as undisturbed as the conservatives they despised, whose thought-saver was: "My father was a Republican, and what was good enough for him is good enough for me." Comfortable mental peace was their form of death.

And some of those who had been thinking desired that same form of rest, a conviction, and found it. I recall vividly meeting Charles Edward Russell and asking him what he had got out of it all. He was one of the most earnest, emotional, and gifted of the muckrakers. There was something of the martyr in him; he had given up better jobs to go forth, rake in hand, to show things up; and he wanted them to be changed. His face looked as if he had suffered from the facts he saw and reported.

"I couldn't keep it up," he said passionately. "It was too fierce, the conditions, the facts, and what was worse, I couldn't understand them. I'd form a theory, then go out and find that the theory was all wrong. I'd set up another theory, see it blow up, and so think again and again, till I couldn't stand it. I joined the socialist party. I had to have something to believe."

As I walked on, reflecting on what Charlie Russell had said and done, I felt the relief he had expressed in a settled creed. That was rest. That would calm all the conflicting thoughts, observations, and feelings. That would give one something to do without any further doubts and worries. But wasn't that the weakness or the strength of religion? Several years after this meeting with Russell I was in Rome, talking with a commanding prelate in the Catholic Church, a wise man, a statesman, a diplomat as well as a priest. A wide-open mind that was aware of all the recent revelations of science, one could talk with him as with a red. He understood everything. It was after the war, when his Church was under a cloud; he was asking me to do an errand to the peace conference, which had excluded the Church. I commented on the weakness of Rome, and he smiled.

"They can never beat us," he said. "There has to be a refuge for the mass of men who cannot think. The Church is that. We say, 'Come to us, all ye that are bewildered and in despair of understanding, and we will tell you what to believe, and do, and think.' "

A belief, a conviction, is all very well for workers. A man of action must not be thinking and learning while he is in motion. Rudolph Spreckels showed me that. He was prophesying one day with such certainty that I halted him to recall the fact that a year before he had made an equally positive prediction, that the Federal Reserve Bank bill, if passed, would precipitate a bank panic.

"Well, what of it?" he demanded.

"Nothing; only the bank bill did pass, and there was no bank panic."

"Well, and what of that?"

"Only this, that if you can be so wrong once you may be wrong again. You should not be so sure of things."

He laid his hand on my arm, and more as a plea than a command, he said, "Don't—don't make me doubt my convictions. I cannot act unless I am sure."

Practical men have a different psychology from that of intellectuals. I think that the brain of a man of action is not like a thinker's or a writer's. Anyway they have peculiar needs; they are unhappy in doubt and unable to act while they are thinking. Perhaps nobody should doubt, think, and consciously learn in action. But practical men, so called, seem to pass through distinct periods; they consult and think till they decide, and then they will not hear or hesitate any more. They shut their eyes and go, blind, like Spreckels.

And so intellectuals like Russell, when they accept a belief, turn to action. He ran for governor of New York State, and he acted. He campaigned, but speeches to put over your propaganda are acts; they are not open-minded thinking in public. Political speeches are not intellectual exercises; they are force. The brain is a muscle to drive something home; it is not a mind. And an intellectual cannot keep it up long. Russell soon was writing again and thinking; he was doubting, too, and suffering. He had got out of his job when he got into action.

My observation was that none of the creed-bound radicals, whether socialists, anarchists, or single-taxers, were thinking and seeing. The spectacle of an evolving world beyond our comprehension was lost upon them, and I did not want to miss the show. I was afraid to join anything. I proposed to play with all of them and work with some, as I did, experimentally. Greenwich Village was the playground, a cheap, rundown part of New York that had in Colonial days been a resort to which people drove in their carriages 'way out from Wall Street, and later a good residence district with neat, well-built houses, which the working poor had taken over and spoiled. In my day the thinking poor and the poor thinkers, the beginners, the youth, were going down there to live and be free.

My home was still in the Connecticut Greenwich. Sad things were happening there. My wife died, and then her mother. A short sentence that, but it covers a long story. My wife, who had, as she thought, given up her life to her mother, stayed home when she might have traveled with me, regulated her whole being in the belief that her mother, so much older than she was, would die first, and then she, the daughter, could venture forth and—live. When Josephine Bontecou took to her bed, knowing she was to die first, she was so enraged that she refused for days to see her mother, and then when she did she reproached her—tragically. For the mother, too, had given up her life, as she thought, to her daughter; she had lived with her, gone with her to Germany when Josephine wanted to study, traveled with her when we traveled and married and traveled—where we wanted to, not always where the mother preferred to go. As I saw it, neither of them had actually sacrificed herself. They had lived as they each wished to live. It was only a thought that made that tragedy, but it was just as tragic for that absurd reason. After my wife died, her mother wished and planned to live on with me; she did not want to go home to her relatives. My mother-in-law and I were as happy together as my wife and I were. She was glad to see her daughter through; she was prostrated when she learned that her daughter grieved that she had not seen her mother through. The mother's consoling thought was that she could now live for me, and when her relatives, distrusting her affection for me, feared she might leave me some of the family property, they took her away. She died in a few months.

If I were a novelist, if I had any understanding of human relations, I would have written the story of those two fine women. And there was a tiny book to thread the story on. Josephine Bontecou left to me a carefully kept diary which gave completely not only her life and pictures of her mother, father, friends, but such a portrait of a husband as I have never seen in literature. The fact that I was the husband did not hinder me from seeing what an ass a "good husband" is in the eyes of an intelligent wife who is thinking of him, who is thinking always of graft or business or—something else; who is always at hand but never at home.

My mother died in this period, and my father, but those were happy deaths; they were the quiet, not unwelcome ends of successful, satisfied living. I felt not much more sorrow than I would at their going to sleep.

The breaking up of my home threw me out into the world as helpless as only a good wife can leave a man. I did not know how to do any of the little, essential things that had always been done for me. I didn't know where to buy my underwear; I didn't know when and how to pay taxes, where our friends lived. I hadn't had anything to do with any such necessaries for twenty years. I was lost, just as those young people were who gathered in Greenwich Village as I did—to be "free." Hell! I soon felt that I'd rather work, fight, talk, for liberty than have it. And license is worse. Assuming that license is the use of liberty, I can say that I did some of the idiocies I had long envied in my loose or bachelor acquaintances, and—there is nothing in them, not for me, nothing but trouble. I am an altruist in all matters of freedom. Let the police have license and anybody else liberty.

One of my experiments was with free speech, and it was a complete success. I was chief of police for half a day; I had command of the New York police force, and I "let 'em talk." And nothing happened.

There was a red meeting in Union Square. I forget the cause; some police outrage had aroused the anarchists, and they assembled to protest. The police were there in full force, mounted and afoot, in uniform and in plain clothes, and they tried to suppress the Constitution and the freedom of speech and assembly. Since the anarchist leaders were looking for trouble, they inspired their orators to speak freely, especially to and of the police, who finally charged at a trot. I was standing talking to an old friend, a police captain in uniform, and we were both struck and almost bowled over. There was some pretty bad clubbing, many arrests, and the meeting was broken up in a rage, both the anarchists and the police hot with unofficial indignation. They both wanted more of it, and the anarchists adjourned the assembly to the next Saturday, when they thought or said they might really start something.

It struck me as a perfect opportunity for a free speech demonstration. I called on the mayor early the next week with a plan. A smiling young secretary, Arthur Woods, stopped me at his door. What did I want? he asked amiably. I told him.

"I want to beat that free speech demonstration next Saturday. You know what's up? The anarchists are planning to show that you and the police don't respect the Constitution, that you won't allow free assembly and free speech, and to win they have to incite the police to charge the mob and start a riot. It is being advertised by the newspaper reports that bombs are to be thrown, and some people are afraid. The malcontents, sensing that, will go there *en masse,* and something might happen—not a revolution, of course, but a riot with some wounded and dead. I think I know how to avoid that."

He asked me how, and I did not like to tell him, a secretary, a subordinate. I preferred to talk to a principal. Colonel Woods was very urgent, however, and finally, after some hesitation, he confided to me that he was about to be appointed commissioner of police.

"I will be in office before next Saturday, and I am worried a bit about what will happen on that, one of the first days of my term. I am as much interested as the mayor in any plan to deal with this emergency; so tell me what you have in mind. What would you do on Saturday?"

"I'd let them speak," I said, and he looked shocked. "They will say terrible things, but what of it? You need not hear them, you and your police."

"But the mob will hear!" he protested. "An already excited mob will hear the speeches made for the purpose of arousing them to action."

"What of that?" I asked. "I have written and spoken to the people of this country for the purpose of arousing them to action, and I never did any harm. I never got action. I think speech is harmless, almost useless, and so do you. The only trouble is with the policemen. They—personally, as human beings—they hear those other human beings saying things that they hate, that make them clutch their clubs and—bang. It's a case of two mobs insulting, taunting, challenging each other till one attacks."

"How would you deal with that?"

"I would have no police present at that meeting. Let the orators orate, let the mob howl only to themselves, with no cops to hear a word."

"On what theory would you take that risk?"

"On the theory that if you and I were advertised to fight next Saturday and you did not want to fight and so stayed away, there would be no fight."

Colonel Woods considered; I could see that he was thinking it over, and his thoughts came out. "I could not have no police preparations," he said. I suggested that he have as large a force as he liked on call. "Stack the back streets and alleys with men," I offered. "Have foot and cavalry all around the blocks back of the Square, but none in sight, none within hearing. It's police feelings that make all the trouble."

He thought on, we talked on, and at last he made me a proposition. He would adopt the plan; he would have his force handy; he must have some one officer in uniform in sight, no more, and I must be there to advise the responsible officer. Who should that be? He asked and I instantly recalled that my old police friend, Schmittberger, was chief of police. I named him, and Colonel Woods agreed.

Two days later Colonel Arthur Woods was appointed commissioner of police, and two days after that we had free speech in Union Square. There was a little old gardener's house with a covered veranda where the orators stood to speak to the hard-packed, standing crowd on the lawn, the sidewalk, and out on the very wide street. Chief Schmittberger in full uniform was on the veranda, but I kept him listening to me and telephoning to Colonel Woods every fifteen minutes. The chief was beaming; all he had to 'phone was "all right, nothing doing"; "yes, they're speaking"; "I don't know what they say." He did hear some sentences, and they seemed to hit him like clubs. Feeling safe and not wanting to be safe, those orators opened their hearts and, as one of them put it, their guts. No matter. The mob soon understood the situation, that you could say what you pleased, and as they heard the orators venture they became intensely moved. But they did not move, of course; they listened. And nothing happened. Nobody heard but the audience. Schmittberger let me "run it"; he watched me, not the meeting, and I thought he was learning what free speech was till along late in the afternoon he pointed to some men pulling up boxes to the outer edge of the crowd. "Who are those butters-in?" he asked. I walked down there, learned that they were socialists who had decided, since speech was free, to talk socialism. I told Schmittberger who they were, and he grasped his stick. "Not your friends!" he exclaimed. He was evidently minded to sock those socialists, but I looked at him, held his eye, and grinned. He got it.

"Well, let 'em speak, hell, let 'em all speak. What do we care?"

And they did speak, more and more of them. I heard the chief telephone to Colonel Woods that there were lots of meetings, not only one. There were orators shooting off their mouths all over the Square, and not the least trouble. How could there be trouble with no police present? Only the organizers of the meeting were in trouble. Toward the end of the day, as it was growing dark, I happened to walk down through the crowd past where I saw the leaders standing in a cross group. They called me a name, the name you don't mention without a smile. Since they did not smile I did, and I asked them what was the matter.

"You're always butting in and spoiling something," they said in various versions.

"But I've got you the free speech you wanted."

"Ah, go to hell! You know damned well that isn't what we wanted."

And it isn't. Why can't the police, the governments, the law-abiding people everywhere learn what the English know—that free speech is what *they* want, not what the reds want? It is their salvation. Liberty to talk, to write, to meet, is a safety valve for feelings which, unexpressed, might cause action.

Colonel Woods learned something like that. He allowed free speech in New York from that day on. I know, because he let— he asked—me to go about when the police might be tempted to interfere, and instruct them. As an old police reporter, the cops knew me by sight, and seeing me with the commissioner and with the chief, they realized that I had some sort of pull, if not authority. I had convinced Colonel Woods that it was the personal reaction of the police as men, not as officers, that incited them to violent action. He asked me once how he could instruct them in the law and the spirit of liberty, and he tried my method—to explain it to them every time he met them face to face on any subject. He did that, but he was a bit too formal. My way was more policelike. He took me in his car one day to City Hall Square to attend a meeting there that had been complained of; the precinct police were being urged to stop it. When the commissioner drove away, I sauntered up near the speaker, and I suffered some shock myself. The speaker was a young woman anarchist, and she expounded her creed of liberty, but she did it with gross obscenity, and, her eyes on the police, she socked them with police profanity. The small crowd did not listen to her; they watched the police, who were angry and in doubt. They came together, the plain-clothes men and the officers in uniform, to consult. By and by I saw one point at me; the others looked, and a good old cop came slowly over to me. I could see that one encouraging word would be enough to have that girl speaker beaten up and arrested.

"Say, Mr. Steffens," he said with a hard eye, "what is this free speech business anyhow? Is that free speech? How can you tell when to let 'em talk and when to—shut 'em up?"

"I'll tell you, officer. Whenever you hear some one saying something that everybody believes, you included, you may beat 'em up. That's not free speech. But when you hear somebody saying something like that pretty girl there that you and everybody else thinks is wrong, then you should draw your clubs, line up in front of the orator, and defend her. For that's free speech."

He looked at me, allowed his face to relax into what might have become a grin, and turned back to his fellow cops. They listened attentively as he reported my interpretation of the Constitution and then laughed and moved apart. The young woman eased her mind in vain; she finished her speech out of breath and had failed to incite a police outrage.

That my interpretation carried was proven a few weeks later one evening when I was passing Madison Square Garden. I stopped to look over a mob at the back door, and seeing a police captain in plain clothes, I asked him what was up. He was laughing as he said, "Oh, nothing. They're giving out some free tickets to make a meeting inside look big."

"But why do you laugh?"

"I was thinking of your definition of free speech that's going around the force. It may not be right, but the cops are saying that you said that anything that was against the Constitution was constitutional free speech."

"That's not accurate," I said, "but it's truer than what I did say; so let it go."

I think that the New York police force that year learned what free speech is. I gave them some pretty good examples. Chief Schmittberger asked me one night to go over on the East Side, where there was a strike and hard times; people were hungry, and the "anarchists" were trying to cash in on it and get action. "Go and tell them and the cops how far they can go," he said.

It was a miserable outdoor meeting in the rain of a pitiful, poor, cold crowd of men and women. The speakers expressed the feelings of the dripping listeners, and the precinct police were for dispersing them. "How far are we to let them go?" they asked me, as they had asked the chief. I said I'd show them. I climbed upon the box under my umbrella, and prefacing my speech by saying that I was to go the limit beyond which no speaker should go, I said: "If I were out of work, down and out, and my wife and children were hungry—if there was food somewhere, anywhere, I would go and I would get it and feed my family."

That was all. The cops were startled. The captain remonstrated: "Say, that means break in and steal."

"Don't you be afraid, Captain. That's only what I'd do. They haven't the guts to do it; they haven't had food enough to—act. Nothing will happen."

And nothing happened. The meeting voluntarily dispersed after that. Other speakers took up and drove in my text, but—I asked the next day—nobody took food for his hungry children that night.

II

EXPERIMENTING WITH PHILANTHROPY AND EDUCATION

J OSEPH W. FELS, of Philadelphia and London, came to Little Point, my Connecticut home, with a purpose. A little bit of a twinkling man—his eyes twinkled, his mind twinkled, his very feet twinkled—he could not keep back anything, not for a minute. When he stepped out of the carriage upon our doorstep, he began: "Say, I've got an excess income of $250,000 a year, which I can't use myself. How can I spend it for others and not do any harm?"

"You can't," I answered.

"I know that," he twinkled. "But I've got to get rid of it; so I ask you: how I can give it away and do the least harm?"

"That is a hard but an answerable question," I said. "But it will take time and thought. Let's sit down on it."

I drew him into the house, to lunch, which did not interest him. He was all nerves; he wanted to eat up his money problem. We agreed that rich men knew how to make money; that was easy; but they had never learned to distribute their riches.

"A proof," he said, "that there's something wrong about riches. It hurts the maker, distracts him from his job. It hurts his children, and it damns the institutions that get it."

"Tainted money," I said, a phrase in common use at that time. "Why not give your money to something you want to hurt or taint?"

He laughed, but he waved away the joke. He agreed in words, but he did not believe literally, that philanthropy was evil, and like most people who ask for advice, he did not want any. I had had enough experience in consultation to be sure that Joe Fels had come there to advise me; he had some scheme for the expenditure of his tainted money, not to hurt, but to help, some cause. I let him talk; he could talk; a born salesman, he was soon selling me his idea to use his excess income to "put over the single tax somewhere." I was to be on the committee that was to manage the Fels Fund.

"We'll hurt your cause," I warned, but I consented to serve; and I noticed that I, too, had, say, half an idea that maybe a careful committee of radicals could spend money wisely. My excuse to myself was that the experiment would be interesting, and it was. The other commissioners were aware of the risk. We all laughed (or wept) at the benevolences of the rich. Could we do any better? Money, mere money, money by itself, could not be bad. Wasn't the fault in the givers, in the methods of giving? Could we not avoid the philanthropists' mistakes and make money a force for good?

The Fels Fund Commissioners were Daniel Kiefer, chairman, Frederic C. Howe, George A. Briggs, Jackson C. Ralston, and myself, with Joe Fels, the founder, and Bolton Hall, as spectators and advisers without votes. Other single-taxers were often present, heard, and followed. We were a humorous group who did not take very seriously what we were doing. The meetings were fun. We were conscientious, careful, hard-working, but not to be disappointed in our failures, which might be as significant as our successes. We agreed that one fault of philanthropy was to give to institutions, such as churches, colleges, parties; the directors of these could not help being influenced by money and by the ideas, real or imagined, of the men who gave it. On the other hand we would not ourselves initiate or manage any undertakings. (The Rockefellers afterward adopted this rule.) We would back men. Our policy was to seek out workers for the single tax, already on the job somewhere, anywhere, and give them money only, not advice, no interference with their methods and programs. We found that we could not do exactly as we wished. The pressure to "help" this or that was too great. "Rules were made," we discovered, "to develop the exceptions that were to be obeyed." And some of our exceptions were successes. We "had to" make up the deficit of *The Public*, the single tax organ, but the exception proved the rule. Louis F. Post, the editor, was too much aware of the danger of money to be influenced by it or us. Backing his paper was really backing a man. We "had to" give to some movements, works, parties, and men that we thought useless if not wrong. In the main, however, we stuck to our loose principle; we gave money to, and otherwise backed, men who had proven their ability to achieve, all by themselves alone. What was the result?

My opinion is, and I think that of most of the commissioners, including Joe Fels, was, that the Fels Fund hurt the single tax. It first speeded up the movement by raising hopes, centralizing efforts, and releasing the workers from the labor of collecting money. As time went on the workers came to want more and more and much more money; they either relaxed their efforts or elaborated their machinery till its purpose was lost sight of or at least diminished. With money to use as a force, they did not depend so much on persuasion. Even the fanatics slackened their propaganda. There were other contributing causes. Differences arose, conflicts of policies (not in the commission; we were always a unit and acted on unanimous votes)—even some bitterness of feeling. Outside events, too, had some influence. By the time the Fels Fund was through, the single tax movement was through—for a long while. It has revived some since, when it was poor again. Henry George, the prophet who saw and promulgated the principle of the tax on land values only, put a great truth into the title of his masterpiece, *Progress and Poverty*. He meant that progress was making poverty, unnecessarily. I can see that poverty makes progress—in a religion or a philosophy. Anyway, my conclusion from my experience in philanthropy was that it is a failure.

Joe Fels got some impish fun out of it, more in England than here. He lived in London half of each year, and he gave away money there, too. In both countries the advertisement of him as a rich philanthropist gave him a certain position. People would listen to him. His personality counted, and his humor had free play. He could say things. When a committee of kind folk called on him to contribute to a fund to feed starving children in the slums of London, he refused. "The children are dying," the spokesman said. Fels answered that charity would not save them; charity solves no problem. "Something fundamental has to be done about the poverty that kills these children, and your unimaginative government by the rich should be moved to do it. I'll help get at their imagination. I'll give ten thousand pounds to pay for the removal of the bodies of the dead children to the lawn of the Houses of Parliament." That offer was refused, of course. But he did rent vacant lots all over London to let them out for market-gardening—this to give employment to the poor and to demonstrate the value of land held out of use. In Boston once, after a handsome offer of money for radical reform, made in the course of a fine, gentle, humorous, but very sincere address, I asked him a question in his mood.

"Mr. Fels," I said, "I can believe that you Jews are the chosen people, but tell me, what were you chosen for?"

"Oh," he answered quick, "to introduce Christianity."

Joe Fels rendered service in America, England, Germany, Denmark, and China. He was an internationalist. But he did what he did, he himself, not his money. His gifts only backed his personality and attracted attention to his ideas and his gestures.

Another experiment I made in this period of my unemployment was the one I have mentioned before, at Harvard. Education was wrong somewhere. Cultured Boston showed that. A community of fixed minds, often refined and scholarly, but satisfied, unquestioning, Boston was inhospitable to new ideas and was dying of its old convictions. And the public opinion of the United States generally, the American mind, was settling into a solid condition. One of the accepted convictions I had heard most frequently was that education was the way to cure our evils. I did not believe that. Educated people were the slowest to move toward any change. It seemed to me that education was a hindrance to reform, but maybe our education was bad. Mine was, and thinking back over my school and college courses, I could see that one trouble with our education was that it did not teach us what was not known, not enough of the unsolved problems of the sciences, of the arts, and of life. It did not aim, apparently, to make us keen with educated, intelligent curiosity about the unknown, not eager to do the undone; it taught most of us only what was known. It gave us positive knowledge when there was no certain knowledge, and worst of all, when we did not particularly want it. We were not curious as students, and we are not curious enough now as men and women. It seemed to me, as I thought and talked it over with others, that curiosity was the beginning and the end of education and that if one could arouse that in the minds of college students, they might reverse their relations with their teachers. The students would be asking questions, not the professors; the students would be learning instead of the teacher teaching. No systematic efforts were made in the colleges I knew, to stimulate first the wish to know, before handing out required knowledge. If this were done, if the students could be sent into the classroom eager to know all about some subject, then the professor's pleasant business would be to offer carefully, not with any certainty, the little uncertain knowledge he has; then to point off at the unsolved problems in that science, with cautious statements of the assumptions and theories with which the researchers were working; and finally, when the students are ready for more, for the unknown, to drill them in the methods of modern research.

The beginning was with the student, as I saw it, and the question was: Could curiosity be planted in a student body? I talked with Walter Lippmann, ever eager to try new things, and I outlined a plan which he fell in with. The plan was to take a university, Harvard, for example; get some picked students to start a spontaneous, voluntary course of lectures in public questions, the speakers all to be non-academic specialists, and all to be instructed to talk in such a way as to leave burning questions instead of convictions in the minds of the student audiences. My model was the Oxford movement in England, in which a theological question caught the interest and the emotions of students and professors alike and spread to Cambridge and other colleges. The question was so profound in its implications that every science, every study, bore on it: philosophy, physics, history, poetry, politics—everything. The effect of the interest in it was to put an intellectual subject in the position that football holds in modern American universities. There were not only debates and essays on it; there were disputes and conversations on this question in classrooms, clubs, at dinners, and in the yards or on the campus. And the final result was not a satisfactory answer to the question but the graduation from the English universities of a lot of educated, interested, thoughtful scholars, statesmen, poets, historians, etc.

We had no such fundamental question; our idea was to excite a searching interest in the common problems of politics and government, discover that those problems had to go to economics for their solution, and then develop an intelligent, practical interest in economics as an unborn science. We conspired with some professors whom we knew, told them our experimental purpose, and set as the test of success that within six months students should be asking questions in class and seeking more, not less, knowledge and work. Twenty-one members of the faculty joined the conspiracy. Lippmann, who did the politics, persuaded a small group of seniors to organize the meetings, and he sent them to me for speakers. I might know some, he said. I did. We had drawn a list, and while I did not show it, I gradually thought of enough lecturers to start with. The students were delighted with my preparedness. They knew nothing, of course, of our instructions to these speakers to avoid all propaganda and to play for questions. I gave the first talk to a large meeting on "The Political Problem," which I stated as clearly and simply as I could; I tried to make it look easy, but I led up to the perception that it wasn't really a political problem at all. The political question was an economic problem and could be answered only by the scientific solution of economics. John Moody, of Wall Street, lectured on "The Financial Problems," stated them, and showed that they waited for their solution on that of the economic problem. A social worker, a woman, described the sociological problem in her city, New York, described the failure and folly of charity, and led up to—the economic problem. By that time there was an interest in the economic problem, and James MacKaye, who understood it radically and had a solution in his own mind, presented it well to a very large meeting of students brought there by hearing the students talk about it who had heard the other lectures. James MacKaye, a trained and a humorous thinker, interested those students; and he did not offer his own solution. He indicated that there were several theoretical solutions, socialism, single tax, etc., but they were only sound, scientific, tantalizing approaches. "The" solution remained to be discovered.

Several professional men followed with lectures designed to show that the ethical and practical difficulties of the law, medicine, etc., were unsolvable by lawyers, doctors, engineers, because of the economic problem which remained unsolved. How could there be "equal justice" in the courts when the rich hire expensive lawyers; the poor, cheap, bad, or none? How could there be ethical and scientific medicine with doctors under the necessity and the temptation to make money first out of their practice and with some patients able to pay, others not? Then came the solutions: the Republican by a Republican, the Democratic by a Democrat, socialism, single tax, anarchism. The Republican and the Democrat were allowed to make propaganda, but by that time their programs looked ridiculous to those students. The radicals did not try to teach their own propaganda. Faithful to the agreement, they, like James MacKaye, presented their plans only as models of honest, intelligent approaches, and even that caution was not necessary. The students who had taken the whole course were critical enough to take care of themselves. They accepted no solution, as their disputes proved.

The experiment was enough of a success to warrant further, improved experimentation. No harm was done; no convictions were taught or learned. And it met the test we had set up. Before the course had gone halfway, at a faculty meeting just before Christmas one of our instructors reported that several members of the faculty had complained that they were having trouble with students who "asked questions out of season," "wanted information beyond the limits of the course," and generally were "critical and troublesome." On the other hand there were teachers who liked what had happened. Some students, they said, "manifested a fresh and pertinent interest in their work, as it seemed to bear upon questions in their minds."

President Van Hise of the University of Wisconsin had noticed this experiment and asked me how he could apply it, "how can we distract the living interest of our students from sport to the intellectual field." My answer was that it was only a matter of throwing into a student body some fundamental question that would take hold. And I still believe that it is questions that should be taught, not the answers; and science is full of questions, not of answers. Why teach knowledge when there is none, when our culture is one of—inquiry and research?

The students at Harvard carried on a course in public questions the next year, but they did not understand the educational purpose of the first year's course, and the lectures they had were to give information. Lippmann had become busy with his own career, and I went to Europe to see if there was any muck to rake and any reforms to copy.

III

SEEING EUROPE WITH BUSINESS MEN— GREENWICH VILLAGE

FREDERIC C. HOWE broached to me at a Fels Commission meeting the idea of going to Europe with a chamber of commerce party which a tourist bureau was promoting. He thought it might be interesting to watch close up the reaction of a mixed lot of American business men to "the sights" of foreign doings in politics and business. He had studied and written books on English, German, and Danish achievements in government and business; he recalled some of the "impossibilities" Europeans had accomplished, and he expected American business men to learn from them. He believed in business men. A lieutenant of Tom Johnson in Cleveland, Ohio, and a good business man himself, he had learned, he said in his quiet way, that there were no business men, any more than there were authors or murderers; there were only men who wrote something or killed some one or happened to go into business. As Fred Howe talked, I agreed that it would be amusing to travel with a chamber of commerce party; but also I thought that it would be interesting to go to Europe with Dr. Howe, an expert. And besides, I was homeless, jobless, and lonely. Yes, I would go abroad with Howe and Mrs. Howe.

The rest of the party was interesting, too, as I discovered on the boat. Marie Howe showed me that. She had the woman's intelligence, which is the novelist's gift, to see people as characters and to hear as they talked, however foolishly, the revelations, in tone, glance, and words, of human traits and relations. Most of the party were just plain, good men of business who had benevolence but had been too busy to develop this good will to any purpose. They and their wives and their attitude to one another fascinated me, as Marie Howe saw and pointed them out. I was a

648

novice in all that side of life. I remember how astonished and humiliated I was when, after a dinner where I had followed only the conversation, Mrs. Howe would make me recall incidents and sayings which carried a story that was going on back of the stage. My wife used to do that, too. She would tell me afterward what had happened, what was back of the talk that had interested me at a social gathering. It annoyed me, made me feel like a blind duffer. Woman's awareness! My man's unobserving concentration! I had come to have a great respect for women and had helped all I could their feminist movement, in which Marie Howe was a leader; but I never learned to understand them, even as voters. The way they fell into the political habits and views of men and the hands of the old parties was one of the griefs of my not very sorrowful life.

My exercise on that trip was baiting those business men and politicians who had come along to learn, they said. I said they could not learn. They said they wanted to see what things were done better abroad so as to do them that way at home. I told them that the best they aspired to was to be good men, not to make better cities. I was told, and I can look back and see, that I was an offense all through that grand tour of England, Belgium, Germany, Switzerland, France, and back. I could not, like Fred Howe, point out the facts and the views to these commercial-political tourists and let them take or leave what they saw. I had to mix it all in. A propagandist, I tried to force them to get it or acknowledge that they were what Sinclair Lewis called them later, much later—Babbitts. No one so far has found a name and a personification for such as I was on that trip, though the members of the party tried to repeatedly.

Robert S. Speer, the then mayor of Denver, was my favorite victim. A genial, earnest, ambitious man of business, he had taken office, to serve his city, from the machine. What could he learn and what could he do if he did learn something in Europe? We both knew Denver, and when I said that it was really run in the interest of the public service corporations he did not deny it, but when I said the first step to free him and his city was to take over and run the public utilities, he answered that that would put them into politics and that politicians would operate them badly. The old cliché. Howe and I tried to make him see that the privately run companies were more in politics than those that were publicly run and that the inefficiency of the publicly managed utilities was due to their operation by disloyal politicians in the pay of the enemy. We cited examples—from Seattle, where public operation of electric light had looked bad till it was shown that the private companies had sabotaged it to make propaganda. Mayor Speer considered all this; you could see him think; so Howe suggested that we take our question to Liverpool, where we were about to land, and let it be answered there.

Cutting some chamber of commerce banquet at Liverpool, we called on the town clerk, who, as Fred Howe said, was the proper head of the city; the titular mayor was a figurehead. The town clerk and a friend welcomed us and our questions.

"Your town has taken over and operates your public utilities, doesn't it?"

"All but gas," he said.

"Are they more in politics now then they were, or less?"

"Less," he said, and his friend echoed, "Much less."

"But gas is still in politics, isn't it?" I butted in.

No answer; I persisted.

"In an American city, if all but one of the public utilities were municipally owned and operated, that one would run the town and its politics and sabotage the others. Doesn't gas own your board of aldermen?"

"No," the town clerk said, and I felt knocked out.

But his friend picked me up. To the town clerk he protested: "Why don't you tell them why gas does not run things? It did, and now it doesn't; but why?"

The town clerk turned to his friend and said, "You tell them, if you like. I'll not do it."

His friend liked to tell us. "You're right," he said. "Gas, left alone, did all the politics and had control of the board, till we beat it—for a while—by an American trick. I don't know how you pronounce the word, but we gerrymandered the election districts and so won a majority and got our self-control. But the gas people still are at work, making progress. They will soon control the board again."

That tour of Europe was like the reports one hears of a trip to Soviet Russia now. Our hosts tried to steer us so that we saw nothing but the good things they wished us to see. We banqueted twice a day, on the average; there were breakfasts also with wine and speakers. Some of us, however, escaped, notably Mayor Bob, Howe, and myself. We saw, as the rest did, London and Paris, Brussels, Frankfort, Munich, Vienna, and Switzerland. We saw the good things to copy that Mayor Speer sought for Denver. He was Denver, that honest, able man; his eyes were Denver's eyes; his ambition was his city's. His interest was the same as our hosts', to see the best. When we came to Düsseldorf, "the best-governed city in Europe," he looked like a painter seeing a paintable landscape. He listened, as to poetry, when he heard leading business men, who were aldermen, telling how the city "worked" property owners who had no use (except for speculation) for houses and lots on the railroad to move out and let shippers in; how they shifted businesses to regroup them for convenience and economy; how—in brief—they ran their city as if business and politics were all one thing, and so built up a community where business, life, and art thrived. There was provision for children, for music and pictures, and the city looked like what it was: one of the great creative art centers of Germany. Airy, sunny—it was beautiful, and it had finish. There were famous statues to tip a conspicuous street corner. Mayor Speer asked how they got the money for all this. I asked how they were able to keep big business under. I got an answer to my question there in Düsseldorf.

"The business of the city is safe, now that it is the biggest business here. We own all the utilities, and we own much more, too. Every man's private business is comparatively small and dependent on the municipality, which everybody is interested in and watches. The only way to prominence and power here is to be in politics and serve the commonwealth."

Mayor Speer's question as to ways and means was not answered till we arrived in Frankfort. Most of these German cities had adopted the city manager idea. Not the honorary, political, underpaid mayor led the public business, but a highly paid, well-trained expert. Like most Americans, Speer began to think there was something in that form, device, or trick. I argued against it, and he, as a mayor, wanted to believe me. Even a city manager, I argued, had to find what a mayor could just as well discover: the sources of revenue to pay for improvements. There was nothing in the mere name and the pay of a city manager. "I insist," I advised, "that some city manager tell you how to get the money." And the city manager of Frankfort, one of the most famous of his profession, pushed by a group of us into a corner, told the secret in a lowered voice, with cautious looks around him.

"We were planning to take a new country district into the city, to subdivide and improve. Speculators began to buy; prices rose; and we were balked. Each speculator wanted the best streets, parks, etc., near him. Why? Because, you see, if the city laid out streets, put in light, water, transportation, the speculator's land would go up from agricultural to city property. He was after a value we, the city, were to add to his land. We were to do all the costly, unprofitable work; he was to get, at very small cost, all the profits. I asked myself why the city should not have the profits as well as the costs of its enterprise and labor. Our leading bankers here are international bankers; our business men live in Frankfort, not on it. They saw what I saw: a rich source of wealth for the city. We did what the speculators wanted to do. We bought the land, improved it, laid it out on a perfect plan. No politics now, no trouble from competing property owners. We made the district first, then sold it out to home builders; and the city made a lot of money, not so much as the speculators would have taken, but—a profit on our turn. And so now we here in Frankfort are keen to get for the city what the city creates of value, all of it, and—the city is rich. All cities and all states—society—would be rich enough to do all their people need in the way of schools, parks, streets, public buildings, playgrounds—if they got the money they make, the values they create, which now go almost everywhere to sharp individuals who become enemies of society."

Mr. Speer heard and sighed, thinking of Denver. Fred Howe smiled and said not a word, thinking of Tom Johnson, Cleveland, and the single tax. I'm afraid I rubbed it in, thinking, as I did, of all the cities I knew at home where the leading citizens lived *on* the people who lived in those cities and States.

What I got in Europe was the suspicion, almost a conviction, that the conditions there were not very different from ours. In spite of the different forms of government and the different methods of their politics, what we called in America "the system" was the same over there. The big difference between Europe and

America was in the "Bob" Speers. On the ship coming home a committee of us sat down to draw a report. Howe and I were the red left; two others were the white right. Mayor Speer was the moderator. He saw practically all that Howe and I saw in Europe, and just as we saw it. When he voted against us with the conservatives, who had seen very little, he argued with them that Howe and I were right in our diagnosis and in our recommendations, but he pleaded with us to make the report practicable, not a fright. As it was we made it too straight and alarming; nothing came of it, of course, except that Mayor Speer returned to Denver with public plans to announce for the city and a private insight into the economics of what he had hitherto considered a moral problem. He was no longer merely good; he was wise. Mayor Speer set his city going in the direction you can see it taking now. It is a physically clean, beautiful city, which owns, not its corrupting utilities, to be sure, but many square miles of mountain parks which Denverites are proud of and use. That city has a playground and a vision of the future, started by "Bob" Speer, who did learn something in Europe.

I came home asking a question Mayor Speer asked: Isn't it possible to "get" big politicians and big business men? If they have imagination they can be made to see, and seeing is doing, with them. My question was, really, whether evolution wasn't possible and revolution unnecessary. I wanted to answer that question experimentally, and I soon had a chance.

My "home" was a room in Washington Square, where youth lived and reds gathered, the young poets, and painters, playwrights, actors, and Bohemians, and labor leaders of a radical trend, like Bill Haywood, socialists like Max Eastman and Floyd Dell, anarchists, and I.W.W.'s. John Reed had a room above mine. His father, U.S. Marshal Charles Reed, whom I had known intimately in the timber fraud cases in Portland, Oregon, had asked me to keep an eye on his boy, Jack, who, the father thought, was a poet. "Get him a job, let him see everything, but don't let him be anything for a while," that wise father said. "Don't let him get a conviction right away or a business or a career, like me. Let him play." I got Jack a job on the *American Magazine*, on condition that he work only for a living, not to become an editor, but to use it as a springboard from which to dive into life. "Do well what you have to do, but keep the job in its second place," I bade him. And he acted on the advice. I used to go early to bed and to sleep, but I liked it when Jack, a big, growing, happy being, would slam into my room and wake me up to tell me about the "most wonderful thing in the world" that he had seen, been, or done that night. Girls, plays, bums, I.W.W.'s, strikers—each experience was vivid in him, a story, which he often wrote; every person, every idea; Bill Haywood, some prostitute down and out on a park bench, a vaudeville dancer; socialism; the I.W.W. program—all were on a live level with him. Everything was the most wonderful thing in the world. Jack and his crazy young friends were indeed the most wonderful thing in the world.

Jack became enamored of Mabel Dodge, who is, in her odd way, one of the most wonderful things in the world; an aristocratic, rich, good-looking woman, she has never set foot on the earth earthy. "A cut flower," Hutchins Hapgood called her. With taste and grace, the courage of inexperience, and a radiating personality, that woman has done whatever it has struck her fancy to do, and put it and herself over—openly. She never knew that society could and did cut her; she went ahead, and opening her house, let who would come to her salon. Her house was a great old-fashioned apartment on lower Fifth Avenue. It was filled full of lovely, artistic things; she dressed beautifully in her own way. "I found out what styles of hats and gowns suited me, and them I wore through all the passing fashions." She read everything; she believed—for a while—everything; she backed everything with her person and her money, especially young geniuses, like Jack and Robert Edmond Jones. She gave "Bobbie" Jones a back room in her flat to play in, and it looked like a nursery of toys. There he slept, worked, and played with the miniature stages and stage accessories he gathered to develop his childlike gift for stage-making and decorating.

Jack Reed had a second room there, when he got home in time to sleep, and either Jack or Mabel Dodge suggested the salon. Anyway we were soon told that one evening a week we might all come there with our friends, anybody, and—talk. A rich, abundant luncheon was laid in the dining-room, apart, and that was visited by some people who were hungry. All sorts of guests came to Mabel Dodge's salons, poor and rich, labor skates, scabs, strikers and unemployed, painters, musicians, reporters, editors, swells; it was the only successful salon I have ever seen in America. By which I mean that there was conversation and that the conversation developed usually out of some one theme and stayed on the floor.

During my newspaper days some society women asked Norman Hapgood to induce some of his friends to come to their dinners and evenings. They had seen in England and France that their kind of people made thus social centers to which writers, artists, and statesmen came for conversation and amusement. Why could not they, the American rich, imitate that? Several writers and wits did go with Hapgood to some swell houses one winter, but soon dropped out. They said they were bored; it was impossible. There was no conversation, only food, drink, and risqué stories. There was no management, no hostess.

Mabel Dodge managed her evenings, and no one felt that they were managed. She sat quietly in a great armchair and rarely said a word; her guests did the talking, and with such a variety of guests, her success was amazing. Practiced hostesses in society could not keep even a small table of guests together; Mabel Dodge did this better with a crowd of one hundred or more people of all classes. Her secret, I think, was to start the talk going with a living theme. She would seize a time when there was an I.W.W. strike to invite, say, Bill Haywood especially. He would sit or stand near her and strike out, in the hot, harsh spirit of his organization, some challenging idea, answer brutally a few questions, and—that evening everybody talked I.W.W. Emma Goldman said something about anarchism one evening when the anarchists were in the news, and that night we discussed anarchism. It was there and thus that some of us first heard of psychoanalysis and the new psychology of Freud and Jung, which in several discussions, one led by Walter Lippmann, introduced us to the idea that the minds of men were distorted by unconscious suppressions, often quite irresponsible and incapable of reasoning or learning. The young writers saw a new opening for their fiction, the practical men a new profession. I remember thinking how absurd had been my muckraker's descriptions of bad men and good men and the assumption that showing people facts and conditions would persuade them to alter them or their own conduct. The new psychology was a feather in the cap of the red who had always held that to change men's minds one must first change their environment. There were no warmer, quieter, more intensely thoughtful conversations at Mabel Dodge's than those on Freud and his implications.

When there was no such theme to make use of, Mabel Dodge would say to Jack Reed or me or—anybody, "Start something, please," and having done so, she and we were expected to bring the general conversation back to whatever it was we had started— if it took hold. The starter was supposed to be moderator and to take the floor now and then. Meanwhile she was backing Jack Reed, Jones, and other young trouble-lovers in a free speech demonstration or a sympathetic appearance for strikers. Once or twice there were elaborate pageants and shows; a new singer who was not getting a hearing got one with a crowd to appreciate—what did not come—a good, unknown voice. There were arrests, releases on her bond.

The highbrow, lowbrow Bohemians had a center in those days. Mabel Dodge's salons were famous in a way and did some good and some harm. There was free speech; there was a release to some pretty tense feelings, especially in the bitter labor conflicts of that time. Greenwich Village, which had been a simple fact, a neglected neighborhood of low rents, became the dwelling-place of students, impecunious artists, and down-and-out reds and the experimental laboratory for little theaters—this picturesque old quarter of the city was ridiculed and romanced into "Greenwich Village," a sort of Latin Quarter. I remember my astonishment on a trip west to hear that the place where I lived in New York was known out there, and as an institution, as a scene in romance and caricature, not as I knew it, but as fiction was making it.

The serious side of Greenwich Village was not noticed by the clever uptown tourists who came slumming down Fifth Avenue. Some of those boys and girls who were agonizing so comically were learning to be writers and painters; some of them, like O'Neill and the Provincetown Players in their dark, dirty little vacant house, were making plays and playwrights, theaters and actors, who later "rose" to Broadway. And among the reds one heard something of the tragedy and the crimes of the labor struggle. I heard, for example, of the plotted blowing-up by the structural iron workers of the steel work of buildings and bridges as a part of the very real war of labor on the U.S. and other steel companies, and I felt something of the passion which prompted a responsible labor organization to turn to the systematic use of dynamite, through which, one later day, I got into the famous McNamara case out in Los Angeles.

DYNAMITE

O N THE terrace of the House of Commons one afternoon, a group of Labor and Liberal members with a few guests were talking very seriously about a threatening coal strike which might start a revolution in England. A revolution! That is what they said; that is how they seemed to feel; and they agreed that the government was in dread of this impending strike which might mean a crisis. All parties shared the fear, and all parties were trying to put it off, Labor too. The conversation had sighed into silence when Kier Hardie, the first and the truest of the Labor members, came out upon the terrace and marched straight up to the group.

"Well," he announced, "we have put off the strike. I come from out there in the fields, and I am relieved to be able to report that we reached an agreement with the men and their leaders to postpone the strike till the spring."

The rejoicing in that group was as real as their concern had been anxious. They congratulated Hardie and one another; they drew out details of the negotiations—Hardie's arguments, the men's answers, the terms of the temporary settlement.

"The government has time," said Hardie. "Let's see what they will do! The conditions which are causes of the strike—and of what the strike may become—remain. All we have gained is time for the government to deal with them. I shall be interested to see what they do with their respite."

"If it were the American government," I said, "it would do nothing. Even if it feared what you all say your government fears and had the time your government has to seek out the causes of trouble and deal with them, it would merely wait and deal with the trouble. Governments, as I have found them, will not anticipate; they cannot see or think of causes of war, of strikes, of other evils. Our culture is against that sort of thinking and acting."

Hardie had been nodding approval of what I was saying, and when I wound up by asking him to write to me if his government did anything, he promised.

"I give you my word," he said, "but I am pretty sure you will not get a letter from me."

The party broke up, and he drew me for a walk down the terrace along the Thames till we were alone. Then he said: "I gather from the papers and from other sources that organized labor is using dynamite in the States to fight your big steel companies. Some fellows have been caught and are to be tried for murder, aren't they? They killed some workers in a Los Angeles newspaper office. Why don't you as a journalist study out the causes of the rage that is so strong that it makes a union—and a labor union, you know, is very, very conservative; any *organization* is conservative —what it is that makes a union appoint men and raise a fund to pay them and their expenses to blow up the steel structures they build? And tell us. And see if you can't make your inquiry more interesting than the question whether the dynamiters are guilty of murder. We have got somehow to consider the causes of strikes and crimes and, as you said, wars—not only the right and wrong of them."

Kier Hardie was a strong, tight-muscled little man, devoted, persistent, but patient, not quick to speech, and, therefore perhaps, impressive. Taking in what he advised me to do, I turned the idea over till the desire came to go and do it. I had come over to muckrake England and other European countries. That could wait. I sailed for home with a purpose: to organize a syndicate of newspapers to send me to Los Angeles to report the McNamara case or, rather, what was back of it, the causes of the dynamiting. Arriving in New York, I went down into Greenwich Village, saw the reds there, and visited labor leaders elsewhere; and to my astonishment they all were taking the view that the McNamaras were innocent and the case against them a frame-up. Some of the very men who had once talked with me about the dynamiting as "action at last, direct action," now declared, and with feeling— even with convincing manifestations of conviction on their part— that organized labor had never done this thing. I reminded one man that he had told me as a joke once how Samuel Gompers and a cabinet of other labor leaders were on a train that was about to pass over a new steel bridge when it blew up. The joke was how near they had come to being blown up by their own petard. The joker's answer was that labor may have blown up some works but not men. The McNamaras had had nothing to do with the explosion and fire which on the night of October 1, 1910, wrecked the Los Angeles *Times* building and killed twenty-one working-men. As a line of defense this absolute denial was acceptable to the friends of labor. "Let capital prove its case" was all right as a fighting slogan, but to believe and make the rank and file of labor believe this lie seemed to me a loss of something true and significant, and I recalled with satisfaction Kier Hardie's equally authentic labor view, that labor had done it and capital and the world should learn why.

The first editor I called on was Henry J. Wright, my old editor on the *Commercial Advertiser*, now the New York *Globe*. He was struck by my undoubting belief that labor, if not the McNamaras, was guilty, and he liked my plan to go to the trial, not to report that, but to find out and show what was behind the act. The Associated Press would cover the trial. His only doubt was whether I could, in the state of feeling existing, get at the truth. And feelings were intense. The case was the news of the day and bade fair to stay on the front page throughout the trial, probably for a year, and the issue was drawing definitely the famous class line. Labor knew its heroes were victims of a conspiracy; capital, the upper and the middle classes, were equally sure the McNamaras were foul, murderous dynamiters. Wright communicated with the editors of the Boston *Globe*, the Chicago *Daily News*, the San Francisco *Bulletin*—twenty-one papers in all—who joined in the assignment of me to "do the story" as I saw it. Good, strong, mostly conservative papers. I went to Los Angeles, feeling well backed.

Going from my hotel straight to the courtroom on the morning of my arrival, I found the attorneys still struggling to complete the jury. I sat down to watch the important, dull business, have a look at J. B. McNamara, the first defendant on trial, the judge, the attorneys, the scene. In a few minutes a clerk of the court came to me to say that the judge, Bordwell, would like to see me in chambers at the next recess. Gladly I went, and the judge

UPPER: CLARENCE S. DARROW. LOWER: FREMONT OLDER.
(FROM BUSTS BY JO DAVIDSON)

greeted me pleasantly; he had known me or my father, knew I was a Californian who had been long away. What had I come there to do? he asked.

"To try this case," I answered, with a light laugh.

"I thought I was to try the case," he smiled.

"How can you?" I questioned. "You think it is a murder case, don't you? And you'll admit as evidence only testimony as to whether the defendants actually committed the alleged crime or not?"

"Why not?" he retorted, but amiably, in the spirit of my self-assertion.

"It is a social manifestation of a condition, not a mere legal offense, this crime. If these men did it, they did it as the appointed agents of labor, and they and their organization of ordinary working-men must have suffered something worth our knowing about to get worked up to a state of mind where they deliberately, as a policy, could carry on for years dynamiting, arson, murder. What were those real or fancied wrongs, what are the conditions which produced this—act of war? That's what has to be gone into."

"Oh, well, I can't go into that," he said, a bit sharply.

"No." I agreed in tone with him. "And that's why I say you can't really try this case, and that I must. And, by the way," I said, "it is the same with most criminal practice. You judges cannot under your rules of evidence look into the always mitigating, sometimes completely explanatory, causes of what you call crimes."

He shook his head. "No."

"Well, that is why we radicals say that one cannot get justice in the courts."

Judge Bordwell afterward called me an "avowed anarchist," and I think he got the avowal from this phrase of mine, "we radicals." Everybody was calling me a red in those days, except the reds; and I accepted the name as I had that of muckraker—as a compliment. People who call such names are only trying to say that, somehow, you are not in the herd; you are different; and that is a compliment, however clumsy. Judge Bordwell did not like my reproach of court justice, I think, and remembered it as from an "avowed anarchist," which was near enough to what I did avow. He asked me how I was going about my trial of the case, and I started to tell him my plan, first to find out whether the Mc-Namaras are guilty or not . . . That's as far as I got. How was I to do that?

"Ask them," I answered. "How long will it take you to find out in your way?" I asked. He thought the trial might last months, possibly a year. "Well," I said, "I'll get the answer this afternoon —if you'll let me go into the jail and interview the prisoners."

He said he would, but would they tell me? "Why will they tell you?"

"Because I won't put on an air of righteousness, climb up on a raised dais, and acting as if I had not and could not ever commit a crime, hale them before me, and threatening to hang them if they tell the truth, swear them to tell it, all of it, and nothing but —evidence."

I hated the law and the courts at that time. I was an anarchist, I guess, but I had been a reporter, remember, in the lobbies of Legislatures where laws were made; and how; and I had reported trials in courts while seeing and hearing the judges, the attorneys, and the prisoners during the intermissions. How can a political police reporter respect law and lawyers?

"How will you ask the prisoners if they are guilty?" Judge Bordwell wanted to know. "And why will they tell you the truth?"

"I will visit them in their prison, sit down hip to haunch with them, and as one crook to another—we'll talk it all over. They'll know that I am no better than they are and that I wouldn't hurt them, that I'd help them if I could. And so they'll see that I am to be trusted, as I am."

It happened like that. When the judge went back to the bench, I spoke to Darrow, who gave me his permission to see his clients, and that afternoon, when court adjourned, I called on them at the jail. There were J. B. McNamara, who was charged with actually placing and setting off the dynamite in Ink Alley that blew up part of the *Times* building and set fire to the rest, bringing about the death of twenty-one employees, and J. J. McNamara, J.B.'s brother, who was indicted on some twenty counts for assisting at explosions as secretary of the Structural Iron Workers' Union, directing the actual dynamiters. He was supposed in labor circles to be the commanding man, the boss; he looked it; tall, strong, blond, he was a handsome figure of health and personal power. But his brother, Jim, who looked sick and weak, soon appeared as the man of decision. They were affectionate brothers, deferred to each other, and J.B. always said "see J.J." about things; "he's the boss." But when they were together it was the other way. J.J. considered, but J.B., the younger, decided, and quick, too. I had never met them before, but when they came out of their cells they greeted and sat down beside me as if I were an old friend. They asked no questions except about mutual friends. They assumed I was to report the trial in court.

"No," I said, and I told them the same that I had told the judge, how and why I wanted to get first from them, then out in the field, the story of what had been done to them and to labor to set them off on an organized policy of dynamiting. "Justifiable dynamiting," I laughed, was to be my defense; but my real purpose was to turn the already pointed general interest in their case to an inquiry into the wrongs done labor, and so to get at the causes of class hate.

"You can't do it," said J.B. "They are after us, not the truth, and us they'll get, if they can."

"I know," I agreed. "It's a doubtful experiment and a risk for you, but it's got to be done sometime. Why not now? Why not help me dig up on the side—while the legal case is going—the case of labor against capital as a parallel, as a background to the case of California versus the McNamaras. I might be able to show why you turned to dynamite, but I can't—I won't—do it without your permission."

"Why not?" asked J.J.

"Because," I answered, "while I don't mean to, of course, I might make a blunder that would give something away and hang you."

Waiting for an answer, we were silent a moment, I watching J.J., who was looking at J.B., who was smiling up at his big brother. It was J.J. who spoke first. "Have you seen Darrow about this?" But J.B. pushed that aside with an impatient gesture.

"If you could do what you propose I'd be willing to hang." That to me; then to his brother he said: "It's for that that we have been working, Joe, to force attention to the actual conditions of labor, and if this man can do it—if this man will only try to do it . . . He means, you see, to go and get the cases of actual black-listing, for example, that have made it impossible for discharged men to ever get work, and—things like that. Why wouldn't I risk my life to get that told? It's what I have been risking my life for right along. Sure, I say; go ahead. Be careful, of course; see Darrow, but—go to it, and luck to you."

"That's J. B. McNamara," said Clarence Darrow, when that night I reported to him and broached my scheme. He would not, he could not, enter into it. He was the attorney whose task it was to resist a conviction in those cases, to save the prisoners from a death penalty. He represented them personally, and he represented also organized labor, which had raised a very large fund, almost dollar by dollar, to prove the innocence of these two labor men. He must do that; he could not have anything to do with my plan, which would not work but might be tried just the same. Meanwhile, however, he asked me to hang around and see how the case was going. I did.

It was going badly, that case. Apparently concerned, both the defense and the prosecution, with the selection of the jury, they were really working on the evidence, finding and forming witnesses; Darrow was building a plant, a building, which he meant to dynamite or fire to prove something. He had his experts, as the other side had. He had his spies, too, who reported what the other side was doing and finding out. He knew the other side had its detectives, of course. The trial of a criminal law case is often a dirty business—outside of court. But Darrow's spies were reporting, not only what the prosecution was doing, but what they were finding out about what the defense was doing. You had the sense all the time that, as some of their spies were your spies also, so some of yours were theirs. You never can be sure which side a spy is serving the better. Anyway Darrow learned that the district attorney was learning so much and so promptly of what the defense was up to and what the defense was afraid of that he was frightened.

When people ask me what sort of man Darrow is, I ask them the apparently irrelative question: When? And my answer is that at three o'clock he is a hero for courage, nerve, and calm judgment, but at 3:15 he may be a coward for fear, collapse, and panicky mentality. A long, lean, loose body, with a heavy face that is molded like an athlete's body, he is more of a poet than a fighting

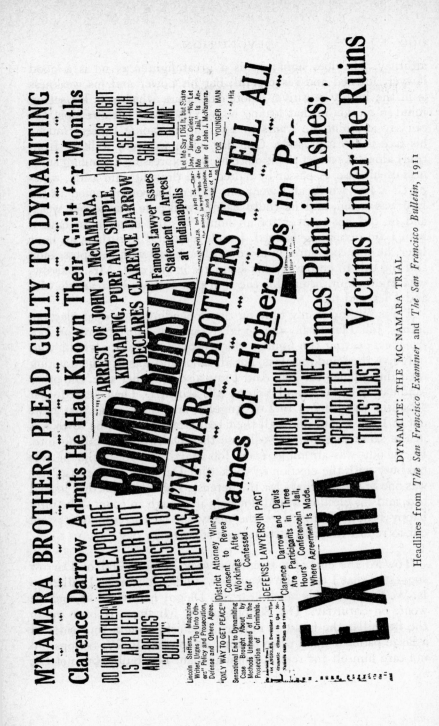

DYNAMITE: THE MC NAMARA TRIAL

Headlines from *The San Francisco Examiner* and *The San Francisco Bulletin*, 1911

attorney. He does fight; he is a great fighter as he is a good lawyer, learned and resourceful, but his power and his weakness is in the highly sensitive, emotional nature which sets his seeing mind in motion in that loafing body. His power is expression. He can say anything he wants to say, but he cannot conceal much; his face is too expressive. One day when we were walking from court along the street to his office he was expressing a winning sureness of his case. A passer-by halted, and drawing him aside, whispered a few words and went on. When Darrow rejoined us his face was ashen, and he could hardly walk; he was scared weak, and he did not recover for an hour. "I can't stand it to have a man I am defending hanged. I can't stand it." And then, an hour later, he was cock-sure, humorous, almost gay with self-possession and the call to encourage his associates in the case. Mrs. Darrow, who knows him, listens for the sigh that follows his leader's wit; and I learned to.

I was putting in my time on the impending municipal election, seeing Job Harriman, the socialist candidate for mayor of Los Angeles, hearing the figures which proved the party would win: only five thousand socialists, but all labor and lots of others voting their discontent—for Job. And I saw also the other side, the other candidates, backers, and voters, all alarmed. They feared that socialism was coming to Los Angeles, and think what that news out in Iowa would do to all their real estate plans! The town was in the same state of near-collapse that Darrow kept falling into. Everybody was atremble, even Job Harriman, for while he was too busy with the election to work with Darrow on "the case," he was one of the attorneys for the defense. He knew that that looked bad, and his election would not help it enough to count. The only happy fellows I met were the many special correspondents sent out to report the case, a front-page story every day.

Toward the end of a strenuous week, some friend of Darrow suggested that I take him away over Sunday for a rest. I called up E. W. Scripps on his ranch near San Diego; he invited us, and we went, on Saturday. The Scripps ranch, Miramar, is back up in the foothills; the house is modern, Spanish, around four sides of a large patio. A good place to rest, except that E. W. Scripps did not care himself for rest. A singular man. Big, bulky, but not fat, his hulking body, in big boots and rough clothes, carried a large gray head with a wide gray face which did not always express, like Darrow's, the constant activity of the man's brain. He was a hard student, whether he was working on newspaper make-up or on some inquiry in biology. That mind was not to be satisfied. It read books and fed on the conversation of scientists, not to quench an inquiry with the latest information, but to excite and make intelligent the question implied. E. W. Scripps had "made" a newspaper, then gone on with a method he discovered to found a long string of "little papers" which were bound to grow, as they did, into a newspaper system called the Scripps-MacRae, later the Scripps-Howard papers. But that was his fun; his business, his chief preoccupation, was to study life in all forms: human, animal, astronomical. Always alone. He did his own thinking, and he had some thoughts: independent, bold, his.

"I'm a rich man, and that's dangerous, you know," he once said. "But it isn't just the money that's the risk; it's the living around with other rich men. They get to thinking all alike, and their money not only talks, their money does their thinking, too. I come off here on these wide acres of high miles to get away from—my sort; to get away from the rich. So I don't think like a rich man. I think more like a left labor galoot, like those dynamiters. They talk about the owner of newspapers holding back his editors." He laughed. "It's the other way with me. I get me boys, bright boys, from the classes that read my papers; I give them the editorship and the management, with a part interest in the property, and, say, in a year or so, as soon as the profits begin to come in, they become conservative and I have to boot them back into their class, and even then—Corruption? Yes, but it's they that corrupt me and my papers, those bright boys from off the streets."

Some day some of those bright Scripps boys who have succeeded as editors should gather, arrange, and publish the letters they all got from "the old man" who introduced mass production into journalism, turning out newspapers and editors as Henry Ford made cars.

The old man received Darrow and me at the station, and on the drive up the hills to the ranch house he acted on my hint that Darrow was to rest. Scripps steered the talk away from the case.

By the time we had settled into chairs in his study, Scripps saw
that that was the wrong treatment; Darrow wanted to talk about
the case or its meaning to him, and he did; he was monologuing
about violence in the labor conflict. Scripps pulled out a sheaf of
typewritten stuff. "Here," he said, "is a thing I have just written
about direct action. I'll read it." It was a defense of the use by
labor of force, dynamite. We, the employers, have and use every
other weapon, he argued. We have the jobs to give or withhold,
the capital to spend or not, in production, for wages, for ourselves;
we have the press to state our case and suppress theirs; we have
the bar and the bench, the Legislature, the governor, the police,
and the militia. Labor has nothing but violence and mob force.
Smiling, he read his Philosophy of Force and then chucked it
back in the drawer as Darrow sighed. It was no use to him; he
could not defend dynamite; he had to defend two prisoners accused of murder, and he described bitterly the lay of the evidence
for and against him.

"I wish we could get a settlement out of court," he said.

"Oh, it can't be as bad as that," Scripps protested, but he glanced
up at me, and a few minutes later, while Darrow was out of the
room, he said: "Darrow is in no state of mind to try that case.
He is beaten by it. Why don't you take him up on the settlement
and see what you can do?"

"That wish," I said, "was only the expression of one mood.
He'll have another when he comes back."

And sure enough, when Darrow rejoined us he laid out his case
as a sure winner; for an hour he proved his case, cynically but
boldly, even humorously. That night he was in the depths again,
and as we were parting for the night, he repeated, "I wish we
could settle it somehow." The next day, Sunday, Scripps made
busy with drives and walks, his plans for the ranch, his newspapers, his ideas—and Darrow was cheerful most of the day,
which seemed to do him good. Scripps took me aside once to urge
me to try for a settlement; he was concerned for Darrow, and he
was concerned for the prisoners and for labor.

"Have you any hunch as to how to go about it?" Scripps asked.

"Yes," I said. "I have." And I told him about an idea that had
been in the background of my mind.

"Fine," said Scripps. "It—might—work. And Darrow's line of

defense won't. You tackle it, and if I, or my papers, can help, give me a ring."

"I can't act like that," I said, "not on what Darrow says in a mood. I'll tackle him when he is normal, some morning; men's minds are clear and responsible in the morning. I'll sound him after breakfast some day."

"Right, and the morning after a railroad trip is a good morning," Scripps urged, with a little chuckle.

That night in the sleeper I lay awake, as Darrow said he did; only I was seeing something. I saw a chance to make an experiment with "big, bad men" and with Christianity.

SETTLING THE DYNAMITERS' CASE. AN EXPERIMENT WITH "BIG, BAD MEN"

T HE idea that lay awake with me on the train to Los Angeles that night was to try out Christianity as a working principle—among sinners. I have told how impressed I was with the testimony in a Wisconsin bribery case that the confessing briber could not buy up the socialist wards in Milwaukee and called them bum wards. My inference was that not only the socialists, anarchists, single taxers, I.W.W.'s, but that all men with a definite hope of a better world and a plan to reach it are unpurchasable. A vision then was the thing to "change human nature." Most men had none. Hence the respectable wards in Milwaukee were not bum. And yet they, too, had a vision. They were Christians, and I read the New Testament to discover the vision and the plan of Christ. It was astonishing, radical, complete, but when I went to the churches I did not hear it preached, and of course the Christians did not practice it. I preached Christianity, and the effect was a shock to the congregations. I preached in Christ's spirit, too, quietly, literally, with none of the force with which I had heard Christian ministers proclaim righteousness and denounce sinners. My sermons were as loving as the Sermon on the Mount, for, verily, I believed then that the righteous can be and must be saved if we are to have a heaven on earth—not only the sinners. No use. The regular members of the Christian churches, thinking they have Christianity, can no more get it than the righteous, thinking they are good, can be made good—for anything. Christianity will not work with Christians.

But, as Jesus learned by hard experience and taught so clearly, Christianity does work with sinners. I proved that for myself. I preached Christianity. Whenever I wanted to get something done I appealed to sinners for help, and the help came. I made Wall Street men contribute to Brand Whitlock's campaigns for mayor of Toledo; I made Wall Street—knowingly—pay for many a radical campaign, plan, and purpose; I got machine pull for reds in many an emergency. Political bosses and business bosses, out-and-out crooks, hard-boiled editors, rough-neck rascals—they never failed to respond to the (unnamed) Christian appeal, especially for mercy. And that is sound. Mercy is scientific, as Christianity is. If our evils have causes, if there are diseases to account for individual crimes of weakness, if there are deliverable temptations to account for individual felonies of strength, if there are removable causes for bribery, corruption, poverty, crime, and war —then the doctrine of forgiveness instead of punishment for the sinner is sound, scientific, and—it is natural. It appeals to some instinct in man.

Having proved this to my own satisfaction by many small private experiments—with sinners—I had long been looking for a chance to try it more openly in a more spectacular situation which all men could see. This long-looked-for emergency seemed to have arrived with Darrow's wish to settle the McNamara case out of court. I could not tell this to Darrow; I had to be fair to him and to the prisoners. I would sound Darrow only when he was unemotional, in the morning, the next morning.

When we crept out, cold, tired, and uncomfortable, from that sleeping-car and in silence ordered and ate our breakfast at the station, Darrow was at his cynical norm when, lighting up a cigarette, I said, "Darrow, you were talking yesterday about a settlement of the case. Do you mean that?"

"Yes. I'd like to settle it, but it's impossible, of course."

"I think not. I think I could work it out, if you'd let me."

"What! And save the boys?"

"Yes." And I outlined my plan: to get a group of employers or, anyhow, capitalists to do it.

He reflected, tempted, no doubt, but he soon threw up his hands. "Do you think for one moment that the local employers would consent to let those prisoners go? And if they did, would the eastern employers who have suffered from dynamite let them? It's impossible. Impossible."

He was dismissing the idea. But I asked him to take a chance and let me try it. He sat back, and we went more into details. Could I do it and not give away the case, not make an implied concession of guilt?

"What's the difference what I say or concede? I'm not an attorney in the case. I can sound out the kind of men I'm thinking of and see and tell you, and you can then decide."

Could I do even that without implicating him and the prisoners? One mistake, and—I answered that he could repudiate me, even denounce me, if I got him in bad. Would I stand for that? he asked. He'd have to do it pretty fiercely. I offered to act without his consent, but he must know, and then if it broke badly he could do whatever he liked. It was a longish talk, and Darrow, with no hope of my success, agreed to let me go ahead and, bit by bit, report progress, leaving him free to repudiate me in any form he felt necessary. He went to his office, I to the office of Meyer Lissner, who was a sort of political boss for the reformers, then in power in Los Angeles. I knew him pretty well personally.

"Lissner," I said, "why don't you Los Angeles people settle this McNamara case and get it out of your system?"

He was sitting all cool and fresh as the morning itself when I spoke. When I stopped, abruptly, he looked as if the sun were breaking through the fog. "What?" he spluttered. "What's that you say? Settle the McNamara case? How? Why?"

"Well," I said, "here it is, tearing your city to pieces—for a year, perhaps; arousing hate, intensifying the class war which you don't believe in. However it turns out, whether you hang those men or not, you won't settle anything or satisfy anybody. A law fight is a fight, perjury, suborning of witnesses, jury bribery, and when one side wins there is no public conviction, only a running sore left. Why not try the other, the kinder, the finer way? Call together the leading men of your city and say to them, 'Here, we've got labor down; we can hang two dynamiters who the workers think are innocent if we want to. But let's not. Let's let labor up and let their heroes go. And then have a conference of leading employers with labor leaders and see if we can't handle our labor problem in such a fashion that we can afford to make Los Angeles the best instead of the worst town in the country for labor.' "

There was more of it. I can't remember our words. Lissner

had to hear my proposition repeated a few times to adjust his mind to the idea. Then he got it, and he liked it. He stood up, went to the window, came back, and he said enough to show that he was for the finer way. "But," he objected, "you can't put it over on the kind of men you need. They are as bitter as labor. They want these men to hang, and you want them to let them go—free? No."

"You think," I said, "that you and I can see this, but nobody else; that we are exceptional men. Sit down and make me a list. Write the names of the few men who actually govern this town, the big, bad men; I mean the kind of men who act off their own bats, don't have to consult others, and who, when they set out to do something, good or bad, put it over. Imagination, courage, strength we need, not goodness. If you get a single good citizen— you know what I mean—if you get a reformer or a heeler on the list, we'll be done. What I ask you to write down is the names of your principals."

He began to jot down names, and each time he wrote he sniffed. "Think of getting him," he said once.

"Who?" I asked, for I was not looking over his shoulder.

"General Otis," he answered. "Harry Chandler—any of them."

"Go on. Write," I said. "And be careful not to put down any of your good reformers. Only men, now; hard-boiled, un-scrupulous fellows who act." I was overexpressing it to keep off names I was sure he would be tempted to add to a list to perform an "idealistic deed," as he called this. He obeyed as well as he could. He finally tossed me some seventeen names, which I knew was wrong.

"There are not in a town the size of Los Angeles so many as seventeen commanding men of the sort I mean, actual dictators, free independent rulers of themselves and other men."

Lissner scratched off a couple. I did not know all the men on his list, but some were right, the very ones he regarded as hopeless for our purpose. In a word, I felt that the men I wanted were on the list with a lot of the kind I did not want. I would start with it. He said I couldn't get one of them, not one. But I challenged him to "let's try it now." I asked him to pick the most likely one, and he chose Thomas E. Gibbons, a free-lance capitalist, like

Lissner himself, and a sportsman, a good fellow, a good mixer, who was very popular.

Gibbons came on a telephone call, and he balked at first; but I reminded him, as I had Lissner, who listened, of San Francisco, where the fierce prosecution of capitalists had left the class line and many wounds all raw and open, and of other cities where the class struggle had been made the preoccupation of the people. "You have it here," I said. "You have socialists and labor men lined up against the other class. You have hate all through your system. That's bad. It may be that the class war is never to end, but why not try some other way, first, in Los Angeles? An act of generosity to these two heroes of labor who are in trouble, with all men looking on, might lead to a really productive rearrangement of labor relations."

Gibbons saw it, but he, too, said that we would fail, that nobody else would agree to such a proposition as letting the prisoners go —free.

"Only you, Lissner, and I can be wise and fine!" I exclaimed, and I challenged them there and then. "I don't want to get all your men. That's your job. But since you are so skeptical I'll show you. You pick out the hardest man on the list to get, and I'll get him."

I was balked by their response. They both named General Otis, and I had not thought of him. Otis was a lifelong labor-baiter. His paper, the *Times*, was notorious all over the country as the most persistent and the fiercest of all the fighters of organized labor. That's why the dynamiters had turned aside from the destruction of steel structures to "hand Otis one." It was his building and his employees that had been blown up and burned to death. Also General Otis bore me a personal grudge for having got him into my syndicate when I was reporting Washington; I wrote everything he did not believe. I would never have chosen Otis to prove that all men were generous if appealed to aright.

And then there was Harry Chandler, General Otis's son-in-law and the business manager of the *Times*—"a hard-headed, materialistic money-maker without a sentiment in all his make-up." Somebody had to "get" him. He and Otis were political powers, bosses; they "controlled" the district attorney, I heard. It did look impossible, but Gibbons was game. He undertook Chandler, I Otis. It did not come out exactly that way.

Otis was "out" when I called, and I found myself talking to Mr. Chandler, whom I did not know by sight. He asked what my business was. Whether Gibbons had seen and told him I did not know, but Harry Chandler demanded my business with Otis in a tone that tempted me. I made my little speech to him, and when he was neither astonished nor expressive, I added more. "Let the men you've got down go, absolutely, you, the *Times*. Say you don't want to punish, say you don't want revenge, say you don't hate labor; say it when you've done it, and then take up the labor situation, hear labor for once; really listen and consider their case and see if you can't by some combination of efficient management and willing labor make this the best-paid labor town in the United States."

Harry Chandler silently listened, and I could see no sign of any reaction till, after a long moment of thought, he said, "Were you going to say that to General Otis?"

"Yes."

Another long pause, and he said: "Do you know, that is the finest proposition that was ever put up to me, and I'm for it. And we can put it over, you and I. I can get the district attorney, I'm sure; you can talk to Darrow. Yes, it can be done. Anyway I'll give it all my time till we get it done. But I'll do this only on one condition: that you don't drag in those others you say you were to see. Certainly not General Otis. Otis? Say, if he ever hears of this he will— No. Not General Otis; and not the others, because they'll tell Otis. When the time comes, when it's all fixed, I'll tell him myself and have it out with him. But for the present, you work by day, call on me at midnight, and—I'll work by night. This will be done."

I agreed, of course. I reported to Lissner, who was amazed and for the first time believed that maybe . . . Then I reported to Darrow, the afternoon of the day when we had had our talk at breakfast. And Darrow believed. He considered the specific terms of settlement; he said he would wire to the American Federation of Labor (his client in the case), then in session, to send a representative to consult with him in the matter; and he expressed his doubt about the Erectors' Association, which was the national organization of the steel employers as against the workers' organization. "Somebody ought to see them," he foresaw.

As to the terms, I told Darrow, as I had told Lissner, Gibbons, and Chandler, that my proposition was to let the McNamaras go unpunished, to call off all further pursuit of the other suspects, and then to call a conference of the leading local employers and the wisest labor leaders to take up and settle somehow, without fights and strikes, the Los Angeles labor problem. Darrow smiled; he thought me a fool, but he shrugged his loose shoulders and said nothing but "Go ahead." He would see the prisoners and tell them what was being done and take their reactions.

Chandler, who was in communication with Captain Fredericks, the district attorney, reported each midnight some progress. Fredericks was willing to settle the case; he held out for terms. He could not let all the prisoners and suspects go scot-free; somebody must be punished. Well, Darrow reported that J. B. McNamara was willing to plead guilty himself, but would not consent to his brother's doing likewise. He said that his brother, John, being an officer in the Structural Iron Workers' Union, represented labor and would not and should not plead guilty, since that would convict labor officially. Jim, as Darrow called the younger brother, was not an officer of the union; he was only an individual. His plea would involve only himself. Chandler took this as possible of acceptance by Fredericks. He was impatient of the district attorney's insistence on some punishment; he, Chandler, would have taken my terms, which I meant still to work for. It seemed sufficient at the moment to have an agreement by both sides to settle somehow without any hangings. I felt sure that, in a final meeting of us all, I could make the Los Angeles gesture complete, and I still believe that that could have been done if we had had only that city to deal with.

But one afternoon I happened to go to Chandler's office just as the night hawk arrived, and he was disturbed. He had read a long telegram from the Erectors' Association head office in Indianapolis to General Otis, warning him of what we were doing and demanding that not one alone but both the prisoners should get long terms.

"I have destroyed that wire," said Chandler, "but what's the use? The game is up. When Indianapolis gets no answer from the general they'll wire again, and I'm not here always as early as this."

"Well, be early tomorrow," I suggested, "and meanwhile let's hurry."

I reported to Darrow, who proposed that I go to Indianapolis and see the officials there, but realized right away that I had to be in Los Angeles. I was sure a few words in the east to the right men would have brought the Erectors' Association in; and I was right, as I'll show later.

The next day, when I called "early" on Chandler, he met me with hands up. "A wire came, as I feared, and the general has it. That will end us." And having said that, he looked down a long aisle and instantly turned and ran into his inner office. I looked where he had looked, and I saw General Otis marching menacingly at us with a telegram waving in his hand. He paid no attention to me.

"Harry," he called, still coming, "what is this, Harry?"

Harry Chandler came like a bad little boy out of his office, but I spoke first.

"Wait a minute, General Otis, I can tell you about this matter; I know more than Mr. Chandler does about it."

"I know you do," said the general, with a glare.

"Will you let me tell it you?"

He nodded.

"It will take five minutes. That's a long time to listen without speaking. Five minutes."

"Go ahead; I'll listen."

"Well, this is a proposition to stop a fight, a fool fight, and try another, better way to settle a difference. How do you stop a fight? By stopping the fellow who has just been struck from striking the next blow. In this fight it's capital's turn. Labor hit you hard, with dynamite, fire, killings. And now you've got labor down where you can give it some legal dynamite and a bit of legal murder. What would happen if, now, you, the *Times* that was blown up, and Los Angeles, should say, 'No. No hangings, no force, no wrongs. We'll not only let your agents go; we will sit down with your picked labor representatives, and we'll see together if we can't do something no city has ever done, plan together for the highest-paid, most productive labor and management in the world'? And this plan is based, General Otis, on the theory, which is probably true, that you can win this case hands down and so hang these and other labor men and have your revenge with all the world looking on to admire—on that theory and this, that, labor-baiter as you are called, you won't do it."

The time wasn't up. I was going on, but General Otis turned from me.

"Harry," he said, "who's stopping this?"

It took Harry, it took me, a moment to get it, that Otis was for it, that in his fierce way he was out to find out who was blocking this plan.

Harry Chandler was recovering. "Why, General, it's the district attorney—Fredericks—he is negotiating for terms—"

Otis was swelling with wrath, and I broke in.

"I can tell you about that, too, General Otis. Fredericks is up against it. He has a reason for his course. He is willing to settle, with the leaders of this county behind him, but the Erectors' Association, who haven't heard our plan straight, they are demanding some punishment, more and more; and Fredericks—"

"But what's that got to do with us?" Otis exploded.

"This," I said. "Fredericks says that the Erectors' Association raised fifteen thousand dollars toward the costs of getting the evidence and that therefore he is their attorney, too. Los Angeles County is not his only client."

"Harry," said Otis, "you go and tell the —— —— that we'll refund that fifteen thousand dollars."

Whether this was ever done I don't know. It may not have been necessary. All I know is that the editor and the business manager of the Los Angeles *Times* were that kind of men, that they backed the settlement of the case, and that the paper stood for it to the end, even when others in Los Angeles ran away before the outcry all over the United States against it.

THE CHURCHES DECIDE AGAINST CHRISTIANITY

WHEN Darrow heard that General Otis was for the settlement of the case, he was so convinced that he called in his associate attorneys for consultation: Le Compte Davis, Joseph Smith—all but Job Harriman. It was hard to tell the socialist candidate for mayor; a settlement with a plea of guilty would mean his defeat. Ed Nockels arrived from the east to represent the American Federation of Labor. And there were the two prisoners, who had to consent to each step taken. And the judge —I had to tell him.

The case was proceeding, of course; they were completing the jury, and one day when I went to court to report something to Darrow, Judge Bordwell called me into his chambers and asked me what was going on. I gave his attentive ear the whole short story up to date and then suggested that perhaps he would better know nothing about it for a while. He looked up sharply and agreed: "Yes. Perhaps you are right there. I'd rather not know about this till . . . Yes."

He afterward said he knew nothing about it, and I remembered this incident years later, when President Wilson said he had no knowledge of the notorious secret treaties of his war allies. The man may know about something the official may take no cognizance of.

We were sailing smoothly toward the end when something happened that felt to me like an explosion. Darrow was accused of an attempt to bribe a juror. A man who was said to be in his pay and was suspected also of being in the pay of the district attorney was supposed to have been seen taking money on a crowded sidewalk, in broad daylight, from Darrow. There was something queer about it, "something fishy"; public bribery isn't very clever, and the witnesses were not very creditable. So people remarked who did not know what I knew, that Darrow was so sure of a settlement that he had no clear motive for "getting" jurors. No matter, however; this incident, published as front page news, made the settlement seem impossible again. We all stuck to it just the same, and the only bad effect was to harden and hasten the negotiations. Other influences worked toward the hardening of the prosecution.

Evidently all men who respond to a generous sentiment themselves think that other men won't. I have shown some of that. No one could believe that Harry Chandler would work for the release of the dynamiters who blew up his newspaper plant. He did, but he would not ask General Otis to; and when his father-in-law and chief came in for a generous settlement, Chandler was dumbfounded. But I think now that even after the revolution of good will, Mr. Chandler still could not credit Captain Fredericks with any such magnanimity. I should have talked to Fredericks to make sure that he heard the proposition in the spirit in which it was broached to and accepted by Chandler and others; the district attorney should have had his chance. But Chandler said so positively that he would "attend to the district attorney" and my associates were so sure that Fredericks was a *Times* man, who would respond to Otis or Chandler and no one else, that I left that end to Chandler. My theory is that Chandler gave Fredericks shrewd instead of idealistic reasons for the settlement, and so, with the Erectors' Association working for victims, the district attorney was driving a hard bargain—a life term for J. B. Mc-Namara, some punishment for J. J. McNamara.

J. B. McNamara resisted these terms. He wanted to take all the punishment. His proposition was that he be hanged and all others go free. But Darrow would not stand for any hanging; nobody must die. J.B. answered that he would rather die than have his brother take any punishment, and it was only when Darrow, the other attorneys, a priest, and, finally, J. J. McNamara all agreed and insisted upon it that Jim consented to a life sentence for himself and a short term for his brother. But even then J.B. stood out for my other terms: the abandonment of the pursuit of the other suspects and the calling of a capital-labor conference in Los Angeles. He seemed to wish for the conference. not because he believed it would do any good; he was a hard skeptic toward all my faith in human nature; but he liked me; he wanted to see my experiment carried through if only to show me that everybody believed in force, so long as it was on their side. I came to share the respect Darrow had for the realism, strength, and loyalty of Jim McNamara.

Darrow was pretty good, too. One afternoon at a conference in jail he showed his feelings and expressed his regret that the two prisoners, especially Jim, would have to be "the goat" for an organized act.

He was more depressed than his clients, and Jim said quietly: "But John and I will not be the only ones to suffer, you know, Darrow. Labor thinks us innocent; the rank and file have paid their hard-earned moneys to prove our innocence. When we plead guilty there will be a shock, and when men are shocked they look for a goat. Sure. I'll get mine, John his, but everybody concerned in the settlement will get his. You, too"—he pointed to me—"and you, Darrow. I've been wondering who will be the real goat, and sometimes I think it will be Darrow."

And Darrow nodded; that was possible. The revulsion of feeling against the chief attorney, an old friend of labor, might be overwhelming. Few people knew how desperate the case was, how sure Fredericks was to win it and hang the dynamiters. And there was the charge against Darrow which would have to be tried, unless we included it in the settlement. Jim McNamara's remark about the goat struck Darrow hard; I saw it strike. But on the way out of the jail, Darrow drew me aside and said: "Tell the prosecution to leave my case out of the settlement. They can have me —to try, if they'll let these prisoners off."

This may have been an expression of his assurance that he could not be convicted, but as a lawyer he knew that a criminal case is not a matter of fact, but of evidence. Innocent or guilty, he might be convicted and sent to prison; and Darrow would die in a prison cell. He was determined, however. He gave me his orders, and I did leave his case out of the settlement. And Fredericks rejoiced; he said that it was all the compensation he desired for giving up the trials of the McNamaras, to have the chance to "get" Clarence Darrow.

When the negotiations were approaching a conclusion it was

deemed advisable by all sides to take up the matter with a larger body of representative business men. Some twenty or more, Lissner's original list and some others, were hurriedly invited to Lissner's office, Wednesday night, November 29. Among those who responded were Stoddard Jess, leading financier of Los Angeles; J. A. Koepfli, former president of the Municipal League and a large employer of labor; R. W. Burnham, local manager of R. G. Dun and Company; Edwin T. Earl, founder of the great Earl Fruit Company and proprietor of two newspapers; Fred Baker, of the Baker Iron Works, who had seen his plant measured for demolition by dynamite; M. T. Synder, banker, former mayor; T. E. Gibbon, a member of the Harbor Commission; Paul Shoup, vice president and general manager of the Southern Pacific electric lines in Southern California; James Slauson, president of the chamber of commerce; H. W. Frank, a prominent merchant; Hon. Frank P. Flint, ex-U.S. senator; W. I. Washburn, banker and member of the city council; Meyer Lissner, and Captain Fredericks.

All practical men of business and politics, not idealists and reformers, no friends of labor; and Senator Flint told me afterward that he and a couple of others were there "under instructions from the east" to bust my scheme. I had had a talk with Mr. Earl. Most of the men there had no idea what the meeting was for, and Lissner, who opened it, said only that I had a statement to make. I repeated my little speech, closing with an appeal not only to settle the case but to do it handsomely, with no punishment of individuals at all, no further pursuit, etc.

Now, it is one thing to speak thus to one man alone. There is no audience, so to speak; the one man doesn't have to think about what the others may say. I could see, as I finished my three-minute address, that some of my auditors thought for themselves and spoke off their own bat, natural-born principals; others looked about at one another and at the principals. One can pick out the leaders and the heelers on such an occasion. Everybody there who heard the proposition for the first time was shocked, and it would not have gone with a big mixed crowd, but fortunately the first one to speak after me was a hard-headed business leader, Fred Baker, who had suffered, as they all knew, from labor troubles. He passed right by the proposition as if that were acceptable, if—

He expressed for the whole crowd the resentment against the dynamiting outrages, the labor conflicts and business losses, but his mind went on to his, the real, question: What next? It was all very well to settle this battle, but the war—the labor war—what was to be done about that?

Mr. Earl, a temperamental man, flamed at Mr. Baker's "bargaining"; but I spoke for Baker, explaining that my purpose was to try out a conference of labor and business leaders on the labor problem and that the reason for a handsome settlement with no punishment was to start such a conference in the right spirit. Mr. Baker's interest in "what next" was mine, and I thought it should be that of Los Angeles. Earl subsided, and Baker and I really got the whole group to agree on the settlement of the case as a step toward a settlement of the labor troubles in Los Angeles. The district attorney, seeing the drift, protested that he must have some penalties, and they all listened to him, but the final statement of the sense of that meeting was that all those present would consent to and defend and help to carry out afterward whatever agreement the district attorney might make with the defense.

The next day some eight or ten other leading citizens who were regarded as necessary to complete the list of insiders to put the matter over on the city were sought, and four were found: William Mulholland, the chief engineer of the Los Angeles Aqueduct; J. B. Lippincott, his assistant; W. B. Matthews, their attorney; and Charles D. Willard, the man who, more than any other, represented the public spirit and ideals of Los Angeles, and personified, led, and managed that city's long fight for good government. They were for the proposition at the first statement of it, "of course." But they were too public-spirited to count big in my experiment as an experiment. Among them all, however—this four and the twenty-four or -five other men consulted, there were enough of the "bad men" not only to control that city for good or for evil but to justify my theory that there is enough good will in all men of imagination and power to do any good, hard job, even if it is not obviously in their own selfish interest. They are not often asked to do any such thing; they are asked chiefly for money for charity or show; and they give that. If they were asked, the worst of them, to serve a good cause, they would give themselves as freely as they give their money.

Thanksgiving Day was the crucial day. Harry Chandler was seeing Fredericks; we on our side were at the jail. That evening while I waited in a car Le Compte Davis, one of the attorneys for the defense, went in to call on Fredericks with the final terms: pleas of guilty with no confessions from J.J. and J. B. McNamara, a life sentence for J. B. McNamara, a very short sentence for J.J., the abandonment of the pursuit of all other suspects, and an agreement to a labor-capital conference afterward. Mr. Davis came out satisfied; we drove to Darrow's house, where he, Ed Nockels, and others were waiting, and Davis reported that Fredericks had accepted the terms definitely. The district attorney had still to see Judge Bordwell, but—"that would be all right," he said.

The next day in court there was a sense of "something doing"; the reporters were alert, anxious, inquiring, but they and the public had no inkling. This was bad management. There is a political, a psychological, use for "leaks" and rumors. The American people were trying J. B. McNamara and divided, some sure he was innocent and some sure he was guilty. Los Angeles was hot with the question; the election was going strong for the socialist party. The minds of men were being made up; most of them were made up and half of these minds were to be proved wrong, all of a sudden. And no inkling of the crash coming. When J. J. McNamara was brought into court with J.B., who alone was on trial, the reporters saw that something was up, but they could not guess what. The district attorney came up to Darrow, who was talking to me, and said that he would have to change one item in the agreement. J. J. McNamara must take a longer term, and he named fifteen years. Darrow spoke to the defendants; they agreed. And Fredericks demanded of me not to write my dispatch that day, not till the other reporters had had a full chance to get my story as well as the news. I agreed, except that I, too, must send a bulletin. All this huddling excited comment and questions. But it was not till the district attorney arose and said, dully, that he understood that the defendants wanted to change their pleas from not guilty to guilty that first the reporters, then, as they sprang to the telephones, the public, got the news, all in a flash. It was too much. The human mind cannot change so suddenly.

That court seemed to fly apart; the people in the room scattered with the news, which flew through the crowded streets. On my way to my hotel everybody was talking about it, angrily. The fact no doubt was that the angry voices were the loudest; one did not hear the other emotions; but I got definitely the sense of an angry mob which seemed to move toward the hotel, where it thickened till, in the lobby, it was packed into a milling herd of excited men who were not telling—they were all apparently asking—what had happened and why. But there was more rejoicing there than in the streets. My part in it was known enough to keep my name sounding—a most unpleasant, almost frightening experience which came to a climax when I was recognized and the lobby moved apart in a hostile fashion to let me pass. There was resentment even there, where the pleas of guilty were good news. And I was relieved when Harry H. Tamen, one of the two owners of the Denver *Post*, came up to me, and aloud, with the crowd closing in to hear, made me a proposition, an amazing proposition, which was, for me at least, a diversion.

"Listen," he said, "if you will come to Denver and show me up in my own paper I'll pay you any price you like and get you all the space you need for a serial. I'll lodge you in my house; you'll have a valet to take care of you, a horse to ride, a car to drive, and nothing to do but investigate me and write. And I'll furnish you the facts, the evidence, for a sensational series of scandals, I myself."

I laughed. No one else did. The crowd was astonished naturally, but not amused. They wondered, as I did, and Tamen saw that and said that he meant it, that it would advertise him and his papers; and then and afterward on the quiet he convinced me that he would have enjoyed such an exposure as he pictured of "all the tricks by which an ex-circus man, advertiser, and newspaper publisher—all that it cost for one man to make a success of his life." I refused his curious offer; I ran away from that mob which even Tamen could not jar out of its distressing effort of readjustment to a shocking piece of sudden news. I went up to my room to write my dispatch to my syndicate of papers, leaving word at the desk that I would receive any newspaper men that called. That was my promise to the district attorney and my obligation to the press. Having the whole inside story of the event of the day, and having only evening newspapers to report to for the next afternoon, I was bound to give the morning men the stuff to beat me with. And they came, one by one, and I told each one the whole story. And this is something for psychologists to explain. They could hardly get it. There was the mass of details to account for the difficulty—in part, but only in part. The trouble was that that news required a complete change of mind on a subject or a situation upon which opinions had been formed. I don't mean that the newspaper men did not gather and report the news, the gist of it, only that they could not, did not, readily grasp the whole of it and its significance. The *Examiner*, for example, which had a good report finally, sent first one man who must have failed, for he was followed by another who took notes fully, but toward midnight one of the news editors himself came, and remarking that "by God, I'll get it," heard the whole story over again and went away to write it.

My own account, a newspaper page in extent, was written brokenly and filed during the night for publication that Saturday afternoon. The morning newspapers had called the settlement a confession. My story began by saying that both capital and labor had pleaded guilty, and showed that the McNamaras had made no confession which involved other persons but had entered into an agreement by which, without force, the labor problem was to be reconsidered in the most anti-labor city in America and, possibly, settled to the advantage of both employers and employees. Whether I expressed in my report the spirit and purposes of the settlement is not for me to say. I did not mention Christianity, either in that dispatch or personally, till some reporters somehow caught the idea and came to me to ask if "the Golden Rule" had not played some part in the negotiations. My answer was evasive, that the Golden Rule was applied in all decent agreements among men. But they "played it up," as we say; it was reported and commented on all over the country. This is an important fact, and it is important to know that Judge Bordwell was apprized explicitly of the nature of our experiment with the common faith and spirit of the Christian religion, in view of what happened.

J. B. McNamara had expressed some doubt about the judge. He had been studying him, as prisoners will as they sit day after day, idly watchful, in a court. Defendants come to know their judges and jurors, and J.B. kept saying to me, "Look out for that judge. He'll bust your whole plan." The dynamiter's theory was that everybody believed in force, nobody in mercy and reason, and that Judge Bordwell would sock him and his brother, if not in the sentences he gave, then in his address from the bench. "Better see the judge," said Darrow, and I called on him that Saturday night, the day after the news was out, but before the echo had come back to us. I called at his club, and he received me in his private rooms there. We talked of judges in general and their job—how lone they are, and remote, dignified; and I said that it was only their superiority that hurt, their affectation or the appearance of a goodness above all human frailties. A judge, I suggested, should never sit in judgment on a crime that he had not done or, at the least, been tempted to do, because understanding was the thing. The ideal would be for only a murderer to try a murder case, an ex-burglar a burglar, a rapist to deal with rape. He demurred, of course, at that, but he listened attentively to my appeal that, in this case of dynamiting, he should show in some way that he had some human understanding of how labor and these two working-men might have been driven by the use of force and black-listing and the violent defeat of strikes to resort to dynamite. The sentences having been agreed to, with the consent of the prisoners, it would be wise and gracious, it would be in tone with the negotiation, to express from the bench with the penalties the judge's understanding of the crime and the good will of the settlement.

"Men who commit a crime," I said, "know the risk they run of punishment, and they stand up and take their medicine. That's all right. But when the judge sits on his raised bench and speaks down to them like a god in terms that suggest that he thinks he is faultless and that the prisoner is beneath all comprehension—that sounds like bunk; it inspires not respect but the contempt of the prisoner and of us reporters, too. We know the judges and how they are made. And the fact is that no human being should ever be forced beyond the pale."

Judge Bordwell asked me how I would say what he had to say, and I advised him to speak as one man to another, as one criminal to another, with imagination, so that the prisoners might go off to the penitentiary feeling that they and the judge were human beings. Something like this I said, and I remember his answer: "I think I can do that."

Anyway I went back to the jail the next day, when the priest was there and the attorneys, and I declared my belief that the judge would be "all right."

That day was Sunday, the decisive day. The churches spoke, and we heard or read on Monday what they said all over the United States. And what they preached was hate and disappointed revenge. Los Angeles was not so bad. The streets were still strewn with the socialist party buttons which voters had thrown away when the news came; the revulsion of feeling was violent. But some inkling of the meaning of the settlement got around. Job Harriman, the socialist candidate, heard all about it from Darrow and me; he accepted it as the only thing to do; and he went forth, proclaiming to his followers that it was all right with him. He would rather have had the case closed on the terms stated than be elected mayor of Los Angeles. And the Los Angeles papers all reported the news with some understanding, enough to let the people know that something better than a revengeful victory had happened. But even then, the local churches did not grasp what they called "the Golden Rule," and as for the churches elsewhere, none of them sensed the fact that Christianity had been applied and had worked. I received afterward hundreds of clippings, a trunkful, and as I labored through them I realized that it is no cynical joke, it is literally true, that the Christian churches would not recognize Christianity if they saw it. Their voice was the voice of righteousness and justice, and they won. The sermons of that black Sunday turned the tide against us. They came like the cries of a lynching mob and frightened all the timid men who had worked with us—and the judge. The men I call principals, the leading capitalists and employers who really are leaders, stood fast. But the men I call heelers, the mere followers who will not think or act without a leader to direct them, they revealed themselves on my too big committee; they ran. Judge Bordwell expressed them, the churches, and public opinion.

When the judge rose in a small courtroom to sentence the McNamaras, he denounced them. He was the righteous judge who never erred or sinned, and he said—well, when he had finished his denunciation, J. B. McNamara turned to give me a look, a smiling, cynical stare, and as he and his brother were being led out to their prison, J.B. said to me, "You see? You were wrong, and I was right. The whole damn world believes in dynamite."

The socialist ticket was beaten. The city felt safe again; public opinion, even the labor vote, was against labor and the settlement. Judge Bordwell made a statement to the press that the idealism of the negotiators had nothing to do with the sudden closing of the case, that he mitigated the punishment the little he did out of "wisdom"; "the court was not swayed by the hypothetical policy favored by Steffens (who, by the way, is a professed anarchist) that the judgment of the court should be directed to the promotion of compromise in the controversy between capital and labor." He said that I had had nothing to do with the matter; the district attorney acted entirely without regard to me. The implication of the judge's view and the district attorney's was that the case had been terminated to save costs to the county!

Pretty bad? Yes, the experiment was a failure. Darrow was indicted and tried twice, but there was no local conference between labor and capital; and two other alleged dynamiters, Matt Schmidt and Dave Kaplan, were arrested three years later, tried, and sent to the penitentiary. The contract we made between capital and labor was broken by the employers, who should be reminded of that when they complain of labor's breaches of contract. But I was not— I am not—through, and there were some results to encourage my theory that good will is a force among strong men.

As I was walking along Fifth Avenue in New York one day a few weeks later I was stopped by Mr. Drew, the secretary of the Erectors' Association, the organization of the employers in the steel industry.

"Say," he said, "what the deuce were you trying to do out there in Los Angeles? We couldn't make head or tail of it." I told him. "So that was it!" he said. "Why didn't you take us in on it and tell us? We would have been for that."

VII

I BECOME A GOAT

WHEN I went home to New York, I felt defeated, disgraced somehow, and helpless. No editors would give me work, and my manuscripts were regularly returned, often unread. I understood that. Having identified myself with a "cause," my name suggested propaganda, labor propaganda to capitalists and treason, interference, folly to labor. I understood how labor took it. At the first flash of the news that the McNamaras had confessed, the friends of labor were shocked and the labor leaders were frightened, especially those who had guilty knowledge of the dynamiting. Some of them fled and hid in a panic. One, I heard, had run to a rich woman's apartment and stayed there till my complete account appeared the next evening. Even then his nerves were "jumpy." Jack Reed, "my own boy," wrote a fierce poem, "Sangar," denouncing me. It was good poetry, however, one of his best, so that was worth while. Jo Davidson describes how, at a gathering of writers, artists, radicals, they all hated me, but expressively, well. One famous labor leader, Tveitmoe, of San Francisco, who was on his way with a group of labor delegates returning to Los Angeles, was so dark and still that Anton Johannsen asked him what he was brooding. His muttered answer was that "first I am going to kill that Golden Rule fellow." Tveitmoe was capable of murder and Johannsen was so alarmed that the moment they reached Los Angeles he came to me with a warning to keep away. I did for a day or two, but I cannot stand the menace of danger. I called at the labor hotel one afternoon and sent up a card penciled "Golden Rule." Invited up, I was greeted noisily, nervously, by all the men there except Tveitmoe. He was sullen, silent. The others, to gain time, joshed me. By and by I said that they had had enough fun with me; it was my turn. I also had something to say, but I'd prefer to say it to Tveitmoe. Drawing up a chair, I sat down close up to the big, black Norwegian and laid out the situation briefly for him to see, but abstractly, with facts and reason. When I had finished Tveitmoe nodded. "Jo," he said to Johannsen, "order the beer." We had a quiet talk, all of us, and I left relieved, as the rest were.

"THE NEW YORK 'TRIBUNE'S' IDEA
OF LINCOLN STEFFENS AFTER HAV-
ING PLAYED PEACE-MAKER"

"But, Tveit," said Johannsen, "I thought you were going to kill the Golden Rule."

"No," Tveitmoe bumbled in his chest, "I would not kill that fellow. He's all right. He ain't got no pope." And it appeared that what had won him was that I had not quoted Marx or any other authority but had appealed to reason, his and mine. It was a lasting understanding, too. Tveitmoe was a trusting friend of mine the rest of his life. He would let me into the most sacred of labor confidences in every emergency. I was a friend of labor to him and to a few, a very few, other such. But to labor, as to capital and to editors, I was an outcast for years. As J. B. McNamara had warned, I, too, was a goat; I was black-listed, but they could not starve me to death. I could live, I had my graft—the unearned money I had picked up in Wall Street and some that I had inherited. I realized then the importance of economic independence; money was more than money; it was liberty. I was physically free. But I was full of a sustaining hatred, too, a relief, only I did not like it. My pleasure in life was in straight seeing and reporting, and here I was so blinded by hate that I could not see. I must deal first with the state of my own mind. How?

That reason was no approach to the minds of other men I had learned. After a few attempts with logic on myself, I had seen to my surprise that it was no use reasoning with myself. The way to influence others was to appeal to their emotions or change their environment or both. I would try that on myself. After some weeks of the most confusing and uncomfortable bitterness, I decided that, since it was capitalists whom I was prejudiced against, I would associate with none but capitalists; I would see no reds, liberals, or labor men, but only employers of labor. And to set my mind right, I assigned to myself the task of listening sympathetically to those "enemies of labor" with a view to getting such a grasp of their difficulties that I could state their side to their complete satisfaction. And I began with Judge Gary, the president of U.S. Steel.

He received me on my card, without any introduction. His evident curiosity was enough, and to point that I said I wanted to see Judge Gary the labor leader, not the captain of industry.

"Yes? Sit down. As a labor leader, you say?"

"Yes. When the steel company beat the unions in the Homestead strike, the officers of the company became the leaders of the workers. For the workers have to have leaders just as the financiers and engineers have, and you, having abolished all their own leaders, left your labor with no leader but you. Right?"

"Yes, I can see that there is something in that."

"All right," I said. "Now I come to you to ask you, as the leader of the steel workers, what you have done for them. We know what you have accomplished for the stockholders, for the

From a Portrait in Oils by John Young-Hunter in 1922

EDWARD WYLLIS SCRIPPS

When Lincoln Steffens heard that Jo Davidson had been commissioned to make a bust of E. W. Scripps, he wrote:

"You must do a great thing with Scripps. He is a great man and an individual. There is no other like him: energy, vision, courage, wisdom. He thinks his own thoughts absolutely. He sees straight. He sees the line he is on and his thinking sticks to that. I regard Scripps as one of the two or three great men of my day.

"He is onto himself and the world, plays the game and despises it. He is sincere and not cynical. Really, he should be done, but as a full length standing figure, so as to show the power of the man, the strength he took care of to keep from being refined; he avoided other rich men, so as to escape being one; he knew the danger his riches carried for himself, for his papers and for his seeing.

"Rough, almost ruthless force, but restrained by clear, even shrewd insight; an executive capable of fierce action, restrained by the observation that a doer must not do too many things himself, but use his will to make others do them."

(Scripps-Howard News)

industry, for the capitalists. What have you to show as a labor leader?"

"Well, we have done something for them, you know. You may not think it much, but it's something. We have begun to make them stockholders—"

He didn't say this with the assurance he put into his reports, and when he hesitated, he evidently expected me to say something like what I did say: "Yes, you have got some workers with a small stock interest, not much, but enough to separate them from the mass of labor and have them on your side."

He said the policy was to give as many as possible of the employees ownership and interest in the company and so increase their pay. It had turned out well for the company. We argued it a bit. I wasn't very serious, and by and by I shunted the argument by asking what he had done as a labor, rather than as a company, leader. He hesitated again before he said: "Well, we have done a lot of welfare work."

"Welfare!" I exclaimed. "You can boast of that? You must know what labor calls that—hellfare work."

"Yes, I know, but I don't understand why."

"I can tell you why," I said, and he seemed really eager to know.

"If you can explain that to me," he said, "you will render me a service, for I have never understood the bitter prejudice of labor against our appropriations for the improvement of the shop conditions."

"You don't understand why the wage workers, who want higher wages, are not pleased with cold showers, soap, and clean towels, neat dressing-rooms, lawns and flowers?" He demurred at my list, but he passed it with a laugh, and accepted my revised question: "You want me to tell you why, when your workers want whatever is coming to them in money for beer, they are not happy when you give it them in white toweling?"

"Y-y-es," he frowned and smiled. "Yes."

"You have, I hear," I began, "a fine corner apartment in the Waldorf?" He nodded. "Well furnished, to your taste, and a lot of paintings on the walls—all of your choosing, all to your taste?" He nodded; he was a patron of art, and it was said that he did his own buying and collected pretty good things.

"Do you ever leave your apartment for a vacation?"

Yes, he did.

"Good," I said. "I'll make you a proposition. The next time you are going away for a period, let me know, leave me a sum of money, your own money, and give instructions in the hotel office to admit me to your quarters with permission to do whatever I choose to do."

Puzzled, interested, he screwed up his handsome face and asked, dubiously, "What will you do?"

"I will throw out that terrible furniture you like, and put in what I like, furniture to my taste. I'll take out your rugs and choose carpets in tone with the walls and the room generally. And the pictures—I haven't seen the paintings you have been collecting, but I am sure they are to your taste, not to mine; and I will replace them with good things, art, the sort of work I like. I'll do it all conscientiously, but I will completely alter and really improve the conditions in which you live, making them what I think they should be. And all with your money, the money you are wasting on your taste, which cannot be as good as mine. And—"

"Wait," he said, laughing. "I can't allow that, and even if I did Mrs. Gary would not stand for it. But I get you." He sobered. "That's it, is it?"

"Yes," I said. "That's welfare work." And I told him about a rich employer I had seen a few nights before at the Brevoort restaurant, tipsy himself, but telling some of us that the reason "we won't pay labor more is because they'd drink it all up Saturday and Sunday and be no good for work on Monday."

Judge Gary seemed to see something new to him. He kept saying, "So that's it, is it?" "That's why." "Well, you have really done me a service, but I don't see what we can do." And he talked at length about his labor problem, inviting comments. He was interested in my inquiry, named me a list of employers and experts to see, and bade me call again, as I did. I came to like Judge Gary. I said so once to Ann Morgan, who did not then like him. "Oh, he's too plausible," she said. "He has taken you in as he does others." She did not know, I did not tell the able daughter of J. P. Morgan, that what I was after was a cure of my hate, but the point was that I did get over hating Judge Gary and the other employers, even those who were not plausible and were as full of blind hate as I was. They could no more see the labor side than labor could see the employers' side; they were as blind as peoples at war. I am not going to tell the details of my experience with these employers; they were interesting but not very new. What interests me more is that this experiment worked perfectly; I rid myself of a prejudice, learned to state the employers' case; I tried it on a chamber of commerce audience once; I got it so that I could say it—without accepting it. I had regained my mental balance.

My avocation during this period was to go wherever I was called by labor to explain the Los Angeles incident, which troubled the workers greatly. Anton Johannsen, an American Federation of Labor official and himself one of the suspected dynamiters, was doing the same thing. We met sometimes and spoke together at closed meetings of unions. A refreshing man, Johannsen. Short, round, and jolly, he was indeed the very spirit of labor, as Hutchins Hapgood called him in a book with that title, a piece of fiction based on Johannsen's life and character. A young carpenter with a mind that tried to understand the conditions under which he lived and loved and worked, he tasted all the philosophies rampant in the underworld: anarchism, socialism, I.W.W., and failing to find the clew—laughed. And he could laugh, loud, happily, sarcastically, bitterly, exultingly, always expressively and always loud. It was said that his laughter in the anteroom saved him from indictment by a grand jury inside. Too hearty, healthy, and unafraid for a guilty man, and when he heard the story he laughed again. He liked my statement of the case of the employer against labor, but he laughed at my hope that capitalists would ever act on their intelligence. At Seattle, where we both told labor our McNamara stories one night, I addressed the chamber of commerce the next day. Jo followed me in and took a back seat. My talk was to the effect that the workers were the consumers also and that employers should pay as high wages as the productivity of labor and the management of business would permit, not to be kind to labor, but to improve the market. The audience seemed to accept my exposition, but at each of three points, when I spoke as if they, the employers present, could and would act upon this view, Jo laughed aloud—three times. The first time I was startled and said nothing, as the men present turned to look at the laugher. The second time also I paused, but the third time, toward the end, when he roared out his laugh, I said: "I notice that you all turn to see who the man is who laughs that way. It is not a man; that is no individual. That is the laugh of labor, laughing at me for thinking that capital can see and pursue its own obvious interest."

But the rollicking humor of Anton Johannsen could laugh at labor, too, at the idea that the workers could act in their own interest, intelligently. He could laugh at himself, but then, he could and did laugh at me as much as I did myself. I remember dropping in at the rear of one of his labor meetings while he was telling his McNamara story, just in time to hear him say of me, "And then this son of a ——" But he said it with such a laugh that the audience and I laughed. He was indeed the laugh of labor. I once urged Sam Gompers, the president of the American Federation of Labor, to send Johannsen about to every place where the labor problem was being discussed: to the gallery of the U.S. Senate, to the anteroom of the U.S. Supreme Court, to political, reform, social, and all other gatherings, including the annual sessions of the A. F. of L., where intellectuals were trying to do "something for labor" or capital—to laugh.

Another intelligent man I met at that time was Matthew Schmidt, better known as Schmidtie. He was a fugitive from justice then. One of the labor men indicted with the McNamaras, he had hidden himself, like David Kaplan, and in the Los Angeles settlement their pursuit was to have been abandoned; and some of the rewards offered were taken down. But one of $25,000 was left standing; I did not know of it. Schmidtie had a job in New York under another name, and he kept pretty well under cover. He saw no one who knew him. A niece of Emma Goldman introduced me to him one evening on Broadway, and he wanted to hear all about the settlement. I told him, of course; I told him, too, how he was included in it.

"Would you advise me to come out in the open or stay under cover?"

It was a test question, and my answer showed me what I really thought. I said, "Stay under." I did not believe that agreement would be kept any more than he did. And a few months later he and Kaplan were arrested by William J. Burns, sent to Los Angeles, tried, and convicted. Schmidtie had gone to a party at

Emma Goldman's house, and not an anarchist, as was reported, but the son of an anarchist, a young man in Burns's pay, betrayed him. (The son of an anarchist is no more an anarchist than the son of a Christian is a Christian or the son of a clergyman is a good man. Only a convert is a true believer.)

I had seen a good deal of Schmidtie, a quiet, observant, able man, philosophic, thoughtful, and, above all, an artist. He was a highly skilled mechanic, who really loved to make and handle fine machinery. When he was arrested, his astonished employer, who had not known who Schmidtie was, called on me to ask if he could do anything to help him in his trouble.

"He was the best workman I ever had," he said. "He mastered our machines, every process of their manufacture; he could make, he could sell, them; and what delighted me was that when he delivered a machine, he stayed and taught its use and, if you will understand me, its beauty. He made the buyer like it and treat it right—all on his own responsibility. A workman, he was as good as a partner. What a waste to lock him up in a prison!"

But Schmidtie is not a waste, even in the penitentiary. He has a philosophy, and he practices it in San Quentin, where he was sent for life. Warden Smith told me that Schmidtie was soon discovered to be a skillful, thorough workman and was promoted to ever more and better work till he had charge of the whole technical, mechanical establishment of the penitentiary, the lighting, the machine shop, etc. "He treats it as if he owns it, and he makes the other convicts assigned to a department of his work carefully, skillfully, *con amore*." I know from other sources that he will take out a new man and say to him: "We work in this shop. It is no snap, and if you loaf on the job, we'll get you out—somehow. You can't express your hate of the prison here. We don't love these walls either, but we do respect ourselves, and we know that to live here and not lose our minds here we have to get into our jobs, take an interest, and work perfectly. And there's another reason for doing it. We are workers, and the hope, the future of the workers depends on our developing to the highest degree our love of work, our skill, our productivity. Working in that spirit, we are a not unhappy family, and we won't let any bum break us up."

I saw the sentiment, but I did not see the revolutionary foresight of Matt Schmidt's attitude toward work till I got to Soviet

Russia later. I have read letters he has received from fellow prisoners after their release, thanking him for having taught them the saving satisfaction to be taken in their skill, in thoroughness, in a fine piece of machinery. But when in Russia I heard of the difficulty the Workers' Republic had with ill-trained, undisciplined, habitually slacker labor, I realized that Schmidtie had been looking ahead always to the time when the workers would be working for themselves. And I recalled then a decision of the I.W.W. leaders in a Massachusetts strike, that if there had to be any sabotage at all, it must be only of the most difficult kind and done only by a few men of supreme skill. General slacking or bad work would hurt labor, teach them bad habits. The purposely bad work planned to hurt the bosses must be so done that it exercised and developed the ingenuity and efficiency of the saboteurs.

This is an illustration of the thoughtful philosophy of the art of labor, which Schmidtie enjoys and teaches in his penitentiary, that you work always for yourself, to whom you owe your very best, everywhere, all the time. Warden Smith offered to do all in his power to have Schmidtie paroled out of his life sentence, but, he said, "The prison and the prisoners will miss that man." Los Angeles County owes it to its self-respect to let both Schmidtie and J. B. McNamara out; the word was given, a contract made and broken. J. J. McNamara is out; so is David Kaplan—their sentences served; but the others are still in—for life.

My preoccupation for two years was with the case against Darrow, their attorney, who was tried in Los Angeles two summers in succession on the charge of bribing jurors. I went out there to testify that the settlement had been agreed to before the date of the alleged act and that Darrow knew it; there was no motive for jury-fixing. This was the substance of the matter, but there was some fun in the first trial. Darrow, his own attorney, called me as his witness and finished with me in a very short time. The district attorney and his assistants took me over; they were "laying for" me, and they contended among themselves as to who was to have the privilege of "skinning me alive." I had heard about all this, and I was eager for the fray. As a reporter of many court trials I had a highly developed contempt for the crude, obviously cunning, browbeating methods of forcing a witness to tell, not the truth, but the attorney's side of the "evidence." A district attorney

"HARPOON" ~~MISSING~~ CUTTE

STEFFENS OUTWITS DISTRICT ATTORNEY

Parrying Dist. Atty. Frederick's questions with rapid repartee and quick retorts, and often with biting sarcasm concealed under a soft cloak of deferential courtesy, Lincoln Steffens, the magazine writer, matched his wits against those of the state's attorney during his cross-examination in the bribery trial of Clarence Darrow, Friday afternoon. He proved a star witness for the defense.

STEFFENS TELLS OF NEGOTIATIONS WITH FREDERICKS

Excites Ire of Darrow Prosecutor by Refusal to Be Trapped.

SAN FRANCISCO, SATURDAY EVENING, JULY 20, 1912.

POLICE, 'FIXED.'

Steffens Holds Courtroom Spellbound

When Quizzed By Darrow Prosecution

Declares Mercy and Understanding Alone Can Solve Problem Raised by McNamara Case, and Tells Why He Worked to Save Defendants.

Testimony Shows Darrow's Only Thought Was for Clients When Franklin's Arrest Placed Him Under Suspicion of Having Bribed Jurors.

Lincoln Steffens

M'NAMARA DEED ACT IN SOCIAL REVOLUTION

—LINCOLN STEFFENS.

Writer Expresses Views During Cross-examination in Trial of Darrow

The Darrow trial at Los Angeles has furnished the setting for one of most remarkable scenes ever witnessed in an American courtroom.

For four hours the judge, jury, attorneys and spectators listened intently and respectfully while Lincoln Steffens explained from the witness who prosecutions can never solve the problem of poverty and of the warfare

REPORT OF THE FIRST DARROW TRIAL

is supposed theoretically to be an officer of the court; like the judge, sworn to do justice, to protect as well as to prosecute the defendant and his witnesses. A just, dignified, intelligent attitude, it is a wonder more prosecutors don't take it. But no, they prefer to fight, as they say, and they do fight to win. And so, in this case, since Darrow was a distinguished attorney from the east, the district attorney was out to beat him and, perhaps, win the prize possible for a winner—the governorship of California. Since I was Darrow's star witness, the game of the cross-examiner was to "make a monkey" of me somehow. Captain Fredericks was not the trial attorney in the case, but he came into court and insisted on his right to break me down. I was glad. I kind o' liked Fredericks.

When Darrow bowed and waved to the prosecution to take the witness, Fredericks rose, and to fix all eyes upon him, he stepped back to the rail, raised his hand, and loudly began: "Mr. Steffens," and he walked slowly, forcefully toward me, with hand high in the air, and step by step, word by word he threatened, "are—not—you—" and he was now close up to me; he threw his pointing finger into my face and finished—"an—avowed—anarchist?"

His play-acting really amused me. There was the typical lawyer, the conceited, unfair prosecutor whom I had seen abusing his power over weak witnesses all my life. I smiled, and slowly, very quietly, I answered: "Oh, I am worse than that."

He staggered as if I had struck him. "Worse than that!" he muttered.

"Yes, I believe in Christianity."

He stepped back, flustered, and it was minutes before he could go on. He did not know what an anarchist was: a man that is opposed to all force, including government. Fredericks thought an anarchist was the opposite: a bomb-thrower. And as for Christianity, Fredericks was a churchman. By and by, when he recovered, he came at me again on that point. What did I mean by calling myself a Christian? I hadn't, but I let that go. I swept my hand around at the audience of labor men, socialists, anarchists, and dumb morons, and said: "Well, you see, Captain Fredericks, those people out there, they are anarchists, socialists, labor men, and they believe, like you, in justice; but I'm a muckraker, and I tell you that things are so bad in this world that justice won't fix them. It's too late for that. I believe that nothing but love will do the job. That's Christianity. That's the teaching that we must love our neighbors."

"And that's worse than anarchy?" he was muttering.

"Yes." I smiled as affectionately as I could. "That means that, for example, you and I should love each other. And you will admit, won't you, that that is going some?"

The judge, who, I learned afterward, was a Christian Scientist, passed me his fan. I fanned myself cool, then handed it back to the judge. We kept that gentle fan going coolly all through that silly, blustering cross-examination—hours of it, while Fredericks consulted his assistants and tried to sock me. He couldn't. I had his goat, as he would say; he could not get mine, he and his advisers. They had their own ideas of the line of attack, and he tried some of theirs till I heard him say to one of them, "No, no. Every time I asked him one of your questions he socked me."

I enjoyed that day in court; so did the judge and the jurors. At a dinner they gave to Darrow afterward, they said they had the time of their lives. Picked for their anti-labor prejudice, these men, mostly small employers, said that they had got the philosophy of labor in that trial. And well they might have, for Darrow gave it and I gave it pretty fully in my testimony, which was made up of elaborate, philosophic addresses to the jury. Fredericks protested, but his questions were fine openings for all that I had to say. He really was a great help to us, and so, though he did not, the rest of us enjoyed that trial.

The next summer there was another judge, a man who, we heard, was not going to allow me to make red speeches to the jury. And he spoiled the fun. But he was fair. Once when the district attorney asked for a yes or a no answer to a question I could not truthfully reply to with a monosyllable, I appealed to the judge.

"You have sworn me to tell the truth, the whole truth—I'll answer that question 'No,' but I warn you that it is perjury; 'No' is not the whole truth." He said that I should have been an attorney at law, and he let me round out my no. And "we" won that case as "we" did the first one. But later one day when I was seeing Fredericks about something else and got to talking about those days, he said, "Anyhow, it was a good fight."

And that's all it was; that's what our whole Christian civilization is—a good fight, as we were about to find out.

VIII

EUROPE: A PROCESSION OF NATIONS MARCHING TO WAR

BETWEEN trips to the Pacific coast I was commuting to and from Europe, and now when Darrow's fight was finished, I spent most of my time abroad. I thought I had business over there, the muckraking of England, France, Germany, Italy, which had been put off for so many years. An excuse, perhaps. I was so lazy or tired that I did not work hard. Like the typical American tourist I liked to be over there where I could enjoy the fruits of the evil done in the interest of the leisure class to which the tourist belongs at least while traveling. The lower classes are humbled to serve you with respect or politeness. They are cheap. You can buy almost anything. It isn't beautiful or right, but it is comfortable, pleasant, and it's none of your business if things are wrong. You may tip or bribe foreigners with a light conscience and a good excuse—"do in Rome as the Romans do" —and enjoy to the full the privileges you pay for. It's not your country. Tourism is a moral rest.

My muckraking was to be, not in the interest of the countries I was to report, but for my own country, to see what light they had to throw on our conditions and our destiny. For I still saw all these older countries as a procession of nations all ahead of us on the hill called civilization, some, like Germany, climbing up just beyond us, others, like England, on top, the rest going over and down the road we all are traveling. Nearest the top on the down grade: Austria, France, Spain, Italy, all stealing down to such bottoms as old Rome and old Greece reached, or India or China. An interesting study, and I did some work on it. But it was hard work. The press was despised; a reporter was "a press man," a person lower than an underservant. He could not walk in on a politician or a business man, and as the eyes and ears of popular curiosity, demand an accounting. That was American. The reporter personifies his paper and the public here. Over there the politician in a mess will refuse to receive the press man and go and see the owner of the paper. And in most European countries the owner of the paper is a friend of the questionable politician or financier. The press in Europe is gone the way the newspapers are going in the United States, into the hands of men who buy and run newspapers, not to protest evils, but to get in on them. I had to introduce myself, not as a reporter, but as a man who was trying to do in Europe what, for example, Mr. James Bryce had done for the United States. That helped some, not much. Mr. James Bryce himself did not do any such investigating in England as he did in America. He inquired into the atrocities of the Germans or Belgians early in the war, and he "fell down" on that, as we would say in our journalism. But he did not and he probably could not have studied European corruption as he did ours. We told him about ours; the English would not have told him about theirs. My impression was that they did not realize theirs, as a general thing. An Englishman in a position to know will tell you that there is no such political corruption in his country as there is in the States—and mean it. The expression on his face, the tone of his voice, all the signs indicate that he is an honest man telling the truth as he sees it. So he will deny all corruption. And then he will entertain you with stories of political methods which, in the States, we would call corrupt. A party whip related that he and the other managers of his machine (which to him is not a "machine" but the party or the organization) had to stop letting young gentlemen stand for Parliament and prefer young, rising solicitors and professional men, because "the young gentlemen will not always be in their seats when we want them and the solicitors will; and when the young gentlemen are told how to vote, they sometimes have ideas of their own; the young professional men, with an eye to business and their careers, can be counted upon."

"I see," I answered; "you, like our bosses, want legislators who will take orders."

"What!" He was not a boss; a whip is a—whip. And "party

discipline" was not "machine subservience." He simply could not generalize.

The English are in the state of mind Americans were in when muckraking began; they are aware of this fact and that wrong; but they do not know how common, how typical, and what is the general effect of their facts. The English say, as we said then, that this man is bad and that act was evil and this practice occurs; but that there are many such men and acts and that the occasional practice is the method by which the British government is corrupted into a class government they do not seem to realize. But there is something else to note about them. The English, from top to bottom, accept their class government, and just as you will find a political gentleman speaking of himself as in the governing class, so you will hear the lower classes speaking with respect of "our governing class." There are members of Parliament who are known and expected to represent the brewers, the coal mine owners, the railroads—even certain railroads—and the banks. That is to say, a member of Parliament may openly do something which, if we could prove it on a U.S. Senator, would have disgraced and might have defeated him in our muckraking days. The English call "privileges" the special interests we call grafts—franchises, special laws, etc. They have no such word as graft, but they do have privileges; and a gentleman may, of course, defend his—privileges. Indeed an Englishman will stand up for his privileges, wherever he is, with the same sense of virtue that an American will defend his rights.

I am not going to muckrake England and Europe here. I can't do it right. It should be done, and by an American newspaper man. An English press man would not know that a scandalous transaction in politics was news, and our American scholars revere and study British government as an ideal. One of the needs of Americans is to be rid of their belief that the British government is better than the American government and so be shunted from our tendency to develop into an accepted class government. The stuff is there; a persistent young American reporter could get it; and a fair report of it, from the American point of view, would be a step toward world peace or, at any rate, toward an understanding of what makes wars. I mean that the actual British government is a world government and, of necessity, therefore a war-maker, as all European governments are empire-makers.

All that I did was to move about for years, a few months at a time, making what I told myself was a preliminary survey, such as I used to make when I first went to an American State or city, to see what the conditions were, in general, and where to dig for particulars. I never reduced my findings to documented evidence. All I can give, therefore, is what foreign visitors to America call "Some Impressions."

The skeletons of all the governments of Europe that I saw into were as like one another and as like the skeleton of American government as the bony structures of human beings are alike—and as unlike the apparent, constitutional framework. A diagram of the government of the United States would fit Great Britain, France, Germany, Italy, as it would Boston, Ohio, or Alaska, and it would look as little like the constitutions of those organisms. The flesh upon those bones and the dress upon the flesh make them look different. There were kings in England and Italy, an emperor in Germany, presidents in France and the United States; but there were premiers, too, and parliaments, and bosses. In England and Italy the kings were notoriously figureheads, hats or crowns upon the actual heads of the premiers, who in their turn were the agents of the temporarily adjusted economic interests which composed the throne and literally dominated the government, just as in the United States a boss like Mark Hanna directed, when he would, his president—just as political bosses controlled governors, mayors, legislators, in the interest of the most active businesses which the boss represents. The German government was most like its theoretical self; the Kaiser was a dictator, but even he and his advisers and the Reichstag had to dictate in the interests of the privileged.

These and other differences were the signs of that growth which I had taken at home to account for the differences between new States and old States, between Colorado, for example, and Connecticut. The European states were, like American States, living organisms in different stages of the process of what we had been calling corruption. The English king had once been a dictator like the German emperor and had then represented agriculture and the landed aristocracy, in the main. The rise of the business and industrial class to economic supremacy was followed by the rise of business to political power. And this was the period of that gross bribery and corruption which the English have forgotten in England and have found and deplored in the United States, as we have. We shall come on through it as the English have; Alaska will become like Pennsylvania; Pennsylvania will become like New England, which is now getting to be more and more like old England; and England may go on into the condition of France or Italy. Germany was going, quietly, almost consciously, into the big industrial stage without any very gross political conflict with the Junkers' agricultural power. Of Italy, where I spent most of my time, I prefer to speak later, when I came to understand it in the American sense—after the war.

Now, the disturbing conclusion of all these observations that I was making abroad and comparing with my own country was one that had occurred to me before: that if the process of corruption was so universal, wasn't it natural, inevitable, and, in the scientific historic evolutional sense, right? Wasn't political corruption of the very essence of the life of a state, the necessary accompaniment of its development? Industry with its machinery, coming into an agricultural social organization, finds the constitution, laws, customs, and the culture of a community of farmers a hindrance to the new breath of life; so it must make changes in the old order to admit the new. As I suggested before, the new railroads have to tunnel the old state as they do the mountains in their way. Captains of industry have to lick the southern planters, "get" the government, "give" to the schools, colleges, and churches, and buy the newspapers. And they do, and that makes the changes historians describe later as progress. The new power does not want to sit on the throne—too busy; they let the old kings, politicians—anybody, keep or take the crown, so long as they can do what they like in business. In England the rulers let the gentlemen of the ruling class govern; in the United States the professional politicians govern, but the liberal opposition, with their old democratic principles, are really working all the time to substitute good or better men for the old-type politicians. And that is happening. My prophecy, from the British peak of Europe, is that we also shall have a government of the people by gentlemen for the business men.

I know and like a political boss of the old school in a progressive city who was finally beaten by the reformers there and had
a city council of young, college-bred gentlemen. Dropping off a
train one day, I called on and laughed at him.

"So," I said, "they have beaten you at last, and you have a
majority of gents for aldermen."

"Yes," he confessed, "and I been a damn fool all these years.
Why, say, those nice boys will put over for nothing for me deals
the old gang used to make me pay and pay high for."

That's England, and France, Europe, and our future. That is
why, I think, the English can see our corruption and not their
own. With the same old moral Greco-Christian culture that we
have, we both see and act in terms of right and wrong. It is not
the granting of a franchise or a protective tariff that is wrong, but
the bribery for which it is voted. A good man may do the same
thing that a bad man does, but if the good man is honest and sincere and gets nothing out of it for himself, he is not at all in the
same category as the intelligent crook, who knows it's a steal, and
makes the thief (who regards himself as an honest business man)
give him a cut of the loot. And you can get such honest men to do
such uneconomic things by a part of the process of corruption:
by education; I mean the kind of education we give today. The
English governing class have so mastered and standardized their
school and college training that they turn out whole generations
of young men who are so alike in appearance, manners, speech,
thought, character, and conduct that any one anywhere can recognize the type. Very strong boys escape and develop an individuality
all the more distinct because of the drilling they survive, but even
these are marked, and very few. What the world knows and what
the world admires and bows to is the typical Englishman produced
in quantity by a system of mass production as wholesale and as
regular as the Henry Ford automobile factories pour forth Ford
cars. They are all so obedient that they have little imagination,
little initiative; they are brave unto death; they are despisers and
drivers of all inferior (un-English) peoples, and persistent promoters and formers of British power, forms, ideas, and customs
all over the world. It is these public school boys, not the British
army and navy, that conquer the earth and expand the British
empire. No less an authority than T. E. Lawrence said to me that

it was individual subjects like himself who made the empire. He was referring to his efforts with the Arabs. "I did the work, laid the plans, and achieved the position where I could have brought in an Arabian kingdom, and I had a hard time to force the navy to coöperate; the army wouldn't. The generals had no orders." And no initiative, I will add; and this also: the British navy is more anarchistic than the army.

Cecil Rhodes was another example of the Englishman who goes out from England and, functioning honestly as the English public school boy with force, makes British empire and, if necessary, war; and Rhodes had some sense of what had made him what he was. He founded the Rhodes scholarships for American boys so that they also would go out with formed minds, which could do innocently what the fine intelligent captains of industry and empire-makers of England want done—for the empire. Americans of the same sort might blunderingly do the very same thing, but it would be less sure and it would be for the good of the backward nation. Germans would do it, but deliberately and, therefore, ruthlessly. But the French, who would be willing to do it if it were not so difficult, would know what they were about, cynical, perhaps, or humorous, but aware of their iniquity.

France is as corrupt, in the American sense, as the United States would be if there were no exposures of graft and no more reforms. The bribery system is accepted in France; there is as much corruption and politics and pull in French business as in French politics. There is corruption in the theater, in the art salons, in the publishing business, the press, the railroad and ticket offices—everywhere. The two or three men in full dress who sit at the entrance to the theater and opera house and scrutinize your tickets are there to watch one another and the manipulations of the ticket office. They and the old women who take you to your seat and hold you up symbolize France, which, unexposed and unreformed, has so completely accepted the graft system that a young revolutionary socialist deputy upon election is made a director of some great corporation and by and by can become a premier of France and a defender of business and privilege against the next wave of revolutionists. Clemenceau, the war premier of France, Briand, the premier later, and other conservative leaders were radicals originally.

The great corporations, called syndicates, are essential parts of the business political machinery in France, where the tendency to merge business and politics has gone further than anywhere else. We in America have what all those countries once had, a dual government, the political establishment and business, and the theory is that the government exists to regulate, control, and adjust the conflicting interests of these businesses as against one another and as against the people. Apparently this is a theory in conflict also with the facts of economic growth. The economic forces, therefore, cause in the United States that political corruption which we regard as an exceptional evil, which in England has gone on to the point where it is quiet, decent, and accepted, but which in France has succeeded in uniting the management of business and the direction of political policies into one government. The syndicates have divided France into spheres of influence, financial, industrial, and political, which are not identical with but as governmental as departments; and in practice, a political leader can have a man appointed to a business job just as he can to a political office. The effect on business is the same as on political administration with us: inefficiency, dishonesty, the retardation of enterprise. But this is due also to another force that we do not feel fully yet. The ownership of big business in France (in England, in Europe, too, but most clearly you see it in France) is in the hands of the third and fourth generation of the descendants of the great founders and builders. There are literally princes of business in France as there were princes and descendants in politics, and they are alike, these two kinds of privileged descendants. They want security, income, profits; not adventure, enterprise, new machinery and methods. How the Europeans ever came to say that Americans worship money when they sell everything for money— the state, honors, business, the arts—is a mystery; and another is how they can see standardization "in the States," when they have it in their very bones. The general effect of European political business corruption has been to make everybody think of money, and not as with us as capital to build with and give away, but as cash to get, hold, or waste, to standardize dress, conduct, customs, and all thinking. The worst danger to America I saw abroad was that the process of corruption which affects our politics finally reaches the minds of men, so that, by the habit of justifying "what is done," they come finally to think right what used to be regarded as wrong. The French, the Latins, escape this, and the Germans may.

The French, corrupt as they are, have saved their minds. Not being so moral as we and the English are, they have not been constantly justifying their actions. They have not called good or right the evil that they have done, and so they have that charm which I felt always in "bad men" in America, in the "honest crooks" in politics and business. A Frenchman of the caliber of Clemenceau will see with you that something he or France is doing is wrong and agree with you as to what is right and yet yield to the compulsion to do wrong, knowingly. You can sit down with him, as you can with an American political boss, and learn all about things as they are, see corrupt acts as typical, hear that what the English call exceptional are the methodical acts that are dooming France; and then you can realize with your French bribers that no exposure and no one reform can change things. The French are what they are—incomprehensible to the rest of us, because they see that what they and we all want is security, that security means the maintenance of things as they are, that things as they are are evil and impossible, and that they think that the only possible outcome is wars and degeneration as in the old worlds of Rome, Greece, Egypt, or—revolution. They see this, with clear, logical, unlying minds, the intellectual French; and they have, therefore, the wit to fight off—to postpone—wars, revolution, and the fate of nations.

My superficial muckraking in Europe gave me the killing sense that I could not write what I was finding out, even if I clinched it all with evidence, because it would be impossible to tell it so that Americans would even consider it. How could one make a young, vigorous, optimistic people on a virgin, rich part of the earth's surface look ahead to those old peoples on old ground and see that the road we were on would lead up over the hill and down to Rome, Egypt, or China? How be heard saying that the process of political corruption we were reforming here and there was a mighty force that was, in Europe, making for the control of trade routes, spheres of influence, empire, war, and that the cost of war, economically and morally, would precipitate the revolution, which alone could change our course and our minds and save us? That's

what I saw eye to eye with far-seeing, wise old conservative statesmen in Paris and Berlin. In London I could see that the fine boys,
the gentle, honest poets and scholars of the Round Table, were the
pawns of the emperors back of the foreign affairs department and
that the Colonial Office was the scepter of the actual sovereign of
the British Empire which was to be the world. They saw, the
British emperors, and they showed me, that the Monroe Doctrine
was our announcement that we were going to Cape Horn when we
got ready and that when they got ready they and we together
would fight our common bloody or bribing way, innocently, un-
knowingly, to the conquest of the planet—for the good of all the
peoples of the earth. You couldn't print that, in English; you
might in French; but the American people can't read French.

IX

MEXICO: THE FIRST REVOLUTION

I was in Italy when the war broke, the long-expected, well-prepared-for, sudden world war, and I headed straight away to Mexico. On a theory. My theory was false, of course. My theory was that the inevitable war would bring on the inevitable revolution. The peoples of the civilized world were living under a system which was so unintelligent and so economically unsound that it could not stand the strain of war any better than it could that of peace. Many people said that in those days. Some people say it today, and curiously enough, now as then, they will argue that, therefore, war is impossible. Assuming that statesmen and rulers are guided by intelligence, these theorists (the practical men) think that the danger seen ahead will lead our leaders to avoid it. Nobody did any such thing in those days. It was only the reds who saw that we were not steered by human intelligence, but were borne along by economic forces. All the conservative, practical theorists, statesmen, and business men were all the while accepting and defending the economic arrangements which were making for the world war, and they were preparing and training to fight it, honestly, as now. I can understand this.

My own thinking was like theirs. I thought I knew that the financiers of London, Paris, Berlin, and New York were dividing the world into spheres of influence and disagreeing over the disposition of some regions. Some trade routes and some oil and other deposits of natural resources were not, finally, allotted. The Bagdad Railroad, building to beat the waterways to India, was temporarily German, and there was the oil of Mesopotamia to be disposed of some day—somehow; probably by war on the day when the German railroad was finished. When the war happened a little ahead of time, I thought I knew what its causes were and its purposes. I listened to the high principles spoken by the chancelleries of foreign affairs, but I knew, didn't I? that state departments represent imperial, war-making business just as police departments represent brewers, liquor dealers, and law-breakers. And so far I was right. The world war, started by an unimportant, apparently irrelevant incident, was caused and directed by the conflicts of the various financial imperial expansions, and its purpose and its achievement was to check one growing empire and leave the four or five others to wait for the next war to reduce the number.

But I thought also that this inevitable war would put such a strain on the economic and political organizations of the already heavily indebted, overtaxed, unhappy countries that their peoples would rise in revolts which would merge in "the inevitable European Revolution." I also assumed something about the limits of human endurance and the uses of human intelligence.

My error served one good purpose, however; it saved me from the war psychology. I did not become "patriotic" and rush to the front. The war was not the thing to watch. To go and be a war correspondent would have been as silly as to go on muckraking Europe. It was helpful to sanity to be where I was when war broke out—in northern Italy. I felt the thrill of fear; I felt—I could almost see—the Italians crouch at the news. But they were not aroused as the French were; they had no immediate attack to face. They could keep their heads, and on the street, in our kitchen, in the cafés, and in the newspapers, they considered whether they should be forced to go in, and on which side.

There was fear, certainly, but there was time, too. And there was the hopeful thought that maybe they could keep out if the war did not last too long. The popular and the business interest of northern Italy was with Germany, which had been penetrating the country financially and socially. But I heard no passionate expressions of partisanship, and as the conflagration of war spread up north from the east to the west, we caught the rumor that the government of Italy was receiving bids from both sides and dickering for terms to throw her weight this way or that. Here was an atmosphere in which to reflect. It quieted the masses, awed the newspapers; it calmed me. The only passionate outbursts I heard were those of the reds, who were numerous in Italy then.

And what they said in those whispered shouts was what I was thinking.

"The Revolution! The Revolution will come out of this."

Like Edward J. Bok, who said that the *Ladies' Home Journal* did not recognize the Cuban war, I would not "recognize" the European war. I would wait for the European revolution, and meanwhile prepare myself to report it. Remembering that I could not understand one city alone but had to see several cities to distinguish between what was general and what was peculiar, I guessed that I would have to experience at least two revolutions to understand one. I looked around for a revolution, and there was Mexico in the throes of one. I would go to Mexico. Ships were few and full, but in Florence I bid for and bought passage on a Greek steamer about to sail from Venice to New York. She stopped at her home port for a few days, and I joined a tourist party to Athens. It was a short trip, but interesting and relevant.

To Athens and back was for me a visit to a part of the earth's surface where a famous race of men had risen to an Acropolis of civilization, developed a culture which is an essential strain in the culture of the world today, and then had fallen, the race and the civilization, to—this modern Greece, almost a desert, and the modern Greeks. There was something wrong with that culture which is so much ours. Old Greece was an experiment with it, and the experiment failed. The Greek civilization was such that, not the poets and the philosophers, not the aristocrats of grace and beauty, but only the modern Greeks were fit to survive. Athens recalled Rome, old Rome and new, the old Romans and their survivors, the modern Romans, the Italians. Looking out of the car window on the way back through Greece, all stripped and bare, I was thinking of Egypt, old and new, and Mesopotamia, when an old man of science, who was seeing what I saw, remarked bitterly that "every desert on earth was man-made." Was that true? Was that the end of what we called in America the development of the natural resources of a country? I thought of and said, "China." "The Chinese survive," he said with a shrug. "They did not exploit China. We are about to develop China's natural resources. Then . . . Anyhow the human choice is Greece or China."

Greece, to my imagination, was a beautiful, empty, ruined antechamber to a revolution.

Arrived in New York, I learned very quickly that the Mexican revolution was in the civil war stage and that one must be careful which side to go in on. Two new leaders, Venustiano Carranza and Pancho Villa, were rising against Victoriano Huerta, the dictator whom President Wilson was refusing to recognize. He was doomed, but Carranza and Villa, both fighting him, were fighting each other, too. The reds in New York who were watching Mexico were on Villa's side, but the only reason they gave was that he was at least a bandit, a Barabbas, whereas Carranza was a respectable, land-owning bourgeois. Jack Reed talked that way, and he later went in on Villa's side. I thought of a trick I used to practice in making a quick decision in politics at home. I'd ask Wall Street, which is so steadily wrong on all social questions. If I could find out which side Wall Street was on, I could go to the other with the certainty of being right. So I inquired down there for the big business men with Mexican interests, called on and invited several of them to luncheon. They came eager to "start me off right." And they agreed that Villa was the man. Their reason?

"Well, you see, we have tried out both of them and Carranza, the —— —— ——, we can't do a thing with him. He won't listen to reason. Obstinate, narrow-minded, proud as hell, he has thrown us out again and again. Whereas Villa . . . You mustn't get the idea that just because he's a bandit he's no good. We have had him seen and—he's all right, Villa is."

Villa was operating in northern Mexico, along our border, which was his base. Carranza was in Vera Cruz, which he took when our troops, just withdrawn, evacuated. I sailed via Havana for Vera Cruz, out of the ice and snow of New York through a storm off Hatteras into the sunshine of those southern seas with the golden islands all quiet in their violet waters. It was beautiful, that slow, peaceful voyage in the backward world, with nothing to disturb one but the war news from the civilized front. And the most beautiful port of all was Vera Cruz, the old Spanish city, with its cruel, romantic history, all told in the ruined monuments of the Conquest, the old palaces and prisons. A star of the tropics, it is, a burning, lazy fixed star.

The inhabitants, Indians, Mexicans, half-breeds, Spanish, U.S. Americans, were getting over the American invasion and settling down, in no great haste, to the government of Carranza and his

barefooted army. Quiet, smiling hate, grasping caution, skeptical
hope, were the emotions I felt in the air as I hung about my
darkened hotel, sat on the dampened café sidewalks, and paid
stiff, suspicious calls. The American invasion was friendly; President Wilson certainly meant well; he thought he was saving the
Mexicans from a murdering tyrant who represented American and
foreign investors and not his own people. But our troops were
rough, literal, and sharp-shooting on duty. Off duty they were

THE MEXICAN REVOLUTION

"Cucaracha" (the Mexican Revolutionary Song). Drawing by José Clemente
Orozco. Courtesy of the Delphic Studios

contemptuous of the greasers, who paid back the gringos with
hate, suppressed, impotent, and, therefore, hot. They understood.
Whatever President Wilson intended, however innocent of imperialism the American people were, the Americans who were at
all interested in Mexico coveted the country, wanted to change its
laws and the people, and to possess or anyhow to govern Mexico.
Yes, they understand us, those backward Mexicans, and we don't
understand them or ourselves. As I said to President Wilson once
when he was asking me why the friendly landing of troops was
resented as an invasion, we Americans don't seem to get it, that
you can't commit rape a little.

Vera Cruz was a hard atmosphere to work in. That I came after the army of soldiers and correspondents left helped some. Luis Cabrera, Carranza's secretary of state, who had been the English-speaking attorney for Americans in Mexico, was the first to believe that my interest was in the revolution, not in Mexico or in American business. He took time to talk to and sound me. He introduced me to the Jefe, Carranza the unapproachable, who received me but did not for months open up. What I wanted, to start with, was the revolutionary history of the revolution. The Americans did not know that; they told the story from their point of view, which was petty, prejudiced, and not revolutionary. They called Carranza a crook, after money, and to prove it, told me that he had "here, just the other day, stolen out of a bank the deposit, some $45,000, of the Mexican treasury in Vera Cruz." I had that in mind when I first met the revolutionary chief. He was speaking of some of his projects, and I asked him what moneys he had to finance them. He indicated sources of funds and wound up by saying, "And then, for cash, there is $45,000 that was lying in bank here. I drew that, and I have it in my possession."

The Americans' suspicion that Carranza had stolen this sum and was out only for money is an illustration of how men expose their own psychology when they attribute motives to others. If Carranza was a thief he would not have volunteered the information that he had the "stolen money." Getting money was not "the" aim of the best of the revolutionary Mexican leaders that I knew. Many of them did, wisely, first make a deposit somewhere (usually out of the country), a get-away fund, money they could run to and with, if they lost out and had to escape. But once having provided for flight, they fought on for principles and their revolutionary program for Mexico. I met some true patriots in Mexico and some true revolutionaries. But was the Mexican a true revolution?

A committee of Latin revolutionists, who were in Vera Cruz when I arrived there, said no. French, Italian, and Spanish delegates sent over here to see, they had been several weeks in Mexico and were about to sail for home to report that the Mexican revolution was not a "veritable" revolution; it was not going according to Marx. As they talked, I realized again that it takes an experience of several revolutions to understand one and that a theory which has grown into a conviction is a hindrance rather than a help to the observing mind. And theories do harden. It is almost impossible to remember always that a theory is only a working hypothesis. I entered into that Mexican revolution in a state of mental doubt and confusion, which did not clear up till I was out of the Mexican into the Russian revolution. And yet there was a basis for comparison in Mexico, and Carranza and other Mexican leaders saw it.

Carranza, as he came gradually into power, took the capital, Mexico City, and felt surer of his sovereignty, talked more to some of us who were near him, and I soon found that he kept constantly in mind the parallel of this, the so-called Maderista revolution and that of Benito Juarez, which occurred in the middle of the last century. This was interesting as a sign that man could use history as an applied science. I had never before been associated with leaders who had or could learn from the past. American reformers were guided only by unclear consideration of right and wrong, or of expediency weighed on the spot. The result was that city after city, State after State in the United States, kept repeating experiments that had failed over and over again. But these historical experiments were not written and were not regarded as experiments. If they were referred to at all, previous failures were laid to the character or the inability of previous leaders, not to the reform policy itself. The real trouble with us is that we Americans are not taught the experimental method of the sciences in politics; our culture is not experimental. We say that "history repeats itself" as if it were a fatalistic law of nature.

To hear Carranza and his colleagues in backward Mexico looking for tendencies in themselves to repeat the errors made in the Juarez revolution and resisting them consciously, even anxiously, was a revelation to me. I remember that in conversation with President Wilson once, I said that the purpose of the Mexican revolution was to avoid the repetitions of history. As an historian I thought that he would like the idea that the repetitions of history might be the anchorage for a science of history; a study of them, with a search for the common causes of them, might lead us out of a linear, chronological narrative of historical events to a comparative consideration of parallel events. Instead of a mere tale of the rise or fall of the Greeks, we might make a study of the rise or the fall of nations, and so discover the why, and, perhaps, avoid the fall of the French, English, or American peoples. Wilson did listen; he asked some interested questions about Carranza's parallel, but he made no comment. I think he was the statesman, not the historian, when we talked. And that was true of Carranza, too. His uses of history were very practical. When he saw Madero call in his rich relatives and the leading citizens of Mexico to advise him, Carranza remembered what had happened to Porfirio Diaz when he did the same thing, and he, Carranza, acted; he warned Madero and went home and began to raise his army. But I am ahead of my story, which will suggest a little deeper parallel.

Benito Juarez, a Mexican, led his people in revolt against the (mostly) Spanish possessors of the land and natural resources of Mexico who had enslaved the people. He won, but he did not alter the economic conditions; a simple, courageous, wise, but not very "wise" native, he set up a political constitution as a barrier against a repetition of slavery and put himself and his kind of good, patriotic Mexicans or Indians in office. He, the liberator, passed, and his successor was one of the best of his men, Porfirio Diaz, also an Indian. But the causes of the evils they had fought remained; the old process began again, and Diaz, the good Indian, the patriotic Indian, began to listen to the "big" land-owners and the leaders of such enterprises as there were in Mexico. This is what Carranza remembered of the old revolution. These leading citizens were not yet bad men in Carranza's sense; they merely knew what they wanted and remembered how they had got things before. Their advice was probably the best they had to give. But their policy was to give to themselves and their kind more and more land from the public domain, more and more mines, and since land and mines are no use without labor, and the Mexicans, living in a hot climate on fat lands, were lazy, it became necessary for those owners who would not work themselves to revive, not slavery, but peonage. They took Diaz into their enterprises, organized companies which invited foreign capital and brains, and finally formed the famous Porfirio Diaz Scientificos, who grew richer and richer while the Mexicans grew poorer and poorer. The foreign capitalists, Spaniards at first, with French, English, German, and finally U.S. Americans, won Diaz, the president and dictator, and the government came gradually but literally to represent them. The paper constitution was interpreted—it was torn to pieces—by their actual government. To free labor, Diaz confiscated the common lands which Juarez had given the towns, villages, and tribes. It was said that those lands were taken for and by the landlords, but there is evidence to show that the motive was to deprive the people of all free land so that they could not work for themselves but would have to work for the landlords. The land seizure served another purpose, however. It caused revolts, fights, banditry, and excused the capture of prisoners, the arrest of "criminals," who were driven by troops from one part of Mexico to another, wherever labor was needed. And this became necessary. Northern Mexicans removed to southern plantations, sickened and died under the heat, the mosquitoes, and the hard conditions of their labor; they died in a few years, and fresh labor had to be found. The system of Mexican peonage is well known. The Indians, a trustful, improvident race, were allowed to run up small debts in the landlord's store, and the law provided for the arrest of debtors. The Mexican people were slaves. Life for the foreign and higher Mexican owners was rich, romantic, and beautiful; for the natives it was miserable and hopeless. Mexico under the Juarez constitution and the Diaz dictatorship repeated the same conditions which caused their revolution and now was causing another revolution. Diaz was blamed and hated, but an outsider could see that it was no man, no men, no party, no class, that was at fault; only the established conditions did it.

Another thing I noted was that it was not revolutionists who caused the revolution which was coming, and coming fast, toward the end of the reign of Diaz. There were revolutionists. I knew the Magoun brothers, who were educated, fanatical revolutionary leaders with a theory and a plan, such as the labor committee in Vera Cruz demanded of a revolution. But I knew the Magouns in American prisons where President Diaz had them held by the U.S. government, which represented the same kind of people he did. The Magouns and all other enlightened revolutionists were helpless in Mexico. They were "agitators," "conspirators," "traitors," and as such were shot or suppressed. No. Revolutionists did not cause or even start the Mexican revolution, and I think that revolutionists cannot make a revolution. Only a government, only the established order, can make a revolution, and the Mexican revolution was all ready made long before an incident started it. A revolution is, in this respect, like a war.

What started the Mexican revolution, which was all ready to go, was the Diaz Jubilee in 1910, a celebration of the very long dictatorship of the president. To it came princes, ambassadors, prelates, and world-famous business men from all the countries which Diaz and the Mexican ruling ring had served so well, and the miserable, barefooted Mexican people saw it. There were processions, audiences, balls, operas—for the foreigners, for a few of the rich Mexicans. Pictorially it was beautiful; the Mexicans are an artistic people. But politically it was a mistake; it was like holding up a great painting of the government of Mexico, so realistic and so dramatic that no imagination could fail to see what it meant. And Mexicans of all classes, even some of the rulers—it is said that even Diaz—saw it. This was Mexico, a parade of grateful, prosperous foreigners through standing masses of ragged Mexicans, to and from the palace of the president. Mexicans are proud; it hurt, and they all suffered and were humiliated and angry at once.

After that, Diaz shipped to a bank in Spain his security fund and soon fled himself from Mexico. "The revolution was on," the Maderista revolution, led by Francisco Madero.

X

CARRANZA AND MADERO

FRANCISCO J. MADERO was the "queer" son of a large, rich, very powerful family of Jewish origin which lived on a vast landed estate in northern Mexico. He did not, as a boy, take to business; cared nothing for lands, cattle, mines, and politics. He saw and he felt the deplorable conditions of the peons, but was taught to regard all that as natural, inevitable. He could not change anything. His ambition was to paint, and he clamored to go to Paris. The family shook their heads but finally yielded to his wish. He was no use anyhow. They let him go, and he did study art. But also he sat around the cafés, listening to the talk about art and about capitalism, socialism, anarchism, and recalling, as he heard these revolutionary remedies, the state of things at home in Mexico.

Now all this talk may have been to most of those Paris students the chatter of youth, but to Madero it meant that there was something to do, something that not he but his father, brothers, neighbors, might do for the Mexican people, something that they did not know about. He sailed for home to tell them, and I heard funny stories of the ridiculous performances of Francisco, the art student, when he rushed in upon his family to deliver his message from Paris, his glad tidings. Pointing to what was going on in Mexico, he told his father and brothers that "things don't have to be the way they are; there is a better way."

Apparently he expected them to rejoice with him over his good news that there were such things as socialism, anarchism, and he was appalled when they laughed at him. They knew all about socialism, and they hooted at it and at him. His family did not want to make things better! No, and when he went with the family to court at Mexico City, he discovered that other men who could introduce a better system would not. The Scientificos jeered at him as his own family had; they indulged the "queer" Madero, but it was a joke on the family, who were properly ashamed. It was said that he even tried to convert Porfirio Diaz.

When there was no joy anywhere in his own class over his good tidings Madero turned to the people, and as has happened before, they heard him, and gladly. At that time free speech was suppressed in Mexico. Agitators were arrested, imprisoned, shot, but young Madero was allowed some leeway, because he was of good family, but also because he was a harmless fool. So he spoke in the streets, and he came to speak with more and more eloquence; his naïveté helped him. A rich, educated, "decent" young man, his mind did not seem so different from the minds of his hearers. He was not a superior person. His message clicked, and the peon and the suppressed agitators were able to repeat it to others. It spread. And the Diaz spies and the police got it, too, and repeated it higher up. Madero was warned; his family was warned. Their "queer" son was not merely queer; he was dangerous. He was arrested, but let go. The family pull got him out of his first scrapes. But he would not listen to reason, and no one could stop him. He was thrown into prison, and he escaped; he ran away, and under cover he preached his message, here, there, all over Mexico; and not only the people but the very jailers listened to him. He could be arrested, but he could not be held. Not his family now, not his father's powerful friends, the petty officials, the other prisoners, the people—somebody always let Madero get away. I asked a jailer once how he came to turn the man out.

"Oh," he said, "when he spoke in the prison to the other prisoners, I heard, and what he said, Señor—what he said was so—so beautiful; and he—he was beautiful too."

Some of Madero's escapes were regarded as miracles; the jailers, called to account by the government, adopted the miracle explanation, which, by the way, may account for similar escapes in biblical and legendary history. But not only the other prisoners, their keepers, and the people, other kinds of men came to look to Madero for leadership. He soon personified all the many forms of discontent in Mexico: the peons and their hope for land, labor and its wish for liberty, the small traders and the petty land-owners and their hopes for free business, the minority groups in the ruling class who were dominated and often despoiled by the Scientificos, and some groups of foreign investors who were not in strong with the dictator and his ring. All of these saw their chance with Madero, and none of them was afraid of him; he was honest, sincere, almost fanatical; but he looked as if he could be controlled, and then, when he was achieving power, his one clever brother appeared beside him and took over the business end of the revolution. Business men found that they could do business with him. But the following that set the revolution off were the patriotic leading Mexicans who, besides their hope of a better position and more privileges under a new dictator like Madero, really resented, as all the people did, the implications of the Jubilee with foreigners appearing openly as the privileged class with Porfirio Diaz as *their* representative, *their* president.

The Diaz government crumbled from within. When the fighting began, Madero led it, but not as a revolutionist and not even as a general. He was the saintly prophet whom the people and the soldiers trusted, he and no other; and—this also is to be noted—nobody distrusted him, not even the non-revolutionary, utterly insincere plotters who joined Madero to pick up the privileges the Scientificos would have to drop. Diaz fled to Spain, where he had deposited his safety fund. Mexico City, which seemed to be taken, really was surrendered to the revolutionists. Madero became the head of the first revolutionary government, which, called the triumphant end, was the beginning of the revolution.

When there is discontent in an American city or a European government, we have agitation, discussion, reform organization, some emotion, a political fight, and an election. If the reformers win, what they have gained is the opportunity and the power to make changes. Usually there are few reforms proposed, and even those are rejected or blunted, because neither the voters nor the reformers have a program. They are content to have ousted the rascals and put honest men in office. That is our moral conception of politics. In Europe they may make some one or two slight economic changes, but not enough to alter the system. The same privileged interests which controlled the old "rascals" find ways to influence, moderate, and gradually to control the new reformers, and things go on as before. That is the curve of reform, and the same curve occurred in Mexico and I think in all revolutions. The

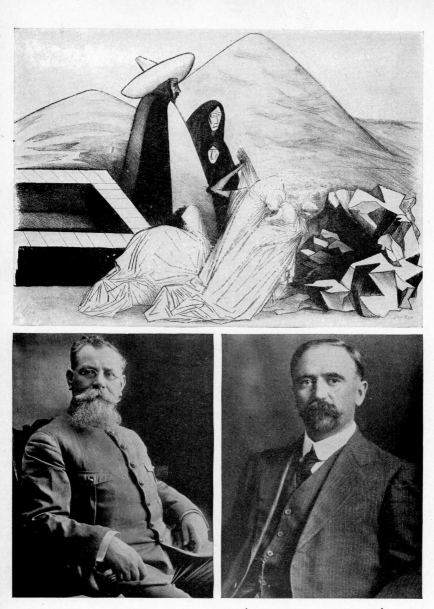

UPPER: THE MEXICAN REVOLUTION (LITHOGRAPH BY JOSÉ CLE-
MENTE OROZCO, COURTESY DELPHIC STUDIOS). LOWER LEFT: VENUS-
TIANO CARRANZA (N.Y. WORLD NEWS SERVICE). LOWER RIGHT:
GENERAL FRANCISCO MADERO (N.Y. WORLD NEWS SERVICE).

difference is one of dimension. A reform curve is short, a revolutionary curve is longer. But the tendency is to form a complete circle back to the starting-point, and there is progress or, at least, change only when the return misses the starting-point and forms a spiral.

Madero was a devoted reformer, and there were sincere men with him, Carranza, for example; and Carranza saw enough of this to show it to me. He told me how, when Madero became president dictator, he, Carranza, thought the revolution had triumphed. He went back to his lands in northern Mexico, leaving Madero to govern the country they had "saved." Madero had his ideas, which were radical, and Carranza agreed with them. He wanted nothing for himself. Mexico for the Mexicans, land for the people, and some political reforms, were enough for Carranza. But neither Madero nor Carranza was a well-grounded radical; they were not clear economists, and they did not see that to carry out the many drastic political and the superficial few economic changes they proposed would require great political wisdom and profound, revolutionary reforms. Carranza said that he soon saw from his estate that the privilege-seekers, old and new, gathered around Madero in Mexico City and that they were coming to control him. The saintly prophet was not able to cope with the worldly wise men. The Madero family was ruling in the person of their "queer son."

"I went to Mexico City," said Carranza. "After watching it and hating it all for months, I went to Madero, and I saw what was happening. The interests we had risen up against and defeated, some of the very men we had fought and defeated, were back in power as Madero's advisers, and I protested to him. He was half aware, but he was altogether confused and helpless.

" 'What can I do?' he pleaded. 'I don't know how to do those political things. I don't understand finance and laws. These men do. I had to ask their advice, and they prove to be not such bad men as we thought. My brothers and their friends, them I can trust, can't I? They are helping me.'

" 'But,' I said, 'whether they are good or bad does not matter. They know no other way of doing things than the old way they are accustomed to, and so, inevitably, if you follow their advice, you and they will restore the old ways, the old evils, and we'll have it all to do over again.'

"Madero was persuaded, but he was only excited and at a loss. 'What can I do? It is too late. I can't get rid of them now, and—they can help me and no one else can.'"

Carranza said that he looked at Madero, saw that he was utterly unfit for the task, and—"I sorrowed," he said. "I warned Francisco Madero. 'Listen,' I prophesied, 'these men around you are not only rapacious grafters of property and privileges; they are not to be satisfied, not all of them. You may give to them all something, but not all equally, and as they begin to taste the loot they will kill you, my friend. They will put you to death to take all, all.'"

Carranza said that he went back home and began at once to raise an army to avenge Madero and save the revolution. So sure was he of his prophecy! "Sure?" he exclaimed. "Isn't assassination the fate of all weak and generous dictators?" His historical prophecy came true. Madero was killed; so was his brother, and by their unrevolutionary friends and admirers.

There was a plot. The Americans were in it. Some of the meetings of the conspirators were held in the American embassy. Our privilege-seekers were Maderistas; they were getting favors from Madero for the high financing they had done for the revolution. But, as Carranza said, not enough. Madero, the weak, was disposed to be fair, and his fairness showed his weakness. We wanted all, we Americans; so we did not join in the killing; oh, no, we were only in on the plot which anybody who knew Mexico knew would lead to the killing of Madero, as it did, "for attempting to escape," as the lie goes. Some picked men, taking him to prison, turned on and shot him in his carriage, and their smiling excuse was the classic Mexican joke: "The prisoner started to flee."

No matter, however, about this, and no matter that there was a slaughter in Mexico City of Madero's loyal revolutionary troops. The paralleling point is that the reactionaries, Americans included, who had accepted Madero and were getting along pretty well with him, were not satisfied with him. He was too honest, too idealistic; so, having "made" the revolution, they made the counter-revolution and pinned their hopes on Victoriano Huerta, who, notoriously a drunken crook, was the general in command of the Maderista army of occupation. He became their general, too. Massing the forces he had gradually brought over secretly to his personal leadership, he sent against them the Maderistas in small enough contingents to be utterly slaughtered, day by day, battalion by battalion, making the infamous Ten Bloody Days in Mexico City. It was a battle in which one general commanded both sides, and it resulted quite naturally in a complete victory for Huerta and the reactionaries who made Huerta the president dictator of Mexico. And this was the man the Americans, other foreigners, and the anti-revolutionists labored so hard to have recognized by the United States. The scandal of the assassinations and double-drilled massacre was so great that the world, busy though it was with the war, saw through it, and President Wilson would have none of it.

It is not revolutionists, it is the anti-revolutionists, who not only make but carry on a revolution. And it is the revolutionists, not the anti-revolutionists, who unmake a going revolution, or, rather, circle it back to defeat at the starting-point. So I theorized.

When after this scandal and long pressure from President Wilson, Huerta went out, the reactionaries, as we have seen in Wall Street, turned to Pancho Villa, who was a grossly illiterate, unscrupulous, unrevolutionary bandit. But Carranza won. He marched into Mexico, D.F., soon after I met him in Vera Cruz, and was in a position to do what Madero had left undone. And he was the type to do it.

Orators start movements and lead them for a while, whether in labor, reform, or politics. When they succeed to power, the walking delegate Sam Gompers, the executive organizer Hiram Johnson, comes to the top. Carranza was a mute executive, unemotional, unsentimental, hard. There was no compromise in him. All that he knew, however, was political history and his own experience. He acted on that. Having seen how the reactionaries "got" poor Madero, he feared that they would "get" his cabinet and other leaders. He trusted only himself, which is characteristic of this kind of dictator. He saw that in Mexico City, where the foreigners and Mexican reactionaries were gathered, his officers were being influenced. He ordered up a railroad train, loaded his government on it, and went traveling all over Mexico. The stated and the apparent purpose of this government on wheels was to enable the

Jefe to see and be seen by the people and so establish communication with them. And he did indeed make speeches at each stop, and he listened to the wishes of the people. But that was not his sole purpose, as he told me one day.

He had invited me to the train as a correspondent, and I was with him throughout his whole months-long journey. The occupation of the travelers was the making of the new constitution and corresponding with the U.S. State Department, which was acting as if it were the responsible government of Mexico. For a while Carranza was cold and mute to all the correspondents, but he gradually warmed to me, on the side. I think it was because I made him laugh, and he gave another reason.

"There," he said, "read that," and he threw on the table of the correspondents' compartment a communication from the American Secretary of State. It was a protest, which originated in Los Angeles, at gambling, prostitution, dancing, and the general wide-openness of Tia Juana, across the California border in Lower California. Lower California is a part of Mexican territory, but it was in the control of American business men and Mexican generals who were opposing Carranza. The American government must have known that Carranza had no power there, but they sent him the protest as if he were responsible. It was but one of the absurd, annoying interferences of our government in Mexican affairs, and Carranza, who knew some of the Americans in Mexico and in Washington and Texas, had a very healthy hatred of us. When we had all read the foolish letter, I remarked that it was easy to answer. Carranza heard and instantly demanded what I meant.

"Oh," I said, "I would reply to that letter, offering to close up Tia Juana if the United States will close up Los Angeles, San Francisco, Chicago, and New York."

He stared at me a moment; then the faintest twinkle smiled in his eyes, and he picked up the note and walked off with it as if he meant to make mine his answer.

After that he would draw me aside and talk to me about revolutionary and political ideas, through an interpreter. I did not speak Spanish, and he pretended to speak no English. He understood it; he often answered me before the interpreter had put what I said into Spanish. The other correspondents wondered, and some of the veterans resented his attitude to me.

"Why," they asked him one day, "why do you talk to Steffens, who doesn't speak Spanish, and not to us, who do?"

"Because," he answered, "that man speaks our language and you don't."

He meant, I interpreted to the correspondents, that I could talk revolution, and they could talk only business. Anyway he came up to me and said: "Do you know, you are the only American in Mexico who never helps us, never tells us what to do?"

"I am here," I answered, "not to help you but to get help. I want to understand a revolution so as to understand others when they come; to see what you do that works and avoid what you do that fails." I smiled and added, "I am here as a patriotic American to learn how to see my country through a revolution we need as much as you do."

"Yes," he said, "but I hear that you have studied the corruption of your country and should know something about government. I am going to ask you to sit in with our constitutional committee and help us make a government."

I said that I would like to watch that committee work but, again, not to advise but to learn. He took me to the committee, told them to consult me, and I did sit with them after that. I never spoke except when I was spoken to, which eased their obvious first suspicion; but they seldom took my advice. They asked me once how I would charter cities and towns, and I answered that I would adopt in the written law the actual form of government as I had found it everywhere: I would make the boss, their Jefe Politico (political chief), the legally responsible head (and dictator) of the government and let him appoint advisers and lieutenants, but with no elected aldermen. They could not see that; it shocked them; and I did not argue it. I wasn't sure myself, and, as I said, that scheme would work only if they removed the chief sources of corruption. The committee were not nearly so trustful of me as Carranza; he believed in me, more and more, with some reason.

The American State Department, and some diplomats and secret service men, and a lot of American business men in Mexico have held it against me that I was the author of the famous Article XXVII which has given them so much trouble. I never denied the charge; it was so creditable that I would have been proud to have drawn that good law. I am sorry now to have to give up that honor and tell the truth.

One day the train stopped for lack of fuel for the engine, and Carranza came up to the constitutional committee in a rage. "What do you think of a situation," he demanded, "where, in an oil country like Mexico, the government cannot get enough oil to keep its own train moving? What can we do? You ought to be able to tell us that," he blazed at me.

I was startled, but I answered quietly, "Maybe I can. Have you a map of the oil regions?"

He changed his aspect. He was evidently curious. He called for the Tampico map, and I traced the line of a road. "What's that?" I asked.

"A road," he answered.

"Public domain?"

"Yes," he said.

"And this?" I pointed to other lines on the map. "And this? And this?"

"Streams," he said, "or stream beds."

"Also government property? Also not private property?"

"Yes, yes."

"Well," I said, "they go right over the oil fields. You could sink wells in them, and they'd be on your property; the oil would be your own government fuel."

Carranza stood there eyeing me a moment; then he said, "Right. At once." And he ordered an officer to take an engine and go and start drilling for oil. But I stopped him.

"One moment, Jefe," I said. "You won't have to drill. The oil men will see what you are up to, and they will offer you all the oil you want if you will stop boring."

The officer sent on the engine came back with oil and the assurance of all the oil that Mexico might need thereafter. Carranza, impressed, took me into his room, and we talked about taxes and constitutions. We studied the old Mexican constitution which had kept one principle in the old royal Spanish charter that is wiser economically than any property principle in American or English law. A land grant gave the surface, the soil, to the farmer or rancher homesteader, but the title did not carry the ownership of what was underground. If gold, silver, coal—if any mineral deposits were discovered, they belonged to the crown and later to the Republic. Mining claims, then, did not go to the farmer, but had to be granted separately, and the state kept the king's share. I advised Carranza to retain this law in principle, and I advised him also to tax back the land and the mines—all national resources—at their full rental value. He saw these points, and he and his successors accepted and enacted so much as they understood of the theory back of them. Naturally the foreigners and the big land-owners resented the principle. Most of their troubles in Mexico came from this policy. It is that which lies at the bottom of the oil disputes. The foreigners who found oil in Mexico, English and Americans, assumed that the English principle prevailed. They bought the surface, the farming rights, of the land over the oil deposit and only later discovered that they did not possess an indisputable claim to the "mineral rights." They appealed to Diaz, who for and after consideration, proclaimed that oil was not a mineral, but the dictator's legislature and Mexico's courts never approved his decree. Carranza's constitution kept the old principle, and oil is still a mineral. The American government and the foreign oil men's lawyers contend that, under American law, the foreign capitalists own the oil deposits with the land, and, in effect, our State Department acts upon the theory that American and English law, not Mexico's ancient and established law and custom, prevails in Mexico.

And they were fighting for this theory all the while I was in Mexico. They made headway, too. They could, by lobbying methods, introduce American ideas into Carranza's cabinet. And he knew it, and that is where his government on wheels came in. We had been several weeks in Guadalajara; the constitution was growing, and I was very comfortably settled, when all of a sudden one night we received word to be on the train early the next morning. We obeyed of course, but we were unhappy about it, and I complained.

"Why?" I asked Carranza that day. He was long silent, embarrassingly silent, but when he did answer it was to give me the philosophy of the train.

"When we were at work, in Mexico [City], I noticed that my associates, some of them, changed their minds; they began to express foreign ideas, American aims. You foreigners are very tempting, you know. I felt the American influence, remembered Madero, his friends, his fate. I decided to come to Guadalajara. The train we came on is the only train running these days; so we escaped your lobby and had time to work for Mexico till the foreigners could get to Guadalajara on foot or a-horseback. I could tell when they arrived. I could hear the news in the debates; so I ordered you to the train, and here we are bound for the next town. And there we shall stay till the Mexicans begin to talk as if they had heard American money talking." He was angry.

"Jefe," I commented, "you have heard me say that I came to Mexico to get ideas for better government in the United States?"

"Yes." He bowed, wondering.

"Well, the idea of a government on wheels is one to introduce in my country. Only, if our government were to keep ahead of our corruption, it would have to be a very fast train and make no stops."

The trouble with Carranza as a revolutionary leader was that he had no economics. He might have been a good statesman; a statesman does not typically know what is moving him, but a revolutionary leader must. Carranza did not, like Madero, give the land, the mines, and other privileges to the old privileged class, but he did give them to his revolutionary leaders and to the people, as individuals; and, of course, these privileges did corrupt the new possessors of them into a privileged class with a privileged class psychology. He did not abolish privileges and close up the sources of corruption; so his "good" men soon became "bad" men. They turned against him and the aims of the revolution. And he himself, being a landlord and an employer of labor, developed under the strain of strikes the psychology of a capitalist, shot into and put down fighting labor. This was after I had gone from Mexico. The revolution had not run its course; so a revolutionary party of labor and unsatisfied leaders and followers rose against Carranza, caught and shot him, and went on.

XI

WILSON AND MEXICO

ALL the while I was in Mexico, the great war was going on in the remote distance, in sight, but out of hearing. The noise of the revolution drowned that of Europe, and, apparently, it is hearing rather than seeing that stirs one. Whenever I came home to New York, Washington, and even to Laredo, I heard the din of the war and felt the excitement enough to visualize it. But not as a menace to us. My friends, mostly pacifists, were fighting the war like soldiers. Their psychology was that of war, just as the pro-war people's was. I did not feel it at all. I joined in meetings and movements to keep us out of war, but the war I feared was with Mexico. I was seeing President Wilson, who made me sure we would not go fighting in Europe and that he had no intention of intervening in Mexico, but he might. The pressure on him was almost irresistible, and he was getting it all, his own and Carranza's, too.

Once when I happened to be home, in Washington, I went during a Mexican crisis to the State Department. I met in the hall outside the secretary's office a lot of my American friends from Mexico. One glance, and I saw that they were the oil, mining, business men who had been lobbying in Mexico City and following Carranza's too slow-moving train around the country, trying to pick off his advisers with reason and with bribes. Yes, bribes. In Guadalajara, Luis Cabrera had accused them to their faces. He had a meeting with them; I was there. He spoke English perfectly, and he spoke it then slowly and quietly. Every Mexican is an eloquent orator.

"You are bribers," he said. "You know it, and I know it; and you know I know it. Don't forget that in the good old days I was your attorney in many a dubious transaction. Recall some of them,

733

gentlemen; do you remember? Well, then, recall also what we did and how we did it."

There was silence till Cabrera went on, just as quietly, to warn them against applying those methods to a revolutionary government. A revolution, somehow, changes human nature, and bribe-takers of old won't take bribes in a period when there is some hope of something better than profits.

The sight of those men in Washington suggested to me something that filled me with such rejoicing that I expressed myself. I said I was glad to see them there, and I must have shown my joy, for one of them asked why I was so extraordinarily happy to see them.

"Oh," I blurted, "your presence here means that Carranza is an honest man, and that you have found his government incorruptible. It means that you could not get the crooked, backward, illiterate Mexicans; so you have had to come to get your own government. The only shadow on my happiness is that I fear you may get it."

There were protests, of course, and some little anger, but they probably recalled also our meeting in Guadalajara. They wanted intervention. Most of the Americans in Mexico did. Naturally. An American who had bought a million acres of land in Mexico at from five to twenty-five cents an acre knew that if we took the country over as we had Porto Rico or even as we had Cuba, his land would be worth $2 to $10 and more an acre. The price of business blocks in Mexico City would double, and houses and lots. The oil men would be rid of a bad government and bad laws—bad for them—and come under "good" government and laws that they understood. So with mining; so with all business. Mexico is full of potential Los Angeleses and has one or two Californias and Floridas. No wonder they inspire and finance trouble. I made, in a lecture delivered all over the United States from New York to Texas to California, this statement, which was never challenged, though several times there were in the audience captains of American industry and diplomatic officers from Mexico; I said that there had not been in all my time in Mexico a single revolution, counter revolution, or raid across our border by Mexicans that was not engineered and paid for by Americans in Mexico. I could not prove that now, but I could have proved it then.

I remember going late one forenoon into the American Club in Mexico City and finding the place crowded with my drinking, hilarious countrymen who grabbed me and shot me up to the bar to drink. "Drink, man, drink. It is coming."

"What? What's the matter?" I asked.

"Haven't you heard the news?"

I had not, and they told me that seventeen Americans had been shot down by Mexicans in northern Mexico.

"Seventeen of 'em!" they shouted. "Seventeen of 'em slaughtered in cold blood!"

"But why," I staggered mentally, "why do you celebrate the killing of Americans?"

"Don't you see?" They explained: "It means intervention. You don't suppose that those blankety-blank pacifists in the Wilson administration can refuse now to send the army, do you?"

Such was the temper and the force of the pressure on Woodrow Wilson, who, like other executives, was without the information needed to hold to his course. The State Department has the duty and the machinery to furnish facts, but it furnishes news instead. I saw in Mexico, and I have seen since, the embassy officials in competition with newspaper correspondents, trying to beat them, asking them to let them wire something first. But the chief trouble with our foreign secret service is that the spies see and report with prejudice and the thought of feeding the prejudice of the State Department. I never found President Wilson informed on anything that I knew about in Mexico. Some facts he had, but none of the color, no background, no such interpretive facts as an executive has to have to act upon, and not nearly enough of what I will call personal impressions. Wilson evidently knew that, for he sent out personal representatives; ex-Governor Lind of Minnesota "covered" Mexico for him, and Lind got things right, as I often observed. But he was alone.

President Wilson inherited from President Taft an army on the Mexican border, which Taft put there ready for the invasion he would not himself order because that act would force a policy of war upon his elected successor. The Americans interested economically in Mexico demanded that the army move, and when Wilson would not attack, then that it stay there. An oil magnate told me that that standing, menacing army enabled the oil companies to evade the Mexican oil tax. "Yes," he said, "it cost the government millions, but it saved us some money. We could put Mexican oil down in New Orleans at a cost of, say, ten cents a barrel; if we had paid the tax it would have cost us, say, twelve or fifteen cents a barrel, and we sold oil then at $1.10 a barrel." And he laughed.

Now, Wilson had no love for the oil men; he despised them and their methods. He used to say that all business men who went into foreign countries should go at their own risk, not at the risk of the nation, not at the risk of war. And he held and he proclaimed the right of revolution, a principle which he had learned in his State of Virginia. If any president could withstand the pressure upon his office, Wilson was the man to do it. He was a liberal, an old-fashioned liberal. But once when I was in New York he was on the verge of war with Mexico. I hurried to Washington. Other pacifists were there. The country generally felt the menace, and the papers were pretty sure the army was going over. The president would not see me, and the cabinet members told me I was too late. Secretary of War Baker said war had been decided upon; he was preparing for the march. Why? The president was informed that Carranza wanted war; he needed it to rally his people to the support of his falling government! Absurd—all lies. I had just come from Carranza, and I knew that Carranza dreaded war; it would be the end, not only of the revolution, but of Mexico for Mexicans. But Carranza had been told, and he believed—he could not be budged from the belief—that Wilson wanted the war for his American purposes.

Misinformation. Criminal misinformation, but what could one do? What was needed was information, and not only information, but facts that would convince Wilson. I gave up. The president would not see me, and if he did, how could I convince him that he was wrong? Besides, I was convinced myself that war with Mexico was inevitable, and I still am. Having seen in Mexico how wars are made, watched the forces at work that make them, and got a glimpse of the economics of empire, I am convinced that the American flag will go to Cape Horn.

In despair I went in to the law office of Charles A. Douglas, the American attorney of Carranza in Washington. We often held hands in mutual sympathy. He tossed me a deciphered private wire from Carranza. It was a message of despair and sorrow. No use. The war was come. A thought struck me. That private wire was convincing.

"Have you any more like that?" I asked. He had, he said.

"I've got a stack of them stuck on a spike, but I have to go to court myself."

He got up to go, but he took me into another room, picked out his spike of recent letters and telegrams from Carranza, and said: "You can read them. They are all sorts, on business mostly, and very private, but some will interest you. You read them. I have to go, fast."

Another bit of evidence that Carranza was honest. But I knew that already. I read those communications, turned out all those that indicated Carranza's innocence of warlike intentions, and went over to the White House. Since I could not see the president, I dictated to his stenographer a message, saying I had seen documents he should see, and—I'll quote: "A war due to irresistible causes is bad enough, but a war made by misinformation is unforgivable, and I, for one, will never forgive it." So I dictated.

A silly note, but I was indignant, and expecting no answer, I went off about my business. David Starr Jordan and Moorfield Story were in Washington to see the president and to protest the war for some peace society. I told them what I knew. Then I called on some men who were organizing a league for peace, a league to enforce peace, which Edward A. Filene was promoting. I pointed out to them that here at our door was a war to prevent, but they were thinking of big wars, and—"Besides," Mr. Filene said, "the new league is too young to act now." I sang him the song which I think should be our national anthem:

> "Mother, may I go out to swim?"
> "Yes, my darling daughter,
> Hang your clothes on a hickory limb,
> But don't go near the water."

It's all right to organize labor, but don't use the union to strike. It's very proper to write free speech into the Constitution, but don't take any liberties. It is highly creditable to form a peace society, but you must not strain it by opposing a war.

Mr. Filene perfected his league, and it was the inspiration for—the League of Nations. One of the successes of this millionaire who failed.

These footless errands done, I went up into the Senate press gallery and watched something I liked to see: the graceful courtesy of the Senate. When I got back to my hotel they said the White House had been calling me all day; I must go there early next morning—"not to the office; to the House."

The president received me at the head of the stairs. "What is this information, this misinformation, you speak of?" he demanded, hard, but smiling, and he stayed my answer till we were in his library and were seated. "Now, then?"

I told him that members of his cabinet had said that war with Mexico was inevitable because he, the president, was convinced that Carranza wanted and was forcing it. That was misinformation. Carranza did not want war but was convinced that he, Wilson, did. Then I recounted the incident with Douglas, how he let me read alone his private correspondence with Carranza, and I quoted the pertinent letters which showed his regret and sorrow.

"Those are private letters and telegrams," I said. "I have separated those that bear on the war and prove my contention; I'll go and get them for you. I am sure Douglas will let me have them for this purpose. I believe he will let me have the whole file. Anyway I offer them all to you."

"No," he answered. "I cannot ask for any of those communications, and they are not necessary. Do you now quote to me again those that struck you as pertinent; be as careful as you can. That will be enough."

I quoted as accurately as I could several of Carranza's private telegrams and was going on to his letters, when the president stopped me.

"That's enough," he said. "Quite enough." While he was reflecting I mentioned the mission of President Jordan and Moorfield Story.

"Keep them away," he said. "Don't let them come near me. I won't see them. Those pacifists make me feel warlike. You believe in Carranza, don't you?"

"As an honest man and a liberal," I said. "Not as a revolutionist."

He smiled, started to say something. "A revolution—" But he checked himself.

"What makes you so sure of Carranza?" he asked.

I related the indirect evidence I had, the incidents told in the last chapter, Douglas's openness about the Carranza letters. "And," I added, "I have looked the man in the face, as you should."

Wilson spoke of the difficulties of a meeting with the Mexican president as if he had thought of one. I spoke of the difficulties a president cooped up in the White House had in getting information. He nodded thoughtfully, and I reproached him. "Why didn't you let me see you yesterday? You knew I had been down there on Carranza's train and must have seen something of him and the facts and his feelings."

His answer gave me an idea that accounted for many things Wilson did, and explained other men, too.

"An executive," he said, "is a man of action. An intellectual—such as you and I," he smiled—"an intellectual is inexecutive. In an executive job we are dangerous, unless we are aware of our limitations and take measures to stop our everlasting disposition to think, to listen, to—not act. I made up my mind long ago, when I got into my first executive job, to open my mind for a while, hear everybody who came to me with advice, information—what you will—then, some day, the day when my mind felt like deciding, to shut it up and act. My decision might be right; it might be wrong. No matter. I would take a chance and do—something."

He laughed, rose, and escorted me out to the head of the stairs. There he paused and turned to me and said: "You have given me information, very valuable information, information which prevents a war."

I must have jerked with my joy. "Yes," he smiled, "there will be no war with Mexico. But when your card came in it suggested nothing. It was your message about misinformation that set me thinking: that after all you were just back from Carranza and might . . . I decided to reopen this, these"—he tapped his forehead, touched his ears—"and—and it was right for once. You had some facts I lacked."

I was shaking with the good news for Mexico; I blurted out a fair request in foolish words. "Well, now, Mr. President, won't you let me in every time when I see you are making a mistake and think I have information—"

"No, no, no," he laughed, and he laid his hand on my shoulder. "I cannot have you running into the White House every time I am making a mistake. You would be coming many times a day every day."

He pushed me down a stair, but I halted there out of reach and asked to amend my request. "Can't I come when it's an emergency and in my line?"

"Ah, that's different," he laughed. "If, with your name, you send the message that it's an emergency, I will see you."

He waved me out, and I went down to Messrs. Jordan and Story, and reported: "We, you and I between us, have stopped a war. We can go home." I told them my story—all that did not concern them personally, and they checked out, those two fine men. Dr. Jordan reported in his *Life* this incident, not exactly as it was, but as he got it from me.

XII

TO RUSSIA: A SECOND REVOLUTION

I spent the first two years of the war commuting between Washington and Mexico, Cuba and Porto Rico, the West Indies, a beautiful part of the world, out of the war zone, at peace, but concerned—unconsciously—as prizes of the conflict of empires. More and more I became aware that I was seeing, in those sunny lands, war in the making, the purposes and the processes of empire, and the only thing that could save the West Indies from conquest—a revolution in Europe. For the great war was a fight among the European conquerors to reduce the number of empires and to advance toward the decision as to which of them is finally to rule the world and bring the backward countries into our system.

I got around pretty much all over Mexico, realizing gradually that the Mexicans, the Indians, are an artistic people, like the Greeks, and that we Americans are so Roman, so moral, that any understanding between us is well-nigh impossible.

American employers could not make Mexicans work. They tried the American method, raising wages, only to see their labor quit earlier each week. When the peons earned enough to eke out their living on their tiny farms they quit. One man, Smith of Guadalajara, an American in charge of a silver mine which operated throughout the revolution, found the way. He taught them the tricks of a trade, the art of carpentering, mining, driving an engine. That fascinated them. Business, which is business to us, is a game to the Mexicans, who don't distinguish between work and play as we do. All is fun to them, or a bore. They enjoyed the revolution. They must enjoy everything or hate it and neglect it. And so in Cuba and in Porto Rico, where the Americans were striving against despair to teach the natives the idea of private property. It looked

741

to me as if man were born an artist and had to be made over into a profiteer. Those natives whom I saw suggested the idea that our "human nature," which we say you "can't change," has been changed in us and has to be changed all over the backward world to make it like us.

Anyhow the conflict between Mexico and the United States appeared to be inevitable, fundamental, and as pitiful as that between Greece and Rome. Poor Mexico, it is so rich! Unhappily for the Mexicans, their country is rich in natural resources which the world needs and which the Mexicans can't or won't develop, except as peons under slave-drivers.

It was to see what will happen to Mexico after the conquest (which President Wilson only postponed, I thought) that I went to Cuba, Porto Rico, San Domingo, Haiti. And, by the way, I went with the U.S. Commissioner to the Danish islands to witness their delivery by a Danish governor and a Danish man-o'-war to the United States under a president who was an anti-imperialist and a pacifist; he bought those islands for war uses—only. Men don't make empires, evidently, or wars, or tyrannies, any more than they corrupt their cities. They say in Cuba that we have corrupted the Cuban masters who have enslaved the Cuban people. Well, something corrupted them. And in Porto Rico you can see how it happens. The first Christians who landed there sought only land, but in that climate the conquerors could not themselves work so much land as they took. They "had to" take the people also to work the land. The early wars among the conquerors were, not for one another's lands, but for the slaves. And so we Americans are in there with our police to put down strikes, to make the natives work their country for us. One could see in Porto Rico that while what we think we want in Mexico is the oil, the mines, the plantations, what we will have to do is to force the playful, artful Mexican "children" (as we call them) to mass labor for use only, and for our use. The Mexican revolution was to save the Mexican people from our slow-growing but very promising culture. In vain, I think. We surround them, in Cuba, in Central America, and in the north. Our State Department does, and it must, govern Mexico as it regulated the Mexican revolution, in the interest of the same kind of American investors who have corrupted the United States.

President Wilson, who believed in the right of regulation and despised corrupting, compromising business men, protected Mexico from us as he protected us from Europe—for a while. He kept us out of war. Seeing something of him in this period, I felt that Woodrow Wilson was not only a well-grounded liberal of the old school of Jefferson; he was the strongest liberal whom we could have had in his place. He was liberalism personified, and when he failed liberalism failed. And he did fail. He did not understand Mexico or the Mexican revolution, and he did not understand the economics of his situation. He did invade Mexico a little; he blamed Carranza and the revolutionary leaders for not controlling a revolution, which is as uncontrollable as a war. He would have blamed himself, as the liberals blamed him, for letting us into the war; only radicals and philosophers realize the power of the forces that move men. I have told how the bosses of New Jersey, having tried all their usual temptations on young Governor Colby, asked what he wanted. They just had to get him, and all they needed to know was what his price was. So England sent man after man over here to get Wilson, till finally they found in Arthur Balfour a man, a liberal who could, as the president said, "talk his language," the liberal language, principles—bunk. Then Germany, unwittingly helping, of course, and the economic forces pressing upon him—then we went in with our leader.

That kept me at home long enough to feel the terror and the strain of the war and to remember that I had once expected it to explode in "the" revolution. And it did, at last, but most unexpectedly, in Russia. Radical theory looked for it in some highly developed capitalist system, such as that of Germany, Austria, Italy, France, or England. But no, it had come in a backward, half-developed capitalistic state, where, as in Mexico, the people were illiterate and labor unorganized. Organized labor is one check upon revolution, literacy another, apparently. But I answered this observation with the thought that Russia was only the beginning and that "the" revolution would soon spread all over Europe. My problem was to get to Russia, across or around those war fronts, past the secret service lines. Rather hopeless; my sole chance to go there for my purpose, to see the revolution, was Wilson. He would understand, but he was busy. I could not gain admission to him. This emergency was mine, not his or Mexico's.

Halted in the street by a passing carriage, I looked into it, and there was Charles R. Crane. I hailed him. Where was he going?

"To Russia," he said, quietly. "I am going to the State Department now to get a passport. Get in and come along."

I stepped into the carriage, and four or five days later we were on a Swedish steamship, bound for Stockholm and points east. The passenger list was long and mysterious. Trotzky was in the steerage with a group of revolutionists; there was a Japanese revolutionist in my cabin. There were a lot of Dutch hurrying home from Java, the only innocent people aboard. The rest were war messengers, two from Wall Street to Germany; and spies; and war business

"FROM RELIABLE SOURCES WE LEARN THAT
LINCOLN STEFFENS IS STILL IN EUROPE RUN-
NING A DAY NURSERY FOR REVOLUTIONS"
Cartoon by Art Young in *Good Morning*,
October 8, 1919

men; one war correspondent, William G. Shepherd. No tourists. Anxiety reigned, the first part of the voyage, to Halifax, the British port we had to make for inspection. I called on Trotzky and his friends, and we talked some, but—"Wait," they said; "let's wait till we get by Halifax." And that was the general sentiment. "Let's not make acquaintances; let's keep still and apart till after Halifax." Somebody knew and had passed the word. At Halifax we and the ship were searched, and we saw good cause for anxiety. The harbor was full of ships, German, Norwegian, Swedish—all sorts of ships that had not got by the search, which was indeed pretty thorough. Having gone through us once and given us the impression that that was the end, having given us time to bring out of hiding whatever we had to conceal, the British searched us again—and again, and yet again. And the British take command and order you about as if they really ruled the waves. They held us for a week or more, an anxious week during which everybody worried except the Wall Street messengers to Germany. They, with their trunkload of "bonds, etc." (we heard), were not inconvenienced. I asked one of them afterward, in a warm moment of confidence, how they got by, they of all people.

"Oh," it was explained, "when you are in the business you study it and you fix it."

So all but the professional guilty are in danger from the secret service as from any other police. War intensifies everything; it doesn't change anything. Suspicion, for example, becomes patriotic and the grafters patriots, and the reds, not the crooks and traitors, are the victims. The German box of "bonds," valuables, and information got by Halifax; but Trotzky was taken off and held for weeks—this though the United States recognized the new revolutionary Russian government, and the British had not yet decided not to. After Halifax that Swedish ship steamed far to the north, nearly to Iceland, and came down darkened into the war zone, where the German and the British ships were fighting. The passangers sat up one night, singing, drinking, playing boisterously —frightened—and the ship's officers fanned the fright. But the spies and the smugglers smiled, and the captain's eyes twinkled. Somehow I got the impression that there was some bunk about it all. That ship's passage across the war front was "fixed" with both sides, and the risk was only of an accident; some warship might collide with us or shoot without inquiry. We got safely across, saw sturdy Norway with its arctic evening, its blazing hot hotels, and its men speculating in ships, Sweden under the blazing sun of winter, Stockholm the beautiful; and we played around a bit with the American minister, Ira Nelson Morris, and with the people who go out and enjoy their winter sports till they are sun-blacked with the light which burns them two ways: directly from above and indirectly by the reflection from the hard snow and ice.

Then, our papers and pulls fixed, we traveled by train up the east coast of Sweden, Crane, Shepherd, and I, all night to the Russian frontier, sledded across it, surviving examinations, and so dropped down over some Finnish territory to Petrograd, till recently St. Petersburg, where we arrived at night in a wintry cold, deserted, grand station and were driven over vacant bumpy streets that felt like a battlefield—to our dark, cautious, whispering hotels.

We were among the first outsiders to get to the Russian Revolution, and as for the insiders, Lenin had but just arrived; Trotzky was delayed at Halifax; and others who were to lead that revolution were still to come.

XIII

THE RUSSIAN REVOLUTION

THE great leaders of the Russian revolutionary movement were not in Russia when the Russian Revolution began; they were in exile; and the lesser leaders who were there did not expect it to happen. Somebody did. On the roofs of buildings that commanded the main thoroughfares, the grand boulevards and squares, we found still standing the machine guns planted to deal with the revolution that the revolutionists did not know was going to happen. And we had a look at the plans drawn to put down mobs of people who did not know they were going to rise in revolt. Government blue prints. Government preparations. It was the government that anticipated, prepared for, started, the revolution in Russia, as in Mexico.

Getting to the scene so soon after the beginning, we had—Crane, Shepherd, and I—the opportunity I craved to find out exactly how a revolution is made. Shepherd also had been in Mexico. Crane had seen the world. We were not to be distracted by the outrages, the inefficiency, the confusion, of such a crisis. Crane had old friends to see; Shepherd, a regular correspondent, had to cover the news; I, unattached, was absolutely free to pursue any line of inquiry I pleased. Our first job was to catch up on the history of the events that had occurred while we were at sea. We worked together; Shepherd and I shared one room, and the moment we were settled, we set forth in those menacing, empty, apparently frightened streets to call with Crane on his old friend, Miliukoff, who was the head of the "provisional government," to pay a visit to our genial Ambassador, ex-Governor (of Missouri) David R. Francis, who had achieved the recognition by the United States of the new Russian government, and to see other friends of Crane's, mostly associates of Miliukoff: reformers in the American sense, who had taken the resignation of the Czar, his throne, and the crown, but not—not the power. They all told us their several stories, fascinating stories, too, of personal adventure, of Rasputin, of the street fighting, of the victory of democracy, and of their plans. But other correspondents arrived or were found, like Dosch-Fleurot, already at work. We hired an interpreter to read us the Russian papers, and we went out ourselves among the people, to the Soviets, and, I remember, Bill Shepherd suddenly began to laugh.

The revolution was still going on. The Miliukoff government, which our government recognized, was not the actual government. The stinking mob of delegates in the All-Russian Soviet was the government. It was milling around in confusion, that revolutionary democracy, but it was conscious of power and was organizing to seize the throne. We pointed it out to our ambassador.

"There, Governor, there is the real thing. That is what you should watch. There is where you should send your observers for information and for liaison."

He shook his head, and Bill Shepherd laughed again.

"No," said the governor. "Our relations are with the government. I cannot recognize, we can't have anything to do with, the Soviet."

"Not even for information?"

"No. You boys cover that, and I'd like to hear about it, of course. But I cannot recognize its existence."

And as if to illustrate our disconnection with reality, we were all summoned to the front window and finally to the front door of the embassy one day to meet a mob shouting: "Muni!"

"Muni! Muni!" the governor repeated. "Who or what is Muni?"

We all wondered a bit till Shepherd, I think it was, guessed. "Why, that must be Mooney, Tom Mooney, that they are asking about." And he had to explain to the ambassador that Tom Mooney was a labor man convicted on false evidence of exploding a bomb in a preparedness parade in San Francisco at the beginning of the war. President Wilson, feeling the world-wide concern, had besought the governor of California to retry Mooney; labor the world over was making a martyr of him.

The ambassador put off the red mob; he would report to his

government and see. He was busy. He was busy with the new Russian government which the revolution was leaving high and dry, to go its own revolutionary way, unrecognized. Its little leaders had their own history to make, and we had to hear and report it if we could. History? How can you get history in the making, on the spot, as it happens? There were several histories all going on together, unconnected, often contradictory narratives that met and crossed, and—they were all "history." We heard aplenty of them; we must have missed many more. Nobody could, nobody will, ever hear them all. History is impossible. Putting together the stories I heard, the stories of the old government, of the new government, of odd witnesses, of soldiers, sailors, workers, of the Soviets, I lay, not the history, but my history, straight like this. It is not the truth; it is my compact version of some truth and some lies that counted like facts; for rumor is a revolutionist and a historian.

The Czar's ministers, busy with the war, knew that the troops at the front were not warlike. They did not hate the Germans; they fraternized with them when they could; and meanwhile they suffered from lack of supplies, food, clothing, and ammunition. Evil reports of the evil conditions were leaking back to the people in the country, in the towns, in the cities; and the spies heard some exaggerated but not wholly untrue stories of catastrophes, corruption, and disloyalty. The people heard that ammunition for the guns on the right was sent to the left and that the ammunition to fit the guns on the left went to misfits on the right. They heard, and, true or false, they believed, that by force of bribery high up, the Russian high command had let the German high command actually direct the movements of Russian armies. In one battle the Russians had been deliberately marched into a swamp and there drowned and slaughtered. One can recognize there one of Hindenburg's victories. There were many such stories, some of them blaming Rasputin, some blaming individual generals. Call them the usual wild rumors of war, as you will; the ministers of the Czar in prison told us they were believed by the people, who meanwhile were as hungry as they were afraid.

The ministers felt they must do something; a revolution was due; and they must deal with it in advance. They decided to handle the menace as they had handled the threatening discontent in other crises, notably in 1905. They would get the people out into the streets of St. Petersburg and shoot the fear of God into them, as we do in strikes.

Starting with the bread lines, they held back the bread. The women, children, and old men assembled and formed in queues leading up to the police stations for bread. One day there was no bread. A lie: the bread was found rotting afterward in the cellars of the stations. The line formed at three, four o'clock, grew all morning, and waited—all that day, that night, the next day. Men came to relieve the waiting, weary women and children. The police jostled them, moving the line here, there, and back till the rumor spread that "there was something wrong." More men came out, more women; the police came out and were more active. Three days this continued till all the people of the multitudinous city were out on the streets.

Ready! The Cossacks were summoned. These most loyal mounted troops did come out, and they rode in and out through the packed masses of men and women, but it was noted that as they rode, gently, among the people, they did not draw their swords or their knouts. On the contrary they moved carefully, and they used the polite Russian word, "Pajalista," which means "If you please" or "By your leave." Cossacks saying "Please"! The crowd whispered, "The Cossacks are with us. The Cossacks!" And they understood that this meant that all the soldiers were with them. So far had the sufferings of the troops at the front affected the army, the main support of the government. Not propaganda.

The government was making a mistake.

There were other supports of the government, but there were other mistakes of the government—Rasputin, for example. The Czar's government looked like, and was supposed to be, an autocracy, but it was not a literal dictatorship, any more than an American boss-ship is. The boss has backers, and his backers are and must be the chief special interests that pay for, own, and direct his power. A boss is an agent. So with the Czar, who may seem to have granted at will privileges—oil sites, mines, franchises, contracts, etc.—but who had to distribute his grants to the proper people. Rasputin, the queer priest, was a simple soul. He probably thought, like the Russian people, that literally the Czar ruled and that, having the Czar's confidence, he could literally sell a bishopric to whom he pleased; he could grant a contract to a contractor not in the ring, a title of nobility to an ignoble person, bankers' privileges to other than bankers. Rasputin, by selling out to his personal favorites privileges needed to bolster the throne, cut off and undermined the sovereign system of corruption in Russia. The church, the nobility, the financiers—all the upper classes hated him and withdrew their support from the Czar. Rasputin was shot and poisoned, but by a prince, and the actual rulers of the country buried him and defied the Czar to punish the assassins. The Czar was suspended in the air when his ministers were making their big mistakes with the army and the people.

In other words, the conditions for the explosion were there; the causes of the revolution were there. And they, the rulers, made a revolution. Not propaganda, I repeat. Revolutionary propaganda, which stable governments suppress with the violence of fear, can only prepare the discontented minds of a people to speak and act when the time comes, after the mob has been formed and the government mistake has started—something; as we shall see.

On the afternoon of the third day of the bread riot—which was no riot—out in the great square in front of the Moscow railroad station an infantry officer was trying to command and incite his men to shoot across the open into the quiet mob. They would not. A student standing by jeered at the officer, who, in a rage, thrust the student through. A Cossack in line on the opposite side of the square saw this; he put spurs to his horse, charged from the ranks, and drawing his sword as he rode, he cut that officer down. There was a cry: "The soldiers *are* with us!" and then there was another cry: "The revolution! The revolution is on!"

That was the call of propaganda. The people knew what those words meant as the Germans knew what *der Tag* meant. If some one had cried, "Loot!" or "Bread!" "Kill and burn!" that crowd might have become a mob just the same, but it might only have sacked St. Petersburg. It was ripe for anything and any suggestion, but there had been many years of propaganda in Russia, all sorts of teachings which had but one phrase in common: "The revolution." That word, naturally, was the one that leaped to men's lips, and it means something big, hard, serious, slow. The mob moved with it, not against the troops; and the troops moved with it, not to put down the mob. Soldiers and people united into one mob with a direction. There was fighting—not much, not nearly so much as there was later in the October revolution when there were leaders. The leaderless mob of the spring did some looting, very little, and mostly of provision shops, for food. The people were hungry. The fiercest fighting was in the army barracks when the street troops returned in the spirit and with the name of the revolution and were resisted by the cool, normal, loyal companies not yet in it.

The Russian Revolution, started thus in the metropolis, was spread by the world word, "The revolution," which gave point, program, and an objective to the fire that burned through the city out into the country up to the Russian front, which called it as good tidings across to the Germans, who hailed it as peace and sat down with the Russian peasants to rejoice that the war was over and "the" world revolution had begun. "Begun," they thought. It had begun in Russia and would sweep the world, armies, governments, the "system."

The propaganda had gone all over the world. All countries, especially in Europe, had been hearing for years about "the revolution," and the propagandists had long been teaching all the peoples who would listen to them what to do when the time came. Now that the time was come the propaganda began to work, but not in the countries where the revolution had not been started. The Germans were stirred, but not moved; so with the Italians, the French. The propaganda could not, it cannot, "make" a revolution. The propaganda worked only in Russia, but the use of it there justifies revolutionary preparedness just as preparedness for war is justified by the event. In Russia, after the start, at the word, all men began to function as they had all more or less consciously anticipated. The Czar in his train quit the front to come home to meet his generals and ministers and together put down the revolution. The democrats and liberals met and agreed on a course to pursue, now that they had their chance. They took train to meet the Czar to tell him all was over, to request his resignation, and legally, regularly, to receive power. Lomonosoff, the director of the railways, told me how the railroad men and the telegraphers all became revolutionary and, under his direction, drew on the Czar's train, hindered the trains of the generals and the ministers, and let the new government pass. They were careful, those railroad men; they were covering their tracks; but every time the

Czar's train passed a junction, a wreck happened behind it to cut off retreat. And there were wrecks or something behind and ahead of the generals' trains and the old ministers' train. The way was clear ahead only for the new government and for the Czar, who heard of the approaching meeting and tried to back out, in vain. He was surrounded by wrecks, except ahead. Those railroad and wire men managed the maneuvers of those trains all that night till, quietly, with everybody else sidetracked, the Czar and the democrats met. The rest was easy. The Czar "signed there"; he was made a prisoner; and the democrats returned with their precious paper and their lawful right to form the provisional government, which their propaganda, which their years of study of other liberal governments, had prepared them to create out of the chaos. When we saw them they were writing on paper a constitution, a description of a representative democracy in the republican form, which would cut out and correct the worst abuses of old Russia and some of the defects of our western republics but would maintain otherwise intact the capitalist system. Those fine, honest, highly educated gentlemen never understood that our liberalism is only an attempt to moderate the workings of a system which was then at war. Their culture, their propaganda, had never attempted to visualize what might be done if the system itself were wiped out and they had a clean slate on which to draw another system. They were reformers about to reform something that had gone past reform and reformers.

The new government of Miliukoff and the good men associated with him had not studied revolutions. They did not know that this one had only begun. They thought it was all over, and they functioned in the air, while the revolution flowed on, turgid, underneath them. The people were functioning, and they acted also upon propagandas. Untaught by the Czar, illiterate, vague, they had heard of democracy, socialism, anarchism, and many other teachings, all of which came up now to confuse them in their literal simplicity. The idea of democracy prevailed, but they thought it meant that they, the people, all of them, were to govern. I was to see pure democracy for once in my life.

Shepherd and I, sitting before the fire we had to bribe to get, would hear a sound we came to recognize, a sound as of cattle coming along the street. "There they go again," Shepherd would grumble, and looking out the window, we would see them, the herd of them, silent, not shouting, not singing, not even talking, only their hooves on the stones resounding. We hated it; the cold in humid Petrograd froze through our clothes, and it was March. The arctic winter was still heavy and dark upon us. Hunching into our overcoats, we would take some Russian and go down to interview the mob. You can interview a mob; it's a solid mass all of one mind, one mood, concentrated, going somewhere, up to some one thing. We would pull one individual, any one, out of the herd and ask our question; he would come to, wake up as from sleep or a daze, and give us the answer any other individual in that mob could have given, vague, but clear enough.

"Where you going?"

"Don't know."

"What do you mean? A million of you out here going somewhere, and you don't know where? Nonsense! What's the matter now?"

"Oh, nothing, only we heard there was something wrong in Petrograd, and we came out to attend to it."

That was democracy, simple, stupid, literal, but conscientious. That was government by the people in Russia.

The night before Miliukoff fell they came out thus. There was something wrong with Miliukoff, and they were out to attend to it. We shuddered along to the square in front of Miliukoff's headquarters, and we learned bit by bit that when the German and the Russian soldiers were fraternizing over the revolution, the German high command put their soldiers up to telling the Russians about the secret treaties for the division of the world and its loot.

"And Russia has one, too," the Germans said. "You get Constantinople."

The Russians could not believe that. Their cause was just, somehow. The Germans bade them investigate. "You have the revolution; you have the archives. Look into them, and you'll see." The word was passed to the soldier and sailor delegates going to Petrograd for the Soviet. They started an inquiry, and sure enough, Russia had a secret treaty with her allies, and it was rumored that Miliukoff had said that, yes, we were to get Constantinople, and we wanted it. Russia must have a warm water port as an outlet all the year round. The mob was out, masses of them, to get it from Miliukoff himself. He was "a nice man," "a gentleman," and they would hear him first.

They stood there, that packed mob, as usual, silent; and we stood with them till after midnight; then some one reported that the minister would not speak, and we went home and to bed. The next morning we returned to the square, and there was the mob, as packed as cattle, waiting on Mr. Miliukoff. The correspondents went off in groups to see the minister, to cover other points. Once we heard that there was shooting in front of the leading hotel for foreigners, and the whole group of reporters left me to cover that, the news of that day. I was fascinated by this quiet, patient mob which took itself and its sovereignty so seriously. Speaking had begun, here and there, to small circles of the crowd. A man near me took off his coat, folded it, and stood on it to speak. Somebody told me what the man was saying, and I recognized it as German propaganda. I asked my volunteer interpreter to sound the people near us: why did they permit German propaganda? At the end of a long, serious Russian conversation he said that his people justified the pro-German on the principle of free speech.

"Then," I said, "your people don't understand the difference between liberty and license."

He reported my remark, and again there was a long, a very long, general discussion, which the interpreter summed up.

"True," he said. "We don't know the difference between liberty and—what is it?—license. In fact, we never heard of license. We would like you to tell us what is liberty and what is license. And what is the difference?"

"The distinction in America is very important," I said, trying to think quick of a definition, which came to me at last. "Liberty," I defined, "liberty is the right of any proper person—I mean anybody in a good social position—to say anything whatsoever that everybody believes."

The interpreter translated, and I expected his hearers to laugh. But no, they threshed out my definition in all sobriety at great length with never a smile, and the conclusion interpreted was: "Yes. We understand that. And now what is that other thing— license?"

"License," I said, "is not a right. It is an impertinence. License is the impudence of some son-of-a-gun, who has no right to live on earth anyhow, to say some damned thing that is true."

Now they would laugh? Wrong. They considered my definition of license at greater length than the other, debated it; they seemed to dispute it hotly, but they finally all agreed on a conclusion, which I got thus:

"They ask me to tell the Gospodin that they understand and that if my definitions are right, then it is license we Russians believe in and not liberty."

That night, late, Mr. Miliukoff came out on his balcony and addressed that sober mob of literal people, and he told them— that honest man confessed—that, yes, he was for the secret treaty; that the Russians must have a warm water port through which to pass, themselves and their goods, back and forth, the year round. In perfect silence the people heard; they stood as if in thought or in sorrow a moment, then turned and melted away. There was no protest, no act; but the next morning, when we called on the minister, he was packing up. He had fallen. Kerenski was to form a government. The people believed in the great orator, and the people ruled.

UPPER: ST. BASIL'S CATHEDRAL, MOSCOW (MARGARET BOURKE-WHITE). LOWER LEFT: WILLIAM C. BULLITT (COPYRIGHT LEDGER PHOTO SERVICE). LOWER RIGHT: ALEXANDER KERENSKI (N.Y. WORLD NEWS SERVICE).

XIV

KERENSKI

ALEXANDER KERENSKI, the Russian orator, like Madero, the Mexican agitator, came to the leadership of revolution because he expressed the feelings—fear, faith, hope—of the people. He was, however, like Miliukoff, the choice of a committee of liberals, and the mob knew that, and when Crane, Shepherd, and I called on the new, emotional leader, he complained that he was powerless. He could but follow; he could not lead; and he was astonished. The throne was nothing but a chair. I had never heard a man express with such searching frustration as Kerenski did his distress at the emptiness of "the palace of the Czars." Kerenski in Russia explained Madero in Mexico, and Madero, Kerenski. They were the first leaders of revolution.

Not an executive and with no plan of his own, Kerenski did what Madero did. He turned for advice to his committee and to other prominent leaders, whose ideas had been formed in moderate, reform movements under the Czar. He was for a republic, a representative democracy, which in his mind was really a plutocratic aristocracy. Meanwhile he was to carry on the war. These were not the ideas of the mob in the street. The people were confused, too; they did not know what a republic was; democracy, as we have seen, was a literal impossibility; but they were definite and clear about peace and no empire. So Kerenski, like Madero, represented the people emotionally, but not in ideas, and like Miliukoff, he felt the revolution, which he named public opinion, sweeping him along and passing him by.

Kerenski could not even manage that public opinion. There were other orators trying to do that, and the people listened to them as they did to Kerenski. The Russians heard everybody, anybody, heard and believed and—were lost in the conflict of counsels.

757

They were making progress, however; they were congealing, as one could see a pure democracy must. They moved on to a representative democracy with Kerenski's government left out. Crane described Kerenski's dilemma of isolation to Governor Francis, who wired long explanations and appeals to Washington. Crane himself was cabling for understanding of the situation and patience with Kerenski, who, nevertheless, was getting mad demands from all the allies and their representatives to go on with the war, to strike with a battle, if not for victory, then hard enough to keep the Germans engaged on the Russian front. And Kerenski was doing his best to represent—the foreigners, at home and abroad, in St. Petersburg and at the front. It was a comic and also a tragic show, that provisional government's efforts, at our behest, to force a people who, newborn to freedom, as they thought, interested in a revolution full of possibilities—land, liberty, justice, and permanent peace with all the world—to carry on a war that they were through with against their very good friends, the German workers and peasants. The dumb mob, listening to the appeals to them to fight, were dazed; and they were moved. They seemed to wish to do whatever they were asked to do, but they would trudge away from the war propaganda to go and hear about peace and democracy, socialism or anarchism. They could not be stampeded.

They could not be stampeded, partly because every call was countered by some opposite call, but it was mostly because they had formed a center, a nucleus, of government. Here again pre-revolutionary propaganda and practice had taught them something to do. They had chosen representatives early.

Having no wards and no idea of geographical representations, they met in the only groups that they knew anything about: in their unions, clubs, associations, regiments. These existing organizations had no idea of numerically equal representation; they chose men and women at random to go and represent them at soviets; one union sent three men, another a score of men and women, another one woman; one regiment sent back twenty-four soldiers, another a trainload, a battleship a crew of ten or two hundred—just as it happened. These delegates came with their credentials and with their wives, women, friends, and swarming in to the Soviet, they organized and went to work. They laid out their baggage, food, beds, and began the debate which was constant, interminable. And while the delegates debated inside, the masses of the mob stood outside to hear the conclusions, judge of the decrees, and move off in herds to report or to execute them. The Russian democracy in the making was a sight—and a smell.

The first time I went to the immense hall where the first Soviet met I was halted, as by a blow, by the stink of the mob inside, and I could see the steam rising, as from a herd of cattle, over those sweating, debating delegates. They lived there. Once inside they stayed inside. They cooked and they ate there, and you saw men sleeping in corners and around the edges of the hall. No hours were kept. When delegates were tired, they lay down, leaving the majority to carry on; when they were rested, they woke to keep the endless, uninterrupted debate going. But they did come to conclusions, that mob of Man, and their conclusions were a credit to the species.

The first law passed by that representative, stinking mass put them ahead of our clean, civilized leading nations. It was against capital punishment. As if Man in the natural state wished not to kill. And the second law was against war and empire: the Russian people should never conquer and govern any other people.

It was while we were watching the spectacle of this primitive representative assembly with its ring of common people striving for peace that we Americans were invited to a tea or a luncheon by Hugh Walpole, the English writer. He and other English gentlemen had come to Petrograd to help restrain the revolution and keep the Russians at war. A standardized Englishman, he did not give us any reasons, and he did not ask us whether we would help and how; he told us what we were to do. No doubt he assumed that we were gentlemen, like him, and would function naturally against the revolution, the people, and peace. Well, we were not gentlemen—I mean I was not. Looking at him and looking at that stinking, earnest, high-aspiring Russian mob, it seemed to me that the mob was the gentleman, not the British novelist-lobbyist. Surely the hope of the race steamed up out of the Soviet, not from Hugh Walpole and his crew of instinctive imperialists. They went to Kerenski; I went back to the mob at the Soviet, where Russian sovereignty was coming into being.

Watching that mass meeting of delegates was like seeing the historical development of human government out of chaos. One could see that there was good will in men, plenty of it, and that, left to itself, its ideals and purposes were noble. Contempt for man, pessimism, melted away. Primitive, untaught men are good. The laws that they could agree upon were noble, and the delegates instinctively wished to make their acts representative. When they were approaching a decision on something in doubt, the leaders of the debate would send out an orator or a leader to explain it to the mob in waiting and ask for, almost pray for, its approval. One day we saw a speaker haranguing the crowds, and we heard that he was the third man sent out to present some proposition. "The others could not make them see it," they told us.

"How do they show their opposition?" I asked.

"Only by silence. They just stand dumb, but we know."

But they had another recourse. A mob in doubt would turn away, and leaving one crowd to stay and watch, the committee of hundreds would march off across the city, picking up other crowds to go and stand in front of the palace of the Czar's mistress, where "a man named Lenin," seeing them, would come out and speak. He spoke briefly, in a quiet tone of voice, so low that few could hear him. But when he had finished, those who had heard moved away; the mass closed up; the orator repeated his speech, and so for an hour or two the man named Lenin would deliver to the ever-changing masses his firm, short, quiet message. The day I got close enough to hear him, the crowd evidently had been troubled by the inactivity of Kerenski and some advice to them to go home and work, not to give all their time to their self-government. My interpreter repeated Lenin's manifolded speech afterward, as follows:

"Comrades, the revolution is on. The workers' revolution is on, and you are not working. The workers' and peasants' revolution means work, comrades; it does not mean idleness and leisure. That is a bourgeois ideal. The workers' revolution, a workers' government, means work, that all shall work; and here you are not working. You are only talking.

"Oh, I can understand how you, the people of Russia, having been suppressed so long, should want, now that you have won to power, to talk and to listen to orators. But some day, soon, you—we all—must go to work and do things, act, produce results—food and socialism. And I can understand how you like and trust and put your hope in Kerenski. You want to give him time, a chance, to act. He means well, you say. He means socialism. But I warn you he will not make socialism. He may think socialism, he may mean socialism. But, comrades"—and here he began to burn—"I tell you Kerenski is an intellectual; he *cannot* act; he can talk; he cannot *act*. But," quietly again, "you will not believe this yet. You will take time to give him time, and meanwhile, like Kerenski, you will not work. Very well, take your time. But"—he flamed—"when the hour strikes, when you are ready to go back yourselves to work and you want a government that will go to work and not only think socialism and talk socialism and mean socialism—when you want a government that will do socialism, then—come to the Bolsheviki."

So that was the Bolshevik propaganda we had been hearing about and been steered away from. The cultivated lady who read the Russian newspapers to us correspondents would not read the Bolshevik paper. Any other paper, any other party, but she would not let the Bolshevik sheet into her house. It was Bill Shepherd who discovered the Bolsheviks to us and to the American papers, and he, I think, was caught by the word. At the sound of it he was fascinated.

"Just the word," he shouted in glee. "Bolsheviki! It sounds like all that the world fears. Bolsheviki! We must find out enough about the Bolsheviki to carry the word. Can't you see it in the headlines? It will stick. It will crackle in everybody's mouth, ear, and brain. Bolsheviki!" He rejoiced in it, and he cabled it, with a story of the party. The word meant nothing—"majority"; the Bolshevik party was not a majority; it was a small minority party, but it was a left party that was most demandful. And that's what Bolshevik meant to the Russian lady and came to mean all over the world, the party that demanded the most, all, and would take nothing less. And Lenin personified the Bolsheviki, and his speech expressed the patience, determination, and wisdom, practical and ideal, of the small minority which won finally in October.

I could not stay to see the second, so-called real, revolution, but I grasped enough to hold the key to it and to what followed— "the seizure of power" by the Bolsheviki that saved the Russian Revolution from repeating the history of the Mexican and all the known revolutions. The milling herd of the All-Russian Soviet, both inside and out in the street, never had a majority in command. It legislated, as we have seen, well; but there was no other action. Its laws aimed deep, but nothing happened, and there was much to do. The pressure to act was acute, and it grew as the hunger and the threats of war and famine increased. But split up into parties to begin with, the divisions increased, and the inactivity. Men of liberal minds, radicals, socialists, democrats, have wondered since how that democracy happened to go so straight to a dictatorship. I think I understand, not only how that happened, but that it had to happen, that it always will happen.

Think of a herd of wild cattle, restless, troubled, sensing danger. They mill and mill, round and round, as those Russians did, looking for a direction in which to stampede. Because those people were in earnest and in fear, as they debated they could not compromise; they split their several minority parties or groups into smaller, not larger, groups, and went on milling. You could see —I mean that I could see—that there could be no majority and that some one minority had to win and lead the whole herd off in some one direction, adopt, all, one plan, and so throw up one minority government that would rule the whole.

Now the minority that decided which degree of the circle was to be taken, the Bolsheviki, was not a unit. They presented a united front; they appeared to be a unit; but those of us who were interested in them knew that they also had debates and disagreements that were intense and lasting. But they had a man, that man Lenin, who could and who did always, finally, close the debate and command action, united and planned. They had a dictator, and the dictator had a plan. That's why the Bolsheviki came into power, not because they were the nearest right (or, if you please, the nearest left), but because they were the nearest ready. Lenin's speech had the idea. He knew that a time would come when the mob would tire of indecision and not only let Kerenski fall, but themselves ask for the czar they were used to, a ruler; and he made his propaganda and prepared his organization and his plans for that day, which he, a mob psychologist, would choose, to "seize power" (his phrase). Lenin had studied; he knew his history.

I remember somebody said, as a joke, but with some truth in it, that the high commands in the war, on all the fronts, carried Baedeker's guidebooks in their hands like tourists. Lenin and his revolutionary staff carried in their hands the history of the French Revolution. I heard disputes of strategy settled by references to the turns of that and other revolutions. But the historical lesson I got out of this was that these men had marked well, and so they avoided repeating, the mistakes made in other revolutions. They knew that they would have sometime at the ebb of the democratic movement, when the people were giving up in despair—they would have to take the throne, by force if necessary, to carry on the revolution.

This I saw from afar. I left for home in May, but I carried my key to the news, and the perspective of distance and freedom from the confusion of details was an advantage for a while. Anyhow I was not surprised by the events there. I understood it when the pure democracy of Russia peaked into a dictatorship, called "the dictatorship of labor," as it was and is, but also, in fact, the dictatorship of one man.

XV

KERENSKI TO WILSON

I QUIT Russia to carry a verbal message from Kerenski to Wilson. Charles R. Crane asked me to. He and the American ambassador had cabled, as Kerenski had, in vain; they could not make the president understand that public opinion reigned in Russia and that the new government had no power to do what the allies wished. Kerenski could not with all his eloquence inspire the Russians to fight Germany, and with all his appearance of power he could not force them to. Yes, yes, he would try, but he knew he would fail. It was an old story to us; Kerenski was forever explaining it to his callers.

One day when we were in the palace, Crane turned from the orator to me to say that he and Kerenski and the ambassador wished that I would go to Washington and tell the president just how it was and what Kerenski thought Wilson might do. It was a good deal to ask of me. I was intensely interested in the course as well as the spectacle of the Revolution. But I, and I alone, was unattached and free to go, and I was of no use there. I considered; we talked it over with Governor Francis. Shepherd, my roommate, said he would cry if I left him all alone there in the cold red terror; but he laughed and laughed. Crane said I could travel on the royal train across Siberia with the new Russian ambassador to the United States, Bakhmetieff, and his staff, and see what was going on out there. I consented, and my first reward was the instructions I got from Kerenski: his message to Wilson.

There were two interviews at different times, but they covered the same ground, and they merge in my memory as one cry. Kerenski couldn't force the fighting; he wasn't a dictator or a czar; he wasn't even a government. "Tell the president that there really is a public opinion in Russia now and that that public opinion rules." The old stuff. But then came some news. Public opinion in Russia might be directed, Kerenski thought, but not by him. The president might steer it back to the war—he and the allies, if Wilson could manage the allies.

"The secret treaties are the nub of the situation," Kerenski said. "Ever since the Russian workers, peasants, and soldiers learned from the Germans at the front that there were secret treaties, showing that we, the allies, also were out for conquest, they won't fight. If, then, the president could call a public conference in some conspicuous place like London and abrogate the secret treaties, I might get our people to go on with the war. But the conference and the act of tearing up those treaties must be so open, so conspicuous, the voice of the allies must be so loud and clear that it will carry to the remotest village in Russia. My voice won't be heard so far. Let the president picture it. When the Russian army heard from the German army that this was a war of conquest, they broke ranks, millions of them; they went home; and in a million places they planted the belief that we were fighting, not to make the world safe for democracy, not for justice, not against empire, but for—just what the Germans were at war for. Nobody but President Wilson can answer that German charge and destroy that belief in the simple minds of the Russian peasants."

I thought, and I think Kerenski knew, that the Russian people not only were against empire and the imperial secret treaties, but were for peace and for the revolution which was to give them land and liberty; but I promised to deliver his message, and he promised, meanwhile, to go to the front and make a warlike demonstration. An American correspondent—Jack Reed, I think it was—told me how Kerenski did his part. He went to the front, and when the soldiers there said it was no use to fight, that the war was over, he said that their allies, English, American, French, and Italian, did not understand this, they were still at war, and were begging for help. With his magnetic eloquence Kerenski appealed to them not to go back on their old allies.

"But we have no ammunition," the soldier delegates pleaded on one front.

Startled by this likely truth, Kerenski begged them nevertheless to make an attack, just as a demonstration of good faith, and the delegates said they would talk it over. The next day a committee appeared and said all right; they would attack; they would not make a feint, but a charge. "Yes," said Kerenski, "club your rifles and go in." "No," they answered, "we have agreed to leave the useless guns behind and go in unarmed. Maybe that will show the allies."

I don't know how to verify this; it may be only one of those queer, incredible tales that came so often from the front. But the story this correspondent told me had it that some twenty thousand volunteers did make an attack for Kerenski on that front and were slaughtered—just to enable Kerenski to report it to us.

The provisional government came down to the station to see off on the Czar's own train Backmetieff and his grand mission of some fifty men and women, across Russia and Siberia—across Asia, to the Pacific Ocean, an eight- or ten- or twelve-day journey. We were short of provisions, but Lomonosoff, director of railways, was on board. He was a famous amateur cook and a knower of cooks. He told us how he spied a poor devil in a huddle of refugees on the railroad station, went up, and pointing his finger at him, said, "Are not you a cook?" The man sprang to his feet and saluted. He was a cook; he had a record; and Lomonosoff took him. "He is our cook." Lomonosoff, a jolly round belly of a man, and this cook gathered our food along the way, and we fed well. We had ptarmigan and other game; we had the best the stripped country could find, all well cooked. I felt that we lived high. But Lomonosoff and the cook fretted and were not satisfied till we crossed the line into China, and after the first stop we were proudly served with some pork. No more game, no more delicious ptarmigan. Pork!

A monotonous but a very busy railroad journey we had. Backmetieff and his economists, diplomats, industrial engineers, and—all, we were preparing for the work of that mission to America with a thoroughness like that of President Wilson's organization under Colonel House and Walter Lippmann later for the peace without victory and conquest. And the result was the same—nothing. I spent my time taking from each man on that train his own individual experience in the revolution. Lomonosoff's was the best; it was on the train that he described to me, with drawings, time tables, and maps, how the railroad men and telegraphers moved the Czar's, this same train, to ultimate capture and the Czar's abrogation. But each of all the other stories added some details and some light to the picture I had of the fall of the old government, the rise of the new government, and the release of the people, who were still carrying on the revolution—as we could see from the train. At every stop, where there was time, we, several of us, gathered up the stories of the revolution in that region, and what struck me was that the same course of events occurred everywhere. At the word, "The revolution is on," the mobs rose; they did not pillage, but they drove out the old, local government, let a new government take the offices, but went right on, those people, to literal, democratic, mob rule. Soviets were formed everywhere, and the debate, the endless debate, began, with the delegates and the crowds whirling in a herdlike circle. Minorities everywhere, no majority anywhere; but the Bolsheviki always a unit, the only one, with a plan, the same old plan to seize power and set up literal socialism, the dictatorship of the proletariat in the sense of the soldiers, peasants, and workmen, in a soviet of delegates, chosen not geographically, but by unions, by associations, by groups. Sometimes I was sure this was the result of propaganda; there certainly was instructed organization all along the line; but sometimes I felt that it was all a sign of some instinct of the Russian people that made them all—clear across Russia and Siberia—behave in the same way. All I feel sure of now, after the program is carried out, is that the Bolsheviki had a plan and that everywhere they had trained leaders to act together on the instant the wired instructions came to them. The Bolshevik preparation for the revolution, the discipline, program, and propaganda, was perfect, but it was based in part on the psychology of the Russian people.

The Bolsheviki knew, for example, that our train carried a democratic, bourgeois, not a revolutionary, mission. Crowds might gather to see us pass, and there were some cheers for Backmetieff, but there were some shots fired at us, too. "Bolsheviki," the ambassador would mutter. Once a troop train of soldiers and sailors, halted to let us pass, raked us with rifle fire. "Bolsheviki." You might think that our journey was an exciting adventure. It was not; it was too long, too monotonous, too like the steppes we passed over, all one tedious reel. No scenery, none. The last two days I was car-sick. The glimpses we had of frontier China cheered us up, but the only joy was to get to Vladivostok and end that stage of the journey.

Vladivostok, a crude young city of the future, was politically only a larger picture of all the places we had seen on our way—a provisional government, like the one our mission represented, sitting not very pretty, over a coagulating democracy. We got news again, instructions from Petrograd and from the west. But all that is left to me of the scene there is a picture of that moblike people expressing themselves, not only politically, but culturally. And how? In a burst of theaters. There were some twenty or more little theaters all over the city, in all sorts of buildings, halls, rooms. I remembered then that we had had a flowering of the drama in Petrograd, too, and in towns all across the continent. What it means I don't know, but that people, released, free, self-governing, flowered into theaters, and theaters of players, too. Some of them had no audiences. Only players, all players, but, spectators or no, the Russians at that time and since have displayed a passion for the theater as a place to play in, to act in and make a show, a child's play of life.

From Vladivostok we had to cross to Japan to catch our Pacific Ocean liner, but there would be diplomatic courtesies to exchange —a nuisance. We arrived at Sakai late at night, and I saw dimly a common sight—the unloading of a boat at a dock—that was beautiful. Just columns of tiny Japanese women, all clean and each marked, daintily, with the letters of her owner or renter, carrying out our cargo. The special train we boarded looked small, but neat, clean, and beautiful, and early the next morning, when I lifted the curtain of my window to look out, I saw—beauty. Rice fields, with mountains in the distance behind them, a familiar picture. And so at Tokio: beauty, taste—Japan is a thing of beauty. I had never imagined that any civilized country, any civilization, could be so lovely as Japan, and I corrected my picture of Greece, old Greece, which may have been something like Japan. That, I thought, is the way all civilized countries will look when every detail of their life is brought up into harmony with their culture.

We played around in Tokio for a week or so; the ambassador had his polite business to attend to; all of us rude Russians and westerners were brought up standing against the grace of the Japanese, in palaces, in shops, in the tea house of the Japanese dancing-girls. We felt the contrast of our present with our future, for Russia and the United States may be like Japan when we are done. But I sailed away from Japan with such a sense of graceful perfection as no poem, no works of art, no city, state, or nation had ever given me before, either in fact or in history. If there should be a war between Japan and the United States, I would secretly pray that it might be a war without victory. Japan may be socially and economically all wrong, as the left Russians sneered, and they pointed to evidence that it was; but Japan proves that right and wrong are not the only tests of excellence.

The voyage across the wide Pacific was, among other things, a rest from the Russians. We had come to know one another. I knew that they, most of them, were against their revolution; they were conservatives who represented a government, fortunately provisional, that had already gone faster than they liked. They had begun to realize that I wanted them to go on and on; and a British secret service man from India was so astonished that I, a white man speaking English, did not care to carry on the British Empire to the conquest of the world that he whispered warnings to Bakhmetieff against me. Little I cared. There was a group of official Chinese delegates on board, bound for Paris, where later I saw their poise at the peace conference. They were stately, philosophic gentlemen who saw straight, however crooked they might talk and walk. They were our allies, sure; we discussed the war and empire, machinery and trade.

I used to pace the deck with those of them who spoke English or German, and one day I summed up a polite conversation with a laugh: "But you don't seem to hate the Germans. You fight them; you are on our side; but you don't hate the Huns. Why not?"

They laughed, too, and they chatted together in Chinese, but one of them, speaking for them all with permission, said: "We are your allies, and we are faithful in our alliance; but it is true, we do not hate the Germans. And I will tell you why. You all rob us. You take our cities, you seize our customs and our trade, you Americans, the English, French—Germans, all. But there's a difference. When the Germans came to us, demanding a port and the city of Kiaochow, I was at the conference of settlement, and I myself, I asked the Germans how they, a Christian nation, justified the taking from us of a port city. And they answered that they did not justify it, but that the British had taken things, the Americans, and the others; so they must have something. And having the power, they would take what they wanted." He paused; then he laughed and added, "And you see, we liked that. They, and they alone, did not do it for our good."

When we arrived at Seattle, Mr. Bakhmetieff drew me aside and said that the British secret service man had protested my presence and demanded that I quit the party, that we travel to Washington by different routes. I consented, of course. Some of the Russian party were annoyed, but not Bakhmetieff. I never saw him again.

In Washington I called with my letters from Crane and Governor Francis on President Wilson, who had been led by cables from Petrograd to expect me. I delivered my message to a silent, thoughtful man.

"Kerenski says, and he says truly, that he cannot make war, that he is only in the seat of power; he is not the actual, ruling government." I described the real, the mob government of the Soviet, and the good will of that democracy, "which Kerenski feels might be satisfied if you, the president, could persuade the heads of the other allied governments to meet conspicuously, say in London, and publicly abrogate the secret treaties.

"Kerenski asks you to clear away their suspicion of loot and conquest so conspicuously and so clearly that the sight and the sound of it will reach to the uttermost villages of Russia and be known to every peasant, soldier, sailor, and worker throughout Russia and all over Asia."

The president's answer to me was the statement that he was so much criticized for afterward: that he knew nothing about the secret treaties. But the way he said it and what he meant was clearly understandable to me. He evidently knew what I was talking about. He knew of those secret treaties, not as an ally, not officially as a party to the making of those treaties, but only as I and the public knew of their existence. No ally had ever communicated the fact to him, but there was no surprise at my reference to "those secret treaties."

He said, as if thinking aloud, and looking past me, "I know nothing of those secret treaties, you know. That makes it difficult

Croton-on-Hudson, N.Y. June 9

My dear Steff -

...As for me, I am doing - nothing. I have been making many
speeches about Russia, and tomorrow go to Chicago and Detroit to
address meetings there. I started a big newspaper syndicate series,
like Louise's, but the newspapers were afraid to touch them ; some of
them sent the stuff back after it was in type. Then Collier's took
a story, put it in type, and sent it back. Oswald Villard told me
he would be suppressed if he published John Reed !

I have a contract with MacMillan to publish a book, but the
State Department took away all my papers when I came home, and up
to date has absolutely refused to return any of them, although promising to do so " as soon as they are examined ". It is now more
than two months.

I am therefore unable to write a word of the greatest story
of my life, and one of the greatest in the world. I am blocked. Do
you know any way to have my papers sent to me ? If they don't come
pretty soon it will be too late for my book - MacMillan's won't take
it.

I was arrested the other day in Philadelphia, trying to
speak on the street, and am held for court in September on the
charges of " inciting to riot, inciting to assault and battery, and
inciting to seditious remarks. "

I feel sort of flat - and stale. My kidney isn't well - I
suppose that is why. Mother writes daily threatening to commit suicide if I continue to besmirch the family name. My brother is going
to France next week. I believe that Intervention in Russia will be
pulled off.

Excuse the depression. I don't see why I chose this low,
grey moment in which to write you. I felt pretty good this morning,
and probably will tomorrow morning.

Yours as ever

Jack

PART OF A LETTER FROM JACK REED

for me to do what Kerenski and Governor Francis ask. If we had such a treaty ourselves, if we were a party to their making, then I could say to our allies, 'Let us abrogate our treaties.' That would be easy, human, diplomatic, polite. But having no such treaty and having no knowledge of those treaties, I would have to say, 'Here, gentlemen, do you meet openly before the world and tear up those secret treaties of yours!'—No, that is hard. That I cannot very well do."

He did not tell me, of course, what he would do or what his answer to Kerenski would be. He asked me many acute questions about Russia, the revolution there, the parties, the prospects, and I answered as best I could. He was disturbed. He got up, walked to the window, and forgot me in his reflections. When he recalled my presence, he asked a few more pointed questions about Russia, one or two about my personal plans and ideas, and thanking me, bade me good-by.

XVI

PREPARING FOR PEACE

O NE of the questions President Wilson asked me after my delivery of the message from Petrograd was whether I had any suggestions to offer for the terms of peace in Europe after the war. I was so struck by this intimation that the war might end that I could hardly gather my wits. When I did I dictated a term, an idea I had heard him express once.

"Let all the peacemaking nations agree that any citizen of any country on earth shall be free to go to any other country on earth, himself and his money and his schemes, provided, however, that he go at his own risk and be subject in the foreign country to the laws and the conditions of that country. In plain language: that all men shall have the run of the earth to risk their own lives and money, but that these adventurers shall not be backed up by their home governments and shall not, therefore, run their own countries into the risk of war."

He smiled. "You got that idea in Mexico," he said. "It's an anti-imperialist principle, and it's sound. I've been acting on it. That's one of the points in my foreign policy that I am criticized for: I don't back up our investors abroad. But I can't put that principle over on other governments. I can see them rising from the table to snarl at the idea of taking away their best excuse for intervention and empire. No," he laughed, "you go out and talk and write up that idea, and if you can show me that it will go, I'll take it to Europe with me. But you can't put it over, and I can't."

I did talk the idea. I was lecturing on the revolutions, Mexican and Russian, and made it part of my argument against intervention anywhere. But I soon learned that the public were not interested in peace; the people were at war. And the Administration learned it too. One day at the end of 1917 or early in 1918, Colonel House sent for me, and I had another intimation of peace. He said that the war was going to end—sometime, and that the president had come to realize that there had been no thought of terms, there had been no propaganda for peace, only for war, and that when he should go to Europe to make peace he would have no intelligent backing for peace in his own country. So, I perceived, the president himself was going to make the peace! But I said nothing about that; I remarked only that they had overdone that war propaganda.

"Yes," said House, "and now we have got to go at our peace propaganda."

"What are you thinking of doing?" I asked.

"Well, we have made a list of speakers to go out and talk up the president's peace terms." He showed me the list of speakers and a copy of the president's peace terms. Jane Addams headed the list of well-chosen speakers.

"Good," I said. "Why don't you start them out?"

"We're afraid to," he answered. "In the present state of the popular mind they might be lynched."

"Well," I said, "what do you want me to do?"

"I thought," he said, "I thought that you might try it first."

I uttered an exclamation, and he laughed himself, but he said that in my lecture on Russia I was giving the Bolshevik peace terms. Why couldn't I go on for ten minutes more and state the president's peace terms? He said I must do it at my own risk, couldn't appear to speak for the Administration, couldn't be backed up or rescued from arrest. I had to stand for official repudiation, but it was a patriotic service, etc.

I was about to lecture across the country and back; so I took on the patriotic service, very gingerly, tentatively. At Buffalo, my first stop, I thought I said nothing that was clear, but at Detroit, the next stop, the U.S. District Attorney, having heard from Buffalo, called on me to warn me that he might have to arrest me. I said: "All right, but I am going to ask you to attend the meeting yourself, and yourself hear what I say. I'm afraid only of the reports of your secret service. They are bum reporters." He went with me to within sight of the hall and then left me to enter by himself. There was no arrest. But there was something else; there was pain on the faces of some of the people who looked up as I said that a permanent peace meant no victory, no punishment; that we would have to sit down with the enemy, we allies, and settle the causes of war in all fairness, leaving no rancor and wrongs to bring on another war. In Chicago some of my audience got up and ran out of the hall, not in anger evidently, but in pain. One woman who ran told me years afterward that she "simply could not stand it to think of making peace like that with the Germans, the Huns." She was at war, and as I went on west I realized more and more that the people with sons at the front were psychologically fighting a war with the Germans, and they could not —literally it was impossible for them to—think of the president treating fairly with the Germans as human beings and with Germany as a civilized country.

Stanford University, Santa Barbara, Los Angeles, were not only fighting; they were frightened; and their fright, especially Santa Barbara's, was wired ahead to San Diego, where they were ready for me. They let me speak in a church on the Russian Revolution, but the next night, when I was to discuss peace and peace terms, the army, the navy, the police, all were out, surrounding the church and the waiting audience. I was forbidden to speak. The pastor of the church was a leading liberal of the town and a member of the city council. I was so sorry for him, a reformer whom the patriotic grafters were after anyhow, that I told him in the presence of the officers the truth: that I was trying for Colonel House to start the propaganda for reflection upon the terms of the peace the president was to make. No use. I must not speak, and afterward that reverend councilman was recalled from office. So I gave up; I reported to Colonel House that I could not talk on peace and that I thought no one else could, unless the president himself would take the lead. But my own conclusion was that there is a limit to free speech. I had always stood for utter liberty, and I would not now set any legal limit. Speech, thought, writings, however free, are too impotent to be dangerous. As I think, however, of the pain I caused those audiences, I feel that mercy or, say, courtesy should be a limit upon individual liberty. It is cruel to talk peace to a people at war, especially if they are not actually fighting. Soldiers at the front might stand it, but the frightened masses in the rear—they must not be tortured with thought and reflection. And for the same reason conscientious objectors are wrong; they are heroes, of course; but they are torturers, and as heroes and torturers, they should be willing to take what they get.

The time to make for peace is not when a war is on; the only time to prepare for peace is before war begins.

REPORTS OF AN ADDRESS ON PRESIDENT WILSON'S PEACE TERMS

Colonel House accepted my report. He did not send out his pacifist speakers, and his fear was realized. President Wilson went to Paris to make an ideal peace with no intelligent peace opinion to back him in America. And one of the causes of his failure was that the secret services of his allies knew that he was alone, that his people, the Americans, were not with him for a fair and a permanent peace.

I got my reward, however, for my dangerous experiment. I got my punishment, too. It has not been forgotten that I spoke for peace when there was war; many communities will not read, hear, or heed me. But when Colonel House sailed for Europe to prepare the way for the president to make peace, he gave orders, which

Lincoln Steffens Esq.

    National Arts Club, New York.

Dear Mr. Steffens;

        I am distressed to read what you have to say in your letter of May 8th concerning your experience in San Diego. Unless your views have undergone a radical change since we talked, I cannot believe your speech justified the criticism which seemed to have been heaped upon it.

        I know you regret having involved the Rev. Mr. Bard and Mr. Templeton Johnson, but I cannot see how they can be properly criti cized for getting a man of your prominence to speak before their people.

        Sincerely yours,

115 East 53rd Street, New York.

May 14, 1918.

COLONEL HOUSE HEARS THE REPORTS

were very reluctantly obeyed, that I was to be permitted to go to Paris to witness the civilized governments end the war that was to end war, the governments whose condition and purposes and limitations I thought I understood.

XVII

THE PEACEMAKER

ARMISTICE DAY—and night—was a spectacle of joy in Paris. The French government let the people have their way, and their way was singing and dancing, madly, gladly, sadly. There were regrets and doubts, but the rejoicing prevailed. And the next days—after joy—came hope, the hope for peace, a real peace. Was it possible? No more wars? The sophisticated sneered, the newspapers mocked, but there was a chance. President Wilson was coming; and the people, the French, the Germans, the English—all the common peoples were putting their hope in the American president whose advent was Messianic.

Wilson came on a ship, with a cargo of commissioners, secretaries, secret service men, and correspondents, all in the ordinary, but *Le Temps*, the leading government organ, described his approach as the French people saw it. The great American prophet of peace was sailing on a cloud through the air to save the Old World, and the cynical editor predicted that the savior would come down to earth for his landing. But there were some fears even in that quarter that he might not fall so hard, that he might indeed make the peace without conquest that he had promised. The Germans had so understood his words; the French folk did; you could hear that in what they were saying all about you. And the Italians—the simple masses, who wanted peace, believed that he had said and meant peace. Our American propaganda, the masterly work of George Creel and the president, had lifted to the pitch of faith the simple, blinding hope of a continent. No European leader, whether reactionary or radical, could have won such trust; the old peoples have had experience of their own leaders; but "Meester Wilson" was a new kind of leader, and his kind of people, the American soldiers, had kept their word. The Europeans believed in us, in our president, but they feared for him. And they prayed for him. Literally. When Wilson traveled by train from his port of landing to Paris, by night, we heard that peasant families had been seen here and there all along the way kneeling beside the track in the dark to pray for him and his mission. And in Paris, when he arrived and had rested, the streets were packed mile on mile to watch him pass in parade, quiet crowds who wanted to look into his face to see, as they said, whether he meant and had the strength to do what he promised.

It was said that he understood this and that he wished to make those hops of his to London and to Rome to gather up the confidence and the strength of the people. I went along with him on those trips; the press was invited in mass, and we could see and hear and feel that the American president was making himself the world leader of all the democracies, the hope of the race. He succeeded in that. When he returned to Paris to go to work with the premiers and peace delegates, Woodrow Wilson was the spokesman of public opinion and the potential ruler of Europe. Whether he realized it or no, we newspaper men knew it, and we knew, too, that the statesmen of Europe knew it and feared it. They had to yield to his first demands: for open sessions of the peace conference, for open covenants openly arrived at. If he had gone on to his other terms! But open sessions was enough; even that was impossible, they said, in Europe, as impossible as open sessions of a Legislature or a political convention in America! How could burglars plan burglary, how could conquerors divide the loot of empire, in public? The imperialists had to agree to open sessions, but Mr. Wilson had to agree to private meetings of the "big four" to prepare for the formal, public meetings. The correspondents fought for press tickets, and they reported solemnly the staged shows which the world watched till we learned what they were. After that the correspondents hung around the lobbies, traded gossip, cultivated leaks, and so watched as best they could the private, very secret sessions of the four or five peacemakers in fact; even the little allies' representatives were excluded from these sessions and depended in part at least upon the press for information. The commanding victors alone made that treaty of peace. They were dividing the earth, and their problem was to manipulate and, if possible, break the American president, break his plan, break his personal strength, which they called his obstinacy, break his power and popularity. And the French led in this process of attrition. Clemenceau was the man who broke Wilson. Wilson was pitied, Clemenceau was execrated or adored, for this; but the conflict of these two men goes deeper, I think. It was a struggle of American idealism and good will against French realism, of the American reformer, the Anglo-Saxon liberal, against the intelligent French radical; and when the good American president fell before the wicked French premier, it was our moral American culture that went down under the clear, logical, conscious intelligence of French culture.

On the afternoon of the third day of the private meetings of the premiers two French newspaper men came in to the American press room at the Hotel Crillon. There were only a few American correspondents there. It was teatime, as the Frenchmen remarked in some surprise, and no tea; they did not know that tea is an English, not an American, institution. We were working when they marched in like a couple of gendarmes, but I rose to meet them, and others came up to make them welcome. They were polite for a few moments; then they said that they had come to verify a bit of news. Had we heard of a little scene at the meeting of the president and the premiers? We looked at one another, we Americans, and I said, "No, nothing. Why? What had they heard?" They exchanged glances, and one of them spoke for them both.

"We heard—but only from French sources, and we can't use it unless we get American confirmation of it—we heard that M. Clemenceau challenged M. Wilson to make a permanent peace. Have you heard anything about the scene?"

"No," I said for myself, and the other Americans present nodded no. "Tell us about it," I urged. "Describe the scene."

Then one of them told how, when the president and the premiers sat down at the table that morning and were about to proceed to business, M. Clemenceau, who was fiddling with his gray silk gloves, said, "One moment, gentlemen. I desire before we go any further to be made clear on one very essential point." The French reporter was entering into his story; he mimicked Clemenceau, drawing tight and smooth his little silk gloves, and bowing sweetly and smiling sardonically. And the reporter acted the parts he quoted.

The president and the premiers halted and looked up expectantly at M. Clemenceau, who said: "I have heard something about a permanent peace. There has been a great deal of talk about a peace to end war forever, and I am interested in that. All Frenchmen would like to make permanent peace. But I would like to know—all the French would like to know—whether you mean it, the permanent peace."

He looked at his colleagues and they nodded.

"So," Clemenceau said, "you really mean it! Well, it is possible. We can do it; we can make the permanent peace. And we French need, we very much need, the permanent peace. Every time you, our neighbors, get into a fight, France is the battlefield, and our population, our armies, do not increase. If there is not an end of wars we French may be all wiped out some day. So, you see, it is we French more than you remote Americans, Mr. President, more than you safe islanders, Mr. Lloyd George, who require the security of the real peace. But we French cannot quite believe that you, our friends, neighbors, allies—that you really mean what you say. Do you, Mr. President?"

Mr. Wilson did.

"And you, Mr. Premier?"

Mr. Lloyd George did.

And the Italians did, of a certainty, yes.

"Very important," M. Clemenceau muttered, as if convinced, as if the whole prospect were changing, and his whole policy. "Very important. We can make this a permanent peace; we can remove all the causes of war and set up no new causes of war. It is very, very important what you say, what you have been so long saying, Mr. President. We here now have the opportunity to make a peace that shall last forever, and the French people, diminishing, will be safe. And you are sure you propose to seize this opportunity?"

They did, they emphatically did.

Clemenceau clucked in his throat; he pressed tight down the fingers of his gloves. "And—you have counted the cost of such a peace?" he asked.

There was some hesitation at that. "What costs?"

"Well," said the French intelligence, "if we give up all future wars—if we are to prevent war, we must give up our empires and all hope of empire. You, Mr. Lloyd George, you English will have to come out of India, for example; we French shall have to come out of North Africa; and you Americans, Mr. President, you must get out of the Philippines and Porto Rico and leave Cuba alone and—Mexico. Oh, we can all go to these and other countries, but as tourists, traders, travelers; we cannot any more govern them or exploit or have the inside track in them. We cannot possess the keys to trade routes and spheres of influence. And, yes, we shall have to tear down our tariff walls and open the whole world to free trade and traffic. Those are some of the costs of permanent peace; there are other sacrifices we, the dominant powers, would have to make. It is very expensive, peace. We French are willing, but are you willing, to pay the price, all those costs of no more war in the world?"

The French correspondents became personal; they smiled. They said that the president and the premiers protested that they did not mean all that, that that was not necessary, not all at once. "No, no, they did not mean that, exactly."

"Then," said Clemenceau, sitting up straight and fisting the table sharply once, "then you don't mean peace. You mean war. And the time for us French to make war is now, when we have got one of our neighbors down; we shall finish him and get ready for—the next war."

The French correspondents rested a moment, smiling; they asked again if we had heard this. When we repeated that it was news to us, they were sorry. "We can't print it—from French sources only. It would be discourteous." They bowed and went out. We Americans separated, without comment, and I assumed that the story would be investigated and reported. I wasn't attached to any news service myself, but if I had been I would have reported the incident just as we got it. For those French correspondents were certainly "inspired" to sound us with that story. I thought that some one very near Clemenceau had sent them to us, but whether it was authentic or not, their gossip was significant. French correspondents, coming as a couple, one to talk, the other to bear witness, were acting on orders from some editor, statesman, or party leader. Some French mind as French, as intelligent, and as representative as Clemenceau's had made that story, if not the Tiger himself. In a word, it was the French view of the peace and of American and English ideals. It is in this sense a true story; it has served me as the key to all the French maneuvers then and since; it flashed out the difference between Wilson and Clemenceau, and it explained Wilson's typical failure.

Wilson did not mean peace, not literally; nor do we Americans, nor do the British, mean peace. We do not want war; nobody in the world wants war; but some of us do want the things we can't have without war. That's what the French see. And they see that we wish, like them, for peace; we will work and we will pray for it, but we have not noted and we will not give up the things that cause wars. Clemenceau and the French would, I think, if we would. But Clemenceau, like so many of the leading French politicians, had seen things as a radical once. As a young man he learned that there are causes of war and that the way to end war is to prevent war: by dealing with the causes thereof. No treaties, no scraps of paper, no partial and no complete disarmament, can hold off very long a war that we have planted in our maladjustment of conflicting economic interests. That was, that *is*, the French view, and so obvious is it to those clear minds that they think we are hypocrites; we must see it, too, they think. And we don't.

The making of the peace of Versailles was a long, slow, secret process, the progress of which came out to us spectators as gossip. But gossip is the color if not the substance of history, and I heard good inside stories of what went on, with rich comment. Jo Davidson, the American sculptor, was on my boat, coming over. His occupation was "busting"; he was to make a record in bronze and marble of the generals and statesmen of the war and the peace. We roomed together; we played together. I heard what his sitters said, from General Foch, the first, the French, commander-in-chief, down through the whole list of French, American, and English insiders; and with the sculptor and his friends we heard what lesser men of all countries were saying, whether they were reporting or only commenting, in the cafés, in the lobbies, in the press rooms. If I got behind on the news, if the newspaper men lost patience with me for grafting on them for the news, I used to fall ill and go to bed. Then they and others would come up to my room and tell me everything. All these details of direct and indirect facts formed in my mind a moving spectacle that reminds me of my muckraking days when, from the outside, I had to visualize what was going on inside a political convention, a city council, or a State Legislature. And the pictures of home and of Paris were much the same; the one was a key to the other.

The picture of the Paris peace conference was of Wilson, the reformer, trying to make a just peace, with Lloyd George nodding approval and the French asking, "What is just?" And there was Clemenceau, like an American boss, with Lloyd George voting with him and the imperialist interests behind him, trying to finish the war, complete the victory, and collect and divide the booty. The Frenchman had all the advantage of clearness of purpose. Having decided that Wilson and Lloyd George did not mean to make a real peace and establish security, Clemenceau set out to rid France of one or two enemies. The French comment was, "Of course; since you would not march to Berlin, we'll ruin the Germans now, and then we'll prepare to defend ourselves against our —other—neighbors later." And they meant "you Americans and the English," and they meant also that we should have no Germany to combine with against them then. And the French candor assumed, however politely, that we English and Americans must see, as they did, that since we were not willing to abolish war and empire there will be a next war and that in it France may have to defend herself against both of us, with what is left of the Germans on our side.

There was a bridge there that I could never persuade a Frenchman to cross. He could not believe that Wilson did not foresee that maybe we would be fighting France, that he could not regard a peace-making as a war-making. The night the Freedom of the Seas was to have been discussed by the peace-makers, we were all laughing over a story that somebody got somebody to tell the president and the premiers of a prison boat-load of Huns lying in a British harbor. Some British sailors rowing past were hailed by the German prisoners, who spat on the water and cried, "To hell with your King George." No answer from the British. The Germans called, "To hell with your Lloyd George," and again they spat. The British rowers rowed on while the Huns spat down a long list of English captains and kings, till finally the English sailors rested and shouted back, "Hey, Fritzies, you may say what you like about King George and Lloyd George and the rest of 'em, but you look out whose sea you're spittin' in, see."

We laughed as we told that to the French as a tale that Mr. Wilson and Mr. Lloyd George had laughed at; but the French did not laugh. They only sneered or wondered. "But Mr. Wilson and Mr. George, they did proceed to discuss the freedom of the seas? And they did let Britain rule the waves? Then you do see what you are doing?"

How was one to answer that? We are both hypocrites, the French and the Anglo-Americans, but the difference is that the French are conscious hypocrites, playing hard and knowingly and therefore well, a crooked game, whereas we are not constantly aware of what we are doing. We really don't face facts. So Clemenceau kept pushing Wilson off the straight and narrow path on to the crooked course of empire, and the French kept thinking that Wilson (and Lloyd George) knew what he and they were doing. Why did not we acknowledge it, why not come out honestly with our mutual actual purposes? It would be so much easier and pleasanter. Didn't we know what the breaking up of Austria was for? No. Didn't we know what mandates were for, that a mandate is an invention with which, without a war and a conquest, we dominant nations could rule and exploit backward nations? No. We were against empire, really and truly, and Clemenceau was forcing us back into imperialism. He was making a just peace impossible, but Wilson had another invention to save the world. We always have a way of retreat, what our underworld calls a get-away. Mr. Wilson, worsted in the treaty, broached our League of Nations. And Clemenceau and the French, amazed, read the covenant, amended it here and there, and shrugging their shoulders, accepted it. But honestly now, here in the café, among gentlemen, friends, and allies, did we really think for one moment that France, for example, or England or any sovereign state would surrender its sovereignty to a League of Nations? If the League was his price for the treaty, all right, but did not Mr. Wilson and did not we realize that such a League would become an instrument in the hands of England and France and—perhaps—less so —the United States for the extension of power over both backward and forward nations? And that otherwise we would not join it? No. We did not. And Mr. Wilson did not. He was sincere. He meant well. He may not have meant all that he said, but he thought he did; he meant honestly what he felt he was saying and doing.

But he agreed to a warlike division of the defeated countries; he made a treaty of peace that was full of war. How could he do that, he, an historian, a highly intellectual man, a very enlightened democrat? The French asked that; they ask it still about him and about us, and their contempt for "the" American president grows as we prove his sincerity. My answer was that Wilson was a righteous man and, as such, personified us, his people. He had ideals; they were high and they were sincere, but they were so high that he did not expect to realize them. He worked for them, but as a practical man he could yield to facts, and so long as he could feel that he had done his best, he was satisfied. I cited other Americans of this type, reformers who fought for the right, drove out the rascals, and came into power—and themselves fell. And never knew it.

Wilson, as we all saw him outmaneuvered, bit by bit, could not, would not, fail. Since he could not make a perfect treaty, he did make the League of Nations. Unable to abolish war and establish peace among the nations, he set up the League to regulate the imperfect treaty and its unjust peace and the economic struggles of the nations. We heard of his mental sufferings after some of his surrenders, but we heard, too, that he justified each one. It sometimes seemed to me in Paris that the most important step for us Americans to take next is to learn to do wrong knowingly. Wilson could not. He had to be, so he was, right. It was as if every night he thought, talked, prayed, over what he had done that day till he could go to sleep feeling that he had not sinned or erred, that there was ever a good reason for his acts.

History will long remember one day when, in desperation, President Wilson ordered his ship, the *George Washington,* to be made ready to take him home. A gesture? A bluff? The French thought so; Clemenceau did not budge. The Americans in Paris thought it a bluff, but we knew he had cards to show, and we were glad. He was calling at last to the people of Europe, so long prepared for this moment. And I happen to know that that was in the mind of the Administration; Wilson would arouse the public opinion of Europe to overthrow the ministries which were thwarting him.

And Lloyd George, the politician, frightened, went to work with his associates and his information. They warned Mr. Wilson that a call from him to the peoples would cause the downfall of governments, not merely ministries; and this was revolution.

Colonel House sent for me. I was supposed to know the revolutionary movements, plans, and possibilities of Europe. House said that the president wanted to know whether, if he boarded his boat and announced that he was through, that he could not make with the present peace delegates the peace he proposed, and that he was sailing for Washington where—only—hereafter he would discuss peace— "Will that cause the downfall of governments or will it precipitate revolution?"

My answer was that no revolution seemed possible then in any country but that such an act by Wilson would probably overthrow every ministry in all the allied countries—unless their peace delegates came to our terms. House looked pleased; he agreed with my judgment. He said all his information was to that effect. He was evidently for the sailing. Many observers then and since have said that Wilson might have won out with his great gesture if he had carried it to Washington or even to the boat. But Wilson took British and French information. He surrendered. He canceled the sailing of the *George Washington*. He stayed with the peacemakers, and I heard from House his, to him, all-sufficient justification. He could not take the responsibility for precipitating revolutions in Europe.

When the Treaty of Versailles was printed and published, the world was shocked. Nobody expected it to be so bad as it was. Americans in our peace delegation resigned—the younger men; Clemenceau and the French had had a triumph. Lloyd George and the British were satisfied. Invitations were issued to attend the signing of the treaty at Versailles. The demand for them was desperate. I got one in an amusing way. The American press received a certain limited number, and as the small executive committee of correspondents were sorting them, they found themselves one short. Larry Hills, the editor later of the Paris *Herald*, and Herbert Swope, later the managing editor of the New York *World*, accused each other of swiping the lost ticket. There was some feeling about it, but as it eased and both gave up hope of recovering the precious card, Hills said he was sorry it was lost because he had wanted to give it to me. "What!" said Swope. "You meant to give it to him. Well, I'll be damned! That's the man I swiped it for." And it was given up—to me.

I did not use my well-got card to the spectacle of the signing of that treaty. As I explained at the time, I had to take a bath at that very hour. An English correspondent who left the scene before it was over expressed my sentiment. "It was an unpleasant sight," he said. "I could not stay. All of our victorious statesmen and generals standing over two or three of the defeated Germans, making them sign there. It was—it was so unsportsmanlike. I ran away."

I said something impulsive in appreciation of the liberal Englishman, but this fine liberal Englishman said bitterly: "Oh, yes. We English, we have always a minority for the right."

The British shared the victory with the French—the English majority. What did the Americans have, we whom the French, the British, the Italians, the Poles, and the rest had defeated— we had no territory, no loot, no glory—what did we have? We, and our president, might have had one of the most inspiring failures in this world of successes. If Wilson had said that he had failed and told why and pointed to a future of such glorious failures—to compromise, his story would have gone down in history as a classic, as one of the most magnificent and significant failures in the story of man. And we need some great failures, especially we ever-successful Americans—conscious, intelligent, illuminating failures. But no, Woodrow Wilson chose success; so he goes down in history as just one more successful American, the founder of the League of Nations, the beginner of world government!

Just before his departure from Paris he gave all the war and peace correspondents of Europe a mass interview at the Crillon. There must have been two hundred reporters there. We asked questions freely. Hoping to hear that the president, whom I admired, was aware of what he had not done, I asked whether he was satisfied with the peace that he had made.

"Yes," he said.

I could not so easily give up hope, my belief in his integrity of mind. Other questions intervened, but I got my chance to repeat.

"Mr. President, do you feel that you achieved here the peace that you expected to make?"

UPPER: THE RUSSIAN REVOLUTION (AMKINO). LOWER: THE PEACE
CONFERENCE (N.Y. WORLD NEWS SERVICE).

He turned and looked at me. I had his attention, his mind. He answered, after a pause, slowly, thoughtfully, sincerely.

"I think that we have made a better peace than I should have expected when I came here to Paris."

I allow that he was counting more on the League of Nations than on the scrap of Versailles paper, but—well, that's what the American messiah to the peoples of Europe said of his own work.

XVIII

THE BULLITT MISSION TO MOSCOW

A T ONE stage of the peace negotiations President Wilson proposed to seek some understanding with Russia. The
premiers objected; they could not risk the contamination
of a direct touch with the Bolsheviki. Wilson suggested an American commission to meet a Russian commission at a distance, and
Prinkipo, an island resort near Constantinople, was named as the
place. As masters of the world, the big four let a summons be
wirelessed to Moscow. It was a victory for Wilson; it was an act
of condescension on the part of his allies; it was a shocking, unofficial, but necessary acknowledgment of the existence, rights, and
powers of an ex-ally, who must desire to come into the comity of
nations. But no. The Bolsheviki wirelessed back only suspicious,
contemptuous questions. Wilson was hurt. His cynical associates
laughed. The Prinkipo arrangement had to be abandoned.

"Your friends don't help a fellow at all," said Colonel House
to me.

"What do you expect?" I answered. "You are fighting them,
hating them, and all of a sudden you invite them to a parley. What
for? Why, if you want to deal with them, why don't you do as you
would to any other government: send in a secret sounding commission first, to see that they understand what you are up to and
so make sure that they will come in the desired state of mind to an
official meeting with your full-powered delegates?"

"That's right," said House thoughtfully. "That is the way to
do it. We'll see. I can have a commission sent in secretly." Then
he thought of something else. He looked up at me aggressively,
and he declared quite unnecessarily, "But not you. You shan't be
on it." I laughed. He knew that I ached to go to Russia then. Much
had happened since I was last there, and he had heard me won-

dering what it all meant. I could not go alone; nobody but spies and armies could enter Russia at that time. Colonel House evidently suspected my advice as a scheme to get myself into Russia.

"No. We'll not send you," he repeated. "I know whom to nominate."

A few days later William C. Bullitt, a special assistant in the State Department, came bouncing up to ask me how I'd like to go to Russia. It was a secret, but Colonel House had got him commissioned to visit Russia and arrange some business there with Lenin. He was to choose his own companions and not tell anybody who they were. Captain Petit had consented to go, a soldier but an ex-social worker who would be able to see how conditions really were, and a naval secretary named Lynch. Would I go as a sort of political observer and liaison man? I would.

"All right," said Bullitt. "We leave Paris tomorrow morning for London, whence we travel via Norway, Sweden, etc., to Petrograd."

Colonel House asked me what questions I would ask in Russia, and he mentioned some that he would like to have answered, especially by Lenin. I noted them well, while he was explaining that Bullitt would concentrate upon the more essential, diplomatic points, which Lloyd George would give him. My interpretation of this subterfuge was that House, knowing I was regarded as a friend of Russia, wanted me to go unofficially as a friend of Bullitt, capable of official repudiation. On the train to London Bullitt showed penciled on a sheet of paper the seven items which Philip Kerr, secretary to Lloyd George, had given him as the terms for the Bolsheviki to agree to. Bullitt's instructions were to negotiate a preliminary agreement with the Russians so that the United States and Great Britain could persuade France to join them in an invitation to a parley, reasonably sure of some results. Colonel House had proposed, Lloyd George had planned, the visit; and Bullitt's instructions came from House and from the British prime minister. And the British paved our way. They had reserved our places on trains and boats and at the London hotel. When we called for our tickets on the boat to Norway they were delivered to us "all paid." British consuls met and speeded us through Norway, Sweden, Finland, on our amusing, beautiful journey.

Bullitt had brought along his secretary Lynch, apparently to play with. On trains and boats they skylarked, wrestling and tumbling like a couple of bear cubs all along the Arctic Circle. A pretty noisy secret mission we were, but Bullitt knew just what he was about; nobody could suspect us of secrecy or importance; and at formal moments and in emergencies the head of our mission was all there with the form, the authority, and the—audacity. The sunburned Swedes and Norwegians let us pass at salute over their sunny winter snow; we were the United States. There was something like a meeting of conspirators in Stockholm the beautiful, where U.S. Minister Morris put us in touch with Bolshevik agents, whom he could not himself touch—to communicate with Russia and arrange for a diplomatic guide to Petrograd. Mrs. Morris was in touch with the King of Sweden, whom we could not touch. I had to tell her a story a day to repeat to His Majesty at dinner. He liked American stories and asked for more and more of them.

The name of the Swedish Red we got to guide us was Kil Baum, which, added to Bullitt and Lynch, made a murderous peace commission. Our conspiracy was to get on through Finland. A new country with new officials is always difficult, and the Finns (and the Poles) felt that they were guardians, not only of their borders, but of European civilization. Bullitt managed the Finns. He laid wires as we proceeded slowly; there was always some one for us to appeal back to; and when at the Russ-Finn border an arrogant Finnish officer drew up to stop and search us, Bullitt outdid him in arrogance—"Hands off, you. Telephone for orders. We pass." The man wilted, and the cordon of troops opened. We sleighed across the line to the special two-car train that was to take us to Petrograd, where Bullitt's work began—delicate, hard work.

Petrograd was a deserted city when we got there at night. Nobody at the station, nobody in the dark, cold, broken streets, and there was no fire in the vacant (American packer's) palace assigned to us. I, being known to the Russians, and mistaken for the head of the mission, was called out by our Swedish and Russian guides to go looking through dead hotels for officials at midnight teas. The rest of our party went gladly to bed to be warmed. I was led from one tea to another till at last the guide found and presented me to Zinoviev, one of the three commissioners appointed to deal with us. Unwillingly, without greeting, he snapped one question at me in German: "Sind Sie bevollmächtigt?"

"No," I answered, and I began to explain the preliminary nature of the mission. He would not listen. When he heard that we were not plenipotentiaries he turned away abruptly, and we never saw him again. Apparently there was some dispute among the Russians as to the purposes of the Bullitt mission and whether to deal with it. Also they differed as to whether Bullitt or I was the actual head. Lenin had to send Tchicherin, Secretary of Foreign Affairs, from Moscow to see, and he saw. He saw that Bullitt was the man, and he heard from me that the Russians' part was to give Bullitt not the least but the most that they could in order to enable Wilson and Lloyd George to win over the French. Often we had to repeat this. When we had it understood by Tchicherin and he had wired it to Lenin, we received an invitation to come on to Moscow to carry on under Lenin's eye.

We had seen some sights that interested us in Petrograd: deserted factories, factory buildings with machinery for thousands of workers struggling along with a few hundred, closed shops and houses, straggling crowds on dead streets—and always cold. But we saw, too, a parade of a red army which Captain Petit and other military observers said would be hard to beat. "Troops with religion in their feet, shoulders, and eyes will fight." As I was watching these soldiers, a rude voice called to me in English, and Bill Shatoff, an I.W.W. from Chicago, greeted me. He knew what I was there for. I asked what he was doing.

"I'll tell you if you won't give me away to the Wobblies at home: I am chief of police of Petrograd." Also, he was civil commissioner of one army and head of a railroad. The revolution had so few executives that every man who could command, organize, and get results had many jobs. Bill Shatoff had had a command in the October revolution and been occupied ever since in holding the control over the city. He was a happy man. He had seen "the" revolution; it had won; and he had seen a light. He was the first man to show me that after a revolution has happened you see everything in a new way. An anarchist, then, may be a chief of police—"the police are over on our side." He took us into his high-powered, fine automobile. "Where'd you get it, Bill?" "Confiscated; we took all the cars." I wondered a moment. "How do you decide here who has cars and who hasn't?" I asked. "I'll tell you, if you'll tell me how you decide at home who has the cars." He took my blundering answer, reframed it, and summed it all up: "In America your fast cars go to people of leisure with lots of time to kill. In Soviet Russia we assign them to busy people in a hurry."

We had left Lynch outside of Russia; we left Captain Petit in Petrograd to see and report on the conditions there, while Bullitt and I entrained with Tchicherin and Litvinov for Moscow. Such a relief. Colder than foggy, humid Petrograd, Moscow is sunny, dry, and seemed warmer. We had a warmed palace, with servants. There was very little food, but we had brought with us mail pouches full of canned stuff; and we liked the piles and piles of caviar they provided: caviar and black bread and tea. It was all they had, we guessed. Anyway the Russians came gladly, promptly, to our meals of canned food, and sometimes they just happened in at meal hours. Tchicherin, a shy, little, serious man, blushed one evening when he called, he said, to ask a question of fact, and I answered, "Yes, Mr. Secretary, supper is about ready." But he stayed to supper. Evidently the leaders were sharing the hardships of the country in this period when we had heard in Paris of their banquets and high living. We had opera and theaters and music; we had the Czar's box one night; but we never had a meal outside our own house, and the Russians were frequently at our table.

Bullitt and Tchicherin, and Litvinov, with Lenin near by, negotiated daily, keeping office hours, while I moved about here and there, seeking information and ideas. There were questions to answer, House's and others of my own. On the train somewhere I had put down on paper all the questions in all our minds. It bored the party. "Why write down such vivid questions?" they protested. "Because," I said, "we'll forget them when we get to Russia." All foreign correspondents know how, when they get into a country, other, local questions supersede those that they came to ask. And so with us, when, after ten days in Russia, I read off at luncheon one day the list we had made, we not only had forgotten, we laughed at them; we did not want the answers to most of them. "How had the Czar and his family been killed?" for example. We were not interested then in the fate of kings. But some of our inquiries had to be made and our new curiosity had to be satisfied by me, who had the time. I was told of the Czar's end, precisely. I was taken to the art galleries to see that the treasures there had been, not stolen, but greatly increased by the official stealing from private galleries. The organization of politics and government and the plans for the development of industry into one great corporation which would some day supersede the political state were explained to me. Not that I "got" it all. How could I, a liberal, grasp the idea of an evolutionary society, which was beginning as a dictatorship to establish a new order, force the people to form new ideas and habits, and defend this growing thing from conspiracies and corruption inside and from wars outside, till its various industries could evolve into one united productive whole, a self-governed, highly disciplined business government which would destroy the political state and be the only government? "You have dual governments," I heard. "You govern men politically, and you govern men industrially. We have to begin there, but we know that there is such a thing as evolution; so we plan to evolve from the socialist state on to anarchism." And they quoted Lenin, who in speeches said: "Support this state that I represent, this beastly political bureaucracy; it is needed now to make wars, civil and foreign. But observe that alongside of this thing that I bid you hate and obey, temporarily, we are building an organization of all industry, and when that is ready, then smash the state. Live only in and by the industrial organization which will subject you for a few hours a day or a year to the severest discipline of absolute government in the shop, but outside the shop, after you have done your part, it will not govern you at all. Outside of your working hours you shall be free."

It takes time to put ideas like that through one's head. I could not get it as I listened. I could repeat what I heard; I could say that Russia, having cleared the ground for it, was laying a new foundation for an evolutionary society, which was to pass through foreseen and planned-for stages of growth from an absolute and political dictatorship through industrial socialism to a liberty, a democracy and peace, to which there would be no opposing interests. The only idea that I could make my own was this that my muckraking had brought me to:

Soviet Russia was a revolutionary government with an evolutionary plan. Their plan was, not by direct action to resist such evils as poverty and riches, graft, privilege, tyranny, and war, but to seek out and remove the causes of them. They were not practicing what we and they preached. They were not trying to establish political democracy, legal liberty, and negotiated peace—not now. They were at present only laying a basis for these good things. They had set up a dictatorship, supported by a small, trained minority, to make and maintain for a few generations a scientific rearrangement of economic forces which would result in economic democracy first and political democracy last.

It was a new culture, an economic, scientific, not a moral, culture. And the Russians we were conversing with, the heads of the Soviet government, were talking out of a new philosophy. No wonder it was confusing and difficult.

Bullitt steered his way through to an agreement with Lenin and Tchicherin. The seven points of Lloyd George's memorandum, and House's points as well, were accepted with very slight verbal modifications. Feeling that he had what we came for, a basis upon which the allies could treat with Russia, Bullitt decided to hurry back to Paris. He arranged for me an interview with Lenin, so that I could ask my undiplomatic questions and get a sense of the man. I had my questions at my finger tips when I was sent in to the great room where Lenin sat behind his desk at one end.

A quiet figure in old clothes, he rose, came around in front of his desk to greet me with a nod and a handshake. An open, inquiring face, with a slight droop in one eye that suggested irony or humor, looked into mine. I asked whether, in addition to the agreement with Bullitt, I could not take back some assurances: that, for example, if the borders were opened, Russian propagandists would be restrained from flocking over into Europe.

"No," he said sharply, but he leaned back against the desk and smiled. "A propagandist, you know, is a propagandist. He must propagand. When our propagandists for revolution won, when they saw the revolution happen, they did not stop propaganding. They went right on propaganding. We had to give them propaganda work to do among the peasants and workers. If our borders are opened our propagandists will go to Europe and propagand, just as yours will come here and propagand. We can agree not to send them to you, and we can agree that if they do go, they shall be subject to your laws, but we—nobody can make a propagandist stop propaganding."

"What assurance can you give that the red terror will not go on killing—"

"Who wants to ask us about our killings?" he demanded, coming erect on his feet in anger.

"Paris," I said.

"Do you mean to tell me that those men who have just generaled the slaughter of seventeen millions of men in a purposeless war are concerned over the few thousands who have been killed in a revolution with a conscious aim—to get out of the necessity of war and—and armed peace?" He stood a second, facing me with hot eyes; then quieting, he said: "But never mind, don't deny the terror. Don't minimize any of the evils of a revolution. They occur. They must be counted upon. If we have to have a revolution, we have to pay the price of revolution."

Lenin was impatient with my liberalism, but he had shown himself a liberal by instinct. He had defended liberty of speech, assembly, and the Russian press for some five to seven months after the October revolution which put him in power. The people had stopped talking; they were for action on the program. But the plottings of the whites, the distracting debates and criticisms of the various shades of reds, the wild conspiracies and the violence of the anarchists against Bolshevik socialism, developed an extreme left in Lenin's party which proposed to proceed directly to the terror which the people were ready for. Lenin held out against them till he was shot, and even then, when he was in hospital, he pleaded for the life of the woman who shot him.

I referred to this, and he acknowledged it and said: "It was no use. It is no use. There will be a terror. It hurts the revolution both inside and out, and we must find out how to avoid or control or direct it. But we have to know more about psychology than we do now to steer through that madness. And it serves a purpose that has to be served. There must be in a revolution, as in a war, unified action, and in a revolution more than in a war the contented people will scuttle your ship if you don't deal with them. There are white terrors, too, you know. Look at Finland and Hungary. We have to devise some way to get rid of the bourgeoisie, the upper classes. They won't let you make economic changes during a revolution any more than they will before one; so they must be driven out. I don't see, myself, why we can't scare them away without killing them. Of course they are a menace outside as well as in, but the émigrés are not so bad. The only solution I see is to have the threat of a red terror spread the fear and let them escape. But however it is done, it has to be done. The absolute, instinctive opposition of the old conservatives and even of the fixed liberals has to be silenced if you are to carry through a revolution to its objective."

He foresaw trouble with the fixed minds of the peasants, their hard conservatism, and his remark reminded me of the land problem. They were giving the peasants land? "Not by law," he said. "But they think they own the land; so they do."

He took a piece of paper and a pencil. "We are all wrong on the land," he said, and the thought of Wilson flashed to my mind. Could the American say he was all wrong like that? "Look," said Lenin, and he drew a straight line. "That's our course, but"—he struck off a crooked line to a point—"that's where we are. That's where we have had to go, but we'll get back here on our course some day." He paralleled the straight line.

That is the advantage of a plan. You can go wrong, you can tack, as you must, but if you know you are wrong, you can steer back on your course. Wilson, the American liberal, having justified his tackings, forgot his course. To keep himself right, he had changed his mind to follow his actions till he could call the peace of Versailles right. Lenin was a navigator, the other a mere sailor.

There was more of this rapid interview, but not words. When I came out of it, I found that I had fertile ideas in my head and an attitude which grew upon me. Events, both in Russia and out, seemed to have a key that was useful, for example, in Fascist Italy, in Paris, and at home in the United States. Our return from Moscow was less playful than the coming. Bullitt was serious. Captain Petit was interesting on the hunger and the other sufferings of Petrograd, but not depressed as he would have been in New York or London. "London's is an old race misery," he said. "Petrograd is a temporary condition of evil, which is made tolerable by hope and a plan." Arthur Ransome, the English correspondent of the *Manchester Guardian*, came out with us. He had been years in Russia, spoke Russian, and had spent the last winter in Moscow with the government leaders and among the people. He had the new point of view. He said and he showed that Shakespeare looked different after Russia, and, unlike some other authors, still true. Our journey home was a course of intellectual digestion; we were all enjoying a mental revolution which corresponded somewhat with the Russian Revolution and gave us the sense of looking ahead.

"So you've been over into Russia?" said Bernard Baruch, and I answered very literally, "I have been over into the future, and it works." This was in Jo Davidson's studio, where Mr. Baruch was sitting for a portrait bust. The sculptor asked if I wasn't glad to get back. I was. It was a mental change that we had experienced, not physical. Bullitt asked in surprise why it was that, having been so elated by the prospect of Russia, we were so glad to be back in Paris. I thought it was because, though we had been to heaven, we were so accustomed to our own civilization that we preferred hell. We were ruined; we could recognize salvation, but could not be saved.

And, by the way, it was harder on the real reds than it was on us liberals. Emma Goldman, the anarchist who was deported to that socialist heaven, came out and said it was hell. And the socialists, the American, English, the European socialists, they did not recognize their own heaven. As some wit put it, the trouble with them was that they were waiting at a station for a local train, and an express tore by and left them there. My summary of all our experiences was that it showed that heaven and hell are one place, and we all go there. To those who are prepared, it is heaven; to those who are not fit and ready, it is hell.

It was a disappointing return diplomatically. Bullitt had set his heart on the acceptance of his report; House was enthusiastic, and Lloyd George received him immediately at breakfast the second day and listened and was interested. Of course. Bullitt had brought back all the prime minister had asked. And that same morning I was received and questioned, very intelligently, by "British information, Russian section." I had learned to despise the secret services; they were so un- and mis-informed; but these British officers knew and understood the facts. They asked me questions which only well-informed, comprehending, imaginative minds could have asked, and my news fitted into their picture. All a long forenoon they probed and discussed and understood so perfectly that when

I was saying good-by at noon I begged leave to compliment them and to contrast their British information with our American secret service. And, by way of a true jest, I said to them: "You have proved to me that my government is honest and that yours is not."

"But why that?"

"Well," I said, "your government, like mine, talks lies, but evidently your government knows the truth. Mine does not. My government believes its own damned lies; yours doesn't."

No action was taken on the proposal Bullitt had brought back from Moscow, and after a few weeks of futile discussion the Bullitt mission was repudiated. I heard that the French, having got wind of it, challenged Lloyd George; he and Wilson had gone back of the French to negotiate with the Russians, they charged. And Lloyd George took the easiest way out. He denied Bullitt in Paris, and when there were inquiries in London, he crossed the Channel to appear before the House of Commons to declare explicitly and at length that he knew nothing of the "journey some boys were reported to have made to Russia." I have had it explained to me since that this is not so weak and wicked as it seemed to us. It was a political custom in British parliamentary practice to use young men for sounding or experimental purposes, and it was understood that if such a mission became embarrassing to the ministry, it was repudiated; the missionaries lay down and took the disgrace till later, when it was forgotten, they would get their reward. But Bullitt would not play this game. He tried to appeal to President Wilson. When Wilson would not see him I remembered the old promise to me after the Mexican affair to receive me if I should send in my name with the words, "It's an emergency." I did that, and my messenger, a man who saw the president every day, described the effect.

"When I said that you wanted to see him and that you asked me to add that it was an emergency, the president sprang to his feet. 'No,' he said, and he walked across the room, where he again said, 'No.' Then he came back to me, and though I had not uttered a word, he defied me. 'No; I will not see him. I won't see that man. No, I won't see that man. That's the man that convinced me on Mexico.'"

This sounded preposterous till I recalled Wilson's theory that the intellectual must sometimes close his mind and act. He and the premiers had probably just had it out on Russia and the Bullitt mission. They were probably back on the general treaty. If he heard me I might reopen his mind on Russia, as I had done on Mexico. So he would not see me.

But he went out of his way to make it up to me personally. I had been pretty outspoken in my hopefulness of the Bolshevik government, and our secret service was suspicious and active. They had shadowed me. Once I invited to our table the young officers who followed me and Jo Davidson into a restaurant and set about converting them to Bolshevik communism. I could not quite win them over, but they reported, I heard afterward, that there was no use shadowing me; I would tell them more to their faces than they could possibly overhear. And another time Secretary of War Baker, who was in Paris, invited me to his room and asked me to tell him just what I had seen, heard, and thought about Russia. I did. I had noticed that there was somebody in his bathroom stripped to the waist and shaving, but I let Baker draw me out, and when I had ended my story a colonel in full uniform appeared, all shaved and fine, to be introduced as the chief of one branch of the secret service. I think this was Baker's characteristic way of dealing with his officer's suspicions; he disarmed by confirming them. Maybe the president had put the secretary of war up to that. Anyway, when my amusing troubles were at their height, soon after the president had refused to see me in "an emergency," he was coming, with Lloyd George and Clemenceau, into the Crillon one day. I had been caught in the front line of the crowd who stood to see the great men arrive, and Wilson, spying me, slipped aside, laid his arm around over my shoulder, and flustered into my ear. He said nothing. It looked as if—I think he was pretending that he was saying something very confidential to me, but I am sure he was saying nothing at all. Anyway I caught not one word of what he said. He slipped back and with a very intimate little understanding nod to me, passed on. And it had the effect that I think the president and Secretary Baker had intended. It gave me some immunity from the detectives and spies who must have seen and reported the incident.

Bullitt was not to be mollified. He waited on his peace job for the treaty to be finished. Then he broke all bounds. He was one of the group of aristocratic young American liberals who were so outraged by the treaty that they met to protest by some united action. I was at that meeting. I was the only older man there to see that significant scene; all those conscientious, high-bred, mostly rich young gentlemen and their wives, who wanted to do right and had to decide then and there whether to sacrifice their careers, as they honestly believed, by an open challenge to the wrong done by their government, by their department, or yield and play the game. They asked my advice, sure, I could see, that I would be for the heroic course. And I would have been in the old muckraking days. But, as I said, I had seen the Russian Revolution, the war, and this peace, and I was sure that it was useless—it was almost wrong— to fight for the right under our system; petty reforms in politics, wars without victories, just peace, were impossible, unintelligent, heroic but immoral. Either they and we all should labor to change the foundation of society, as the Russians were doing, or go along with the resultant civilization we were part of, taking care only to save our minds by seeing it all straight and thinking about it clearly. I only stated, I did not urge, this view; and some of those fine young men resigned in a round robin of protest; others remained in office.

Bullitt resigned and went home to make his report and mine to the United States Senate. My report was only technical: to the effect that the destructive period of the Russian Revolution was over; the constructive process had been well begun. The Senate used the report of the Bullitt mission only to fight President Wilson and the Democrats and to help elect the Republicans.

XIX

THE PEACE THAT WAS NO PEACE

PEACE settled upon Paris when the peace-makers went home, the thousands of them: the premiers and the president, their delegates, secretaries, experts, secret services, lobbyists, and the special correspondents, and the soldiers—all the foreigners. Only the Parisians were left, and the regular correspondents and the reparation officials—and the bankers. Just people. No uniforms, no guests, no poses. We were all very intimate and comfortable and quiet. A street girl accosted me near the Crillon one afternoon, and I reproached her.

"I have passed this way every day for a year, and you have never spoken to me before. Why not? Why now?"

She smiled, frowned, began to apologize. "Mais, Monsieur—" but she laughed instead and said: "Oh, well, you see the boys are all gone now, and the officers, and the foreigners. So you—so I. Come," she invited, "I will just walk a block with you, just for fun, just us French." And we talked about the foreigners, especially the Americans, "who don't know how to play, to whom everything is business, even love."

I stayed behind in Paris because I wanted to watch the consequences of the treaty. And the consequences of the peace were visible from Paris. There were wars, revolutions, distress everywhere. I challenged a group of war correspondents to name all the wars, big and little, that were going on in the world, and they could not do it. They could not, among them, list more than a score. Real wars, I mean; the economic conflicts were universal. I traveled all over Europe, to Berlin, Vienna, Rome, following correspondents to the news, which they could not altogether cover, and we passed by spectacular scenes of "readjustment" which were never "covered" to get to the big story the editors wished reported.

We came to have contempt for those statesmen, the peace-makers, and their ignorance. They had drawn on the map straight lines that cut off peoples from their markets, towns and villages from their fields and industries, put communities that spoke one language under rulers who spoke another, sometimes carelessly, sometimes at the behest of malicious or grasping lobbyists. Paris was quiet, but the rest of the world was not quiet. The poor peasants of Europe who had prayed that the American president might not be like their own politicians prayed no more. They were hard, too, bitter, disillusioned, grasping. The French peasants presented bills for the water, light—the improvements the Americans and English had put into their houses. Other peasants and workers were mad enough to revolt if they could find leaders. Revolutions were occurring or menacing; Germany had had one, and defeated, the revolutionists were inciting to another, a real one, with the experienced Russians pointing the way and giving advice.

Convinced as I was then that nothing but revolution would save us, I was back on the job that took me to Mexico and Russia, a study of revolution, and there was something to learn. Old revolutionary theories were being exploded. One of those that went first was the idea that "when things get bad enough, the revolution is bound to occur." Things were so bad in Germany that the revolution could not occur. The instinct to repair and rebuild, to plant, harvest, and eat, was so strong in distress that the people were busy. They could not stop long to listen to the leaders, who could not themselves agree. Socialists, even German socialists, and anarchists —revolutionaries—are not revolutionists. They are liberals, most of them, who only talk and think revolution—Kerenskis, Mensheviks. Lenin alone knew that in time to act upon his knowledge. He had split the Russian Marxians early into Bolsheviks and Mensheviks, so it seemed; but really he was separating the men of action in his movement from the intellectuals. That was never done consciously in Germany, and the leaders who wanted to "do socialism" (in Lenin's phrase), the revolutionists, and the evolutionists who wanted to talk and gradually to approach their goal, differed and distracted the German people, who were in a bad way, hungry and frightened. I heard there, from the left, the old theory that things must get still worse. I went to Vienna, where they were still worse. The Viennese, labor, middle class and nobles—practically all of them were so poor, so hungry, that their little children's legs were bent into bows, and when their doctors broke and reset them straight (as was done) they bent again. And the people there saw this, and they wept, but they did not revolt. They were so weak themselves that they could not think, then, of revolution. They did not turn to their socialism till things got better, and even then they chose the evolutionary course. My observations in Austria and Germany suggest that that old theory be reversed, that there is a better chance of revolution in a country like the United States where labor is very well off. A sudden precipitation into hard times might cause an uprising almost impossible in a state of continuous misery.

Over in Hungary they were exploding another, a liberal, theory: that you can have a revolution without a red terror. Lenin himself had thought that and said so: we might avoid the actual killings; and I heard in Buda-Pesth that he was advising Bela Kun, who was the head in that city of the victorious red revolution in Hungary. Anyway Bela Kun suppressed the red terror there, both the slaughter and the fear, and he lost out. The reds let the whites stay in Hungary, and they wiggled and wangled, got help from abroad (Hoover, who was feeding the people, used his charity for the whites against the reds), and finally rose and conquered the red revolutionary government, driving Bela Kun to Moscow, where, by the way, having learned his lesson, he became so ruthless that the Bolsheviki themselves demoted him. The terror, red or white, is inevitable in a revolution or a civil war, just as outrage and death are unavoidable in a foreign war and as bribery and corruption are natural elements in a political conflict of economic forces.

South of Hungary and east and west, in the Balkans there were revolutions, but they turned, as in Austria, into struggles between the workers and the peasants, and with no considered plans and no revolutionary but only political purposes, the peasants won and were soon deceived, corrupted, or defeated by the old reactionary interests, kings, nobles, business. The failure of all radical programs to understand and plan for the peasants was the outstanding weakness exposed by the war and its consequence in Europe—that and the prevalence of liberal instincts and doctrines. This last appeared in the well-nigh universal reaction of all the peoples and most of the socialists and radicals against Bolshevism, as too literal, too ruthless and logical. The Russian Revolution undoubtedly helped to stay the revolutionary spirit of Europe. Organized labor discovered that the workers were capitalistic, but all organized interests and groups, economic and political, shrank before the spectacle of the Russian Revolution and its civil wars. Nobody meant that when they spoke of socialism and revolution. And the Russians knew it. They had to change the name socialism to communism to distinguish between liberal and literal Marxism, very much as Christians have had to acknowledge Protestants and Catholics.

I went to Russia again in 1923, with Senator Robert M. La-Follette, his son Bob Jr. (who succeeded him in the Senate), and Jo Davidson. That journey brought out the difference between an American liberal, called at home a radical, and a real radical. Senator LaFollette was very friendly to the Russians, who liked him well, but he deplored their excesses, both in the terror and in the lengths to which they had gone to change the foundations of life and government. I heard him tell the Russians that they need not have gone so far; if they had only introduced into Russia the reforms he had carried through in Wisconsin they would have got what Wisconsin had; and he invited them to send a group or a committee to his State to learn what to do. Wisconsin! It's about the best we have to show, but the system is intact there, and his son, Senator Robert M. LaFollette Jr., still fights it, and he knows that his State has not so much to teach Russia as Russia has to teach Wisconsin. Young Bob is not a radical; he certainly is not a Russian radical, but there was a generation between him and his fine old father, and the present senator could see and learn on that journey.

But what interested me on that fascinating trip was to see that the Bolshevik government was making good, and without compromise, too. They retreated. Their so-called New Economic Policy was a backing up, but it was temporary, a step back for a moment along the line they would soon renew the advance upon. The peasants, taxed according to their production, had reduced their harvests, and the Bolsheviki, having no sense of the land problem as we know it, having no idea that they might tax the land and not the harvest, had been forced to let the peasants sell what they reaped over and above what they needed. This required the government to let private traders buy the surplus and sell at retail other things that the farmers wanted to buy or exchange. So there was free exchange and private business on a small scale—for a while. But the Bolsheviki explained that they intended later, when they were quite ready for it, to dispossess the kulaks (rich farmers) of their lands, establish and make understood the law, as it then stood, that all the land belonged to the state and that the peasants paid rent for it (not taxes). But also they proposed, next, to sweep all the peasants off their own holdings and put them to work as labor on the great Soviet farms to be managed on a grand scale by experts who would direct all operations, as in the industries, in syndicates under central control for the common good. In other words the Bolsheviki, who are socialists, who are psychologically the proletariat, intended to transform the farmers from proprietors into laborers and then solve the farm problem as a part of the labor problem.

And to anticipate, they are doing that now in the summer of 1930. They waited a long time; they let the peasants, who are a powerful majority of some 92 per cent. of the population, play along in possession of the land under the incentive of profits, and as was expected, the thrifty among them accumulated more and more land and, illegally but actually, made wage-workers out of their neighbors. The so-called "rich peasants" or kulaks were recommencing the process of capitalism; in time there would have been rich and poor again, land-owners and farm laborers, capitalists, employers, and employees. It was this process that Trotzky was so impatient to put a stop to that he broke the Bolshevik law against open debate, appealed from the government to public opinion, and was banished. But Stalin, Lenin's successor, a peasant himself, was waiting for two developments:

(1) For a conscious, political division of the peasants into poor and rich, so as to have the poor majority with him against the rich.

(2) For a demonstration in prolonged practice that industry could be developed without the incentive of profit.

When the Bolshevik government was convinced and ready on these points, Stalin gave the order for the abolition of the kulak, land-ownership, and farming for individual profit. All farmers in Russia are to be workers on state-owned and -managed grand estates, which, like the industries, are to be parts of the machinery for mass-production.

To my American-bred mind the revolutionary by-product of all this was the Russians' conclusion that their experiment had demonstrated that, just as in all other countries, labor would work without the driving force of individual profit, so farming, business, and management generally could be inspired by—let us say vanity or pride, the ambition to excel in service. The art motive worked, and it worked pretty well.

In between these visits to revolutionary experiments, I was running with the pack of correspondents to the peace conferences— San Remo, Lausanne, Genoa—where the unsolved political problems left by the Paris peace-makers were being negotiated, but not settled. We could not make peace. Turkey was the apparent enemy at Lausanne and Genoa, but oil was the real devil. That did not appear on the surface. The peace delegates talked for the correspondents and the peoples about principles and politics, but they spent their days and nights in closed rooms whispering about the oil of Mesopotamia. This, the truth, the cause of war and corruption and lying diplomacy, came out but twice, once in a mere rumor, once in print. The first time was when Mussolini came to Lausanne. He had refused to attend the peace conference, and the delegates said, "No matter"; they affected to despise the Italian dictator. But when he suddenly changed his mind and was coming —for a visit—I noticed that everybody was excited. Even the dignified diplomats were curious to see this mighty menace to democracy. They marked the stages of his approach and were astonished when he halted a few miles out of Lausanne, ordered his dinner, and declared his intention to stay the night at a little, friendly inn. We heard afterward what happened—the lobby rumor, which was never verified. When his secretaries remonstrated with him, saying that Mr. Lloyd George and the other premiers and ambassadors were waiting at Lausanne to see him, he said, "Oh, they will see me; they will come here to see me." And they did, we heard. The prophets drove out to meet the mountain and welcome him to the peace conference. But he is said to have said, "No, I am not going to your peace conference. It is not necessary. I can tell you here, now, in a few words, the Italian position. We have no quarrel with Turkey, and if you make a fair peace with her, Italy will agree and sign."

Very gratifying to Mr. Lloyd George and his colleagues. "But," Mussolini is said to have said, in his rude, realistic, hard Italian manner—"but, gentlemen, you are not seeking peace, I hear. You are out for the loot, for oil— Well, so be it. Italy is clear on that, too. If it is peace you make we will do our share, but if it is loot you get, if it is oil you take, then—Italy wants her share."

Authentic? I don't know. We laughed in the lobbies over that story, which we believed. Like so many rumors, it was truer than the records; whether Mussolini said it there is no way to prove, but somebody said it, somebody who understood what it was all about, that Lausanne peace conference and the other peace conferences—all the peace conferences and all the wars.

The Genoa peace conference was made clear by a reporter, Sam Spewack, who knew nothing about foreign affairs; all he knew was police and political news, but he was a star at that, and some editor of the New York *World*, probably Herbert Swope, sent him abroad as an experiment, just to see what a hard-boiled, contemptuous boy would do to European diplomacy. There was no risk for the paper, which had its regular correspondents. Spewack came straight to Genoa and was a lonely scab. Jo Davidson discovered him in our hotel.

"You ought to see him," said Davidson. "He's about six feet six, as thin as he is long, and associates with no one. The first thing he did when he got here was to go out and buy a violin. He's sitting down there now in his room playing the fiddle. I guess he misses his wife or—something."

I went down, saw Spewack, and heard him. His contempt for Europe, the peace conference, diplomacy, and journalism was based on his experience in the underworld. There could be no difference between jury-fixing and peace-making, between political graft and international loot, between politics and diplomacy, and as for foreign correspondents, he knew without looking that they were just ordinary plain reporters who ran in a pack. And he acted on that knowledge. I joined him. I was substituting on the Hearst papers for Karl von Wiegand, who had to go to Holland to get the Kaiser's book; so I kept in touch with the regular correspondents, but Jo Davidson and I followed Sam Spewack around to see him work, alone. He played his fiddle, got up, and went out to see somebody; read the papers, buttonholed lobbyists, not delegates, and called on a premier or an ambassador.

"Say," he said one day, "this is all about oil."

I nodded. "Sure." He played the fiddle awhile. Then he asked, "Why monkey around with conference debates on Turkey when oil's the stuff?" He fiddled, went out, came back, and fiddled. I don't recall his ever going to a conference. He was in the lobby with the lobbyists, hearing the rumors about oil and Mesopotamia, and he did attend the daily sessions of the press with Lloyd George or his British spokesman. And he sent some dispatches, and these made the front page at home. They were unusual, not stuff the regular correspondents were sending, and therefore beats. He was creeping up on oil. One day he burst into action. He got hold of a tentative oil agreement, which, if signed, would have settled the division of the oil fields among the big oil companies. He believed that if the oil men made peace the peace delegates would make peace, and that if the oil men could not agree the diplomats would not agree. The diplomats were the political agents of the oil companies just as legislators are representatives of the oil, the public service corporations, the railroads at home. He sent me out to ask diplomatic questions. He himself buzzed lobbyists who never appeared in the lobbies, the big attorneys who stayed in their rooms, and he decided: "Let's go," he said.

He cabled the tentative agreement of the oil companies for the division of the loot in Turkey and exaggerated it into a final settlement. The agreement had been initialed; he said it was signed. I cabled, too, but I stuck to the facts which Spewack interpreted the truth of. That agreement was, as he made it, a settlement of the graft, which awaited only the sure confirmation of the peace delegates in a treaty with Turkey. My cable was buried. Spewack's was the news of the day, but, "premature," it made a sensation, a scandal, and broke up both the agreement and the Genoa peace conference. Diplomacy could not admit openly that it was the division of the oil that the peace-makers were talking about. Lloyd George himself met the press to deny Spewack's story; none of his official staff had the courage or the strength to meet that emergency. English gentlemen do hate to lie when everybody knows the truth. But Mr. Lloyd George fixed his beautiful violet eyes on Sam Spewack and said without quailing just what he wished to have reported, and the New York police reporter looked back at that world statesman with the same unquailing contempt that he would have shown an American chief of police. He knew, did Sam Spewack, that business, politics, diplomacy, are all one thing. That peace conference faded away; Spewack went on to Berlin, Moscow, Paris; and he carried American newspaper methods and his reporter's scorn wherever he went. And the statesmen of Europe bowed to this irreverent boy and gave him scoop after scoop. He had finally to be fired from the *World* because he showed for his editors, or some of them, the disrespect premiers and presidents had wilted before.

Some magazine or some newspaper syndicate owes it to the world to report, to muckrake, European countries as the United States has been "covered." Spewack could do it. I could not. As Spewack said to me in the packed lobby after we had both "exposed" the oil of Mesopotamia at Geneva, when his story was the news of the day and mine was buried—before all the correspondents, statesmen, and lobbyists that evening he came up to me, laid his great hand on my shoulder, and looking down from his mental and physical height, he said, "Stef, you know news, you can get news, but you can't write it, boy, you can't write it."

XX

MUSSOLINI

LET this, the truest chapter in this narrative, my story of Italy and Mussolini—let it be also the purest fiction, romance; there's a girl in it, by the way. She was assigned by the London School of Economics to an American peace group in Paris, and as she went dancing about among the delegates, lobbyists, and correspondents, it seemed to me that she was one of the happiest things I had ever seen. She was as joyous as Jack Reed was when he came out of Harvard to see and sing life. He only sang. This girl danced. Her eyes danced, her mind, her hands, her feet danced as she ran—she literally trotted about on her errands. I was fascinated by this personification of the younger generation which had been profiteering behind the war front on their neglect by the older generation, preoccupied with the war. She was not for me, of course. Too young. But I felt something which I smothered by likening her to a boy. Her name was Ella Winter, but I called her Peter. I was only helping this bright Professor Peter to see through what was going on all around her. She was a radical, she thought. A university organizer of the British Labor party, she and another girl who afterward married a son of H. G. Wells, later managed the novelist's stand for Parliament. But she was English, educated English. She "saw through" nothing, not even the economics she lectured on at her college. It was fun, and it was an excuse to be with her, to point her eager eyes through the diplomatic front of peace to the war in the rear.

When the peace-making was over and she returned to London, I visited her and eased her anxious parents by showing them that, to me, she was only Youth. Soon after that I was barred from England, from the British Empire and possessions. I never learned why, and my inquiries embarrassed my liberal English friends, who knew that, unfortunately, I was not dangerous. They heard that Lloyd George had done it, but they could not believe that for no stated reason an inhabitant of the earth could be ruled off so large a part of it as, unfortunately, the British Empire is. The English don't know their own government. They don't know, for example, that the American institution of "pull" is an English political practice. My son, Pete, will know it. He will always be four or five years younger than he might have been because somebody postponed his birth by the pull that kept his father out of England. There were compensations, however. I had to describe post-war Europe to his unintending mother in letters which forced me to clear my own mind while I was clearing hers, not only on politics, but on how to choose a husband from among her several suitors in England. It was a queer mix-up, this innocent romance, but looking at it backward, I can see that it was Peter who made me see what I was looking at—she and Mussolini.

He, too, appeared as a romantic figure. Benito Mussolini came like thunder on the right. It was just as if the Author of all things had looked down upon this little planet of His, and seeing the physical, mental, moral confusion here, said to Himself, "How can I, in a flash, clear up these poor humans? I haven't much time for so small a ball of mud, but I must somehow help them to change their minds and catch up with the changes I am making." And "I know," He said; "I will have a political thunderstorm, big enough for all men to notice and not too big for them to comprehend, and through it I will shoot a blazing thunderbolt that will strike down all their foolish old principles, burn up their dead ideas, and separate the new light I am creating from the darkness men have made." And so He formed Mussolini out of a rib of Italy.

Anyway, that's how I saw the Duce and his Fascismo, as lightning that illuminated, in flashes, Russia and Germany, France, England—all Europe and, later, the United States. Mussolini took the method, the spirit, the stuff, of Bolshevism and used it to go— right. The method! Was that what the divine Dictator meant us to see—that there was a method, good either way? I, a broken liberal, had to answer that to explain it to my liberal girl, who believed, as I did still, a little, in majorities, in democracy, in liberty; and I had to see it as it happened, close up. I was there when Mussolini leaped into sight.

With England closed to me I had been going to Italy for my breathing-spells between peace conferences and warlike explosions. It was quiet, comfortable, cheap; and there was a revolution to watch for. The Italians were sore. Humiliated by defeat in the war and by the slights of their allies in the peace-making, they were in trouble economically, too. There was discontent enough for a revolution and socialism enough to guide one, but no leader, not like Lenin, no master mind to separate the talkers from the doers and lay a course. The debate persisted. Some red labor did rise and take over some factories, but the owners, wise in leadership or in neglect, let the workers run things. Business was bad. It was a good time to have labor try its hand at management. Nobody could succeed. Labor failed, quit, making another defeat for the people, who turned to politics with the sullen soldiers organizing to lead them. I went from northern Italy to the south, looking for parallels with Mexico and Russia. It was time for the government mistake that might precipitate the revolution. The black shirts were forming and looking for a leader to march on Rome. That was "imminent revolution," but the leader was Gabriele d'Annunzio, an intellectual; he could talk and write, but he could not act. He wouldn't even march to Rome. The black shirts marched on ahead, without him. What would Rome do?

Whether it was a mistake or a wise act, that weak, distracted government did not oppose; it either invited or encouraged the march. The troops were held off, the police tipped to inactivity, and the invaders came peacefully and took possession with powerful consent. And when D'Annunzio would not come to head this curiously leaderless conquest of power, this helpless mob, Mussolini was sent for. "Who was Mussolini?" we asked, and we soon had the answer.

Benito Mussolini came (by a night train) to Rome, and he seized power, not only the leadership but the throne, which he filled to overflowing. He let the king stand, aside, but he suppressed him and his ministers, and the parliament, and liberty, democracy, and aristocracy; he commanded the army, the navy, the police; he occupied the ministries—all by force, by the threat of the force of his personality, his decision, his activity, by the fear of his power to throw his small, organized minority of armed youth into violent action. It was a spectacle, so swift, so quiet, so tense but orderly; amazing; so easy—for the right man at the right psychological moment. And on Mussolini's part, it was so understood. He evidently knew something. He knew something we did not know. Put it this way: Mussolini knew something which we did not know that we knew. He said so.

I asked him, later, how he came to seize power. "You know," I explained, "you were not elected; you did not seek election. You just jumped into the throne; you seized it and power."

His answer showed that he understood my question and me, that I was a liberal with preconceived liberal principles and the liberal's inquisitiveness about the way to do—whatever you want to do. His fierce face expressed his contempt for me and my kind and our dead logic.

"You're a correspondent?" I nodded. "Yes," he mocked, and he asked and answered: "You saw the war? Yes. And the peace? Yes. And the revolution in Russia? Yes.

"Well," he sneered, "did you learn anything?"

God's question to man, that! Could we, could I, learn from experience, from history, from events, he meant, as he could and did. Or did I stick to my principles, theories, in the face of the plain facts? My muttered reply was that yes, I had learned some things.

"Some things!" he exclaimed. "Some?" he bored. "Listen. Do you think now any of the things you thought before you saw the war, the peace, and the revolution?"

What a question! Did I? I did till Mussolini shot that searching question into me. I carried some of my old ideas as a creed in one compartment of my brain, while I stowed away in another compartment the news I saw and reported. There was no bridge in my sight until I beheld this man of action and of mind throw away his baggage and strut across Russia's revolutionary experience from his old white ideology to the new red ideology. He, an ex-socialist of the left, almost an anarchist, had watched the war, as a soldier, to see how you get obedience unto death out of the people; he had watched the peace as a red to see what the war was about; he had watched Russia, as a leader seeking a way to do—whatever you want to do. And he had learned because, no mere intellectual, he could change his mind, deep down, to the depths where it would change his acts, his every impulse.

I—and my kind, the intellectuals—must learn to do that, else we'll never lead, and some day, as in Soviet Russia, we'll be killed as obstacles. We know too much. We know that there is no absolute knowledge, that there are only theories; but we forget this. The better educated we are, the harder we believe in axioms. I asked Einstein in Berlin once how he, a trained, drilled, teaching scientist of the worst sort, a mathematician, physicist, astronomer, had been able to make his great discoveries. "How did you ever do it?" I exclaimed, and he, understanding and smiling, gave the answer.

"By challenging an axiom."

Mussolini was challenging axioms, which brain-bound me, which spiked Europe to the past. As bold as Einstein, Mussolini, the willful man of action, saw by looking—at Russia, for example—that the people there in power were distracted by conflicting counsel and helpless. They wanted to follow, not to lead; to be governed, not to govern themselves. Democracy enthroned went straight to a dictatorship. He saw also that about the same time, in a similar emergency—in the fright of war which is like that of a revolution—the western nations turned to dictatorship. England made Lloyd George a dictator; France made Clemenceau a dictator; the United States suppressed its Constitution and made Woodrow Wilson absolute. But I, too, saw that. We all saw it, as Mussolini did. What was the difference? I—we—judged what we saw. We said Wilson weakened, Lenin did wrong. Mussolini saw it all; he said it, but also he acted upon it. He really learned it all. When he withered me with his contempt for learning only "some things," I answered by asking him roughly, "And what did you learn?"

"I learned"—he came back still superior, still on top—"I learned that there is an empty throne in every country and that, given the emergency, the bold men can seize it—and hold it."

He saw this, and he pointed out to his friends in Italy that they could do there what the Bolsheviki did in Russia. His friends said no, that that was all very well for backward, illiterate Russia, but not for Italy.

"I said," he said, "that what was done in Russia and in old Rome could be done in new Rome. And I did it. And now—I know what you will say: you will say that yes, it was done in Italy and Russia, but it could not be done in France, England, America. I say that what has been done—in one place—can be done everywhere."

The powerful way Mussolini says things is deceptive. As he said this, with force, like a threat, I felt that it was only he, this one man, who could see and say and act thus. But Mussolini's power and his triumph came not only out of his strength and his character and his frightening contempt, but from his faith, his scientific confidence, in facts and in history. Like Lenin. These new, revolutionary leaders read history, and not as the scholars do, for love of a growing body of knowledge, not even as scientists seeking the laws that govern events, but as men of action, reading a record of human experimentation to find out what can be done and how. They detect, they think, the workings of elemental forces, and they hitch their wagons to these—not to stars, but to historically discovered and experimentally proved going concerns. They don't judge men and events; they try to understand them to prophesy and steer by. History, both current and classic, told Mussolini that he was historically due—he and Lenin. There was the mob coming, the crisis of revolution to take possession of and turn as he would. He had taken it, and he was doing one of the two things that had to be done, as Lenin had done the other.

They were opposite or at any rate different things. But never mind that. The method is what we lack and need, a way to do what I had seen reformers at home (and in history) begin in vain to do. Where were we to learn how to succeed? Lenin had learned from history; Mussolini had learned from the news, confirmed by history, a way to do—whatever it was that they were doing, he and Lenin. Two different experiments, then, with one and the same method. What was it in general? Well, they had both abandoned the democratic method and were using a dictatorship supported by a very small, instructed, disciplined, armed minority of rebellious but really romantic, obedient youth.

What they were doing is another question, and it is important. Lenin and his successors, the Bolsheviki, were sweeping away a culture, an organization of society, which they named capitalism and hated as a failure which threw up a few rich, many poor, and all grasping, cowardly, mean. Their theory was that human nature can be, if not changed, then so cultivated and selected by economic conditions that the more desirable parts will survive, the undesirable instincts be discouraged. They were founding on the revolution, on the cleared bottom of society, a new system without any incentives to or possibilities of riches and poverty, graft, war, injustice, tyranny. They were abolishing private property and making labor the owner and governor of all things and all men.

What was Mussolini doing? He would not tell me. The refusal was absolute. Why?

"You would publish my plan."

"Only in America."

"It would be republished here."

"Well, but what of that?"

"My people don't want to know my plans. They wouldn't, they couldn't, but they don't want to have to try to, understand a plan that involves difficult economic problems. They want me to do the work, and when I tell them I will, they are satisfied to let me and they go back to work."

There was a fact in this. Like the Russians, the Italians were worried and debating about what to do till Mussolini came along, as Lenin did, and said, "Let George do it." I witnessed this. I was there. When Mussolini said that they, the people, might stop governing and go to work—he would do it all—it was almost as if all Italy sighed and said, "Amen." And the people did go back to work, and they worked as they had not worked before. Is democracy a false theory? It may be an end, but is democracy the way to democracy? The Russians say no, political democracy is not the way to economic democracy; economic democracy is the way to political democracy.

And liberty? Mussolini abolished free speech, free thought, free assembly, a free press. But so did Bolshevik Russia, and so did Germany, France, England, and the United States; they, the governments and their peoples—we all—abolished liberty in our emergency of war. Don't we always abolish liberty when we are afraid or in trouble? Isn't liberty a psychological matter? Isn't it something that depends, not upon laws and constitutions, but upon our state of mind? Isn't liberty a measure of our sense of security and nothing else? Like democracy, like honesty, like peace, liberty has to be founded in economic arrangements that abolish fear.

The first time I saw Mussolini he showed his hand on this question. It was at Lausanne, the day after he had met the other premiers at his inn outside of the city and told them his position on the peace-making with Turkey. He came to town, took a hotel suite, and received, among others, some of us correspondents. He was seated in a great armchair, holding before his eyes a little book. He rose, and we were introduced, one by one. Then he sat down as we did, and he pretended to resume his reading, but his eyes were sizing us up, one by one. It was embarrassing, insulting, and apparently to make sure that we got his contempt for us, he turned the book upside down and went on—eyeing us over the top of it. I grinned, enjoying the scene; the others were indignant, and when at last he threw down the book and challenged us direct, no one was ready for him.

"Well," he charged in French, "you wanted to interview me. Why don't you begin?"

The first man to recover was the correspondent of *Le Temps*, the Paris organ of the French government that had criticized Mussolini a good deal.

"Do you think, Mr. President," he stuttered, "that we may—perhaps—achieve peace—some measure of peace at this Lausanne Conference?"

"*Le Temps*," sneered Mussolini, "*Le Temps!* Thinks you can make peace at a peace conference!"

It was fierce, the way he said it, an attack. And he sat up, leaned forward, and bored his scorn into the French correspondent. Then he turned to the rest of us. "Oh, ask me something, somebody."

He was asked, haltingly, several questions. What was he going to do about his parliament? He laughed. "It will do what I say." But it's a deliberative body, with power? "It will obey." And that's all he would say. He was curt, brief; the interview was very short, but I came out of it sure that here was a man and that that man knew something and meant something and had the will and the way to do something. I would go and live in Italy to see if I could not complete the changes occurring in my mind by watching this dictator work.

A beautiful, romantic country, Italy. I could not enjoy it alone. My English girl had given up lecturing at the London School of Economics and was conducting an old Wundt-like experiment in psychology at Cambridge. A waste. She could learn more in Italy. And she had not decided which of her suitors would suit her. I got a passport somehow, by pull, slipped over to England, and, in short, I disapproved of all the other candidates for husband and recommended myself, with reasons, for a while. We went to San Remo, took a villa, and there in the fall of 1924 my son, Pete Stanley Steffens, named after his mother, Peter, was born. There were trips to Germany, Austria, France, Czecho-Slovakia, but Italy was the best show. We lived the second year at Alassio, in a cracking palace in a wild, big, neglected garden. But, together now, we watched Mussolini and the world. It was all romance, and Wall Street paid. I saw in the news that stocks were down, in fear that LaFollette might be elected president—when a Coolidge was running against him. I bet on Wall Street and won, in the boom, my garden on the Riviera, the laughter of my baby boy, and the education of his mother—and, by the way, a fresh view of my own country.

THE LATIN QUARTER

UPPER LEFT: JO DAVIDSON (EDWARD WESTON). UPPER RIGHT: JOHN DOS PASSOS.
LOWER LEFT: ERNEST HEMINGWAY (HELEN BREAKER, PARIS). LOWER RIGHT:
GERTRUDE STEIN (STATUE BY JO DAVIDSON).

XXI

EXPERIMENTAL EUROPE

THE next few years were rather personal, *en famille*. The two villas we lived in so happily on the Italian Riviera (1924-1926) were, one at old San Remo, the other at Alassio, both back up on the hills overlooking the town, Italy, the sea, the world. And we who sat or played about in our quiet gardens, I, my young wife, and the infant child, were of three generations. I often felt like a sudden grandfather with a grown daughter and a grandson to bring up to see things and to live with them as they are becoming. How was that to be done? I was not wounded or bitter; I was neither a cynic nor a believer. I had my girl to disillusion and my little boy to start off with none of our illusions and yet with interest and self-confidence.

That meant giving them other illusions.

Yes, but there is progress that way. I would not tell the child any of my new illusions, on authority, as certain. We would answer his questions by "going to see," and sometimes I'd be right; sometimes he'd be right and I wrong. To his mother I offered the old rule of my experience: to look at facts, let them destroy an illusion, and not be cast down, but go on studying the facts, sure that in those very same facts would be found constructive material with which to build up another—illusion, no better, perhaps, but other than the old one. Despair over a bad, negotiated peace which merely divided the loot and dominion of the world might show that that very loot and that dominion were the purposes, and, therefore, pointers to the causes, of war. True, the idea of making peace by removing the causes and incentives might prove an illusive theory, but it was an advance over the old one: that the statesmen of old, corrupt governments could write a peace on paper. There was a thought in my theory, too, and it was thinking that misled us. If we could only learn to see, to think only enough to help us to see, we might learn ourselves and teach Pete, our boy, to learn without convictions, without thinking to conclusions, and therefore without too many fixed illusions. "Maybe," I said, smiling, but seriously. My child sobered me. With him in mind I was slower, more careful, than I would have been in reporting for a newspaper. For his sake, in part, I looked again and again; we all looked and looked again, and it was a sight that we saw from the garden above the cities and the sea.

There was the world before us, in motion, and we were there, not only to play, but to watch the news, without blinking. If there were happenings we could not read enough about, we were handy to Rome, Paris, Berlin, where we went for more. And guests were coming and going, all sorts of travelers from all sorts of places with all sorts of views and experiences: correspondents and business men, artists, writers, tourists. The American reporters from Rome came, denouncing the press censorship, the frightening tyranny of the dictatorship. Pretty bad, and my English liberal wife was inflamed. But was there liberty in England? Was Mussolini pretending to give us liberty? What was he driving at? We should not judge him by what we wanted, but by what he wanted to do. I had seen American correspondents judging the revolution in Mexico against foreign business control by asking whether foreign business was good there! The Russian Revolution was tested by its treatment of the Czar, the capitalists—the classes it was trying to get rid of. That was not seeing.

Theron and Netta Cooper, of the Walden Book Shop, Edwin Kuh, from the wheat pit, and his wife; Max Epstein, big business, and Mrs. Epstein, came over from Chicago with the flush of American prosperity to shine on us. Jo Davidson and his wife, Yvonne, the *couturière,* and Mme. Robert Castro, the French writer, came down from Paris. Sinclair and Grace Lewis, he trying to get into rage enough at Europe to lay a novel somewhere abroad; Fred and Marie Howe, he making a study of the history and the practice of banking, she full of George Sand; the Whelpleys, Americans from London, called. Frederick C. O'Brien, of the South Seas, lived near us at Alassio, planning to "do" Liberia down on the Africa west coast. While the Davidsons were with us at Alassio, Mrs. Harry Payne Whitney, the sculptress, drove over from Bordighera to dinner, full of humorous complaint that artists and writers were all snobs who held her off as a rich woman instead of taking her in as an artist. Fay Lewis, his niece, and Margaret Johannsen (the most eager, grasping, grateful tourist I ever saw) brought us a new view of American labor, and Janie Hollister of Santa Barbara and New York brought us perplexed and perplexing problems of the American younger generation of aristocrats. Mrs. Richard Washburn Child, the wife of the American ambassador at Rome, called and let us see Mussolini and Fascism as she saw them close up. Mrs. Jack London passed our way just for fun. Max Eastman and Eliena Krylenko, his young Russian wife, came direct from Russia with news and with light on dark spots there. Dosch-Fleurot, his wife, and his dog called and laughed. Hayden B. Harris, the American banker in Paris (who had been the American financial observer in Italy during the armistice), and Mr. and Mrs. Leon Graves, came to rest, play, and chat. We, on our part, drove over to Nice to call on Brand and Mrs. Whitlock, to Florence to spend a rich week with Charles Erskine Scott Wood and Sara Bard Field. We had vacations in Switzerland, where we saw Colonel Arthur Woods, the ex-commissioner of police of New York, then a director of a Rockefeller fund, and in Carlsbad, Vienna, and at Salzburg (for the plays) with Edward A. Filene, whose account of America was simply incredible.

Those were sight-seeing years, the two in Italy, and such sights, and, best of all, such happiness. It seems to have been spent all in those Italian gardens in an atmosphere of play. Even our Italian servants were happy, as I demanded and would recommend. When they were engaged, these servants, I warned them that they might lie, politely; loaf, some; steal, the regular percentage; be careless, not overclean, and not too efficient; we'd stand for all that, and more. But if any one of them was ever or even appeared to be unhappy—out. They understood, laughed, and none was ever discharged by us. Another American family that bid for and won (with my "pull") our good cook at Alassio put her out in a month for overgrafting, lying, neglect. "How could you keep such a woman?" she asked, and our answer was that she was happy with us and never did those things. Honor among thieves.

It was from the servants and their families and our humbler

neighbors that we got the local but typical "feel" and experiences of Fascism, the fear and the pride of the Italians. It was tyranny, and their inborn anarchism deeply resented the domination of Mussolini and Youth. The young men who were, and the boys and girls who meant to be, Fascists ruled the families, the towns— everything, like the young communists in Russia. It was a bracing sight to see the young black shirts walk through the streets, into an inn, or down the aisle of a railroad train, heads up, shoulders back, in command of the world. They were insolent. Youth is hard. The Fascists abused their power over their neighbors; they murdered, tortured, in some places. We heard the tales told in our garden and were stirred by them, but the Italians themselves were patient, because, they said, Mussolini was restoring Italy to its rank as a first-rate power; they could be proud again; he was tackling their internal problems with vigor at least; and he and Fascismo were no harder on them, labor, than they were on their employers. Which was true. The local bankers and business men showed us as much fear and as much pride as our servants did, and with cause. Our local Garibaldi Bank was suddenly closed one day, and we read in our Genoa newspaper that the Garibaldi banks all over Italy were all simultaneously—punished. We on our hill must be as patient as the Italians in Italy. We must not judge and, like the correspondents and foreigners, say that because we believed in free speech, a free press, in liberty, democracy, justice, we will have none of Mussolini. Liberty, justice, etc., may be only our illusions. We must look for Mussolini's illusions.

One day we read that Mussolini had gone before his parliament, announcing a financial crisis. The lira was sinking. It must be pegged somewhere, immediately. "You," he said in effect, "you parliamentarians couldn't solve this problem in months. You would talk, debate, disagree, and you'd finally only compromise, too late. I can settle it, now, and I will. I invite you, therefore, to do what you can do very well: Go to your cafés, sit down, and cuss out Mussolini, while I, Mussolini, will do the job in a week." And in a week or so he did, somehow, stabilize the lira.

To my wife, a member of the British Labor party, thinking of getting into Parliament, this was a shock. But I tempted her to pause and consider that maybe Mussolini was right, that parliamentary government had been tried and failed, that maybe labor in power in the British Parliament would be made to go slow, not, as was said, by any vague "sense of the responsibility of power," but by the "interests" which had made the other parties conservative. These causes of corruption had not been removed; therefore they might do to labor what they had done to liberalism. I described to her the labor government of San Francisco as a prophecy of a labor government in England. Where, as in Russia, these causes had been removed, a labor government, even a dictatorship, was continuously radical and loyal to its purposes. Soviet Russia owned and operated all those businesses which, in the United States (and in European countries, too), find that they must corrupt politics and control government. There was none but petty political corruption in Russia. The dictator was never asked to do wrong. His troubles were only with men who differed as to the way to carry out their common plan or the pace of progress. Maybe, then, if the sources of evil were closed up, a king might govern England, the Republican party govern the United States, a parliament reign in Italy. Maybe the form of government does not matter. Perhaps we should teach that to our little Pete and not teach him that if he is a good boy and grows up to be a good man, he will be able to give a people a good government. He must be intelligent, not virtuous. We were bringing it home thus to us, ourselves, his parents, that we should watch and learn from Italy and Europe and America, where all sorts of experiments are being carried on in several different theories, from the results of which we perhaps —but our boy surely—might be able to learn things we don't know and even draw, not conclusions, not new illusions, but workable theories, to try out with intelligence.

The mother followed all this, but Ella Winter and most of our guests balked at Mussolini. "If we are to tolerate his tyrannies for the sake of his end, we must ask what his end is," so they argued, and that balked me. For Mussolini was not closing any sources of corruption, like Russia; he was trying to regulate, control, govern them all, like the United States and the rest. Mussolini was reestablishing the actual sovereignty of the state, an old, old experiment, but the Italian experiment was under new, modern conditions and with temporary success and meaning.

We could see from our hill that one form of the conflict in Europe was against dual government, political and industrial.

There was the state, which, theoretically supreme, governed all men and all things in all countries, but, in fact, landlords, industries, business, also governed some men and some things, including a part of the state. An individual citizen was subject to the politically enacted laws that prescribed conduct, but as an employee on the land, in a shop or a factory, the same individual was subject to the rule of his employer, who told him what to do in his working hours, whether he could work at all or not, and how much he could have to live on. This industrial government was more powerful in his life than the political government was. If he was discontented with his wages, hours, and the laws of industry, he might protest and appeal to the state, but then he found that the industry which governed him was a partner, a sharer, in the sovereign power of the state. So with his employer. If his workers resisted his power, he sometimes found that the state was a rival power which might act for his employees as citizens or subjects. Or an industrialist, with an influence over the sovereign state, often found that the financial interest was more potent in the state and could decide against him. The result of this confusing conflict of interests for control of the state is what we call in the United States political corruption, but the tendency of it is to unite into one sovereignty the dual and sometimes manifold powers within a nation. It is old, this conflict, but after the war it was becoming conscious, as a short story of Hugo Stinnes may illustrate.

This great German industrialist was the third of three generations of business bosses. He was an instinctive, brainy, unintellectual man of action and will. He appeared as a merger of trusts after the war, and his reach was across the borders of his enemy countries, France and Belgium. He was following the vein of coal in the ground, the lines of least resistance in economics above ground, and some of us in Paris became interested in him when we heard that he was negotiating there for the merger of his German industrial combinations with the French cartels in the same fields. Our interest then was in peace. If Stinnes could merge the competing interests of French and German mines and industries he would make permanent peace between France and Germany. For the great French industrialists had corrupted and controlled France: French politics, press, and finance; and we assumed that Stinnes, with his horizontal and his vertical trusts, which were approaching a combination of all the business in Germany, controlled Germany, politics, press, finance. It was to have been a merger of the corrupting, controlling, actually sovereign interests of both countries, and our theory was that while Stinnes was looking only for a union of business, he would, whether intending it or not, be uniting two competing, warring countries. And his reported terms were sensible, practical, and peace-making. Stinnes was proposing that, in principle, the Germans should have 51 per cent. of the control, the French 51 per cent. of the profits. This was on the theory that the French were more interested in money, the Germans in production and management. The centralized, international business directorate would, in the pursuit of this policy, move managers, inventors, and foremen from Germany into France, and financiers and skilled workers, high and low, from France into Germany. There would be a gradual crossing of both business and breeds, and, for the purposes of peace-making, these negotiations seemed more important to economists than the parleyings of the premiers and peace delegates and the fighting of the lobbyists at the peace conferences. I went to Germany to learn more about Stinnes, the peace-maker.

It was impossible to see him, and his associates said that he could not talk. Talking was not in his line; he was inarticulate about what he could only do. But they, those friends of his, told amusing and significant stories about him. He had always been restless over his necessary political activities. Intent only on the building of an organization of all business, he had, as Americans like him complained that they had to do—he "had to" do politics. He hated it; he hated to corrupt the government, and he asked a profound question, "Why should there be two governments, one the state, the other of business?" They should be one, and Stinnes, in his blundering, ununderstanding way, had himself elected to the Reichstag so that he, the master builder, might be also a master statesman. I saw him in the Reichstag, and I heard amusing anecdotes about this executive as a deliberative parliamentarian. He was driven almost crazy by the debates. He could see what to do at a glance, and he wanted to do it immediately, but there were hundreds of other members, and—"They only talk," he complained. As Mussolini had said: "These parliamentarians talk, talk, talk, and to no definite end. They only agree on a compromise, which satisfies more or less their conflicting views, but does not do the job."

Stinnes wanted to abolish the state. He was not allowed to say it, and his motive was not ambition to rule, but his perception was that all business, all industry, even all agriculture and finance, might be united into one great trust and that that could, would, and should be the one and only all-sufficient government! This reminded me of the old I.W.W. slogan in the United States, "one big union." It was anarchism, but it reminded one also of socialist Russia, where also the conflict of the dual governments was felt as absurd and confusing. There the adopted, evolutionary plan was, by stages, first to set up a state as sovereign in political and in industrial power—like the Fascist state; or, since Mussolini had learned it from Russia, his establishment was like the Soviet state in that it achieved one united government. But the Russian wanted the political state only as a scaffold to build Stinnes's industrial establishment. Starting with a state that not only governed Russia and protected it in war against its foe, the world, but actually owned all property, land, forests, natural resources, railroads, industry, business, and houses, the Soviets planned to organize those building businesses and properties into divisions to be merged into one great all-comprehensive combination which should finally abolish the political state and be left standing as the government of Russia and of all men and things Russian. There would be no privileged, no propertied, persons; all men and women would be subjects of industry, directed absolutely, disciplined hard—governed in the few working-hours required for production every year, but outside of that—free, not governed at all.

Stinnes and his Germans, then, were driving, unconsciously perhaps, at the same end which the Bolsheviki, philosophically and deliberately, were driving at. Peace was only a by-product. The difference was that, while Stinnes's blind movement was to leave the capitalist in command, the open-eyed purpose of the Russians was to put and keep labor on the throne, the workers, producers, and consumers, who are to be merged into one and the very same people. Mussolini, by comparison, was leaving all the old competing blind interests, capital and labor, politicians and industrialists, and trying by force to subject them all equally to the state. France was proceeding conservatively in the old way, by the business corruption of politics carried to a logical extreme, to make business and the state one. In England they were preparing to let a so-called Labor party take the throne, trusting, however fearfully, that a Labor ministry would be liberal, conservative, safe. And, by the way, when my radical English wife saw how "safe" the first Ramsay MacDonald government was and went home to hear the members of her party say they wanted to prove that a Labor government was "safe," she asked, "Safe for what?" and she was half convinced that the English "radical" way was indeed safe for privilege.

She should not, no one should, be fully convinced, because one meaning of all this was that political corruption was not only an inevitable, it was a useful, necessary process. I thought over all my work as a muckraker, and I was willing to ask, but not yet to say that I was all wrong, the bribers right. If in Europe, as an outsider, I could see that there was an economic drift to merge industrial trusts into one combination of all business and that that tendency, encountering old, liberal laws passed at a time when we all believed in competition, had to corrupt its way through politics and government and become "the" government, then—it was time to go home and to look again and see, and let my boy Pete grow up where he might see, that maybe—maybe bribery and corruption are acts of God, and his father and muckrakers in general the agents of the Devil.

XXII

A EUROPEAN VIEW OF AMERICA

AFTER Italy, France again. Jo Davidson offered us for a winter residence his country place, Bêcheron, in Touraine. I can see now that I was on the way home. I was working on a *Life of Satan,* and down in the country we were busy and looked settled. But I was attentive to American news, interested in all I heard from and about the United States, the growing bigness of us, the feeling and the comment of Europe. Evidently we had won the war—not as our soldiers said, not in a military sense. Nobody won the war in that sense; everybody lost it. But spiritually we were undefeated, unlicked. When the fighting front came down and one could cross all lines, we found the whole world dancing to American jazz—the Germans, too. And economically they all were dancing to our pipers. We went into the war a conceited, but secretly rather humble, second-rate country; we came out self-assured. Our soldiers, our engineers, our organizers and managers, our industrialists and financiers—we had measured ourselves with our European competitors and discovered our competence; we were beaten only in diplomacy. In actual fighting, in work, in resources, riches, management, we were a first-rate people, "the" first world power! The criticism of us, the hate and envy, proved that and swelled our magnitude. We were the creditor country and, in industry, the pace-maker. The English, Germans, French, said it to one another in their newspapers. Even Soviet Russia, which despised our ideals and our culture, saw something in us to admire, covet, and copy. And most convincing of all, our own American correspondents in Paris, the hardest-boiled, least sentimental of observers, were reporting—something new. At the Anglo-American Press Association, American correspondents who went home for short business visits came back and in short, unaccustomed speeches tried to say that we had grown, that we were wonderful—one man blushed, stammered, and blurted that something was "beautiful at home."

There was, there must be, a new United States to see. It was not all new. There were scandals and familiar brutalities. In the late Wilson and the Harding administrations there were obvious grafts, but the Senate itself was doing some muckraking, and I was tempted to take the other side now. Something had happened to me, something that had begun in San Francisco, when I ended my muckraking with "An Apology for Graft," pleading that the prizes we offer for successful stealing from the public, the riches, honors, prestige, are too much for strong men. When the news accounts came to Europe of the Sinclair oil scandal, I wrote "An Apology for Oil," and Glenn Frank, then editor of the *Century*, first accepted, set, and advertised, then rejected it. We punished (a little) Sinclair and his associate, a cabinet member who yielded to the temptation to take our navy oil fields and operate them for us. My feeling about this incident showed me that I could no longer be a muckraker, not of business graft. I would have liked to muckrake the reformers; I was tempted to do that when the Senate, the liberals, and the people were killing President Wilson as they would have liked to "kill the Kaiser." Americans were still lynchers. Disturb them, disappoint or shock them, and they rise up in wrath, to ask who is the matter. And him they take criminal vengeance on. Wilson failed in Europe, but he was, perhaps, the greatest liberal we had. What liberal among all his critics could have done better under the circumstances?

The circumstances! It was the circumstances, the conditions, in European politics and business that were at fault. And liberalism. To have defended Wilson's failure would have been to take the light of Russia and Italy to America and show that liberalism was a failure; to remind my liberal friends that it was liberals who, in the liberal sense, made the war in all the allied countries, and who made the peace, too. That was why liberalism was fading out practically after the war; it had been tried and found wanting. The people of Europe were choosing between the extreme right and the extreme left. The English people, for example, were voting for the Tories or for Labor, and once at the House of Commons a group of Liberal party leaders asked me, at a luncheon, why this was so and what they could do to recover their place as, at least, an alternative party. I asked them, as I would have liked to ask the liberals in America, if they realized that they were not liberals; that liberalism was no longer an attitude and a philosophy, but a creed; that that creed had been exposed as false; and that, unlike truly liberal men, they had not learned anything from their war and their peace and probably could not learn even enough to consider a dictatorship and a minority as a method to do by evolution what revolutionary Russia had done: remove the causes of corruption and war; take and publicly own and operate all the business, which in private hands, always, everywhere, corrupted politics, grafted on industry, and led us into war? They had no answer, those English liberals. They had "principles"; they stuck to their convictions; so I recommended to those British liberals a study of Mussolini, as a leader trying by Bolshevik methods to avoid a revolution and by evolution to establish the state as the sovereign ruler of private business, privileged classes, and labor. They shook their heads, no; they could not do that. I must be pulling their legs. When the conservative English people elected the Labor party to do, liberally, what Mussolini was doing, many of those liberals went over into the Labor party, to be one of the influences that made it merely liberal. Ella Winter, my own household Labor party member, had hope. She knew now the history of the labor governments in California and in Mexico. But Lenin, Marx—some radical authority had said that if evolution was possible anywhere it would be in England. England, then, might be taken as a continuing experiment in evolution, with Labor as the agent of capital and the liberal minority as a check upon the excesses of both capital and labor.

I was still of the opinion that only revolution could do the job, and the spectacle of the Europeans of all countries and all classes going to work after the war like ants to restore everything as near as possible as it had been was convincing. "Reparations" was the word, repair the dominating idea. No basic changes. No new elements added, no old chemicals omitted from the combination that had exploded in the war. Nobody, in Mussolini's phrase, had learned anything. We were instinctive animals, not intelligent men; not the best of us. I had been seeing statesmen and financiers; now I was playing around with artists, writers, and it was pretty much the same: there was no concern about the war that had struck us, no asking why, no thought of prevention. Bitterness, cynicism, drink, sex—aplenty, but no science. There was a revolutionary spirit, but it shot off in the direction of art, morals, conduct. The war had had its effect, but not on the minds of men, only on their emotions.

Recalling my old theory that the war would cause revolutions, and how I had come to Europe to watch for them, you can imagine my slow disappointment to see and hear that sex was the thing. The revolutionary spirit of Germany, where conditions were the worst, turned to sex perversions and the establishment of a cult with newspapers to defend and promote the vices. In all Europe there was license. In America, where economic conditions were the best, we heard that all classes and ages had loosened up on drink and sex and that youth, which had found other outlets in Europe, were smashing through all the old moral inhibitions at home.

Some of that was to be seen around us in Europe, but among the writers and artists from home in Paris, the revolution was only subjective. Market writers and illustrators played to the new demand for "sex stuff," but the rest, the best, turned in on themselves. James Joyce, who moped silent at his restaurants, published his profound study of the subconscious, *Ulysses*. He and Ezra Pound were internationalists in language, and Ezra Pound, the American, was seeing and seizing all the world for his. Pound was a private, professional propagandist, as Gertrude Stein was. They both encouraged the younger artists to despise the old forms and the old stuff, to rebel, break away and dare. William A. Bird, an American correspondent, and his wife provided a place for the rebels to conspire and play in. The cafés in the Latin Quarter were for the mob, and there had been a "mob" of American and English young artists in Paris ever since the war. At "Billy Bird's" beautiful little old apartment, he and his gay wife, Sally, gathered in the workers, writers, painters, musicians. That's where I saw the best of them. George Antheil and Ezra Pound met, and the musician and the poet showed us the new music there, both of them, for that rebellious poet was a musician, too. Ezra Pound hated, and he charged, all fences in art; he incited the younger men to jump the barriers. He was a good revolutionary influence, but himself had been hurt somehow at home, deeply wounded. Gertrude Stein was another powerful revolutionary leader who was content to be herself, do her own work, but when the young men and women came to her, she gave them all they would take. Jo Davidson put her in marble as she was, a massive, serene Buddha, and while he was doing her, talking as usual, she did him in words. I heard the "Portrait of Jo Davidson" read at a distance one evening, and, unable to hear distinctly all the words, the reading sounded like the sculptor monologuing at his work—but exactly. Gertrude Stein struck me not only as a genius, but as a wise woman. She accepted herself as she was. She was large; she dressed as a large woman. Yvonne Davidson, one of the most creative of the famous French *couturières* of the day, made for Gertrude Stein, at her behest, a great flowing fat gown to wear when she was called by the Sitwells to read at Oxford, England. "Dress *me*," ordered the writer, and Yvonne dressed *her*, beautifully. Gertrude Stein made her Ford car over to fit her, and her home befitted her, the furniture, the great paintings she had bought, the perfect little dinners served there. You felt there her self-contentment and shared her composure, but, best of all, the prophetess gave you glimpses of what a Buddha can see by sitting still and quietly looking. Ernest Hemingway sat at her feet and took "not much," she said, but it was all he could use, and he wished it were more.

Hemingway was the surest future over there. He dawned upon me one night at the Lausanne peace conference, or perhaps it was in Rome, when he showed me a dispatch as from Greece. He had just come back from the exodus of the Greek fugitives from Turkey, and his cable was a short but vivid, detailed picture of what he had seen in that miserable stream of hungry, frightened, uprooted people. I was seeing the scene and said so. "No," he corrected, "read the cabelese, only the cabelese. Isn't it a great language?" And it was, and I recall later, much later, that he said: "I had to quit being a correspondent. I was getting too fascinated by the lingo of the cable." At the time I asked to read all his dispatches, for the pictures; got from him his rejected manuscripts, and read short stories, since published, which made me, as they did Guy Hickok and other reporters, sure of Hemingway. He could, he would, do it some day. Walking along the street with him, he would go boxing in the air, fishing, bull-baiting—all the motions. In Paris, where they approve all eccentricities, nobody noticed except to smile with this big, handsome boy, squaring off to phantom-fight you. He was gay, he was sentimental, but he was always at work. Like Sinclair Lewis, like my little boy, Pete, he was forever playing he was what he was writing. And he was straight, hard-boiled honest, too.

Guy Hickok warned me one day that Mrs. Hemingway was about to have a child. How did he know? "Oh," Guy said, "Hem was sitting by the window in my office while a visitor and I were talking about birth control, and all of a sudden Hem up and grumbled, 'There is no sure preventative.' " A little later Mrs. Hem bore, laughing, their great, big Bumbi Hem, who was brought up in his first year or so by the humorous old concierge woman of the house which was their address. His parents were away skiing in the Alps or bull-fighting in Spain, partly for the sport, partly for the phrases, the very words.

Dos Passos and Hemingway inspired and troubled my wife in a Chinese restaurant in Paris one night by their perfect agreement that anybody can write. "You can," Hem told her with a left to the jaw. "It's hell. It takes it all out of you; it nearly kills you; but you can do it. Anybody can. Even you can, Stef." And Dos Passos backed up the surer man only a little less surely. Great boys, those. Hemingway, when he had heard some of my stories, wanted to write my life, and when much later in New York he had seen my chapter on T.R. as a politician, he rejected it utterly as "foully written," wished he had had it to do, but declared: "You can do it, Stef. You can write. Anybody can. It's hell, and I haven't done it yet, but I will." I think he thought that writing was a matter of honesty and labor, and maybe it is, utter honesty and hard labor, but my association with writers like Hemingway has persuaded me that it is a mere matter of genius, not any moral or intellectual gifts; authors are seldom even intelligent; art is evidently the effect of some fairy's wand waved over the wrong infant before even the fairy could judge.

Jo Davidson is the only artist I have met who was consciously in the stream of life as I knew it. The others, certainly the young Americans in Paris, had been in the water, some of them had been nearly drowned by the flood of the war, but they saw and felt only the waves that broke over them. Hemingway had been wounded and pretty badly hurt, physically and emotionally, but he never asked what had loosed the furies. He blamed the Italians, with whose army he had served; he talked about them, but only as the American soldiers in France spoke of the French. Jo Davidson had been at the front, though only as a correspondent, but he never dwelt on those experiences. Like Jack Reed, he saw and felt the big forces that had done it once to us and might do it again to "our boys." His art saved the sculptor. "Busting" generals, statesmen, financiers, he talked to them, and he listened to them, and so saw the war and the peace from the perspective of headquarters, the capitals, and the markets. Jo Davidson was in the stream of art too. I have heard him say that the war had no influence upon art, only upon some of its themes. It had turned him from nudes and decorations to heads, mostly of great men, and he often regretted that. He also yearned for "mere beauty," wished he could be more than a "portrait buster," as his critics charged. I was with him all through his post-war busting; I heard his delight when he was making a panel, a lovely female figure or the life-size figure of my two-year-old child, "a human not yet erect." But Jo Davidson was all there, with all his faculties at work, when he was seeing and hearing and doing his Foch or John D. Rockefeller. He came back from such jobs with more than a likeness. He had conversations to repeat, and such conversations! Hemingway would have asked to write them. They were the expression in words of the character and the drama he had thumbed into the clay; they were richly appreciated by the sculptor, who enjoyed artistically the telling, the acting, of them; and the artist learned from those experiences, which gave him a growing grasp of men and the forces that moved them. There is some relation between Jo Davidson and his day. Dos Passos felt, saw, and he represents economic situations in his novels, and Upton Sinclair has economics at the bottom of all his writings. But Jo Davidson knows and has put into his great gallery of our times the sympathetically understood victors and victims of a critical period of the world's history.

It was Jo Davidson who first uncovered to me the new America. While I was living so pleasantly in his old manoir in the château district of Touraine, seeing the American tourists sight-seeing in their loaded busses, Jo was in New York and Oklahoma doing some work for E. W. Marland, the oil magnate, and, of course, hearing and seeing his country from a peak of big business. He wrote me letters about the energy and the adventure he felt, of the prosperity, the industry, the mass movement, which was so alive with fearless imagination that he himself was stirred by business. "You must come and see it," he said. The artist who should shun, my friend who knew how I had denounced big business, was asking me to come and see what had inspired his imagination as the old popes and princes of the Middle Ages had inspired their architects, sculptors, painters—not to despise but to work. There was a day when I would have said that the process of corruption had reached even the arts, and maybe that is what was happening. But another warning thought halted me. I remembered that in Soviet Russia, they, the reddest of reds, had seen and shown me a similar view of the United States; through all their contempt for our capitalism and their hateful resentment of our dull enmity to their communism, they had respect for our efficiency; they coveted, not our reformers and good men, but our big, bad captains of industry; and they envied and planned to imitate our mass production, not our Constitution, laws, and customs, not our justice, liberty, and democracy, not our respectability, good intentions, and law-abiding morality—none of our ideals, not even our business ideals, but only our machinery, our big business production, our chain stores and other beginnings of mass distribution.

Yes, there was something new to see in my own country, and I had something new to look it over with, not an old muckrake.

PART V
SEEING AMERICA AT LAST

I

THE DYNAMITERS AGAIN

THE date (March 1927) of my return from Europe was fixed by Clarence Darrow and Fremont Older, who wrote me that it was about time to call the old broken agreement that settled the McNamara dynamiting case in Los Angeles. Two of the prisoners, J. J. McNamara and David Kaplan, had served their terms and were out; two others, J. B. McNamara and Matt Schmidt, were in San Quentin for life. Under the agreement Schmidt and Kaplan should never have been arrested. Other items of the settlement had not been kept. Los Angeles employers never made the voluntary effort promised to deal openly and generously with labor for a rational, community arrangement with the workers there. Labor had not resented this in any way. The violent, the dynamiting, phase of the labor struggle was over. There were strikes here and there over the country. But organized labor, rank and file, had repudiated dynamite and was working with organized capital, contentedly and well, on a policy of contracts. Peace had come at home as abroad, and an agreement broken by capital was a bad precedent to leave standing. It was time for a pacific gesture. I had tried for one before, twice.

At the end of the war, when President Wilson was leaving Paris, I proposed to Colonel House a general amnesty by the president and the governors of States for all war and labor prisoners. That would have included the dynamiters. Colonel House rose to the suggestion as he always did to any liberal idea. And he acted on this one himself right away.

While I was writing for him a memorandum to present to the president on the boat going home, Robert Minor, the American writer and cartoonist, was arrested, charged with Bolshevik propaganda among the American troops during the Armistice. He had been playing around with me in Paris till suddenly he was gone, and by the time I had traced him he had been condemned to be shot. I protested to House that a summary shooting of a man as well known as Bob Minor would rearouse ill will and spoil our amnesty plan. House was an old friend of Bob Minor's father, a judge in Texas, who was cabling House to act.

"How can I stop it?" House asked.

"Well, it's the army that has Bob in its clutches," I reflected. "Evidence is no use; justice is vain. An order, a direct command, pull, is all that will function. You can't, not legally, but—you can get a commanding man to convey your command. The army taught to obey will obey."

"But who? Who can do it?"

"Get a very prominent man—a good man—a lawyer"—I was thinking out loud, slowly—"a Wall Street lawyer who knows politics and acts politics—who has a front and can speak as with the voice of—"

"Colby!" House exclaimed. "Bainbridge Colby! And he's in Paris now."

He telephoned the next secretary of state, made an appointment for me, and I was soon at the Ritz, telling all about Bob Minor.

"But is he guilty?" Mr. Colby asked.

I knew nothing of the case, but I answered my lawyer.

"Does not an attorney always work better if he knows his client is innocent?" I asked.

"Um—yes," said Colby.

"Well, then, I assure you that Bob Minor is as innocent as Adam, Eve, and the serpent."

Mr. Colby went to work. He was making progress when he bade me get out of Paris. There were rumors of pull in the Bob Minor case, and it might be traced to and through me. I went to Switzerland with a jaunting party of correspondents, and by the time we got to Geneva, Colby wired me that Bob was released to go home.

And by the way, the next time I saw Bob Minor he said something lots of men have felt and left unsaid. He came up uncomfortably to me in the street and—"Say, Stef," he said, "you did what you did in Paris that time—you didn't do it for me, did you? You did it for the Cause."

"Sure, Bob," I assured him, "but why are you so anxious about that?"

"Oh," he said, "I do hate this damned feeling of gratitude."

President Wilson received and read on his boat our amnesty memorandum, but he rejected the idea of it sharply, totally. He was in a fighting, acting mood, bitter and executive. And the American people were not ready for anything like peace. It looked better when Harding was president. After he had been in office awhile I went to him with a similar proposition, and to be sure of my ground, I sounded first a small number of governors to see if they would join in a general act of clemency for war and labor prisoners. Right away I got the reaction familiar to me: the politician governors would pardon their prisoners if the president would pardon his; the better men, the good, business governors, were most unwilling. Well, Harding was a politician; rumor had it that he was a sinner.

President Harding heard me out, his handsome face expressing his willingness and his doubt. He nodded, smiled, wagged his head. "Make peace at home," I said. "We've got it abroad. Let all the prisoners go who are in jail for fighting for labor, for peace, for—anything. Let 'em all out, with a proclamation, you and the governors."

"That's all right," he said, "for fellows like you and me, but— but They won't let me do it." He had the case of Eugene V. Debs, the socialist leader, before him; we all knew that, and I had asked his permission to visit Debs in Atlanta.

"I am going to pardon Debs," he said. "I have put that over, but a general amnesty?" He shook his head; then he perked up. "I'll tell you what I'll do," he said. "I'll make you a fair, sporting proposition. You get my cabinet and I'll do it. No. You get Hoover and—and my secretary of labor, and I'll get the rest myself, and we'll do it." And when I rushed out, quick, and came back, quick, with the most emphatic refusals of Hoover and the secretary of labor, Harding laughed. He did not say what he found so funny, but his laughter was so loud and sardonic that a secretary ran in and ran out.

The president had in his hand a typewritten paper which he pushed at me. "Here, look at this." It was a declaration his attorney general had dictated for Debs to sign when pardoned, a dirt-eating promise. "What would you do about that?" Harding asked, and when I looked up from reading it and said, with some feeling, that I would not pardon any man who would subscribe to such a statement, he nodded.

"I thought so," he muttered, and he crumpled the paper and dropped it. He pardoned Debs without any humiliating conditions.

When I visited Debs at Atlanta and told him what was coming, he was not elated. He was a happy man in prison. He loved everybody there, and everybody loved him—warden, guards, and convicts. Debs wanted to hear "all about the Russian Revolution," the outrages of which he had denounced. It was not socialist, he pleaded, just as Emma Goldman declared it was not an anarchist revolution. Like so many reds who rejected Bolshevism, Debs the socialist could not abide the violence, bloodshed, tyranny. They all had had their mental pictures of the heaven on earth that was coming, and this was not what they expected. As I told Emma Goldman once, to her indignation, she was a Methodist sent to a Presbyterian heaven, and naturally she thought it was hell. I was asking Debs to wait and hear more about it, even to go to Russia and see it for himself, before judging the Soviet Republic. He described the horrors he had heard of, and he could describe; Debs had eloquence, but when he finished his fiery speech to me on the rude, wild ruthlessness of the Russians, I said very quietly: "True, 'Gene. That's all true that you say. A revolution is no gentleman."

He sprang to his feet. "Of course," he exclaimed. "I forgot." And he promised me then and there never again to denounce the Russian Revolution on any charge without first hearing my answer to it. He did. When he got out he made a speech denouncing, as the socialist leader, the revolution and all its works, and he did not answer a letter of protest I addressed to him. I offered to go to Indianapolis to see him. I never saw Debs again, but he was never again very well.

The war psychology, which in America was also an anti-labor, anti-radical mass psychology, was still too strong in Harding's day for any pacific gesture, and my general amnesty scheme was too sweeping. I returned to Europe. In 1927, with Coolidge in the White House and prosperity everywhere, it looked, as Darrow and Older wrote, as if something might be done in one State, California, where we had a claim. I went home hopeful, therefore, traveling slowly, zigzag, westward, stopping to look and listen for the news; and we got some that bore upon my purpose.

The spirit of labor had changed utterly. Prosperity, high wages, plenty of work, and some propaganda had taken the fight out of the workers and their leaders. President Greene of the American Federation of Labor was preaching that to maintain high wages and raise them, the workers must work more, produce more. There was none of the old stress on the conflict between capital and labor. And the organized workers heard this willingly, as if it were understood. Like the socialists, organized labor listened sympathetically to denunciations of Bolshevik Russia, although the same doctrine of productiveness was preached there. What it meant to me was that the revolutionary spirit was dead or quiescent. The interest in, the memory of, my dynamiters was almost gone. Organized labor might not care to help get McNamara and Schmidt out of prison, but changed conditions would likewise have removed the employers' reason for continuing their punishment. It was psychologically the time to ask for their pardon.

Darrow in Chicago felt this, and he was hopeful also because the Progressives were in power in California. I was present at the birth of the Progressive movement in Republican California, saw the fine young reformers take away from the Southern Pacific the old machine control of the State. The Progressives were honest men and liberals, and Darrow, who knew that, showed by his hopefulness that he also believed in honesty. When I arrived in California and saw the heads of the administration, I was chilled. They talked of justice, the right, their honesty. I knew what that meant: no generosity, no mercy, no human understanding, and no wise politics. Fremont Older, big, kind, but realistic, was not so optimistic as Darrow, but he had the facts, the names, the men. "There's a chance," he said. I found that the prisoners, J. B. McNamara and Schmidt, were out of touch with the world. They thought that organized labor, having abandoned dynamite entirely, might be willing to say so and work to get them, its dynamiting agents, out of prison! They had no idea how completely they were forgotten, "and," as J. J. McNamara said in Chicago, "I can't tell them so that they realize it." But my hope was not in labor; it was in the men who had suffered from the dynamiting and made the settlement with me.

I went to Los Angeles, saw Harry Chandler, the successor of General Otis, deceased, and made to him my proposition to have McNamara and Schmidt pardoned.

"Of course," he said. "That's the thing to do, and I and the *Times* will be for it. But I can't help you do it. I am out of it, you know, now. We have no influence with this administration. All I can say is that you may quote me to them as willing to stand for keeping the old contract and pardoning those men and that if they are let go, the *Times* will approve."

It was the *Times* that was blown up, remember.

I saw the new district attorney, Asa Keyes, who had to remove certain technical obstacles to an act of clemency. He remembered the settlement. He consented at once. "I'll do it," he said, "and right away. I'll do anything else I can, but that's not much, I guess."

Keyes has since been sent to the same prison with Schmidt and McNamara for practices not uncommon in a district attorney's office.

Backed by these sinners, I called next on the governor and his prison board. Governor Young heard my plea. He was very liberal, and personally he was kind. He showed me through the Governor's Mansion, which was once my father's house, my home. And he said that he would do whatever the prison board recommended. But I watched him dealing with the case of Mooney and Billings, both innocent, as I knew, and both convicted on perjured testimony, as he knew. A man so inexecutive with innocent prisoners would be slower still with my guilty friends. Anyway, Charles W. Neumiller, the chairman of the prison board, made it plain that he would recommend no leniency, to say nothing of a fine gesture toward labor. He had some feeling, some class prejudice. "Too much has been done already for these dynamiters," he said.

These officials represent the new State of California—new to me. The moderately successful, the well-to-do, the respectable people from the east and the middle west, had poured into sunny California, drowned out the old spirit, and the righteous, the good, people whom I had seen in action in the cities and States I had muckraked were the dominant Californians. The sunshine there may ripen them some day as it did the old Forty-niners, but California today is not a western, it is a middle western, State. I gave up my decent purpose—for the present. If the reformers are defeated and men with imagination ever get back into power, I shall try again. Meanwhile I recall a story Brand Whitlock told me long ago when he was mayor of Toledo.

A drunken bum walked unsteadily into his open office, drew a chair up to the mayor's desk, and said, "Brand, what do you stand for?"

"Oh," the mayor answered, "I can't stop work to tell you that. It would take too long."

"Ah, say, you ought to be able to put it in one word."

"Well, if I had to put it in one word, I'd say I stood for justice."

"Oh, no, not justice. I voted for you, and I wouldn't 'a' voted for you if I thought you stood for justice. Why, say, if I got justice I'd get it in the neck, and I don't believe even you would like it if you got justice."

The mayor, amused, asked the bum what he thought he should stand for. "You don't like my one word. What's your word?"

"Oh, I don't know, but I've always had a kind of a stinkin' notion that you stood for mercy."

Brand Whitlock liked that word and that story. He was that way. At the height of the rumpus over the dynamite settlement he wrote me a sympathetic little note, saying he understood and adding that as he lived he kept shortening his philosophy till he had it down now to two words, "Judge not." "Fine," I answered, but his philosophy was too long and too negative. I had got mine down to one short, positive word, "Wiggle." I must not judge a State like California. "You cannot indict a nation," said Edmund Burke. But—we must learn, we Americans, to understand the guilty; they are in so many ways superior to the innocent.

Matt Schmidt said it in the warden's office of the penitentiary. Tom Mooney was stating his case, proving his (undoubted) innocence, and as he talked, we all felt that he was not only innocent; he had become righteous, a bore, an offense with his rights and his wrongs. Schmidt must have sensed what I sensed, for I heard him whisper to J. B. McNamara, "Thank God, Jim, we are guilty."

Another plea for strength: walking with Fremont Older through the yard of Folsom Prison, a convict, Bill English, a famous old stage-robber, came up to the big editor with a remonstrance.

"You are making a mistake with your paroles, Mr. Older. They are letting out the convicts who have good prison records, the fellows that are 'good' in here and stand in with the prison officials. They are no good, you know. They go out and break parole. That hurts us all; it hurts the parole. You can't trust good people in here any more than you can outside. They go back on you."

"Well, but whom can we trust?" asked Older. "Who should be paroled?"

"Oh, take the hard guys, the bad men. If they will accept parole they'll keep their word and the system will grow."

"How about you, Bill?" I challenged.

"Well," he retorted, "you can trust me. I'm not ready yet, but if I ever send you word that I'll take parole, you can betcha life I'll stick."

A year or so later he sent his word; he was paroled, and that was the last ever heard of Bill English. He stuck his parole, as Older knew, to the end.

II

THE NEW UNITED STATES

INSTEAD of my showing America to my wife, it was she who
began showing it to me. Youth can see, and Ella Winter had
another advantage. She carried on one wall of her mind the
European picture, made in England, of the United States and its
people. She saw what she saw with the surprise of sharp contrast,
starting as we sailed up the harbor of New York. "Why! It is
beautiful," she exclaimed. Robert Dunne, who stood beside her,
nodded, moved also as I was by the bursting power of it all, the
daring, the triumph of a new expressive art. Fifth Avenue the
next day was clean, handsome, orderly. The traffic was, as expected, dense, but it was slow, a regulated flow up and down,
and no hurry.

"Look," she pointed, "the crowd is great, the movement lively,
but no individuals are excited. There's no rush. There is leisure
here." And, as she indicated, this individual was walking along
quietly, that one pausing at a shop window, a couple halting to
greet and chat. It was true. The "surging crowds" and the close
column of cars were made up of quiet, leisurely individuals. And
it was so downtown, even at Broad and Wall Streets.

She saw less standardization and better dressing than in London
or Paris. Of course Americans shop all over Europe, and they wear
what they buy everywhere, all styles, all fashions. How can
Europeans see standardization here and not at home? What have
we as true to type as a French, German, or English child, nurse, or
schoolboy? How can an Oxford- or Cambridge- or Sorbonne-
formed gentleman find Americans all alike? With "the" American in her mind's eye, she met not him or her, but such an endless
variety of individuals in dress, manners, ideas, that she thought
she was seeing only exceptional people, as indeed she was, but

so many of them that they, the untypical Americans, must be representative. It took her a year or more to get down to the types and feel the standardization that is coming to us, also, as it has to Europeans.

Her key observation came after she had visited schools. Her inquiry was personal, anxious; she had her own child in mind, and like the researcher she was, she went around New York, seeing all that was being done about the education of children. When she had seen all the nursery schools there were, she came back to the hotel and said: "Well, you Americans may not have education now, but it doesn't matter. You will have it. All the schools I have visited are consciously experimenting, and in different ways. They are watching one another, noting results, changing their methods according to their experience, and learning how to treat children and to grow them. Some day you will have here an educational system or systems built up on experimental knowledge."

And a little later, when she had heard captains of industry talk and my reports of conversations with old friends in business, journalism, politics, she broadened her observation: "I wonder if that is not the vital point about America, that this is an experimenting country. Anybody can see anybody. Everybody is willing 'to try anything once,' as they say. Nothing is final or fixed. Everything, from high buildings to automobiles, from railroad coaches to cooking stoves and factory machinery—all but your Constitution—is tentative, temporary, to be scrapped some day for the next good thing. Nothing is done."

My impressions tuned in with hers. I felt afresh the power, the momentum, of America as a going concern. The force of us had increased. There could be no stopping or turning us now. We were on the way; we might not know where we were going, but, for better or for worse, we were going, going. Whither? It would be worth trying to find out where we were bound, just as I had learned to see what foreign countries were tending to do. And I began to sense a direction here, a direction new to me. My wife's pointing finger, my old friends' cynical or sad hopelessness, and the contrast between the fixity of old Europe and the vigor and ever-changing movement of the United States braced me to see and to acknowledge that my country was not going my way, not the liberal, not the red radical, but also not exactly the English,

French, or German way. It was going its own way. What way was that? I asked, but I could not credit the answer that occurred to me.

The American way was not the Russian way, no; ours was in the opposite direction, but—but, yes, Bolshevik Russia and the mass machine-making United States were more alike, essentially and politically, than any other two countries that I had seen. Wasn't it this, that these two young peoples, the Russians and the Americans, are driving, the one consciously, the other unwittingly, toward the same end?

My wife's observation about experimenting was the point. Mr. Owen D. Young told me one day something about the General Electric Company's big experimental plant where chemists, physicists—all sorts of scientific researchers—were gathered to carry on, partly for the company, but partly for science and themselves, their intensive specialized work. All that he said went to show that big business was absorbing science, the scientific attitude and the scientific method. Cocksureness, unconscious ignorance, were giving way to experiment, and alert patience was waiting "to see." About that time E. A. Filene came along, reporting that he had heard a vice president of General Motors, whose largest single plant was an experimental-research plant, say: "We don't think any more in business. Oh, we may have our opinions; we may think up how we can do or make something we need. We may think up a theory, but we don't act on our theories any more. We send our theory or our need into the laboratory and so have it tried out. If it doesn't work, we change the theory, scrap it. But if a theory, modified, works, we may make it into an engine or a car and put it out for trial on the market, but—even then, it's only a sort of working hypothesis. We go on monkeying with that and other theories and hunches to improve the car on trial."

This is revolutionary. If this spirit had got out of the science laboratories into business in a business country, it would seal the doom of our old Greek-Christian culture. It would spill over into politics, economics, life. No more thinking; no more right thinking; no more believing or logical reasoning from premises to conclusions. We would not have one city after another trying a commission form or some other fool idea of government and, whether it succeeded or failed, going right on believing in it. Wondering would supplant convictions, insight inspiration; experiment would blow up argument; and as for our conclusions, they would not be uplifted into principles and creeds but tried out as working cars or working hypotheses. No wonder my old liberal friends were sore and obstinate. A new, the new, culture was sweeping down over us, and big business, and the old root of all evil!

How far had it gone, this new way of thinking? Mr. Filene himself, who told me about it, was there to ask me to write his life, the "failure of a successful millionaire." His failures, as I have said, were first, to get his employees to take over his business, and second, to achieve himself and see general such a reduction in the costs of distribution as had come in production. He wanted some one to go through his story to find out what his mistakes were, whether in theory or in practice, so that his failure might not be repeated. I could not do it, but the point I make here is that this was a "successful" American business man looking back over his whole life as an experiment. And quite consistently, Filene, as a significantly unsuccessful experimenter in the field of distribution, admired—he came pretty near adoring—Henry Ford as a pioneering, triumphant experimenter in production. He showed me Samuel Crowther's book on Ford's life, and it is indeed a revolutionary story. It might well be the Bible, as Ford is the prophet, of business.

No intellectual, only a man of brains with no "education," Ford had set out instinctively to make something for use. It happened to be a car, a new thing. Filene quoted Ford as having said once to him that if he had known what he was doing, if he had been thinking intellectually of his grand purpose, he would have made something already in universal use, like shoes. But he was a mechanic; he got to pottering around with the horseless carriage, and he made one finally that would "get you there, get you back." It was good enough for common use; it had to be cheap enough for everybody to have one. That's what use meant to this man whose head was working like a red's. He aimed at the mass market. His was not to be a luxury car for a few at a high price, but a vehicle for any and everybody in the world to climb up off the earth on and ride—ride on wheels, fast. According to his disciple, Filene, Ford did not fix his price by taking the cost of a car and adding his profit. That was the old business way; he chose a new way; he set his price at

Ewing Galloway, N.Y.

NICOLAI LENIN

P. & A. Photo

WOODROW WILSON

DICTATORS

Wide World Photo

BENITO MUSSOLINI

what the common mass of men—business men, laborers, farmers—could pay, and trusted to his hunch theory that if all who needed a car bought one the total would be so great that his overhead would be reduced to practically nothing. It worked, this experiment, and as it worked, he kept cutting his price and increasing his sales till the automobile became a handy tool, a common necessity in universal, democratic use.

This done with cars could be done with other things, and other men, seeing however dimly what Ford was doing, applied his practices as principles, to other cars first, then to other things, until now one can foresee the application of the method and of machinery to the mass production of a machine age. A conscious age, conscious, too, of its beauty as well as of its democracy. Garet Garrett, the writer, the economist, told me how a foreman in Ford's works, joining quietly in his admiration of the beauty of a great piece of machinery for mass production of a Ford part, said: "Yes, and such a machine will make not only the thing we want. Thus anything, everything anybody wants can and will be made." They see it, these prophets in action, and there are scribes to hear and report, like Garet Garrett, like Samuel Crowther.

It seemed to me, fresh from Europe where nothing new is doing, that Henry Ford, the industrial leader in a land of industrial pioneering, was a prophet without words, a reformer without politics, a legislator, statesman—a radical. I understood why the Bolshevik leaders of Russia admired, coveted, studied him. He was a labor leader, for example. With no sentiment at all about the workers, handling labor as he did raw material, he learned by experience to stand for high wages. He discovered that, to get the best working-men, he had to compete with other employers by paying more wages. He outbid his rivals and so discovered that high wages improved the market for cars. He met obstacles, of course. One he could never overcome: the landlord. His wage-earners had their rents raised to all the traffic would bear. Something will have to be done about that some day—not by Ford. No wage-payer can deal with that. Only mass action can meet the rent problem. Another obstacle that Ford did deal with prophetically was his stockholders. He had started out in the usual thoughtless standard way with partners and later stockholders to raise capital, and his partners, typically, were men whose interest was not in making cars cheap for universal use but in making money. They had not seen what he saw, that good wages to labor, good earnings to farmers, prosperity in the masses, made a good market for cars. They were for dividends, stock melons. Ford saw that dividends were a leak, a waste upon the rich who bought fancy cars and luxury articles. His stockholders, being naturally for the division of profits among themselves, not among the workers and consumers, resisted Ford. He bought them out. He paid high, but he did what his followers will all have to do some day; he abolished his stockholders to remove an obstacle to progress. He still had to pile up profits into a surplus, but this was to protect himself against the banks, which were after him as they are after all industry and business. Also he needed, in this stage of our civilization, a surplus as an experimental fund to finance, himself, the big changes he saw ahead.

This was Russian and revolutionary. A captain of industry, the salaried head of one of our greatest manufacturing companies, asked me once to tell him, in his terms, just what it was that Soviet Russia was doing. I said: "If we should do here what they are doing over there, you, for example, would be rid of the old, fine, but now conservative owner-founder of this company and all the other owners and lien-holders, all the stocks and bonds. And you would be free of the private bankers and landlords." I spoke slowly, watching his face, and the expression of released joy on it was a sufficient comment. But what he said was expressive, too.

"My God, is that it? Why, that would free business!"

He meant that with these limits removed, he and the other young managers of business could take risks and adventure forth as the old founders and owners had in the days of their youth, when they were managers, before they became owners, retired, soft, rich, and interested in money and security. Well, Ford had freed himself by his re-purchase of his stock. And that is what E. A. Filene had not done. He, the democrat in business, had given shares to his young partners, and they became interested, not in management, not in a democratic experiment, but in profits, salaries, dividends, honors, charities, public services, philanthropies— riches. Ford's story, and E. A. Filene's, and E. W. Scripps's, might show why American business had taken such long and illuminating strides toward the solution of the problem of production and so few and such mincing steps toward the distribution of "goods." I say few. Filene had invented what he called "the basement," where the surpluses of overproduction were sold into use at whatever price they would bring. But he himself was more interested in two young competitors of the big department store: mail-order houses and chain-stores, which threatened to win out—as he pointed out with glee—because he saw in them the beginning of the systematic solution of economic distribution to follow economic production of goods—not yet of wealth.

But that, too—the distribution of wealth—was within sight in my amazing country. As we traveled westward to California, the sense we had that business was driving full power ahead went with us. Men talked about it; you felt it; and it seemed to be general. Labor was getting some of it. My wife was struck by the streams of automobiles everywhere, city after city, towns, villages, and country. Seeing a big bunch of automobiles parked in a road near the fields, she would ask what they were doing there all alone, and when I suggested that they were the cars of the farm hands she could hardly believe it. And yet there they were all through Indiana, Iowa, Nebraska, Colorado, even in the desert of Nevada. Sometimes we saw the owners of them at work. And in California seven or eight cars stood in front of our house one day when an English woman, meaning to call, passed us by. "I thought," she explained afterward, "that all those cars meant that you were having a reception." They were the cars of the workers who were putting in order the house we had just bought. Ella Winter knew in pounds and shillings what we were paying these workers and servants; she added the cars and put the final touch to her revised picture of the United States.

"This country has," she said, "what the socialists in Europe have always said they wanted, and more. You have food, shelter, and clothing for all the workers and—and a car!"

There was the political point in what we were seeing and hearing, the connection with what I had been doing all my life. But wait. There were some workers who did not work. We had some unemployment, too. And worse was coming. The American experiment was still in the making. We were seeing only the direction. High wages, compared with Europe, we had, and the meaning and the effect was understood. It was the result of an unconscious experiment. Wages had gone up during the war. The mass of well-paid men made business good. When peace came and the soldiers returned to work, business hesitated, then went on into the Coolidge boom, and some big business managers and many commentators saw and said that it was our high wages that gave us our buying-power. Never mind how right or wrong this is. To us, here, now, it is an approach to a new view of labor, a new sense of democracy. Not a sentiment, but a sense, not taught by strikes and radical propaganda, but a perception by our rulers, the big business men. The climax and the test came with the end of Coolidge and of the Coolidge boom, in the business crisis of 1929, when President Hoover faced the problem of cutting the curve of a panicky depression.

Then emerged the idea, as a hard-boiled business perception, that mass production and mass distribution required mass prosperity, not individual riches—not a few, not even a lot, of rich people, but the general distribution of wealth in the form of wages, salaries, and earnings among men and women who are both workers and consumers. Only mass consumption by the masses can maintain mass production by machinery. Henry Ford, as usual, saw, said, and alone he did it, first.

"Let's meet the depression by raising wages," he advised at the White House conference, and he set the example no one could quite follow. He ordered a raise in his shops.

That meeting of the heads of industry and finance with the heads of the U.S. government under President Hoover struck me as an historical event of some significance. It was a recognition, however informal and unaware, of the truth Stinnes had seen in Germany, Mussolini in Italy, and the Bolsheviki in Russia, that the government of business and the political government should be one. It confirmed the impression I got when I came home from Europe that big business had won in the long struggle which we muck-rakers had reported only the superficial evils of; we and the liberals, progressives, and reformers had been beaten. The process of corruption had culminated in the comfortable establishment of the big bribers in power. The summoning of big business men to the White House to a public conference in broad daylight was a logical acknowledgment of the meaning of the election that chose Hoover for president.

That presidential election with Governor Smith, a Jeffersonian Democratic politician, running to defeat against Hoover, an engineer in business, seemed to mark the end of a period, my period, and perhaps of a culture, the moral culture. Hoover was the Hamiltonian, who had no democracy in him, none, neither political nor economic. He has shown no sense of the perception that privileges are a cause of our social trouble. He is a moralist in that. He believes in the ownership and management by business men of all business, including land and natural resources, transportation, power, light. Good business is all the good we need. Politics was the only evil, and he has no sense of politics. When he came home from his years and years of professional service in foreign lands, he did not know or care whether he was a Democrat or a Republican; he was a candidate and won some votes for the nomination for president at a Democratic convention. He stood four years later as the Republican candidate of and for business against an able, successful Democrat who was a philosophic, political democrat. And the people believed, as they voted, with Hoover. Food, shelter, and clothing, plus the car, the radio—prosperity interested them more than any old American principles, which were all on the Democratic side with Smith. I went through that campaign, sensitive, interested, non-partisan. What little I said was in the Jeffersonian tradition, but I was watching to report, not playing to win. I can assert that everybody was for business; even the Democrats who voted for Smith, were for good business, of course; they, too, expected Smith to carry on the good times and favor business. It seems to me that there are many more Republicans in this country than voted for Hoover, that our southern Democrats, party-bound by their traditions, are unconscious Republicans who only think that they are Democrats, who don't know that they are Republicans. In California, where I was living, there were no politics or principles at all. It was all business. In brief, that was an economic election which sent to the White House Herbert Hoover to do what he is trying to do: to represent business openly, as Coolidge and other presidents had covertly.

PROHIBITION: A HANG-OVER

THERE was another, a characteristically moral, issue, which was a hang-over from my day: prohibition. But that was submerged, evaded, kept in the background, and the prohibitionists were on the side of big business, as they have been for years. The big business men who were employers accepted prohibition very generally, not for themselves, but for their workers. And in that they behaved as the socialists in Belgium did, for the same reason. They both want sober labor. But the prohibition issue was dealt with in the presidential campaign as a moral issue usually is and must be dealt with—hypocritically, dishonestly, immorally. Smith, the prophet of old principles, was not frank, and Hoover, the spokesman of the new experimental era, called prohibition— however insincerely—a noble experiment.

Passing laws to enforce morality is an old experiment that has failed over and over again, but it would be worth trying again if President Hoover and big business would openly regard it as an experiment and lead people so to watch it, willing to drop prohibition if it cannot be enforced and resolve never again to apply force to morality. So much honesty of mind is hardly possible. Our law books are cluttered with blue laws that are dead but unrepealed. Some of these were dug up to embarrass Police Commissioner Roosevelt when, to reform the police, who were corrupted by the liquor business, he tried to make the cops enforce the laws regulating saloons. His plea, like Hoover's no doubt, was that laws proved unenforceable would be repealed. Roosevelt had less drastic liquor laws than Hoover, and he was closer to his smaller field, with nothing else to do. He failed, and two of his ablest successors, General Greene and Colonel Woods, failed. I have told some of this story and offered my explanation. When the moralist calls the cop, he is turning his fine moral duty over to a man who has no sympathy with and no fitness for the job. It may be made the policeman's duty, and he is paid to do it, say, $300 a month. But the liquor business man offers him as much, or more besides, not to do his duty; backs him, praises, gets him promoted for doing nothing, lets him have both wages and bribes, and helps him if he gets into trouble. On the other hand, if he does his duty, the policeman is apt to be discharged from the force for any little fault and so lose his pay, his bribe, and his job. My intimate experience with this sort of thing had about convinced me that all sumptuary legislation, like all uneconomic regulation and, indeed, our whole penal system, was unpractical, unscientific, and immoral. There is a better way to all morality, and the temperance movement shows it.

I used to eat lunch with the Wall Street brokers at a bar in a basement back of the Stock Exchange. That long bar had once been for drinks, with a free lunch counter at one end. The space for drinking shrank; the lunch counter, no longer free, grew, till in my time the drink section was narrower than the free lunch used to be. Later I saw the eating-space spread over the counter and off upon tables and, finally, into many dining-rooms. The brokers and clerks who drank did not survive; they died off or were discharged, and the habit of temperance came, everywhere. That shrinking Wall Street bar was the measure of what I found happening all over this country. Temperance, without police aid, with the force only of propaganda and the rise and spread of prosperity, was coming fast. But the growing number of temperate people was an increase also of votes for prohibition, and a man appeared to use them. I came upon him when I was muckraking Ohio.

In every little community there I found that there was a solid little anti-saloon vote for local option, which the politicians, especially the "bad actors" among them, respected. When I asked why, the answer was that there was a fellow in Columbus named Wayne or Wheeler, or was it Wayne Something Wheeler, who ran the politics of this movement, and—"say, he knows the game." I called in due course at his small upstairs office in Columbus, and there was Wayne B. Wheeler, glad to see me, a friend, of course, a fellow reformer. He told me what he was up to and how far he had succeeded. Amazing.

"How do you do it?" I asked.

He bent forward, fiery will in his keen eyes, and he hissed his shrewd, mad answer: "I do it the way the bosses do it, with minorities. There are some anti-saloon voters in every community. I and other speakers increase the number and the passion of them. I list and bind them to vote as I bid. I say, 'We'll all vote against the men in office who won't support our bills. We'll vote for candidates who will promise to. They'll break their promise. Sure. Next time we'll break them.' And we can. We did. Our swinging, solid minorities, no matter how small, counted. The pols came to us, volunteered promises, which, by and by, were kept. We are teaching these crooks that breaking promises to us is surer of punishment than going back on their bosses, and some day they will learn that all over the United States—and we'll have national prohibition."

"By crooks!" I exclaimed. "You'll sacrifice everything else?"

"Yes. One thing at a time."

A powerful, determined, cunning realist, Wayne B. Wheeler. When I objected that he was blunting Tom Johnson's fight against big, privileged business, he said: "We have no quarrel with business. The employers of labor are with us."

"So you are with them."

"One fight at a time," he repeated.

I did not expect to see his prediction come true, but I did admire his method. I was so struck by it, his account of his use of the minority, that I described it to Mayor Johnson as a method to achieve some of his more fundamental ends. A democrat, he would not touch it. I recommended it to the woman suffragists and they applied it, but only as a last resort, not steadily and clearly as Mr. Wheeler did. I have since suggested it to the colored voters and to labor. Any strong minority can use it with effect. But I did not myself grasp the full political significance of the minority till it appeared as the conqueror of the Russian Revolution and the Bolshevik ruler of the Soviet Republic and, again, as the Fascist weapon that put Mussolini on the throne of Italy.

Prohibition, however achieved, is not an unmixed evil, just as it stands. Its habitual violation has spread high and far a contempt for man-made laws that may turn our attention some day to natural laws of economics and psychology. Its partial enforcement has tended to sober labor and to injure only the rich and their children, thus hindering the development of a governing aristoc-racy out of our plutocracy. The enactment of the prohibition laws has set a precedent for the confiscation or annihilation of wealth and property; English law would not so lightly permit such a ruin of the business of invested capital as prohibition has written into our constitutional law. The brewers, the liquor and saloon interests, richly earned what has been done to them; they were always deep in the worst of politics. If prohibition succeeds we might logically proceed to take over all the property and functions of all the other businesses that are deep in politics. But prohibition is far from a success. The conflict for and against enforcement is still waging, and the liquor business, driven underground, is only burrowing deeper and higher into politics and government, with a following of bold bands of gunmen, corruptionists, and straight-out felons. One hears people wondering at the open outrages of bandits and professional killers who fight with machine guns on the city streets, commit murders freely and safely, and generally defy and teach defiance to law and order. My English wife exclaimed with ad-miration that "that could not happen in England; we have been reduced to respect for law." She thought that our American initia-tive and our turn for experimentation came from the same source. There may be something in that, but our American banditry and machine-gun fighting are "protected." Bootlegging is the sales department of a big business, probably our biggest single business. The liquor business is at least as big and as profitable as the brewery and saloon businesses combined were before prohibition. No such monster industry can exist illegally without the protection of the police, the connivance of courts, and the moral support of a power-ful public opinion. It is in a noisy stage of its development now. Starting out afresh as a competitive business, with many little organizations, the new liquor trade is forming pools and mergers which divide the field with the understanding of the police. Taking a city like Chicago or New York, the bootleggers buy the police and some judges at any price asked. Then come attempts to invade one another's territories or to force combinations, and with no recourse to law, the bootleggers have to fight it out in the streets. The police agree to the division of territory; they do all they can to have the faith kept, but they cannot arrest one bootlegger for encroaching on another's field. Hence the bootleggers have to arrest one another with sawed-off shotguns and quiet murders. "But why can't the police detect the murderers and the law hang them? Is murder protected?" The murderers are often known to the authorities, but they are good customers and pals of the police, who will not go back on a friend. Murder is not explicitly protected; manslaughter is not in the agreement made. Homicide is only thrown in to carry out a good bargain.

But this, the criminal stage of the development of the new liquor business, will pass as it did in oil, in mining, in railroads, when competition among the many syndicates has been reduced to a trust, with the whole business under one central head. That won't happen till the bootleggers have bought their way all through politics to a place beside the power trust and the railroads, in government, to a voice in the press and in the management of parties, a foothold in the banks, and a "fair deal" in the schools—in brief, when the prohibition liquor business is a respectable vested interest.

The liquor business was not represented at President Hoover's economic conference, but it was there as the enforcement issue was in the presidential campaign. The moralists back of it were on the side of big business and so helped to make the election a triumph of corruption. When I say that, however, I am not implying that the president is corrupt, only that I am; that I am adjusting my mind, like Boston and Philadelphia, to the acceptance of that which I have been calling political business corruption as a natural, well-nigh universal process of change; that bribery is just one of the ways our instinctive, absent-minded industrialists had to take to make over an agricultural state, people, and culture into an industrial, machine-driven organization of society; that bribery is in a very pious sense an act of God; and that all the various forms of corruption should be regarded, not as felonies, but as evidences of friction in the process of pouring new wine into the narrow necks of old bottles. Anyhow this is literally and scientifically true: when our old moral and liberal culture sets up such obstacles as prohibition, whether of drink or of trusts, growing, spreading, powerful business is forced by some blind urge to buy or lie its way through Legislatures, courts, press, schools, churches, and public opinion to its end, whatever that is.

I am recording here that my lifework had brought me so far, consciously. I had come unconsciously to that point before. When

I arrived home from the war, the peace, the revolutions, and the reparations, I heard what everybody now knows, that dirty political grafting had risen up into the very White House. A group of business men had actually chosen, nominated, and put over a president for their big business purposes, and like the Southern Pacific Railroad in California, like the business bankers of Tammany, and like the life insurance bosses, they had had to let the little politicians get theirs by the direct, scandalous, mean stealings of their (the Ohio) school. Would I please muckrake that? I would if I could begin with those big business men first and report last what made them do it. No. That was not wanted; only the old muck was wanting to be raked. Some strong instinct prompted me to decline that opportunity. And I was right politically and journalistically.

The scandals of the Harding Administration, which clouded the Coolidge Administration, which had to do something about them, had no effect. Hoover was in both cabinets, the noisy and the quiet one, but he came through to the presidency. Which was "normalcy." He represented big business, honestly. The Harding way was the old, the politician's, way. The Coolidge way was the new American, the old English, the respectable, businesslike way of representing business, and that Hoover personified. No need of bribing him, no excuse for any graft in the White House. Bribery and corruption were over. President Hoover, like Coolidge, honestly believed that the government should favor big business, without price. And so, when the economic crisis came, President Hoover could call together the big business men to counsel and agree with him on a business political policy which he and they should join in carrying out. All in the open. It matters not that this president and these captains of industry did not know what to do; we have not yet got to science and scientists in government. The engineer president was bringing to the throne, formally and publicly, the potential heads of our two actual governments: the industrial government and the political government; the government which fixes the people's wages, working-hours, and conditions and therefore governs their lives in the shop and in the kitchen, and the political government which manages them socially; the government which decides what they shall eat and that which decides what they shall drink. A victory. A marriage. One can't sneer any more that Washington is the kept woman of Wall Street. They are man and wife, and that changes everything; it makes the old wrong right. It makes Washington a decent woman.

What about the children of the union that ends so well the long and rather scandalous romance we have been talking about? What is to be the end or objective? The high contracting parties may not know or intend any end, but I think we outsiders can detect a direction and, perhaps, foresee some results—some to further, some to hinder, a little—from the high Alps of European experience.

I V

PROPHECY

I N RUSSIA the ultimate purpose of this conscious process of merging politics and business is to abolish the political state as soon
as its sole uses are served: to make defensive war abroad and
at home and to teach the people by propaganda and by enforced
conditions to substitute new for old ideas and habits. The political
establishment is a sort of protective scaffolding within which the
temporary dictatorship is building all agriculture, all industries,
and all businesses into one huge centralized organization. They will
point out to you from over there that our businesses, too, are and
long have been coming together, merging trusts into combines,
which in turn unite into greater and greater monopolies. They
think that when we western reformers and liberals resist this
tendency we are standing in the way of a natural, inevitable economic compulsion to form "one big union" of business. All that
they have changed is the ownership, which they (and Henry Ford)
think is about all that's wrong. Aren't they right to encourage the
process? Aren't we wrong to oppose it? Anyway President
Hoover's conference of the masters of mergers to meet a business
situation was a call to them to put a head on business, see it as a
whole, and act upon it with him as a unit. What they proposed was
not enough to stay the general depression, which has causes beyond their ideas and habits of thought, but it did take them out
of themselves for a moment. They agreed to list the large expenditures they were going to make anyhow and add to it as much other
building, buying, and improving as they could safely venture upon
—this was for the psychological effect. But it was a recognition of
the plain truth that good business as a whole is for the common
good and requires the coöperation of the people as a whole. It
was propaganda. It was a Plan.

It was then that Henry Ford raised his wages, as an example, and saw and said why the others could not heed. They had stock-holders to consider, and the stock market. Ford had neither of these to contend with. He had just been scrapping his old car and the machinery that made it. That had used up many millions of his cash capital. But he was able financially, and, a dictator in his busi-ness, he was free, to declare that a large part of his profits should go to his workers to enable them to go on buying and consuming; there were no stockholders to demand that it go into dividends. The other business bosses were not dictators but representatives, and they represented stockholders or stock which has rights, some-times prior rights. Our culture, theirs, teaches that when there's a crisis and something has to be cut, when the choice is between the non-producing stockholders and the producing wage-workers, it is "naturally" wages, not dividends, that we reduce first. At that White House conference which contemplated the wage-workers as the consuming market, those business men saw that this natural readiness to cut wages must be checked. They would not raise wages with Ford, but they realized that wages must not be cut. And they taught that. And that is a sign, I think, of a direction in which this mammoth movement we cannot stop or turn is going.

I heard employers out west saying that they must not cut wages. I pressed the question of what they would do when the test came: "Will you cut dividends or wages?" And in the words of one of them, they answered, "Oh, but we can't cut wages." They did, some of them, and they discharged workers till unemployment became a nervous problem. Business men could not this time act upon the idea, but they had and they could utter the idea that good wages were at the bottom of good business and a good market. This is progress. American business has come, market-wise, to the idea that Bolshevik Russia is putting into its unwritten constitu-tion, that the producers and the consumers are one and the same people and that production and consumption must about balance; else there must be foreign markets and empire and panics.

But there's that other reason why seeming masters of business could not follow Ford and raise wages—the stock market. At a time long ago when there were a lot of railroad disasters, I asked a shrewd New York banker, just for the fun of it, what the matter was.

"Have you financiers no railroad men to operate your railroads?"

"Yes," he said. "We have them. We have men trained in operation from the ground up, and some of them have been promoted clear to the top. But we find that when we take a crackerjack of a division superintendent from somewhere out west, bring him here as a vice president, and raise his salary from—nothing to $25,000 and over $50,000, he—and his wife, who came here feeling rich and well paid, soon learn that no fifty thousand a year, no salary a year, is in it with what they can make on the side, in Wall Street; so they begin to get rich, prominent, and neglectful of railroading."

This is generally true. All the great corporations suffer somewhat from the distracting discovery of their ablest managers that, being in on the game, they can make more in Wall Street than they can in manufacturing. Some companies have dealt with the problem of keeping their managers' minds on the business by forming them into pools and letting them tell off some one of their number to do the gambling for all. Even then they all are interested in the stock market as much as in the goods market, and this speculative interest keeps the managers of industry more or less on the side of the capitalists, big and little.

In France, less so in England, business generally is in the possession of stockholders and others in the second, third, and fourth generation. These owners employ managers, who are held back from scrapping old for new machinery and methods by the conservative interest of the stockholders in profits which they take out of the business and spend on their lives of leisure. I have heard foreign corporation officers complaining of the way the resources of their factories are absorbed to no business uses, and I have seen the mouths of American industrialists water at the sight of famous, great, but backward foreign plants. "How I would like to get hold of those works! By putting in our new machinery and methods and cutting out the waste in dividends—for a while—I could make millions of dollars where the French now make millions of francs."

The shortest story I ever heard of the state of England today was told me in the smoking-room of a ship by an American business man who had been called for consultation on the bad condition of a fine old manufacturing concern in England.

"I showed them that their machinery and methods were antediluvian and suggested scrapping them all and reorganizing completely. They could see that that should be done, but they held back, and I could not make out what was the matter till at last one of them said:

" 'We could persuade our stockholders to rebuild and reorganize once. They would forgo dividends and pay for one such change to bring us up to your degree of efficiency. But would not you in the next few years be inventing new machinery, and would not we, to keep up with you, have to scrap again and again?'

"When I said, 'Yes, probably,' they threw up their hands and said, 'We could never draw our stockholders into any such constant policy of periodic improvements.' And there was nothing doing."

The Americans who talked thus did not see, apparently, that there was an inevitable conflict of interest between ownership and management. One of them came home and stood for the multiplication of his company's stock issue. That put up the price of the shares, and he had a lot of shares. He made a fortune, but he was binding his company to pay dividends on a capital increased to represent profits earned in good times but not likely to be earned in bad times. He would want later to cut wages to keep up the payments to the wasters who own his shares and would be asking for economies, conservatism in adventure, like the older, foreign profiteers. All the speculating managers in the Coolidge boom were tempted in this direction by their own gambling interests.

But I think I saw the wedge go in that will show them the split between owners and managers. The banks are, economically, the representatives of ownership. They speculate, too; they sometimes deal in, they always hold, shares. When they thought they had Ford once, he sounded them, and they said that what they wanted was the treasury, not the presidency, not the managers of plants and makers of cars, but the place where they could handle the money and own and manipulate the stock. And what a good time they would have had issuing a new lot of Ford shares!

Now bankers are stock-market-wise, and they normally govern it. But in the late Coolidge boom, when the managers of industry were bulling stock prices against the opposition of the banks, they discovered that they contributed to the power of the banks over them by first depositing, then borrowing, their own companies' money. They stopped this. They very generally put their moneys directly into the call loan market, freed it for the moment, and learned for all time that they could share the power of the banks, and not only over the stock market.

This and other signs suggest that financial sovereignty, and therefore business, and therefore political sovereignty, in the United States, may be passing from the banks to the management of industry—the management, not the ownership. Indeed it looks as if the fundamental issue may be between management and ownership—not, as in my day, labor and capital, but producers and owners.

Henry Ford at the White House conference blurted a parallel prophecy of the prospect when he said to a reporter that business will all be run for a living some day, without any profits to divide. An industry would have to pay, of course, but the money made could not be wasted in dividends, melons, and big salaries to enrich the owners. It would have to be put back into the business. Business men would have to work as he does now, for a living. This must come generally, he foresaw, because he was doing it; and if one did it his competitors would have to, and not only in one industry.

For another perception, new, true, and fecund, by the industrial mind, is that all businesses are in competition. That two grocery stores, two railroads, several oil concerns compete was obvious, and business men acted on it. They formed trusts to establish monopolies, but they did not realize, till mass production came, that railroads compete also with automobiles, that all transportation competes with the radio, with the power and light business, with the grocery trust, and with the landlord. They are all in a struggle for their shares of the average wage. It is amusing and it is encouraging to have a big oil man sit down with you to explain that if labor is getting, say, ten dollars a day, then oil and the movies have to compete for the lion's share of ten dollars.

With this articulate perception goes another, still more far-reaching, whispered "hunch" or insight that the poor rich, the middle class of quiet leisure, does not count in this machine age of mass production. These people do not buy staples like the Ford cars; they are not important in business. The people who live in large part on dividends and interest would be wiped out or driven back to work if the profits of industry were to go back into the business for wages, new machinery, and improvements generally.

But that is what is happening everywhere in the western world. The Russian Revolution consciously abolished the middle class. The great war ruined—all wars ruin—whole layers of the middle class. The crash of the Coolidge boom—all panics, depressions, and disasters reduce the leisure class. Every great change, every economic crisis, the whole movement of civilized life, tends to concentrate riches in the hands of a few, who, in a generation or two, have to hire and depend upon managers, who acquire thus the power which they are beginning to feel, seize, and use—to reduce the world to workers, all.

The good people whom I have found to be "no good," who carry through no reforms, who oppose all change as soon as they understand it—these, the great obstacle to all progress, whose incomes are a wasteful graft on business, in which they are a useless hindrance, whose "moral" influence in art, literature, education, culture, and business is as "bad" as it is in politics, these people are doomed outside as they are in—Russia. I could see it in small towns in the west, where the chain stores, for instance, were threatening the retail livings of the local merchants, who cried out that they, the leading citizens as well as the leading business men, might have to give up their businesses and go to work for salaries or even wages; they and their children.

A tragedy this, for the middle men, the middle class, who, in all countries, call themselves the backbone of society. But there is a bright light to be seen through the darkness. We are coming to the seven-hour day of the five-day week. Leisure, as well as wealth, is to be distributed, apparently, again, by the same process as in Russia. There the Soviet government, with a plan, foresees that in a country where there are only workers and managers, with no owners and grafters—in an economic democracy the workers with machines will have short and shorter hours. That means leisure. So care is taken now to develop in labor the habits and taste to use well the probably many idle hours each day or the many idle days of every year of the masses. Workers are encouraged, therefore, to go to concerts, operas, theaters, ballets; they are guided through art galleries, where I heard them instructed in the craftsmanship of painting and sculpture. The problems, skill, and technique of the artist were described in terms of carpentry for a carpenter's union, and other trades heard the same lesson in terms of their own handicrafts.

The preparation in America for the dawning future is not so intelligent, conscious, and purposeful, but it is evident. The old arts of the theater, literature, painting, have got too far ahead of the crowds to be understood by them, but business is doing its blind best by what we call contemptuously commercial art to show the work of painters, for example, in all sorts of advertising. That gives painters a conspicuous, big place to hang their pictures. But the blindest, most characteristic art movement of our age of machinery is the movie and the talkie-movie, a new art that can include all the other arts. And mass producers, who are business men and not reformers, philanthropists and (not conscious) prophets, run their art for the consuming masses, who rush in crowds to see and support it. As they must. In Hollywood I have heard with my optimistic grin the imported writers and artists grieving and cursing because, with such a wide market as they have to serve to meet their extravagant costs, they could not "raise" the cinema any faster than "the mob" could go in appreciation. They tried, but they failed. They complained eloquently, and my kind of men and women sympathized with them, but I thought that I was seeing something new and wonderful under the sun through their tears and rage: that this new machine mass art cannot develop for its own sake; it is so tied to the democracy that it cannot rise to its obviously potential heights without lifting and being lifted by the human race.

V

FALLING OUT OF BED

SEEING is one motion; believing is another. As I see my own country last, after seeing the rest of the world, I think I believe what I have been seeing all my life and telling over and over in this my biography. I have been contending, with all my kind, always against God. He had plans, too. All countries, all life, all being—are chapters in His book of revelations. The United States is making an experiment second in hopefulness only to Russia, a revelation of evolution as against revolution. Revolution has the advantage in that it clears the ground. It swept away in Russia one detected cause of what we call evil; it opened the door to such human intelligence as a few thoughtful, feeling individuals had developed to lay out consciously and carry through ruthlessly a plan so to arrange the conditions of social living and so to adjust the forces of economic life that not the cunning, grasping possessors of things but the generous, industrious producers and the brave, imaginative leaders of the race shall be the fit to survive. Russia is the land of conscious, willful hope.

But the United States of America, which the Russians recognize as their chief rival, is, however unconsciously, moving with mighty momentum on a course which seems not unlikely to carry our managing, investing, ruling masters of industry, politics, and art—by our blind method of trial and error—in the opposite direction around the world to the very same meeting-place, as they, some of them, are beginning to see and say. Our poets and muck-rakers might well watch what they do, and sing or prattle the message of their acts.

Some change in me, this? It is. I have not lived in vain. The world which I tried so hard, so honestly, so dumbly, to change has changed me. It took a war, a peace, and a couple of revolutions to do it, but it is done. My spiral-like story ends as it began: by my being thrown out of bed by the shocks of an earthquake which has laid me out, not crying, however, but smiling. My life was worth my living. And as for the world in general, all that was or is or ever will be wrong with that is my—our thinking about it.

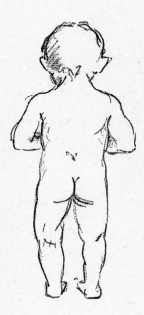

INDEX

BY WINTHROP PARKHURST